SMALL BUSINESS TAXATION

Planning and Practice

Third Edition

Gary L. Maydew

CCH INCORPORATED
Chicago

Editorial Staff

Technical Review . . . . David Gibberman, J.D.

Copy Editor . . . . Mary Konstant

Production . . . . Diana Roozeboom

Index . . . . Lynn Brown

This publication is designed to provide accurate and authoritative information in regard to the subject matter covered. It is sold with the understanding that the publisher is not engaged in rendering legal, accounting, or other professional service and that the author is not offering such advice in this publication. If legal advice or other expert assistance is required, the services of a competent professional person should be sought.

ISBN 0-8080-0741-6

©2001, **CCH** INCORPORATED

4025 W. Peterson Ave.
Chicago, IL 60646-6085
1 800 248 3248
http://tax.cchgroup.com

To my parents, Kermit and Lelia Maydew,
who taught all their children
a respect for work
and a love of learning.

Preface

Small Business Taxation, Third Edition, provides clear explanations and analysis of the tax law affecting small businesses. The book provides enough detail to satisfy accountants, attorneys, tax preparers, bankers and other professionals who consult small businesses, but there is much in the book that offers direct value to the astute business owner and manager. Concepts are illustrated with a generous amount of examples, and helpful tax planning tips and pitfalls are featured in this tax planning guide and reference. Footnotes provide authority for those who need to reference source materials.

Teachers will also find the Third Edition extremely helpful and one that covers "all the bases" for a course focused on small business tax and planning. The First and Second Editions of *Small Business Taxation* also found great favor with continuing education providers.

Incorporating the fact that many medium and small businesses are doing business in foreign countries, the Third Edition includes a new chapter covering taxation of international transactions. A new chapter on estate planning is also included, as well as expanded coverage of sole proprietorships. Changes brought about by the Economic Growth and Tax Relief Reconciliation Act of 2001 are reflected throughout the book.

Six distinct topics are covered: (1) tax entities—including the formation and operation of partnerships, LLCs, C corporations and S corporations; (2) income, deductions, and credits that relate to the entities; (3) corporate tax law focusing on penalty taxes and reorganizations; (4) business entity distributions and liquidations; (5) taxation of international transactions; and (6) income tax planning and estate planning for the individual and the family.

It is the author's hope that readers will benefit from the book's logical organization, straightforward coverage, and practical features that have grown out of decades of practical experience educating students and consulting business owners and advisers.

Gary Maydew

November 2001

About the Author

Gary L. Maydew, Ph.D, C.P.A, received his doctorate from the University of Illinois at Champaign-Urbana. A retired accounting professor at the College of Business at Iowa State University, Professor Maydew has published several books and more than 50 articles on taxation. His background in public accounting and his experience in teaching, consulting and researching small business taxation make him very qualified to write on tax planning for small business.

Contents

Contents in Detail

Chapter 3 *Corporate Operations*

Chapter 5   Gross Income—General Concepts

Chapter 6   Deductions—General Concepts and Business Applications

Chapter 8   Cost Recoveries

Chapter 9   Gains and Losses

Chapter 10   *Deferred Compensation*

Chapter 11   Penalty Taxes

Chapter 12   Corporate Reorganizations

Chapter 13   *Partnership Sales, Distributions, and Liquidations*

Paragraph

Chapter 17   Taxation of International Transactions

Chapter 18   Estate Planning

Chapter 1

Sole Proprietorships and Single Owner LLPs

¶ 101 General Characteristics

For federal taxation purposes, the entity is disregarded for sole proprietorships and single owner LLPs that are not incorporated. The income and deductions are not taxed at the entity level, but are reported by, and taxed to, the owner. In effect, the conduit rule applies to such entities (i.e., the sole proprietorship or single owner LLP is a mere conduit for the owner), and revenue and expenses flow through to the owner retaining the same characteristic that they had at the proprietorship or LLP level. If the activity constitutes a trade or business, the revenue and expenses are reported on Schedule C (Schedule F for farmers and fishermen).

When a sole proprietor sells his or her business, for tax purposes the sale is not of a single asset, but rather of each individual asset. For example, if the business assets consisted of inventory, equipment worth more than book value, a building, land, and goodwill, the sale would yield:

- Inventory—ordinary income;

- Equipment—Code Sec. 1245 gain to the extent of depreciation taken; Code Sec. 1231 gain for the remainder of the gain;

- Building—Code Sec. 1231 gain (assuming straight-line depreciation);

- Land—Code Sec. 1231 gain;

- Goodwill—Capital gain.

Consistent with the fact that the entity is disregarded for tax purposes, a sole proprietor's business must be on the same tax year as the sole proprietor is for his or her other activities. Generally, this would be the calendar year.

In other instances however, something similar to the entity concept applies. A sole proprietor may use a different accounting method for his or her business than he or she uses for other activities. If inventory is material to the business, the accrual method must be used for such business.[1] However, small businesses with $1,000,000 or less in gross receipts are allowed to use the cash method of accounting. See ¶ 507 for details. If a taxpayer is engaged in more than one business, he or she may use different

---

[1] Reg. §§ 1.446-1(a)(4)(i) and 1.446-1(c)(2)(i).

accounting methods for each business (subject to the requirement that income must be clearly reflected). Also, a taxpayer is not required to use the same method to report his or her nonbusiness income as the method used for business income.[2]

¶ 103   Computation of the Self-Employment Tax

Net income from a sole proprietorship or single person LLP is subject to self-employment tax. The self-employment tax is based on the net income from the business.[3] However, if gross income from the business is $2,400 or less, the sole proprietor may instead (for Social Security and Medicare purposes only) base his or her tax on two-thirds of his or her gross income.[4]

>   **Example 1-1.** Sue Hanratty had gross income from her business of $1,800 and net income of only $500. She may base her self-employment tax on either $500 or $1,200.

If the businessperson has net earnings of less than $2,400, but gross income of more than $2,400, he or she may use as self-employment income the greater of $1,600 or the net income.[5]

>   **Example 1-2.** Edward Tate had gross income from his business of $9,500, but net earnings of only $1,100. He may use either $1,100 or $1,600 as his self-employment income.

The combined Social Security and Medicare rate for the year 2001 is 15.3 percent. However the Social Security rate of 12.9 percent is levied only on the first $80,400 of net income in 2001. The Medicare rate of 2.9 percent is levied on the entire net income. However, in computing both the self-employment tax and taxable income, the self-employed taxpayer may deduct one-half of the Social Security taxes.

>   **Example 1-3.** Fredrica Smith has self-employment income of $61,000 in the year 2001. For Smith, self-employment income subject to the self-employment tax is $61,000 × .9235 = $56,334. The tax is $56,334 × .153 = $8,619. One-half of the tax, or $4,310, is deducted for adjusted gross income.

>   **Example 1-4.** Harry Jones had self-employment income of $100,000 in the year 2001. For Jones, self-employment income subject to the self-employment tax is the lesser of $80,400, or $100,000 × .9235 = $92,350. The tax is computed as follows:

$$\begin{array}{rcl} \$80,400 \times .153 & = & \$12,301 \\ (\$92,350 - 80,400) \times .029 & = & \underline{347} \\ & & \\ \text{Total} & & \$12,648 \end{array}$$

---

[2] Reg. § 1.446-1(c)(1)(iv)(b).
[3] Code Sec. 1402(b)(2).
[4] Code Sec. 1402(a)(15)(i).
[5] Code Sec. 1402(a)(15)(ii).

¶ 105   Self-Employment Income Defined

Self-employment income is defined as the net earnings from any trade or business, including a partner's distributive share (whether or not distributed) of income or loss from a partnership.[6] However, excluded from the definition are:[7]

1. Rentals from realty and personalty unless the landlord materially participates,

2. Dividends and interest,

3. Capital gains and losses and involuntary conversions (if the converted property is not held for resale),

4. The deduction for net-operating losses is not allowed (cannot reduce self-employment income),

5. The deduction for personal exemptions is not allowed,

6. The exclusions for income from U.S. possessions under Code Sec. 931 and the exclusion for foreign-earned income under Code Sec. 911 are not allowed,

7. The distributive share of partnership income to a limited partner is excluded except to the extent it represents guaranteed payments for services.

¶ 107   Net Operating Losses Resulting from a Sole Proprietorship

The starting point in computing a net operating loss (NOL) is taxable income (in this case a loss) on line 39, Form 1040. Several additions must be made to the taxable loss (resulting in a reduced NOL). These are:[8]

•   No net operating loss deduction is allowed (this would be from a carryback or carryover from another tax year).

•   Nonbusiness capital losses may not exceed capital gains. The Code Sec. 1202 exclusion for gain on certain small business stock is not allowed for this purpose.

•   Nonbusiness deductions may be deducted only to the extent of nonbusiness income and net nonbusiness capital gains. Nonbusiness income consists of interest, dividends, annuities, and certain royalties. However, wages and rental income are considered business income for this purpose. Nonbusiness deductions consist of all deductions not attributable to or derived from a trade or business except personal casualty and theft losses. In the

---

[6] Code Sec. 1402(a).
[7] Code Sec. 1402(a)(1)–(15).

[8] Code Sec. 172(d); Reg. § 1.172-3(a).

event that the standard deduction is taken, it is treated as a nonbusiness deduction.

- Business capital losses are allowed only up to the sum of business capital gains and any excess of nonbusiness income and net nonbusiness capital gains over nonbusiness deductions.

- No deduction is allowed for personal or dependency exemptions.

Example 1-5. Roger Workers had a taxable loss as follows in the year 2000:

Salary	$19,000	
Loss from Schedule C	(40,000)	
Net long-term capital gain from the sale of business property	3,000	
Interest income		1,700
Exemptions (4)		(11,200)
Standard deduction (joint return)		(7,350)
Taxable income		($34,850)

His net operating loss for the year 2000 is as follows:	
Taxable income	($34,850)
Add:	
Exemptions	11,200
Excess of nonbusiness deductions over nonbusiness income ($7,350 − $1,700)	5,650
Net operating loss	($18,000)

Once a net operating loss is determined, it may be carried back two years to offset income, or, if not used in the two carryback years, forward as far as 20 years.[9] An election can be made to skip the carryback years and instead carry the loss forward.[10] In Example 1-5, absent an election, Workers would carry the loss back first to 1998, then 1999, or forward to 2001 and beyond.

The net operating loss deduction is treated as a deduction to arrive at adjusted gross income (AGI) in a carryback year. Since it reduces adjusted gross income, all deductions based on AGI except for the contributions deduction must be recomputed in a carryback year. For example, the medical expense deduction and casualty losses are increased due to the lowered AGI.

If the loss is not entirely used up in the carryback year, the carryover to the next year must be computed. In determining the carryover, the

[9] Code Sec. 172(b)(1)(A).   [10] Code Sec. 172(b)(3).

following adjustments must be made to the taxable income of the year in which the loss is taken:[11]

- Personal exemptions are added back.

- Any net capital losses must be added back.

- Except for charitable contributions, an adjustment for deductions, the computation of which is dependent on AGI, must be made. The procedure is to add back to original AGI the net operating loss, compute the deductions based on that AGI, and then deduct the amounts deducted once the carryback is applied.

Example 1-6. Assume that the net operating loss is as determined in Example 1-5 ($18,000). Assume that, in 1998, Worker's taxable income was as follows:

Business income (from Schedule C)			$ 25,400
Capital losses			(400)
Adjusted gross income			$ 25,000
Less: medical expenses	$2,275		
Less: 7.5% of AGI	1,875	$ 400	
Contributions		1,600	
Taxes and interest		8,200	(10,200)
Exemptions (4)			(10,800)
Taxable income			$ 4,000

Since the carryback exceeds the taxable income, it is obvious that the income of the carryback year will be fully absorbed. On the net operating loss carryback form (Form 1045), the recomputed income for 1998 would be less than zero, and all of the total tax for 1998 would be refundable.

The taxable income *after* the carryback would be as follows:

AGI		$ 25,000
Less: net operating loss		18,000
Redetermined AGI		$ 7,000
Less: medical [$2,275 − ($7,000 × .075)]	$1,750	
Contributions	1,600	
Taxes and interest	8,200	(11,550)
Exemptions (4)		(10,800)
Recomputed taxable income		($15,350)

---

[11] Code Sec. 172(b)(2).

However, as previously mentioned, another issue concerns the portion of the original $18,000 NOL that can be carried to another tax year (1999 in this example). The three adjustments previously mentioned must be taken into account, and the taxable income modified by these adjustments must be computed. Computation of the carry-over to 1999 would be as follows:

Recomputed taxable income		($15,350)
Exemptions		10,800
Net capital loss		400
Adjustment for medical expenses		
$2,275 − [.075 ($25,000 + $400)]	$ 370	
Less: medical expenses included in recomputed taxable income	(1,750)	1,380
Net operating loss carried to 1999		$ 2,770

Although net operating loss carrybacks can be obtained by filing an amended return (Form 1040X), the process is expedited if Form 1045, Application for Tentative Refund, is filed.

Tax Tips and Pitfalls

Often it is impossible to avoid a net operating loss. If possible, however, a net operating loss should be avoided, due to the large loss of deductions. The taxpayer's personal exemptions are always lost, as is any net capital loss deduction. Also, the excess of nonbusiness expenses over nonbusiness income is lost. Hence, it is advisable to accelerate the collection of income and/or to defer the payment of expenses if by doing so a NOL can be avoided. If a net operating loss is inevitable for a given year, there are some useful strategies to be undertaken. Capital losses should not be created and neither should long-term capital gains. Since nonbusiness deductions in excess of nonbusiness income are lost, it is best to defer contributions and medical expenses into the next year. If the taxpayer already has incurred substantial nonbusiness deductions, he or she should consider increasing nonbusiness income if possible. For example, Series EE bonds could be cashed in.

Chapter 2

Partnerships

¶ 201   Partnership Defined

A partnership is an association of two or more persons formed to conduct a business for profit as co-owners.[1] The operation of partnerships is governed by the partnership agreement, and, in most states, by the Uniform Partnership Act.

The Internal Revenue Code ("Code") defines partnerships in a fairly broad context, stating that "the term 'partnership' includes a syndicate, group, pool, joint venture or other unincorporated organization through or by means of which any business, financial operation, or venture is carried on and which is not . . . a corporation or a trust or estate."[2] The intent to carry on a business is critical to the existence of a partnership for tax purposes. For example, the regulations state that a joint undertaking merely to share expenses does not constitute a partnership; neither does mere co-ownership of property unless the co-owners actively carry on a trade or business.[3]

.01   *Exclusion from Partnership Status*

Code Sec. 761(a) permits unincorporated organizations to elect exclusion from partnership status provided that the organization is formed:[4]

- For investment purposes only and not for the active conduct of a trade or business, or

- For the joint production, extraction, or use of property, but not for the purpose of selling services or property produced or extracted.

The members must be able to compute their income without the necessity of computing partnership taxable income.[5]

¶ 203   Characteristics of Partnerships

The partnership form of organization has certain features not present in other entities, although some characteristics are common to other entities.

---

[1] Sec. 101(6), Revised Uniform Partnership Act (1997).

[2] Code Sec. 761(a).

[3] Reg. § 301.7701-1(a)(2).

[4] Reg. § 1.761-2(a).

[5] Code Sec. 761(a); Reg. § 1.761-2.

- *Limited life.* The life of a partnership may be terminated by the withdrawal of a partner; the bankruptcy, death, or retirement of a partner; or even the mental or physical incapacity of a partner. The admission of a new partner also formally dissolves a partnership. A distinction should be made between the *dissolution* and the *liquidation* of a partnership. For example, the death of a partner or admission of a new partner may dissolve the partnership, but will not necessarily *liquidate* the partnership, since the business may continue with a new partnership arrangement. The actual liquidation of a partnership entails converting the assets to cash, paying the debts, and distributing the remaining cash to the owners.

- *Unlimited liability.* If the partnership is a *general partnership*, each partner is personally liable for the liabilities of the partnership. If the assets of the partnership are not sufficient to pay the debts, creditors can take the individual assets of the partner. In a *limited partnership*, while at least one partner must be a general partner (with an unlimited liability), other partners may be designated as limited partners. Their liability cannot exceed the amount that they contributed to the partnership.

- *Mutual agency.* Every partner is an agent of the partnership, so long as the activity falls within the normal scope of business of the partnership. If the partner is dishonest or negligent, this feature can be a severe drawback.

- *Ease of formation.* The formation of a corporation constitutes a formal process; in contrast, it is very easy to form a partnership. All that is really required is an agreement, oral or written, between two or more persons. However, a written agreement can eliminate much misunderstanding.

- *Conduit rule of taxation.* A partnership is not an income tax paying entity.[6] Instead, the partnership is a conduit for the partners; i.e., the income is passed through to the partners, who include the income on their individual income tax returns.

.01 General vs. Limited Partnerships

It is often useful to organize limited partnerships. Whereas a general partnership has only general partners, a limited partnership has at least one general partner and at least one limited partner. General partners are subject to unlimited liability for partnership debt, participate in the management of the partnership, and are subject to self-employment taxes

---

[6] A few states levy a state income tax on partnerships.

on partnership earnings. Limited partners, however, are subject to liability only up to the amount that they contribute to the partnership, do not participate in the management of the partnership, and their share of the partnership profits is not subject to self-employment tax.

¶ 205   Formation of a Partnership

Two important issues connected with the formation of a partnership are the partnership agreement and the tax implications of the contribution of assets to the partnership.

.01   The Partnership Agreement

Although an oral partnership is binding, the partnership agreement should be in writing. Ideally, an attorney should draft the agreement. Typical features of a partnership agreement are as follows:

- Name and address of the partnership and each partner;

- Nature of the business;

- Starting date of the partnership, length of time of the partnership (if not indefinite), and accounting year of the partnership;

- Provisions for allocations of profits and losses, salary allowances to partners, and withdrawals by partners;

- Amounts and types of assets to be contributed by each partner and valuation methods to be used on noncash assets;

- Duties, rights, and authority granted to each partner and indication of time devoted to business by each partner;

- Provisions for the retirement or withdrawal of an existing partner and provisions for the admission of new partners;

- Provisions for an annual audit (especially important if there are inactive partners);

- Provisions for continuing the business in the event of death of a partner, including life insurance policies on the partners and buy-back agreements from the estate of the deceased;

- Disclosure of important tax and accounting policies to be followed; and

- Provision for resolving disputes.

.02 Tax Implications of the Contribution of Assets

Generally, no gain or loss is recognized to a partnership or any of its partners when property is exchanged for an interest in a partnership.[7] The capital interest must be in exchange for property; if services are exchanged for a partnership capital interest, the exchange is taxable to the person performing the services. It is reported as compensation for services.[8]

What if the transferor of services receives a partnership profits interest, but not a capital interest? Generally, the receipt of a profits interest is not a taxable event. However, the receipt of a profits interest may be taxable if:[9]

- The profits interest relates to a substantially certain and predictable stream of income from partnership assets, such as income from high-quality debt securities or a high-quality net lease;

- The partner disposes of the profits interest within two years of its receipt; or

- The profits interest is a limited partnership interest in a publicly traded partnership under Code Sec. 7704.

The determination of whether an interest granted to a service provider is a profits interest is tested at the time the interest is granted, even if at that time the interest is substantially nonvested, if two conditions are met:[10]

1. The partnership and the service provider must treat the service provider as the owner of the partnership interest from the date of its grant, and the service provider must take into account the distributive share of partnership income, gain, loss, deduction, and credit associated with that interest in computing the service provider's income tax liability for the entire period during which the service provider has the interest.

2. Upon the grant of the interest or at the time that the interest becomes substantially vested, neither the *partnership* nor any of the partners may deduct any amount (as wages, compensation, or otherwise) for the fair market value of the interest.

In a case decided by the Tax Court, a general partner received a one percent capital interest in a partnership determined to be worth in excess of $80,000 in exchange for services provided to the partnership. The capital interest was required to be included in taxable income. The partnership

---

[7] Code Sec. 721(a).
[8] Reg. § 1.721-1(b)(1).

[9] Rev. Proc. 93-27, 1993-2 CB 343.
[10] Rev. Proc. 2001-43, 2001-34 IRB 191.

interest was valued at the time that it was transferred. Although the taxpayer was obligated to perform some minimal services after the transfer, the Tax Court ruled that the transfer was not conditioned on performance of those future services.[11]

If the partner receives money or other consideration, the transfer becomes taxable.[12] Also, if the partner transfers property subject to a liability in excess of the basis, gain is recognized to the extent that the portion of the liability assumed by the noncontributing partner exceeds the basis of the contributing partner.

> **Example 2-1.** In exchange for a one-third interest in the partnership, Allen Shultz contributed land worth $60,000, but subject to a mortgage of $30,000, which the partnership assumed. Shultz's basis in the land was $16,000. Shultz is relieved of the responsibility of $20,000 of the mortgage ($30,000 × 2/3). He has a taxable gain of $4,000 ($20,000 − 16,000).[13]

.03 Disguised Sale Rules—Partner and Partnership Transactions

Contributions to partnerships by a partner are generally nontaxable under Code Sec. 721. Nonliquidating distributions from a partnership to a partner are also generally nontaxable to the extent of the partner's basis in the partnership interest. Thus, there is an incentive for a partner to contribute property to a partnership and soon after receive a partnership distribution.

Under Code Sec. 707(a), such a transaction can be categorized as a disguised sale. Regulations issued in September 1992 address disguised sales.

The regulations require two conditions to be met before a transfer of property to a partnership followed by a partnership distribution is treated as a sale of property in whole or in part:[14]

- The transfer of money or other consideration by the partnership to the partner would not have been made except for the transfer of property, and

- If the transfers are not made simultaneously, the subsequent transfer is not dependent on the entrepreneurial risk of partnership operations.

Facts and Circumstances Indicating a Sale

The regulations list 10 factors that may tend to show the existence of a sale:[15]

---

[11] *R. Johnston v. Commr.*, 69 TCM 2283, Dec. 50,558(M), TC Memo. 1995-140.
[12] Reg. § 1.721-1(a).
[13] Reg. § 1.752-1(c).
[14] Reg. § 1.707-3(b)(1).
[15] Reg. § 1.707-3(b)(2).

1. The timing and amount of a partnership distribution to a partner are determinable with reasonable certainty at the time of the original partner contribution to the partnership.

2. The transferor has a legally enforceable right to the subsequent distribution.

3. The partner's right to receive the distribution is secured in any manner, taking into account the period during which it is secured.

4. Any person has made or is legally obligated to make contributions to the partnership so as to permit the partnership to make the distribution to the partner.

5. Any person has loaned or has agreed to loan the partnership the money or other consideration required to enable the partnership to make the distribution, taking into account whether any such lending obligation is subject to contingencies related to the results of partnership operations.

6. The partnership has incurred or is obligated to incur debt necessary to permit it to make the distribution, taking into account the likelihood that the partnership will be able to incur that debt (considering such factors as whether any person has agreed to guarantee the debt).

7. The partnership has sufficient money or other liquid assets, in excess of the reasonable needs of the business, that are expected to be available to make the transfer (taking into account the income that will be earned from the assets).

8. Partnership distributions, allocations, or control of partnership operations is designed to effect an exchange of the burdens and benefits of ownership of the property.

9. The distribution to the partner is disproportionately large in relationship to the partner's general and continuing interest in partnership profits.

10. The partner has no obligation to return or repay the distribution, or has such an obligation but it is likely to become due at such a distant future date that the present value of the obligation is small in relation to the distribution.

The regulations contain a two-year presumptive rule. If a distribution occurs within two years of the contribution of property, the transfer is presumed to be a sale unless the facts and circumstances clearly indicate that the transfer was not a sale.[16] On the other hand, if a distribution to a partner and a contribution by the partner are more than two years apart, the transfer is presumed *not* to be a sale unless the facts and circumstances clearly establish that the transfer was a sale.[17]

Guaranteed Payments and Preferred Returns

The regulations provide that "reasonable" guaranteed payments for capital or preferred returns paid within two years are not treated as part of the sale of property to the partnership (i.e., they will not create a disguised sale).[18] Guaranteed payments for capital are payments for the use of capital that are not based on partnership income. Preferred returns are preferential distributions of partnership cash flow with respect to capital contributed that will be matched, to the extent available, by an allocation of income or gain. The "reasonable" requirement is met if the sum of any preferred return and any guaranteed payment for capital payable for that year does not exceed an amount determined by multiplying either the partner's unreturned capital at the beginning of the year or, at the partner's option, the partner's weighted average capital balance for the year by the safe harbor interest rate for the year.[19]

The safe harbor rate for a taxable year is 150 percent of the highest applicable federal rate, at the appropriate compounding period(s), in effect at any time from the time that the right to the return on capital is first established pursuant to a binding, written agreement among the partners through the end of the partnership tax year.[20]

Operating Cash Flow

The regulations permit distributions of "operating cash flow" without creating a disguised sale of contributions of partnership property. "Operating cash flow" for this purpose equals taxable income or loss from partnership activities increased by tax-exempt interest, depreciation, amortization, and cost recovery allowances and decreased by debt payments, property replacement or contingency reserves actually established by the partnership, capital expenditures when made other than from reserves or from borrowings the proceeds of which are not included in operating cash flow, and any other cash expenditures not deducted in determining such taxable income or loss.[21]

Liabilities Transferred

Liabilities transferred by a partner may be treated as consideration given by the partnership (and thus part of a disguised sale). If the debt transfer is treated as consideration, the amount of the consideration is the excess of the liability over the partner's share of the liability immediately

---

[16] Reg. § 1.707-3(c).
[17] Reg. § 1.707-3(d).
[18] Reg. § 1.707-4(a).

[19] Reg. § 1.707-4(a)(3).
[20] *Id.*
[21] Reg. § 1.707-4(b).

after the transfer. If the debt is recourse debt, the partner's share of the debt is determined under Code Sec. 752 and the corresponding regulations.[22] If the debt is nonrecourse debt, the partner's share is determined by applying the same percentage used to determine the partner's share of the excess nonrecourse debt under Reg. § 1.752-3(a)(3).[23] The regulations distinguish between "qualified" and "nonqualified" liability.

If a transfer of property by a partner to a partnership is not otherwise treated as part of a sale, the partnership's assumption of or taking subject to a qualified liability is not treated as part of a sale. However, if a transfer of property by a partner to the partnership is treated as part of a sale without regard to the partnership's assumption of or taking subject to a qualified liability, the partnership will be treated as transferring consideration pursuant to a sale equal to the lesser of the amount of consideration that the partnership would be treated as transferring to the partner if the liability were not a qualified liability or the amount of the qualified liability multiplied by the partner's net equity percentage with respect to that property. If a partnership assumes or takes property subject to a nonqualified liability, the partnership will be treated as transferring consideration to the extent that the liability transferred exceeds the partner's share of that liability.[24] "Qualified liability" is a liability assumed or taken subject to by a partnership in connection with a transfer of property to a partnership by a partner to the extent that the liability:[25]

- Is a liability that was incurred by the partner more than two years prior to the earlier of the date that the partner agrees in writing to transfer the property or the date that the partner transfers the property to the partnership and that has encumbered the transferred property throughout the two-year period;

- Is a liability that was incurred in anticipation of the transfer of the property to a partnership, but that was incurred by the partner within the two-year period prior to the earlier of the date the partner agrees in writing to transfer the property or the date the partner transfers the property to the partnership and that has encumbered the transferred property since it was incurred;

- Is a liability that is allocable under the rules of Reg. § 1.163-8T to capital expenditures with respect to the property; or

- Is a liability that was incurred in the ordinary course of the business in which the property transferred to the partnership was used or held, but only if all of the assets related to that

---

[22] Reg. § 1.707-5(a)(2).
[23] *Id.*

[24] Reg. § 1.707-5(a).
[25] Reg. § 1.707-5(a)(6).

business are transferred other than assets that are not material to a continuation of the business.

If the debt is a recourse liability, only the amount of the liability that does not exceed the fair market value of the transferred property is counted as qualified liability. A liability incurred within two years of the transfer of property is presumed to be in anticipation of the transfer unless the facts and circumstances clearly indicate to the contrary.[26]

Basis of the Contributing Partner's Interest

Basis of the partner's interest in the partnership is essentially a carryover basis, i.e., it is equal to the sum of the money contributed, the adjusted basis of property contributed, and any gain recognized to the contributing partner.[27]

Example 2-2. Joe and Roger Anderson are investing the following items to form a partnership:

	Contributed by Joe		Contributed by Roger	
	Basis to Joe	Fair Market Value	Basis to Roger	Fair Market Value
Cash	10,000	10,000	35,000	35,000
Machinery and equipment	—	—	30,000	45,000
Buildings	—	—	20,000	20,000
Land	140,000	100,000	—	—
Mortgage on land . . .	30,000	30,000		
	120,000	80,000	85,000	100,000

The basis of Roger's partnership interest consists of the $35,000 cash contributed, the $50,000 basis of other assets, and his $15,000 share of the mortgage, or a total of $100,000. The basis to Joe is the $10,000 of cash plus the $140,000 basis of the land, reduced by the $30,000 mortgage, but increased by his $15,000 share of the mortgage. Thus, his total basis is $135,000.

¶ 207   Contributions of Property to a Partnership[28]

In recent years Congress has made three changes to Code Sec. 704(c), which deals with allocation of gains, losses, and write-offs of assets contributed by a partner to a partnership. The most important change was made in 1984. Prior to then, allocations among partners, unless the partnership provided otherwise, were made as if the partnership had purchased the

---

[26] Reg. § 1.707-5(a)(7).
[27] Code Sec. 722.
[28] Adapted from: Gary L. Maydew, "New Rules for Partnership Allocations," *Taxation for Accountants*, Vol. 52, No. 5, May 1993.

property. If the partnership agreement so provided, the various allocations could be shared among partners so as to take into account the variation between the basis of the property and the fair market value at contribution.[29] The Tax Reform Act of 1984 (P.L. 98-369) made a major change in this rule, *requiring* that income, gain, loss, and deductions with respect to property contributed to the partnership by a partner be shared among the partners so as to take account of the variation between the basis of the property to the partnership and its fair market value at the time of contribution.[30] The Code also provided that similar rules be applied to determine the deduction for zero basis payables and other accrued but unpaid items contributed to a partnership by cash basis partners.[31] Congress felt that the failure to take into account the variation between basis and fair market value would result in a shifting of income or losses among partners that would not reflect the economic burdens borne.[32] The bottom line was that Congress was concerned that the artificial shifting of tax consequences between partners was occurring, to the detriment of Treasury revenues.[33] The intent of Congress was to leave considerable latitude to the Secretary in developing regulations covering the law. Congress was concerned that the rules might turn out to be overly complex with respect to allocation of depreciation and depletion; hence, the Secretary was provided with suggestions for ways in which flexibility could be maintained, especially for small partnerships. Specifically, the Senate Finance Committee suggested that:

1.   Aggregation of appreciated properties contributed by a single partner and aggregation of depreciated properties contributed by a single partner be permitted;

2.   Differences between fair market value and basis of less than the lesser of 15 percent and $10,000 be permitted to be accounted for under prior law; and

3.   Differences between fair market value and basis to be eliminated more slowly than required by the new rules through allocation solely of gain or loss on the disposition of such properties (without requiring special allocations of depreciation or depletion).[34]

The Revenue Reconciliation Act of 1989 (P.L. 101-239) amended Code Sec. 704(c), applicable to distributions of property, to read that if any property so contributed is distributed (directly or indirectly by the partner-

---

[29] Code Sec. 704(c) (prior to amendment by the Tax Reform Act of 1984).

[30] Act Sec. 71(a), Tax Reform Act of 1984, amending Code Sec. 704(c).

[31] *Id.*

[32] Committee on Ways and Means, Report, P.L. 98-432, part 2, March 5, 1984, p. 1209.

[33] *Id.*

[34] Senate Finance Report, P.L. 98-169, April 2, 1984, p. 231.

ship (other than to the contributing partner) within five years of being contributed—

i.   The contributing partner shall be treated as recognizing gain or loss (as the case may be) from the sale of such property in an amount equal to the gain or loss which would have been allocated to such partner under Code Sec. 704(c)(1)(A) by reason of the variation described in subparagraph (A) if the property had been sold at its fair market value at the time of the distribution,

ii.   The character of such gain or loss shall be determined by reference to the character of the gain or loss which would have resulted if such property had been sold by the partnership to the distributee, and

iii.   Appropriate adjustments shall be made to the adjusted basis of the contributing partner's interest in the partnership and to the adjusted basis of the property distributed to reflect any gain or loss recognized under this subparagraph.[35]

The Energy Policy Act of 1992 (P.L. 102-486) amended the same subsection of the Code slightly to make clear that the distribution could be made directly or indirectly.[36]

The Taxpayer Relief Act of 1997 (P.L. 105-34) extended the period in which a partner recognizes precontribution gain with respect to property distributed by the partnership from five years to seven years.[37]

.01   *The Regulations*

The regulations attempt to provide guidance to implement the purpose of Code Sec. 704(c) by preventing the shifting of tax consequences among partners with respect to built-in gain or loss. The regulations allow different methods to be used for different items of contributed property so long as the overall combination of methods is reasonable.

.02   *Covered Property*

Code Sec. 704(c) property is the excess of the partnership's "book value" over the partner's adjusted basis at the time of contribution. "Book value" is fair market value at the time of contribution and is subsequently adjusted for cost recovery and other events that affect the basis of the property.[38]

"Built-in gain or loss" is the difference between the property's book value and the partner's tax basis at the time of contribution. The built-in

---

[35] Act Sec. 7642(a), Revenue Reconciliation Act of 1989, amending Code Sec. 704(c).
[36] Act Sec. 1937(b)(1), Energy Policy Act of 1992, amending Code Sec. 704(c)(1)(B).

[37] Act Sec. 1063, Taxpayer Relief Act of 1997, amending Code Secs. 704(c)(1)(B) and 737(b)(1).

[38] Reg. § 1.704-3(a)(3)(i).

gain or loss is thereafter reduced by any decrease in the difference between book value and the partner's tax basis (e.g., depreciation).[39]

Accounts payable and other accrued items of a partner who was using the cash basis method of accounting are Code Sec. 704(c) property for allocation purposes.[40] These regulations apply only if the transaction is governed by Code Sec. 721; i.e., to the extent that a transfer to a partnership is treated as a sale under Code Sec. 707, Code Sec. 704(c) does not apply.[41]

.03 Revaluations

Ongoing partnerships may revalue their assets in connection with such events as the contribution of money or property to a partnership or a distribution of money or property to a partner, using the principles of Code Sec. 704(c).[42] Partnerships, however, are not required to use the same allocation method for these revaluations as for Code Sec. 704(c) property, although the method must be reasonable and consistent with the purposes of Code Sec. 704(b) and (c).[43] Basic adjustments made by partnerships under the Code Sec. 743 election or under Code Sec. 751 (a sale or liquidation of the partner's Code Sec. 751 property) must also be made under the principles of Code Sec. 704(c).[44]

Allocations are also required under Code Sec. 704(c) for the following transactions:[45]

- The transfer of a partnership interest by a contributing partner. In that event, the transferee partner steps into the shoes of the transferor.

- The disposition of Code Sec. 704(c) property by a partnership in a nonrecognition transaction (e.g., a nontaxable exchange). In that case, the substituted basis takes up the built-in gain or loss.

- The contribution of Code Sec. 704(c) property to a second partnership by a partner, or the contribution of a partnership interest to a second partnership by a partner who has contributed Code Sec. 704(c) property to the first partnership. The upper-tier partnership must allocate its distributive share of lower-tier partnership items with respect to that Code Sec. 704(c) property in a manner that takes into account the contributing partners' remaining built-in gain or loss.

---

[39] Reg. § 1.704-3(a)(3)(ii).
[40] Reg. § 1.704-3(a)(4).
[41] Reg. § 1.704-3(a)(5).
[42] Reg. § 1.704-1(b)(2)(iv)(f).

[43] Reg. § 1.704-3(a)(6).
[44] *Id.*
[45] Reg. § 1.704-3(a)(7), (8), and (9).

.04 Anti-Abuse Rule

Finally, the regulations contain an anti-abuse rule, stating that an allocation is not reasonable if the contribution of property and allocations are made with a view to shifting the tax consequences of built-in gain or loss among the partners in a manner that substantially reduces the present value of the partners' aggregate tax liabilities.[46]

¶ 209   Allocation Methods

The regulations contain a description of three methods considered reasonable: the traditional method, the traditional method with curative allocations, and the remedial allocation method. Only the first two are discussed here.

.01 Traditional Method

The traditional method has three essential requirements:[47]

1. Upon the taxable disposition of Code Sec. 704(c) property, any built-in gain or loss must be allocated to the contributing partner.

2. For Code Sec. 704(c) property that is subject to cost recovery (i.e., depreciation, depletion, or amortization), deductions attributable to such items must be allocated to take into account any built-in gain or loss. Generally, the allocations to the noncontributing partners must be based on book value (i.e., the fair market value at time of contribution).

3. The total allocations cannot exceed the "ceiling," i.e., the total deduction based on the partnership's tax basis.

Example 2-3. Brown, Smith, and Williams form an equal partnership. Brown and Smith each contribute $12,000 cash and Williams contributes equipment having a fair market value of $12,000, but with a tax basis of only $7,000. Assume a five-year life and straight-line depreciation. Generally, Brown and Smith would be entitled to annual depreciation of $800 each ($12,000/3/5); however, the total depreciation cannot exceed the ceiling of $1,400 ($7,000/5). Accordingly, Brown and Smith each are allocated $700 of depreciation and Williams is not allocated any depreciation. Williams has an original built-in gain of $5,000 ($12,000 − $7,000). The adjusted book value for the partnership at the end of the first year is $9,600 ($12,000 − book depreciation of $2,400). The tax basis of the asset at the end of the first year is $5,600. Williams has a built-in gain at the end of the first year of $4,000 ($9,600 − $5,600). The partnership sells the property

---

[46] Reg. § 1.704-3(a)(10).   [47] Reg. § 1.704-3(b)(1).

at the start of the second year for $9,000. Because the total gain of $3,400 ($9,000 − $5,600) is less than Williams's remaining built-in gain of $4,000, all of the $3,400 gain must be allocated to Williams.

Example 2-4. Assume the same facts as in Example 2-3 except that at the start of the second year the property is sold for $11,100. Of the gain of $5,500 ($11,100 − $5,600), $4,000 is built-in gain and is allocated solely to Williams. The remaining $1,500 of gain is allocated equally between the three partners.

.02 Traditional Method with Curative Allocations

A curative allocation is an allocation for tax purposes that differs from the allocation of the item as reflected on the books of the partnership. A partnership may limit its curative allocations to one or more particular tax items even if the allocation of those available items does not offset fully the effect of the ceiling. The regulations allow reasonable curative allocations to reduce or eliminate disparities between partners. The purpose of these allocations is to correct distortions created by the ceiling rule.[48]

Curative allocations must be consistently applied from year to year.[49] Further, the curative allocation must be reasonable in amount, timing, and type.[50]

Example 2-5. Assume the same facts as in Example 2-3 and that the partnership has gross sales of $4,200 and no expenses except depreciation. To make up for the effect of the ceiling, a curative allocation (for tax purposes only) of an extra $200 of sales could be made to Williams. If this were done, the effect on both tax and book capital at the end of the first year would be:

	Brown		Smith		Williams	
	Tax	Book	Tax	Book	Tax	Book
Original basis ..	$12,000	$12,000	$12,000	$12,000	$ 7,000	$12,000
Sales	1,300	1,400	1,300	1,400	1,600	1,400
Depreciation ...	− 700	− 800	− 700	− 800	-0-	− 800
End of yr. 1	12,600	12,600	12,600	12,600	8,600	12,600

Without the curative allocation of sales, the ending tax capital accounts would have been $12,700, $12,700, and $8,400 respectively. Thus, the curative allocation reduced the difference between the partners' tax and book capital balances. Assuming that sales income remained constant for the next four years, by the end of the fifth year, their tax capital accounts would all have equal balances of $15,000.

An allocation in excess of the amount needed to correct the disparity caused by the ceiling is an unreasonable curative allocation. For example,

---

[48] Reg. § 1.704-3(c)(1).
[49] Reg. § 1.704-3(c)(2).

[50] Reg. § 1.704-3(c)(3).

assume the same facts as in Example 2-5 except that a curative allocation of an extra $1,000 of sales is allocated to Williams. Because the curative allocation is in excess of the $200 needed to correct the disparity brought on by the ceiling, the allocation would be unreasonable and the IRS would adjust the allocation. Also, if in the previous examples, Williams contributed the equipment because he had unused net operating loss carryovers and could benefit from the extra sales income allocated, the allocation would be deemed by the IRS to be unreasonable because it "is used with a view to shifting a significant amount of partnership taxable income to a partner with a low marginal tax rate and away from a partner with a high marginal tax rate."[51] A better strategy in that event might be to *sell* the assets to the partnership and report the gain to offset the net operating losses.

.03 Exceptions and Special Rules

The IRS generally followed the intent of Congress with respect to small disparities. Generally if there is a "small disparity" the partnership may do any of the following:[52]

- Use a reasonable Code Sec. 704(c) method,

- Disregard the application of Code Sec. 704(c) to the property, or

- Defer the application of Code Sec. 704(c) (i.e., allocate gain or loss with respect to the property only upon the disposition of the property).

A disparity between book value and adjusted tax basis is a small disparity if the following two conditions are met:

1. The difference between book value of all properties contributed by one partner during the partnership tax year does not differ from the adjusted tax basis by more than 15 percent of the adjusted basis.

2. The total gross disparity does not exceed $20,000.

Example 2-6. Tamara Grant contributes property to the partnership with an adjusted basis of $30,000 and a fair market value of $45,500. In the same year, she contributes property with an adjusted basis of $60,000 and a fair market value of $53,000. Even though the difference between the adjusted basis and book value is not more than 15 percent ($8,500/90,000, or 9.4%), and the net difference between basis and fair market value is only $8,500, the gross disparity, as defined in the regulations, is $22,500 ($15,500 + $7,000). Hence, the

---

[51] Reg. § 1.704-3(c)(4), Example 3. [52] Reg. § 1.704-3(e)(1)(i).

allocations required by Code Sec. 704(c) and the regulations will be applicable.

The regulations permit aggregation of all property, other than real property, that is included in the general asset account. It also permits aggregation of zero basis nonrealty, inventory (provided that the specific identification costing method is not used), other types of property designated in guidance published in the Internal Revenue Bulletin, and other property as permitted by letter rulings.[53]

Tax Tips and Pitfalls

It is generally best to avoid contributing property that has a liability in excess of basis since a taxable gain may result. This trap is easy to fall into because the value of land and buildings often greatly exceeds the basis of the property. Paying down the mortgage to an amount below basis is often advisable. In the case of depreciable property, the gain could result in ordinary income, due to the depreciation recapture rules.[54]

¶ 211   Basis of Contributed Property to the Partnership

The general rule for determining the partnership's tax basis in contributed property (often called the inside basis) is incorporated in Code Sec. 723, which states that the basis to the partnership is the basis in the hands of the partner.[55] A limited exception to this rule exists for gain recognized on property contributions to a partnership which would be an investment company (under Code Sec. 351) if it were incorporated. Such gain would increase the basis of the property to the partnership.[56] Obviously, this exception does not apply to the formation of business partnerships. An application of the general rule follows.

In Example 2-2, although the machinery has a fair market value of $45,000 at the time the partnership is formed, the basis to the partnership is carried over from Roger (i.e., only $30,000).

When *personal use* property is contributed to a partnership, the basis to the partnership is the lesser of the basis to the partner or the fair market value at the time of contribution.[57]

Example 2-7. Bob Throckbottom contributed two assets to a partnership in exchange for a partnership interest. Both were held by him for personal use purposes. Results are as follows:

---

[53] Reg. § 1.704-3(e)(2), (4).

[54] See Chapter 9 for details.

[55] Code Sec. 723.

[56] Id.

[57] *Lawrence Y.S. Au v. Commr.*, 40 TC 264, Dec. 26,110, aff'd per curiam, CA-9, 64-1 USTC ¶ 9447, 330 F2d 1008.

	Basis to Throckbottom	FMV when Contributed	Basis to Partnership
Automobile	$12,000	$ 8,000	$ 8,000
Building	65,000	100,000	65,000

The basis to the partnership of *services* contributed to the partnership is the fair market value at the time of contribution (also the amount of income recognized to the contributor of the services). Depending on the nature of the services, they may be deductible as a business expense or may be capitalizable.

Example 2-8. The Adler-Baer partnership has $40,000 of assets which have a basis of $25,000. Campbell contributes legal services worth $4,000 in connection with a lawsuit in exchange for a 10 percent interest in the capital and profits. The partnership is considered to have sold assets with a basis of $2,500 for $4,000 and will have a recognized gain of $1,500. The partnership will also have a deduction for legal fees of $4,000.

.01 Holding Period and Characteristics of Gains/Losses

The holding period of the partnership for property contributed to it includes the period during which it was held by the partner.[58] This rule logically follows because the basis is also determined by reference to the partner's basis.

Generally, the *type* of gain or loss on the sale of partnership property is determined by the use to which the property is put by the partnership. However, to prevent abuse of this general rule (i.e., converting capital losses to ordinary losses and ordinary income to capital gains), Code Sec. 724 (applicable to property contributed to a partnership after March 31, 1984) requires three types of assets to retain the same characteristic as they had in the hands of the partner, *regardless* of the use to which they are put by the partnership. The three types of assets are:

1. Unrealized receivables (defined by Code Sec. 751(c) as ordinary income or loss to the partnership *whenever* sold or exchanged);[59]

2. Inventory (defined by Code Sec. 751(d)(2)), which is automatically classified as ordinary income or loss property for only the first five years after the contribution;[60] and

3. Capital loss property, the taint on which is also removed after five years.[61]

---

[58] Reg. § 1.723-1.
[59] Code Sec. 724(a).
[60] Code Sec. 724(b).
[61] Code Sec. 724(c).

Hence, if inventory and capital loss property are held by the partnership for more than five years, the use to which the partnership put the property would determine the type of gain or loss on sale.

> **Example 2-9.** The Block and Wasson partnership sold at a loss on June 7, 2001, land which was contributed by Block to the partnership on August 1, 1996. The land was a capital asset to Block, but was used by the partnership in its trade or business. The partnership *must* recognize a capital loss even though it was a Code Sec. 1231 asset in the hands of the partnership. Had the land been held until August 2, the loss would have been a Code Sec. 1231 loss.

¶ 213   Organization and Syndication Fees

Organization and syndication fees are not deductible, but instead must be capitalized.[62] Syndication fees may not be amortized; they are considered to be an asset possessing an indefinite life.[63] However, organization costs may, at the election of the partnership, be amortized over a period of time not less than 60 months, beginning with the month that the partnership begins business.[64] Syndication expenses are incurred in connection with the issuing and marketing of interests in the partnership and therefore include such items as brokerage, registration, legal, and accounting fees, as well as printing costs of the prospectus and other selling and promotional material.[65] Organization costs normally must be expected to benefit the partnership throughout its entire life. They include legal and accounting fees connected with organizing the partnership and filing fees.[66]

¶ 215   Depreciation Recapture

To the extent that the contribution by the partner is tax free under Code Sec. 721, there is no depreciation recapture at the time depreciable property is contributed to a partnership.[67] If the transfer is partly taxable (e.g., if liabilities in excess of basis are assumed), then depreciation recapture is recognized to the extent of the lesser of the gain recognized, or the depreciation recapture potential. The depreciation recapture potential is not forgiven, but merely shifts over to the partnership.[68]

Tax Tips and Pitfalls

Transfers of services in exchange for a partnership interest result in taxable income to both the partner providing the service and the existing partners (who are considered to have sold part of their interest). However, subjecting the capital interest to *restrictions* would bring the transfer under Code Sec. 83, and would avoid income recognition until the restrictions are lifted.

---

[62] Code Sec. 709(a).
[63] Reg. § 1.709-2(b).
[64] Code Sec. 709(b).
[65] Reg. § 1.709-2(b).

[66] Reg. § 1.709-2(a).
[67] Code Secs. 1245(b)(3) and 1250(d)(3).
[68] Reg. §§ 1.1245-2(c)(2) and 1.1250-3(c)(3).

A prospective partner holding appreciated property who expects a net operating loss for the year might prefer to sell the property to the partnership instead of contributing the property for an interest in the partnership. The realized gain may offset the net operating loss, and the partnership would have a higher tax basis in the asset than if contributed. (However, see a subsequent section of this chapter which discusses the tax status of sales between partners and partnerships.)

Transfers of partnership property which are subject to liabilities in excess of basis may require the contributing partner to recognize gain. Possible strategies to avoid or mitigate this outcome include: paying down the debt before contribution, leasing the property to the partnership instead of contributing it, or contributing other property instead.

¶ 217 Taxable Income of a Partnership and the Partners

For federal income tax purposes a partnership is not required to pay tax. Instead, the conduit rule applies, i.e., income flows through from the partnership to the individual partners. Generally, the income has the same characteristics in the hands of the partners as it had at the partnership level.

For information purposes, a partnership is required to file a return. From the perspective of the partner, the most important part of the partnership return is Schedule K-1, which tells the partner how much income he or she has and where on Form 1040 it should be reported. The partnership return (Form 1065) is due on the 15th day of the fourth month after the close of the partnership year. Thus, calendar year returns are due on April 15, although individual partners appreciate receiving a copy of the return earlier so that they may file their own returns.

Partnership income and expenses, depending on their nature, are either aggregated to form "net ordinary income" or are reported separately.

The following items are required to be reported separately from net ordinary income.[69]

---

[69] Code Sec. 702; Reg. § 1.702-1; 2000 Instructions, Form 1065.

	Item	Code Section Describing
1.	Net income (loss) from rental real estate activities	61(a)(5) and 469
2.	Gross income and expenses from other rental activities	61(a)(5) and 469
3.	Portfolio income	163 and 469(e)
	Interest income	61(a)(4) and 469(e)
	Dividend income	61(a)(7) and 469(e)
	Royalty income	61(a)(6) and 469(e)
	Short-term capital gains and losses	1222 and 469(e)
	Long-term capital gains and losses	1222 and 469(e)
	Other portfolio income	469(e)
4.	Section 1231 gains and losses	1231
5.	Charitable contributions	170
6.	Expense deduction for recovery property	179
7.	Deductions relating to portfolio income (not including investment interest)	163
8.	Interest expense on investment debts	163
9.	Taxes paid or accrued to a foreign country (partners may take a deduction for foreign taxes or may take them as a credit)	901
10.	Recoveries of bad debts, prior taxes, and delinquency amounts	111
11.	Gains and losses from wagering transactions	165
12.	Soil and water conservation expenditures	175
13.	Nonbusiness expenses	212
14.	Medical and dental expenses	213
15.	Alimony	215
16.	Amounts representing taxes and interest paid to cooperative housing corporations	216
17.	Intangible drilling and development costs	263
18.	Various exploration expenditures	616 and 617
19.	Income, gain, or loss to the partnership from a distribution of unrealized receivables	751
20.	Any items of income, gain, loss, deduction, or credit subject to a special allocation under the partnership agreement which differs from the allocation of partnership taxable income or loss generally.	

Partners are also required to take into account separately their distributive share of any partnership item, which if separately taken into account by any other partner, would result in an income tax liability for that partner different from that which would result if that partner did not take the item into account separately.[70] Because of this requirement, the various tax credits, i.e., credit for income tax withheld, the low income housing credit, qualified rehabilitation expenditures related to rental real estate, the work opportunity credit, credit for alcohol used as a fuel, the nonconventional source fuel credit, orphan drug credit, credit for increasing research activities, and the investment credit, all flow through to the partners. Tax preference items used to compute the alternate minimum tax for individuals are also passed through.[71]

If one is in doubt about whether to report an item of income, expense, or credit separately, a good decision rule is to determine whether the item would have some special characteristic in the hands of the partner. If the answer is yes, the item should generally be reported separately. For example, Code Sec. 1231 gains and losses have a special characteristic because the net gains may qualify for capital gain treatment. On the other hand, Code Sec. 1250 gains on property used in an active trade or business have no special characteristic; hence, they are included as part of ordinary income of an individual. Therefore, using this decision rule, one would expect to report Code Sec. 1231 gains and losses separately but include Code Sec. 1250 gains in the ordinary taxable income of a partnership.

In determining ordinary taxable income, the following deductions are not allowed:

- Personal exemptions;
- Foreign taxes;
- Charitable contributions;
- Net operating losses;
- Miscellaneous itemized deductions; and
- Depletion of oil and gas wells.[72]

The various revenue and expense items which make up net ordinary income or loss are all reported on page 1 of Form 1065. These items include revenue and expenses from farms and businesses, net ordinary income or loss from either partnerships or from fiduciaries, ordinary gains or losses from the sale of assets used in a trade or business, and other income or loss from business operations.[73] Note that neither passive income or loss nor portfolio income or loss is included in net ordinary income. However, interest on trade accounts or notes receivable is not considered portfolio income. Therefore, it *is* included in net ordinary income. Guaranteed payments to partners for such items as salaries and interest on capital are deducted to arrive at net ordinary income. Other commonly encountered

---

[70] Reg. § 1.702-1.
[71] See Chapter 3 for a discussion of the alternate minimum tax.

[72] Code Sec. 703.

[73] 2000 Instructions, Form 1065.

expenses include salaries and wages to employees, rent expense, interest expense incurred on trade or business activities, taxes, bad debts, repair and depreciation, depletion, retirement plans, employee benefit plans, and other deductions such as supplies, utilities, travel and entertainment, insurance, amortization, janitorial services and the like.[74]

Example 2-10. The Johnson-Lincoln partnership, sharing profits 50/50, reported the following information for the calendar year 2000:

Sales	$900,000
Cost of sales	670,000
Interest income	
Trade notes	7,500
Savings certificates	6,000
Gain on sale of machinery	9,000
Gain on sale of bonds	2,000
Guaranteed salary to Johnson	35,000
Guaranteed interest on capital	
Johnson	9,000
Lincoln	12,000
Contributions	1,500
Other expenses	86,000

Net ordinary income would be determined as follows:

Sales		$900,000
Cost of sales		670,000
Gross profit		230,000
Interest income		7,500
Form 4797 gains—depreciation recapture		9,000
Total income		$246,500
Guaranteed payments to partners	$ 56,000	
Other expenses	86,000	142,000
Net ordinary income		104,500

Separately Reported Items

Interest income—savings certificate	$ 6,000
Gain on sale of bonds	$ 2,000
Contributions	$ 1,500

Thus, Johnson would report on his Form Schedule E income from the partnership of $96,500 ($35,000 + $9,000 + $52,500). In addition, he would report $3,000 of interest income on Schedule B, $1,000 of capital gains on Schedule D, and $750 of contributions deduction on Schedule A.

---

[74] *Id.*

¶ 217

¶ 219 Self-Employment Income of a Partnership

Guaranteed payments to partners for services rendered, whether received by general or limited partners, will generally qualify as income from self-employment. The extent to which other income and deductions count as self-employment income depends on three factors:

1. Whether the partner is a general or a limited partner. A limited partner excludes from self-employment income everything *except* guaranteed payments for services rendered to the partnership.[75]

2. Whether the partnership is engaged in a trade or business. If the partnership is *not* involved in a trade or business (e.g., rents out a building as its only activity), again, only guaranteed payments to the partners qualify as self-employment income.[76]

3. Whether a particular item of income or deduction is related to income from a trade or business in which the partnership meets the standard of "material participation." Income derived by the owner or tenant of farm land in subject to the self-employment tax if the owner or tenant materially participates in the production or management of the production of agricultural or horticultural commodities.[77]

General partners in a partnership which is engaged in a trade or business add their share of net ordinary income to their guaranteed payments. Net losses from Form 4797 are added and net gains are deducted to get to self-employment income. Any passive income or loss or portfolio income should have previously been excluded from ordinary net income; if not, adjustments should be made to exclude these items from ordinary net income.

Example 2-11. Refer back to Example 2-10. Johnson's self-employment income is computed as follows:

Net ordinary income of partnership	$104,500
Less: Form 4797 gains	9,000
	95,500
Add: Guaranteed payments	56,000
Net earnings from self-employment	$151,500

---

[75] Code Sec. 1402(a)(13).
[76] Code Sec. 1402.
[77] Code Sec. 1402(a)(1).

Self-Employment Income to Partners

	Johnson	Lincoln	Total
Distributive share of net ordinary income as adjusted.............	$47,750	$47,750	$ 95,500
Guaranteed payments............	44,000	12,000	56,000
Total	$91,750	$59,750	$151,500

¶ 221   The Partner's Share of Taxable Income

For tax purposes, the partnership agreement for income allocation generally holds. There are two important exceptions, however:

1. The partnership agreement does not state how a given item of income, gain, loss, deduction, or credit is to be allocated. In that event, the item is allocated in the same manner as general profits and losses are allocated.

2. The allocation to a partner lacks "substantial economic effect."[78] An agreement will lack a "substantial economic effect" if the main purpose is to avoid or evade federal income tax.[79] For an allocation to have economic effect, it must be consistent with the underlying economic arrangement of the partners, i.e., in the event that there is an economic benefit or economic burden corresponding to an allocation, the partner to whom the allocation is made must receive such economic benefits or bear such economic burden.[80] In general, an economic effect is substantial if there is a reasonable probability that the allocation will affect substantially the dollar amounts received by the partners independent of tax consequences.[81] However, the economic effect of an allocation is not substantial if, at the time, the allocation becomes part of the partnership agreement:[82]

    a. The present value of the after-tax consequences of at least one partner may be enhanced, and

    b. There is a strong likelihood that the present value of the after-tax economic consequences of no partner will be substantially diminished.

As mentioned previously, effective for contributions after March 31, 1984, income, gain, or loss, and deduction on property contributed by a partner to a partnership must be shared among partners so as to take into account the difference between basis and fair market value at the time of contribution.[83]

Example 2-12. Link and Sage form a partnership in which the income is allocated 60:40. If the partnership agreement is silent as to

---

[78] Code Sec. 704(b).
[79] Reg. § 1.704-1(b)(2).
[80] Reg. § 1.704-1(b)(2)(ii)(a).

[81] Reg. § 1.704-1(b)(2)(iii)(a).
[82] *Id.*
[83] Code Sec. 704(c).

how the general business credit should be allocated, it should be allocated using the 60:40 ratio.

Example 2-13. Matson and Bender form a partnership and agree to divide income equally. Since Matson is a high income taxpayer, the agreement stipulates that he is to be allocated all of the capital gains from the partnership and that Bender will be allocated an extra amount of ordinary income to make up the balance. This agreement would lack substantial economic effect and would be disregarded by the IRS.

In *Vecchio*, the Tax Court refused to allow a special allocation of gain on the sale of property because the partnership agreement lacked substantial economic effect. The agreement did not reflect the entire book gain realized in the year of sale. In addition, the agreement did not require that liquidating distributions be made in accordance with partner's positive account balances, and there was no required restoration of deficit balances.[84]

Limited partnerships with nonrecourse debt on realty are subject to some special distributive share rules. Allocation of nonrecourse deductions (i.e., those attributable to nonrecourse liabilities) have no economic effect because no partner bears an economic risk in connection with the deductions. Therefore, allocations of nonrecourse deductions generally must be made in accordance with the partners' interests in the partnership.[85]

As the nonrecourse deductions decrease the basis of the property, "partnership minimum gain" is created. Partnership minimum gain is the gain that would be created if the partnership disposed of the property for the amount of the liability, i.e., it is the excess of the nonrecourse liabilities over the adjusted basis of the property. Partnership minimum gain decreases as reductions occur in the amount by which the nonrecourse liability exceeds the adjusted tax basis of the encumbered property.[86]

If there is a reduction in partnership minimum gain, there must be a "minimum gain chargeback," i.e., each partner must be allocated items of partnership income and gain for that year equal to that partner's share of the net decrease in partnership minimum gain.[87] To avoid impairing the economic effect of other allocations, allocations pursuant to a minimum gain chargeback must be made to the partners who either were allocated nonrecourse deductions or received distribution of proceeds attributable to a nonrecourse borrowing.[88] If a limited partnership plans to use nonrecourse debt, the partnership agreement should be carefully drafted to take into account the effect of this complicated set of regulations.

[84] *S.J. Vecchio v. Commr.*, 103 TC 170, Dec. 50,027 (1994).

[85] Reg. § 1.704-2(b)(1).

[86] Reg. § 1.704-2(b)(2).

[87] Reg. § 1.704-2(f)(1).

[88] Reg. § 1.704-2(b)(2).

.01 Special Allocations

The special allocations required that are mentioned above for contributions after March 31, 1984, prevent inequities among partners from developing due to the contribution of appreciated or depreciated property. These special allocations are essential to prevent one partner from benefiting at the expense of others. Refer back to Example 2-3 for an example of a required special allocation.

¶ 223 When to Report Income from a Partnership

A partner reports income from a partnership (whether or not distributed) for any taxable year of the partnership that ends within or on the taxable year of the partner.[89]

> **Example 2-14.** Paul Sheffen, a calendar year taxpayer, belongs to a partnership with a September 30 fiscal year. For the year ending September 30, 2001, his share of the partnership income is $18,000. The income is reported on his 2001 return even though three months of the income was earned in 2000.

The potential for tax deferral through the selection of a fiscal year is obvious. As a result, there are severe restrictions on a partnership's choice of a fiscal year.

¶ 225 Fiscal Years of Partnerships

Effective for tax years beginning after 1986, partnerships generally must conform their tax years to the tax years of their owners. The specific requirements are as follows:[90]

- A partnership must use the same tax year as that of its partners who own a majority interest in partnership profits and capital. If that majority interest tax year changes, the partnership is not required to change its tax year for either of the two taxable years following the change.

- If partners owning a majority interest have different tax years, the partnership must adopt the same tax year as that of all of its principal partners (those who own five percent or more of profits of capital).

- If a tax year cannot be determined under either rule, a year must be used which results in the least aggregate deferral of income to the partners.[91] Generally, the calendar year would result in the least aggregate deferral.

An exception to the above rules is permitted if partnerships can establish a business purpose for having a different year.

---

[89] Code Sec. 706(a).
[90] Code Sec. 706(b).

[91] Reg. § 1.706-1T(a)(1).

The business-purpose exception is developed by the IRS. Rev. Proc. 87-32[92] states that a desire to change an accounting period to coincide with the natural business year of the entity, as defined in Rev. Proc. 74-33,[93] is not the sole factor used to determine if there is a business purpose for a change in accounting period. Rev. Rul. 87-57[94] indicates that there is a business purpose for using a natural business year in the following circumstances:

- The taxpayer can establish that it has two natural business years and one results in less deferral of income than the other (in this case, the taxpayer may use the natural business year that results in less deferral of income);

- The failure to meet the natural-business-year test is due to unusual circumstances or to an unusual event, such as a strike;

- The end of the taxpayer's operating cycle is not within the taxpayer's control; or

- The taxpayer has a natural business year and changes to the accrual method of accounting at the same time it changes its accounting period.

Responding to outcries from tax practitioners and small business owners, Congress passed in the Revenue Act of 1987 (P.L. 100-203) a provision allowing an election to retain a fiscal year, or, in the case of a new entity, to adopt a fiscal year.[95] This election need not be made if the business-purpose exception can be used. For existing partnerships, the election may be made to retain the same year-end as it had for its year beginning in 1986.[96] New partnerships are allowed to elect a fiscal year so long as the deferral period is not greater than three months (generally, the year-end would have to be no earlier than September 30).[97]

The election is made by filing Form 8716, "Election to Have a Tax Year Other Than a Required Tax Year." For existing partnerships wishing to retain their fiscal year, the due date of the election was July 26, 1988. The IRS ruled that a partnership that elected to retain its June 30 tax year under Code Sec. 444 could not change or amend its elective June 30 year-end to September 30. The IRS noted that the Code Sec. 444 election is binding until a termination event occurs.[98]

The election is not without cost. A partnership making the election is required to maintain with the IRS a refundable, but non-interest bearing deposit, called a "required payment."[99] The "required payment" equals the "net base income" of the partnership multiplied by the adjusted highest

---

[92] 1987-2 CB 396.
[93] 1974-2 CB 489.
[94] 1987-2 CB 117.
[95] Act Sec. 10206(a)(1), Revenue Act of 1987, adding Code Sec. 444.
[96] Id.
[97] Id.
[98] IRS Letter Ruling 8943012, July 24, 1989.
[99] Act Sec. 10206(b)(1), Revenue Act of 1987, adding Code Sec. 7519.

Code Sec. 1 rate. Such product is reduced by the amount, if any, of the required payment for the preceding year.[100] "Net base income" is the sum of net ordinary income plus/minus the various separately stated items for the year immediately preceding the election year, divided by the number of months in that tax year, times the number of months in the deferral period (the number of months preceding December 31).[101] The adjusted highest Code Sec. 1 rate is set at one percentage point above the highest individual rate; hence, the 2002 rate is 38.6 percent.[102] The due date of the payment is April 15 of the calendar year following the calendar year in which the applicable election year begins.[103] No payment need be made unless the required payment exceeds $500.[104]

¶ 227   Partnership Losses

Partnership losses are deducted by partners using the same timing rules as for income inclusion. In order to deduct losses, however, the partner must have a basis in the partnership. If losses exceed basis, the excess losses are carried forward indefinitely, to be used whenever the partner's basis gets above zero.[105]

> **Example 2-15.** Bill Hastings had a basis of $40,000 in a partnership before his share of the loss for the year, which was $52,000. He may deduct only $40,000, thus reducing his basis to zero; the remaining $12,000 loss constitutes an indefinite carryover.

Each type of loss (ordinary, short-term, or long-term) must be allocated if the total loss exceeds the partner's basis.[106]

> **Example 2-16.** Justin Mills had a basis at the end of the year, without regard to any losses, of $20,000. His share of the partnership losses amounted to $12,000 of short-term capital losses and $18,000 of ordinary losses. Only two-thirds ($20,000/30,000) of the losses are deductible. Thus, Mills could deduct $8,000 of short-term capital loss and $12,000 of ordinary loss.[107]

A new partner has been precluded (since the Tax Reform Act of 1976 (P.L. 94-455)) from deducting partnership losses incurred by the partnership before he entered the partnership. Prior to April 1, 1984, an entering partner could have the various items of income, loss, gain, credits, and deductions allocated in one of two ways:

1.   The partnership year could be closed when the new partner entered the partnership; or

2.   The income, loss, etc., could be prorated evenly over the entire year.

---

[100] *Id.*
[101] *Id.*
[102] *Id.*
[103] *Id.*
[104] *Id.*

[105] Code Sec. 704(d).
[106] Reg. § 1.704-1(d)(2).
[107] If Mills had no other capital transactions, only $3,000 of the short-term capital loss could be deducted.

However, Congress felt that cash basis partnerships were getting around these rules by delaying the payment of expenses until the end of the year, and then admitting a new partner immediately prior to the payment of those expenses.[108] Hence, effective for periods after March 31, 1984, "cash basis items" must be prorated over the period to which the items are attributable.[109] "Cash basis items" are items which the partnership accounts for using the cash receipts and disbursements method. Specifically, they are:[110]

- Interest;

- Taxes;

- Payments for services or for the use of property; and

- Any other item prescribed by the IRS.

Tax Tips and Pitfalls

In the two preceding examples, the tax benefit of a loss deduction was partially lost for that particular tax year. However, as discussed in the next section, there are a number of ways in which a partner's tax basis is increased. For example, a partnership can borrow money, or a partner can make additional capital contributions. Either technique could increase the basis to the extent that all losses are currently deductible.[111]

.01 Adjustments to the Basis of a Partnership Interest

The original basis for a partner's interest in a partnership most likely stems from the purchase of a partnership or from the contribution of assets to the partnership. In either case, the original basis consists of the sum of the money contributed, the adjusted basis of property contributed, the partner's share of any partnership liabilities, and any gain recognized at the time of the entrance into the partnership.[112] If the partnership is acquired through other means (such as a gift, for example), the basis is determined by the rules discussed in Chapter 9.

Once the original basis is determined, it is adjusted for the following income and expense events:

1. Increased by the partner's distributive share of:

    a. Taxable income of the partnership (both ordinary taxable income and items required to be allocated separately);

    b. Tax-exempt income of the partnership; and

    c. The excess of the deductions for depletion over the basis of the property.

---

[108] Committee on Ways and Means, Report No. 98-432, March 5, 1984, part 2, p. 1213.
[109] Code Sec. 706(d)(2)(A).
[110] Code Sec. 706(d)(2)(B).

[111] However, if money was borrowed at year-end for no apparent business reason, the IRS might assert the lack of a business purpose.
[112] Code Sec. 722.

2.   Decreased by the partner's distributive share of:

  a. Losses of the partnership (both ordinary taxable losses and items required to be allocated separately);

  b. Nondeductible expenses of the partnership; and

  c. The partner's deduction for depletion of oil and gas wells.[113]

Example 2-17. Jim Allen's share of income and expense items of a partnership were ordinary taxable income, $6,000; long-term capital loss, $1,200; municipal bond interest income, $1,400; charitable contributions, $400; and fines and penalties, $250. His basis adjustment would be $5,550 ($6,000 − $1,200 + $1,400 − $400 − $250).

The IRS has ruled that when a partnership makes a charitable contribution of property, the basis of each partner's interest in the partnership is reduced, but not below zero, by each partner's share of the adjusted basis of the property contributed.[114]

In addition to income and expense items, changes in the liabilities of a partnership affect the basis of a partnership interest. Specifically, an increase in a partner's share of the liabilities of a partnership increases the basis of the partnership interest, and a decrease in a partner's share of liabilities decreases the basis of a partnership interest.[115] Even nonmonetary liabilities of a partnership affect a partner's basis. In a letter ruling, the IRS said that deferred prepaid subscription dues should be included in the bases of the partners' interests.[116]

A partner's share of a decrease in partnership liabilities is treated as an advance draw to the extent of the partner's distributive share of income for the partnership year. The deemed distribution is taken into account at the end of the partnership taxable year, rather than when the deemed distribution occurs.[117]

Although the basis of general partners is affected by changes in both recourse and nonrecourse debt, limited partners may take into account only their share of nonrecourse debt (if the debt is nonrecourse, the lender may take back the property that is security for the debt, but has no other recourse to the partner's property). On the other hand, partners are *personally liable* for recourse debt. If the partnership has nonrecourse debt, the amount of losses deductible is limited to the amount "at risk," which may be less than the basis.[118]

---

[113] Code Sec. 705(a).

[114] Rev. Rul. 96-11, 1996-1 CB 140.

[115] Code Sec. 752.

[116] IRS Letter Ruling 9823002, February 5, 1998.

[117] Rev. Rul. 94-4, 1994-1 CB 195.

[118] Code Sec. 465(a).

.02 Allocating Recourse and Nonrecourse Debt to Partners

Recourse debt created after December 28, 1991, is allocated according to a constructive liquidation scenario. Under this scenario it is assumed that:[119]

1.   All partnership liabilities are payable in full;

2.   All partnership assets, including cash, but not including property contributed to secure a partnership liability, have a zero value;

3.   The partnership disposes of all of its property in a fully taxable transaction for no consideration (except relief from liabilities for which the creditor's right to repayment is limited solely to one or more assets of the partnership);

4.   All items of income, gain, loss, or deduction are allocated to the partners;

5.   All partners with negative cash balances contribute cash to restore their balances to zero; and

6.   After paying liabilities, the partnership liquidates and cash is paid to partners having positive capital balances.

The needed cash contribution in step five comprises the allocation of recourse debt.

> **Example 2-18.** Baker and Hesson each contribute $40,000 cash to a partnership which incurs a $120,000 recourse debt to buy a $200,000 building. Baker and Hesson share profits and losses in a 70:30 ratio. Under the constructive liquidation scenario, the $200,000 loss would be shared $140,000 and $60,000 respectively. Thus, Baker would have a negative balance in his capital account of $100,000 ($40,000 − $140,000) and Hesson a negative balance of $20,000 ($40,000 − $60,000). Baker is allocated $100,000 of the debt and Hesson $20,000. Therefore Baker's basis in the partnership is $140,000 ($40,000 + $100,000) and Hesson's basis is $60,000 ($40,000 + $20,000).

A partner's share of a partnership's nonrecourse liabilities is the sum of the following amounts:[120]

1.   The partner's share of partnership minimum gain;

2.   The partner's precontribution gain that would result under Code Sec. 704(c) if the property were disposed of in a taxable transaction; and

---

[119] Reg. § 1.752-2(b).   [120] Reg. § 1.752-3(a).

3.   The partner's share of the partnership's excess nonrecourse debt (the amount remaining after allocations 1 and 2), determined in accordance with the partner's share of partnership profits. Excess nonrecourse liabilities may be allocated either according to the partner's share of partnership profits, or the manner in which the partnership agreement calls for allocations of deductions attributable to the nonrecourse liabilities. The partner's interest in partnership profits is determined by taking into account all facts and circumstances relating to the economic arrangement of the partners. The partnership agreement may specify the partners' interests in partnership profits for purposes of allocating excess nonrecourse liabilities provided the interests so specified are reasonably consistent with allocations that have substantial economic effect of some other significant item of partnership income or gain. Alternatively, excess nonrecourse liabilities may be allocated among the partners in accordance with the manner in which it is reasonably expected that the deductions attributable to those nonrecourse liabilities will be allocated. Additionally, the partnership may first allocate an excess nonrecourse liability to a partner up to the amount of built-in gain that is allocable to the partner. To the extent that a partnership uses this additional method and the entire amount of the excess nonrecourse liability is not allocated to the contributing partner, the partnership must allocate the remaining amount of the excess nonrecourse liability under one of the other permissible methods. Excess nonrecourse liabilities are not required to be allocated under the same method each year.[121]

If the partnership has only general partners and has no nonrecourse debt, allocation of liabilities is relatively straightforward. However, in all other instances, the regulations must be read carefully to determine partnership liability allocations.[122]

Finally, cash and property contributions by the partner increase basis, while cash and property distributions reduce basis.

Example 2-19. Judy Ronson, a 40% general partner in the REU partnership, began the calendar year with an $80,000 basis in her partnership interest. At that time, the partnership had total debt of $120,000. The following events transpired:

July 1 . . . .   Ronson made an additional contribution of $20,000
September 30 . . .   Ronson withdrew $15,000
December 31 . . .   Partnership debt totaled $150,000

---

[121] Reg. § 1.752-3(a)(3).
[122] For a good discussion of special problems attendant to the allocation of partnership liabilities, see Robert C. Ricketts, "The Allocation of Partnership Liabilities Under Sec. 752," *The Tax Advisor*, May 1991, pp. 288-294.

Year ended December 31	*(Ronson's share)*
Net ordinary income	$ 16,000
Long-term capital gains	3,000
Guaranteed salary (withdrawn monthly)	12,000
Code Sec. 1231 losses	(4,000)
Charitable contributions	(1,000)

Her basis at December 31 is determined as follows:	
Basis (January 1)	$ 80,000
Contributions to partnership	20,000
Distributive share of:	
Net ordinary income	16,000
Long-term capital gains	3,000
Guaranteed salary	12,000
	$131,000
Distributive share of:	
Code Sec. 1231 losses	(4,000)
Charitable contributions	(1,000)
	$126,000
Withdrawals:	
September 30 withdrawal	(15,000)
Salary withdrawals	(12,000)
Basis before considering change in partnership liabilities	99,000
Share of increase in partnership liabilities	12,000
Basis December 31	$111,000

¶ 229 Transactions Between Partners and Partnerships

Generally, when transactions occur between partners and partnerships, other than in the partner's capacity as a member of the partnership, the two are considered to be separate entities; i.e., the transaction can be considered to have occurred between the partnership and one who is not a partner.[123] However, there are a number of exceptions, limitations, and other ramifications to this general rule. Examples of transactions where the partner *is* considered to be an *outsider* include:[124]

- Loans of money or property by the partnership to the partner, or by the partner to the partnership;

- The sale of property by the partner to the partnership;

- The purchase of property by the partner from the partnership;

---

[123] Code Sec. 707(a)(1). [124] Reg. § 1.707-1(a).

- The rendering of services by the partnership to the partner or by the partner to the partnership; and

- The partnership using property owned by the partner to obtain credit or to secure firm creditors by guaranty, pledge, or other agreements.

Code Sec. 707(b)(1) prohibits the deduction of losses from the sale or exchange of property, directly or indirectly between:[125]

- A partnership and any person who owns either directly or indirectly more than 50 percent of the profits or capital interest; or

- Two partnerships in which the same persons own, directly or indirectly, more than 50 percent of the profits or capital interest.

Some relief from this harsh rule is provided if the transferee later sells the property at a gain. In that event, the gain is reduced (but not below zero) by the previously disallowed loss.[126]

Example 2-20. Walter Ebert sells for $70,000 land with a basis of $100,000 to a partnership in which he owns a 70 percent interest. The partnership later sells the land for $92,000. The $30,000 disallowed loss of Ebert's sale reduces the partnership gain down from $22,000 to zero. Had the partnership sold the land for $115,000, the gain of $45,000 would be reduced to $15,000.

In addition to disallowing losses where the partner has an over 50 percent interest, Code Sec. 707(b)(2) acts to convert capital gains to ordinary income where the transferee does not use the property as a capital asset.[127] This provision will apply even if the property is used in the trade or business and would thus qualify as a Code Sec. 1231 asset.[128]

Example 2-21. Richard Dixon sells at a gain an auto and land to a partnership in which he owns a 55 percent interest. Both items were capital assets in the hands of Dixon. The partnership plans to hold the auto as inventory and will build a business building on the land. Dixon must treat the gain on both items as ordinary income.

In applying the loss disallowance and gain conversion rules above, the constructive ownership rules of Code Sec. 267(c)(1), (2), (4) and (5) are used.[129] These rules provide that:[130]

1. Stock owned directly or indirectly by or for a corporation, partnership, estate, or trust is considered owned *proportionately* by or for its shareholders, partners, or beneficiaries;

---

[125] Code Sec. 707(b)(1).
[126] Code Secs. 707(b)(1) and 267(d); Reg. § 1.707-1(b)(1)(ii).
[127] Code Sec. 707(b)(2).
[128] Reg. § 1.707-1(b)(2).
[129] Reg. § 1.707-1(b)(3).
[130] Code Sec. 267(c).

2.   An individual is considered to own the stock owned, directly or indirectly, by or for his or her family (brothers and sisters, spouse, ancestors, and lineal descendants); and

3.   Stock constructively owned by a person by reason of the first rule is treated as actually owned by that person for the purpose of *again* applying the first and second constructive ownership rules, but stock constructively owned by an individual by reason of the second rule will not be treated as constructively owned by that individual for the purpose of again applying that second rule.

Example 2-22. The XYZ partnership is owned by the following entities:

Name	Percent Owned	
Sara..................	35	
Sara's husband	10	
Sara's father-in-law	8	
XY Partnership	30	(a partnership owned 40 percent by Sara and 60 percent by Pat)

Sara owns 35 percent directly, 10 percent indirectly through her husband's ownership, and another 12 percent indirectly through the XY partnership (40 percent × 30 percent), for a total of 57 percent. Sara's husband owns 10 percent directly, 47 percent indirectly through Sara (35 percent + 12 percent), and another 8 percent through his father for a total of 65 percent. Sara's father-in-law, however, owns only 18 percent, 8 percent directly, and 10 percent through Sara's husband. Note that the ownership of Sara's husband that is constructively owned because of marriage to Sara is *not* attributed to Sara's husband's father.

Another exception exists when depreciable property is sold to or bought from a controlled partnership. The partnership is considered to be "controlled" if the partner owns (directly or indirectly) over 50 percent of the capital interest or profits interest in the partnership.[131] Any gain on the sale of the property then becomes ordinary income.[132] The constructive ownership rules under Code Sec. 267(c) (other than (c)(3)) are also applied here.[133]

If a cash basis partner renders services to an accrual basis partnership, and the payment for the services does not fall into the category of "guaranteed payments," the expense may not be deducted by the partnership until the year in which it is includible in the income of the partner.[134] This is true

---

[131] Code Sec. 1239(c)(1).
[132] Code Sec. 1239(a).
[133] Code Sec. 1239(c)(2).
[134] Code Sec. 267(a)(2).

of all partnership interests (it applies to partners owning less than 50 percent as well as to majority partners).[135]

Example 2-23. Ned Smithson, a cash basis taxpayer, rendered $500 of services to the Barrow-Smithson partnership in December 2001. The services were not in the nature of guaranteed payments. The partnership paid him in February 2002. Even if the partnership is on the accrual basis, the expense is not deductible until 2002, the year in which Smithson reports the income.

¶ 231   Guaranteed Payments

To the extent that payments made to a partner for services or the use of capital are determined without regard to the income of the partnership, such payments are characterized as "guaranteed payments."[136] They are considered as being made to one who is not a member of the partnership for purposes of computing net ordinary income of the partnership; i.e., unless required to be capitalized, they are deductible to arrive at net ordinary income.[137] However, for purposes other than computing net ordinary income, guaranteed payments are considered a partner's distributive share of ordinary income.[138] Therefore, for purposes of income tax withholding and federal payroll taxes, the partner is not regarded as an employee.[139]

Partners report guaranteed payments as income for the taxable year within or with which ends the partnership taxable year in which the partnership deducted such payments as paid or accrued under its method of accounting.[140]

Example 2-24. Wayne Verde, a partner in the D-V partnership, is on the cash basis. The partnership is on the accrual basis and has a September 30 year end. His guaranteed salary for the year ended September 30, 2001, was $24,000 ($2,000 per month). The September salary was unpaid as of September 30. Despite the lack of receipt of the salary, Verde would report $24,000 of guaranteed salary on his calendar year 2001 return.

It is not always clear as to whether a payment to a partner is a guaranteed payment. The Tax Court has held that payments based on gross rentals *could not* be considered guaranteed payments since "gross rentals constitute partnership income."[141] However, the IRS has stated that "the term 'guaranteed payments' should not be limited to fixed amounts."[142] Instead, payments that are primarily compensatory in nature will be treated as guaranteed payments, even if based on gross income, if the facts and circumstances warrant.[143]

[135] Code Sec. 267(e)(1).
[136] Code Sec. 707(c).
[137] Reg. § 1.707-1(c).
[138] Id.
[139] Reg. § 1.707-1(c); Rev. Rul. 69-184, 1969-1 CB 256.
[140] Reg. § 1.707-1(c).
[141] E.T. Pratt v. Commr., 64 TC 203, Dec. 33,189, aff'd, CA-5, 77-1 USTC ¶ 9347, 550 F2d 1023.
[142] Rev. Rul. 81-300, 1981-2 CB 143.
[143] Id.

.01 Computing Guaranteed Payments

Although computing guaranteed payment is usually easy, complications can arise under at least three different scenarios: minimum guaranteed payments, guaranteed payments when there are partnership losses, and guaranteed payments when the partnership has capital gains and losses.

.02 Minimum Guaranteed Payments

If the partnership agreement specifies that a partner is to receive a certain percentage of partnership profits, but in any case is to receive at least a certain amount, then the guaranteed payment is the excess of the minimum guaranteed payment over the partner's distributive share of profits.[144]

Example 2-25. As provided by the partnership agreement, Jane Dorsey is to receive 25 percent of the profits, but no less than $15,000. Partnership profits for the year are $40,000. Of the $15,000, $15,000 − (.25)($40,000), or $5,000 is a guaranteed payment. The remaining $10,000 is considered to be a distribution of profits.

Example 2-26. Assume the same facts as in the previous example, except that the partnership profits are $80,000. Dorsey's share of partnership profits is $20,000. However, the guaranteed payment is $15,000 − $20,000 = zero. Thus, there is no guaranteed payment for this particular year.

.03 Guaranteed Payments in Loss Years

Guaranteed payments are deducted to arrive at net ordinary income. Therefore, if the guaranteed payments exceed ordinary income, a net ordinary loss is created.

Example 2-27. Fred Kugler, a partner in the KLM partnership, is to receive a guaranteed salary of $25,000 plus one-third of the profits. Partnership losses before deducting the guaranteed salary were $35,000. The total net ordinary loss is therefore $60,000. Kugler would report a guaranteed salary of $25,000 and his share of the net ordinary loss, $20,000.

.04 Guaranteed Payments and Capital Gains

Guaranteed payments can be made only from net ordinary income. Therefore, capital gains and losses are not affected by guaranteed payments; instead they are allocated according to each partner's distributive share under the partnership agreement.

Example 2-28. Assume the same facts as in Example 2-27, except partnership losses before deducting the guaranteed salary were $45,000, and the partnership also had capital gains of $10,000. Kugler

---

[144] Reg. § 1.707-1(c).

would report a guaranteed salary of $25,000, an ordinary net loss of $23,333, and capital gains of $3,333.

If there are capital gains in a partnership which guarantees a minimum payment to a partner, additional complexities can result.

Example 2-29. Assume the same facts as in Example 2-25, except that the partnership profits of $40,000 consist of net ordinary income of $30,000 and capital gains of $10,000. The $10,000 that is a distributive share of profit is allocated pro-rata between the remaining net ordinary income of $25,000 and the capital gain of $10,000.[145]

	Ordinary income	Capital gains	Total
Before guaranteed payments	$30,000	$10,000	$40,000
Guaranteed payment	5,000	—	—
	$25,000	$10,000	$35,000

Distributive share to Dorsey:			
10,000 / 35,000 × 25,000	=	7,143
10,000 / 35,000 × 10,000	=	2,857
Total		10,000

Distributive share to other partners:			
25,000 / 35,000 × 25,000	=	17,857
25,000 / 35,000 × 10,000	=	7,143
		25,000

¶ 233 Partnership Elections

The entity concept governs most partnership elections; i.e., most elections must be made at the partnership level.[146] For example, election of accounting methods, depreciation methods, and the option to expense intangible drilling and development costs are made by the partnership rather than by the individual partners.[147] Elections made at the partnership level do not affect the nonpartnership interests of a partner.

However, three elections must be made separately by each partner. They are:[148]

1. The election under Code Sec. 901 (to claim as a credit or deduct as an expense) with respect to the partner's share of foreign taxes;

2. The election under Code Sec. 617 to deduct certain mining exploration expenditures; and

---

[145] Rev. Rul. 69-180, 1969-1 CB 183.
[146] Code Sec. 703(b).
[147] Reg. § 1.703-1(b)(1).
[148] Code Sec. 703(b).

3. The election under Code Sec. 108(b)(5) to apply basis reductions required in bankruptcies or insolvencies first to depreciable property or the Code Sec. 108(c)(3) election to treat certain indebtedness as qualified real property business indebtedness.

¶ 235 Limited Liability Companies

Limited liability company (LLC) acts have been passed in all of the states. It is possible to organize an LLC in virtually every state.

LLCs are taxed like partnerships. Thus, the conduit rule and single taxation characteristics are present. However, the owners (members) have the limited liability feature of corporations, i.e., the most that can be lost by the member is the investment in the business.

.01 IRS Requirements for an LLC to Be Taxed as a Partnership

Prior to 1997, the IRS position on LLCs was contained in Rev. Rul. 88-76.[149] The ruling required at least two of the four corporate characteristics be lacking in order for the entity to be taxed as a partnership. Under the "check-the-box" regulations (discussed in ¶ 237), the default rules allow entities to have the classification they would be most likely to choose. The filing of an election is not required. For example, a newly formed domestic entity with at least two members is automatically classified as a partnership.

.02 Other Features of LLCs

An LLC must have at least two members to be characterized as a partnership for federal tax purposes. However, those members can be individuals, partnerships, corporations, trusts, estates, or other LLCs.

.03 Uncertainties in the Taxation of LLCs

The fact that an LLC is something of an amalgamation of limited partnerships and general partnerships makes several tax issues less than clear-cut.

Self-Employment Tax

In a general partnership, both guaranteed payments and distributive shares of partnership income are subject to self-employment tax. However, in a limited partnership, limited partners are subject to self-employment tax only on guaranteed payments. Because partners in an LLC have limited liability, but often participate in the management of the partnership, what should be the self-employment status of their distributive shares of income and loss? The IRS has addressed this issue in proposed regulations. The proposed regulations state that generally a member of an LLC will be subject to self-employment tax on his or her distributive share of business income or loss of the LLC. However, a member would be treated as a

---

[149] 1988-2 CB 360.

limited partner (thus subject to self-employment tax only on guaranteed payments) if:[150]

- The member does not have authority to contract for the LLC;

- The member does not participate in the LLC's trade or business for more than 500 hours during the taxable year; and

- The member does not provide more than de minimis services for an LLC that performs substantially all of its activities in the fields of health, law, engineering, architecture, accounting, actuarial science, or consulting.

Share of Liabilities and At-Risk Rules

As previously discussed, recourse debt and nonrecourse debt are allocated to partners using different rules. Because, under state law, the liability of an LLC member is limited, it would appear that all debt would have to be allocated using nonrecourse debt rules. This issue awaits clarification by the IRS.

A partner's share of partnership losses is deductible only to the extent that the partner investment is "at risk." Because an LLC member is at risk only to the extent of his or her capital investments, presumably his or her share of partnership debt, though increasing basis, will not increase the amount the partner has at risk. Again, this issue awaits clarification.

.04 Converting to an LLC

When a partnership is converted to an LLC, generally there should be no gain or loss to the partners. The conversion is *not* treated as a sale or exchange; therefore, the partnership is not considered terminated.[151] Also, the tax year is not terminated, basis of partnership assets is unchanged, and the basis of the partner's interest in the LLC is unchanged unless the partner's share of the partnership liabilities changes.[152] However, if the partner's share of the partnership liabilities changes, there will be either a deemed contribution of money by the partner to the partnership or a deemed distribution of money by the partnership to the partner. In the latter case, gain will be recognized by the partner to the extent that the deemed distribution exceeds the adjusted basis of the partnership interest.[153]

The conversion of a C corporation or an S corporation to an LLC unfortunately is treated as a liquidation of the corporation. Therefore, under Code Secs. 331 and 336, there will be both gain at the corporate level (passed through to the shareholders of an S corporation) and gain to the shareholders. The tax on liquidation makes conversion of a corporation to an LLC generally not an attractive option.

---

[150] Prop. Reg. § 1.1402(a)-2(h)(2), (5)(i).
[151] Rev. Rul. 95-37, 1995-1 CB 130.
[152] *Id.*
[153] *Id.*

.05 Advantages of LLCs Compared to Other Entities

Although at first glance it would appear that LLCs are taxed in the same manner as S corporations, LLCs have considerably more flexibility with respect to the formation, operation, and disposition of the business than do S corporations.

1. *Contribution of assets.* In at least two instances, Code Sec. 721 rules for partnership formations are more liberal than are Code Sec. 351 rules for corporate formation. While Code Sec. 351 requires the transferors to have "control" of the corporate stock (at least 80 percent), there is no such control requirement in Code Sec. 721. And while the contribution to a corporation of property whose debt exceeds basis requires gain recognition under Code Sec. 357(c), the corresponding requirement under Code Sec. 721 requires gain recognition only if the *debt relief* exceeds basis.

   Example 2-30. Eugene Clark contributes property having a basis of $85,000 and a mortgage of $100,000 to a corporation in exchange for 80 percent of the stock. He would have to recognize a gain of $15,000. If he had contributed the property to a partnership in exchange for a 20 percent interest, his debt relief would have been only $100,000 × .80, or $80,000. Since this does not exceed basis, no gain recognition would be required.

2. *Special allocations.* LLCs have the flexibility to make special allocations of income, losses, credits, etc., in the agreement, although under Code Sec. 704(b) the agreement must have "substantial economic effect." S corporations do not have that flexibility; special allocations would create a second class of stock which would terminate the S election.

3. *Built-in gains.* C corporations that switch to S status after 1986 are subject to the built-in gains tax at the corporate level. There is no such tax for LLCs. However, if a C corporation is converted to an LLC, it is considered liquidated and would be subject to the double tax. Therefore, converting a C corporation to an S corporation would generally be much better than converting to an LLC.

4. *Basis adjustments.* When an LLC membership is sold or liquidated, the LLC could elect to make favorable basis adjustments under Code Secs. 754, 743, and 734. S corporations cannot make these elections.

5. *Ownership restrictions.* S corporations cannot have as owners partnerships, corporations (other than qualified subchapter S

subsidiaries), nonresident aliens, and in some instances, trusts. There are no restrictions on LLC owners.

6. *LIFO recapture; passive income.* C corporations electing S status must recapture as income the difference between LIFO and FIFO inventory amounts and pay the tax in three installments. Also, if the C corporation has accumulated earnings and profits, it can be subject to a corporate level tax on excessive passive income even though it is an S corporation. Too many years of excessive passive income can cause loss of S status altogether. These provisions are not applicable to LLCs.

7. *Greater loss deduction possibilities and tax-free distribution possibilities.* S corporation shareholders can offset losses only against the basis of their stock and loans made to the corporation. Depending on how the IRS applies the at-risk rules, LLC members may be able to add their share of the LLC debt to their basis. This potentially higher basis would also permit larger distributions to be free of tax.

8. *Property distributions treated more favorably.* Although S corporations must always recognize gain on distributions of appreciated property, LLCs can, in many cases, distribute property without gain to either entity.

.06 Drawbacks of LLC status

The sale of S corporation stock will result in capital gain; however, when an interest in a partnership is sold or liquidated, part of the gain is usually ordinary due to the presence of Code Sec. 751 assets on the partnership books. Other drawbacks include the uncertainties discussed above.

¶ 237 Simplification of Entity Classification Rules (Check-the-Box)

On December 18, 1996, the Treasury issued final regulations governing check-the-box rules, which had been proposed on May 13, 1996. The IRS believed that the rules governing classifying entities as partnerships or corporations were too complicated and too formalistic.

.01 Classification for Federal Tax Purposes

Whether an organization is an entity separate from its owners for federal income tax purposes is a matter of federal tax law, not the entity's classification under local law.[154]

A joint venture may create a separate entity if the participants carry on a business and divide the profits. However, merely sharing expenses or

---

[154] Reg. § 301.7701-1(a)(1).

co-ownership of property that is leased does not necessarily create a separate entity.[155]

.02 Classification as Corporations

An entity is classified as a corporation if it is:[156]

- A business entity organized under a federal or state statute, or under a statute of a federally recognized Indian tribe, if the statute describes or refers to the entity as incorporated or as a corporation, body corporate, or body politic;

- An association (as determined under Reg. § 301.7701-3);

- A business entity organized under a state statute, if the statute describes or refers to the entity as a joint-stock company or a joint-stock association;

- An insurance company;

- A state-chartered business entity conducting banking activities, if any of its deposits are insured under the FDIC, or a similar federal statute;

- A business entity wholly owned by a state or any political subdivision thereof;

- A business entity that is taxable as a corporation under a provision of the Code other than Code Sec. 7701(a)(3); and

- Certain foreign entities.

.03 Wholly Owned Entities

In general, a business entity with a single owner that is not automatically classified as a corporation under the rules listed above, is disregarded as an entity separate from its owner.[157] These entities are classified under default rules. However, an eligible business entity with a single owner can elect to be classified as a corporation.[158] For single owner entities in existence prior to January 1, 1997, the entity's claimed classification will generally be respected unless it claimed to be a partnership.[159]

.04 Two or More Owners

In general, a business entity with two or more owners that is not automatically classified as a corporation under the rules listed above is considered to be a partnership under the default rules.[160] However, all eligible entities with two or more members may elect to be treated for tax purposes as corporations or as partners.[161] For an entity with two or more

---

[155] Reg. § 301.7701-1(a)(2).
[156] Reg. § 301.7701-2(b).
[157] Reg. § 301.7701-2(c)(2).
[158] Reg. § 301.7701-3(a).

[159] Reg. § 301.7701-3(b)(3).
[160] Reg. § 301.7701-3(b).
[161] Reg. § 301.7701-3(a).

owners that was in existence prior to January 1, 1997, the entity's claimed classification will generally be respected.[162]

.05 Deemed Liquidation of Associations

The IRS has issued proposed regulations providing that associations electing to convert to partnerships are deemed to distribute all of their assets to the shareholders who then immediately contribute all of the assets to a newly formed partnership. The plan of liquidation is deemed to be adopted immediately before the deemed liquidation incident to an elective change in entity classification, unless a formal plan of liquidation that contemplates the filing of the elective change is adopted earlier.[163]

¶ 239 Transition Rules for Existing Entities

Generally, an existing eligible entity's claimed classification will be respected for all periods prior to January 1, 1997, if three conditions are met:[164]

1. The entity had a reasonable basis (within the meaning of Code Sec. 6662) for its claimed classification;

2. The entity and all members of the entity recognized the federal tax consequences of any change in the entity's classification within the 60 months prior to January 1, 1997; and

3. Neither the entity nor any member was notified in writing on or before May 8, 1996, that the classification of the entity was under examination.

The regulations provide detailed guidance on how to elect classification or to change classification.[165]

---

[162] Reg. § 301.7701-3(b)(3).
[163] Prop. Reg. § 301.7701-3(g)(2)(ii).

[164] Reg. § 301.7701-3(f).
[165] Reg. § 301.7701-3(c).

Chapter 3

Corporate Operations

¶ 301   C Corporations—Organization and Operation

Corporations which do not elect to be taxed like partnerships are taxed under Subchapter C of the Internal Revenue Code. Although the Tax Reform Act of 1986 (TRA '86) generally decreased the relative desirability of "C" status as opposed to "S" status, there are still a number of scenarios in which "C" status is preferable. In addition, much of corporate tax law applies to both C and S corporations. Hence, the reader can assume that the material in this chapter also applies to S corporations unless the context in the succeeding chapter (which covers S corporations) indicates otherwise.

¶ 303   Characteristics of a Corporation

A corporation is an entity created solely by law. It is separate and distinct from its owners, i.e., it is a separate, albeit artificial, person. Being a legal entity, a corporation may own property, enter into contracts, borrow money, and sue and be sued, among other rights. The following features are commonly present in the corporate entity:

- *Unlimited life.* The life of a corporation is independent of its owners, and is perpetual, in the absence of insolvency or unless a deliberate decision is made to liquidate the corporation.

- *Limited liability.* The liability of corporate investors (stockholders) is limited to the amount of money they invest.[1] Creditors cannot attach the personal assets of stockholders.

- *Centralized management.* Unlike sole proprietorships, owners may not be involved in the management of corporations. Professional managers are hired to run most large corporations. However, most small corporations are family corporations. Owners usually manage such corporations.

- *Difficulty of formation and operation.* As mentioned, corporations are created by law; a corporate charter must be obtained from the pertinent state. Most states require annual reports to be submitted to an officer of the state, usually the secretary of state. In addition, many states have laws prohibiting distributions out of paid-in capital.

---

[1] However, stockholders in closely held corporations often find it expedient or necessary to co-sign or otherwise guarantee debt of the corporation. Also, the model professional corporation act adopted by all of the states mandates unlimited liability for professional service corporations. Therefore, the feature of limited liability may be more apparent than real for many closely held corporations.

- *Double taxation.* The corporation is subject to a tax on its income. In addition, if the income is distributed to the stockholders, they must include the dividends on their personal income tax returns.

- *Ease of transfer of ownership.* When a partnership interest is transferred, the partnership may be dissolved. In contrast, corporate stock may be transferred without having any effect on the continuity of the business. Also, most shares have a fairly small value, often less than $100; hence, the transfer via gift is facilitated.

¶ 305   When Is an Entity Taxed as a Corporation?

Although to be a corporation in a legal sense, the organization must be recognized as such by state law, for federal income tax purposes state law is not controlling. Instead, the Code and the courts take a broader view of corporate status, sometimes recognizing entities as corporations when state law does not and sometimes even disregarding the corporate status.

.01   Disregarding the Corporate Status

If the only purpose of a corporation is tax avoidance, the corporation may be disregarded as a sham. The Supreme Court has stated, "The Government may look at actualities and upon determination that the form employed for doing business or carrying out the challenged tax event is unreal or a sham may sustain or disregard the effect of the fiction as best serves the purpose of the tax statute."[2]

The lack of a business function can also be critical; for example, where the only apparent function of a corporation was to pay overriding royalties to its stockholders, a business deduction was denied to the corporation (thus rendering the corporation ineffective for federal income tax purposes).[3] In another case where the shareholder controlled and managed bank accounts of the corporation so as to have the funds paid directly to him, the Tax Court concluded that ". . . the corporation involved here is nothing more than bones without flesh" and disregarded the corporate entity.[4]

.02   Upholding the Corporate Entity

The *presence* of a business purpose is equally important in conveying corporate status. The Supreme Court has also held that "so long as that purpose (a useful purpose in business life) is the equivalent of business activity or is followed by the carrying on of business by the corporation, the corporation remains a separate taxable entity."[5] Giving great flexibility and a wide latitude to the IRS, the Supreme Court, in *Higgins v. Smith,*

---

[2] *Higgins v. Smith,* SCt, 40-1 USTC ¶ 9160, 308 US 473.
[3] *Ingle Coal Corp. v. Commr.,* CA-7, 49-1 USTC ¶ 9267, 174 F2d 569, aff'g 10 TC 1199, Dec. 16,469.

[4] *S. Pollack v. Commr.,* 45 TCM 12, Dec. 39,466(M), TC Memo. 1982-638.
[5] *Moline Properties, Inc. v. Commr.,* SCt, 43-1 USTC ¶ 9464, 319 US 436.

suggested that if the IRS determines that the corporate form is a sham, it may either sustain or disregard the corporate status as it sees fit.[6]

Tax Tips and Pitfalls

The taxpayer should be very cautious about setting up a corporation that does not have an obvious business purpose. The IRS will certainly seek to disregard the corporate status if deemed to be in the government's interest. On the other hand, if circumstances should change and the corporate status becomes a drawback to the taxpayer, the IRS may seek to uphold the corporate entity.

¶ 307   When Is a Corporation Dissolved?

The expiration or cancellation of a corporate charter does not necessarily eliminate taxable activities. If the corporation, or a successor entity, continues to carry on a business, a taxable entity will also continue to be in evidence. The actual tax status of the particular business will depend on the type of successor entity. If after the charter revocation the business is owned by only one individual, it will likely be taxed as a sole proprietorship.[7] If the corporation itself continues to conduct business after expiration of its charter, corporate status will most likely continue.[8] However, if the owners intended to form a partnership and took steps in good faith to conduct the business as such, the entity would likely be treated as a partnership.[9]

The date that the stockholders agree to dissolve does not necessarily determine the end of the corporate life; more important is the date of dissolution under state law.[10]

What if the corporation ceases all business operations, yet retains a small sum of cash merely to pay state taxes to enable it to retain its corporate charter? Since the purpose is to retain its corporate charter, not to wind up its affairs, the IRS requires the filing of federal income tax returns.[11]

¶ 309   Entities Taxed as Corporations

A business entity is any entity recognized for federal tax purposes that is not classified as a trust or that is not otherwise subject to special treatment.[12] A business entity having two or more members is classified as either a corporation or a partnership.[13] A business entity with only one owner may be classified as either a corporation, or the entity may be disregarded in which case the entity is taxed as a sole proprietorship.[14] See

---

[6] *Supra*, n. 2.

[7] For example, see *Knoxville Truck Sales & Services, Inc. v. Commr.*, 10 TC 616, Dec. 16,336.

[8] *J. Crocker v. Commr.*, CA-7, 36-2 USTC ¶ 9335, 84 F2d 64.

[9] *E.M. Burleson v. Commr.*, 12 TCM 932, Dec. 19,849(M).

[10] *R.A. O'Connor v. Commr.*, 26 TCM 820, Dec. 28,586(M), TC Memo. 1967-174, aff'd, CA-2, 69-2

USTC ¶ 9453, 412 F2d 304, cert. den'd, 397 US 921; *Nat'l Metropolitan Bank of Washington v. U.S.*, CtCls, 65-1 USTC ¶ 9420, 345 F2d 823, 170 CtCls 617.

[11] Rev. Rul. 56-483, 1956-2 CB 933.

[12] Reg. § 301.7701-2(a).

[13] *Id.*

[14] *Id.*

¶ 237 for a list of entities classified as corporations under the check-the-box regulations.

¶ 311   General Rules of Incorporation—Code Sec. 351

Code Sec. 351 provides that an incorporation is generally a tax-free exchange, i.e., gain or loss is not recognized by either the transferor or the transferee.[15] This general rule is consistent with the idea that a mere change in the form of doing business should not be taxable. Otherwise, forming a corporation, a trust, or a partnership could be prohibitively costly. Tax-free status is not automatic, however. The parties to the incorporation must meet three key requirements:[16]

1. The items transferred must be "property;"

2. The transferors must receive only stock in exchange; and

3. The transferors must "control" the corporation immediately after the transfer.

"Property" is defined in a wide-sweeping sense, generally constituting every item transferred, both tangible and intangible, except services. Cash is considered property,[17] as are unrealized receivables of cash basis taxpayers.[18]

"Stock," in the context of Code Sec. 351, can be either common or preferred, but cannot include stock rights or warrants.[19] The Revenue Reconciliation Act of 1989 (P.L. 101-239) narrowed the type of consideration that the stockholder could receive. For transfers on or before October 2, 1989, securities (e.g., bonds and long-term notes) as well as stock could be received in a Code Sec. 351 transaction. However, for transfers after October 2, 1989, only stock can be received by the stockholder.[20]

Code Sec. 351 is not necessarily inapplicable merely because no stock is issued in exchange for the property. In *Lessinger*, the Tax Court said that ". . . an exchange of stock is a meaningless gesture where the proportionate ownership of the transferor and transferee is identical."[21] Stock received does not have to be in proportion to the property transferred. However, a disproportionate transfer would generally imply that either a gift, compensation, or debt payment was made.[22]

Example 3-1. Carlos Gomez and his son formed a corporation. Gomez contributed land worth $200,000 and his son contributed equipment worth $120,000. Each received 50 percent of the stock. The corporate formation is nontaxable under Code Sec. 351, but Gomez is

---

[15] Code Sec. 351(a).
[16] *Id.*
[17] See *G.M. Holstein v. Commr.*, 23 TC 923, Dec. 20,881; Rev. Rul. 69-357, 1969-1 CB 101.
[18] See, for example, *Hempt Brothers, Inc. v. U.S.*, CA-3, 74-1 USTC ¶ 9188, 490 F2d 1172.

[19] Reg. § 1.351-1(a)(1)(ii).
[20] Act Sec. 7203, Revenue Reconciliation Act of 1989.
[21] *S. Lessinger v. Commr.*, 85 TC 824, Dec. 42,489.
[22] Reg. § 1.351-1(b)(1).

considered to have made a gift to his son of $40,000 ($200,000 − (50% × $320,000)).

"Control" means that the transferors must own at least 80 percent of the voting stock and at least 80 percent of all other classes of stock in the corporation.[23] The phrase "immediately after the exchange" does not require simultaneous exchanges by two or more persons, but does include a situation where the rights of the parties have been previously defined and the execution of the agreement proceeds with an expedition consistent with orderly procedure.[24]

.01 Exceptions to Code Sec. 351 Nontaxability

There are three exceptions to the nontaxability rules of Code Sec. 351: provision of services by the transferor, assumption of excess liabilities, and tax avoidance or lack of business purpose in connection with the assumption of liabilities.[25]

If services are transferred by the shareholder, the transaction is taxable to the shareholder.[26] The shareholder reports income equal to the fair market value of the services and has a basis in the stock equal to its fair market value. Depending on the nature of the services rendered, the corporation will either have an asset to be capitalized or an expense to be written off.

> **Example 3-2.** In connection with the formation of Hilltop Farms, Inc., Allan Kincaid rendered legal services and received stock worth $750. Kincaid has income of $750 and stock with a basis of $750. The corporation has incurred organization costs (to be amortized over 60 months) of $750.

The individual transferring only services cannot be counted in determining the 80 percent control requirement. But what if an individual contributes *both* stock and services? Generally, in this instance, the transferor may count all of the stock received in meeting the control requirement.[27] However, if the amount of property transferred is nominal compared with the value of services transferred, and the primary purpose of the property transfer is to qualify for Code Sec. 351 treatment, then none of the stock counts for control purposes.[28] The IRS will not issue favorable advance rulings in this area unless the value of the property is at least 10 percent of the value of the services.[29]

> **Example 3-3.** Ted Connell contributed $15,000 of property and $25,000 of services to a corporation in exchange for 25 percent of the stock. Jim Harvey contributed property for the other 75 percent of the stock. Since the value of property contributed by Connell is at least 10

---

[23] Code Sec. 368(c).
[24] Reg. § 1.351-1(a)(1).
[25] Code Secs. 351(d) and 357(a) and (b).
[26] Code Sec. 351(d).

[27] Reg. § 1.351-1(a)(2), Example 3.
[28] Reg. § 1.351-1(a)(1)(ii).
[29] Rev. Proc. 77-37, 1977-2 CB 568.

percent (in this case it is 60 percent) of the value of services, all of the stock received by Connell is counted in meeting the 80 percent requirement. Thus, the 80 percent requirement is met (Connell and Harvey together own 100 percent of the corporation). However, Connell's transfer of services is taxable.

Example 3-4. Assume the same facts as in the previous example, except that Connell contributes only $2,000 of property. Since the 10 percent test is not met, none of the stock received by Connell counts for control purposes, and Code Sec. 351 requirements are not met, since Harvey received only 75 percent of the stock. Thus, the transfer would be taxable to both Connell and Harvey.

Generally, the assumption of a liability by the transferee corporation does not affect the nontaxability of the exchange.[30] However, if the liabilities assumed by the transferee corporation plus the liabilities to which the transferred property is subject exceed the basis of property transferred to it, the excess is deemed to be a gain from the sale of those assets.[31]

Example 3-5. Pat Sullivan transferred equipment with a basis of $40,000 and land with a basis of $60,000, but encumbered by a $135,000 mortgage, to a corporation in exchange for all of its stock. Sullivan must recognize a gain of $35,000 ($135,000 − ($40,000 + $60,000)).

The character of the gain depends on whether the assets transferred are capital gain, Code Sec. 1231, or ordinary property. If more than one type of asset is transferred, gain is allocated among the assets according to their respective fair market values.

Example 3-6. Assume the same facts as in the previous example and also that the equipment is worth $50,000 and the land is worth $150,000. Also assume that $20,000 of depreciation has been taken on the equipment and that all of the assets have been held over one year. Of the $35,000 gain, $8,750 [$50,000/($50,000 + $150,000) × $35,000] is ordinary income. The remaining gain of $26,250 is Code Sec. 1231 gain.

Not all liabilities are counted for this purpose. Liabilities that would give rise to a deduction when paid (e.g., accounts payable of a cash basis taxpayer) and liabilities giving rise to a deduction under Code Sec. 736(a) (distributive shares of income or guaranteed payments owed to a retiring partner or a deceased partner) do not count for this purpose.[32] However, a

---

[30] Code Sec. 357(a).

[31] Code Sec. 357(c).

[32] Code Sec. 357(c)(3)(A).

liability, which when paid would be capitalized, would count for this purpose.[33]

If the principal purpose of the assumption of debt is for a tax avoidance purpose or the transaction lacks a business purpose, then the total liabilities transferred are considered to be cash boot.[34] This scenario may result in a different consequence than if excess liabilities are transferred. If excess liabilities are transferred, gain to the extent of the excess must be recognized even if there is a realized loss on the transaction, i.e., even if the property transferred had depreciated rather than appreciated. However, if tax avoidance is considered present, then all liabilities are treated as cash boot. In that case, the lesser of the liabilities or the realized gain would be taxable gain. If the property transferred had depreciated, there would be a realized loss and tax avoidance would not result in any recognized gain.

.02 Basis of the Stock and the Property Transferred

The basis of stock received in a Code Sec. 351 transfer is essentially a substituted basis, i.e., the basis of the property substitutes for the basis of the stock. Basis of the property is decreased by any money or other boot received (liabilities are considered the same as money for this purpose) and is increased by any gain recognized on the transaction.[35]

Example 3-7. Assume the same facts as in Example 3-5. Sullivan's basis in the stock is $60,000 + $40,000 − $135,000 + $35,000 = zero. In this instance, the zero stock basis is no coincidence. Anytime the liabilities transferred exceed the basis of property transferred, basis of the stock will be zero.

The corporation has a carryover basis in the property received. Only one adjustment is made to the carryover basis—the corporation adds any gain recognized by the transferor to the basis of its property.

Example 3-8. Assume the same facts as in Example 3-7. Total basis of the property to the corporation is $60,000 + $40,000 + $35,000 = $135,000.

How should basis resulting from excess liabilities be allocated? The regulations are silent on this issue. Several allocation methods are possible. For example, allocation of the extra basis could be based on the *pro rata* share of either the basis or the fair market value of the various assets. One would think that the latter is more defensible, but the acceptable method is in doubt.

---

[33] Code Sec. 357(c)(3)(B).
[34] Code Sec. 357(b).
[35] Code Sec. 358(a).

.03 Depreciation Recapture

A Code Sec. 351 transfer does not trigger depreciation recapture.[36] However, the recapture potential carries over to the corporation. Thus, the depreciation must be recaptured when the corporation disposes of the assets. As for depreciation taken after the transfer, the corporation "steps into the shoes" of the transferor to the extent that the adjusted basis to the transferee does not exceed the adjusted basis in the hands of the transferee.[37] Thus, the method and life years will be unchanged by the transfer.

For the year of transfer, the allowable deduction is prorated between the transferor and the transferee on a monthly basis. The transferor's share of depreciation is the depreciation for the entire year multiplied by a fraction, the numerator of which is the number of months in the transferor's year before the month of transfer.[38] Thus, the transferee corporation gets depreciation for the month of transfer.

Example 3-9. Nate Jamison placed into service in 2000 farm equipment costing $50,000. On April 10, 2001, he transferred the equipment as part of a Code Sec. 351 transfer to a corporation. Depreciation for the entire year (year 2) for seven-year assets, using 150% of straight-line and the half-year convention, would be $50,000 × .1913 = $9,565. Jamison would take depreciation of $9,565 × 3/12 = $2,391 on the equipment. Since $5,355 of depreciation was taken in 2000, the basis of the equipment to the corporation is $50,000 − $5,355 − $2,391 = $42,254. However, depreciation to the corporation would be based on the original cost and would be $9,565 × 9/12 = $7,174.

Any basis to the transferee corporation in excess of the transferor's basis is subject to a fresh start for depreciation purposes.

Example 3-10. Assume the same facts as in Example 3-9, except that due to gain recognized by Jamison resulting from an excess liability transference, the basis of the equipment to the corporation is $47,254. Depreciation to the extent of $42,254 would be as in Example 3-9, i.e., $7,174. However, depreciation on the other $5,000 of basis would be based on the first year of acquisition, i.e., $5,000 × .1071 = $536 (seven-year life, half-year convention, first year, 150%).

---

[36] Code Sec. 1245(b)(3); Code Sec. 1250(d)(3).
[37] Code Sec. 168(i)(7); Prop. Reg. § 1.168-5(b)(1).
[38] Prop. Reg. § 1.168-5(b)(4)(i).

¶ 313 Tax Rates

The corporate tax rate schedule has eight brackets. These rates are as follows:[39]

Taxable Income		
Lower end of bracket	Upper end of bracket	Tax Rates
$ 1	$ 50,000	15 percent
50,001	75,000	25 percent
75,001	100,000	34 percent
100,001	335,000	39 percent
335,001	10,000,000	34 percent
10,000,001	15,000,000	35 percent
15,000,001	18,333,333	38 percent
18,333,334 and over		35 percent

Example 3-11. Kar Auto, Inc. had taxable income of $80,000 for the calendar year 2001. The tax is:

$$
\begin{array}{rcl}
\$50,000 \times .15 & = & \$\ \ 7,500 \\
25,000 \times .25 & = & 6,250 \\
5,000 \times .34 & = & \underline{1,700} \\
\text{Total} & & \underline{\$\ 15,450}
\end{array}
$$

Example 3-12. Pleasant Valley Grocers Co. had taxable income of $1,050,000 for the calendar year 2001. The tax is:

$$
\begin{array}{rcl}
\$\ 50,000 \times .15 & = & \$\ \ 7,500 \\
25,000 \times .25 & = & 6,250 \\
25,000 \times .34 & = & 8,500 \\
235,000 \times .39 & = & 91,650 \\
715,000 \times .34 & = & \underline{243,100} \\
\text{Total} & & \underline{\$357,000}
\end{array}
$$

Tax Tips and Pitfalls

The existence of the 39 percent and the 38 percent "bubbles" may make smoothing of income very desirable. For example, a corporation that normally has taxable income of $90,000 per year should be reluctant to sell property or investments if doing so would push them into the 39 percent bubble. Use of the installment sales method might prevent the marginal tax rate from intruding into the "bubble."

Certain corporations may, in lieu of the regular corporate tax rates, be required to pay the alternate minimum tax (AMT). See a later section of this chapter for a discussion of the AMT computations.

---

[39] Code Sec. 11(b).

¶ 315   Controlled Groups

Absent Code Sec. 1561, corporations would find it very advantageous to split into two or more corporations so as to take advantage of the two tax brackets that have lower marginal tax rates.

> **Example 3-13.** Tatum County, Inc., estimates taxable income for 2001 to be $180,000. The tax would equal ($50,000 × .15) + ($25,000 × .25) + ($25,000 × .34) + ($80,000 × .39), or $53,450.

> **Example 3-14.** Assume the same facts as in the previous example, except that the corporation splits into two corporations, each of which has $90,000 of income. The total tax would be ($50,000 × .15) + ($25,000 × .25) + ($15,000 × .34) = $18,850 × 2 = $37,700. The tax savings would equal $15,750 ($53,450 − $37,700), a significant tax savings.

Code Sec. 1561 prevents taxpayers who are members of a "controlled group" from achieving this tax savings.

.01   Definition of Controlled Groups

The term "controlled group" covers two distinct types of ownership arrangements: "parent-subsidiary controlled groups," and "brother-sister controlled groups."[40] Parent-subsidiary groups consist of one or more chains of corporations connected through stock ownership with a common parent corporation if two conditions are met:

1. One or more of the corporations own either a minimum of 80 percent of the total *combined voting power* of all stock eligible to vote, or a minimum of 80 percent of the total *value* of shares of all classes of stock of each of the corporations other than the common parent corporation; and

2. The common parent corporation owns directly stock (options are counted as stock for this purpose) possessing at least 80 percent of either the total *combined voting power* of all stock eligible to vote, or at least 80 percent of the total *value* of shares of all classes of stock of at least one of the other corporations.[41]

> **Example 3-15.** The LC Corporation owns 80 percent of the only class of stock of MM, Inc., and MM owns 40 percent of the only class of stock of Orange Co., Inc. LC also owns 80 percent of the only class of stock of Nusbum Co., and Nusbum owns 40 percent of Orange Co., Inc. LC is the common parent of a parent-subsidiary controlled group of which the members are LC Corporation, MM, Inc., Orange Co., Inc., and Nusbum Co. LC Corporation has *direct* control of MM, Inc. and Nusbum Co., and *indirect* control of Orange Co., Inc.

---

[40] Code Sec. 1563.   [41] Code Sec. 1563(a)(1); Reg. § 1.1563-1(a)(2).

Example 3-16. Assume the same facts as in Example 3-15, except that LC Corporation owns only 75 percent of Nusbum Co. In that event, Nusbum Co. drops out of the controlled group as does Orange Co., Inc.

In determining whether or not the parent owns at least 80 percent of one or more of the corporations, stock owned directly by the other companies (intercompany holdings) is not included, i.e., not treated as being outstanding.[42]

Example 3-17. Brant Co. owns 70 percent of the only class of stock of Cory Inc. and Dalton Co. Cory owns the remainder of Dalton and Dalton owns all of the remainder of Cory. Since intercompany holdings are excluded for purposes of the 80 percent test, Brant Co. is considered to own *all* of the stock of both Cory Inc. and Dalton Co. Hence, the three corporations form a controlled group.

.02 Brother-Sister Groups

A brother-sister group exists if five or fewer persons (defined as individuals, estates, or trusts) own:

- At least 80 percent of the total *combined voting power* of all stock eligible to vote, or at least 80 percent of the total *value* of shares of all classes of stock of each corporation; and

- More than 50 percent of the total *combined voting power* of all stock eligible to vote, or more than 50 percent of the total *value* of shares of all classes of stock of each corporation, taking into account the stock ownership of each such person only to the extent such stock ownership is identical with respect to each such corporation.[43]

The five or fewer persons who are counted for the 80 percent test must be the same persons as those who are counted for the over 50 percent test.[44] This means that in applying the 80 percent test, stock is counted only for those shareholders who own stock in *each* corporation.

The 80 percent test is often called the vertical test, and the over 50 percent test is called the horizontal test; putting the stock ownership in matrix form can result in vertical addition to determine if the 80 percent test is met, while the over 50 percent test is determined by selecting the lowest ownership across the row for individual ownership, and then adding down to determine if the least common ownership exceeds 50 percent.

---

[42] Code Sec. 1563(a)(1)(B); Reg. § 1.1563-1(a)(2).

[43] Code Sec. 1563(a)(2).

[44] Reg. § 1.1563-1(a)(3).

Example 3-18. The stock of Diamond, Coal, and Tar Corporations is owned by the following unrelated individuals:

Individuals	Corporations			Lowest Ownership
	Diamond	Coal	Tar	
Jones	30%	45%	52%	30%
Smith	20	31	18	18
Brown	35	15	26	15
Green	15	9	4	4
	100%	100%	100%	67%

Adding vertically, the 80 percent test is met, while selecting the *least* common ownership of individuals, the over 50 percent test is also easily met. Hence, all three corporations are members of a brother-sister controlled group.

Example 3-19. Assume the same facts as in Example 3-18, except that the ownership takes a slightly different configuration, as follows:

Individuals	Corporations			Lowest Common Ownership
	Diamond	Coal	Tar	
Jones	21%	45%	56%	21%
Smith	20	31	18	18
Brown	35	15	26	15
Green	24	9	0	0
	100%	100%	100%	54%

Although the over 50 percent test appears to be met, in applying the 80 percent test for all three corporations, Green's ownership must be dropped out as follows:

Individuals	Corporations			Lowest Common Ownership
	Diamond	Coal	Tar	
Jones	21%	45%	56%	21%
Smith	20	31	18	18
Brown	35	15	26	15
	76%	91%	100%	54%

The 80 percent test is not met, so Diamond, Coal, and Tar Corporations, considered as a threesome, are not members of a controlled group. However, other combinations must also be tested:

Individuals	Corporations		Lowest Common Ownership
	Diamond	Coal	
Jones	21%	45%	21%
Smith.......................	20	31	20
Brown	35	15	15
Green.......................	24	9	9
	100%	100%	65%

Diamond and Coal appear to be members of a brother-sister controlled group, but applying the same tests, so would Diamond and Tar, and Coal and Tar. If this is so, in what manner would the tax brackets be allocated? Unfortunately, the regulations are silent with respect to this question.

.03 Combined Groups

Combined groups are defined as three or more corporations each of which is either a member of a brother-sister group or a parent-subsidiary group, and one of which is both the common parent of a parent-subsidiary controlled group and a member of a brother-sister controlled group.[45]

Example 3-20. Toy, Inc. and Soldier Toy, Inc. are both 80 percent owned by Thompson. Toy, Inc. is also the 100 percent owner of a subsidiary, Big Toy Co. All three corporations are members of a combined group since all three are members of either a brother-sister (Toy, Inc. and Soldier Toy, Inc.) or a parent-subsidiary group (Toy, Inc. and Big Toy Co.), and at least one member (in this case Toy, Inc.) belongs to a brother-sister group *and* is a parent.

.04 Determining Stock Ownership—Direct Ownership and Attribution Rules

Various stock attribution rules (stock is considered constructively owned) apply in determining whether control exists for both brother-sister and parent-subsidiary groups. For parent-subsidiary groups, stock, in meeting the 80 percent requirement, includes stock directly owned by the corporation as well as options to acquire stock, options to acquire options, and so on.[46] In turn, these two categories of "stock" will be considered indirectly owned by any parent of the owning corporation, provided that such parent has control of the owning corporation.

Example 3-21. Watts, Inc. owns 90 percent of the stock of Light Bulb, Inc., and 480 of the 1,000 shares of stock outstanding of Ohms Co. Light Bulb, Inc., owns 300 of the shares of Ohms Co., but has an option on 200 more shares (it is the only option holder). For control purposes, Light Bulb, Inc., owns 500 out of 1,200 shares of Ohms Co. Since it is controlled, however, its parent, Watts, Inc. owns 480 shares

---

[45] Code Sec. 1563(a)(3); Reg. § 1.1563-1(a)(4). [46] Code Sec. 1563(d)(1) and (e)(1).

directly and 500 shares indirectly (constructively), or a total of 980 shares out of the 1,200. Hence, the 80 percent test is met, and Ohms Co. is a member of the controlled group.

The attribution rules are necessarily quite different for brother-sister groups. Stock owned by a "person" (an individual, estate, or trust) includes stock owned directly as well as stock owned under the following attribution rules:

1.   Options to acquire stock, options to acquire options, and so on;

2.   Stock owned either directly or indirectly by or for a partnership is considered to be *proportionately owned* by a partner provided that the partner has at least a five percent interest in either the capital or profits of the partnership;

3.   Stock owned directly or indirectly, by or for a corporation, is also considered to be *proportionately owned* provided that the person owns at least five percent of the *value* of the stock.[47]

Example 3-22. Mayberry owns 20 percent of the M-D partnership and 30 percent of the stock of BMA, Inc. In turn, M-D and BMA, Inc., own 40 percent and 35 percent of LMM, Inc. Stock ownership of eight percent (40% × 20%) is attributed to Mayberry from the M-D partnership and another 10.5 percent (30% × 35%) from LMM, Inc.

4.   Stock owned directly or indirectly by or for an estate or trust is considered owned by a beneficiary to the extent of the person's "actuarial interest," provided that the "actuarial interest" is at least five percent. The "actuarial interest" of a person in stock owned directly or indirectly by or for a trust is determined in accordance with Reg. § 20.2031-7 (these regulations contain, among other items, tables used to value life estates and remainder interests). The actuarial interest of each beneficiary is determined by assuming both the *maximum* exercise of discretion by the fiduciary in the beneficiary's favor and the *maximum* use of the stock to satisfy the beneficiary's rights.[48]

Example 3-23. The fiduciary of the Whitaker Trust has the authority, under the trust agreement, to invade corpus for the benefit of J.J. Whitaker, one of the beneficiaries, up to $40,000. Total trust corpus is $100,000, including $30,000 of stock in Whitaker, Inc. All $30,000 of the stock is attributed to J.J. Whitaker.

If, under the terms of the estate or trust, neither the stock itself nor the income from the stock could be distributed to the beneficiary, then the beneficiary does *not* have an actuarial interest in the stock.[49]

---

[47] Code Sec. 1563(d)(2) and (e).
[48] Reg. § 1.1563-3(b)(3).

[49] *Id.*

¶ 315.04

Example 3-24. Assume the same facts as in the previous example, except that under the terms of the trust, J.J. Whitaker cannot receive the stock or the dividends from the stock. J.J. does not have an actuarial interest in the stock.

5. Blood relatives are divided into two categories: spouses and other relatives. Generally, spouses are considered to own stock in a corporation by or for the spouse. Ownership is not attributed to spouses who are legally separated or are under a decree of separate maintenance, whether the decree is final or temporary. Spousal attribution is also not considered if all four of the following conditions are met:[50]

    1. The individual does not at any time in the tax year own directly any stock in the corporation;

    2. The individual is not a director or employee of the corporation and does not participate in corporate management at any time in the tax year;

    3. No more than 50 percent of the corporation's gross income for such tax year was from passive sources, i.e., royalties, interest, rent, dividends, and annuities; and

    4. The stock is not at any time in the tax year subject to conditions substantially restricting or limiting the spouse's right to dispose of the stock and which run in favor of the individual or children under age 21.

Attribution rules for minor children (under 21) work both ways, i.e., stock owned directly or indirectly by the children is attributed to the parents and stock owned by the parents is attributed to the children. However, with respect to adult children and grandchildren, stock ownership is attributed to the individual *only* if the individual owns (not counting this attributed stock) over 50 percent of either the total combined voting power or the total value of all classes of stock. A legally adopted child is considered a blood relative for this purpose.[51]

Example 3-25. Jason Gregory owns 30 shares of the 100 shares of stock outstanding of Gregory & Children, Inc. His daughter Beth, age 26, owns 15 shares, while his son John, age 18, owns 22 shares. The stock of John is attributed to Jason since John is under 21. Thus, Jason directly and indirectly owns 52 percent. In turn, since Jason owns over 50 percent, he must also count the stock of the adult offspring Beth; hence, Jason constructively owns 67 shares. Beth, however, owns only 15 shares (under 50 percent); therefore, the stock of Jason is not attributed to her and the stock of her brother is never attributed to her. Therefore, her total actual and constructive ownership is only 15

---

shares. John, the minor son, owns directly and indirectly his stock and · that of his parent (52 percent). However, he does not attribute the stock of his sister.

¶ 317   Impact of Controlled Groups

Members of controlled groups must share only one of each of the three corporate income tax brackets.[52] The result of this sharing or allocation of the income tax brackets is to give the corporations no more of the benefit of the lower marginal rates than if only one corporation had all of the income.

Example 3-26. Adams Co. and Baird Co. have taxable income of $110,000 and $120,000, respectively. They allocate the income tax bracket equally. Their tax computations are as follows:

	Rate	Adams Co.	Baird Co.	Total
First $25,000	15%	$ 3,750	$ 3,750	$ 7,500
Next $12,500	25%	3,125	3,125	6,250
Next $12,500	34%	4,250	4,250	8,500
Excess..............	39%	23,400	27,300	50,700
Total		$34,525	$38,425	$72,950

The income tax brackets are allocated evenly unless the members consent to an apportionment plan providing for an unequal allocation of such amounts.[53] Consent with respect to a particular December 31 must be made by means of a statement signed by the duly authorized representatives of each corporation which sets forth the name, address, taxpayer account number and tax year of each corporation; the amount apportioned to each member; and the service center where the original of the statement is to be filed.[54] Each member then attaches a copy of the consent form to its tax return.[55]

Tax Tips and Pitfalls

Unless each corporation has taxable income at least equal to $100,000 divided by the number of corporations in the group, it is important to file an apportionment plan so as to utilize all of the three income tax brackets.

Example 3-27. Mill, Inc., and Wright Co. are brother-sister corporations. In the current year they have taxable income of $40,000 and $120,000, respectively. If they do not file an apportionment plan, their respective income taxes are shown in columns A and B. Columns C and D reflect an equal apportionment of the first two brackets, and $2,500 of the third bracket to Mill, Inc., and the remaining $22,500 to Wright Co.

---

[52] Code Sec. 1561(a)(1).
[53] Code Sec. 1561(a).

[54] Reg. § 1.1561-3(b)(1)(i).
[55] Id.

Tax on	Column A Mill	Column B Wright	Column C Mill	Column D Wright
First $25,000	$3,750	$ 3,750	$3,750	$ 3,750
Next $12,500	3,125	3,125	3,125	3,125
Next $2,500	850	850	850	850
Next $10,000	—	3,400	—	3,400
Next $10,000	—	3,900	—	3,400
Next $60,000	—	23,400	—	23,400
	$7,725	$38,425	$7,725	$37,925
Total		$46,150		$45,650

Since Mill, Inc.'s $40,000 of taxable income is less than $50,000 ($100,000/2), an apportionment would be expected to save tax—in fact, $500 in tax. It is important to note that the brackets *could* have been apportioned differently, had the corporations desired it, while still achieving the optimum tax savings.

¶ 319   The Alternative Minimum Tax

In lieu of the regular income tax, corporations, like individuals, are subject to an alternative minimum tax (AMT) if such tax exceeds the regular tax.[56] However, the AMT will not apply to small business corporations after 1997. Small business corporations are defined as corporations having gross receipts of no greater than $5 million for their first three consecutive years after 1994. Once a corporation meets the $5 million test, it will not be subject to the AMT until its average annual gross receipts for all three-taxable-year periods ending before the taxable year exceed $7.5 million.[57]

The starting point for the calculation of the AMT is taxable income before any net operating loss deduction but after special deductions.[58] In order to arrive at the tax base, taxable income is adjusted by four items: preferences, adjustments, book income, and the exemption.

The four tax preferences listed below constitute additions to taxable income for AMT purposes. These preference items were generally present in the old add-on minimum tax which existed prior to TRA '86. The preference items are:[59]

1. *Accelerated depreciation of real property placed into service prior to 1987.* This is the excess (if any) of the depreciation taken on the property over depreciation using straight-line rates, the half-year convention and no salvage value, but using the same life years (generally 15, 18, or 19) as the ACRS statutory years. Excess depreciation is determined separately

[56] Code Sec. 55(a).
[57] Act Sec. 401(a), Taxpayer Relief Act of 1997, adding Code Sec. 55(e).
[58] Instructions, Form 4626. "Special Deductions" consist of the dividends received deduction, certain

income from controlled foreign corporations, and, for public utilities, a deduction for dividends paid on certain preferred stock.

[59] Code Sec. 57; Instructions, Form 4626.

for each property rather than aggregated. Hence, if straight-line depreciation exceeds ACRS on one Code Sec. 1250 property, the excess may not be used to offset the tax preference from another Code Sec. 1250 property. **Note:** If the corporation used a longer recovery period than the ACRS statutory life, no preference will result.

Example 3-28. The Watson Company placed into service a building on January 3, 1981, and a second building on July 3, 1986. The respective costs were $90,000 and $120,000. For 1989, the accelerated depreciation and straight-line amounts were:

	ACRS	S/L	Excess
Building acquired on 1/3/81	$5,400	$6,000	None
Building acquired on 7/3/86	8,760	6,316	$2,444

Thus, there is a tax preference of $2,444 resulting from the building acquired on July 3, 1986.

2. *Tax-exempt interest from private activity bonds issued after August 7, 1986.* The amount to be added back is the excess of such tax-exempt interest reduced by any expenses attributable thereto (which would not have been deductible for regular income tax purposes).[60]

Example 3-29. The Watson Company in 2001 received $12,000 from municipal bonds issued in 1998, the proceeds of which were used to finance construction of a factory building. Expenses incurred by Watson Company in 2001 in connection with the tax-exempt interest amounted to $3,500. For AMT purposes, $8,500 must be added as a preference.

3. *Intangible drilling costs.* The tax preference here is the portion over 65 percent of the "net income from oil, gas, and geothermal activities" of the excess (if any) of intangible drilling costs deducted during the year over the amount that would have been deducted had the costs been capitalized and depreciated over either 120 months or depleted under the permissible rules for cost depletion, starting in any case, in the month in which production begins. **Note:** The costs of drilling dry holes does not constitute intangible drilling costs. "Net income from oil, gas, and geothermal properties" is defined as the excess of gross income over all deductions, except that the excess drilling and development costs are not deducted for this purpose.

Example 3-30. Watson Company in 2001 spent $180,000 of intangible drilling costs to bring in an oil well which began production

---

[60] A detailed discussion of private activity bonds is outside the scope of this book. The reader is referred to Code Sec. 141 for details.

in July. The deduction allowable if the costs had been amortized is ($180,000/120) × 6 = $9,000. However, if cost depletion for these costs had been used, eight percent of the estimated reserves were sold in 2001; hence, eight percent of the drilling and development costs, or $14,400, would have been deductible. Watson elects to use this cost depletion for AMT purposes; therefore, excess drilling and development costs are $180,000 − $14,400, or $165,600. Gross income from all oil properties amounted to $2,000,000. Expenses, including the $180,000 of drilling and development costs, amounted to $1,950,000. "Net income" is $2,000,000 − [$1,950,000 − ($180,000 − $14,400)] = $215,600. Tax preferences from drilling and development costs are $165,600 − ($215,600 × .65) = $25,460.

4. *Depletion.* Here the tax preference is the excess of the depletion deduction over the adjusted basis of the property at the end of the year (determined without regard to the depletion deduction), figured separately for each property.

> **Example 3-31.** Watson Company had an adjusted basis in a gravel pit at the start of 2001 of $27,000. Gross income from the pit in 2000 amounted to $800,000. Percentage depletion taken for 2001 was $800,000 × .05 = $40,000. There were no other items affecting basis in 2001. The tax preference amounts to $13,000 ($40,000 − $27,000).

¶ 321 Adjustments

There are 11 adjustments required by corporations in determining AMT. These are considerably more complicated than the preferences previously discussed. While preferences all result in additions to the AMT base, adjustments may result in either additions or subtractions to the tax base. A discussion of the 11 adjustments follows:[61]

1. *Depreciation of property placed into service after 1986.* For personal property being depreciated under MACRS methods, depreciation for AMT purposes is computed at 150 percent of straight-line, switching over to straight-line for the first tax year in which that method gives more depreciation, and using the alternative life as specified by Code Sec. 168(g). For real property, whether commercial or residential rental, straight-line and a 40-year life are used. If personal property has no class life, 12 years is used. If depreciation is included in inventory, the inventory is refigured based on the depreciation adjustment. The difference between depreciation for regular income tax purposes and for AMT purposes, whether plus or minus, is entered as an adjustment.

---

[61] Code Sec. 56; Instructions, Form 4626.

For property placed in service after December 31, 1998, the Taxpayer Relief Act of 1997 conforms the recovery period used for purposes of the alternative minimum tax depreciation adjustments to the recovery periods used for purposes of the regular tax.[62]

Example 3-32. Diamond Company in 1995 had four assets subject to depreciation. The depreciation for regular and for AMT purposes is as follows:

| | Depreciation | | Regular | | | AMT | | |
| | Date | Original | | | | | | |
Description	Acquired	Basis	Life	Rate[a]	Amount	Life[b]	Rate[c]	Amount
Building	1/3/93	$150,000	31½	3.2%	$ 4,800	40	2.5%	$ 3,750
Personal Property A. . .	1/5/93	60,000	7	17.5%	10,500	12	10.25%	6,150
Personal Property B. . .	7/2/94	20,000	5	16.0%[d]	3,200	5	12.75%[e]	2,550
Personal Property C. . .	1/6/95	30,000	7	14.3%	4,290	10	7.5%	2,250
					$22,790			$14,700

[a] Rates taken from ACRS table.
[b] Life for AMT purposes is the alternative depreciation system as provided in Code Secs. 168(g) and 167(m) and Rev. Proc 83-85, 1983-2 CB 6.
[c] Rates based on original cost given the life year and 150 percent method.
[d] Sold on 10/5/95. One-half year depreciation allowable.
[e] Sold on 10/5/95. One-half year depreciation allowable.

Thus, the adjustment to taxable income is $22,790 less $14,700, or an addition of $8,090.

2.   *Mining exploration and development costs paid or incurred after 1986 (Code Secs. 616 and 617).* For each mine or other natural deposit (not including oil, gas, or geothermal wells), the expenses are refigured by amortizing them over 10 years beginning with the year in which the expenses were made. The adjustment is determined by subtracting the refigured amount from the deduction taken after the 30 percent deduction (see Code Sec. 291). Special rules exist for losses from mining properties (see Code Sec. 56(a)(2)(B) for details).

3.   *Long-term contracts entered into after February 28, 1986 (Code Sec. 460).* The amount of the adjustment is equal to the difference between taxable income that would have been recognized had the percentage of completion method been used and the amount of taxable income recognized for regular tax purposes.

Note: "Home construction contracts" are not subject to this adjustment. For short-term contracts (those to be completed within two years or less of the contract commencement date) of small contractors (those whose average annual gross receipts for the three taxable

---

[62] Act Sec. 402(a), Taxpayer Relief Act of 1997, amending Code Sec. 56(a)(1)(A).

years preceding the taxable year of the contract are not over
$10,000,000), the percentage of completion is determined using the
simplified procedures for allocating costs outlined in Code Sec.
460(b)(3). "Home construction contracts" are contracts where at least
80 percent of the estimated total contract costs (as of the close of the
taxable year in which the contract was entered into) are reasonably
expected to be attributable to the building, construction, reconstruc-
tion, or rehabilitation of:

   a. Dwelling units in buildings with no more than four dwelling
      units; and

   b. Improvements to real property directly related to such
      dwelling units and located on the site of such dwelling
      units.[63]

Example 3-33. Baymore Company in July 1997 entered into a
contract to construct a building with more than four units. The
contract price was $50,000,000, and estimated costs were $40,000,000.
Costs actually incurred in 1997 and 1998 were $5,000,000 and
$12,000,000, respectively. Taxable income in 1998, using the percent-
age of completion method, is ($12,000,000/$40,000,000) ×
$50,000,000 = $15,000,000; $15,000,000 − $12,000,000 =
$3,000,000. This rule applied to long-term contracts entered into after
June 21, 1988, but before July 11, 1989. Assuming that Watson
Company uses percentage of completion-capitalized cost for regular
income tax purposes and that its taxable income under that method is
$2,700,000, the adjustment for AMT purposes is a $300,000 addition
($3,000,000 − $2,700,000).

   4. *Pollution control facilities placed into service after 1986 (Code
      Sec. 169).* For certified pollution control facilities placed in
      service after 1986 and before 1999, amortization for AMT
      purposes is determined by using the alternative life as provided
      in Code Sec. 168(g) and using straight-line depreciation. For
      facilities placed in service after 1998, the AMT deduction is
      determined under MACRS using the straight-line method. The
      difference between this computation and the amortization
      taken for regular income tax purposes is then added to or
      deducted from taxable income.

   5. *Circulation expenses of personal holding companies (Code Sec.
      173).* This adjustment is the difference between total circulation
      expenses deducted and the amount that *would* be deductible if
      all circulation expenses paid or incurred after 1986 were capi-
      talized and amortized over a three-year period beginning with

---

[63] For more details concerning the above discussion, see Code Sec. 460.

the year the expenses were made. Special rules apply if a loss is incurred with respect to these expenses.[64]

6. *Merchant marine capital construction funds (Code Sec. 7518).* Certain amounts deposited in a "capital construction fund" under Section 607 of the Merchant Marine Act of 1936 are permitted as a deduction for regular income tax purposes. In addition, income (including gains and losses) earned by the fund may be excluded from income. However, for AMT purposes, these preferences are not permitted and, therefore, must be added back.[65]

7. *Code Sec. 833(b) deduction (Code Sec. 833).* This pertains to deductions permitted for certain insurance companies for regular income tax purposes. The deduction is not permitted for AMT purposes.

8. *Basis adjustment.* For AMT purposes, depreciation, amortization of mining development costs, pollution control facilities, and circulation expenses will all be different (usually lower) than for regular income tax purposes. In turn, the generally lower write-offs will result in a higher basis for AMT purposes. The purpose of this adjustment is to refigure gains and losses resulting from the sale of property placed into service after 1986. Generally, this amount will be negative (a deduction) since the AMT gain will be less (or the loss more) than for regular tax purposes.

Example 3-34. Refer to Example 3-32. Assume personal property B was sold for $12,000. The adjusted basis for regular income tax purposes is ($20,000 − $4,000 − $3,200) = $12,800. Thus, the *loss* for regular income tax purposes is $12,000 − $12,800 = $800. However, for AMT purposes, the adjusted basis is ($20,000 − $3,000 − $2,550) = $14,450. Thus, the *loss* for AMT purposes is $12,000 − $14,450 = $2,450. Hence, $1,650 ($2,450 − $800) will be *deducted* to arrive at AMT.

9. *Certain loss limitations (Code Secs. 465 and 704(d)).* For regular income tax purposes, partnership loss deductions are subject to two limitations: (1) the amount at risk, and (2) the adjusted basis in the partnership before the loss deduction. If any of the other adjustments or preferences affect the loss for AMT purposes, the amount at risk, or the adjusted basis, or any combination of the above, then the recomputed loss may be different from what was reported for regular income tax purposes.

---

[64] See Code Sec. 56(b)(2)(B).
[65] Also, basis of certain assets may be affected; see Code Sec. 7518(f) for details.

Example 3-35. Assume that for regular income tax purposes, the Watson Corporation's share of partnership loss from the W-Y partnership was $90,000, but the adjusted basis before the loss was only $65,000, so that only $65,000 was deducted for regular tax purposes. The AMT adjustment reduced the loss from $90,000 to $55,833. Without any adjustment here, however, only $30,833 of the loss ($65,000 − $34,167) would be deducted. Since the loss of $55,833 is less than the basis, all of it should be deducted for AMT purposes. Therefore, this adjustment would be a deduction of $25,000 ($55,833 − $30,833).

10. *Tax shelter farm activity of personal service corporation.* An adjustment is required for personal service corporations that have gains or losses from a tax shelter farm activity (as defined in Code Sec. 58(a)(2)). The adjustment required here involves refiguring the gains and losses, and taking into account any AMT adjustments and preferences which would change the loss or gain (e.g., depreciation adjustments). The difference between the loss allowed for regular tax purposes and for AMT purposes is then added or deducted to arrive at AMT.

11. *Passive activity losses of closely held corporations and personal service corporations (Code Sec. 469).* Two reasons exist for this adjustment. First, the various other AMT adjustments and preferences may have changed the amount of the loss. Second, for AMT purposes, the transitional rules (which allow a partial deduction for the years 1987-1990 for passive activity losses and credits attributable to passive activity interests held on October 22, 1986) do not apply.

¶ 323 Book Income Adjustment (For Years After 1989)

For any tax year beginning after 1989, a corporation's alternative minimum taxable income (AMTI) is increased by 75 percent of the excess (if any) of the "adjusted current earnings" over the AMTI (determined without regard to the adjustment based on adjusted current earnings and the alternative tax net operating loss deduction).[66] "Adjusted current earnings" (ACE) is defined as AMTI before the "alternative tax net operating loss deduction" and the adjustment based on adjusted current earnings but subject to the following adjustments:[67]

1. *Depreciation.*[68] The adjustment for depreciation depends on the tax year in which the assets were placed into service. For property placed into service after 1993, ACE depreciation is the same as depreciation for AMT purposes. Therefore, no adjustment is required. Depreciation for property placed into service

---

[66] Code Sec. 56(g)(1).
[67] Code Sec. 56(g)(3).

[68] Code Sec. 56(g)(4)(A).

in a tax year beginning after 1989 but before 1994 is determined under the alternate system of Code Sec. 168(g). The depreciation deduction for property depreciated under the original ACRS or MACRS is determined by computing the adjusted basis as of the close of the first tax year beginning before 1990 and dividing that by the remaining life years that would exist had the property been depreciated under the alternative system. Finally, for property placed into service before 1981, the method used for computing taxable income applies unless book depreciation would yield a smaller present value.

2.   *Items included in E&P.*[69] Generally, an adjustment is required for items which are excluded from gross income for purposes of computing AMTI but included in earnings and profits (E&P). However, deductions which would have been allowable had the amount been included in gross income can be taken. Special rules apply to insurance contracts. Income from insurance contracts is as determined by Code Sec. 7702(g)(1)(B), i.e., income is the excess of the sum of the increase in the net surrender value and the cost of the life insurance protection provided under the contract over the net premiums paid during the year.

3.   *Items not deductible in computing E&P.*[70] Generally, if an item is not deductible for E&P purposes, it is not deductible for purposes of determining adjusted current earnings. The 70 percent dividends-received deduction constitutes an example of a deduction that is not allowed for E&P purposes, and, therefore, not for AMTI purposes. However, an exception exists for the 80 percent dividends-received deduction as well as for the 100 percent dividends-received deduction allowable under Code Secs. 243 and 245 (members of affiliated groups and dividends distributed out of E&P while the distributing corporation was a foreign sales corporation (FSC)). This exception applies only if the dividend payor and receiver could not file consolidated returns by reason of Code Sec. 1504(b), i.e., one of the companies was an exempt corporation, an insurance company, a foreign corporation, and so on. Furthermore, a deduction is permitted only to the extent that the dividend is attributable to income of the paying corporation that is subject to tax after Code Secs. 30A (the Puerto Rico Economic Activity Credit) and 936 (the exclusion for foreign trade income of an FSC) are applied. A special rule, outside the scope of discussion of this book, exists for dividends from Code Sec. 936 companies.

---

[69] Code Sec. 56(g)(4)(B).   [70] Code Sec. 56(g)(4)(C).

4. *Other E&P adjustments.*[71] Generally, the several adjustments made to taxable income specified in Code Sec. 312(n) to arrive at E&P apply for AMT purposes for tax years beginning after 1989. Required items for which to adjust include: intangible drilling costs, amortization of circulation expenditures and organizational costs, LIFO inventory adjustments, and installment sales.

5. *Loss on exchange of debt pools.*[72] For AMT purposes, no loss is recognized on the exchange of debt pools for another pool of obligations if the second pool has substantially the same effective interest rates and maturities.

6. *Depletion.*[73] The allowance for depletion for any property placed into service for a tax year beginning after 1989 is determined by computing cost depletion as provided by Code Sec. 611.

7. *Other adjustments.*[74] Other adjustments may be required for certain ownership changes (as defined by Code Sec. 382) occurring in a tax year beginning after 1989.

¶ 325   Alternative Tax Net Operating Loss—Deduction

The starting point for the alternative tax net operating loss deduction (ATNOLD) is the net operating loss (NOL) determined for regular tax purposes, with the following three exceptions:[75]

1. For a loss year beginning after 1986, the regular NOL must be reduced by the positive AMT adjustments and increased by the negative AMT adjustments. The only tax preferences taken into account are those that increased the regular NOL; they serve to reduce the ATNOLD.

2. In determining NOL carrybacks and carryforwards for tax years beginning after 1986, only 90 percent of AMTI is used to reduce the carrybacks and carryforwards.

3. Once ATNOLD is computed, the amount that may be taken as a deduction is the lesser of ATNOLD or 90 percent of AMTI (computed before ATNOLD). Any excess ATNOLD may be carried back or carried forward.

---

[71] Code Sec. 56(g)(4)(D).
[72] Code Sec. 56(g)(4)(E).
[73] Code Sec. 56(g)(4)(F).
[74] Code Sec. 56(g)(4)(G).
[75] Code Sec. 55(d).

¶ 327   The Tax, Exemption and Credits

The AMT rate is a flat 20 percent. The alternative minimum tax foreign tax credit is the only credit allowed against the tentative minimum tax.[76]

The tentative exemption allowed corporations for AMT purposes is $40,000.[77]

However, the exemption is reduced by $.25 for every dollar of AMTI above $150,000.[78] Thus, the end of the phase-out range for the exemption is $310,000 of AMTI.

¶ 329   How the AMT Limits the General Business Credit

The general business credit may not be used to offset the alternate minimum tax. The general business credit is limited to the excess of the corporation's net income tax over the greater of:[79]

1.   Its tentative minimum income tax, or

2.   25 percent of its regular tax liability in excess of $25,000.

> **Example 3-36.** In 2001, Microblade, Inc., had a net regular tax liability before credits of $200,000. The tentative minimum tax was $80,000. General business credits amounted to $225,000. The general business credit is:

Net income tax		$200,000
Less: greater of:		
(1) .25 ($225,000 − $25,000)	$50,000	
(2) tentative minimum tax	$80,000	80,000
General business credit limitation		$120,000

¶ 331   Minimum Tax Credit[80]

When the tentative minimum tax exceeds the regular income tax (and therefore there is an alternate minimum tax paid), the difference is most often due largely to timing differences, i.e., income for AMT purposes is recognized earlier than for regular tax purposes, and/or deductions are allowed later for AMT purposes than for regular tax purposes. In order to prevent these items from being taxed twice, a minimum tax credit is allowed. The minimum tax credit (the amount of the AMT) may be carried forward indefinitely and offset against the regular income tax in any years in which the regular income tax exceeds the tentative minimum tax. For tax years beginning after 1989, the entire AMT (that due to both permanent and timing differences) is allowed as a credit. The minimum tax credit cannot be carried back to previous tax years, and, when carried forward,

---

[76] A detailed discussion of this credit is outside the scope of this book. See Code Sec. 59 for details.
[77] Code Sec. 55(d)(2).
[78] Code Sec. 55(d)(3).
[79] Code Sec. 38(c).
[80] Code Sec. 53.

can only be used in years in which the regular tax liability exceeds the tentative minimum tax.

> **Example 3-37.** In 2000, Engineering Products, Inc., had a regular tax liability of $180,000 and a tentative minimum tax of $200,000. In 2001, its regular tax was $260,000 and its tentative minimum tax was $245,000. It may use $15,000 of its minimum tax credit carryover in 2001. Thus, its tax in 2001 will be $245,000. The remaining $5,000 of minimum tax credit is carried forward to 2002 and later years.

¶ 333 Filing Requirements

Although individuals and fiduciaries need to file returns only if certain gross income levels are reached, every corporation in existence must file a return, regardless of its taxable income or gross income.[81] A corporation is not considered in existence after it ceases business and dissolves, provided that it retains no assets. State law is not controlling for this purpose. However, if a corporation has valuable claims for which it will bring suit, it is considered as having retained assets and is, therefore, still in existence.[82] A corporation that has obtained a charter, but which has never transacted any business nor derived any income, may request the district director to relieve it from filing a return. Otherwise, a return must be filed.[83]

¶ 335 Forms

Form 1120A is a simpler, shorter form than Form 1120. It has only two pages, instead of four, and does not have Schedule A (Cost of Goods Sold), Schedule C (Dividends and Special Deductions), or Schedule E (Compensation of Officers). All C corporations, except for certain special corporations, may use Form 1120. However, to use Form 1120A, a corporation must meet all of these eleven requirements:[84]

1. Its gross receipts, total income (net receipts plus other items of income), and total assets must each be less than $500,000;

2. Its only dividend income is from domestic corporations and those dividends qualify for the 70 percent dividends-received deduction and are not from debt-financed securities;

3. It does not have any of the "write-in" additions to tax listed in the Instructions for Form 1120, Schedule J, line 3 or line 11;

4. It must not own any part of a foreign corporation or foreign partnership; nor must any foreign shareholders own directly or indirectly 50 percent or more of its stock;

5. It is not a member of a controlled group and is not filing a consolidated return;

---

[81] Code Sec. 6012(a)(2); Reg. § 1.6012-2(a)(1).
[82] Reg. § 1.6012-2(a)(2).
[83] *Id.*
[84] 2000 Instructions, Form 1120A.

6.   It must not have any ownership in or transactions with a foreign trust;

7.   It is not undergoing a dissolution or liquidation nor is it filing its final tax return;

8.   It is not a personal holding company;

9.   It has no nonrefundable tax credits other than the general business credit and the credit for prior year minimum tax;

10.   It is not making an election to forego the carryback period of an NOL; and

11.   It is not required to file a special tax return (e.g., Form 1120-PC).

¶ 337   Filing Dates

The due date for the corporate return is the 15th day of the third month following the corporate year end. However, an automatic six-month extension is granted upon the timely filing of Form 7004.[85] The estimated unpaid tax liability must be remitted on or before the date of filing the extension. The form must be signed by one of the following:[86]

• An officer of the corporation;

• A duly authorized agent holding a power of attorney;

• A person currently enrolled to practice before the IRS; or

• An attorney or certified public accountant qualified to practice before the IRS.

If the return to be filed is consolidated, the form must be signed by a person eligible to sign for the parent corporation (see four eligible persons listed above), and the name, address, EIN, and tax period of each member must be shown on Form 7004.

The IRS may terminate the automatic extension at any time by mailing a notice of termination, in which case the corporation has 10 days to file the return.

Tax Tips and Pitfalls

It is important to pay the estimated unpaid tax liability at the time of filing the extension. Failure to pay by the date of the extension request will result in the imposition of the failure to pay tax penalty, which is, like all penalties, nondeductible. However, this penalty is avoided if the corporation has paid 100 percent of its tax at the time of filing the extension.

---

[85] Code Sec. 6081(b); Reg. § 1.6081-3.   [86] 2000 Instructions, Form 7004.

If the corporation needs additional time, an additional extension of time request may be filed. This extension, however, is not automatic.

Effective for determining interest rates after December 31, 1990, corporations having a large underpayment of tax (in excess of $100,000) must pay interest at the federal short-term rate plus five percent.[87] This relatively high rate of interest will likely spur corporations to avoid large underpayments and, once a 30-day letter of proposed deficiency is received upon audit, to pay promptly.

¶ 339   Estimated Tax Payments

Corporations (including S corporations) are generally required to stay current on their tax liability, i.e., they are required to make payments of estimated taxes in four quarterly installments. For calendar year corporations, the due dates of the installments are April 15, June 15, September 15, and December 15.[88] Fiscal year corporations must pay by the 15th day of the 4th, 6th, 9th, and 12th months.[89]

> **Example 3-38**. Henson Co. has a September 30 fiscal year. Estimated tax payments are due January 15, March 15, June 15, and September 15.

Failure to pay a sufficient amount of estimated tax payments may result in the imposition of an underpayment penalty. The amount of payment required to *avoid* the underpayment penalties depends on whether or not the corporation is deemed a "large corporation." "Large corporations" are defined as having had taxable income of $1,000,000 or more during any of the three tax years prior to the current year.[90] In determining the $1,000,000, net operating and capital loss carrybacks and carryforwards are not taken into account. Also, if the corporation is a member of a controlled group, the $1,000,000 must be divided.[91]

Small corporations may avoid the underpayment by paying, in each installment, 25 percent of the lesser of:[92]

- 100 percent of the eventual tax liability; or

- 100 percent of the prior year's tax.

The corporation's payments cannot be based on last year's tax if there was *no* tax liability or if the return was for less than 12 months.[93]

Tax Tips and Pitfalls

If the tax liability is expected to increase, the corporation may be considerably underpaid (thus having the use of the money) and yet still avoid the penalty. For example, if the tax liability is expected to

---

[87] Act Sec. 11341, Revenue Reconciliation Act of 1990, amending Code Sec. 6621(c).
[88] Code Sec. 6655(c).
[89] Code Sec. 6655(i)(1).

[90] Code Sec. 6655(g)(2).
[91] *Id.*
[92] Code Sec. 6655(d)(1).
[93] *Id.*

increase from $100,000 to $150,000, timely payments of $25,000 for each installment will retain the use of $50,000 and still avoid the underpayment penalty. On the other hand, if the tax liability is expected to fall, for example, to $80,000, the corporation should aim at the 100 percent of eventual tax liability requirement, keeping in mind, however, that falling below the 100 percent will result in a healthy nondeductible penalty. Given a 34 percent marginal tax rate, a 10 percent nondeductible penalty is equivalent to a *deductible* interest rate of over 15 percent. Therefore, it would usually be less expensive to pay the installment with short-term debt.

Large corporations must generally pay in each installment an amount equal to 25 percent of 100 percent of the eventual tax (hence, 100 percent will have been paid in). However, for the first installment (a time in which it is obviously difficult to estimate the total tax for the year), large corporations may pay in 25 percent of last year's tax.[94] If the first installment is short, the next required installment is increased to make up for the shortfall.[95]

Example 3-39. Bison, Inc.'s tax liability for the calendar year 2000 was $600,000. On April 15, 2001, the corporation estimates that its total tax liability for the 2001 calendar year will be $800,000. It would avoid the underpayment penalty for the first installment by paying $150,000. If by June 15 the corporation still expects an ultimate tax liability of $800,000, it should pay in ($800,000 × .25), or $200,000, plus the shortfall from the April 15 payment ($200,000 − $150,000), for a total of $250,000.

¶ 341 Annualized Income Installment and Adjusted Seasonal Installment Alternatives

The requirement that corporations have 100 percent of each installment paid or 100 percent of last year's tax could work a hardship on corporations with fluctuating income or those with seasonal income. Thus, the Code allows two alternatives to the 100 percent rules. The annualized method allows a corporation to annualize its income for every payment period and pay in a specified percentage of the tax on the annualized income. The applicable percentages are:[96]

Installment	Percentage
1	25
2	50
3	75
4	100

---

[94] Code Sec. 6655(d)(2).
[95] *Id.*

[96] Code Sec. 6655(e)(2)(B)(i).

Tax Tips and Pitfalls

The annualized method is advantageous for corporations which earn more of their income during the latter quarters of the year.

Example 3-40. Kirkland Co., a calendar year corporation, had taxable income of $500,000 for the first 3 months, $900,000 for the first 5 months, $1,800,000 for the first 8 months, $3,000,000 for the first 11 months, and $3,500,000 for the entire year. The corporation had few AMT adjustments; therefore the tentative minimum tax was less than the regular tax liability. Assuming no credits, the tax due for each installment *without* the use of the annualized method would be $1,190,000 × .25 = $297,500. The estimated payments due under the annualized methods, however, would be as follows:[97]

	First 3 Months	First 5 Months	First 8 Months	First 11 Months
Taxable income	$ 500,000	$ 900,000	$1,800,000	$3,000,000
Annualization multiple . . .	4	2.4	1.5	1.09091
Annualized income	2,000,000	$2,160,000	$2,700,000	$3,272,730
Tax	680,000	734,400	918,000	1,112,728
Applicable percentage	25	50	75	100
Cumulative payments	170,000	367,200	688,500	1,112,728
Less: previous cumulative payments		170,000	367,200	688,500
Payment due	$ 170,000	$ 197,200	$ 321,300	$ 424,228

Note that the first required payment is $127,500 less and the second is $100,280 less than under the regular 100 percent requirement.

The adjusted seasonal installment method may be helpful to companies that operate their business on a seasonal basis, or that derive most of their income during only a part of the year. However, in order to qualify for this alternative, the corporation's "base period percentage" for any six consecutive months must be at least 70 percent.[98] The "base period percentage" is the average percent of six-month taxable income to yearly taxable income for the relevant six-month period for the three preceding tax years.[99]

Example 3-41. A miniature golf course, on the calendar year, received the following percentage of total yearly income during the six-month period April through September of 1998, 1999, 2000: 72 percent, 68 percent, and 76 percent, respectively. The average percent for the three-year partial period is 72 percent. Since this exceeds 70 percent, the corporation qualifies for the seasonal installment method.

The required amount of each installment payment is determined as follows:[100]

---

[97] 2000 Instructions, Form 2220.
[98] Code Sec. 6655(e)(3)(B).

[99] Code Sec. 6655(e)(3)(D).
[100] Code Sec. 6655(e)(3)(C).

1. Take the taxable income for all months during the tax year preceding the filing month (the month the installment is due);

2. Divide the taxable income by the base period percentage for all months during the tax year preceding the filing month;

3. Determine the tax; and

4. Multiply the tax by the base period percentage for the filing month and all months during the tax year preceding the filing month.

Example 3-42. Small Golf Course, Inc., had the following amounts of taxable income for the years 1998-2001.

	1998	1999	2000	2001
First 3 months	($300,000)	($320,000)	($350,000)	($400,000)
First 4 months	(115,000)	(170,000)	(172,000)	(200,000)
First 5 months	35,000	40,000	45,000	50,000
First 6 months	305,000	310,000	355,000	400,000
First 8 months	960,000	1,090,000	1,180,000	1,300,000
First 9 months	1,150,000	1,230,000	1,350,000	1,500,000
First 11 months	1,040,000	1,140,000	1,250,000	1,360,000
Entire year	925,000	1,000,000	1,110,000	1,200,000

The first step is to arrive at the base period percentages for the total months before the filing month. Since the filing months are months 4, 6, 9, and 12, the months before the filing months are months 1-3, 1-5, 1-8, and 1-11. Hence, the requirement is to divide income for each of the above periods by total income for the entire year for all three base years, and then take a simple average of those percentages. For example, the ratio of taxable income for the first eight months to taxable income for the entire year for 1998, 1999, and 2000 is $960,000/$925,000 = 1.0378, $1,090,000/$1,000,000 = 1.09, and $1,180,000/$1,110,000 = 1.0631. The base period percentage for months 1-8 is, therefore, (1.0378 + 1.09 + 1.0631)/3 = 1.0636.

Doing the calculation for all four periods yields base period percentages as follows:

	First 3 months	First 5 months	First 8 months	First 11 months
Base period percentage	0	.0394	1.0636	1.1301

The income for the periods for the current year (2001) is then annualized by dividing such income by the above percentages.

Taxable income	($400,000)	$ 50,000	$1,300,000	$1,360,000
Annualized income	0	$1,269,036	$1,222,264	$1,203,433

Then the tax is computed on the annualized income.

Tax (annualized)	0	$ 431,472	$ 415,570	$ 409,167

Next, the base period percentages for the months through and including the filing periods (1-4, 1-6, and 1-9) are computed the same way as was done previously. They are as follows:

	First 4 months	First 6 months	First 9 months
Base period percentage	0	.3198	1.2298

Then the tax previously computed on the annualized income from the 1-3, 1-5, and 1-8 periods is multiplied by the base period percentage to arrive at a tax for the 1-4, 1-6, and 1-9 periods as follows:

	First 4 months	First 6 months	First 9 months
Base period percentage	0	.3198	1.2298
Tax (annualized).	$0	$431,472	$415,570
Tax for each installment	$0	$137,985	$511,068

The actual installment payment which would avoid a penalty, however, is the lesser of the regular payment of 25 percent of the total tax for the year reduced by credits, or the amount shown above reduced by the total of all preceding payments. Total tax for the year would be $408,000, and 25 percent of that would be $102,000. Thus, the required payment for the first quarter is the lesser of $102,000 or zero, as shown above, or *zero*. Required for the second quarter is the lesser of $137,985 — zero or $204,000, or $137,985. Required payment for the third quarter is the lesser of $511,068 − $137,985 = $373,083 or $102,000 + $66,015 = $168,015, or $168,015. Note that in this quarter the regular $102,000 is used because it is less, but when a corporation switches from either the annualized income or the seasonal installment method to the regular method, any shortfall resulting from the use of these methods must be recaptured. Had the corporation used the regular method for the first two quarters, $204,000 would have been required to be paid. Since the required payment for the first two quarters is only $137,985, the difference between $204,000 and $137,985, or $66,015, must be added to the regular payment of $102,000. Finally, in the fourth quarter the lesser of $409,167 − $306,000 = $103,167, or $102,000, is required. To summarize, the required payments are $0, $137,985, $168,015, and $102,000, respectively.

¶ 343 Gross Income of Corporations

Gross income of corporations is computed essentially the same way as it is for individuals. Code Sec. 61, in listing the most frequent sources of income, does not distinguish between corporations and individuals. Thus, one would expect that a corporation could derive income from, among other sources:[101]

- Compensation for services, including fees, commissions, fringe benefits, and similar items;

[101] Code Sec. 61(a).

- Gross income derived from business;

- Gains derived from dealings in property;

- Interest, rents, royalties, dividends, and annuities;

- Income from life insurance and endowment contracts;

- Income from discharge of indebtedness; and

- Distributive shares of partnership gross income.

On the other hand, certain items listed as gross income would not, due to their nature, typically be encountered by corporations. They include:[102]

- Alimony and separate maintenance payments;

- Pensions;

- Income in respect of a decedent; and

- Income from an interest in an estate or trust.

Code Secs. 72–90, which discuss specific inclusions in gross income, generally do not differentiate between corporations and individuals. Again, however, certain inclusions would be typically encountered by corporations, while other items would not generally be encountered at the corporate level.

Code Sec.	Topic

Inclusions applying equally to corporations and to other entities include:

72	Annuities; certain proceeds of endowments and life insurance policies
74	Prizes and awards
75	Dealers in tax exempt securities
77	Commodity credit loans
83	Property transferred in connection with services
84	Transfer of appreciated property to political organizations
87	Alcohol fuel credit
90	Illegal irrigation subsidies.

Inclusions applying only to corporations include:

78	Dividends received from certain foreign corporations by domestic corporations choosing the foreign tax credit
80	Restoration of value of certain securities
88	Certain amounts with respect to nuclear decommissioning costs (theoretically this could also apply to other entities).

Inclusions applying only to individuals include:

73	Services of child
79	Group term-life insurance for employees

---

[102] *Id.*

¶ 343

Code Sec.	Topic
82	Reimbursement of moving expenses
85	Unemployment compensation
86	Social Security and tier 1 railroad retirement benefits.

The exclusions applying to both corporations and other entities include:

101	Death benefits
102	Gifts and inheritances
103	State and local bond interest
108	Discharge of indebtedness
109	Improvements by lessee on lessor's property
110	Qualified lessee construction allowances
111	Recovery of tax benefit items
126	Certain cost sharing payments
130	Certain personal injury liability assignments
136	Energy conservation subsidies.

An exclusion applying only to corporations is:

118	Contributions to the capital of a corporation.

Exclusions applying only to individuals include:

104	Compensation for injuries and sickness
105	Amounts received under accident and health plans
106	Contributions by employer to accident and health plans
107	Rental value of parsonages
112	Combat pay of members of Armed Forces
117	Qualified scholarships
119	Meals or lodging furnished for the convenience of the employer
120	Group legal services
121	Gain on residence exclusion
122	Certain reduced services retirement pay
123	Amounts received under insurance contracts for certain living expenses
125	Cafeteria plans
127	Educational assistance programs
129	Dependent care assistance programs
131	Certain foster care payments
132	Fringe benefits
134	Certain military benefits
135	Income from U.S. savings bonds used to pay higher education tuition and fees
137	Adoption assistance programs
138	Medicare+ Choice MSA.

¶ 345   Capital Gains and Losses

As contrasted with individuals, corporations do not receive favorable treatment for capital gains. The treatment of capital losses, however, is different for corporations than for individuals. Individuals have a net capital loss deduction allowable of $3,000 per year. Corporations cannot deduct net capital losses.[103] They can, however, carry net capital losses back three years and forward five years.[104] Regardless of the characteristic of the capital loss (short-term or long-term), a capital loss carryback or carryforward becomes short-term.[105] Capital losses carried back or forward can be used to offset capital gains during those years but only to the extent that a net operating loss is not thereby created or increased.[106]

¶ 347   Additional Depreciation Recapture on Buildings

Although depreciation recapture rules are generally the same for corporations as for individuals, Code Sec. 291 contains an important exception. Corporations that sell depreciable realty at a gain (Code Sec. 1250 property) may have to recapture more depreciation than is required under Code Sec. 1250. In essence, 20 percent of the excess of the gain that would have occurred had the property been Code Sec. 1245 property over the Code Sec. 1250 gain constitutes an additional recapture.[107] The computational steps are as follows:

1. Compute the ordinary income, assuming that the property is Code Sec. 1245 property (such as machinery or equipment);

2. Compute the actual Code Sec. 1250 gain;

3. Take 20 percent of the excess of (1) over (2) (this is the Code Sec. 291 gain); and

4. Add the amount determined in (2) to (3) (this is the total ordinary income).

Example 3-43. On January 4, 1983, Jay, Inc. acquired an apartment building at a cost of $300,000. The corporation held the building until January 3, 1991, selling it for $380,000. It took ACRS depreciation of $192,000; straight-line would have been $160,000. Ordinary income on the sale is computed as follows:

---

[103] Code Sec. 1211(a).
[104] Code Sec. 1212(a)(1).
[105] *Id.*

[106] *Id.*
[107] Code Sec. 291(a).

Total gain ($380,000 + $192,000 − $300,000) = ... $272,000

Ordinary income if the property was Code Sec. 1245
property (lesser of $272,000 or $192,000) 192,000

Code Sec. 1250 gain (lesser of $272,000 or $192,000 −
$160,000)* 32,000

20 percent × ($192,000 − $32,000) 32,000

Total ordinary income: ($32,000 + $32,000) 64,000

---

* Code Sec. 1250 gain for residential rental property being depreciated at accelerated rates is the lesser of the total gain or the excess of ACRS depreciation over straight-line.

Tax Tips and Pitfalls

This provision is currently of little importance since corporations presently receive no preferential treatment on capital gains. However, if a preferential treatment for capital gains *is* restored, it would be especially applicable to any buildings acquired after 1986 (since only straight-line methods can be used, there would be no Code Sec. 1250 gain, but 20 percent of the straight-line depreciation up to the total gain would have to be recaptured under Code Sec. 291). For property acquired after 1980 and before 1987, Code Sec. 291 has no application to commercial real property depreciated under accelerated rates since in that event all of the depreciation is recaptured anyway. The example above covered an example of residential rental property; Code Sec. 291 had a moderate impact on the type of gain. Finally, the sale of pre-ACRS property can result in significant Code Sec. 291 gain. Hence, if preferential capital gain treatment is restored and *if* taxpayers contemplate the transfer of appreciated buildings to corporations, the Code Sec. 291 impact would be as follows:

- Pre-ACRS property—Considerably more ordinary income potential

- ACRS commercial realty—No additional ordinary income potential

- ACRS residential realty—Moderate additional ordinary income potential

- Post-1986 commercial realty—Considerably more ordinary income potential

- Post-1986 residential rental—Considerably more ordinary income potential

¶ 347

¶ 349   Charitable Contributions

Generally, the rules governing charitable contribution deductions for corporations follow those for individuals. Exceptions relate to the deduction limit, the amount deductible for certain contributions of inventory, and the year of deduction of accrual contributions.

Corporations are subject to a much lower limit on contributions, i.e., a 10 percent limit rather than 50 percent. The deduction cannot exceed 10 percent of taxable income before contributions and also before the dividends-received deduction, net operating loss carrybacks, and capital loss carrybacks.[108] However, the net operating loss and capital loss carryforward *are* deducted before arriving at the taxable income base.

> **Example 3-44.** Weary Fox, Inc., had taxable income of $200,000 before the charitable contributions deduction and before an NOL carryforward. It has an NOL carryforward of $60,000 and contributions of $18,000. The contribution deduction is limited to $14,000 (10% × ($200,000 − $60,000)).

Contributions in excess of the limit may be carried forward for up to five years. Current year contributions must always be used before any carryforwards.[109]

The deduction rules for corporations are very similar to the rules for individuals, with one exception. Generally, deductions for contributions of inventory are limited to basis, i.e., the appreciation must be deducted from the fair market value. However, for contributions to exempt organizations caring for the ill, the needy, or infants, only one-half of the appreciation need be deducted.[110]

> **Example 3-45.** Lewis, Inc., a clothing store, donated clothing with a basis of $2,000 to the Boy Scouts and clothing with a basis of $3,000 to an organization caring for the homeless. Respective fair market values were $4,500 and $5,000. Only $2,000 could be deducted for the Boy Scouts contribution. However, $3,000 + .5 ($5,000 − $3,000), or $4,000, of the homeless organization contribution can be deducted.

The Tax Court has held that a bakery that donated 4-day-old bread to food banks could base the deduction on the full retail price less one-half the appreciation, rather than beginning with a discounted price. The IRS had asserted that the 4-day-old bread should be valued at only 50 percent of retail.[111]

The regulations require that the taxpayer receive from the donee a written statement that includes a description of the property, the date of

---

[108] Code Sec. 170(b)(2).
[109] Code Sec. 170(d)(2).
[110] Code Sec. 170(e)(3)(B).

[111] *Lucky Stores, Inc. v. Commr.*, 105 TC 420, Dec. 51,059 (1995), aff'd CA-4, 98-2 USTC ¶ 50,662, 153 F3d 964.

receipt of the contributed property, and a statement representing that the property will be used in compliance with Code Sec. 170(e)(3) and Reg. § 1.170A-4A(b)(2) and (3).[112] The IRS has ruled that a statement from the donee organization received before the donation that indicated its intent to use the property for the ill, needy, and infants was insufficient to fulfill this requirement.[113]

C corporations are allowed a deduction equal to the fair market value minus one-half the ordinary income for computers and computer technology donated to primary and secondary schools.[114] This provision is effective until December 31, 2003. Qualified contributions are limited to gifts made no later than two years after the date the taxpayer acquired or substantially completed the construction of the donated property. Such donated property could be computer technology or equipment that is inventory or depreciable trade or business property in the hands of the donor. The original use of the donated property must begin with the donor or the donee.

Tax Tips and Pitfalls

Corporations should generally seek to make contributions in the form of property rather than cash. Appreciated inventory should be given to charities caring for the ill, the needy, or infants. Tangible property other than inventory should only be given if the charity will use it in its exempt function. If the tangible property is subject to considerable depreciation recapture, the advantages of gifting it are reduced. Intangible property (stock, bonds, etc.), however, may be given to any public charity; the important requirement is to ensure that the holding period exceeds one year.

¶ 351   Organizational Expenditures

Though organizational expenditures have an unlimited life, Code Sec. 248 permits the election of a ratable amortization over a period of not less than 60 months.[115] The election must be made by attaching a statement to the corporate return for the first year that the corporation conducts business. The statement must give the description and amount of the expenditures, the date such expenditures were incurred, the month in which the corporation began business, and the number of months to be written off.[116]

The amortization period must begin with the month that the corporation begins business, not necessarily the same month as when the corporation begins its existence.[117]

---

[112] Reg. § 1.170A-4(b)(4)(i).

[113] IRS Letter Ruling 9621005, April 29, 1996.

[114] Act Sec. 224, Taxpayer Relief Act of 1997, adding Code Sec. 170(e)(6).

[115] Code Sec. 248(a).

[116] Reg. § 1.248-1(c).

[117] Code Sec. 248(a); Reg. § 1.248-1(a)(3).

Organizational expenditures are defined as expenditures which meet all three of the conditions listed below:[118]

1.   They are incident to the creation of the corporation;

2.   They are chargeable to the capital account of the corporation; and

3.   They are of a character which, if expended incident to the creation of a corporation having a limited life, would be amortizable over such life.

Examples of organization costs include legal services incurred in connection with the organization of the corporation, i.e., drafting the corporate charter and bylaws, preparing minutes of organizational meetings, and drafting the terms of original stock certificates. Also included would be necessary accounting services, expenses of temporary directors and of organizational meetings of directors or shareholders, and fees paid to the state of incorporation.[119]

Organization costs do *not* include expenses connected with the sale or issuance of stock, expenses connected with the transfer of assets to the corporation, or expenditures connected with the reorganization of a corporation (unless directly incident to the creation of a corporation).[120]

Tax Tips and Pitfalls

In order to be amortized, organizational expenses must be incurred in the first tax year of the corporation. This should be kept in mind in planning for the incurrence of organizational expenses. If the costs are significant and the tentative choice for a tax year end results in a short-period return the first year, consideration should be given to selecting a subsequent month for the first year end.

¶ 353   Dividends-Received Deduction

In order to prevent the possible imposition of triple taxation, the Code permits corporations to take a deduction for dividends received from a U.S. corporation. The percentage allowed as a deduction depends on the percentage of stock owned. It is:[121]

- 100 percent if received by a corporation which is in the same affiliated group as is the paying corporation;

- 80 percent if the receiving corporation owns 20 percent or more of the distributing corporation;

- 70 percent if the ownership is under 20 percent;

- 40 percent of dividends on public utility preferred stock; and

---

[118] Code Sec. 248(b); Reg. § 1.248-1(b)(1).
[119] Reg. § 1.248-1(b)(2).
[120] Reg. § 1.248-1(b)(4).
[121] Code Secs. 243(a) and (c), 245, and 247.

- A partial deduction for certain 10 percent or more owned foreign corporations.

There are three modifications to the dividends-received deduction.

.01 Debt-Financed Portfolio Stock

The dividends-received deduction renders much of the dividends nontaxable. If a corporation could borrow the money to purchase the stock and deduct the interest expense, a very favorable arbitrage situation would be created. Code Sec. 246A plugs this loophole by disallowing the dividends-received deduction to the extent that the stock is debt-financed. The permitted dividends-received deduction is equal to the relevant percentage (70 percent or 80 percent) times 100 percent — the "average indebtedness percentage."[122] The "average indebtedness percentage" equals, for the "base period," the average "portfolio indebtedness" divided by the average adjusted basis of the stock.[123] "Portfolio indebtedness" is only debt *directly* attributable to investment in the stock. The "base period" is the shorter of:[124]

- The period beginning on the ex-dividend date for the most recent previous dividend on the stock and ending on the ex-dividend date for the current dividend, or

- The one-year period ending on the day before the ex-dividend date for the current dividend.

The reduction in the dividends-received deduction is not to exceed the interest deduction.[125] Also, the disallowance does not apply (the deduction is allowed in full) if:

- As of the beginning of the ex-dividend date the corporation owns at least 50 percent of both the total voting power and the total value of the stock, or

- As of the beginning of the ex-dividend date the corporation owns at least 20 percent of both the total voting power and the total value of the stock and five or fewer corporate shareholders own at least 50 percent of both the total voting power and the total value of the stock.[126]

The disallowance also does not apply if the corporation is eligible to receive the 100 percent dividends-received deduction.[127]

Example 3-46. Bowman Co. received a $20,000 dividend in 2001 from a company in which it has a 40 percent ownership. The adjusted basis of its stock is $200,000; the average portfolio indebtedness during the base period was $50,000. The dividends-received deduction equals

---

[122] Code Sec. 246A(a).
[123] Code Sec. 246A(d).
[124] Code Sec. 246A(d)(3) and (4).

[125] Code Sec. 246A(e).
[126] Code Sec. 246A(c)(2).
[127] Code Sec. 246A(b).

$12,000 ($20,000 × .80 = $16,000; $16,000 − ($16,000 × $50,000 / $200,000) = $12,000).

The Tax Court has ruled that where funds were borrowed by a subsidiary and distributed to the parent company for the purpose of purchasing portfolio stock, the dividend disallowance rules under Code Sec. 246 do apply.[128]

.02 Extraordinary Dividends

Code Sec. 1059 was enacted to prevent corporations, through the declaration of large dividends, from recovering, without any effect on taxable income or basis, a substantial portion of the cost of the stock. If the corporation receives an "extraordinary dividend" and the stock has not been held more than two years before the dividend announcement date, then the basis of the stock must be reduced by the nontaxable portion of the dividend.[129] The dividend is deemed "extraordinary" if the amount equals or exceeds a "threshold percentage" of the greater of the adjusted basis of the stock or the fair market value on the day before the ex-dividend date. The "threshold percentage" is five percent for preferred stock and 10 percent for common stock.[130]

Since this rule applies to a single dividend distribution, taxpayers would be tempted to avoid its application by making a series of distributions. Such manipulation is partly prevented by aggregation rules. All dividends which have ex-dividend dates within an 85-day period are aggregated. Dividends within a one-year period are aggregated only if they exceed 20 percent of the adjusted basis.[131] The aggregation rules cannot be avoided by making nontaxable exchanges of the stock.[132]

Code Sec. 1059 requires a corporate shareholder that receives an "extraordinary dividend" to reduce the basis of the stock by the nontaxed portion of the dividend. A corporate shareholder recognizes gain whenever the basis of the stock with respect to which an extraordinary dividend received is reduced below zero.[133] Prior to May 4, 1995, the excess was not taxed until the sale or disposition of the stock.

> **Example 3-47.** Manning, Inc., purchased for $100,000 40 percent of the stock in York Co. in 2000. In 2001, it received a dividend of $25,000 at the time that the stock was worth $120,000. Since the $25,000 equals or exceeds 10 percent of the greater of $100,000 or $120,000, the dividend is treated as extraordinary. The 80 percent dividends-received deduction of $20,000 is allowable; but the basis of the stock is reduced by the $20,000 deduction, down to $80,000.

---

[128] *H. Enterprises International, Inc. v. Commr.*, 75 TCM 1948, Dec. 52,612(M), TC Memo. 1998-97, aff'd per curiam, CA-8, 99-2 USTC ¶ 50,723, 183 F3d 907.

[129] Code Sec. 1059(a)(1).

[130] Code Sec. 1059(c).

[131] Code Sec. 1059(c)(3).

[132] Code Sec. 1059(c)(3)(C).

[133] Act Sec. 1001, Taxpayer Relief Act of 1997, amending Code Sec. 1059(a)(2).

Example 3-48. Assume the same facts as in the previous example, but that the dividend in 2001 was $150,000 and that the stock was sold in 2003 for $115,000. Although the nontaxable portion of the 2001 dividend was $120,000, only $100,000 can be used to reduce basis. However, in 2002 the stock is deemed to be sold for $20,000. With the basis of the stock now at zero, the gain in 2003 would be $115,000.

Tax Tips and Pitfalls

Assuming that the purchasing company is in a position to control or influence dividend payment, careful attention to the amount and dates of distributions will yield good results. For example, if stock was purchased on April 20, 1995, four dividend payments of six percent on September 1, 1995; February 15, 1996; July 2, 1997; and March 5, 1998 would all have to be treated as extraordinary. On the other hand, three dividend payments of 9.5 percent each on June 21, 1996; June 25, 1997; and June 28, 1998 would not have to be treated as extraordinary, even though they comprise 28.5 percent of the basis as opposed to only 24 percent of the basis.

.03 *Dividends Paid Within 45 Days of Purchase*

Code Sec. 246(c) prevents corporations from purchasing stock shortly before the ex-dividend date, receiving a large nontaxable dividend, and then selling the stock at a loss.

In the case of common stock, the dividends-received deduction is inapplicable if the corporation has held the stock for 45 days or less during the 90-day period beginning 45 days before the ex-dividend date or to the extent that the corporation is obligated (whether pursuant to a short sale or otherwise) to make related payments with respect to positions in substantially similar or related property.[134] The holding period for preferred stock is increased to 90 days.[135]

The holding period is reduced for any period in which the taxpayer:[136]

- Has an option to sell, is under a contractual obligation to sell, or has made, but not yet closed, a short sale of substantially identical stock or securities; or

- Is the grantor of an option to buy substantially identical stock or securities; or

- Has diminished its risk of loss by holding one or more positions with respect to substantially similar or related property.

The dividends-received deduction is limited to the applicable percentage of taxable income computed without regard to the dividends-received deduction.[137] However, if the dividends-received deduction would create or

---

[134] Code Sec. 246(c)(1).
[135] Code Sec. 246(c)(2).

[136] Code Sec. 246(c)(4).
[137] Code Sec. 246(b)(1).

increase a net operating loss, the limitation does not apply, and the deduction is allowed in full.[138]

> **Example 3-49.** Zeon, Inc., had a tax loss from operations of $29,990 but dividend income from 15 percent owned stock of $100,000. The tentative dividends-received deduction is $70,000, but the deduction is limited to .70 × ($100,000 − $29,990) = $49,007. Thus, taxable income equals $21,003.

> **Example 3-50.** Assume the same facts as in the previous example, except that the company incurs an additional $11 of expenses, thus increasing the loss to $30,001. The full $70,000 dividends-received deduction would now be allowed since a net operating loss of $1 would now be created. Thus, $11 of additional deduction would save the tax on $21,003.

¶ 355 Net Operating Loss Deduction

The net operating loss for corporations is essentially the excess of deductions over income; however, no net operating loss deduction (from a carryback or carryforward) is allowed, and the dividends-received deduction is allowed in full.[139] For tax years beginning after August 5, 1997, net operating losses may be carried back two years and forward 20 years.[140] Prior to the Taxpayer Relief Act of 1997, net operating losses were carried back three years and forward 15 years. However, the three-year carryback for NOLs of farmers and small businesses attributable to loss incurred in Presidentially declared disaster areas is preserved. If the taxpayer elects, the entire carryback period may be relinquished and the loss carried forward instead.

Congress extended the carryback time for losses incurred in a farming business to five years.[141] In addition, a "specified liability loss" may be carried back for 10 years.[142] "Specified liability losses" are deductions attributable to:[143]

1. Product liability;

2. Expenses incurred in the investigation or settlement of, or opposition to, product liability claims;

3. Any amount allowable as a deduction which is in satisfaction of a liability under state or federal law that requires:

    a. The reclamation of land,

    b. The decommissioning of a nuclear power plant,

    c. The dismantlement of a drilling platform,

---

[138] Code Sec. 246(b)(2).
[139] Code Sec. 172(d).
[140] Act Sec. 1082, Taxpayer Relief Act of 1997, amending Code Sec. 172(b).

[141] Act Sec. 2013(A), Tax and Trade Relief Extension Act of 1998, amending Code Sec. 172.
[142] Code Sec. 172(c).
[143] Code Sec. 172(f).

d. The remediation of environmental contamination, or

e. A payment under a workers compensation act.

Tax Tips and Pitfalls

Generally, it will be advantageous to carry NOLs back. However, if marginal tax rates in future years are expected to be considerably higher than in the carryback years, an election to forego the carryback may be advisable.

Although net operating losses can be carried forward as long as 20 years, a corporation should seek to produce income so that the net operating loss may be used as soon as possible. The present value of a dollar of deduction 20 years from now is very small.

Chapter 4

S Corporations

¶ 401 Background

The feature of double taxation, present in C corporations, can present a severe drawback to owners and operators of small businesses. On the other hand, partnership status may also be undesirable due to the features of unlimited liability and limited life. Congress addressed these problems in 1958 by adding subchapter S to the Code. Several revisions to subchapter S have been made through the years, the most important being the Subchapter S Revision Act of 1982 (P.L. 97-354).

In passing the 1958 Act, Congress recognized that if the double taxation disadvantage could be removed, other corporate features, such as limited liability and unlimited life would be very attractive to small businesses. The Act could give small businesses the advantages of the corporate form of organization without being made subject to the possible tax disadvantages of the corporation.[1]

S status affects only the federal tax status of the corporation. Depending on state law, a state tax may or may not be required. Also, the S corporation, in a legal sense, is not affected by S status. Corporations are governed under state law and the federal S election in no way affects state law.

¶ 403 Eligibility Requirements

Corporations do not automatically attain S status; instead, the corporation must make an election. In order to be eligible to elect S status, corporations must meet the following requirements:[2]

1. Have no more than 75 shareholders.[3]

2. Have as shareholders only individuals, estates, and certain trusts and exempt organizations.[4]

3. Not have a nonresident alien as a shareholder.

4. Be a domestic corporation.

---

[1] Senate Report No. 1622, 83d Congress, 2d Sess., 119 (1954).

[2] Code Sec. 1361(b).

[3] Act Sec. 1301, Small Business Job Protection Act, amending Code Sec. 1361(b)(1)(A). For years beginning before 1997, only 35 shareholders were allowed.

[4] Act Sec. 1302(a), Small Business Job Protection Act, adding Code Sec. 1361(c)(2)(A)(v); Act Sec.

1302(b), adding Code Sec. 1361(c)(2)(B)(v); Act Sec. 1302(c), adding Code Sec. 1361(e); Act Sec. 1316(a), amending Code Sec. 1361(b)(1)(B) and adding Code Sec. 1361(c)(7); Act Sec. 1316(e), amending Code Sec. 1361(e)(1)(A)(i); and Act Sec. 1303, amending Code Sec. 1361(c)(2)(A).

5.   Not be a financial institution, an insurance company, a domestic international sales corporation, or a corporation electing Code Sec. 936 credits.

6.   Not have more than one class of stock.

.01   Requirements In Detail

1.   *Have no more than 75 shareholders.* For this purpose husbands and wives are treated as one shareholder, regardless of whether the stock is owned as joint tenants, as community property, or separately.[5]

2.   *Have as shareholders only individuals, estates, and certain trusts and exempt organizations.* Corporations and partnerships may *not* be shareholders. The following trusts *may* be shareholders.[6]

   a.   A trust, all of which is treated (under the grantor trust rules of Code Sec. 671 *et seq*) as owned by an individual who is a citizen or resident of the United States. Trusts which are treated for tax purposes as if there were no trust are covered here. Examples would be grantor trusts, such as revocable trusts.

   b.   A trust that is described in (a) that continues in existence after the deemed owner's death. The trust is an eligible shareholder only for a two-year period beginning on the day of the deemed owner's death.[7]

   c.   A testamentary trust to which stock is transferred under the terms of the will, but only for the two-year period beginning on the day on which the stock is transferred to it.[8]

   d.   A trust created primarily to exercise the voting power of stock transferred to it. Each beneficiary of these "voting trusts" is counted as an owner.[9]

   e.   A qualified subchapter S trust. A "qualified subchapter S trust" may elect to be treated as a qualified shareholder. Trusts "qualify" if:

      1.   There is only one income beneficiary,

      2.   Corpus, during the life of the income beneficiary, may be distributed only to such beneficiary,

---

[5] Code Sec. 1361(c)(1).
[6] Code Sec. 1361(c)(2).
[7] Act Sec. 1303, Small Business Job Protection Act, amending Code Sec. 1361(c)(2)(A). For years beginning before 1997, the applicable time period was only 60 days.

[8] *Id.* For years beginning before 1997, the time period was only 60 days.
[9] Code Sec. 1361(c)(2)(B)(iv).

3. The income interest of the income beneficiary terminates on the earlier of his death or the termination of the trust,

4. If the trust is terminated during the life of the beneficiary, all of the corpus must be distributed to him, and

5. All of the income is distributed annually.

If the election is made, all of the income is taxed to the beneficiary. The election is made by the beneficiary's signing and filing with the IRS a statement that:[10]

i. Contains the name, address, and taxpayer identification number of the beneficiary, the trust, and the corporation;

ii. Identifies the election as being under Code Sec. 1361(d)(2);

iii. Specifies the effective date (not earlier than 15 days and two months before the date on which the election is filed);

iv. Specifies the date on which the stock of the corporation was transferred to the trust; and

v. Provides all information and representations necessary to show that:

1. Under the terms of the trust and applicable local law:

   a. During the life of the current income beneficiary, there will be only one income beneficiary of the trust (if husband and wife are beneficiaries, that they will file joint returns and that both are U.S. residents or citizens);

   b. Any corpus distributed during the life of the current income beneficiary may be distributed only to that beneficiary;

   c. The current beneficiary's income interest in the trust will terminate on the earlier of the beneficiary's death or upon termination of the trust; and

   d. Upon the termination of the trust during the life of such income beneficiary, the trust will distribute all its assets to such beneficiary.

2. The trust is required to distribute all of its income currently, or that the trustee will distribute all of its

---

[10] Reg. § 1.1361-1(j)(6).

income currently if not so required by the terms of the trust.

3. No distribution of income or corpus by the trust will be in satisfaction of the grantor's legal obligation to support or maintain the income beneficiary.

f. Effective for years beginning after 1997, certain qualified retirement plan trusts and charitable organizations qualifying under Code Sec. 501(c)(3) will be eligible S corporation shareholders and will count as one shareholder for purposes of the 75 shareholder rule.[11]

g. Effective for tax years beginning after 1996, electing small business trusts are eligible to be S corporation shareholders.[12] Each potential current beneficiary is counted as a shareholder. If there is no potential current beneficiary, the trust itself is treated as the shareholder.[13]

The interests in the qualifying trusts must be acquired by gift bequest, or another nonpurchase acquisition.[14]

Tax Tips and Pitfalls

Many wealthy individuals choose, for estate planning purposes, to transfer a substantial portion of their assets to revocable trusts. Ownership of S corporation stock by these trusts does not disqualify S corporation status.

3. *Not have a nonresident alien as a shareholder.*

4. *Not have more than one class of stock.* Congress has in mind here preferred vs. common. Mere differences in voting rights do not create two classes of stock for this purpose, i.e., one could have class A voting common and class B nonvoting common and, if they were identical in all other respects, two classes of stock would not exist for this purpose.[15] Thinly capitalized corporations have experienced problems in that the IRS has not only treated the debt as equity, but has also asserted that the corporation now has two classes of stock. However, Congress in 1982 enacted safe harbor rules which provide that "straight debt" is not treated as a second class of stock.[16] The regulations clarify what is considered to be debt for this purpose. Instruments or obligations that meet the definition of "straight debt" are not treated as outstanding stock.[17] While a formal note is not required, in order to meet the straight debt requirements

---

[11] Code Sec. 1361(c)(6).
[12] Act Sec. 1302(a), Small Business Job Protection Act, adding Code Sec. 1361(c)(2)(A)(v).
[13] Act Sec. 1302, Small Business Job Protection Act, adding Code Sec. 1361(c)(2)(B)(v).

[14] Act Sec. 1302(c), Small Business Job Protection Act, adding Code Sec. 1361(e)(1)(A)(ii).
[15] Code Sec. 1361(c)(4).
[16] Code Sec. 1361(c)(5).
[17] Reg. § 1.1361-1(b)(5).

there must be a written, unconditional obligation to pay a sum certain on demand or on a specific date for which:

a. The interest rate and payment dates are not contingent on profits, the borrower's discretion, dividend payments, or similar factors,

b. The debt is not convertible, and

c. The creditor is an individual (other than a nonresident alien), an estate, a trust described in Code Sec. 1361(c)(2), or a person who is actively and regularly engaged in the business of lending money.[18]

Subordinated debt is not prevented from qualifying as straight debt.[19] However, an obligation will cease qualifying as straight debt if the obligation is either materially modified or is transferred to a third party who is not an eligible shareholder (i.e., a corporation, a partnership, or certain trusts).[20]

As long as the above requirements are met, an obligation of an S corporation will not be treated as a second class of stock even if the obligation would be considered equity under general principles of federal tax law. The regulations provide that if a straight debt obligation has an unreasonably high rate of interest, a portion of the payment may be recharacterized and treated as a noninterest payment. However, such a reclassification will not result in a second class of stock.[21] Presumably the reclassified payment would be nondeductible to the corporation but taxed to the recipients. However, the regulations do not address this issue.

If a C corporation converts to S status, existing debt, as long as it meets the straight debt requirements discussed above, will not be treated as a second class of stock even if it is considered equity under general principles of federal tax law.[22] Presumably, then, a thinly capitalized C corporation that has had some of its debt recategorized as equity and the interest treated as a constructive dividend could convert to S status without the recategorized debt being treated as a second class of stock.

The regulations state that restricted stock which is issued in connection with the performance of services within the meaning of Reg. § 1.83-3(f) and that is substantially nonvested within the meaning of Reg. § 1.83-3(b) is not treated as outstanding stock of the corporation, and the holder is not treated as a shareholder solely by reason of holding the stock, unless the holder makes an election with respect to the stock under Code Sec. 83(b).[23] Restricted stock for this purpose is stock issued to an employee or an independent contractor (or beneficiary thereof) either in recognition of the performance of services or in the refraining of performance of services.[24]

---

[18] Code Sec. 1361(c)(5)(B)(iii).
[19] Reg. § 1.1361-1(l)(5)(ii).
[20] Reg. § 1.1361-1(l)(5)(iii).
[21] Reg. § 1.1361-1(l)(5)(iv).

[22] Reg. § 1.1361-1(l)(5)(v).
[23] Reg. § 1.1361-1(b)(3).
[24] Reg. § 1.83-3(f).

"Substantially nonvested" means that the stock is subject to a substantial risk of forfeiture and is not transferable.[25]

Deferred compensation plans do not constitute outstanding stock if the plan:

- Does not convey the right to vote;

- Is an unfunded and unsecured promise to pay money or property in the future;

- Is issued to an employee in connection with the performance of services or to an individual who is an independent contractor in connection with the performance of services for the corporation (and is not excessive by reference to the services performed); and

- Is issued pursuant to a plan with respect to which the recipient is not taxed currently on income.[26]

Tax Tips and Pitfalls

The fact that nonvoting stock is not treated as a second class of stock can be very helpful in planning for S corporations. For example, assume that an S shareholder has three children, one of whom is active in the business, and the other two who are inactive and live some distance from the business location. The S corporation could issue voting common to the child active in the business and nonvoting common to the two absent children.

Whether all classes of stock have identical rights to distributions and liquidation proceeds is determined by reference to state law, the corporate charter, articles of incorporation and bylaws (collectively considered the governing agreement).[27] Commercial contracts such as leases, employment agreements, or loan agreements generally would not be a part of the governing provision (and thus would not affect distribution and liquidation proceeds), *unless* a principal purpose is to circumvent the one class of stock requirement. The regulations state that although a corporation is not treated as having two classes of stock as long as the governing provisions provide for identical distribution and liquidation rights, any distributions (including actual, deemed, or constructive) that differ in timing or amount are to be given appropriate tax treatment in accordance with the facts and circumstances.[28]

Example 4-1. An S corporation has two equal shareholders, Arbor and Bush. Under the S corporation's bylaws, shareholders are entitled to equal per-share distributions. The S corporation distributes $50,000 to Arbor during the current year, but does not distribute $50,000 to

---

[25] Reg. § 1.83-3(b).
[26] Reg. § 1.1361-1(b)(4).

[27] Reg. § 1.1361-1(l)(2)(i).
[28] *Id.*

Bush until the next year. The difference in timing of the distributions would not create a second class of stock.

Example 4-2. An S corporation has two equal shareholders, Cooper and Daley, both of whom are employed by the S corporation and have binding employment agreements. The compensation paid to Cooper is deemed excessive; the compensation paid to Daley is considered reasonable. The facts and circumstances of the case indicate that the principal purpose of the employment agreements was not to circumvent the one class of stock requirement. Even though the excessive compensation could not be deducted, these employment arrangements would not create a second class of stock.

Example 4-3. An S corporation has a binding agreement to pay health insurance premiums for its employee/shareholders. The premium payments differ for each employee. The facts and circumstances of the agreements indicate that the principal purpose of the premium payments was not to circumvent the one class of stock requirement. These premium payments would not create a second class of stock.

State law may require the S corporation to pay state income taxes on behalf of some or all of the shareholders. Such laws do not create a second class of stock as long as the outstanding shares confer identical rights to distribution and liquidation proceeds. Timing differences between such constructive distributions and actual distributions to the other shareholders do not create a second class of stock.[29]

Buy-Sell Agreements

The regulations provide that buy-sell and redemption agreements and agreements restricting the selling of stock generally are disregarded in determining whether a corporation has a second class of stock. This is true unless:[30]

- A principal purpose of the agreement is to circumvent the one class of stock requirement; and

- The agreement establishes a purchase price that, at the time the agreement is entered into, differs significantly from the fair market value of the stock.

However, agreements that provide for the purchase or redemption at a price between book and fair market value are not considered to differ significantly from the fair market value of the stock.[31] The regulations state that a good faith determination of fair market value will be respected unless it is shown that the value was substantially in error and the determination of value was not done with reasonable diligence.[32]

[29] Reg. § 1.1361-1(l)(2)(ii).
[30] Reg. § 1.1361-1(l)(2)(iii)(A).
[31] *Id.*
[32] *Id.*

The regulations provide safe harbors for the determination of book value. The book value computation will be accepted if either:[33]

- The book value is determined in accordance with generally accepted accounting principles (including permitted optional adjustments); or

- The book value is used for any substantial nontax purpose (e.g., for credit purposes).

Call Options

In general, a call, warrant, etc., is treated as a second class of stock if, taking into account the facts and circumstances, the call option is substantially certain to be exercised and has a strike price substantially below the fair market value of the underlying stock on the issue date of the option.[34] The regulations provide that the option does not have a strike price substantially below fair market value if the price at the time of exercise cannot, under the terms of the option instrument, be substantially below the fair market value of the underlying stock at the time of exercise.[35]

There are two important exceptions to the above rule:

1. A call option is not treated as a second class of stock if it is issued to a person that is actively and regularly engaged in the business of lending and is issued in connection with a commercially reasonable loan to the corporation.[36]

2. A call option issued to an employee of the corporation or to an independent contractor in conjunction with services rendered is not treated as a second class of stock if:[37]

   a. The call option is nontransferable; and

   b. The call option does not have a readily ascertainable fair market value at the time of issuance.

In addition, a safe harbor is provided to call options if on the date of issuance the price of the call is at least 90 percent of the fair market value of the underlying stock.[38]

Convertible Debt

Convertible debt is treated as a second class of stock if:[39]

- Under general principles of federal tax law it would be considered equity and a principal purpose of issuing the security is tax avoidance; or

---

[33] Reg. § 1.1361-1(l)(2)(iii)(C).
[34] Reg. § 1.1361-1(l)(4)(iii)(A).
[35] *Id.*
[36] Reg. § 1.1361-1(l)(4)(iii)(B)(1).

[37] Reg. § 1.1361-1(l)(4)(iii)(B)(2).
[38] Reg. § 1.1361-1(l)(4)(iii)(C).
[39] Reg. § 1.1361-1(l)(4)(iv).

- It embodies rights equivalent to that of a call option such that if the rules for call options (discussed above) were applied, it would be treated as a second class of stock.

Inadvertent Terminations and Effective Date

If the second class of stock rules are inadvertently breached, the inadvertent termination rules under Code Sec. 1362(f) apply[40] (see the section on terminations). The IRS has been fairly liberal in applying the inadvertent termination rules. The effective date of Reg. § 1361-1(l) generally applies to taxable years beginning on or after May 28, 1992. However, it does not apply to an agreement entered into before May 28, 1992, unless the agreement has been substantially modified. A corporation and its shareholders have the option to apply Reg. § 1.1361-l to prior years.[41]

5. *Be a domestic corporation.* Foreign corporations are not eligible for S status.

6. *Not be certain financial institutions, an insurance company, a domestic international sales corporation, a corporation electing Code Sec. 936 credits, or a subsidiary of a parent/subsidiary group where the parent is a C corporation.* Generally, financial institutions cannot have S status. However, domestic building and loan associations, mutual savings banks, and any cooperative banks without capital stock organized and operated for mutual purposes and without profit *are* eligible to elect S status, as are banks that do not use the reserve method of accounting for bad debts.[42] S corporations may own 80 percent or more of the stock of a C corporation, and they may also have a qualified S subsidiary (QSSS).[43] A qualified S subsidiary is defined as any domestic corporation that qualifies as an S corporation and is 100 percent owned by an S corporation parent.[44] The S corporation parent must elect to treat it as a QSSS.[45] A QSSS is *not* treated as a separate corporation. Therefore, all of its assets, liabilities, items of income, deductions, and credits are treated as belonging to the parent S corporation.[46]

---

[40] Reg. § 1.1361-1(l)(6).

[41] Reg. § 1.1361-1(l)(7).

[42] Act Sec. 1315, Small Business Job Protection Act, amending Code Sec. 1361(b)(2), and Senate Committee Report. For tax years beginning before 1997, all financial institutions to which Code Sec. 585 applied (or would have applied but for Code Sec. 585(c)) were ineligible for S status.

[43] Act Sec. 1308(a), Small Business Job Protection Act, amending Code Sec. 1361(b)(2); Act Sec. 1308(b), adding Code Sec. 1361(b)(3). For tax years beginning before 1997, S corporations could not be a member of an affiliated group.

[44] Code Sec. 1361(b)(3)(B).

[45] *Id.*

[46] Code Sec. 1361(b)(3)(A).

¶ 405   Electing S Status

All shareholders must consent to the election, which is filed on Form 2553.[47] If stock is held as tenants in common, joint tenancy, tenancy by the entirety, or is community property, then all parties must sign.[48] The consent of a minor may be made by the minor, the legal representative of the minor, or by the parent if no legal representative has been appointed.[49] Consent of an estate is made by the executor or administrator, and each deemed owner of a trust must give consent.[50]

A revenue procedure provides automatic relief for late S corporation elections in two situations:[51]

1. The corporation intended S status, income is reported by the shareholders as if it were an S corporation, and the entity was not notified by the IRS of any problem regarding its S status within six months of the due date of the first S corporation return, and

2. For periods before January 1, 1997, the corporation intended to be an S corporation; however, due to a late S corporation election, it was not permitted to be an S corporation for the first tax year specified in the election, the corporation and the shareholders treated the corporation as an S corporation for all succeeding years, and all relevant tax years for both the corporation and all of its shareholders are open.

.01   Effective Date of the Election

The election may be made at any time during the tax year. To be effective as of the start of the tax year, the election generally must be made by the 15th day of the third month of the tax year.[52] However, Congress has given authority to the IRS to treat late elections as timely if the IRS determines there was reasonable cause for the late election.[53] A revenue procedure provides guidance for late S elections for corporations who meet the following criteria:[54]

- The failure to qualify as an S corporation was solely because Form 2553 was not timely filed,

- The due date for the tax return (excluding extensions) for the first S year has not passed, and

- There was reasonable cause for the failure to make the election.

If the corporation does not meet the eligibility requirements above, it can request relief by applying for a private letter ruling.

---

[47] Code Sec. 1362(a).
[48] Reg. § 1.1362-6(b)(2).
[49] Id.
[50] Id.

[51] Rev. Proc. 97-48, 1997-2 CB 521.
[52] Code Sec. 1362(b).
[53] Code Sec. 1362(b).
[54] Rev. Proc. 98-55, 1998-2 CB 645.

The courts tend to interpret the timeliness requirement strictly. In *McLane Land & Timber Co.*, the corporation presented the affidavit of an employee from the accounting firm indicating that the employee mailed the election form. However, a district judge ruled that the "act of mailing is not significant for purposes of establishing a timely mailing." Rather, the proof of the postmark is significant.[55]

Example 4-4. JJ Inc., a calendar year corporation, plans to file an election in 2001. If the election is made by March 15, it is retroactive back to the first of the year; if made after March 15, the election will not be effective until 2002.

If a person held stock at some time during the year prior to the election, and if that person does not consent to the election, the election is not effective until the next tax year.[56]

Example 4-5. Wang sold his stock in Harper Corporation to Guthrie on February 6, 2001. On March 2, 2001, the stockholders file Form 2553. Wang does not sign the form. Harper Corporation will not have S status until 2002.

¶ 407   Terminations

S status may terminate either voluntarily or due to a failure to continue to meet the qualifications for S status. Bankruptcy does not terminate an S election. In *Stadler Associates, Inc.*, the sole shareholder argued that the filing of the bankruptcy petitions terminated the company's S corporation status because the underlying purpose of the subchapter S election was lost upon the appointment of the chapter 7 trustee. However, a U.S. Bankruptcy Court found no statutory basis for such an assertion.[57] A voluntary revocation may be made by a majority of the stockholders consenting to the revocation.[58] If the revocation is filed by the 15th day of the third month of the tax year, it is retroactive to the beginning of the year. If the revocation is filed outside 2½ months after the start of the new year, it is effective for the next year, unless a prospective date is specified in the revocation. In the latter case, the corporation will have two short tax years, one as an S corporation, the other as a C corporation.[59]

Example 4-6. On April 10, 2001, the stockholders of Hilltop, Inc., file a revocation of S status, specifying the prospective date of June 1 as the revocation date. Hilltop, Inc., will have a January 1–May 31 short year as an S corporation, and a June 1—December 31 short year as a C corporation.

---

[55] *McLane Land and Timber Co. v. U.S.*, DC Ark., 97-2 USTC ¶ 50,817.
[56] Code Sec. 1362(b)(2); Reg. § 1.1362-6(a)(ii)(B)(2).

[57] *In re Stadler Associates, Inc.*, BC-DC Fla., 95-2 USTC ¶ 50,589.
[58] Code Sec. 1362(d)(1).
[59] *Id.*

If the corporation fails to meet any of the criteria previously specified as necessary to S status, an involuntary termination is effective as of the date of the event causing cessation of the S status.[60]

> **Example 4-7.** Rhinehart Corporation, a calendar year corporation, has 75 shareholders. On July 10, 2001, Sims sold his stock to two new shareholders. Rhinehart Corporation will file as an S corporation for the period January 1–July 9, and as a C corporation from July 10–December 31.

If an S corporation has previously been a C corporation and also has accumulated earnings and profits for those years, too much passive income can cause the loss of S status. If passive investment income exceeds 25 percent of gross receipts for three consecutive tax years, the S status is terminated as of the first day of the first taxable year beginning after the third consecutive tax year of excess passive investment income.[61]

> **Example 4-8.** Blink, Inc., consented to S corporation status on January 1, 1998, at which time it had accumulated earnings and profits. For the years 1998, 1999, and 2000, it has passive investment income comprising 32 percent, 28 percent, and 29 percent of gross receipts, respectively. The election is terminated effective January 1, 2001.

"Passive investment income" is defined as gross receipts from royalties, rents, dividends, interest, annuities, and sales or exchanges of stock or securities, but only to the extent of gains.[62]

Regulations, later revoked, indicated that "gross receipts" are not the same as gross income. Gross receipts are similar to gross sales, which is defined as the total amount received or accrued from sales, services, or investments *before* reductions for cost, returns, and allowances.[63]

.01 Inadvertent Termination of S Status

An inadvertent termination could result in a severe hardship for corporations since normally a five-year waiting period is required before a new election may be made.[64] However, a corporation which has an involuntary termination may retain its S status if:

- The IRS determines that the termination was "inadvertent,"

- Steps were taken by the corporation within a reasonable time period after the termination date to restore S status, and

- The corporation and shareholders agree to adjustments that the IRS may require for the period.[65]

---

[60] Code Sec. 1362(d)(2)(B).
[61] Code Sec. 1362(d)(3).
[62] Code Sec. 1362(d)(3)(C)(i).

[63] Former Reg. § 1.1372-4(b)(5)(ii), revoked.
[64] Code Sec. 1362(g).
[65] Reg. § 1.1362-4(a).

The corporation has the burden of proof to show that under the relevant facts and circumstances, there was an "advertent" termination. If a terminating event was not reasonably within the control of the corporation and was not part of a plan to terminate, or if the event took place without the knowledge of the corporation, the termination is likely to be deemed inadvertent.[66]

The corporation makes a request for determination of an advertent termination by filing a ruling request.[67] The IRS may require any adjustments deemed appropriate, and all persons who were shareholders during that time period must consent. The granting of S status by the IRS may be retroactive or may be granted only for the period in which the corporation again became eligible for S treatment.[68]

The IRS has been given additional authority to waive inadvertent terminations. The IRS may waive an invalid election resulting from a corporation's inadvertent failure to qualify as a small business corporation.[69] It may also waive an invalid election caused by the failure to obtain required shareholder consents.[70] The IRS is also empowered to treat subchapter S elections that were filed late as timely if there is reasonable cause to support the late filing.[71] These provisions are retroactive, applying to elections for tax years beginning after December 31, 1982.

Divorce can often cause inadvertent loss of S status. For example, if a corporation has 76 shareholders, two of whom are husband and wife (they each own shares), their divorce would cause the loss of S status since there are now more than 75 shareholders.

.02 Election After Termination

Generally, if S status is terminated, a corporation cannot again elect S status until five taxable years have passed. However, the IRS may permit the corporation to make a new election before the five-year time period expires if the corporation shows that a new election would be warranted under the relevant facts and circumstances. The regulations indicate that if the termination is inadvertent and cured, or if there is a transfer of more than 50 percent of ownership after the date of termination, the IRS would tend to restore S corporation status.[72]

¶ 409 Rules of Operation

The conduit rule is generally applicable to S corporations; i.e., income flows through to the stockholders whether or not it is distributed in dividends, and the income retains the same characteristic in the hands of the shareholder that it had at the corporate level.

---

[66] Reg. § 1.1362-4(b).
[67] Reg. § 1.1362-4(c).
[68] Reg. § 1.1362-4(f).
[69] Act Sec. 1305(a), Small Business Job Protection Act, amending Code Sec. 1362(f).

[70] Id.
[71] Act Sec. 1305(b), Small Business Job Protection Act, adding Code Sec. 1362(b)(5).
[72] Reg. § 1.1362-5(a).

Example 4-9. Sue Jenkins is the 100 percent shareholder of Lane, Inc. During its taxable year, Lane, Inc., an S corporation, had ordinary income from its business of $20,000, $4,000 of long-term capital gain, and $600 of contributions. Jenkins received no distributions during the year. For her tax year within which the corporate year end fell, Jenkins would report $20,000 of income on Schedule E, $4,000 of capital gains on Schedule D, and a $600 contribution on Schedule A.

¶ 411   Allocation of Income

Losses also flow through to shareholders who deduct them on their individual returns. If there has been a change of ownership, gains and losses are allocated based on the number of days in the year that each stockholder held the stock.[73]

Two choices are available for computing the shareholders' portion of income and expense items where ownership has changed during the year:[74]

1. The yearly income is prorated over the number of days, and then allocated to the shareholder based on the number of days he or she held the stock.

2. If the shareholder's interest is completely terminated, and if all affected shareholders agree, an election may be made to close the books as of the day before the sale. The election is made by filing a statement indicating that the corporation elects under Code Sec. 1377(a)(2) as if the taxable year consisted of two taxable years. The statement must be signed by all affected parties and is filed with the return for the current tax year. Congress clarified, effective for years beginning after 1996, just who needs to agree to have the books closed. All "affected shareholders" as well as the S corporation must agree to close the books. "Affected shareholders" are the shareholders who sold the stock and the shareholders who bought the stock during the taxable year. If a shareholder has transferred stock to the corporation, then the corporation is also an "affected shareholder" for this purpose.[75]

Example 4-10. As of January 1, 2001, Zucker Co., an S corporation, is owned 60 percent and 40 percent by Frey and Polk. On April 10, 2001, Polk sold all of his interest to Bess. Ordinary income for the year is $48,000, $15,000 earned from the period January 1 through April 9, and the remaining $33,000 earned after April 9. If the proration method is used, the income reported by Polk would be $48,000 × .40 × 99/365 = $5,208, Bess would report $48,000 × .40 × 266/365 = $13,992, while Frey would report $48,000 × .60 = $28,800.

---

[73] Code Sec. 1366(a).
[74] Code Sec. 1377(a).

[75] Act Sec. 1306, Small Business Job Protection Act, amending Code Sec. 1377(a)(2).

However, if the interim book closing method is used, Polk would report $15,000 × .40 = $6,000, Bess would report $33,000 × .40 = $13,200, and Frey would continue to report $28,800.

Tax Tips and Pitfalls

Since all affected stockholders must consent for the interim book closing method to be used, a purchasing or selling shareholder should consider which method will be personally most beneficial. In the above example, Polk would likely prefer the daily allocation method since it would result in less income being taxed to him.

¶ 413 Items Flowing Through Separately

As is true of partnerships, S corporation income and expense items are divided into those entering into ordinary taxable income and the items which need to be reported separately. Items reported separately are shown on Schedule K, and Schedule K-1 is sent to each shareholder. As is true of partnerships, the decision criteria for reporting an item separately is whether or not the item would have a special characteristic at the individual level. Following is a noninclusive list of separately reported items along with the reason for reporting them separately:

Item	Reason
Passive gains, losses and credits	Limitation of passive losses
Capital transactions	Individuals must report separate from other items
Portfolio income	Could affect the deduction for investment interest
Code Sec. 1231 transactions	Are netted; gains become long-term capital gains
Exempt interest	Must be reported for informational purposes on Form 1040
Investment income, expenses	Could affect the deduction for investment interest
Recoveries of tax benefit items	Taxability of the item depends on the extent deduction gave a tax benefit
Tax preference	Included to arrive at individual's minimum tax
Code Sec. 179 expense election	Limitation of $24,000 (for 2001 and 2002) on individual return
Income or loss from rental	Passive activity loss allowance of $25,000 for rental real estate (No limit for real estate professionals)
Charitable contributions	Must be itemized; subject to a 50 percent AGI limit

Item	Reason
Foreign income, losses, and foreign taxes	Foreign tax credit, exclusion
Property distributions	Special basis rules
Distributions from accumulated earnings and profits	Taxed as dividends

¶ 415   Operating Losses

As is true of income, losses flow through to shareholders. The loss in the hands of the shareholder is a deduction for adjusted gross income and therefore can, if sufficiently large, create a net operating loss carryback or carryforward for the individual.

Tax Tips and Pitfalls

The fact that shareholders can derive an immediate tax benefit from net operating losses of S corporations constitutes an important incentive to elect S status at the time of inception of the corporation. NOLs of a new C corporation can only be carried forward; NOLs of an S corporation flow through to the shareholders. An overall limitation exists for loss deductions; losses deducted cannot exceed the sum of the adjusted basis of the stock plus any debt owed to the shareholder.[76] Any excess loss becomes an indefinite carryover, to be used against income in a carryforward year.[77]

Merely guaranteeing a note of an S corporation is not sufficient to allow loss deductions. In *Salem*, the shareholders guaranteed and then later co-signed notes on behalf of an S corporation. However, the stockholders did not pledge any personal property as security, and the bank looked to the corporation for repayment. The Tax Court ruled that the shareholders could not increase their bases in the corporation because they made no economic outlay creating indebtedness of the corporation to them.[78]

Example 4-11. Greene's share of the loss of an S corporation was $40,000. He had a basis in his stock of $25,000 and a note receivable from the corporation in the amount of $20,000. The loss reduces the basis of his stock to zero and his note to $5,000.

Income in subsequent years first restores the basis of the debt, and then the stock.[79]

Example 4-12. Assume the same facts as in Example 4-11 and that Greene's share of taxable income the next year was $17,000. The first $15,000 of income would restore the basis of the note back to its

---

[76] Code Sec. 1366(d)(1).
[77] Code Sec. 1366(d)(2).
[78] *R.J. Salem v. Commr.*, 75 TCM 1798, Dec. 52,572(M), TC Memo. 1998-63. Also see *A. Bean*

Est. v. Commr., 80 TCM 713, Dec. 54,125(M), TC Memo. 2000-355.

[79] Code Sec. 1367(b)(2)(B).

original basis of $20,000; the remaining $2,000 would increase the basis of the stock from zero up to $2,000.

Repayment of the debt before basis is restored will result in income to the shareholder to the extent that the repayment exceeds the basis. Characterization of the income depends on whether the debt is an open account, or is evidenced by a note. If an open account, the income is ordinary; if a note exists, the income is a capital gain.[80]

The stockholder who has used a note receivable to absorb some of the NOL of an S corporation should be careful not to receive any payment on the note until basis is restored, or income will result. Even a partial payment must be allocated between basis and gain.

The loss carryforward is personal to the stockholder; i.e., a new stockholder does not succeed to the loss carryforward. If the corporation terminates S status, the loss must be deducted by the end of the "post-termination period" or it is irrevocably lost.[81] The "post-termination period" is the later of one year after the last day of the corporation as an S corporation or the due date for filing the last S return or 120 days beginning on the date of a determination that the corporation's election had terminated for a previous taxable year.[82]

A sale, gift, or other disposition of S corporation stock is not wise if the basis is zero and there are loss carryforwards. Similarly, S status should not be terminated if there are loss carryforwards. An alternative would be to loan the corporation money before disposing of the stock, thus deducting the carryforward against the basis of the loan.

¶ 417 Differences Between Partnership and S Corporation Income Determination

Although the partnership is never a federal taxable entity, there are four instances in which S corporations must pay a tax. There is a tax on "built-in capital gains" and on "excessive passive income." There is also a LIFO recapture tax and a general business credit recapture. All of these are discussed later. S corporations do not have guaranteed salaries; stockholders are employees, and their salaries are treated the same as other employees. S corporation shareholders do not receive self-employment income from the S corporation. Also, current distributions to partners rarely have current tax implications, so there is no separate section for distributions. However, for S corporations, distributions can present tax problems to shareholders; hence, Form 1120S has a separate section for distributions.

Partnerships are not subject to the depreciation recapture rules under Code Sec. 291; however, C corporations and S corporations which were C

---

[80] Rev. Rul. 64-162, 1964-1 CB (Part 1) 304; Rev. Rul. 68-537, 1968-2 CB 372.

[81] Code Sec. 1366(d)(3).
[82] Code Sec. 1377(b)(1).

corporations for any of the three immediately preceding taxable years are subject to this recapture provision.[83]

Code Sec. 291 gain is equal to 20 percent of the difference between the amount of ordinary income that would have existed had the property been subject to Code Sec. 1245 and the amount of the Code Sec. 1250 gain.

> **Example 4-13.** Langston Enterprises sold an office building for $650,000. The building cost $500,000, and $200,000 of straight-line depreciation was taken. The Code Sec. 291 gain is .20 ($200,000 − $0) = $40,000. The Code Sec. 1250 gain is zero since straight-line depreciation was used. Hence, the results, depending on whether Langston Enterprises is a partnership or an S corporation which had been a C corporation in the last three years are:

	S Corporation	Partnership
1250 gain	—	—
291 gain	$ 40,000	—
1231 gain	310,000	$350,000
Total	$350,000	$350,000

¶ 419   Dealings Between Shareholders and S Corporations

With the exception of property transfers for stock qualifying under Code Sec. 351, dealings between shareholders and S corporations are generally treated as if they were arm's length, i.e., they will be taxable. However, there are three exceptions to this rule. The first two exceptions apply to dealings with "related parties," i.e., corporations and individuals who own, directly or indirectly, over 50 percent of the value of the outstanding stock.[84] They are:

1. Losses on sales to related parties are not deductible.[85] The disallowed loss reduces future gains of the purchaser, but cannot increase losses.[86]

> **Example 4-14.** Higgins sold at a $20,000 loss land to the Doolittle Corporation, an S corporation of which he and his brother together own 70 percent. Higgins's loss is not deductible. Later, the Doolittle Corporation sold the land for a $27,000 gain. Only $7,000 of the gain is taxable. However, if Doolittle had sold the land at a $5,000 loss, the $20,000 disallowed loss would *not* increase Doolittle's loss.

2. Gains on sale of depreciable property between related parties is treated as ordinary income.[87]

---

[83] Code Secs. 1363(b)(4) and 291(a)(1).
[84] Code Sec. 267(b)(2).
[85] Code Sec. 267(a)(1).
[86] Code Sec. 267(d).
[87] Code Sec. 1239(a).

3. The third exception relates to expense accruals on items accrued to cash basis taxpayers who are shareholders. The expense items are not deductible until paid.[88]

Example 4-15. Phelps, Inc., accrued at the end of 2000 a $5,000 bonus to Klaussen, a 60 percent stockholder in the corporation. The bonus was paid on February 2, 2001. It is deductible by Phelps, Inc., in 2001, when paid.

Fringe benefits paid by S corporations on behalf of over two percent shareholders are also subject to special rules. These rules are discussed later in this chapter.

¶ 421 Tax Basis of the Shareholder

The starting point for computing the shareholder's basis is his or her original tax basis. Original basis might arise from a Code Sec. 351 transfer, a taxable transfer, a purchase, gift, or inheritance. Original basis is determined under the rules for those types of acquisitions; for example, if acquired by inheritance, basis would generally be fair market value at date of death. Original basis is affected by results from operations, by additional capital contributions, and by distributions of cash or property. Operations causing an increase in basis include:[89]

- Items of income (including tax-exempt income) which are separately separated;

- Nonseparately stated income; and

- Depletion in excess of the basis of the property.

Operations decreasing basis include:[90]

- Separately stated deductions and losses;

- Nonseparately stated losses;

- Nondeductible expenses not properly chargeable to capital; and

- Deductions for depletion to the extent that the deductions do not exceed adjusted basis of the property.

In a very important case for shareholders of financially troubled corporations, the Supreme Court has ruled that discharge of indebtedness income (DOI), which is excludable from income under Code Sec. 108, is nonetheless an item of income that passes through to S shareholders. Therefore, S shareholders receive an increase in stock basis from the DOI. The Court also ruled that the attribute reduction required under Code Sec. 108 takes place after the pass through of income to the shareholders.[91]

---

[88] Code Sec. 267(a)(2).
[89] Code Secs. 1366(a) and 1367(a)(1).
[90] Code Sec. 1367(a)(2).

[91] *D.A. Gitlitz v. Commr.*, SCt, 2001-1 USTC ¶ 50,147, 121 SCt 701, rev'g, CA-10, 99-2 USTC ¶ 50,645, 182 F3d 1143.

However, as of this writing, legislation to retroactively reverse this holding has been introduced in Congress.

¶ 423   Current Distributions

The treatment of current distributions depends on whether the corporation has earnings and profits accumulated from years in which it was not an S corporation. Distributions by S corporations with no earnings and profits are first treated as a return of capital until the stock basis is reduced to zero and then as capital gains.[92]

> **Example 4-16.** Val Dez, Inc., has always been an S corporation. In 2001, Dez, a shareholder, received a cash distribution of $30,000. His adjusted basis in the stock at the end of 2001 was $25,000. The first $25,000 of the distribution is tax-free, but reduces his basis down to zero. The remaining $5,000 is a capital gain.

Distributions from S corporations reduce the basis of the shareholder's stock before losses are taken into account. Congress has made it easier to make tax-free distributions in loss years. Effective for tax years beginning after 1996, in determining the amount in the accumulated adjustments account, net negative adjustments (i.e., the excess of losses and deductions over income) for that taxable year are disregarded.[93]

> **Example 4-17.** Hastings is the sole shareholder of HH, Inc., a calendar year S corporation with no accumulated earnings and profits. Hastings' adjusted basis in her stock on January 1, 1997, is $5,000. HH, Inc., had in 1997 ordinary losses of $4,300 and Code Sec. 1231 gains of $1,200. It distributed $2,500 to Hastings in 1997. Adding the Code Sec. 1231 gains to the beginning basis results in a stock basis before distributions and losses of $5,000 plus $1,200, or $6,200. The distributions reduce the adjusted basis down to $3,700 ($6,200 − $2,500). Of the $4,300 loss, $3,700 is deductible, reducing Hastings' adjusted basis to zero. Thus, the tax results to Hastings are Code Sec. 1231 gains of $1,200, a nontaxable distribution of $2,500, an ordinary loss deduction of $3,700, and a $600 loss carryforward.

The distribution rules are more complicated if the corporation has earnings and profits accumulated from years in which it was a C corporation. There are four prioritizing items to go through:[94]

1.   The distribution is tax-free up to the accumulated adjustments account (AAA). This account accumulates undistributed S corporation earnings for years beginning after 1982. Stock basis is reduced (not below zero) to the extent that the distribution is from AAA.

---

[92] Code Sec. 1368(b); Reg. § 1.1368-1(c).
[93] Code Sec. 1368(e)(1)(C).
[94] Code Sec. 1368(c). For years beginning before 1997, corporations with S corporation income accu-

mulated before January 1, 1983, had to keep track of previously taxed income (PTI).

2. Any amount remaining after item one is treated as dividends to the extent of accumulated earnings and profits (E&P), i.e., earnings accumulated while a C corporation. These amounts are reported by shareholders as dividend income on Schedule B. Stock basis is not reduced by dividends.

3. Any remaining amount is treated as a reduction of stock basis, and is nontaxable to that extent.

4. Once the stock basis is zero, remaining distributions are treated as capital gains.

Example 4-18. Jack Sewall is the sole shareholder of Happy Farms, Inc., a calendar year S corporation, with accumulated earnings and profits of $5,000 and an accumulated adjustments account of $2,000 on January 1, 2001. Sewall's adjusted basis in the stock on January 1, 2001, is $10,000. During 2001, Happy Farms makes a distribution to Sewall of $6,000, has a capital gain of $3,000, and has an operating loss of $9,000. For purposes of determining the tax status of the distribution, the net negative adjustments of $6,000 ($9,000 − 3,000) are not taken into account. Therefore, $2,000 of the $6,000 distribution is a distribution out of AAA, reducing it to zero. The remaining $4,000 of distribution is out of accumulated earnings and profits, reducing E&P to $1,000. The AAA account is then decreased by $6,000, resulting in a negative balance on January 1, 2002, of $6,000. Of the $6,000 distribution, the $2,000 from the AAA is nontaxable to Sewall, but reduces his basis from $10,000 plus the $3,000 of capital gains, down to $11,000. The other $4,000 of distribution is a taxable dividend but does not reduce basis. Sewall may deduct the entire $9,000 operating loss. His basis on January 1, 2002, is $2,000 ($10,000 + $3,000 − $2,000 − $9,000).

Example 4-19. Wainright, Inc. has the following balances at the end of 2001 before considering the effect of distributions:

Accumulated adjustments account $36,000
Accumulated earnings and profits 19,000

Jim Wainright's stock basis (the sole shareholder) is $40,000. A $58,000 distribution was made in 2001 to Wainright. Of the distribution, $19,000 is taxed as a dividend; the other $39,000 is nontaxable, but reduces his basis to $1,000.

Every S corporation is expected to keep an AAA account, and, if necessary, an other adjustments account. The AAA account includes taxable income but not tax exempt income, and all expenses and losses, including nondeductible expenses unless they relate to exempt income. Cash distributions reduce AAA, as does the fair market value of property distributions. The Tax Court has ruled that adjustments to the AAA for losses and deductions are made prior to adjustments for shareholder distribu-

¶ 423

tions.[95] The other adjustments account consists of tax-exempt income (including life insurance proceeds) and the expenses attributable to tax-exempt income (including premiums on life insurance policies in which the corporation is the beneficiary).

Example 4-20. River Valley Sales, Inc., an S corporation, began 2001 with balances in the accumulated adjustments account and other adjustments account of $80,000 and $12,000, respectively. During 2001 it had the following items of income, deductions, and distributions:

Ordinary income from trade or business	$50,000
Long-term capital gain	12,000
Portfolio interest income	4,000
Tax-exempt interest	7,000
Charitable contributions	2,500
Expenses related to tax-exempt interest	2,600
Penalties	500
Distributions	21,000

A hypothetical 2001 Schedule M-2 of Form 1120S, which reconciles these two accounts appears below:

Schedule M-2
Analysis of Accumulated Adjustments Account and Other Adjustments Account

	Accumulated Adjustments Account	Other Adjustments Account
1. Balance at beginning of year	80,000	12,000
2. Ordinary income from page 1	50,000	
3. Other additions	16,000*	7,000
4. Loss from page 1		
5. Other reductions	(3,000)**	(2,600)
6. Combine lines 1 through 5	143,000	16,400
7. Distributions other than dividend distributions	(21,000)	
8. Balance at end of year	122,000	16,400

* Long-term capital gains		$ 12,000
Portfolio interest income		4,000
** Charitable contributions		2,500
Penalties		500

---

[95] *S.R. Williams v. Commr.*, 110 TC 27, Dec. 52,527.

¶ 425   Property Distributions

Unless in connection with a reorganization, an S corporation recognizes gains on appreciated property.[96] Because of the conduit rule, gains are passed through to the shareholders and reported on their individual returns. The shareholder has a basis in the property equal to fair market value.

If the corporation distributes property with a fair market value less than basis, losses are not recognized. Again, the shareholder picks up the property at fair market value.

Tax Tips and Pitfalls

Property having a fair market value less than basis should generally not be distributed to shareholders. Since the shareholder gets a basis equal to fair market value, the potential loss is irrevocably lost. A better strategy would be to have the corporation sell the property and then distribute the property. In that event, the loss would pass through to the shareholders and would be deductible by them.

¶ 427   Post-Termination Distributions

After a corporation terminates S status, distributions would generally be taxed as dividends to the extent of current earnings and profits. If there were a considerable amount of undistributed income from S years, this result would be very unfortunate. Fortunately, S corporations are allowed a certain post-termination period in which cash distributions may be treated as being from AAA (and thus be nontaxable.) The post-termination transaction period is defined as the period beginning on the day after the last day of the corporation's last taxable year as an S corporation and ending on the latter of :

- One year later; or

- The due date for the last year of the S corporation return (this includes extensions);

- 120 days after any determination pursuant to an audit which follows the termination of the corporation's election and which adjusts an item of income, loss, or deduction arising during the S period;

- 120 days after a determination that the S corporation had terminated for a previous taxable year (this determination could arise from a court decision, a closing agreement, or with some other agreement between the IRS and the S corporation.)[97]

---

[96] Code Sec. 1363(b).   [97] Code Sec. 1377(b).

Tax Tips and Pitfalls

This one-year time period is extremely critical for corporations that have terminated their S status. Distributions within the one-year period will, to the extent of AAA, be nontaxable. However, distributions outside the one-year period will, to the extent of earnings and profits, be fully taxable. For example, a company with $20,000 of AAA loses its S status as of January 1, 2001. During 2001, it has earnings and profits of $18,000. A distribution of $15,000 on or before December 31, 2001, would be nontaxable; a distribution on or after January 1, 2002, would be taxable.

¶ 429   Taxes Incurred by S Corporations

Unlike partnerships, which are never subject to federal taxes, S corporations are subject to tax in four instances:

1.   If it realizes built-in gains;

2.   If it has excess passive income;

3.   If it has general business credit recapture; or

4.   If it is subject to the LIFO recapture.

.01 *S Corporations—Built-in Gains Tax*[98]

When Congress passed the Tax Reform Act of 1986, it recognized that the lower individual rates contained in the Act as well as the repeal of the *General Utilities* rule would create an incentive for corporations to elect S status. Concerned that companies might use the S provisions to avoid a higher tax on previously appreciated assets, Congress in 1988 added new Code Sec. 1374, the "built-in gains tax" (BIG tax). The tax applies to corporations that converted to S corporation status after 1986. Thus, the tax does *not* apply to:[99]

- Corporations that have always been S corporations; and

- Corporations that converted to S corporation status *before* 1987.

The tax applies generally to assets disposed of in the "recognition period," i.e., a 10-year period beginning with the first day of the first taxable year for which the corporation was an S corporation.[100]

The BIG tax is treated as a loss sustained by the S corporation, and as such, passes through to the shareholders.[101] The character of the loss is determined by allocating the loss proportionately among the recognized built-in gains.[102]

---

[98] This discussion is adapted from Gary L. Maydew, "The Built-in Gains Tax—The IRS Issues Proposed Reg.," *Taxes—The Tax Magazine*, May 1993.

[99] Code Sec. 1374(c).
[100] Code Sec. 1374(d)(7).
[101] Code Sec. 1366(f)(2).
[102] *Id.*

Proposed regulations were issued in 1992 and final regulations in 1994 that explain the IRS position on the BIG tax.

.02 The Regulations

The regulations list four steps necessary to compute the built-in gains tax.[103]

1. Determine the "net recognized built-in gain."

2. Reduce the net recognized built-in gain (but not below zero) by any net operating loss or capital loss carryforwards allowable.

3. Apply the applicable tax rate (35 percent for years beginning on or after January 1, 1993).

4. Determine the final tax by reducing the amount arrived at in step three by allowable business credit carryforwards (these must have arisen while a C corporation).

"Net recognized built in gain" for a given year is the lesser of three computations:[104]

1. The "prelimitation amount" is the recognized built-in gain less the recognized built-in losses plus any recognized built-in gain carryover from previous years.

2. The "taxable income limitation" is the taxable income the corporation would have had if it were a C corporation. However, this is computed as modified by Code Sec. 1375(b)(1)(B), under which taxable income is computed without regard to the deductions allowed by Code Sec. 241 *et seq* for dividends received (but with the deduction of organization costs) and without regard to the net operating loss deduction.

3. The "net unrealized built-in gain limitation" is the amount by which the net unrealized built-in gain exceeds the net recognized built-in gain for all prior taxable years.

If the prelimitation amount exceeds the net recognized built-in gain for a tax year, the net recognized built-in gain includes a ratable portion of each item of income, gain, loss, and deduction included in the prelimitation amount.[105] If net recognized built-in gain is equal to the S corporation's taxable income limitation, the amount by which the prelimitation amount exceeds the taxable income limitation is a recognized built-in gain carryover included in the corporation's prelimitation amount for the succeeding taxable year. The recognized built-in gain carryover consists of a ratable portion of each item of income, gain, loss, and deduction not included in the

---

[103] Reg. § 1.1374-1(a).
[104] Reg. § 1.1374-2(a).

[105] Reg. § 1.1374-2(b).

corporation's net recognized built-in gain for the year the carryover arose.[106]

Example 4-21. Western, Inc., elected S corporation status effective January 1, 2001. On that date, a partial balance sheet (the company had no liabilities) was as follows:

	Fair Market Value	Adjusted Basis	Built-in Gain (Loss)
Cash.................	$ 20,000	$ 20,000	$ -0-
Accounts receivable	50,000	56,000	(6,000)
Inventory	70,000	52,000	18,000
Equipment	60,000	63,000	(3,000)
Building...............	100,000	85,000	15,000
Land	50,000	40,000	10,000
Total	$350,000	$316,000	$34,000

Early in 2001, the company sold the inventory for $74,000, collected all of the accounts receivable at a loss of $6,000, sold a machine bought early in 2001 at a gain of $4,000, and sold the land at a gain of $8,000. Since no gains have previously been recognized, the net unrealized built-in gain limitation is $34,000. Total gains are ($74,000 − $52,000) − $6,000 + $4,000 + $8,000 = $28,000. However, the prelimitation amount does not include the gain on the machine and would include only $18,000 of gain on the inventory (the built-in gain at the time of achieving S status). Thus, the prelimitation amount is $70,000 − $52,000 − $6,000 + $8,000 = $20,000. Assume the taxable income that the company would have had as a C corporation is only $9,600. Thus, the net recognized built-in gain is $9,600 (the lessor of $34,000, $20,000, and $9,600). Assuming that the land is a Code Sec. 1231 asset, the recognized built-in gain consists of ordinary income of $8,640 ($18,000/$20,000 × $9,600), ordinary losses of $2,880 ($6,000/$20,000 × $9,600), and Code Sec. 1231 gains of $3,840 ($8,000/$20,000 × $9,600).

Net Unrealized Built-in Gain

The balance sheet example listed above is a simplification of the computation of unrealized built-in gain. The regulations define "net unrealized built-in gain" as the total of five computations:[107]

1.   The amount that would be realized if, at the beginning of the recognition period, the company remained a C corporation and sold all of its assets at fair market value to an unrelated party who assumed all of its liabilities, decreased by

2.   Any liabilities that would be included in the amount realized, but only those for which the company would be allowed a

---

[106] Reg. § 1.1374-2(c).   [107] Reg. § 1.1374-3(a).

¶ 429.02

deduction on payment (generally accounts payable of a cash basis company), decreased by

3. The aggregate total adjusted bases of the assets on the first day of the recognition period, increased or decreased by

4. The company's Code Sec. 481 adjustments (for changes in accounting methods) that would be taken into account on the sale, and increased by

5. Any recognized built-in loss that would not be allowed on the sale under Code Sec. 382, 383, or 384 (limitations on losses arising from changes in the ownership of the entity).

Example 4-22. Assume the same facts as in Example 4-21 and also that the corporation has been on a hybrid basis and has a $100,000 mortgage, accounts payable of $30,000, and that there are no Code Sec. 481 adjustments or loss carryforward limitations. The amount realized would be $350,000 ($220,000 cash received + $100,000 + $30,000). The net unrealized built-in gain would be:

Amount realized	$350,000
Deduction for accounts payable	30,000
Bases of the assets	316,000
Net unrealized built-in gain	$ 4,000

Recognized Built-in Gain or Loss

Any sales or exchanges of assets held as of the date of the election result in recognized built-in gain or loss.[108] But what about collection of income and payment of expenses? The regulations go into considerable detail. Income items constitute recognized built-in gain if the item would have been included in gross income before the effective date of the election had the corporation been using the accrual method.[109] The *amount* of accounts receivable recognized may depend on whether the receivables are sold or collected.

Example 4-23.[110] As of the effective date of the S election, a cash basis corporation has receivables with a face value of $50,000 and a fair market value of $40,000. Later that year, the corporation collects all $50,000 of the receivables. The $50,000 is recognized built-in gain. Assume instead that the company had disposed of the receivables for $45,000. In that case, the recognized built-in gain would be $40,000.

Deduction items constitute recognized built-in loss if the item would have been previously deductible had the accrual method been used.[111]

---

[108] Reg. § 1.1374-4(a).
[109] Reg. § 1.1374-4(b)(1).
[110] Adapted from Reg. § 1.1374-4(b)(3), Example 1.

[111] Reg. § 1.1374-4(b)(2).

Example 4-24.[112] A cash basis taxpayer had a $600,000 lawsuit filed against it in 2000. It elected S status in 2001. It settled the lawsuit for $400,000 in 2001. Since the corporation could not have deducted the item in 2000 even if it had used the accrual method (economic performance would not have occurred), the $400,000 deduction in 2001 is *not* a recognized built-in loss.

Examples in the regulations also cover contingent liabilities, deferred payment income and liabilities, Code Sec. 481 adjustments, deemed distributions, discharge of indebtedness and bad debts, completion of contract, and installment sales.

Partnerships Interests

The corporation's recognized built-in gain or recognized built-in loss limitation from its ownership in a partnership is the total of three computations:[113]

1.   The amount realized if, on the effective date of the S election, the company sold its partnership interest for its fair market value to an unrelated party, decreased by

2.   The corporation's adjusted basis in the partnership interest, and increased or decreased by

3.   The corporation's allocable share of the partnership's Code Sec. 481(a) adjustments that would be taken into account on the sale.

In general, the effect on the corporation's net recognized built-in gain from its distributive share of partnership items is computed as follows:[114]

1.   Determine the extent to which the distributive share would have been treated as recognized built-in gain or loss if the partnership items had originated in the S corporation.

2.   Determine the S corporation's net recognized built-in gain without partnership items.

3.   Determine the S corporation's net recognized built-in gain with partnership items.

4.   If the amount computed in (3) exceeds the amount computed in (2), the excess is the S corporation's partnership recognized built-in gains, and the S corporation's net recognized built-in gain is the sum of the amount computed under step (2) plus the partnership recognized built-in gain. If the amount computed in step (2) exceeds the amount computed in step (3), the excess is the S corporation's partnership recognized built-in loss, and the

---

[112] Adapted from Reg. § 1.1374-4(b)(3), Example 3.

[113] Reg. § 1.1374-4(i)(4).

[114] Reg. § 1.1374-4(i)(1).

S corporation's net recognized built-in gain is the remainder of the amount computed under step (2) minus the partnership recognized built-in loss.

Example 4-25.[115] Snyder Co. elects to become an S corporation on January 1, 2001. On that date, it owns a 50 percent interest in the Powell partnership. Its share of Powell's recognized built-in gain limitation is $100,000. In 2001, Powell sells an asset with a basis of $50,000, and a fair market value on the effective election date of $200,000, for $200,000, and recognizes a gain of $150,000, Snyder's share of which is $75,000. Snyder's net recognized built-in gain without partnership items is $35,000 and with partnership items is $110,000. Because Snyder's partnership recognized built-in gain limitation is $100,000, the $75,000 is not limited, and Snyder's net recognized built-in gain for the year is the total $110,000. However, if Snyder's partnership recognized built-in gain limitation had been only $50,000, Snyder's partnership recognized built-in gain would have been limited to $50,000, and Snyder's total recognized built-in gain would be $85,000 ($35,000 + $50,000).

In general, the partnership recognized built-in gain or loss cannot exceed the excess (if any) of the corporation's recognized built-in gain or loss limitation over its partnership recognized built-in gain or loss for prior taxable years.[116] However, this limitation does not apply if the corporation forms or avails of a partnership with the principal purpose of avoiding the built-in gains tax.[117] If an S corporation disposes of its partnership interest, the recognized built-in gain or loss may not exceed the excess (if any) of the S corporation's recognized built-in gain or loss limitation over its partnership recognized built-in gain or loss during the recognition period.[118]

Small Partnership Interests

Generally, the recognized built-in gain or loss rules for distributive shares of a partnership do not apply to any year in the recognition period if the fair market value of the corporation's partnership interest at the beginning of the recognition period is less than $100,000 and is less than 10 percent of the partnership capital and profits at all times during the year. However, the rules *will* apply if the corporation forms or avails a partnership with a principal purpose of tax avoidance.[119]

Deduction Carryforwards

In general, a corporation can deduct against net recognized gain its net operating loss and capital loss carryforwards, but not other carryforwards, such as charitable contribution carryforwards.[120] However, if the carryforwards are limited because of ownership changes under Code Secs.

---

115 Adapted from Reg. § 1.1374-4(i)(8), Example 3.
116 Reg. § 1.1374-4(i)(2).
117 Reg. § 1.1374-4(i)(2)(i).

118 Reg. § 1.1374-4(i)(3).
119 Reg. § 1.1374-4(i)(5).
120 Reg. § 1.1374-5(a).

382, 383(b), or 384, these sections will limit their use as deductions against recognized built-in gain.[121]

Credits and Credit Carryforwards

The special fuels credit, the business credits, and the minimum tax credit (but not the foreign tax credit) carryforwards from C years are allowed against the built-in gains tax. However, the amount of the carryforwards available for use is subject to the limitations of Code Sec. 38(c) (the business credit allowable cannot exceed the excess of the net income tax over the greater of the tentative minimum tax or 25 percent of the net regular tax liability in excess of $25,000) and Code Sec. 53(c) (the minimum tax credit cannot exceed the excess of the regular tax liability over the tentative minimum tax for the year).[122] For these purposes, both the regular tax liability and the tentative minimum tax are computed by taking into account only the recognized built-in gains.[123]

Example 4-26.[124] Hi Tech Co. is a C corporation which elects to become an S corporation on January 1, 2001. On that date, Hi Tech Co. has a $500,000 business credit carryforward from a C year and an asset with a fair market value of $400,000, a basis for regular tax purposes of $95,000, and a basis for AMT purposes of $150,000. In 2001, Hi Tech Co. sells the asset for $400,000, thus having a net recognized built-in gain of $305,000, and a regular tax liability of $106,750. The tentative minimum tax after the exemption would be $47,000. Thus, the business credit limitation is $106,750 less the greater of:

> 25 percent of the tax liability over $25,000 (.25 (106,750 − 25,000)) = $20,438, or the tentative minimum tax of $47,000

Thus, the limitation is $106,750 − $47,000 = $59,750, and the Code Sec. 1374 tax due is $106,750 − the business credit of $59,750 = $47,000. The remaining business credits of $440,250 are carried forward to future years.

Inventory

Inventory is valued at what it would bring in a bulk sale, i.e., at the amount that a willing buyer would pay to a willing seller for the inventory in a purchase of all of the assets of the S corporation on that day.[125] Generally, the inventory method used by an S corporation determines whether inventory it disposes of during the recognition period has been held on the first day of that period. This means that a company using LIFO will not have any recognized built-in gains unless or until it eats into its LIFO layer. However, if the corporation changes inventory methods to LIFO with a principal purpose of avoiding the built-in gains tax, it must use the FIFO

---

[121] Reg. § 1.1374-5(b).
[122] Reg. § 1.1374-6(b).
[123] Reg. § 1.1374-6(b).

[124] Adapted from Reg. § 1.1374-6(c), Example 1.

[125] Reg. § 1.1374-7(a).

method to identify its dispositions of inventory.[126] Also, at the time a C corporation using LIFO makes an S election, a LIFO recapture amount (the difference between FIFO and LIFO) must be included in income for its last C year. The tax is payable in four equal installments.[127]

Section 1374(d)(8) Transactions

If an S corporation acquires assets from a C corporation and the transaction is wholly or partly nontaxable (so that basis of the assets to the S corporation is determined in whole or in part by the basis in the hands of the C corporation), a tax is imposed during the recognition period on any net recognized built-in gain.[128] This tax must be determined separately from any other Code Sec. 1374(d)(8) transactions and separately from other built-in gains, e.g., loss carryforwards acquired in a Code Sec. 1374(d)(8) transaction can offset only net recognized built-in gains attributable to assets acquired in that same Code Sec. 1374(d)(8) transaction.[129] Even the taxable income limitation discussed previously must be allocated among the various built-in gains determined.[130]

Anti-Stuffing Rules

If a corporation acquires an asset before or during the recognition period with a principal purpose of avoiding the built-in gains tax (e.g., to create a recognized loss), the asset and any loss, deduction, loss carryforward, and credits and credit carryforwards are disregarded in determining the prelimitation amount, taxable income limitation, net unrealized built-in gain limitation, deductions against net recognized built-in gain, and credits against the built-in gains tax.[131]

Effective Dates

Generally, these regulations will apply only for taxable years ending on or after December 27, 1994, but only where the S election or Code Sec. 1374(d)(8) transaction occurred on or after that date.[132] However, if a corporation transfers an asset to a partnership in a transaction to which Code Sec. 721(a) applies (nonrecognition of gain), and the transfer is made in contemplation of an S election, or the transfer is made during the recognition period, Code Sec. 1374 applies on a disposition of the asset by the partnership as if the corporation had disposed of the asset itself to the partnership. This requirement applies as of the effective date of Code Sec. 1374 (conversions after 1986).[133]

The regulations clear up some of the confusion. However, many questions are left unanswered, such as how net unrecognized built-in gains are to be determined. For example, does determination of "fair market value" require an appraisal? Presumably many if not most corporations switching

---

[126] Reg. § 1.1374-7(b).
[127] Code Sec. 1363(d).
[128] Code Sec. 1374(d)(8).
[129] Reg. § 1.1374-8(b).

[130] Reg. § 1.1374-8(c).
[131] Reg. § 1.1374-9.
[132] Reg. § 1.1374-10(a).
[133] Reg. § 1.1374-10(b).

to S status did *not* have their assets appraised. What sort of estimates of fair market value will the IRS accept?

.03 LIFO Recapture Tax

As previously mentioned, if an electing S corporation was previously a C corporation and used LIFO to determine its inventory, then a LIFO recapture amount is included in gross income for the last C tax year.[134] The tax is payable in four equal installments, the first of which is due when the last C corporate return is filed.[135]

In a private letter ruling, the IRS ruled that a C corporation with interests in partnerships that use the LIFO method must include the LIFO recapture amount in income when it converts to an S corporation. The IRS asserted that allowing a corporation to avoid LIFO recapture by holding LIFO inventory in a partnership would circumvent the purpose of the LIFO recapture statute.[136]

.04 Penalty Tax on Excessive Passive Income

As previously mentioned, the presence of excessive passive income can result in the loss of S status. However, in addition, a penalty tax may be imposed on S corporations with excessive passive income. The tax is imposed in any taxable year in which at year's end an S corporation has earnings and profits accumulated from "C" years, and in which gross receipts exceed 25 percent of passive investment income.[137] Thus, a corporation which has always been an S corporation is not subject to this tax. The amount subject to tax (the excess net passive income) is computed as follows:[138]

$$\text{Excess net passive income} = \frac{\text{Passive investment income in excess of 25\% of gross receipts for the year}}{\text{Passive investment income}} \times \text{Net passive income}$$

The amount subject to tax is limited to the taxable income.[139] The terms "gross receipts" and "passive investment income" have the same meanings as in Code Sec. 1362(d)(3) (relating to loss of S status if the corporation has excess passive investment income).[140]

.05 Definition of Passive Income

In general, passive investment income is gross receipts from royalties, rents, dividends, interest, annuities, and gains and losses from sales or exchanges of securities.[141]

---

[134] Code Sec. 1363(d)(1); Reg. § 1.1363-2(a).

[135] Code Sec. 1363(d)(2)(A); Reg. § 1.1363-2(b).

[136] IRS Letter Ruling 9716003, September 30, 1996.

[137] Code Sec. 1375(a).

[138] Code Sec. 1375(b); Reg. § 1.1375-1(b)(1)(i).

[139] Code Sec. 1375(b)(1)(B).

[140] Code Sec. 1375(b)(3).

[141] Reg. § 1.1362-2(c)(5)(i).

Royalties

Royalties include mineral, oil, and gas royalties, and amounts received for the privilege of using patents, copyrights, secret processes and formulas, goodwill, trademarks, tradebrands, franchises, and other like property.[142] However, royalties derived in the ordinary course of a business or franchising or licensing of property are not passive income. Generally the royalties would be derived in the ordinary course of business if the corporation either created the property or performed significant services or incurred substantial costs in developing or marketing the property.[143]

Copyright royalties are not passive income. Neither are mineral and oil and gas royalties as long as the income would not be treated as personal holding company income if the corporation were a C corporation. Amounts received from the disposal of timber, coal, or domestic iron ore to which the special retained economic interest rules apply also are not passive income. Active business computer software royalties as defined in Code Sec. 543(d) also are not passive income.[144]

Rents

In general, rents are defined as amounts received for the use of, or the right to use, real or personal property of the taxpayer. However, rents derived in the active business of renting property are not passive. Generally, in order to meet the active business requirement, significant services must be provided or substantial costs incurred (net leases generally would not meet this requirement).[145]

Interest

Interest means any amount received for the use of money (including tax-exempt interest). However, this does not include interest on obligations acquired in the ordinary course of business from the sale of inventory or the performance of services.[146]

Net Passive Income

"Net passive income" equals passive investment income less deductions directly connected with the production of such income (not including the dividends-received deduction and the net operating loss deduction.)[147]

Example 4-27. Garbo, Inc., an S corporation, has $100,000 accumulated earnings and profits from C years. During the year, it had gross receipts from its business of $150,000, dividends of $60,000, and interest income of $40,000. Deductions attributable to the dividend and interest income amounted to $5,000. Excess net passive income (ENPI) is as follows:

---

[142] Reg. § 1.1362-2(c)(5)(ii)(A)(1).
[143] Reg. § 1.1362-2(c)(5)(ii)(A)(2).
[144] Reg. § 1.1362-2(c)(5)(ii)(A)(3).

[145] Reg. § 1.1362-2(c)(5)(ii)(B).
[146] Reg. § 1.1362-2(c)(5)(ii)(D)(1) and (2).
[147] Reg. § 1.1375-1(b)(2).

$$\text{ENPI} = \frac{(60{,}000 + 40{,}000) - .25\,(150{,}000 + 60{,}000 + 40{,}000)}{100{,}000} \times (100{,}000 - 5{,}000)$$

$$= \frac{37{,}500}{100{,}000} \times 95{,}000 = \$35{,}625$$

The tax would be $\$35{,}625 \times .35 = \$12{,}469$.

.06 Interaction of the BIG Tax and Passive Income Tax

If an S corporation which had converted from C status after 1986 were to sell stocks or securities which had built-in gains, it could be subject to both the BIG tax and the passive income tax. To alleviate this potential double taxation, Congress provided that for purposes of the BIG tax, if the passive income tax is imposed, that each item of passive investment income is reduced by an amount which bears the same ratio to the amount of the passive income tax as the amount that such item bears to the total passive income for the taxable year.[148]

Tax Tips and Pitfalls

As is true of the tax on built-in gains, the excess passive income tax is at punitive rates. Some possible strategies to avoid its implementation are:

- Securities that have built-in losses could be sold and the proceeds distributed to the shareholders.

- Savings accounts could be used to purchase municipal bonds or low-yielding common stocks.

- If an S election is contemplated, excessive passive income is anticipated, and accumulated earnings and profits are not too large, one should consider distributing the E&P *before* the election.

- If a new corporation is being formed and excessive passive income is likely, an S election could be made immediately.

- Since the amount taxed is limited to the taxable income, realizing Code Sec. 1231 losses may be appropriate if there will be excessive passive income.

.07 General Business Credit Recapture

To the extent that an S corporation took general business credits against its tax in years in which it is a C corporation, it is subject to the various recapture rules. Therefore, for example, the low income housing credit and the investment tax credit are subject to recapture if the S corporation fails to meet the various requirements.

---

[148] Code Sec. 1366(f)(3).

¶ 431   Fringe Benefits to Shareholders

Generally, owners of S corporations who work for the corporation are treated as employees, e.g., wages are subject to withholding. This is contrasted with partnerships where partners are not treated as employees. However, exceptions exist for certain fringe benefits paid to "two percent shareholders."[149] "Two percent shareholders" are persons who own directly or indirectly (using Code Sec. 318 attribution rules) on any day of the S corporation year more than two percent of the outstanding stock or more than two percent of the voting power of the stock.[150]

Fringe benefits thereby not available to stockholders/employees include: group-term life insurance, health and accident plans, and meals and lodging. The Ninth Circuit has ruled that distributable income from an S corporation does not entitle a shareholder to establish a Keogh plan. The court stated that the Code contains no language indicating that S corporation pass-through income also constitutes net earnings from self-employment.[151]

There has been much confusion about whether an S corporation can deduct the cost of fringe benefits to two percent shareholders. The IRS has ruled that these fringes are in the nature of guaranteed payments; therefore, the S corporation is entitled to deduct the fringes. The shareholder is required to include the fringes in gross income.[152]

¶ 433   Salaries Versus Distributions to Employee/ Shareholders

Under current law, an S corporation shareholder's share of distributions or undistributed profits is not subject to self-employment tax. On the other hand, wages paid to a shareholder/employee are subject to FICA and FUTA taxes. Therefore, considerable incentive exists for employee/shareholders to take compensation in the form of distributions instead of salaries. To prevent this tax strategy from being effective, the IRS will recategorize distributions as salaries, and will collect back FICA and FUTA taxes, as well as the inevitable penalties and interest.[153] To prevent this outcome, S corporations should pay their employee/shareholders at least a modest salary. The S corporation will be in a much better position arguing that a given salary is adequate, rather than trying to justify why *no* salary was paid to an employee/shareholder.

---

[149] Code Sec. 1372(a).

[150] Code Sec. 1372(b).

[151] *A.R. Durando v. Commr.*, CA-9, 95-2 USTC ¶ 50,615, 70 F3d 548.

[152] Rev. Rul. 91-26, 1991-1 CB 184.

[153] Rev. Rul.74-44, 1974-1 CB 287. The IRS has also been successful in court in this matter. See,

e.g., *J. Radtke v. U.S.*, CA-7, 90-1 USTC ¶ 50,113, 895 F2d 1196; *Spicer Accounting, Inc. v. U.S.*, CA-9, 91-1 USTC ¶ 50,103, 918 F2d 90; *Gale W. Greenlee, Inc. v. U.S.*, DC Colo., 87-1 USTC ¶ 9306, 661 FSupp 642.

¶ 435   Tax Year Ends

Shareholders of S corporations treat their distributive share of income, deductions, and credits as if all the items were distributed as of the last day of the corporation's tax year.[154] For this reason, calendar year shareholders will be able to continually defer income from fiscal year S corporations.

> **Example 4-28.** Scott Fuller is on a calendar year. His 100 percent owned S corporation is on an April 30 fiscal year. Fuller will have a continual eight month deferral of income, e.g., the income for the first eight months of the corporation's fiscal year starting on May 1, 2000, will not be reported until Fuller files his 2001 return.

Congress has placed severe restrictions on the ability of S corporations to select fiscal years. "Permitted" years are:[155]

- Calendar years, or

- Accounting periods for which the corporation can establish a business purpose.

The IRS requires that for a natural business year to exist, more than 25 percent of the gross business receipts must have been earned in the last two months of the fiscal year.[156] This test must have been met for three consecutive years.

The Revenue Act of 1987 (P.L. 100-203) provided an additional option that contains a good news/bad news scenario. The good news is that the S corporation may elect a fiscal year which has a deferral period that is not longer than the shorter of:[157]

- Three months, or

- The deferral period of the tax year being changed.

> **Example 4-29.** An S corporation currently has an April 30 year-end. Its required year is December 31. The deferral period of the tax year being changed is eight months (May–December). Since this is longer than three months, a fiscal year ending September 30, October 31, or November 30 could be elected.

> **Example 4-30.** An S corporation has been using a calendar year, which is also its required year. It desires changing to a fiscal year. However, the deferral period of the tax year being changed is zero, hence, a fiscal year is not allowed.

> **Example 4-31.** A newly formed S corporation began business on May 2, 2001. It desires a fiscal year. It could end its first year on September 30, October 31, or December 31.

---

[154] Code Sec. 1366(a).
[155] Code Sec. 1378(b).

[156] Rev. Proc. 87-32, 1987-2 CB 396.
[157] Temp. Reg. § 1.444-1T(b)(2).

Generally, a Code Sec. 444 election is made by filing Form 8716, "Election to Have a Tax Year Other Than a Required Tax Year," by the earlier of:[158]

- The 15th day of the fifth month after the month including the first day of the new year, or

- The due date (without regard to extensions) of the tax return of the new tax year.

The down side to making a Code Sec. 444 election is that the S corporation must make and maintain a deposit of the amount of income tax that would be deferred by the shareholders of the S corporation.

---

[158] Temp. Reg. § 1.444-3T(b)(1).

Chapter 5

Gross Income—General Concepts

¶ 501   Definition of Income

The concept of "economic income" was developed in the early part of the twentieth century by several economists.[1] "Economic income" is defined as the amount that an individual could have consumed during a given time period and still be as well off at the start of the period as at the end of the period. In effect, income can be measured as the consumption plus the change in net worth from the beginning to the end of the year. Operationalizing the concept is not as easy as it would seem, however. For economists would also include in income the imputed value of possessions, i.e., home, auto, and so on. Also, the value of labor used to grow a garden, build a family room, etc., would be imputed as income. Finally, to determine real income, economists would factor in inflation, a variable that immensely complicates the process.

The accountant's definition of income rests on the revenue principle, also known as the realization concept. For income to be realized, generally there must be an exchange with someone outside the entity. Accountants operationalize the revenue principle by requiring, before income is recognized, that:[2]

1.   An exchange transaction with an outsider has occurred;

2.   Substantially all of the work necessary to complete the earnings process has been completed, i.e.,:

   a. Collection from the purchaser/buyer is reasonably assured; and

   b. The expenses of making the sale can be determined with reasonable reliability; and

3.   The amount of income be capable of being reasonably estimated.

The realization concept is based on the accountant's desire to have an objective basis for measuring income. Therefore, unrealized gains and losses and imputed income are generally rejected as being too subjective to allow recognition.

---

[1] See, for example, Henry C. Simons, Personal Income Taxation, University of Chicago Press (1921).

[2] See Financial Accounting Standards Board, Statement of Financial Accounting Concepts, No. 3, "Elements of Financial Statement of Business En-terprises," (Stamford, Conn., Dec., 1980, para. 64); and "Basic Concepts and Accounting Principles Underlying Financial Statements of Business Enterprises," APB Statement #4, American Institute of Certified Public Accountants, (1970).

¶ 503   Tax Concepts of Income

Income for tax purposes may be defined as all inflows of assets or reductions in liabilities except for a return of capital. Thus, income in the broad sense includes, among other items, gains on sale of property, gross profit on the sale of inventory, gifts, inheritances, and damages.[3] However, for income tax reporting purposes, *gross income* is the more important term.

Gross income is defined broadly in the Code as follows: "Except as otherwise provided in this subtitle, gross income means all income from whatever source derived . . ."[4] This is an all-encompassing definition of gross income. The courts have also interpreted the language of the Code as having a sweeping scope. In *Helvering v. Clifford,* the Supreme Court stated that Congress used this language to exert "the full measure of its taxing power."[5] In *Glenshaw Glass,* the Court stated that "Congress applied no limitations as to the source of taxable receipts, nor restriction labels as to their nature . . ." encompassing "accessions to wealth, clearly realized, and over which the taxpayers have complete dominion."[6]

The regulations add little to the definition except to state that gross income includes income realized in any form, whether in money, properties, or services and, therefore, may be realized in the form of services, meals, accommodations, stock, or other property as well as in cash.[7]

¶ 505   Return of Capital—A Judicial Doctrine

As previously noted, income does not include a return of capital. This is not reflected in the Code, and in fact was a source of some confusion when the Code was first enacted.[8] However, an early Supreme Court case cleared up some of the confusion by stating, "In order to determine whether there has been gain or loss, and the amount of the gain, if any, we must withdraw from the gross proceeds an amount sufficient to restore the capital value that existed at the commencement of the period under consideration."[9]

¶ 507   Accounting Methods

The accounting method used by the taxpayer will obviously have a significant impact on the income subject to tax in a given year. Hence, the IRS is not indifferent to the method used by the taxpayer. In fact, the Code specifies permissible accounting methods.

.01   *Permissible Accounting Methods*

Taxable income must be determined under the accounting method that the taxpayer regularly uses to keep his or her books.[10] However, if the

---

[3] For two landmark cases which shaped the definition of income for taxpayers, see *Eisner v. Macomber,* 1 USTC ¶ 32, 252 US 189, 40 SCt 189; and *Commr. v. Glenshaw Glass Co.,* 55-1 USTC ¶ 9308, 348 US 426, 75 SCt 473.

[4] Code Sec. 61(a).

[5] *Helvering v. Clifford,* 40-1 USTC ¶ 9265, 309 US 331, 60 SCt 554.

[6] *Supra,* n. 3.

[7] Reg. § 1.61-1(a).

[8] 50 Cong. Rec. 513.

[9] *Doyle v. Mitchell Bros. Co.,* 1 USTC ¶ 17, 247 US 179, 38 SCt 467.

[10] Code Sec. 446(a); Reg. § 1.446-1(a)(1).

method used does not clearly reflect net income, the IRS may specify the method.[11] The four methods listed in the Code are: the cash receipts method; the accrual method; any other method permitted by the Code; and any combination of cash and accrual (often called the hybrid method).[12] The courts have given considerable latitude to the IRS in this area; i.e., the IRS has considerable discretion in determining whether a taxpayer's accounting method is proper.[13]

.02 Relationship of Accounting and Generally Accepted Accounting Principles (GAAP) Tax

Tax accounting is based on, and generally follows, GAAP; however, there are numerous exceptions. Practitioners have long been in favor of more conformity between GAAP and tax rules; unfortunately, the thrust in recent years has been away from conformity as Congress, the IRS and the courts have also sought to protect Treasury revenues. A landmark case in which the Court asserted its authority to disregard generally accepted accounting principles was the *Thor Power Tool Co.* case, in which the court stated:[14]

> The primary goal of financial accounting is to provide useful information to management, shareholders, creditors, and others properly interested; the major responsibility of the accountant is to protect these parties from being mislead [sic]. The primary goal of the income tax system, in contrast, is the equitable collection of revenue; the major responsibility of the Internal Revenue Service is to protect the public fisc. Consistent with its goals and responsibilities, financial accounting has as its foundation the principle of conservatism, with its corollary that "possible errors in measurement [should] be in the direction of understatement rather than overstatement of net income and net assets." In view of the Treasury's markedly different goals and responsibilities, understatement of income is not destined to be its guiding light.

.03 Cash Accounting Method—Reporting of Income

Under the cash basis method, income is reported when received, regardless of when earned.[15] Income need not necessarily be received in the form of cash in order to be taxable. If instead of cash the taxpayer receives services or property, the "cash equivalency," i.e., the fair market value, is recognized. Thus, the key is whether the item can be valued in terms of money (have a fair market value).[16] An early court case established that an open *accounts receivable* does not represent property in this context because "it is absurd to speak of a promise to pay a sum in the future as having a 'market value.' "[17] However, *notes receivable*, if unconditioned and negotiable, are regarded as property and are thus included in income at their fair market value when received.[18]

---

[11] Reg. § 1.446-1(b)(1).

[12] Code Sec. 446(c).

[13] See, for example, *Commr. v. J.R. Hansen*, 59-2 USTC ¶ 9533, 360 US 446, 79 SCt 1270; *Commr. v. J. Catto*, 66-1 USTC ¶ 9376, 384 US 102, 86 SCt 1311.

[14] *Thor Power Tool Co. v. Commr.*, 79-1 USTC ¶ 9139, 439 US 522, 99 SCt 773. For more on the *Thor* case, see the section on inventories.
[15] Reg. § 1.446-1(c)(1)(i).
[16] Reg. § 1.446-1(a)(3).
[17] *A.M. Bedell v. Commr.*, CA-2, 1 USTC ¶ 359, 30 F2d 622.
[18] *Appeal of A.W. Wolfson*, 1 BTA 538, Dec. 196.

.04   Accrual Accounting Method

Under the accrual method, income is generally reported when earned, regardless of when collected. In determining when income is earned, two tests must be met:[19]

1. All of the events must have occurred which fix the *right* to receive the income; and

2. The amount thereof must be capable of being determined with reasonable accuracy.

If income is received from the sale of property, generally the all events test is met when title to the property passes to the buyer.[20] In the case of services, the all events test is met when the services have been performed. The accrual method must be used to account for purchases and sales where inventory is a factor, unless the Commissioner authorizes another method.[21] The IRS distinguishes between merchandise inventory and materials and supplies inventory for this purpose. Merchandise is property transferred to a customer (including property physically incorporated in that which is transferred to the customer), whereas materials and supplies are property consumed during the production of property or provision of services.[22]

Exception to Accrual Method for Small Businesses

In an important rule change for small businesses, the IRS allows small businesses (those with annual gross receipts of $1,000,000 or less) to use the cash basis method of accounting even if inventory is a material income-producing factor.[23] Businesses adopting the cash method under the procedure treat inventories as materials and supplies that are not incidental under Reg. § 1.162-3 (i.e., include in expenses only in the amount that are actually consumed and used during the tax year).[24] For purposes of this procedure, inventory is consumed and used in the year in which the taxpayer sells the merchandise. Therefore, the cost of the inventory is deductible in such year, or in a later year if paid in a later year.[25]

Despite the fact that this procedure supposedly allows the cash method, qualifying taxpayers must include in income open accounts receivable due in 120 days or less as accounts are actually or constructively received.[26]

Taxpayers qualify for the cash method if for each prior tax year ending on or after December 17, 1998, its average annual gross receipts for the three-year tax period ending with the applicable tax year does not exceed $1,000,000.[27] For this purpose, gross receipts include net sales, all service income, interest, dividends, and rents, but not sales tax collected for the

---

[19] Reg. § 1.446-1(c)(1)(ii); Reg. § 1.451-1(a).
[20] *Lucas v. North Texas Lumber Co.*, 2 USTC ¶ 484, 281 US 11, 50 SCt 184 (1930).
[21] Reg. § 1.446-1(c)(2).
[22] IRS Letter Ruling 9723006, February 7, 1997.

[23] Rev. Proc. 2001-10, 2001-21 IRB 272.
[24] *Id.*
[25] *Id.*
[26] *Id.*
[27] *Id.*

taxing authority.[28] Controlled groups must aggregate gross receipts in determining eligibility for the cash method.

Taxpayers who have been in existence for less than three years must average gross receipts for the years that they have been in existence. If one of those years is a short tax year, such year must be annualized.[29]

Taxpayers need not conform their book income to taxable income, but are required to maintain adequate books and records, including a reconciliation of book and taxable income.[30]

Taxpayers who adopt the cash method as provided by the procedure are considered to make a change in accounting methods to which Code Secs. 446 and 481 apply. This change is automatic and taxpayers must generally follow the automatic provisions of Rev. Proc. 99-49.[31]

.05 Hybrid Method

A hybrid method may be used if it does not distort net income and is consistently applied.[32] An example of the hybrid method would be using the accrual method for purchases and sales and the cash basis method for all other income and expenses.

If a taxpayer is engaged in more than one business, he or she may use different accounting methods for each business (subject to the requirement that income must be clearly reflected). Also, a taxpayer is not required to use the same method to report his or her nonbusiness income as he or she uses for business income.[33]

> **Example 5-1.** Tom Hawley owns two businesses: a hardware store and an auto repair shop. He uses the accrual method for the hardware store and a hybrid method for the auto repair shop. In addition, he has significant interest and dividend income which he reports on the cash method.

¶ 509 Modifying Doctrines and Other Exceptions

Although the general rules for reporting income under the cash and accrual methods are fairly straightforward, several exceptions exist which are significant. The items covered here are constructive receipt, claim of right doctrine, repayments, discounted government obligations, short-term government obligations, the tax benefit rule, original issue discount, and prepaid income.

.01 Doctrine of Constructive Receipt

Taxpayers who use the cash basis of accounting have many opportunities to shift income into the year that they prefer. A taxpayer may *not*, however, postpone the taxation of income to a future year merely by

---

28 *Id.*
29 *Id.*
30 *Id.*

31 *Id.*
32 Reg. § 1.446-1(c)(1)(iv).
33 Reg. § 1.446-1(d)(1).

refusing to accept the money or to deposit a check. If income is in the taxpayer's control and possession, it is considered to be constructively received by him or her.[34] Thus, if income is credited to the taxpayer's account, set apart for the taxpayer, or otherwise made available to the taxpayer, it is considered constructively received. If the taxpayer's control is subject to substantial limitations or restrictions, there is no constructive receipt.[35] Examples of constructive receipt listed in the regulations are:[36]

- Interest coupons which have matured (taxed in the years matured unless no funds are available to pay); and

- Dividends on corporate stock when made subject to demand of a stockholder (but dividend checks regularly mailed on December 31 but not received until January 1 do not constitute constructive receipt).

However, interest income on savings certificates subject to a lower rate if withdrawn early is not deemed to be constructively received.[37]

If a cash basis taxpayer receives a check on the last day of the year, it is constructively received in that year even if it is not received until after banking hours.[38] Generally, if a check is mailed at the end of one year but is not received until the next year, there is no constructive receipt. Attempts to take undue advantage of this fact will probably fail, however. For example, if a check is available to a taxpayer, but he or she requests that it be mailed (with the objective of delaying receipt), the courts will rule that the income is constructively received.[39]

The mere possession of a check does not always lead to constructive receipt. The check must currently be capable of being converted to cash, i.e., the checkmaker must be solvent and the check must not be postdated.[40] If the maker is short of money and asks the payee to hold the check until after the end of the year, there is no constructive receipt.[41]

.02 Claim of Right Doctrine

The claim of right doctrine stems from a Supreme Court case in the early thirties. The North American Oil Company received in 1917 income from the sale of oil and gas, the title to which was in dispute. The litigation was not settled until 1922 (in favor of the taxpayer). The IRS asserted that the income should be taxed in 1916; the company argued (among other points) that the income was not taxable until 1922, the year that the litigation was settled. The Supreme Court, in ruling for the IRS, said, "If a taxpayer receives earnings under a claim of right and without restriction as to its disposition, he has received income which he is required to return,

---

[34] Reg. § 1.451-2(a).
[35] Id.
[36] Reg. § 1.451-2(b).
[37] Reg. § 1.451-2(a); Rev. Rul. 66-44, 1966-1 CB 94.
[38] C.F. Kahler v. Commr., 18 TC 31, Dec. 18,884.

[39] See, for example, F.W. Kunze v. Commr., CA-2, 53-1 USTC ¶ 9400, 203 F2d 957.
[40] C. Goodman v. Commr., 5 TCM 1126, Dec. 15,549(M).
[41] See, for example, L.M. Fischer v. Commr., 14 TC 792, Dec. 17,636.

even though it may still be claimed that he is not entitled to retain the money, and even though he may still be adjudged liable to restore its equivalent."[42]

Both accrual and cash basis taxpayers are potentially subject to the claim of right doctrine. Note that for an accrual basis taxpayer the all events test may not be met, but the claim of right doctrine overrides the all events test.

The claim of right doctrine applies if the taxpayer's right to the use of the money is unrestricted, whether or not the taxpayer actually uses the money.[43]

Of the many cases litigated, a fair number concern disputes with other parties and condemnation awards. If the retention of the earnings is in dispute, merely segregating the property and holding it in trust will not negate the claim of right doctrine.[44] Income erroneously received because of over-charging is excludable if it is paid back in the same tax year.[45] However, if the mistake is not discovered in the same tax year, the claim of right doctrine *does* apply.[46] Condemnation awards are subject to the claim of right doctrine if the proceeds are available without restrictions, regardless of whether the award is final.[47] On the other hand, if the right to the award is contingent on some future event (e.g., final resolution in court), and because of the contingency the amount is *not* made available to the taxpayer, but is held by some other party (e.g., the court or a governmental body), the claim of right doctrine does *not* apply.

Example 5-2. In May 2001, B&R Lands, Inc., became aware that lease payments received from Far Western Gas Co. for both 2000 and 2001 were excessive. Of the total overpayment of $60,000, $20,000 was overpaid in 2000 and $40,000 in 2001. B&R Lands, Inc. paid back all $60,000 by December 2001. The $20,000 overpayment in 2000 would be taxed in 2000 under the claim of right doctrine. However, the $40,000 overpayment in 2001 is not subject to the claim of right doctrine since it was paid back in the same year.

.03 Repayments

Repayment of income reported under the claim of right doctrine is deductible when paid.[48] However, if the taxpayer is under no legal obligation to pay back the earnings, the repayment may be nondeductible.[49]

---

[42] *North American Oil Consolidated v. Burnet*, 3 USTC ¶ 943, 286 US 417, 53 SCt 613.

[43] *Corliss v. Bowers*, 2 USTC ¶ 525, 281 US 376, 50 SCt 336.

[44] *E.J. Costello v. Commr.*, 50 TCM 1463, TC Memo. 1985-571, Dec. 42,493(M).

[45] *J.W. Gaddy v. Commr.*, 65-1 USTC ¶ 9342, 344 F2d 460 (Acq.).

[46] *E.E. Healy v. Commr.*, 53-1 USTC ¶ 9292, 345 US 278, 73 SCt 671.

[47] *W.Q. Boyce v. Commr.*, 69-1 USTC ¶ 9124, 186 CtCls 420, 405 F2d 526.

[48] See, for example, *E.E. Healy v. Commr.*, 53-1 USTC ¶ 9292, 345 US 278, 73 SCt 671; *A. Teitelbaum v. Commr.*, CA-7, 65-1 USTC ¶ 9440, 346 F2d 266; *S. Lowenstein & Son v. Commr.*, CA-6, 55-1 USTC ¶ 9477, 222 F2d 919.

[49] *E.H. Berger v. Commr.*, 37 TC 1026, Dec. 25,382.

¶ 511   Discounted Governmental Obligations

Discounted governmental obligations having a special tax treatment fall into two types: (1) Series E or EE bonds; and (2) short-term obligations.

.01   Series E or EE Bonds

Series E or EE bonds are issued at a discount. The interest element is the difference between the purchase price and the redemption price. Although the redemption price increases twice a year, cash basis taxpayers are not required to report the interest until the bond matures or is redeemed.[50]

A cash basis taxpayer, however, can *elect* to be taxed on the annual increment in value. Once made, the election applies to all such obligations, and all of the increases in redemption prices for past years must be included in the year the election is made. The election is binding in future years as well. Opting to forego the chosen election would be a change of accounting method, which would require the permission of the IRS.[51] Accrual basis taxpayers do not have an alternative: they *must* report the annual increment in value.

Tax Tips and Pitfalls

Most taxpayers will not profit by making the election to report the annual increment in value. This is true because the additional interest earned resulting from deferring the tax will easily outweigh any increase in tax in one year, although there are exceptions to this general rule. If a taxpayer for several years purchased the maximum amount each year (currently set at $30,000 of face value), and then wished to redeem all of the bonds in *one year,* the bunching of income might be sufficient to push him or her into a much higher tax bracket. In that case, the extra tax paid might more than offset the additional interest earned.

Another instance where it may pay to make the election is where a child (or any individual with no taxable income) is given Series EE bonds. A return should be filed for the first year that there is an increment in value. The return would include the increment as income and contain the election. Thereafter, no return would need to be filed so long as gross income does not meet the filing levels. The bonds can then be redeemed tax free. For additional discussions of the income of children, see Chapter 16.

.02   Short-Term Government Obligations

Noninterest-bearing short-term obligations issued at a discount are subject to special rules. The term "government obligations" here applies to debt issued by the U.S., possessions of the U.S., state or local government, or

---

[50] Code Sec. 454(c).   [51] Code Sec. 454(a).

the District of Columbia.[52] Short-term obligations are those with a fixed maturity date of not more than one year from the date of issue.[53]

Whether the taxpayer utilizes the cash basis or accrual method, the discount element must result in ordinary gain or loss.

However, the *timing* of income recognition will differ. Code Sec. 1281 requires accrual method taxpayers, as well as certain other taxpayers, to amortize the discount on a *pro rata* basis according to the number of days in the discount period.[54] Generally, cash basis taxpayers are allowed to wait until the obligation is sold or redeemed before they need report the discount.

> **Example 5-3.** On October 15, 2000, the L-M partnership, a cash basis partnership, purchased a $10,000, 180-day Treasury Bill at $9,600. The partnership redeemed the bill at the maturity date at par. The entire gain ($400) is ordinary income and is all reported in 2001, the year of sale or redemption.

> **Example 5-4.** Assume the same facts as in Example 5-3, except that the partnership is an accrual method taxpayer. Ordinary income of $171 ($400 × 77/180) would be reported in 2000; the remaining $229 would be reported in 2001.

If the short-term obligation is exempt from tax (e.g., a state or local obligation), the discount element must be separated from any remaining gain or loss because the discount element is excludable while the remaining gain or loss is taxable.

> **Example 5-5.** Assume the same facts as in Example 5-3, except that the obligation was issued by the State of Illinois, and the partnership sold it on January 13, 2001, for $9,890. The discount element up to the date of sale is $200 ($400 × 90/180). This is excludable, but it increases the basis of the obligation to $9,800. Thus, the partnership has ordinary income of $90 ($9,890 − $9,800) from the sale.

¶ 513 Tax Benefit Rule

When amounts deducted in one year are recovered in later years, the recovery is generally taxable, but a portion of the recovery may be excluded from taxation. Amounts recovered after 1983 may be excluded only to the extent that the deduction did not reduce income subject to tax.[55] The theory behind the tax benefit rule is to put taxpayers in roughly the same position as if the refunded deduction had not been claimed on the original return. The tax benefit rule is frequently applicable to state income taxes that were deducted in one year and refunded in a later year.

> **Example 5-6.** A married couple deducted state income taxes of $1,600 in 1996. Their other itemized deductions totaled $5,700. In

---

[52] Code Sec. 454(b).
[53] *Id.*

[54] Code Sec. 1281(a)-(b).
[55] Code Sec. 111.

1997, $750 of the state income tax was refunded. Only $600 of the tax provided a tax deduction (the first $1,000 of the state income tax was needed to get to the standard deduction in 1996 of $6,700). Therefore, $600 of the $750 refund would be taxable, while only $150 would be excludable.

> **Example 5-7.** Assume the same facts as in the previous example, except that their other itemized deductions are $6,200. Since $1,100 of the $1,600 of the state income taxes provided a tax deduction, the entire $750 refund would be taxable.

¶ 515   Original Issue Discount Debt/Imputed Interest

Many business owners have either purchased, issued, or have contemplated purchasing or issuing, original issue discount (OID) securities. Still more businesses will at some time purchase or sell property on installments, and thus be subject to imputed interest rules. Thus, the general rules regarding OID and imputed interest are covered in this section.

The premise behind the OID/imputed interest rules is that the time value of money should be taken into account where certain transactions carry an interest rate different than market rates. OID/imputed interest rules are designed to prevent taxpayers from manipulating the principal-interest balance of transactions so as to: (1) convert one form of income into another form of income; (2) delay recognition of income while accelerating payment of expenses; (3) convert an asset into an expense; (4) convert income into a liability; and (5) present the mismatching of interest income and deductions.[56]

.01   Applicability of OID

OID rules are generally applicable to a transaction if either the stated rate of interest in the debt instrument is lower than the market rate, or the interest is not paid at the same rate as its economic accrual.[57] OID is defined as the excess of the "stated redemption price at maturity" over the "issue price."[58] A *de minimis* rule prevents OID from applying if the OID is less than one-fourth of one percent of the stated redemption price at maturity multiplied by the number of complete years to maturity.[59]

> **Example 5-8.** On October 1, 2001, Jason and Sons, Inc., purchased for $7,000 a newly issued 10-year bond with a face value of $10,000. The *de minimis* amount is $10,000 × .0025 × 10 = $250. Since the discount of $3,000 ($10,000 − $7,000) exceeds the *de minimis* amount of $250, OID rules are applicable.

---

[56] Schuyler M. Moore, "Analyzing the New Proposed Regulations on Imputed Interest and Original Issue Discount," *The Journal of Taxation*, July 1986, p. 14.

[57] James W. Banks and Joseph P. Tyrrell, "Planning Real Estate Transactions Under the OID Rules," *The Practical Accountant*, Vol. 20, No. 3 (1987).

[58] Code Sec. 1273(a)(1).

[59] Code Sec. 1273(a)(3); Reg. § 1.1273-1(d)(2); note that special rules for determining the de minimis amount apply to installment obligations (see Reg. § 1.1273-1(d)(3)).

The "stated redemption price at maturity" is the sum of all payments provided by the debt instrument other than qualified stated interest payments.[60]

Example 5-9. White Brothers, a partnership, borrowed $50,000 from a lender in 2001, issuing a five-year term note. The note provides for annual interest payments of 6 percent in years one through three and 10 percent in years four and five. The interest in years four and five above 6 percent is *not* fixed; hence the stated redemption price at maturity is $50,000 + ($50,000 × [(10% − 6%) × 2]) = $54,000.

Determination of the "issue price" depends upon: (1) whether the loan is a cash loan or a property loan, and (2) whether the debt instrument or the property is publicly offered.[61] In the case of debt issued for money, if it is publicly offered, the issue price of each debt instrument in the issue is the first price at which a substantial amount of the debt instrument is sold for money.[62] If the debt for money is a private placement, the issue price is the price paid by the first buyer (creditor).[63] If the debt is issued for publicly traded property, the issue price is the fair market value of the property.[64] If the debt is publicly traded but the property is not, the issue price is the fair market value of the debt.[65] The last scenario is where both the debt and the property are both nonpublicly traded. Unless Code Sec. 1274 applies, the issue price is equal to the stated redemption price at maturity.[66] If Code Sec. 1274 applies, the issue price is the stated principal amount if there is adequate stated interest and in any other case the imputed interest amount.[67]

Example 5-10. Refer to Example 5-9. The issue price is $50,000 and the stated redemption price was previously determined to be $54,000. Hence, the OID is $4,000.

.02 When Imputation Is Required

Since interest imputation requirements may apply in the absence of OID (and vice-versa), one must distinguish imputation rules between cash loans and seller-financing transactions.

.03 Imputation Required for Cash Loans

The imputation requirements for certain cash loans are covered in Code Sec. 7872, which has the appropriate title of "Treatment of Loans with Below Market Rates."[68]

---

60 Code Sec. 1273(a)(2); Reg. § 1.1273-1(b).

61 Code Sec. 1273(b).

62 Code Sec. 1273(b)(1); Reg. § 1.1273-2(a); note that the term "public" does not include underwriters or wholesalers.

63 Code Sec. 1273(b)(2).

64 Code Sec. 1273(b)(3).

65 Id.; Reg. § 1.1273-2(b)(1).

66 Code Sec. 1273(b).

67 Code Sec. 1274(a); note that special rules exist for points paid from the borrower to the lender, other payments from the buyer to the lender, payments between third-party lenders and sellers, and modifications of debt instruments in connection with assumption of debt (See Reg. § 1.1273-2(g)).

68 Code Sec. 7872 has more general applicability than to the above discussion; it also applies to below-market gift loans (see Chapter 16 for details).

.04 Imputation of Term Loans

Imputation is required in the case of certain term loans (the loan is considered to be a "below market loan") when the amount loaned (amount received by the borrower) exceeds the present value of all payments due under the loan.[69] The present value is determined by discounting, using the "applicable federal rate," as provided in the regulations implementing Code Sec. 1274. These regulations apply the general, well-known principles of present value determination. If the loan carries both periodic interest and a principal payment due only at the end of the loan term, two relatively separate, but uncomplicated, present value calculations are required.

.05 Present Value of Principal Computation

The principal payment present value computation (assuming no "short periods") is determined by the following formula:[70]

$$PV = \frac{\text{Principal amount}}{(1 + i)^n}$$

PV = present value of the payment to be made in the future.

Principal amount = the face value of the note to be paid at the end of period n.

i = interest (the required discount rate, i.e., the APR given the length of the note).

n = the number of periods in the term loan.

.06 Present Value of Interest Payments

The present value computation for interest payments (assuming an equal stream of payments over equal periods) is determined with this formula:[71]

$$PV = PMT \times \frac{1 - \dfrac{1}{(1 + i)^n}}{i}$$

where the other variables are as before, and PMT equals the cash interest payments at *the end of each* period.

Example 5-11. Riggs and Sons sold land on January 2, 1996, receiving a five-year note due on January 2, 2001, in the amount of $5,000,000. The note calls for annual interest payments at 4 percent on each anniversary of the note. Assume an annual discount rate of 6

---

[69] Code Sec. 7872(e)(1)(B).
[70] Adapted from Reg. § 1.1274-2(h), Example 1.

[71] *Id.*

percent. The present value of the $5,000,000 note is the sum of the present values of:

1. The principal payment $PV = \dfrac{\$5,000,000}{(1 + .06)^5} = \$3,736,291$

2. The interest payments $PV = \$200,000 \times$

$$\dfrac{1 - \dfrac{1}{(1 + .06)^5}}{.06} = \$842,473$$

$$\text{Total} = \underline{\$4,578,764}$$

Once it is determined that the present value is less than the face value of the debt, the OID can be computed. In computing the OID, the issue price is generally considered to be the discounted present value of the debt instrument as computed to determine if the loan is below market, using 100 percent of the APR rate for sales or exchanges occurring after June 30, 1985.[72]

Example 5-12. Assume the same facts as in the example above. The OID is $5,000,000 − 4,578,764 = $421,236.

.07 Required Discount Rates ("Applicable Federal Rates")

Generally, the applicable federal rate depends only on whether the debt instrument qualifies for the federal short-term rate, the intermediate rate, or the long-term rate. This in turn depends on whether the term is no more than three years; more than three years, but no more than nine years; or more than nine years.[73]

The federal rates are published monthly in the *Internal Revenue Bulletin* in the form of revenue rulings.

.08 Amortizing Discount—The Lender

Generally, the lender is required to amortize the discount (i.e., take into income) by using the effective interest rate method of amortization. Under the effective interest rate method, the unpaid balance of the loan at the start of each period is multiplied by the effective interest rate (the yield to maturity).[74] Any difference between the effective interest and the interest called for in the contract is added to the unpaid balance.

Example 5-13. Refer to the previous example. Computation of the amortized discount would be as follows:

---

[72] Code Sec. 1274(b); for exceptions to this, see ¶ 515.13.

[73] Code Sec. 1274(d)(1); Reg. § 1.1274-4(b).
[74] Reg. § 1.1272-1(b).

Beginning of Year	Unpaid Balance of Loan	Discount Rate	Total Interest	Contract Interest	Difference (+ to L.B.)
1	$4,578,764	6%	$274,726	$200,000	$74,726
2	4,653,490	6%	279,209	200,000	79,209
3	4,732,699	6%	283,962	200,000	83,962
4	4,816,661	6%	289,000	200,000	89,000
5	4,905,661	6%	294,340	200,000	94,340
6	5,000,001				

Thus, the first year, $274,726 of interest income would be reported.

.09 Exceptions to the Mandatory Accrual Rates—The Lender

Note that in the previous example, the taxpayer is reporting interest income that has not yet been received. A cash basis taxpayer who is also a nondealer may elect to defer reporting the interest income until such is received in cash, provided that the stated principal amount does not exceed $2,918,500 (for 2001).[75]

Also, seller-financed transactions coming under Code Sec. 483(e) are not required to use the accrual method to report the discounts.[76]

.10 Amortizing Discount—The Borrower

Generally, the borrower must also amortize the OID using the effective interest rate method.

> **Example 5-14.** Refer to the previous example. The borrower would deduct as an expense $274,726 the first year and so on. Generally, this expense deduction is taken without regard to whether the taxpayer is on the cash or the accrual method.

.11 Exceptions to the Accrual Rules—The Borrower

There are a number of instances in which the borrower is not required to use the accrual rules to report the amortized OID. They include:

- Borrowers in transactions where the non-dealer-seller-financier has elected to defer the interest income until received in cash;[77]

- Seller financing transactions coming under Code Sec. 483(e);[78] and

- Loans for the sale of personal-use property.[79]

.12 Other Ramifications of OID

The preceding discussion has covered the most common application of OID rules. Special applications or problems include:

- Uneven interest payments;

---

[75] Code Sec. 1274A(c); Rev. Rul. 2000-55, 2000-52 IRB 595.
[76] Code Sec. 1274(c)(3)(F).

[77] Code Sec. 1274A(c).
[78] Code Sec. 1274(c)(3)(F).
[79] Code Sec. 1275(b).

- Aggregation rules;

- Modification of debt instruments;

- Variable interest;

- Contingent interest;

- Acquisition premiums;

- OID debt exchanged in corporate reorganization;

- Retirement of debts;

- Related parties' sales; and

- Options.

Discussion of these items is outside the scope of this book. Interested readers are referred to Code Secs. 1272–1275, and the regulations thereunder, for details of the above matters.

.13 Transactions Not Covered by OID Rules

Certain transactions not subject to the OID rules may nevertheless have unstated interest and require imputation of interest. These transactions are exempted from Code Sec. 1274 but are potentially covered under Code Sec. 483.

Exempted are sales of farmland, if the sales price is not in excess of $1 million; personal residences; and other assets to the extent that the sum of the sales price plus stated interest does not exceed $250,000.[80] Also exempted are exchanges of debt instruments by an individual; testamentary trust; estate; small business corporation (Code Sec. 1244(c)); or a partnership with capital not in excess of that allowed small business corporations for farmland.[81]

Code Sec. 483 rules provide for the same imputation requirements as does Code Sec. 1274. However, if unstated interest is present, the amortization rules are much different.

.14 Code Sec. 483 Amortization Rules for the Seller

Recall that the mandatory accrual rules usually apply to creditors if the debt is subject to Code Sec. 1272. However, these rules do not apply to Code Sec. 483 transactions. Therefore, general tax accounting rules are applied to report the interest income. Specifically, the interest is divided into the stated and the unstated portions. The *stated* interest is reported using the relevant accounting method of the seller (i.e., cash or accrual), while the *unstated* interest is reported when the payment is either due (accrual basis taxpayer) or paid (cash basis taxpayer).

---

[80] Code Sec. 1274(c)(3).   [81] *Id.*

Example 5-15. Assume the same facts as in Example 5-11, except that the loan is subject to Code Sec. 483 instead of Code Sec. 1272, and that the seller is an accrual basis taxpayer. The stated interest of 4 percent would be accrued each year; however, the unstated interest (totaling $421,236) would not be reported until the note is due.

.15 Code Sec. 483 Amortization Rules for the Buyer

The rules for the buyer and seller are not necessarily symmetrical in this case. The buyer's interest expense is limited to the stated rate of interest.[82] This is true even for nonpersonal use property in the case of Code Sec. 483 transactions.

.16 Deferral Rental Agreements

Certain deferred rental agreements for the use of tangible property or for services are also subject to OID. Prior to the Tax Reform Act of 1984, it was possible for rental agreements to provide for increasing rent payments over the life of the lease. This was a benefit if the payor was an accrual basis taxpayer and the receiver of the rent was a cash basis taxpayer, since the accrual basis taxpayer could deduct amounts in excess of what was paid. Both the receiver (even if on the cash basis) and the payor are required to report the income and the deductions on the accrual basis.[83] However, this requirement *only applies to rental agreements with payments in excess* of $250,000.[84] If the payments exceed $250,000, one of the following conditions must be present for the accrual method to be required:

- There is at least one amount allocable to the use of property during a calendar year which is to be paid after the close of the calendar year following the calendar year in which such use occurs;[85] or

- There are increases in the amount to be paid as rent under the agreement.[86]

If the rental agreement does not allocate rents to a given accounting period, what is termed a "constant rental amount" accrues.[87] In computing the "constant rental amount," the rate used is 110 percent of the APR, compounded semi-annually.[88]

Example 5-16. Brady Co. leases plant machinery for a two-year period, beginning on January 1, 2001. The lease calls for a $400,000 payment on December 31, 2001. Assume the relevant federal rate is 5.91 percent. The 110 percent of APR is 6.50 percent. The amount of an ordinary annuity of one dollar for two years at 6.50 percent is

---

[82] Code Sec. 483(d)(3).
[83] Code Sec. 467, effective generally for agreements entered into after June 8, 1984.
[84] Code Sec. 467(d).

[85] Code Sec. 467(d)(1).
[86] *Id.*
[87] Code Sec. 467(b).
[88] Code Sec. 467(e)(4).

2.065. Thus two equal rent payments of $193,705 would be deducted each year, and interest expense of $12,590 would be deducted in 2002.

¶ 517   Prepaid Income

A *cash* basis taxpayer must report prepaid income (i.e., payments received before the income is earned by the recipient) during the year received. This reporting rule is consistent with the conceptual underpinnings of the cash basis method. However, *accrual* basis taxpayers must also generally recognize prepaid income in the year of receipt, even though, for book purposes, the income is properly deferred.[89]

> **Example 5-17.** LaWare, Inc., a calendar year corporation and accrual basis taxpayer, leased a building to tenants March 31, 2001, for a two-year period for $80,000. For book purposes only, $30,000 of revenue would be recognized. The remaining $50,000 would be reflected in a liability account, Deferred Rent Income, and would be recognized as income over the remaining life of the lease. However, for *federal income tax purposes,* the entire $80,000 must be taken in 2001, the year received.

.01   Certain Advance Payments

There is an exception for certain "advance payments." Advance payments for this purpose are defined as any amount which is received in a tax year by an accrual basis or hybrid basis taxpayer and which are to be applied against the sales price in a future taxable year of inventory held primarily for sale to customers in the ordinary course of a trade or business or the sales price of items being built, installed, constructed, or manufactured by the taxpayer but not completed and delivered during the year. The advance payments may be either included in income in the year of receipt, or in the year in which the income would be recognized as being earned for financial reporting purposes.[90]

> **Example 5-18.** D&D Mfg. Co., an accrual basis partnership, entered into a $90,000 contract in December 2000 to deliver custom machinery to a customer in September 2001. The partnership received an advance payment of $15,000, the other $75,000 being due when it delivered the machinery. The entire $90,000 is taxed in 2001.

In certain instances, the deferral cannot extend past the second tax year following the year in which the advance is received. This restriction applies if the taxpayer received "substantial advance payments" and has on hand or could obtain, through his or her normal supply source, a sufficient quantity to satisfy the agreement.[91] Substantial advance payments are received when the advances exceed the taxpayer's cost. Once substantial advance payments are received, then *all* advanced payments

---

[89] Reg. § 1.451-5(b); *M.E. Schulde v. Commr.*, 63-1 USTC ¶ 9284, 372 US 128, 83 SCt 601.

[90] Reg. § 1.451-5(b).
[91] Reg. § 1.451-5(c).

received by the end of the second tax year following the year in which the test is first met must be reported as income. Also, the cost (estimated if necessary) must be included in the cost of goods sold.[92]

> **Example 5-19.** Assume the same facts as in Example 5-18, except that the estimated costs of production are $54,000. The partnership collected advance payments of $30,000 in 2000, $30,000 in 2001, $10,000 per year in each of 2002, 2003, and 2004, the year that the machinery was completed and delivered. By the end of 2001, "substantial payments" have been received. Therefore, in the year 2003, $80,000 of income is reported, and the estimated costs of production of $54,000 are deducted.

.02 Prepaid Income—Services

Generally, prepaid income for services to be performed is taxed during the year received. However, an accrual basis taxpayer may defer reporting the income until the services are performed *if* the services are performed by the end of the year following the year of receipt.[93] If for any reason a portion of the services is not performed by the end of the next succeeding year, the amount allocable to the services not performed must be included in income in such succeeding year.[94]

> **Example 5-20.** The Ty-de Co., an accrual basis corporation, entered into a contract on November 15, 2000, to furnish janitorial services to Crump Towers for 12 months. The services are to begin on December 1, 2000, and run through November 30, 2001. The company received an advance payment of $24,000 on December 1, 2000. The amount to be included in income in 2000 is $2,000 (the amount earned). The remaining amount is reported in 2001. If Ty-de Co. had been a cash basis corporation, all $24,000 would be reported in 2001.

> **Example 5-21.** Assume the same facts as in Example 5-20, except that the $24,000 received is for an 18-month contract beginning on December 1, 2000, and running through May 31, 2002. Even though Ty-de Co. is an accrual basis entity, the entire $24,000 must be reported as income in 2001.

¶519   Gross Income—Exclusions

The U.S. government has a number of reasons to exclude items from gross income. Some items are excluded because they do not or should not fit the definition of income. Other items are excluded by the federal government to accomplish various economic or social objectives. Still other exclusions are enacted into law in order to clear up confusion regarding the tax status of an item.

---

[92] Reg. § 1.451-5(c)(1).
[93] Rev. Proc. 71-21, 1971-2 CB 549.

[94] *Id.*

The statutory exclusions are, for the most part, contained in Code Secs. 101 through 138. The presumption is that an item of income is includible in gross income unless:

- It does not fit the definition of income (e.g., is a return of capital);

- To tax it would be unconstitutional; or

- It is *specifically* excluded by one of the Code sections.

Thus, to infer, either by the application of accounting principles, or through logic, that a given item is excludable from income is very imprudent. Decisions to exclude items from gross income should be based on specific references to the Code and regulations or other administrative authority, or (and one must be even more careful in this respect) on a reading and examination and evaluation of judicial authority.

Many of the statutory exclusions are related solely to individuals. In this book, only those individual exclusions directly related to employment are covered. Those exclusions which apply to partnerships and corporate entities are covered in the most depth.

.01 Employee Wage and Salary Benefits

There are a considerable number of employee benefits that are excludable from the gross income of the employee, though recent tax acts have reduced employee fringes. The essential trade-off between cash salary payments and fringes, from the perspective of the employee, is the reduced freedom of utility versus the reduced income tax burden. To some extent, this trade-off can be minimized through the use of cafeteria plans.

.02 Meals and Lodging

The value of meals and lodging furnished to an employee is excludable from gross income if furnished for the convenience of the employer.[95] However, an additional requirement must be met. In the case of meals, the additional requirement is that the meals be furnished on the business premises.[96] There is a stricter requirement for lodging. The employee must be required to live on the premises as a condition of his or her employment.[97]

The number of meals excludable during the week depends on whether the employee is required to live on the premises. If the employee is required to live on the premises, *all* meals are excludable.[98] Otherwise, meals furnished on nonworking days do not qualify for the exclusion.[99]

Meals furnished by the employer are regarded as furnished for the convenience of the employer if the meals are provided for a "substantial

---

[95] Code Sec. 119(a).
[96] *Id.*
[97] *Id.*

[98] Reg. § 1.119-1(a)(2).

[99] *Id.*

noncompensatory business reason."[100] Examples of noncompensatory business reasons include:

- When the employee must be available during the meal period for emergencies;

- When the business requires such a short meal period that the employee could not be expected to eat elsewhere;

- When there are insufficient eating facilities in the vicinity of the employer's premises; and

- When the meal is furnished immediately after the working hours, and the employee's duties prevent him or her from eating during the duty hours.[101]

The exclusion is available only for employees, not for partners or sole proprietors.

Where the employer did not demonstrate that business necessity restricted its employees to short meal periods or that the employee could not have obtained meals within a reasonable meal period, the IRS ruled that the meals were not furnished for a substantial noncompensatory business reason.[102]

Meals may also be excludable under Code Sec. 132 as a *de minimis* fringe benefit (see the discussion of Code Sec. 132 later in this chapter). The value of a meal provided to an employee is excludable from wages for FICA tax and income tax withholding purposes if the meal is excludable from the employee's income under Code Sec. 119 or 132. If the meal did not meet the requirements of Code Sec. 119 or 132, but it was reasonable to believe at the time the meal was provided that it was excludable under Code Sec. 119, the meal is still excludable from wages for FICA tax purposes; if it was reasonable to believe that the meal was excludable under Code Sec. 132, the meal is still excludable from wages for both FICA tax and income tax withholding purposes.[103]

.03 Health and Accident Benefits and Premiums

Health and accident benefits paid for injury or illness fall into four categories:

1. Compensation for personal injury or illness;

2. Reimbursement for medical expenses;

3. Payment for the loss of a member or function of the body; and

4. Income reimbursement plans.

---

[100] *Id.*
[101] *Id.*
[102] IRS Letter Ruling 9602001, September 15, 1995.

[103] Code Sec. 3121(a)(19) and (20); Code Sec. 3401(a)(19); IRS Letter Ruling 9829001, March 10, 1998.

Compensation for personal injuries or illness, whether received under workmen's compensation laws, as damages, or as payment through health and accident plans purchased by the taxpayer, are excludable from income.[104] Reimbursement for medical expenses under health and accident plans is excludable from income, whether the policy premiums are paid by the employer (if the plan is qualified), the employee, or both.[105] The same is true for payments which reimburse for the loss of a member (e.g., an arm), or function of the body.[106] With respect to income reimbursement plans, however, it is important to know who paid the premiums. If the employee pays the premiums on an income reimbursement plan, the payments are excludable from income; if the employer pays the premiums, the payments are taxable.[107]

.04 Premiums Paid by Employer

A second issue is the tax status of premium payments made by employers on behalf of employees to health and accident plans. Premium payments made by the employer do not constitute taxable income to the employee.[108] Coverage need not be through an insurance company, but can be a self-insured plan, i.e., established through contributions to a fund or trust.[109] Even though disability *benefits* are taxable when received by employees, the premium payment made by employers on their behalf is *not* taxable.[110]

.05 Workers' Compensation

All states have some form of workers' compensation laws. These laws were one of the first forms of "no-fault" insurance, i.e., for work-related injuries, the employee is paid from the workers' compensation funds without regard to fault. These payments are fixed by state law and, though partly to compensate for injuries, have the primary purpose of making up income benefits. Though disability payments are generally taxable, workers' compensation is totally excludable.[111]

.06 Group-Term Life Insurance

Normally, if an employer pays premiums on life insurance policies on which the employee is the beneficiary, the premiums constitute income to the employee. However, there is an exception for group-term life insurance policies purchased for employees (partners and sole-proprietors are not considered employees for this purpose). The premiums on the first $50,000 of coverage are excludable from income.[112] If the policy coverage exceeds $50,000, the taxpayer determines income in the following manner:[113]

1.   Determine the coverage over $50,000;

---

[104] Code Sec. 104(a).
[105] Code Sec. 105(b).
[106] Code Sec. 105(c).
[107] Code Sec. 105(a).
[108] Reg. § 1.106-1.

[109] *Id.* Also see Code Sec. 105 and the regulations.
[110] *Id.*
[111] Code Sec. 104(a)(1).
[112] Code Sec. 79(a).
[113] Reg. § 1.79-3.

2.   Look up in the regulations the uniform cost per month per $1,000 of coverage (the cost is differentiated into 5-year age brackets);

3.   Determine the yearly cost of such coverage; and

4.   Subtract any portion of the premiums paid by the employee.

Example 5-22. Elizabeth Stone's employer purchased $90,000 of group-term life insurance for her. She paid $20 per year of the premium; her employer paid the balance. On December 31, she was 32 years old. The cost per month per $1,000 for age 30 to 34 is $.08. Therefore, the amount of income taxed to her is ($90,000 − $50,000) × .08 × 12/$1,000 = $38.40 − $20 = $18.40.

Various nondiscrimination requirements must be met before the premiums are excludable from income.[114]

Tax Tips and Pitfalls

Providing that the plan does qualify, group-term life insurance is an excellent fringe for employees for three reasons:

1.   Proceeds paid out are exempt from income;

2.   The premiums on the first $50,000 of coverage are excludable; and

3.   Even for coverage above $50,000, the amount includible in income is considerably less than the cost of coverage of individual policies.

A pitfall does exist with respect to a plan that discriminates in favor of key employees. In such an instance, the key employee must include in income the greater of the amount from Table 2001 or the actual premiums paid by the employer. However, the nonkey employees may still exclude the first $50,000 of coverage. Another important consideration is that the coverage can be proportional to salaries and yet be considered to not discriminate in favor of key employees.

Example 5-23. Winkle, Inc., has four full-time employees: the president/sole shareholder paid $60,000 per year; and nonowner employees, each earning $20,000. The group insurance plan provides coverage of $120,000 for the president and $40,000 for each employee. This plan is not discriminatory. However, the president must report income on the premium cost above $50,000.

.07   Child or Dependent Care Assistance Programs

An employee may exclude from gross income amounts paid by an employer for dependent care assistance which, if incurred by the employee,

---

[114] Code Sec. 79(d).

would be considered employment-related expenses under Code Sec. 21(b)(2).[115] The exclusion is limited to $5,000 provided per tax year of the employee ($2,500 for those married filing separately).[116] Any excess over $5,000, must be included in gross income during the year that the services are *provided,* not necessarily in the year paid.[117] There must be a written, nondiscriminatory plan.[118] To be excludable, the payments must not be made to dependents of the employee or the employee's spouse or children under 19 of the employee.[119] The exclusion cannot exceed the earned income of the employee. If the employee is married, the exclusion cannot exceed the earned income of the spouse who earns least.[120]

The term "employee" also refers to self-employed individuals and partners. Hence, if both spouses work in the business (or one spouse is employed elsewhere), a tax advantage may be gained by providing care or paying for care of dependents of the spouses.

Tax Tips and Pitfalls

This is an underused fringe by small businesses. The perceived and actual value of child care assistance looms large in the minds of working couples and single parents. Workers who are not worried about the welfare of their children are more productive workers.

.08 *Employee Achievement Awards*

Employees may exclude from income at least a portion of the value of "employee achievement awards." A full exclusion is allowed if the cost to the employer of the award does not exceed the maximum deduction allowed the employer.[121] The maximum deduction, in turn, depends on whether the plan award is qualified or nonqualified. A nonqualified plan award deduction of up to $400 per tax year for all nonqualified awards combined is allowed. The ceiling for qualified awards is $1,600 per tax year, including all other awards given (both qualified and nonqualified).[122]

"Employee achievement awards" are defined as items of tangible personal property which are:[123]

- Transferred by an employer to an employee for length of service achievement or safety achievement;

- Awarded as part of a meaningful presentation; and

- Awarded under conditions and circumstances that do not create a significant likelihood of the payment as disguised compensation.

---

[115] Code Sec. 129(a)(1).
[116] Code Sec. 129(a)(2)(A).
[117] Code Sec. 129(a)(2)(B).
[118] Code Sec. 129(d).
[119] Code Sec. 129(c).

[120] Code Sec. 129(b).
[121] Code Sec. 74(c).
[122] Code Sec. 274(j)(2).
[123] Code Sec. 274(j)(3).

For a plan award to be qualified, it must be part of a written nondiscriminatory plan or program, and the average yearly cost of all employee achievement awards must not exceed $400 per year.[124] Special criteria exist providing limitations on length of service and safety achievement awards.[125]

.09 Cafeteria Plans

A cafeteria plan is a written plan that offers employees the opportunity to pick among cash and qualified fringe benefits.[126] A qualified benefit is any benefit excludable from an employee's gross income by reason of an express provision of the Code (other than Code Sec. 106(b), 117, 127, or 132). Group term life insurance includible in gross income only because it exceeds the $50,000 limitation of Code Sec. 79 also is a qualified benefit.[127] For example, employees might have the choice of being covered by a health insurance policy or taking the equivalent amount in cash. If employees take the cash, they will be taxed; if they take the medical coverage, they will not be taxed. The advantage of cafeteria plans is that employees have more flexibility—they may select the benefits that best suit their needs.

A plan will not qualify if it discriminates in favor of highly paid employees, either with respect to their eligibility to participate or with respect to contributions and benefits.[128]

.10 Other Fringe Benefits

Generally, for a fringe benefit to be excludable, it must either be excluded specifically under some provision of the Code (e.g., group-term life insurance), or the item must belong to one of the following seven categories:[129]

1. No-additional-cost service;

2. Qualified employee discount;

3. Working condition fringe;

4. *De minimis* fringe;

5. Qualified transportation fringe;

6. Qualified moving expense reimbursement; or

7. Qualified retirement planning services.

A "no-additional-cost service" is defined as any service provided to an employee if the service is offered for sale to customers and the employer incurs no substantial additional cost in providing the service to the employee.[130] The service must be in the line of business in which the employee works.[131] An example would be a free ticket to an airline employee.

---

[124] Code Sec. 274(j)(3)(B).
[125] Code Sec. 274(j)(4)(B) and (C).
[126] Code Sec. 125(d).
[127] Code Sec. 125(f).

[128] Code Sec. 125(b).
[129] Code Sec. 132(a).
[130] Code Sec. 132(b).
[131] *Id.*

A "qualified employee discount" is any discount which does not exceed:[132]

- For property, the gross profit percentage of the price at which the services are being offered to customers; or

- For services, 20 percent of the price at which the services are being offered by the employer to customers.

A "working condition fringe" is any property or service provided to an employee to the extent that if the *employee* paid for the item, it would be deductible as either a business expense (under Code Sec. 162) or as depreciation (under Code Sec. 167).[133] Examples would include the value of use by an employee of a company car for business purposes or the provision of a bodyguard for the employee.[134]

"*De minimis* fringes" refer to property or services which are so small in value as to make accounting for them either unreasonable or administratively impractical.[135] Included are such items as: typing personal letters by a secretary, company picnics, occasional supper money, holiday gifts of property with a low value, and occasional sporting event tickets.[136] Subsidized meals generally are excludable under this provision, provided that the revenue from the eating facility covers the direct costs of operating the facility.[137]

The provision of on-premises athletic facilities such as pools, gyms, tennis courts, and training courses also qualifies for exclusion from income.[138]

A "qualified transportation fringe" is defined as any of the following benefits provided by an employer to an employee:[139]

- Transportation in a commuter highway vehicle provided that the transportation is in connection with travel between the employee's residence and place of employment;

- Any transit pass; and

- Qualified parking.

For tax years beginning after December 31, 2001, the amount excludable from gross income of the employee of the value of transportation in the employer's vehicle and transit passes together cannot exceed $100 per month. The exclusion for qualified parking cannot exceed $175 per month.[140]

---

[132] Code Sec. 132(c).
[133] Code Sec. 132(d).
[134] Committee on Ways and Means Report No. 98-432.
[135] Code Sec. 132(e).
[136] Committee on Ways and Means Report No. 98-432.

[137] Code Sec. 132(e).
[138] Code Sec. 132(j)(4).
[139] Code Sec. 132(f).
[140] Code Sec. 132(f)(2).

Qualified transportation fringes include cash reimbursements by employers to employees. However, cash reimbursements for transit passes qualify only if vouchers or a similar item which may be exchanged only for a transit pass are not readily available for a direct distribution by the employer to the employee.[141]

The ability of an employee to choose between qualified transportation fringes and taxable compensation does not create constructive receipt of income.[142]

A "transit pass" is defined as any pass, token, farecard, voucher or similar item that enables a person to travel on mass transit facilities (whether or not public owned) or is provided by any person in the business of transporting persons if the vehicle used is a "commuter highway vehicle."[143] A "commuter highway vehicle" is any highway vehicle that has a seating capacity of at least six adults in addition to the driver. Also, at least 80 percent of the mileage use must be reasonably expected to be for purposes of transporting employees from their residence to work, and on trips during which the number of such employees is at least one-half of the seating capacity of the vehicle (not including the driver).[144]

"Qualified parking" is defined as parking provided to an employee on or near the employer's business premises or on or near a location from which the employee commutes. However, to qualify the commute must be in a commuter highway vehicle or by carpool. In addition, the parking cannot be on or near property used by the employee for residential purposes.[145]

"Qualified moving expense reimbursements" are amounts received (directly or indirectly) as either payment for or reimbursement of expenses, which if incurred by the employer, would be deductible as moving expenses under Code Sec. 217. However, the term does not include payments or reimbursements of expenses deducted by the employee in a prior taxable year.[146]

Effective for tax years beginning after December 31, 2001, and before January 1, 2011, "qualified retirement planning services" provided by the employer to an employee and his or her spouse are excludable from income of the employee.[147] "Qualified retirement planing services" are defined as any retirement planning advice or information provided to the employee and spouse by an employer maintaining a qualified employer plan.[148] Highly paid employees are eligible for the exclusion only if the services are available on substantially the same terms to all employees of the group who normally receive information and education about the plan.[149]

---

[141] Code Sec. 132(f)(3).
[142] Code Sec. 132(f)(4).
[143] Code Sec. 132(f)(5)(A).
[144] Code Sec. 132(f)(5)(B).
[145] Code Sec. 132(f)(5)(C).
[146] Code Sec. 132(g).
[147] Economic Growth and Tax Relief Reconciliation Act of 2001, Act Sec. 665, adding Code Sec. 132(a)(7).

[148] Economic Growth and Tax Relief Reconciliation Act of 2001, Act Sec. 665, adding Code Sec. 132(m)(1).
[149] Economic Growth and Tax Relief Reconciliation Act of 2001, Act Sec. 665, adding Code Sec. 132(m)(2).

¶ 521   Principal Exclusions from Gross Income— Typically Found at Business Levels

Five exclusionary items are discussed here: life insurance proceeds, state and local bond interest, income from debt discharge, recovery of previous deductions, and leasehold improvements.

.01   Life Insurance Proceeds

Life insurance proceeds paid by reason of death generally are excludable from income.[150] An exception to this rule exists where there has been a transfer of ownership of the policy for valuable consideration.[151] However, the exception does not apply, i.e., the proceeds are excludable from income, if the policy transfer is either:[152]

- To the insured;

- To partner of the insured;

- To a partnership in which the insured is a partner;

- To a corporation in which the insured is a shareholder or officer; or

- One where the recipient of the policy has a tax basis in the policy that is in whole or in part a "substituted basis," i.e., the basis carries over from the transferor.

Example 5-24. Richard Senter died in 2001 and the proceeds of his life insurance policy were paid to his children. The proceeds are excludable from income.

Example 5-25. Senter transferred ownership of his life insurance policy to his sister in 1986. His sister paid him $6,000 for the policy and paid $2,000 in net premiums beginning in 1986. Upon his death in 2001, she collected $20,000, the face amount of the policy. She has gross income equal to $20,000 − ($6,000 + $2,000), or $12,000.

Example 5-26. In 1993, when Senter formed a partnership with his son, he transferred ownership of a life insurance policy with a $10,000 face value to the partnership. Upon his death in 2001, the partnership collected $10,000, none of which is taxable.

If the insured sells or surrenders a policy before death, taxable income results to the extent that the amount received exceeds the net premiums paid.[153] Losses are not deductible.

---

[150] Code Sec. 101(a)(1).
[151] Code Sec. 101(a)(2).

[152] *Id.*
[153] Code Sec. 72(e).

There are two other frequently encountered situations with respect to life insurance. Often the proceeds payable at death are taken in installments rather than in a lump sum.[154]

Example 5-27. Senter's wife was the beneficiary of a $20,000 policy on his life. She elected to take the proceeds in 10 equal installments of $3,200 each. Of the $3,200 yearly installments, $2,000 is excludable as a return of cost ($20,000/10); the remaining $1,200 is income.

Sometimes life insurance proceeds are paid in the form of alimony as part of a divorce or legal separation decree. These proceeds are taxed as alimony rather than as life insurance proceeds and are taxable to the extent that they constitute alimony payments.[155]

The proceeds of an insurance policy received in a property settlement are excluded from taxation.[156]

.02 State and Local Bond Interest

Generally, interest is excludable on so called "state or local" bonds, i.e., the obligations of a state, territory, or a possession of the United States, or any political subdivision of any of the foregoing, or of the District of Columbia, the proceeds of which are used to provide government services such as building roads, providing education, police and fire protection, and so on.[157] Recent tax acts (Deficit Reduction Act of 1984 and Tax Reform Act of 1986 especially) have, however, created several rules for "private activity bonds," which provide exceptions to the excludability rule. Private activity bonds are now generally *taxable*.[158] Private activity bonds are defined as issues which meet two tests:[159]

1. More than 10 percent of the proceeds are used for private business use; and

2. Either:

    a. It meets a private security or payment test (more than 10 percent of the interest or the principal is secured by, or payment will come from, private business use) (Code Sec. 141(b)); or

    b. It meets a private loan financing test (the amount going to private business exceeds the lesser of 5 percent of the proceeds or $5,000,000) (Code Sec. 141(c)).

Certain private activity bonds remain exempt from the regular income tax because Congress has deemed the activities to be worthy ones (e.g., low-

---

[154] Code Sec. 101(d); Reg. § 1.101-4 (note, however, that portions of this regulation were made obsolete by the Tax Reform Act of 1986, P.L. 99-514).

[155] Code Sec. 71.

[156] Act. Sec. 421, Tax Reform Act of 1984, repealing Code Sec. 101(e).

[157] Code Sec. 103(a).

[158] Code Sec. 103(b).

[159] Code Sec. 141(a).

income housing), but the interest on these bonds are nonetheless subject to the alternate minimum tax (AMT).[160]

"Arbitrage bonds" also do not qualify for interest excludability.[161] Arbitrage bonds are issued where the proceeds are used to invest in taxable securities paying higher interest rates than the state or local bond issued.[162]

Usually the prospectus for the bond issue will contain an opinion of an attorney as to whether or not the bond is subject to federal income tax.

Tax Tips and Pitfalls

C corporations in the 39 percent bubble may find it attractive to invest temporary cash in exempt securities. If the securities are issued in the state where business is conducted, an exclusion from state tax (this varies among the states) may also be available.

.03 Discharge of Indebtedness

Generally, when a debtor has a debt forgiven, income results to the debtor, unless the creditor had a gratuitous intent, in which case the forgiveness constitutes a gift. Debt forgiveness may occur in the context of a bankruptcy, a nonbankruptcy insolvency, or the debtor may be solvent. The income tax results are somewhat different for each case.

Debt forgiveness in bankruptcy does not constitute income to the debtor.[163] However, certain tax benefits (called tax attributes) must be reduced to the extent of the gross income excluded. The attributes are reduced in the following order:[164]

1. Net operating losses and loss carryovers;

2. The general business credit;

3. Minimum tax credit;

4. Capital losses and loss carryovers;

5. Reduction of the basis of assets; and

6. Passive activity losses and credit carryovers;

7. Foreign tax carryovers.

Items (2), (3) and (7) above are reduced by $.333 for every $1.00 of excluded income.[165] The reduction in any passive activity credit carryover is $.333 for each dollar excluded.

Insolvent debtors who have debts discharged outside of bankruptcy have no income unless they are solvent *after* the debt forgiveness. In that

---

[160] Code Sec. 57(a).
[161] Code Sec. 103(b)(2).
[162] Code Sec. 148.

[163] Code Sec. 108(a).
[164] Code Sec. 108(b).
[165] *Id.*

event, they have income to the extent that they are solvent afterwards.[166] The reduction of tax attributes listed above also applies to insolvency.

If the debtor is solvent, gain is generally recognized to the extent of the debt forgiven. In measuring insolvency, contingent liabilities cannot be counted. In *Merkel*, a taxpayer was determined to be solvent at a debt forgiveness date because they could not include in the insolvency calculations guarantees on a note.[167]

In a technical advice memorandum, the IRS ruled that when a bankruptcy court discharges a partner from his share of a partnership recourse debt, the partner has a deemed distribution under Code Sec. 752(b). The discharge of debt provisions of Code Sec. 108 are not applicable to the partnership if the partnership is not relieved of debt as a result of a partner's discharge.[168]

For transactions after October 9, 1990, a debt for debt exchange will result in income to the debtor only if the issue price is less than the amount owed. For debt that is not publicly traded, the issue price will be the face amount of the debt if interest is present at the federal rate; if not, the issue price is determined by using the present value calculations provided for in Code Sec. 1274.[169]

.04 Debt Relief for Farmers

Insolvent or bankrupt farmers fall into the previous discussions. However, solvent farmers whose "qualified farm indebtedness" is forgiven by a "qualified person" may exclude from income the amount of the debt forgiveness.[170] The tax attribute reduction also applies to farm debt relief.

.05 General Rules for Income Recognition

If the forgiveness of debt is a taxable transaction, a transfer of property to the creditor is generally treated as two separate transactions: a "sale" (fair market value is the deemed sales price); and a payment of the debt. The deemed sale may result in either gain or loss to the debtor; the debt payment results in income to the extent of the forgiveness.[171]

.06 Purchase—Money Debt Reduction

If the seller reduces the debt of a solvent buyer, then the reduction is treated as a purchase price reduction (reduces the basis).[172] If the basis is exhausted, the remainder constitutes gross income.

.07 Leasehold Improvements

The value of buildings or other improvements constructed by the lessee is generally not includible in income.[173] However, where the improvements are partly or totally in lieu of rent, the value of the improvements is taxed as rental income.[174]

---

[166] Code Sec. 108(a)(3).

[167] *D.B. Merkel v. Commr.*, 109 TC 463, Dec. 52,423, aff'd CA-9, 99-2 USTC ¶ 50,848, 192 F3d 844.

[168] IRS Letter Ruling 9619002, January 31, 1996.

[169] Act Sec. 11325(a), Revenue Reconciliation Act of 1990, adding Code Sec. 108(e)(10).

[170] Code Secs. 108(a)(1) and (g).

[171] Reg. § 1.1001-2(a); also note that results may differ according to whether the debt is recourse or nonrecourse.

[172] Code Sec. 108(e)(5).

[173] Code Sec. 109.

[174] Reg. § 1.109-1.

Chapter 6

Deductions—General Concepts and Business Applications

¶ 601 Introduction

Depending on the nature of the item, deductions are generally classified as expenses, losses, or write-offs. Fixed asset write-offs are discussed in Chapter 8. Deductions and losses are covered in some detail here, with the main emphasis being on: (1) general concepts, criteria, guidelines, and constraints affecting deductibility, and (2) tax planning implications for small businesses.

¶ 603 Distinctions Between Expenses, Losses, and Write-offs

The distinction between these three types of deductions (in tax law, as well as in accounting) is not always clear-cut; however, expenses, losses, and fixed asset write-offs do have some intrinsic differences.

.01 Accounting Definitions

Accountants define expenses as decreases in assets or increases in liabilities during a period resulting from delivery of goods, rendering of services, or other activities constituting the enterprise's central operations.[1] Expenses are costs which have expired because they lack any future value.

Losses are decreases in equity from peripheral transactions of an entity excluding expenses and distributions to owners. Losses result from peripheral transactions which may be beyond the entity's control.[2]

Fixed asset write-offs have the purpose of allocating the cost of the asset over its life in a systematic and rational fashion.[3]

¶ 605 Trade or Business Expenditures—General Concepts Governing Deductibility

For trade or business expenditures to be deductible, five tests must be met:

1.   The expenditures must be ordinary;[4]

2.   The expenditures must be necessary;[5]

---

[1] Financial Accounting Standards Board, "Statement of Financial Accounting Concepts No. 3," ¶ 65, (1973).

[2] *Id.* ¶ 67-71.

[3] Accounting Principle Board, APB Statement No. 4, "Basic Concepts and Accounting Principles

Underlying Financial Statements of Business Enterprises," (1970).

[4] Code Sec. 162(a).

[5] *Id.*

3. The expenditures must be reasonable in amount;[6]

4. The expenditures must be of a current nature, i.e., must not be required to be capitalized; and

5. The expenditures must be paid or incurred (depending on the accounting method used) in the tax year.

.01 *Ordinary, Necessary, and Reasonable*

The Code does not elaborate on the terms "ordinary" and "necessary." The Supreme Court defined "ordinary" as an expense that is typically incurred in the line of business of the taxpayer.[7] The Supreme Court in *Heininger* said that a "necessary" expense is one that is appropriate and helpful to the business, the incidence of which would be considered a normal response to business conditions; it need not be mandatory.[8] The Court also laid down the precept that decisions regarding ordinary and necessary are usually questions of fact as opposed to questions of law.[9]

"Reasonableness" is not defined in Code Sec. 162, but in Code Sec. 212, the regulations state that for an expense to be "reasonable," it must "bear a reasonable and proximate relation to the production or collection of taxable income . . ."[10]

.02 *Capital Expenditures*

Capital expenditures are recoverable only through cost allocations such as depreciation; to permit their deduction currently would distort taxable income.[11] In a landmark case, the Supreme Court in *INDOPCO* said that while a taxpayer's expenditure that creates or enhances a separate and distinct asset must be capitalized, ". . . It by no means follows, however, that *only* expenditures that create or enhance separate and distinct assets are to be capitalized . . ."[12] The Court did not want the tax definition of a capital asset narrowed to the extent that taxpayers could expense all expenditures that did not create separate and identifiable assets. The Court observed that "[t]he notion that deductions are exceptions to the norm of capitalization finds support in various aspects of the Code."[13]

In applying *INDOPCO*, the IRS and the lower courts often arrive at differing interpretations regarding what needs to be capitalized.[14]

---

[6] *Lincoln Electric Co.*, CA-6, 49-2 USTC ¶ 9338, 176 F2d 815.

[7] *Welch v. Helvering*, 290 US 111, 54 SCt 8, 3 USTC ¶ 1164 (1933).

[8] *Commr. v. Heininger*, 64 SCt 249, 320 US 467, 44-1 USTC ¶ 9109 (1933). Mr. Heininger, a Chicago dentist, was a purveyor of "lavishly advertised" false teeth who incurred legal expenses in defending a "fraudulent order" of the U.S. Postal Office.

[9] *Id.* Thus, the circuit courts are supposed to reverse the Tax Court's findings in the ordinary and necessary expense arena only if they can find a misapplication of a question of law.

[10] Reg. § 1.212-1(d). Prior to the codification of "reasonableness," the Sixth Circuit in a landmark case, *Commr. v. The Lincoln Electric Co.*, 176 F2d 815, CA-6, 49-2 USTC ¶ 9388, ruled that the element of reasonableness was inherent in the phrase "ordinary and necessary."

[11] Financial Accounting Standards Board, "Statement of Financial Accounting Concepts No. 3," (1973).

[12] *INDOPCO v. U.S.*, SCt, 92-1 USTC ¶ 50,113, 503 US 79.

[13] *Id.*

[14] See, Gary L. Maydew, "To Deduct or Capitalize: Courts and IRS Interpret INDOPCO," 63 *Practical Tax Strategies*, No. 3 (Sept. 1999). Also see *Wells Fargo, et al. v. Commr.*, 224 F3d 874 (8th Cir., 2000).

.03 Application of the Ordinary, Necessary, and Reasonable Concepts

Provided that the item is clearly a business expenditure, rather than personal, the ordinary and necessary tests are rarely applied. However, the IRS has attempted to apply the ordinary and necessary tests in a wide variety of situations. In *Mann,* the IRS asserted unsuccessfully that advance payments for feed made by a hog farmer lacked the ordinary and necessary criteria.[15] Many cases have dealt with unreimbursed expenses of employees.[16] Many other cases concern deductions for expenses incurred by a closely held corporation where a shareholder may have obtained some personal benefit.[17] The reasonableness test is most often applied when the payer and the recipient are not dealing at arm's length, as in the case of relatives or employee/officers.

> **Example 6-1.** Chuck Denmeyer hired his 14-year-old son to work in his hardware store during the summer. He paid the son $30 per hour compensation. A portion of the wages would doubtless be treated as unreasonable compensation (and thus disallowed) by the IRS.

.04 Paid or Incurred in the Tax Year

Finally, the expenditure must be paid or incurred in the tax year. If the business is on the cash basis, the item must be paid; accrual basis taxpayers need only have incurred the expense.[18] (See later in the chapter for a detailed discussion as to when to deduct expenses.)

¶ 607 Losses—Business Related—General Rules

The general rule for loss deductions (for all types of losses) is provided in Code Sec. 165 which states, "There shall be allowed as a deduction any loss sustained during the taxable year and not compensated for by insurance or otherwise."[19] The regulations provide more general guidance, amplifying "insurance" to include other forms of loss compensation, and cautioning that the general rules permitting the loss deduction are subject to other code sections prohibiting or limiting deductions.[20]

Although Code Sec. 165 does not itself specifically forbid deducting unrealized losses, for losses to be deductible, they must be evidenced by closed and completed transactions, fixed by identifiable events, and, except for disaster losses (discussed later), the losses must actually be sustained

---

[15] *Mann v. Commr.,* 73-2 USTC ¶ 9618, 483 F2d 673, rev'g 31 TCM 808, Dec. 31,480(M) (8th Cir., 1973).

[16] The magnitude of the expenses compared to income generated appears to be a factor with the Tax Court; see, for example, *Strictland v. Commr.,* 43 TCM 1061, Dec. 38,936(M) (1982).

[17] For example, in *Bender v. Commr.,* 43 TCM 808, Dec. 38,864(M) (1982), a partnership was denied a deduction for providing supplies to a relig-

ious camp (expenses were connected with the partner's individual religious beliefs); similarly, in *Akland v. Commr.,* 46 TCM 51, Dec. 40,092(M) (1983), a corporation was denied a deduction for the cost of a seminar on trusts which was of interest to the majority shareholder.

[18] However, see the material following on "economic performance" and the "all events test."

[19] Code Sec. 165(a).

[20] Reg. § 1.165-1(a).

during the year.[21] A deductible loss must be bona fide, with substance over form governing the deductibility of the loss.[22]

.01 *Amount of Loss Deductible—General Provisions*

Generally, the starting point in computing the amount of the loss deduction is the adjusted basis provided in Code Sec. 1011 (see Chapter 9 for details on basis determination). The term "adjusted basis" means that the original basis has been adjusted both up and down to reflect such items as capital expenditures, previous losses,[23] and for the various cost write-offs, e.g., depreciation.[24]

The second step is to determine the amount realized. The "amount realized" from a sale is the sales price less selling expenses. The sales price includes certain items the obligation from which the seller is relieved, such as the relief of debt or taxes.

The third step is to determine the amount of the realized loss, if any, that may be *recognized* for tax purposes. (Chapter 9 contains a detailed discussion of loss recognition rules for transactions other than sales.)

¶ 609   Bad Debts

Code Sec. 166(a) provides the general authority for a bad debt deduction, stating that "there shall be allowed as a deduction any debt which becomes worthless during the year"; while a portion of a partially worthless debt may also be charged off during the year, "in an amount not in excess of the part charged off within the tax year," as a deduction.[25]

.01 *Bona Fide Debt Requirement*

In order to deduct a debt, the debt must be bona fide, i.e., the relationship must be based on a valid and enforceable obligation to pay a fixed or determinable sum of money.[26]

Generally a debtor-creditor relationship does not exist where repayment is based on, or is dependent on, profits earned by the "debtor."[27] If the facts indicate such, the "debt" may be treated by the IRS as a contribution of capital or as an investment, instead of a loan. If previously included in income, the obligation is considered to be enforceable, even if unenforceable under state law.[28]

Example 6-2. Brentor Brothers, an accrual basis partnership, accrued in 2000 an amount of $15,000 of receivables from gambling debts, which are unenforceable in its state. The debt becomes worth-

---

[21] Reg. § 1.165-1(b).

[22] Reg. § 1.165-1(b).

[23] Casualty and theft losses, to the extent deductible, reduce the adjusted basis of property.

[24] Reg. § 1.165-1(c); also proper adjustment must be made in order to reflect salvage value (see Reg. § 1.165-1(c)(4)).

[25] Code Sec. 166(a).

[26] Reg. § 1.166-1(c).

[27] See *Sluss v. Commr.*, 10 TCM 405, Dec. 18,291(M) (1951), and *Barnard v. Commr.*, 22 TCM 1773, Dec. 26,445(M) (1963).

[28] Reg. § 1.166-1(c).

less in 2001. The partnership is entitled to a bad debt deduction in 2001.

.02 Evidence of Worthlessness

The question as to when a debt is uncollectible and therefore worthless is a question of fact and has been the subject of much litigation. Mere refusal of the debtor to pay in and of itself is not sufficient proof of worthlessness.[29] Even adjudication of bankruptcy does not always justify a bad debt deduction for *total* worthlessness. If the debt is secured, or if there exists a reasonable probability that some assets would be available for unsecured creditors, then at most only a partial deduction can be taken.[30]

If the debtor is solvent, bad debt losses due to compromise of the debt may not be deductible unless the reduction is under the terms of a composition agreement.[31]

The actual procedure for dealing with bad debts differs according to whether:

- The taxpayer is on the cash or accrual method;

- The pre-1987 or post-1986 alternatives apply;

- The debt is business or nonbusiness; and

- The asset that has "gone bad" is a signed note or an open account.

.03 Cash Basis Taxpayers—Time of Deduction

Cash basis taxpayers generally will not have reported income due them on an open accounts receivable. Hence, basis of the receivable is zero, and no deduction is allowed when the debt becomes uncollectible. However, income of a cash basis taxpayer that is evidenced by a negotiable note is reportable when the note is received. Therefore, *negotiable notes receivable* of cash basis taxpayers *will* have a basis and would be charged off upon becoming worthless.

.04 Accrual Basis Taxpayers—Time of Deduction

Accrual basis taxpayers normally report income as it is earned; therefore they may take a bad debt deduction on accounts or notes that have become worthless during the year. However, the item must have been included in income either for the year of the deduction of the bad debt or for a previous year.[32]

---

[29] See, for example, *Higginbotham-Bailey-Logan Co.*, 8 BTA 566, Dec. 2901 (1927), and *Tussaud's Wax Museums, Inc.*, 25 TCM 1081, Dec. 28,116(M) (1966).
[30] See *Meyer Tank Mfg. Co., Inc., v. Commr.*, 42-1 USTC ¶ 9346, 126 F.2d 588 (2nd Cir., 1942)

(secured debt), and *Dallmeyer v. Commr.*, 14 TC 1282, Dec. 17,712 (1950) (reasonable possibility of some assets available).
[31] See, for example, *Taylor Co., Inc. v. Commr.*, 38 BTA 551, Dec. 10, 428 (1938).
[32] Reg. § 1.166-1(e).

¶ 611   Business Bad Debts

Business bad debts are deductible as an ordinary business expense. Hence, there are no limitations on the amount of the deduction; the deduction can create or increase a net operating loss, and, for sole proprietors, the deduction is for AGI, i.e., "above the line."

.01 Direct Write-Off Method

Under the specific charge-off method, an entity deducts identifiable bad debts that have become either partly or totally worthless during the tax year.

.02 Totally Worthless Bad Debts

If a taxpayer has determined that an account or note is totally worthless, a deduction may be taken *only* in the year in which it becomes totally worthless. If, however, the taxpayer has previously taken a deduction for a *partially worthless* portion (see the discussion following) of the specific debt, in order to prevent a double deduction, such amount must be subtracted to arrive at the current year's deduction.[33]

.03 Partially Worthless Bad Debt

A deduction for the partial worthlessness of a specific debt is also permitted.[34] The taxpayer must be prepared to substantiate the reasons for writing off a portion of the account or note.[35]

Partially worthless bad debts are deducted for tax purposes at the *discretion* of the taxpayer. In essence, taxpayers have three choices:

1. Deduct a portion of the bad debt in the year in which it becomes partly worthless;

2. Wait until more of the debt is worthless to take a greater partial deduction; or

3. Wait until the year in which the debt becomes totally worthless to take the deduction.

¶ 613   Conformity of Tax and Accounting

Although in the case of totally worthless bad debts, the taxpayer is technically not *required* to charge off the specific bad debt on the books, failure to conform is risky, since the IRS, should it later rule that the debt is only partly worthless, will not allow any deduction.[36]

Strict conformity is required for the deduction of partly uncollectible debts, i.e., the deduction for tax purposes is limited to the amount charged off on the books.[37]

---

[33] Reg. § 1.166-3(b).
[34] Reg. § 1.166-3(a).
[35] Reg. § 1.166-3(a)(2)(iii).

[36] IRS Pub. 535 (2000), "Business Expenses," pg. 42.
[37] Reg. § 1.166-3(a)(2).

¶ 615   Recovery of Bad Debts—Direct Write-Off

Generally, the recovery of a bad debt that has been previously written off constitutes gross income. However, to the extent that the original deduction did not create a tax benefit, the recovery is not income for tax purposes.[38]

> **Example 6-3.** Bronson Brothers, Inc., wrote off on its books, and deducted for tax purposes, a $6,000 bad debt in 1999. Because the corporation experienced a net loss in 1999, the deduction provided only a $3,600 tax benefit. In 2001, the company recovered $4,800 of the debt. Therefore, $3,600 of the recovery will be taxed and the remainder will escape taxation under the tax benefit rule. However, the $1,200 not taxed will reduce any net operating loss carryover created by the bad debt deduction.

Tax Tips and Pitfalls

Generally speaking, a taxpayer using the specific charge-off method should deduct partly worthless debts in the first year that they become partly worthless and should make a book entry for at least that amount. Waiting for the year of total worthlessness can be a risky alternative. If the IRS determines that the total worthlessness occurred *before* the year of write-off, the deduction will be disallowed and administrative and legal appeals may be the only alternatives.

¶ 617   Reserve (Allowance) Method for Bad Debts

Prior to 1987, taxpayers were allowed to use the reserve method to account for bad debts. Elimination of the reserve method for all entities, except for certain small banks and thrift institutions, was accomplished by the Tax Reform Act of 1986.[39]

¶ 619   Nonaccrual-Experience Accounting Method

The Tax Reform Act of 1986 imposed some new limitations on the use of the cash method of accounting for certain entities, requiring that C corporations, partnerships with C corporations as partners, and tax shelters must use the accrual method of accounting.[40] To ease somewhat this draconian requirement, Congress also provided that the above named entities with income from services are not required to use the accrual method to report the service income for any portion of the receivable which, on the basis of experience, will be uncollectible.[41] The performance of activity other than services, i.e., the sale or manufacture of goods, the loaning of money, and the acquisition of receivables from other persons, does not affect the eligibility to use the nonaccrual-experience method;

---

[38] Reg. § 1.166-1(f).
[39] Tax Reform Act of 1986, P.L. 99-514 (1986 Act), § 805, repealing Code Sec. 166(c) and (f).

[40] Code Sec. 448(a).
[41] Code Sec. 448(d)(5).

however, receivables arising from *those activities* would not be eligible for this method.[42]

Even with respect to the performance of services, the nonaccrual-experience method may not be used on accounts where either interest is charged on overdue accounts or if there is a penalty for late payments.[43] However, the method could be used for those accounts that are not charged interest or a penalty. Offering a discount for early payment has a result similar to charging interest for late payments. However, offering a sales discount will not lose the eligibility for the nonaccrual-experience method.[44]

> **Example 6-4.** Fanning, Inc., collects trash for both residential and commercial customers. The residential customers are charged interest for payments made past 30 days; the commercial customers receive a two percent discount if paid within 10 days, but are not subject to an interest charge. The nonaccrual-experience method could be used on the commercial customers, but not for the residential customers.

.01 Applying the Nonaccrual-Experience Method

In applying the nonaccrual-experience method, a taxpayer may use either of two methods: the separate receivable system or the periodic system. Under the "separate receivable system," each accounts receivable is analyzed to determine the amount, if any, of the receivable that is expected to be uncollectible.[45] The amount that is not expected to be collected is a percentage that is derived from taking the ratio of a six-year moving average of bad debts (adjusted for recoveries) to ending accounts receivable.[46] The determination is made only once. The amount not expected to be collected is not reported as income when the receivables are accrued. If more of the receivables are collected than expected, the excess must be included in income when collected.[47]

> **Example 6-5.** Johnson Co.'s six-year average of bad debts to ending receivables is 12.5 percent. At the end of 2001, the company had two receivables arising from the performance of services.

Receivable	Amount	Ratio	Uncollectible Amount
A	$14,000	.125	$1,750
B	6,000	.125	750
	$20,000		$2,500

Of the $20,000 of receivables, $17,500 will be included in income and $2,500 will not be included.

---

[42] Temp. Reg. § 1.448-2T(d).
[43] Temp. Reg. § 1.448-2T(c).
[44] *Id.*

[45] Temp. Reg. § 1.448-2T(e)(3).
[46] Temp. Reg. § 1.448-2T(e)(2).
[47] Temp. Reg. § 1.448-2T(e)(3).

Example 6-6. Assume the same facts as in the previous example and that in 2002 all $6,000 of receivable B is collected. An additional $750 must be included in income in 2002.

The "periodic system" is more like the reserve method in that the aggregate amount that the taxpayer estimates will be uncollectible is estimated.[48] The basis for the estimate is the six-year moving average previously discussed. The amount in the "account" is adjusted upward or downward, as circumstances demand. Thus, the effect could be to increase or decrease gross income. The actual specific bad debts are charged directly to bad debts expense.[49]

The nonaccrual-experience method is treated as an accounting method, and it was generally required that Form 3115 be filled out for the taxpayers' year that began in 1987 for those taxpayers switching to the method. New taxpayers who qualify need only adopt the method.[50]

¶ 621   Recognition of Expenses

The criteria for recognizing an expense and the time period in which it is recognized differ greatly according to whether the taxpayer is on the cash or the accrual method.

.01   The Cash Method

Deductions for a cash basis taxpayer are generally not allowable until the year they are paid.[51] Therefore, purchases on account, unpaid wages, and accrued property taxes, for example, are not currently deductible. Obviously, expenditures of a capital nature must be capitalized and written off over the useful life. The matter of prepaid expenses, however, is somewhat unclear and appears to depend on the *type* of prepaid item as much as anything. Prepaid interest must be allocated over the life of the loan unless the prepayment is in the form of points paid on a mortgage on the primary residence of a taxpayer, in which case they are deductible in the year they are paid.[52] For prepaid rent, an early Board of Tax Appeals denied a deduction for prepayments.[53] However, one circuit court of appeal has held that prepaid rent may be deductible if the prepayment is not for more than one year.[54] For prepaid expenses other than interest and rent, if the prepayment does not exceed one year, the Supreme Court has indicated its approval of the Ninth Circuit's decision in *Zaninovich* which allowed a deduction for prepaid expenses.[55]

Payment is considered made during the year in which a check is drawn and mailed to a taxpayer.[56] Thus, a check dated December 31 is considered

---

[48] IRS Notice 88-51, 1988-1 CB 535.
[49] *Id.*
[50] Temp. Reg. § 1.448-2T(h)(3).
[51] Reg. § 1.461-1(a)(1).
[52] Code Sec. 461(g).
[53] *Baton Coal Co.*, 19 BTA 169, Dec. 5,882 (1930).

[54] *Zaninovich v. Commr.*, 80-1 USTC ¶ 9342, 616 F2d 429 (9th Cir., 1980).
[55] *Hillsboro National Bank v. Commr.*, 83-1 USTC ¶ 9229, 460 US 370 (USSC, 1983).
[56] *Eli B. Witt Est. v. Fahs*, DC Fla., 56-1 USTC 9534, 160 FSupp 521.

paid that year if it has December 31 as a postmark. Having the check certified is a prudent step if the amount is material. Payment by note is not considered payment until the note is paid.

.02 Accrual Method—General Rule for Deductions

If a taxpayer uses the accrual method, an expense is generally deductible during the tax year in which all events have occurred which determine the fact of the liability, the amount can be determined with reasonable accuracy, and economic performance has occurred with respect to the liability.[57] Although the exact amount of the liability may not be determinable, an expense is still deductible if the amount can be reasonably estimated.[58] On the other hand, taxpayers generally cannot deduct reserves for estimated expenses such as warranty costs or sales returns.

¶ 623   Premature Expense Accruals—The Economic Performance Test

In the Tax Reform Act of 1984, Congress enacted a constraint to the all-events test. The constraint, deemed the "economic performance test," was designed to prevent premature accruals. The economic performance test does not so much set the *time* of the deduction as it places a *constraint* on the time of deduction. In certain instances, the deduction may be *later* than the date that economic performance has occurred. For example, deferred compensation for services is deductible only during the period that the service provider reports the income.[59] Similarly, accruals to cash basis-related taxpayers are not deductible until paid.[60]

The economic performance test provides generally that the all-events test is not met until economic performance has occurred. In a substantive sense, the concept of economic performance relates more to the revenue side than the expense side. Essentially, economic performance occurs when the seller/lessor/purveyor of services performs, i.e., delivers the goods, allows use of the property, or provides the service.[61] It is at that point, and generally not before, that the buyer/lessee/user of services may generally accrue the deduction. The Code specifies the performance that must occur, as follows:[62]

Liability Arising Out of	*Occurrence of Economic Performance*
1. The providing of services to the taxpayer by another person.	As the person provides the services.
2. The providing of property to the taxpayer by another person.	As the person provides the property.
3. The use of property by the taxpayer.	As the taxpayer uses the property.

---

[57] Reg. § 1.461-1(a)(2).
[58] *Id.*
[59] Temp. Reg. § 1.404(b)-1T.

[60] Code Sec. 267(a)(2).
[61] Code Sec. 461(h)(2)(B).
[62] Code Sec. 461(h)(2).

4. Any of the first three instances
    and payment by the taxpayer
    are to be made in the form of
    property or services.

    As the taxpayer provides such
    property or services.

5. Workers' compensation or tort
    liabilities of the taxpayer.

    As the payments are made.

.01 Use of Property or Services Provided to the Taxpayer

If the liability of a taxpayer arises out of the use of property or services by the taxpayer, economic performance generally occurs ratably over the period of use.[63]

>   **Example 6-7.** J&J, Inc., signed a contract on December 1, 2000, giving it exclusive use of a hog facility for a four-year period beginning on January 1, 2001. J&J made full payment of $1,000,000 at the time the contract was signed. The payment is deductible at the rate of $250,000 per year, starting in 2001.

An earlier date than the period of use (i.e., the date of payment) may be used to determine economic performance if the property or services can reasonably be expected to be performed within three and one-half months after the date of payment.[64]

>   **Example 6-8.** The Fairview Co. signed a contract on December 2, 2000, with a company to clean up flood damages which Fairview had incurred. Payment was made at the time the contract was signed. If the taxpayer can reasonably expect the services to be performed within three and one-half months after the payment date, the item may be deducted in 1996.

.02 Liability from Services and Property To Be Performed by the Taxpayer

Generally, if the liability requires the taxpayer to provide services or property to another taxpayer, economic performance occurs as the taxpayer incurs the cost.[65]

>   **Example 6-9.** Hilltop Realty, the owner of an office building, on January 1, 2001, enters into a three-year lease with a tenant. The lease calls for Hilltop Realty to provide certain services in connection with the feedlot. In 2001 Hilltop Realty incurs and pays $60,000 of janitorial services. The expenses are deductible in 2001, the year incurred.

>   **Example 6-10.** Wake Corporation, a calendar year, accrual method taxpayer, sells computers under a three-year warranty that obligates Wake to make any reasonable repairs to each computer it sells. During 2000, Wake sells 10 computers. In 2001, Wake repairs, at

---

[63] Reg. § 1.461-4(d)(3)(i).
[64] Reg. § 1.461-4(d)(6)(ii).

[65] Reg. § 1.461-4(d)(4)(i).

a cost of $5,000, two computers sold during 2000. The $5,000 of warranty expense is considered incurred in 2001.[66]

.03 Liability for Property or Services Attributable to Long-Term Contracts

If a long-term contract is taken into income under the percentage of completion method, then economic performance is considered to occur the earlier of:[67]

- The date the property or services are provided, or

- As the taxpayer makes payment for the property or services used in producing the product.

.04 Liabilities for Which Payment Is Economic Performance

There are certain liabilities for which economic performance does not occur until payment is made. Generally, a payment made to a person other than the person owed the money (including payments made in trust, escrow accounts, court administered funds, etc.) does not create economic performance. See a later section of this chapter for exceptions to this rule. Instead, economic performance occurs as payments are made from that other person or fund to whom the liability is owed. These liabilities are as follows:[68]

- Liabilities arising under a workers' compensation act or out of any tort, breach of contract, or violation of law.

- Rebates and refunds—economic performance occurs as payment is made regardless of whether the items are recorded as a deduction, an adjustment to gross receipts, or an adjustment to cost of goods sold.

- Awards, prizes, and jackpots.

- Insurance, warranty, and service contracts.

- Taxes—generally economic performance does not occur until the tax is paid to the relevant governmental body. However, in certain instances, a liability to pay a tax is permitted to be taken into account in the taxable year before the year in which economic performance has occurred under the recurring item exception discussed below.

.05 Recurring Item Exception

To meet the recurring item exception, economic performance must have occurred on or before the earlier of:[69]

- The return due date (including extensions) for the item to be deducted that year, or

- Eight and one-half months after the year end.

---

[66] Adapted from Reg. § 1.461-4(d)(7), Example 2.
[67] Reg. § 1.461-4(d)(2)(ii).

[68] Reg. § 1.461-4(g).
[69] Reg. § 1.461-5(b)(1).

If economic performance occurs outside the due date but within eight and one-half months of the close of the year, an amended return is required if a deduction is sought for that year.[70]

Example 6-11. Lassie Corporation, a calendar year, accrual basis taxpayer, runs a cattle feedlot. Under its method of accounting, Lassie recognizes sales income upon execution of the sales contract, rather than upon shipment. In December 2000, Lassie contracts to pay Dodson Co., a common carrier, $1,000 upon June 2001 delivery of cattle sold by Lassie in November 2000. Lassie generally incurs such shipping costs from one taxable year to the next. Economic performance with respect to the amount paid to Dodson for shipping services occurs in June 2001, as Dodson provides the shipping services. Assume that all the events that fix and determine Lassie's $1,000 liability occur in 2000. Also assume that Lassie files its corporate return on September 15, 2001. If Lassie adopts the recurring item exception, Lassie may deduct $1,000 for its 2000 taxable year, even though economic performance does not occur until June 2001. The $1,000 expense relates to 2000 income from the sale. Thus, better matching results from its accrual in the taxable year preceding the year during which economic performance occurs.

Example 6-12. Assume the same facts as in the previous example, and assume that Lassie files its income tax return for 2000 on March 15, 2001. The costs are ineligible for the recurring item exception treatment because economic performance with respect to the costs does not occur before Lassie files a return for the taxable year for which the item would have been deducted under the exception. However, since economic performance occurs within eight and one-half months after 2000, Lassie may file an amended return.

.06 Adopting the Recurring Item Exception

A taxpayer may adopt the recurring item exception as part of its method of accounting for any type of item for the first tax year in which that type of item is incurred. Generally, in other circumstances, a change would constitute a change in accounting methods.[71]

¶ 625 Disallowed Expenditures

The Code prohibits the deduction of certain expenditures; the deduction for certain other expenditures is limited or restricted. Under disallowed expenditures, the following will be considered:

1. Expenditures against public policy;

2. Political contributions;

3. Personal expenditures;

---

[70] Reg. § 1.461-5(b)(2).
[71] For rules regarding changes in accounting methods, see Code Sec. 446 and the regulations.

4. Expenses related to tax-exempt income; and

5. Unrealized losses.

.01 Expenditures Against Public Policy

Discussed in this section are: (1) bribes and kickbacks; (2) other illegal payments; and (3) fines and penalties.

Bribes and Kickbacks

Payments to officials or employees (even unpaid employees) of any government of the United States, a state, a territory or possession of the United States, D.C., or Puerto Rico are not deductible if the payment constitutes an illegal bribe or kickback.[72] The legality of the payments is determined under the laws of the United States and the states.[73]

The legality of payments to officials or employees of foreign governments, however, is determined by reference to the Foreign Corrupt Practices Act of 1977.[74] Thus, for example, payments made to foreign officials to facilitate routine nondiscretionary decisions may be deductible.

The burden of proof in this instance is on the IRS to establish that the payment is illegal.[75]

Other Illegal Payments

Payments to other than government officials are not deductible if the payment is an illegal bribe, kickback, or other illegal payment under U.S. law, or state law (if generally enforced).[76] Again, the burden of proof is on the IRS. Kickbacks, rebates, and bribes under Medicare and Medicaid are also specifically prohibited.[77]

Fines and Penalties

No deduction is allowed for fines or similar penalties paid to a government of the United States, a state, D.C., a territory or possession of the United States, or Puerto Rico, for the violation of any law.[78] Fines and penalties, for this purpose, include amounts paid:[79]

- Pursuant to a criminal conviction or a guilty plea;

- As a civil penalty;

- In settlement of an actual or potential fine or penalty; or

- Through forfeiture of posted collateral.

---

[72] Code Sec. 162(c)(1); Reg. § 1.162-18(a)(1) and (3).

[73] Reg. § 1.162-18(a)(5).

[74] Code Sec. 162(c)(1).

[75] *Id.*

[76] Code Sec. 162(c)(2).

[77] Code Sec. 162(c)(3).

[78] Code Sec. 162(f).

[79] Reg. § 1.162-21(b)(1).

The regulations cite, as examples of nondeductible fines, amounts paid due to violations of federal environment laws, federal safety laws, state truck laws, and city building codes.[80] Fines and penalties do *not* include legal and related fees incurred in defense of any criminal or civic actions, court costs, or stenographic and printing charges. Compensatory damages are also not considered fines and penalties.[81]

Tax Tips and Pitfalls

Although fines and penalties incurred in connection with a lawsuit are not deductible, legal fees generally may be deducted if incurred to preserve the reputation of the business and/or the businessperson.

.02 Political Contributions

Generally, no deduction is allowed for political contributions. Specifically, Code Sec. 276 prohibits in most cases a deduction for:[82]

- Advertising in a convention program of a political party or in any other publication or for admission to any dinner or program; the deduction is denied if any part of the proceeds directly or indirectly benefit, or were intended to benefit, a political party or candidate; and

- Admission to an inaugural ball, gala, parade, concert, or similar event if the event is identified with a political party or candidate.[83]

Political parties for this purpose are defined rather broadly to include not only political parties and national, state, and local committees of political parties, but also committees, associations, or other organizations which accept contributions or make expenditures for the purpose of influencing or attempting to influence the selection, nomination, or election of any individual to any elective public office.[84]

Two tests (both must be met) are applied to determine whether the proceeds benefit the political process:[85]

1. The proceeds may be used to further the candidate's candidacy; and

2. The proceeds may not be received in the ordinary course of a candidate's trade or business (excepting the trade or business of holding a political office).

Tax Tips and Pitfalls

Taxpayers should be very cautious about making, let alone deducting, political contributions. However, there are limited instances

---

[80] Reg. § 1.162-21(c).
[81] Reg. § 1.162-21(b)(2).
[82] Code Sec. 276(a)(1) and (2).

[83] Code Sec. 276(a)(3).
[84] Code Sec. 276(b)(1).
[85] Code Sec. 276(b)(2).

in which such expenditures may be deductible. Advertising in national convention programs is permitted if the proceeds are used solely to defray the costs of the current or next year's convention, assuming the expenditures are reasonable in light of the benefits.[86]

Although expenditures made in the acquisition of goods or services from a politician who operates a business are not considered political contributions (and are thus deductible), if proceeds received by a candidate exceed substantially the fair market value of the goods or services provided by the candidate, *no portion* of the expenditure is deductible.[87] Thus, strict care should be taken to ensure that any dealings with a business owned by a politician meet the arm's-length transactions criteria.

.03 Personal Expenditures

The entity concept is often and easily violated in small business contexts. It is not unusual for the owner(s) to use business funds to make payments for what are personal expenditures of the owner(s). With rare exceptions (e.g., medical expenses, moving expenses, etc.), these expenditures are not deductible if paid directly by the owner(s).[88] Depending on the type of entity that pays the expenditures for the owner(s), the expenditures may or may not be deductible. However, generally if the entity *can* take the deduction, then the owner(s) will have gross income. Therefore, the expenditures are generally best *not* paid from the business entity.

.04 Expenses Related to Tax-Exempt Interest

Generally, no deduction can be taken for expenses related to the production of tax-exempt income (e.g., municipal bond interest).[89] "Tax-exempt income" for this purpose means income that is wholly exempt from taxation.[90] If an expenditure is indirectly allocable to both exempt and nonexempt income, a reasonable allocation method must be used.[91]

.05 Unrealized Losses

Generally, losses are recognized only if there has been an exchange with a taxpayer outside the entity seeking the loss deduction. This prohibition of unrealized losses is a key part of the realization concept in tax accounting. Thus, decreases in market value (paper losses) are generally not deductible. An exception to the realization concept is provided for certain casualty losses (see the discussion later in this chapter).

¶ 627   Hobby Losses

Many wealthy taxpayers enjoy expensive activities that may have some attributes of a business, yet may possess other attributes typical of a hobby. Common examples include: building, racing, and restoring automo-

---

[86] Reg. § 1.276-1(b)(2); the standards are more strict for institutional advertising, however.
[87] Reg. § 1.276-1(f)(3)(iii) and (iv), Example 4.
[88] Code Sec. 262(a).

[89] Code Sec. 265(a)(1).
[90] Reg. § 1.265-1(b).
[91] Reg. § 1.265-1(c).

biles; breeding and racing horses; collecting art and rare coins; maintaining "show livestock farms"; showing dogs; and so on. If the activity incurs net tax losses, the question arises as to whether the activity is a business or a hobby.

Code Sec. 183 places severe restrictions on the deduction of expenses in a hobby activity. If the activity is an "activity not engaged in for profit" (a hobby), then expenses are deductible in the following order:[92]

1. Expenses which would be deductible in any event (i.e., property taxes and interest).[93]

2. Expenses (except for deductions affecting property basis, such as depreciation) which would be deductible if the activity were a trade or business. Category number two expenses can, after deducting category number one expenses, be deducted only to the extent of gross income from the activity, i.e., the expenses cannot create a taxable loss.

3. Deductions which would affect basis, such as depreciation, partial losses with respect to property, partially worthless bad debts, amortization, and amortizable bond premiums. As with category two expenses, these expenses cannot create a taxable loss.

Note that if category two and three expenses are allowed, they become itemized deductions subject to the two percent floor. Also note that the division of deductions between categories two and three is potentially beneficial to the taxpayer since, if depreciation is not taken, basis is not impaired.[94]

.01 Factors Determining Whether an Activity Is a Hobby or a Business

Code Sec. 183 does not define a hobby. However, the regulations note that the issue is a question of fact and reference should be made to objective standards, nine of which are listed in the regulations:

1. *Manner in which the taxpayer carries on the activity.* A businesslike manner (e.g., good accounting records) would strengthen the case for treating the activity as a business.

2. *Expertise of the taxpayer or taxpayer's advisors.* Extensive study of business, practices or consultation with experts would constitute examples of business-like approach.

3. *The time and effort expended.*

---

[92] Code Sec. 183(b); Reg. § 1.183-1(b).
[93] However, unless the interest is incurred on a qualified home mortgage, none of it is deductible starting in 1991.

[94] Reg. § 1.183-1(b).

4. *Expectation that the assets may increase in value.* Expected "profit" may include appreciation in property as well as in operating income.

5. *Success of the taxpayer in other activities.*

6. *History of income and losses.* A string of losses would generally, unless due to unforseen or fortuitous circumstances beyond the control of the taxpayer, indicate a hobby.

7. *The relation of occasional profit to losses.* A combination of occasional small profit with large losses or large investments could indicate a hobby. However, the potential to earn a substantial profit in a very speculative venture is a strong indication of business intent.

8. *Financial status of the taxpayer.* Generally, the wealthier the taxpayer, the more difficult it is to show business intent.

9. *Element of personal pleasure or recreation.* Although the lack of personal pleasure or recreation from the activity is not *required* to show business intent, the *presence* of personal pleasure or recreational motives may indicate a hobby.[95]

.02 Presumptive Rule

Generally, in IRS-taxpayer disputes, the taxpayer has the burden of proof. However, in the case of hobbies, the burden of proof (to show a hobby) shifts to the IRS if:

- In the case of race horses, a profit is shown in any two out of the seven consecutive tax years ending with the current tax year; or

- In all other cases, a profit is shown in any three out of five consecutive tax years ending with the current tax year.[96]

Example 6-13. Sharon Wilson, a wealthy businesswoman, raises show dogs on an acreage outside her city. During the current year, she has the following items of income and deductions:

Sales		$60,000
Operating Expenses	$57,200	
Depreciation	6,000	
Property Taxes	500	$63,700
Net Loss		($ 3,700)

If the activity is considered a business, all of the expenditures are deductible and the result is a $3,700 tax loss. However, if deemed a hobby, the results are as follows:

---

[95] Reg. § 1.183-2(b).   [96] Code Sec. 183(d).

Sales	$60,000
Less—Property Taxes	500
Remainder	$59,500
Less—Operating Expenses	57,200
Remainder	$ 2,300
Less—Depreciation ($6,000 limited to $2,300)	2,300
Taxable Income	0

However, note that the $57,200 and $2,300 of deductions are subject to the two percent floor on itemized deductions.

¶ 629   Related-Party Transactions

Code Sec. 267 contains two prohibitions on loss and expense deductions where related parties are involved. The purpose of the Code Sec. 267 limitations is to prevent sham transactions from being developed to create artificial losses. The two prohibitions concern:

1.   Losses on sales to "relatives"; and

2.   The accrual of expenses between "relatives" if the payor uses the accrual basis method of accounting and the recipient uses the cash basis method.[97]

Losses on sales to relatives are flatly *prohibited* in the year of sale.[98] However, the losses are in effect suspended until the purchaser sells or disposes of the property. At that time, the suspended losses can reduce the gains (but not create or increase losses) of the relative who purchased from the selling relative.[99]

> **Example 6-14.** Ed Lammey sold property for $200,000 to a corporation that he controlled. Basis of the property to Lammey was $340,000. The corporation later sold the property for $225,000. The $140,000 loss of Lammey is disallowed; however, the $25,000 realized gain of the corporation on the disposition is reduced to zero by the $140,000 suspended loss. Note that in this case much of the suspended loss ($115,000) is lost forever.

"Relatives," for Code Sec. 267 purposes, include:[100]

- Blood relatives—ancestors, lineal descendants, and siblings;

- A corporation and an individual, if he or she controls, directly or indirectly, more than 50 percent of the value of outstanding stock;

---

[97] Code Sec. 267(a).
[98] *Id.*
[99] Code Sec. 267(d).
[100] Code Sec. 267(b).

- Two corporations who are members of the same controlled group;

- Various relationships between trusts and the grantors and/or beneficiaries; and

- A corporation and a partnership, if the same persons own more than 50 percent in value of outstanding stock of the corporation and more than 50 percent of capital interest, or profits interest, in the partnership.

Constructive ownership rules apply in determining indirect stock ownership of corporations, i.e., stock owned by a relative of the taxpayer is constructively owned by the taxpayer.[101]

The expense accrual prohibition applies *only* when the payor utilizes the accrual method and the recipient uses the cash method of accounting. In that event, the accrual basis taxpayer is denied a deduction until the recipient includes the item in income (generally when received).[102] Although, generally, the context of these accruals would be interest, salaries, or bonuses, it is also applicable to unstated interest, as determined under Code Sec. 483, and, in some instances, even to owed but unpaid cost recovery items, such as organizational expenditures and covenants not to compete.[103]

> **Example 6-15.** Hy-Fly, Inc., a calendar year accrual basis taxpayer, accrued a $25,000 bonus to its president and sole shareholder at the end of 2000. The bonus was paid on January 28, 2001. Hy-Fly must wait until 2001 to deduct the bonus.

¶ 631   Lobbying Expenditures

Prior to the passage of the Revenue Reconciliation Act of 1993 (RRA '93), certain lobbying expenses were deductible. However, RRA '93 repealed the deduction for most lobbying expenses.[104] However, Congress, in RRA '93, left three instances in which lobbying expenses are still deductible:

1.   Lobbying of local governing bodies such as city and county governments is still allowed.

2.   A *de minimis* rule is applied to in-house lobbying expenditures. If the expenditures do not exceed $2,000, they are deductible.

3.   A deduction is still allowed for expenditures that involve only the monitoring of legislation.

---

[101] Code Sec. 267(c).
[102] Code Sec. 267(a)(2)(B).
[103] Temp. Reg. § 1.267(a)-2T.

[104] Revenue Reconciliation Act of 1993, Act Sec. 13222(a), amending Code Sec. 162(e).

A taxpayer must use a reasonable method of allocating labor and general and administrative costs to lobbying activities. Reasonable methods include:[105]

- The ratio method;

- The gross-up method; and

- A method that applies the principles of Code Sec. 263A (uniform capitalization rules).

¶ 633   Capital Expenditures

Generally, capital expenditures are not currently deductible. Included are amounts paid out for new buildings or permanent improvements made to increase the value of any property.[106] Items are considered capital expenditures if they either:

- Add to the value or substantially prolong the life of property; or

- Adapt property to a new or different use.[107]

Examples of capital expenditures include:

- The cost of acquiring, constructing, or erecting property having a useful life substantially beyond the end of the tax year;

- Expenditures in securing a copyright;

- Cost of defending or protecting title to property;

- Architect's fees;

- Purchasing commissions for securities; and

- Cost of goodwill in connection with the purchase of the assets of a going concern.

.01   Exception to the Requirement to Capitalize

Code Sec. 263 and the attendant regulations list several categories of expenditures for which an election may be made either to expense or capitalize the items. Included are:[108]

---

[105] See Reg. § 1.162-28 for details.

[106] Code Sec. 263(a)(1).

[107] Reg. § 1.263(a)-1(b).

[108] Code Sec. 263(a)(1); Reg. § 1.263(a)-1(b).

Type of Expenditure	Code Section
1. Development of mines or deposits	616
2. Research and experimental	174
3. Soil and water conservation	175
4. Fertilizer, etc. by farmers.....................	180
5. Removal of architectural and transportation barriers to the handicapped and elderly	190
6. Tertiary injectants	193
7. Those for depreciable personal property used for business purposes and eligible to be deducted	179
8. Circulation expenses	173
9. Organizational expenditures	248
10. Carrying charges.............................	266
11. Exploration of minerals	617

Special rules also exist that require the capitalization and inclusion in inventory of certain expenses.[109]

¶ 635   Search and Start-Up Costs

Generally, no deduction is allowed for start-up expenditures.[110] However, the taxpayer may elect to treat the costs as deferred expenses and amortize them over a 60-month period.[111] Unamortized costs existing at the time of sale or other disposition of the business may be deducted in that year.

"Start-up expenditures" are amounts paid or incurred to:

- Investigate the creation or acquisition of an active trade or business;

- Create an active trade or business; or

- Help get the activity engaged in an active trade or business.[112]

The expenditures must also be of such a nature that they would be deductible if incurred in the operation of an existing active trade or business.[113] The term does not include interest, taxes, or research and experimental expenditures.[114]

Typical examples of business investigation expenditures are those incurred in connection with site selection, engineering and architectural surveys, traffic studies, marketing research, labor input availability, transportation and other infrastructure facilities, and legal fees. The treatment of business investigation expenses depends on whether the business is actually started.

---

[109] Code Sec. 263A.
[110] Code Sec. 195(a).
[111] Code Sec. 195(b).

[112] Code Sec. 195(c)(1)(A).
[113] Code Sec. 195(c)(1)(B).
[114] Code Sec. 195(c).

Start-up expenses include the cost of training workers, obtaining labor and produced inputs, advertising, and professional services. There is some overlap between start-up expenses and pre-opening costs. Generally, pre-opening costs are more site specific and are compressed into a shorter time period than the more general term, start-up expenses. In order to amortize search and start-up costs, the business must become an active going concern.[115]

The tax treatment of the above expenses is as follows:

Taxpayer Already in Line of Business	Business Actually Started?	Tax Treatment
Yes	Yes	Expense currently
Yes	No	Expense currently[*]
No	Yes	Amortize over 60 months
No	No	Not deductible[**]

[*] *York v. Commr.*, 58-2 USTC ¶ 9952, 261 F.2d 421 (4th Cir. 1958).
[**] Rev. Rul. 57-418, 1957-2 CB 143.

Tax Tips and Pitfalls

Taxpayers considering entering a new line of business should consider forming a new Code Sec. 1244 corporation *before* incurring significant search and start-up costs. If the business is *not* entered into, the corporation could be liquidated and an ordinary loss deduction taken on the worthlessness of the stock under Code Sec. 1244. Otherwise, as previously mentioned, no deduction is available.[116]

¶ 637   Losses—Business Related

Code Sec. 165 provides the general rule for deducting losses, stating that, "there shall be allowed as a deduction any loss sustained during the taxable year and not compensated for by insurance or otherwise."[117] Qualified loss deductions for individuals are limited to the following three types of losses:

1. Losses incurred in a trade or business;

2. Losses incurred in any transaction entered into for profit, even though not a trade or business; and

3. Certain casualty and theft losses.[118]

The subject of losses is quite broad, so we will consider only those losses likely to be encountered by a trade or business.

---

[115] *Dailey v. Commr.*, 47 TCM 150, Dec. 41,014(M) (1984) and *C.E. McManus III v. Commr.*, 54 TCM 475, Dec. 44,186(M) (1987).

[116] Donald R. Quinn, "Search and Start-up Expenses For a New Business: When are they Deducti-ble?", The Practical Accountant, May 1984, pp. 77-78.

[117] Code Sec. 165(a).

[118] Code Sec. 165(c).

.01   *Obsolescence of Nondepreciable Property*

A deduction is allowed for business losses incurred due to the sudden termination of the usefulness (obsolescence) of nondepreciable property in any of three instances:

1.   The business is discontinued;

2.   The transaction is discontinued; or

3.   The property is permanently discarded from use.[119]

Although this provision would seem to be rather wide-sweeping, it does *not* apply to:

- Losses on the sale or exchange of any property;

- Losses sustained upon the obsolescence or worthlessness of depreciable property;

- Casualty losses; or

- Losses due to the decline in value of inventory (due to obsolescence or any other factor).[120]

The above exceptions narrow considerably the range of assets subject to these rules, leaving only supplies, various intangible assets, and perhaps land in certain instances.

> **Example 6-16.** Minibus Lines, Inc., acquired a small chain of restaurants in 1986, allocating to goodwill $400,000. By 2001, due to a change in consumer tastes, the business was unprofitable and was abandoned. The corporation could deduct the $400,000 of goodwill.

Even though many of the assets eligible under this provision are capital assets, losses due to obsolescence are *not* considered capital losses; therefore, the capital loss limitations under Code Secs. 1211 and 1212 ($3,000 annual limit for noncorporate taxpayers and limits on carrybacks and carryovers) do not apply.[121]

.02   *Demolition of Buildings*

No deduction is allowed for either the loss on the demolition of a building or for the costs incurred in demolishing a building.[122] Instead, such amounts must be capitalized, i.e., added to the basis of the land.[123]

.03   *Decline in Value of Stock*

No deduction is allowed for the mere decline in value of stock when the decline is due to a fluctuation in market prices or other similar cause.[124] A shrinkage in value, however extensive, does not create a deduction so long

---

[119] Reg. § 1.165-2(a).
[120] Reg. § 1.165-2(b).
[121] *Id.*

[122] Code Sec. 280B(a)(1).
[123] Code Sec. 280B(a)(2).
[124] Reg. § 1.165-4(a).

as the stock retains some value.[125] The above loss prohibition does *not* apply to securities of a dealer which are treated as inventory.

.04 *Worthless Securities*

A loss is permitted when securities become totally worthless during the year. The loss is treated as if it were a sale or exchange on the last day of the year.[126] The character of the loss depends on whether the security is a capital asset. If not a capital asset, the loss is ordinary; however, if the security is a capital asset (generally the case unless the business is a dealer in securities), the loss will be a capital loss.[127]

"Securities" are defined for this purpose as:[128]

- A share of stock;
- A stock right or subscription; or
- Debt such as bonds, debentures, notes, certificates, or other evidence of indebtedness.

The securities of affiliated corporations are not considered capital assets; hence, any loss is ordinary.[129] An affiliated corporation is one where the taxpayer owns directly at least 80 percent of both the voting power and the other nonvoting stock (nonparticipating, nonvoting preferred need not be owned).[130]

¶ 639 Business Casualty and Theft Losses

Casualty losses generally are deductible whether incurred in conjunction with a trade or business or incurred on personal use assets. Our focus is limited to business casualty losses.

.01 *Definition of Casualty Losses*

The code and the regulations mention fire, storm, shipwreck, and theft as being eligible for casualty loss treatment.[131] However, other than that brief description, the code and regulations are silent with respect to the definition.

Thus, it has been left to the courts and the IRS to interpret what are and what are not casualties. Events which have or have not been deemed casualty losses are as follows:[132]

Held to be casualty losses:

- Auto damage due to icy condition of road or freezing of motor,
- Earthquake,
- Sudden sinking of land,

---

[125] *Id.*
[126] Code Sec. 165(g)(1).
[127] Reg. § 1.165-5(b) and (c).
[128] Reg. § 1.165-5(a).
[129] Reg. § 1.165-5(d)(1).

[130] Reg. § 1.165-5(d)(2).
[131] Code Sec. 165(c)(3); Reg. § 1.165-7(a).
[132] 2001 CCH STANDARD FEDERAL TAX REPORTS ¶ 10,005.002.

- Mine cave-ins,
- Subsoil shrinkage of residential property due to drought,
- Unexpected and unusual drought causing loss to residential property,
- Flood,
- Hurricane,
- Freezing and bursting of water pipes,
- Quarry blast,
- Damage to septic tank drain and water pipe caused by tractor,
- Vandalism.

Held not to be deductible as casualties:

- Onion smut,
- Contamination of well,
- Rusting,
- Corrosion,
- Moth damage to fur coat,
- Drying up of well from drought,
- Disease and insect attack to tree.

.02 Requirements to Take a Casualty Loss Deduction

The mere occurrence of the casualty will not necessarily generate a casualty loss deduction. The taxpayer must also provide evidence of the property's basis.[133] If the event does qualify as a casualty, clean-up and repair expenses are also deductible as part of the loss.[134]

.03 Use of Repair Costs to Measure the Deduction

Although the courts often accept the cost of repairs as a measure of the casualty loss, one should be aware of several caveats in this regard:

- The repairs are not deductible as a casualty loss to the extent that they increase the value of the property over what it was before the casualty event;[135]

- The repairs must actually be performed;[136]

- Actual, not estimated costs, must be used;[137] and

- Evidence must be provided to establish the amount spent on repairs.[138]

---

[133] *Rosenthal v. U.S.*, CA-2, 69-1 USTC ¶ 9430, 416 F2d 491.

[134] *Smithgal v. Commr.*, 81-1 USTC ¶ 9121 (Ga. 1981).

[135] Reg. § 1.165-7(a)(2)(ii); *Lamphere v. Commr.*, 70 TC 391, Dec. 35,183 (1978); *Harmon v. Commr.*, 13 TC 373, Dec. 17,196 (1949).

[136] *Bagnol v. Commr.*, 37 TCM 1038, Dec. 35,239(M) (1978).

[137] *Lamphere v. Commr.*, 70 TC 391, Dec. 35,183 (1978).

[138] *Lutz v. Commr.*, CA-6, 79-1 USTC ¶ 9258, 593 F.2d 45 (rev'g and rem'g 35 TCM 661, Dec. 33,812(M)).

.04 *Time of Deduction of Casualty Losses*

Generally, casualty losses are deducted in the year of the casualty event. However, an exception exists for casualty losses for which there is a claim for reimbursement. In such case, the loss cannot be deducted (for the portion expected to be reimbursed) until it can be determined with reasonable certainty, whether or not the reimbursement will be received.[139]

> **Example 6-17.** Dixon Brothers' business automobile was totally destroyed by fire in November 2000. Its adjusted basis at that date was $14,000. As of December 31, 2000, the partnership had an outstanding claim against its insurer of $12,500. In February 2001, the partnership settled the claim for $11,250. The partnership has a $1,500 loss in 2000, and an additional $1,250 loss in 2001.

.05 *Amount of the Casualty Loss*

The amount of the casualty loss deduction for business property depends on whether the property is totally or only partly destroyed. If the property is totally destroyed, the loss is equal to the adjusted basis of the property at the time of the casualty event, less any insurance reimbursement. However, for partial business casualty losses, the deduction is limited to the lesser of:[140]

1. The adjusted basis of the property; or

2. The decline in fair market value of the property.

> **Example 6-18.** Assume the same facts as in Example 6-17, except that the automobile was only partly destroyed, and that the fair market value was $18,000 before the fire, but only $6,000 afterward. The insurance company settled the claim in December for $4,200. The casualty loss deduction is the decline in fair market value of $12,000 (since this is less than the $18,000 adjusted basis), reduced by the insurance recovery of $4,200, or $7,800.

.06 *Aggregation of Property for Computing Loss*

Trade or business losses are determined by reference to single, identifiable items of damaged property. For example, damage to ornamental trees and shrubs is computed separately from any loss to the building.[141]

.07 *Disaster Losses*

To give relief to taxpayers (who after a disaster loss may have severe cash flow needs), Congress enacted an election permitting taxpayers to deduct the casualty loss in the year immediately *before* the year of the

---

[139] Reg. § 1.165-1(d)(2)(i).
[140] Reg. § 1.165-7(b)(1). Note that the rules for personal use casualty losses are more strict: the computed loss must be reduced by both a $100 floor per casualty and by 10 percent of adjusted gross income.

[141] Reg. § 1.165-7(b)(2)(i).

disaster.[142] The disaster must have been such as to warrant assistance by the Federal Government under the Disaster Relief and Emergency Assistance Act (i.e., the area must have been declared a Federal Disaster Area).[143]

---

[142] Code Sec. 165(i)(1).   [143] *Id.*

Chapter 7

Tax Credits

¶ 701   Introduction

Part IV of Chapter One of subtitle A of the Internal Revenue Code breaks down credits into seven subparts. Five of the subparts involve credits while the other two subparts provide rules for computing two of the credits. The five subparts are:

Subpart	Code Section	Type of Credit
A		Nonrefundable Personal Credits
	21	Expenses for household and dependent care services necessary for gainful employment
	22	Credit for the elderly and permanently and totally disabled
	23	Credit for adoption expenses
	24	Child tax credit
	25	Interest on certain home mortgages
	25A	Hope and lifetime learning credits
	25B	Credit for elective deferrals and IRA contributions by certain individuals
B		Foreign Tax Credit, Etc.
	27	Taxes of foreign countries and possessions of the United States; possession tax credit
	29	Credit for producing fuel from a nonconventional source
	30	Credit for qualified electric vehicles
	30A	Puerto Rico Economic Activity Credit
C		Refundable Credits
	31	Tax withheld on wages
	32	Earned income
	33	Tax withheld at source on nonresident aliens and foreign corporations
	34	Certain uses of gasoline and special fuels
D	38	General Business Credit, consisting of:
	40	Alcohol used as fuel
	41	Credit for increasing research activities
	42	Low-income housing credit
	43	Enhanced oil recovery credit
	44	Disabled access credit

Subpart	Code Section	Type of Credit
	45	Renewable electricity production credit
	45A	Indian employment credit
	45B	Employer Social Security credit
	45C	Orphan drug credit
	45D	Markets tax credit
	45E	Small employer pension plan start-up cost credit
	45F	Employer-provided child care credit
	1396	Empowerment zone employment credit
E	46	Investment credit
F	51	Work opportunity credit
	51A	Welfare-to-work credit
G		Credit Against Regular Tax for Prior Year Minimum Tax Liability
	53	Credit for prior year minimum tax liability

Personal tax credits are not covered in this book. Instead, attention is directed to credits that could be incurred by a business, be it a sole proprietorship, partnership, or corporation. Since the credits listed in Subpart D, the general business credits, comprise the vast majority of credits available to a business, those general business credits most likely to be available to a small business are discussed.

¶ 703   General Business Credits

The general business credit may not exceed the sum of the regular tax plus the alternative minimum tax (AMT) less the credits allowable under Subparts A and B, less the greater of: (1) the tentative minimum tax or (2) 25 percent of the net regular tax liability (i.e., regular tax liability reduced by the credits allowable under Subparts A and B) in excess of $25,000.[1]

Effective for tax years beginning after December 31, 1997, unused general business credits are carried back one year and forward 20 years.[2] However, the new small employer pension plan start-up cost credit may not be carried back to a taxable year beginning before January 1, 2002.[3] Prior to 1998, the carryover provisions for the general business credit were back three years and forward 15 years. If any portion of the business credits determined for any tax year remains unused at the end of the carryover period, the unused credits are allowed as a deduction for the first tax year following the last tax year in the carryover period.[4] If a taxpayer dies or

---

[1] Code Sec. 38(c)(1).
[2] Code Sec. 39(a).
[3] Act Sec. 619(c)(1), Economic Growth and Tax Relief Reconciliation Act of 2001, adding Code Sec. 39(d)(10).

[4] Code Sec. 196(a).

ceases to exist before the end of the carryover period, any unused credits are allowed as a deduction for the tax year in which death or cessation occurs.[5] The deduction for unused investment credits is limited to 50 percent of the unused credits. However, the 50 percent limitation does not apply to the rehabilitation credit, or to unused research credits for a tax year before 1990.[6]

If there is more than one business credit, and if the total exceeds the limitation, the credits are used in the following order:[7]

1. Investment tax credit;

2. Work opportunity credit;

3. Welfare-to-work credit;

4. Alcohol fuels credit;

5. Research credit;

6. Low-income housing credit;

7. Enhanced oil recovery credit;

8. Disabled access credit;

9. Renewable electricity credit;

10. Empowerment zone employment credit;

11. Indian employment credit;

12. Employer Social Security credit;

13. Orphan drug credit;

14. New markets tax credit;

15. Small employer pension plan start-up cost credit;

16. Employer-provided child care credit.

¶ 705 Alcohol Fuels Credit

The alcohol fuels credit is actually the sum of three credits: the alcohol mixture credit, plus the alcohol credit, plus in the case of an eligible small ethanol producer, the small ethanol producer credit.[8] The alcohol mixture credit is for each gallon of blended fuel which is either sold by the taxpayer producing the mixture in the course of trade or business to any person for use as a fuel, or is used by the taxpayer producing the mixture in a trade or business.[9]

---

[5] Code Sec. 196(b).
[6] Code Sec. 196(d).
[7] Code Secs. 38(d)(1) and 51A(d)(2).

[8] Code Sec. 40(a).

[9] Code Sec. 40(b)(1).

The alcohol credit is for each gallon of straight alcohol fuel which is either used by the taxpayer as a fuel in a trade or business or is sold at retail and placed in the fuel tank of the purchaser. The credit is reduced for alcohol with a proof of at least 150 but less than 190.[10]

The credit terminates for any period after December 31, 2007. The credit also terminates for any period before January 1, 2008, during which the rates of tax under section 4081(a)(2)(A) are 4.3 cents per gallon.[11]

To qualify as "alcohol," the fuel must have a proof of at least 150 and must not be made from petroleum, natural gas, or coal (including peat). Both methanol and ethanol qualify.[12]

¶707   Credit for Increasing Research Activities

A credit is allowed for certain qualifying research expenditures paid or incurred not later than June 30, 2004.[13] However, there were two suspension periods (July 1, 1999 to September 30, 2000; and October 1, 2000 to September 30, 2001).[14]

A 20 percent credit is permitted for two types of research expenditures: qualified research expenses and, for C corporations only, basic research payments.[15]

If the credit is taken, the deduction for research and experimental expenditures provided by Code Sec. 174 is reduced by the amount of the credit.[16] If the amount of the research expense credit exceeds the amount allowable as a deduction for qualified research expenses, the amount chargeable to capital account for such expenses must be reduced by the excess.[17]

There are two ways to compute the research credit: the standard computation, and a new elective alternative computation. Under the standard method, the credit for qualified research expenses applies only to the excess of the current year's expenses over the base amount.[18]

The "base amount" consists of the average annual gross receipts for the four preceding taxable years times the "fixed-base percentage."[19] In general, the "fixed-base percentage" is the percentage which the total qualified research expenses for the years 1984-1988 is of the total gross receipts for those taxable years.[20] However, the fixed-base percentage is computed differently for "start-up" companies. A "start-up" company is a company that either:[21]

---

[10] Code Sec. 40(b)(2).

[11] Code Sec. 40(e).

[12] Code Sec. 40(d)(1).

[13] Code Sec. 41(h).

[14] Act Sec. 502(d), Tax Relief Extension Act of 1999.

[15] Code Sec. 41(a).

[16] Code Sec. 280C(c)(1).

[17] Code Sec. 280C(c)(2).

[18] Code Sec. 41(a)(1).

[19] Code Sec. 41(c)(1).

[20] Code Sec. 41(c)(3)(A).

[21] Act Sec. 1204(b), Small Business Job Protection Act, amending Code Sec. 41(c)(3)(B).

- Began its first taxable year with both gross receipts and qualified research expenses after December 31, 1983; or

- Did not have both gross receipts and research expenditures during at least three years in the 1984-1988 period.

The fixed-base percentage for start-up companies is three percent for the first five taxable years beginning after December 31, 1983, in which the taxpayer has qualified research expenses.[22] For the sixth taxable year, it is $1/6$ of the percentage which the aggregate qualified research expenses for the 4th and 5th such taxable years is of the aggregate gross receipts of the taxpayer for such years. In the seventh year, it is $1/3$ of the percentage which the aggregate qualified research expenses for the 5th and 6th such taxable years is of the aggregate gross receipts of the taxpayer for such years. In the eighth year, it is $1/2$ of the percentage which the aggregate qualified research expenses for the 5th, 6th, and 7th such taxable years is of the aggregate gross receipts of the taxpayer for such years. In the ninth year, it is $2/3$ of the percentage which the aggregate qualified research expenses for the 5th, 6th, 7th, and 8th such taxable years is of the aggregate gross receipts of the taxpayer for such years. In the tenth year, it is $5/6$ of the percentage which the aggregate qualified research expenses for the 5th, 6th, 7th, 8th, and 9th such taxable years is of the aggregate gross receipts of the taxpayer for such years. Thereafter, it is the percentage which the aggregate qualified research expenses for any five taxable years selected by the taxpayer from among the 5th through the 10th such taxable years is of the aggregate gross receipts of the taxpayer for such selected years.[23]

Special rules exist for short-period taxable years.[24] In computing the credit for increasing research activities for taxable years beginning after December 31, 1989, qualified research expenses and gross receipts taken into account in computing a taxpayer's fixed-base percentage and a taxpayer's base amount must be determined on a basis consistent with the definition of qualified research expenses and gross receipts for the credit year, without regard to the law in effect for the taxable years taken into account in computing the fixed-base percentage or the base amount.[25]

New organizations would have zero base period expenses. The Internal Revenue Code, however, prevents new businesses from taking undue advantage. The minimum base amount is 50 percent of the current year's qualified research expenses.[26]

The alternative method of computing the research credit is elective. Once made, the election is applicable to that and all subsequent tax years unless the IRS agrees to a revocation.[27]

---

[22] Code Sec. 41(c)(3)(B)(ii).
[23] Id.
[24] See Reg. § 1.41-3(b).
[25] Code Sec. 41(c)(5); Reg. § 1.41-3(d)(1).

[26] Code Sec. 41(c)(2).

[27] Act Sec. 1204(c), Small Business Job Protection Act, amending Code Sec. 41(c)(4)(B).

The alternative computation of the research credit is equal to the sum of three tiers of credits:[28]

Tier 1 credit: 2.65 percent of qualified research expenses for the tax year as exceeds 1 percent of the four-year average of gross receipts described in Code Sec. 41(c)(1)(B), but not in excess of 1.5 percent of that average;

Tier 2 credit: 3.2 percent of qualified research expenses for the tax year as exceeds 1.5 percent of that average but does not exceed two percent of that average; and

Tier 3 credit: 3.75 percent of qualified research expenses for the tax year as exceeds two percent of that average.

"Qualified research expenses" may be incurred as in-house research expenses or as contract research expenses, but, in any event, they must:

- Be paid or incurred in carrying on a trade or business;

- Qualify to be expensed under Code Sec. 174;

- Be undertaken for the purpose of discovering information which is technological in nature, the application of which is intended to be useful in the development of a new or improved "business component" of the taxpayer; and

- Substantially all of the activities of which constitute elements of a process of experimentation that relates to a new or improved function, performance, or reliability or quality.[29] Regulations state that research qualifies for the credit only if it is undertaken to obtain knowledge that exceeds, expands, or refines the common knowledge of skilled professionals in a particular field of science or engineering.[30] However, one court has rejected this regulation as being contrary to the intent of Congress, stating that "[t]he purpose of the 'technology' requirement of § 41 is to eliminate the 'soft sciences' from contention for the credit, not to focus on the word 'discovery'."[31] The substantially all requirement is satisfied only if 80 percent or more of the research activities, measured on a cost or other consistently applied reasonable basis constitute elements of a process of experimentation for a qualified purpose. The substantially all requirement is applied separately to each business component.[32] The IRS has delayed the effective date of Reg. § 1.41-4.[33]

---

[28] Act Sec. 1204(c), Small Business Job Protection Act, amending Code Sec. 41(c)(4).

[29] Code Sec. 41(b)(1), and (d)(1) and (3); Reg. § 1.41-4(a)(2).

[30] Reg. § 1.41-4(a)(3)(i).

[31] *Tax and Accounting Software Corporation, et al. v. U.S.,* 2000-2 USTC ¶ 50,672 (N. Dist., Oklahoma, 2000).

[32] Reg. § 1.41-4(a)(6).

[33] IRS Notice 2001-19, 2001-10 IRB 784.

A process of experimentation in the physical or biological sciences, engineering, or computer science may involve:[34]

- Developing one or more hypotheses designed to achieve the intended result;

- Designing an experiment (that, where appropriate to the particular field of research, is intended to be replicable with an established experimental control) to test and analyze those hypotheses (through, for example, modeling, simulation, or a systematic trial and error methodology);

- Conducting the experiment; and

- Refining or discarding the hypotheses as part of a sequential design process to develop or improve the business component.

Expenses paid or incurred prior to commencing a new business (as distinguished from expanding an existing business) may be paid or incurred in connection with a trade or business but are not paid or incurred in carrying on a trade or business. Thus, research expenses paid or incurred by a taxpayer in developing a product the sale of which would constitute a new trade or business for the taxpayer are not paid or incurred in carrying on a trade or business.[35] The trade or business requirement is disregarded in the case of in-house research expenses if, at the time such expenses are paid or incurred, the principal purpose of the taxpayer in making such expenditures is to use the results of the research in the active conduct of a future trade or business of the taxpayer.[36]

The term "business component" means any product, process, computer software, technique, formula, or invention which is either:[37]

- Held for sale, lease, or license; or

- Used by the taxpayer in a trade or business of the taxpayer.

Any plant process, machinery, or technique for commercial production of a business component is treated as a separate business component rather than as part of the business component being produced.[38]

"In-house research expenses" consist of:[39]

- Any wages paid or incurred to an employee for qualified services performed by such employee;

- Any amount paid or incurred for "supplies" used in the conduct of qualified research; or

---

[34] Reg. § 1.41-4(a)(5).
[35] Reg. § 1.41-2(a)(2).
[36] Code Sec. 41(b)(4).

[37] Code Sec. 41(d)(2).
[38] *Id.*
[39] Code Sec. 41(b)(2).

- Any amount paid or incurred to another person for the right to use computers in the conduct of qualified research (except to the extent that the taxpayer receives any amount from any person for the right to use substantially identical personal purpose).

"Supplies" consist of tangible personal property except for land and land improvements and depreciable property.[40] Generally, utilities are considered a selling and administration expense. However, to the extent that electricity expenses are extraordinary (e.g., laser or nuclear research), it may be treated as a research expense.[41]

"Contract research expenses" are amounts paid to persons who are not employees of the taxpayer. Only 65 percent of contract research expenses are eligible for the credit.[42] However, effective for tax years beginning after June 30, 1996, 75 percent of amounts paid to a qualified research consortium is eligible for the credit.[43] A "qualified research consortium" is a tax-exempt organization that is organized primarily to conduct scientific research.[44] Prepaid contract research expenses are deductible in the year that the qualified research is conducted.[45] For purposes of Code Sec. 41, a contract research expense of the taxpayer is not a qualified research expense if the product or result of the research is intended to be transferred to another in return for license or royalty payments and the taxpayer does not use the product of the research in the taxpayer's trade or business.[46]

Certain activities are not eligible for the credit. Excluded are the following:[47]

1. Research relating to style, taste, cosmetic, or seasonal design factors;

2. Research conducted *after* commercial production is begun;

3. Research related to the adaptation of an existing business component to a particular customer's requirement or need;

4. Research related to the reproduction of an existing business component (in whole or in part) from a physical examination of the business component itself or from plans, blueprints, detailed specifications, or publicly available information with respect to such business component;

5. Any of the following types of surveys or studies:

   a. Efficiency surveys;

   b. Activities related to management functions or techniques;

---

[40] Code Sec. 41(b)(2)(C).
[41] Reg. § 1.41-2(b)(2).
[42] Code Sec. 41(b)(3).
[43] Act Sec. 1204(d), Small Business Job Protection Act, amending Code Sec. 41(b)(3)(C).
[44] *Id.*
[45] Code Sec. 41(b)(3)(B).
[46] Reg. § 1.41-2(a)(1).
[47] Code Sec. 41(d)(3)(B) and (4); Reg. § 1.41-4(c).

    c. Market research, testing, or development (including advertising or promotions);

    d. Routine data collection; and

    e. Routine or ordinary testing or inspection for quality control;

6. Research on computer software which is developed by or for the benefit of the taxpayer primarily for internal use by the taxpayer (however, software developed for a qualified research activity or software developed for a production process which is a qualified research activity will be eligible for the credit); costs incurred in merely adapting or modifying existing programs do not qualify for the credit; development of software for internal use in general functions (e.g., accounting or personnel) is not eligible for the credit);

7. Research conducted outside the United States;

8. Any research in the arts, humanities, or social sciences; and

9. Research to the extent funded by any grant, contract, or otherwise by another person or governmental entity.

The following activities are deemed to occur after the beginning of commercial production of a business component:[48]

- Preproduction planning for a finished business component;

- Tooling-up for production;

- Trial production runs;

- Troubleshooting involving detecting faults in production equipment or processes;

- Accumulating data relating to production processes; and

- Debugging flaws in a business component.

.01 Basic Research Expenditures

"Basic research payments" are amounts paid in *cash* by a C corporation pursuant to a written agreement to a "qualified organization."[49] The qualified organization must itself perform the research unless it is a scientific, tax-exempt organization or is a certain grant organization.[50]

"Qualified organizations" are:[51]

- Educational institutions;

- Certain scientific research organizations;

---

[48] Reg. § 1.41-4(c)(2)(ii).
[49] Code Sec. 41(e)(2).
[50] *Id.*
[51] Code Sec. 41(e)(6).

- Scientific tax-exempt organizations; and

- Certain grant organizations.

The key to obtaining the credit is the conducting of basic research. The term means original investigation for the advancement of scientific knowledge which does not have a specific commercial objective. Basic research does *not* include research done outside the United States or research in the social sciences, arts, or humanities.[52]

A 20 percent credit can be taken for the excess of the basic research expenditures over the sum of:[53]

- The minimum basic research amount; plus

- The maintenance-of-effort amount.

The "minimum basic research amount" is the greater of:[54]

- One percent of the average of the sum of the amounts paid or incurred during the base period (the three years immediately preceding the current year) for any in-house research expenses and any contract research expenses; or

- The amount of basic research expense treated as contract research expense during the base period.

However, there is a floor amount for basic research. The minimum basic research amount is never less than 50 percent of the current year's basic research payment.[55]

The "maintenance-of-effort amount" is the excess of:[56]

- The average of the "nondesignated university contributions" paid during the base period, times the cost of living adjustment for the calendar year, over

- The amount of nondesignated university contributions paid during the current tax year.

"Nondesignated university contributions" are amounts paid to an educational institution qualified organization for which a charitable deduction is allowable.[57] The purpose of the maintenance-of-effort amount is to prevent corporations from reducing their normal contributions to universities and substituting basic research payments.

Note: Any basic research payment that does not exceed the sum of the minimum basic research amount and the maintenance-of-effort amount may be treated as contract research expenses (and is therefore eligible for the incremental qualified research expenditures).[58]

---

[52] Code Sec. 41(e)(7)(A).
[53] Code Sec. 41(a)(2), and (e)(1) and (3).
[54] Code Sec. 41(e)(4) and (7)(B).
[55] Code Sec. 41(e)(4)(B).

[56] Code Sec. 41(e)(5).
[57] Code Sec. 41(e)(5)(B).
[58] Code Sec. 41(e)(1)(B).

Example 7-1. The 2-N Company made basic research payments to Iowa State University of $200,000 in 1993, $250,000 in 1994, $250,000 in 1995, and $300,000 in 1996. The company also made nondesignated contributions to Iowa State of $50,000, $50,000, $40,000, and $20,000 during those years. During the same period, the 2-N Company spent on in-house research and contract research the amounts of $1,000,000, $1,100,000, $1,500,000, and $2,000,000, respectively. The cost of living adjustment for 1996 was determined to be five percent. The minimum basic research amount is the greater of:

- 0.01 (($1,000,000 + $1,100,000 + $1,500,000)/3) = $12,000; or

- $300,000 × 0.50 = $150,000

Thus, the minimum basic research amount is $150,000.

The maintenance-of-effort amount is (($50,000 + $50,000 + $40,000)/3) × 1.05 = $49,000; $49,000 − $20,000 = $29,000. Thus, the credit for basic research is 0.20 ($250,000 − $150,000 − $29,000) = $14,200.

The incremental research credit is based on the $2,000,000 spent plus the unused basic research amount of $179,000, or a total of $2,179,000. Subtracted from this amount is the base period expenditure of $1,200,000 (($1,000,000 + $1,100,000 + $1,500,000) divided by 3. Hence the incremental expenditure is $2,179,000 − $1,200,000 = $979,000. The incremental credit is $195,800. The total research credit is $210,000 ($14,200 + $195,800).

The research credit does flow through to individual taxpayers. However, a limitation is placed on the individual taxpayer who:[59]

- Owns an interest in an unincorporated business;

- Is a partner in a partnership;

- Is a beneficiary of an estate or trust; or

- Is a shareholder of an S corporation.

The credit cannot exceed the tax attributable to the portion of a person's taxable income attributable to the interest in the business. In no case could the amount exceed the limitations on general business credits as a whole. Unused amounts may be carried back one year or carried forward 20 years.[60]

Example 7-2. Todd Winvex, an individual taxpayer, had taxable income of $80,000 in 2001 and a before-credits tax of $21,923. Included in taxable income is $8,000 from an S corporation that also generated research credits, of which his share was $4,000. He may use

---

[59] Code Sec. 41(g).   [60] *Id.*

only $2,192 (($8,000/$80,000) × $21,923) of the credit. The unused amount is carried back one year or carried forward to the next year.

All trades or businesses (whether or not incorporated) that are under common control are treated as a single taxpayer, and the credit to each is its proportionate share of the increase in qualified research giving rise to the credit.[61] "Control" exists where the requirements of Reg. § 1.52-1(b)-(g) are met.[62]

Example 7-3. Andrea Johnson owns control of the J-K partnership and two corporations, J Co. and K, Inc. Their research expenses are as follows:

Current Year	Base Period	Current Year	Increase (Decrease)
J-K	$200,000	$280,000	$80,000
J Co.	$100,000	$120,000	$20,000
K, Inc.	$150,000	$100,000	($50,000)
Total	$450,000	$500,000	$50,000

The aggregate increase in research expenses is $50,000.

Therefore, the credit is $10,000, $8,000 of which is allocated to J-K (($80,000/$100,000) × $10,000), and $2,000 of which is allocated to J Co. (($20,000/$100,000) × $10,000).

.02 Reporting Requirements

The credit is claimed on Form 6765, "Credit for Increasing Research Activities." As previously mentioned, the credit is part of the general business credit and is subject to the limit imposed on general business credits.

¶ 709   Low-Income Housing Credit

As previously mentioned, the low-income housing credit is part of the general business credit. Hence, it is subject to the limitation and carrybacks and carryforwards discussed in ¶ 703. The credit had been scheduled to expire at the end of 1991, but The Revenue Reconciliation Act of 1993 removed the expiration.[63] Some unique aspects of the low-income housing credit are:

- The basis for depreciation is *not* reduced by the credit; and

- The credit will be a "passive activity credit" (Code Sec. 469) and thus subject to limitation or disallowance for individuals, closely held C corporations, or personal service corporations. The deduction equivalency of the credit may be taken up to $25,000 for individuals with low-income housing if AGI is not

---

[61] Code Sec. 41(f)(1).
[62] Reg. § 1.41-6(a)(3).

[63] Act Sec. 13142(a)(1), Revenue Reconciliation Act of 1993, striking Code Sec. 42(o).

more than $200,000. The credit is phased out for AGI between $200,000 and $250,000.

The credit may be taken for a certain percentage of the cost of constructing new or rehabilitating certain low-income housing projects. The credit is equal to the applicable percentage times the qualified basis of each qualified low-income building.[64]

A "qualified low-income building" is a building that at all times during the compliance period is part of a qualified low-income housing project.[65] In turn, a "qualified low-income housing project" means any project for residential rental property provided that one of the following two tests is met:[66]

1.   At least 20 percent of the residential units are both "rent restricted" and occupied by individuals whose income is not more than 50 percent of the area median gross income; or

2.   At least 40 percent of the residential units are both rent restricted and occupied by individuals whose income is 60 percent or less of area median gross income.

The election to use one of the above tests, once made, is irrevocable.

"Rent-restricted units" are those units where the "gross rent" does not exceed 30 percent of the income level (50 percent or 60 percent of the area median gross income) selected.[67] Gross rent does not include rental assistance programs, but does include any utility allowance determined under regulations.[68] If the tenant's income increases so that it is above the 50 percent or 60 percent test, whichever is applicable, the unit may still be treated as a rent-restricted unit if the unit continues to be rent-restricted. However, if the tenant's income rises above 140 percent of the income limit, the next comparable unit must be rented to someone whose income is below the limitation.[69]

Generally, a building will be treated as a qualified low-income building if the project of which the building is a part meets the rent restriction and low-income resident requirements by the end of the 12-month period in which the building is placed into service.[70] If the first building placed into service does not itself meet the requirements, other buildings placed into service *after* the first building may be counted to see if the project qualifies only if the later buildings meet the requirements within 12 months after the first building is placed into service.[71]

Eligibility is not affected merely because an occupant of a residential unit voluntarily pays a *de minimis* amount toward the purchase of the unit if all amounts paid are refunded to the tenant if he or she should move out

---

[64] Code Sec. 42(a).
[65] Code Sec. 42(c)(2).
[66] Code Sec. 42(g)(1).
[67] Code Sec. 42(g)(2)(A).

[68] Code Sec. 42(g)(2)(B).
[69] Code Sec. 42(g)(2)(D).
[70] Code Sec. 42(g)(3)(A).
[71] Code Sec. 42(g)(3)(B).

and if purchase is not permitted until after the close of the compliance period. The amounts paid toward equity must be included in gross rents for purposes of determining if the rent restriction requirement is met.[72]

.01 Qualified Basis

As previously mentioned, the base for determining the credit is the qualified basis. "Qualified basis" is the portion of the "eligible basis" that is allocable to qualified low-income buildings.[73] Allocation is determined by taking the lower of the unit fraction (the fraction of units which is low-income units) or the floor space fraction (the fraction of total floor space of the residential units occupied by low-income units).[74]

Example 7-4. A newly constructed building with 20 units and 180,000 square feet devoted to rental apartments has 12 units totaling 95,000 square feet which are rented to low-income tenants. The building cost $1,000,000. The qualified basis is $1,000,000 times the lesser of:

- 12/20 = 0.60; or

- 95,000/180,000 = 0.52778.

Thus, the qualified basis is $527,780.

The "eligible basis" of a new building is its adjusted basis as of the end of the first year of the credit period.[75] The eligible basis of an existing building also is its adjusted basis as of the dose of the first year of the credit period if the building was acquired by purchase, at least 10 years have elapsed since the building was last placed in service or the date of its most recent nonqualified substantial improvement, and the building was not previously placed in service by the taxpayer or any person related to the taxpayer at the time previously placed in service. Otherwise, the eligible basis of an existing building is zero.[76]

Relationship generally is determined under Code Sec. 267(b) or 707(b)(1) (substituting "10 percent" for "50 percent").[77] The requirement that at least 10 years elapse since the building was last placed in service or its most recent nonqualified substantial improvement may be waived by the IRS if it determines such a waiver is necessary to avert an assignment of the mortgage to HUD or the Farmers Home Administration or to avert a claim against a federal mortgage insurance fund.[78] "Substantial improvements" are capital improvements made within any 24-month period if the costs are at least 25 percent of the adjusted basis (determined without regard to depreciation) of the building as of the first day of the 24-month period.[79] A substantial improvement is a "nonqualified substantial improvement" if Code Sec. 167(k) (as in effect on November 4, 1990) was

---

[72] Code Sec. 42(g)(6).
[73] Code Sec. 42(c)(1)(A).
[74] Code Sec. 42(c)(1)(B) and (C).
[75] Code Sec. 42(d)(1).

[76] Code Sec. 42(d)(2)(A) and (D).
[77] Code Sec. 42(d)(2)(D)(iii)(II).
[78] Code Sec. 42(d)(6)(A).
[79] Code Sec. 42(d)(2)(D)(i).

elected with respect to the improvement or the improvement was depreciated under ACRS.[80]

If the building contains non-low-income units which are above the average quality standards of the low-income units, the eligible basis of the building must be reduced. The reduction is equal to the portion of the adjusted basis which is attributable to those non-low-income units.[81] However, if the cost per square foot of the non-low-income units does not exceed 115 percent of the cost of the low-income units, the taxpayer need not apply the reduction if the excess cost is excluded from the eligible basis of the building.[82]

The eligible basis of a building has to be adjusted as follows:[83]

- Decreased by the portion of any grant funded by federal funds; and

- Decreased by any cost for which an election was made to amortize rehabilitation expenses as provided by Code Sec. 167(k) as in effect before November 5, 1990.

If the building is purchased by a second taxpayer before the end of the first taxpayer's compliance period, the second taxpayer is not entitled to a new credit, but instead succeeds to the remaining credit which would have been available to the first taxpayer.[84]

For purposes of determining when a building was last placed into service, the following acquisitions are not counted as a placement into service:[85]

- Where the basis is a carryover basis (in whole or in part);

- If the property was acquired from a decedent;

- If it was acquired from a government or from a nonprofit institution whose acquisition of the property was at least 10 years after it was placed into service and all income from the property is exempt from federal taxation;

- By any person who acquired it by foreclosure of any purchase-money security interest held by that person at least 10 years after it was placed into service if the property is resold within 12 months after the date that the person foreclosing it placed it into service;

- Of a single family residence by an individual who owned and used the residence only as his or her principal residence.

---

[80] Code Sec. 42(d)(2)(D)(i).
[81] Code Sec. 42(d)(3)(A).
[82] Code Sec. 42(d)(3)(B).

[83] Code Sec. 42(d)(5).
[84] Code Sec. 42(d)(7).
[85] Code Sec. 42(d)(2)(D)(ii).

.02 Applicable Percentage

For qualified low-income buildings placed into service after 1987, "applicable percentage" means the appropriate percentage determined by the IRS for the earlier of:[86]

- The month in which the building is placed into service; or

- At the election of the taxpayer, the month in which the taxpayer and the housing credit agency enter into a binding agreement as to the housing credit amount to be allocated to the building; or

- In the case of a building financed by tax-exempt bonds (Code Sec. 42(h)(4)), the month in which the bonds are issued.

The credit percentage is over twice as much for units that are *not* federally subsidized as for the units which receive a federal subsidy. For nonsubsidized buildings, the credit rate is computed so that the present value of the 10 annual credit amounts equals 70 percent of the qualified basis. The comparable credit rate for subsidized buildings is set so that the present value of the 10 annual credit amounts equals only 30 percent of the qualified basis.[87]

The credit with respect to any building for the first tax year of the credit period is limited to that computed for the full year multiplied by the number of months over 12 in which the building was in service. Any credit disallowed because of the application of the partial year fraction is allowed in the 11th year of the credit period.[88]

If the qualified basis increases after the close of the first year of the credit period, the applicable percentage that applies to the increase in qualified basis is two-thirds of the applicable percentage that would otherwise be used. This two-thirds rule applies to all remaining years in the credit period.[89]

.03 Limitation on Total Credit

The total credit available is limited for each state to $1.25 times the population of the state.[90] However, the limitation does not apply to the portion of any credit attributable to eligible basis financed by exempt state or local bonds which are subject to the volume cap on private activity bonds provided by Code Sec. 146. The principal payments on the debt are also required to be applied within a reasonable period to redeem obligations, the proceeds of which were used to provide such financing.[91]

The appropriate state agency (usually the housing agency) allocates the state credit to individual taxpayers. Therefore, the credit can be taken

---

[86] Code Sec. 42(b)(2)(A).
[87] Code Sec. 42(b)(2)(B).
[88] Code Sec. 42(f)(2).

[89] Code Sec. 42(f)(3).
[90] Code Sec. 42(h)(3)(C).
[91] Code Sec. 42(h)(4)(A).

only to the extent of such allocation.[92] Generally, the allocation must be made by the close of the calendar year in which the asset is placed into service.[93] There are, however, three exceptions:[94]

1. If by the close of the calendar year that the asset is placed into service the state agency has made a binding commitment to allocate a specified credit amount to a later year, then the credit is allowed;

2. If there is an increase in the qualified basis, the credit is allowed beginning in the year in which the increase occurred; and

3. If the taxpayer's basis in a project at the end of a year exceeds 10 percent of the reasonably expected basis, the credit may be taken starting that year. The expenditure must involve either new construction or a substantial rehabilitation.

Even though the credit will be taken over a 10-year period, once the state agency grants credit, it cannot be retracted.[95]

.04 Rehabilitation Expenditures

Rehabilitation expenditures paid or incurred for a building are treated as a separate new building.[96] However, the qualified basis attributable to such expenditures, when divided by the low-income units in the building, must be at least $3,000. The computation of the average rehabilitation expenditures per unit is made as of the close of the first tax year of the credit period.[97] "Rehabilitation expenditures" are defined as capitalizable amounts incurred for property (or additions or improvements to property) subject to depreciation.[98] The term *does not* include the acquisition cost of the property nor does it include the portion of the property which is not residential rental property or the eligible portion reduced because of above-average cost of non-low-income units.[99]

If the rehabilitation expenditures are treated as a separate building, the expenditures are considered placed into service at the close of the 24-month period in which the average expenditures per unit are determined. The applicable fraction (discussed previously) is used to determine the qualified portion of eligible basis.[100]

.05 Credit Period

The term "credit period" means the 10-year period beginning with the tax year in which the building is placed into service. However, the taxpayer may elect to use the next tax year if the building is a qualified low-income building as of the first year of such period.[101]

---

[92] Code Sec. 42(h)(1)(A).
[93] Code Sec. 42(h)(1)(B).
[94] Code Sec. 42(h)(1)(C), (D), and (E).
[95] Code Sec. 42(h)(2)(A).
[96] Code Sec. 42(e)(1).

[97] Code Sec. 42(e)(3).
[98] Code Sec. 42(e)(2)(A).
[99] Code Sec. 42(e)(2)(B).
[100] Code Sec. 42(e)(4).
[101] Code Sec. 42(f)(1).

.06 Recapture of Credit

Recapture occurs in any tax year in the "compliance period" in which the qualified basis is less at the end of the year than at the start of the year.[102] A reduction could occur in qualified basis if there is a reduction in the number of low-income units in the building. A total credit recapture amount results if:

- The taxpayer disposes of the property;

- The project no longer has sufficient rent-restricted units;

- The project fails to meet either the 20-50 test or the 40-60 test (Code Sec. 42(g)(1)); or

- Financing is obtained from either federal subsidies or from the proceeds of tax-exempt bonds.

Not only must the credit be recaptured, but interest at the overpayment rate must also be paid from the due date of the return in which the credit was paid. The interest is not deductible.[103] To the extent that the credit did not reduce the tax in the year in which the credit was allowed because of either the general business credit limitation, or because the credit exceeded the tax due, the credit need not be recaptured. Instead, the carryover is reduced.[104]

The "credit recapture amount" is the total decrease in the credit which would have resulted if the accelerated portion of the credit were not allowed, plus the interest previously discussed.[105] The "accelerated portion of the credit" is the excess of the total credit allowed over the prior tax years over the credit which would have been allowed if the credit were taken equally over the 15-year period.[106] If there has been no previous recapture, the recapture is:

Year of Recapture	Portion Recaptured
2-11	one-third
12	four-fifteenths
13	one-fifth
14	two-fifteenths
15	one-fifteenth

Example 7-5. In 1998, Salem Construction Co. placed into service a qualified low-income housing project. The project qualified under the 40-60 rule and 50 percent of the units were low-income units. However, by the end of 2001, the percentage of units occupied by tenants with income below 60 percent of the median for the area had dropped to 30 percent. Hence, one-third of the credit taken must be recaptured.

---

[102] Code Sec. 42(j)(1).
[103] Code Sec. 42(j)(2)(B).
[104] Code Sec. 42(j)(4)(A).

[105] Code Sec. 42(j)(2)(A).
[106] Code Sec. 42(j)(3).

.07 Certification Requirements

By the 90th day after the end of the first tax year of the credit period, the taxpayer must certify on Form 8609, "Low-Income Housing Allocation Certification," the following information:[107]

- The tax year, i.e., the calendar year in which the building was placed into service;

- Both the adjusted basis and the eligible basis of the building at the close of the first year of the credit period;

- Authorization from the credit agency of the maximum applicable percentage and qualified basis permitted to be taken into account;

- The election under Code Sec. 42(g) which is used to qualify (the 20-50 test or the 40-60 test); and

- Any other information that the IRS may require.

.08 Reporting Requirements

Form 8609, "Low-Income Housing Credit Allocation Certification," must be used to obtain a housing credit allocation from the housing credit agency. Part I must be filled out by the authorized housing agency for the state. The computation of the credit is made on Form 8586, "Low-Income Housing Credit." Low-income housing recaptures are reported on Form 8611.

¶711 Disabled Access Credit

The disabled access credit was designed to aid small businesses that were required to modify their buildings to comply with the Americans With Disabilities Act of 1990. The credit is 50 percent of the eligible access expenditures for the taxable year that exceed $250, but do not exceed $10,250.[108] Small businesses eligible for the credit must have either had gross receipts for the preceding taxable year of not more than $1,000,000, or must have employed no more than 30 full-time employees.[109] However, the credit is not available for buildings placed into service after November 5, 1990. Presumably, most businesses have already complied with the Act and have already used the credit to the extent possible.

¶713 Indian Employment Credit

The Indian employment credit is equal to 20 percent of the excess of:[110]

1. The sum of:

   a. The "qualified wages" paid or incurred during the tax year, plus

---

[107] Code Sec. 42(l).
[108] Code Sec. 44(a)

[109] Code Sec. 44(b)
[110] Code Sec. 45A(a).

b. The qualified employee health insurance premiums paid or incurred during the tax year, over

2. The sum of the qualified wages and qualified employee health insurance premiums paid or incurred during the calendar year 1993.

"Qualified wages" are wages paid or incurred for services rendered by a "qualified employee."[111] They do not include wages for which the Work Opportunity Credit is taken.[112] "Qualified employees" are any employees if:[113]

- The employee is an enrolled member of an Indian tribe or the spouse of such;

- Substantially all of the services performed during the period by such employee are performed within an Indian reservation; and

- The principal place of abode of the employee is on or near the reservation where the services are performed.

Employees *not* eligible for the credit include:[114]

- Individuals receiving wages in excess of $30,000 (indexed for inflation for years after 1994);

- Individuals described in Code Sec. 51(i)(1);

- Any five percent owner; and

- Individuals who perform services in connection with a gaming activity.

¶ 715   Employer Social Security Tax Credit

The employer Social Security credit is the excess employer Social Security tax paid or incurred during the tax year.[115] The term "excess employer Social Security tax" is any tax paid by an employer with respect to tips received by an employee during any month, to the extent such tips:[116]

- Are deemed to have been paid by the employer; and

- Exceed the amount by which the wages (excluding tips) paid by the employer are less than the total amount which would be payable at the minimum wage rate established by the Fair Labor Standards Act.

---

[111] Code Sec. 45A(b)(1)(A).

[112] Act Sec. 1201(e), Small Business Job Protection Act, amending Code Sec. 45A(b)(1)(B).

[113] Code Sec. 45A(c).

[114] *Id.*

[115] Code Sec. 45B(a).

[116] Code Sec. 45B(b)(1).

For this purpose, only tips received at food and beverage establishments are taken into account.[117] However, effective for services performed after December 31, 1996, the credit applies as well to tips received in connection with the delivery or serving of food or beverages, regardless of whether the food or beverages are consumed on the establishment's premises (e.g., a credit is allowed for tips in connection with delivery of food).[118]

¶ 717 Credit for Contributions to Community Development Corporations (New Markets Tax Credit)

A taxpayer who holds a qualified equity investment on a credit allowance date which occurs during the taxable year may take a new markets tax credit.[119] The credit rate is five percent for the first three credit allowance dates and six percent for the remaining credit allowance dates.[120]

The "credit allowance date" is defined as the initial date of the investment and the next six anniversary dates.[121] A "qualified equity investment" is a cash investment in a qualified community development entity.[122] "Qualified community development entities" are domestic corporations or partnerships who have as a primary mission serving, or providing investment capital for, low-income communities or low-income persons.[123]

¶ 719 Credit for Small Employer Pension Plan Start-up Costs

Effective for tax years beginning after 2001, a credit is allowed to small employers for 50 percent of the qualified start-up costs of a new pension plan.[124] The credit may be claimed for the first three years beginning with the tax year in which the plan becomes effective. The credit is limited to $500 per year.[125] "Qualified start-up costs" are defined as any ordinary and necessary expenses of an eligible employer paid or incurred in connection with the establishment or administration of an "eligible employee plan," or the retirement-related education of employees with respect to the plan. In addition, the plan must cover at least one non-highly paid employee.[126]

To qualify as a small employer, an employer must meet the requirements of Code Sec. 408(p)(2)(C)(i), i.e., have employed a maximum of 100 employees earning $5,000 or more in compensation in the preceding year.[127] The credit taken reduces what would otherwise be deductible by the

---

[117] Code Sec. 46B(b)(2).
[118] Code Sec. 45B(b)(1)(A).
[119] Code Sec. 45D(a)(1).
[120] Code Sec. 45D(a)(2).
[121] Code Sec. 45D(a)(3).
[122] Code Sec. 45D(b).
[123] Code Sec. 45D(c).
[124] Economic Growth and Tax Relief Reconciliation Act of 2001, Act Sec. 619(a), adding Code Sec. 45E(a).

[125] Economic Growth and Tax Relief Reconciliation Act of 2001, Act Sec. 619(a), adding Code Sec. 45E(b).

[126] Economic Growth and Tax Relief Reconciliation Act of 2001, Act Sec. 619(a), adding Code Sec. 45E(d)(1).

[127] Economic Growth and Tax Relief Reconciliation Act of 2001, Act Sec. 619(a), adding Code Sec. 45E(c).

amount of the credit. However, a taxpayer may elect to not take the credit, in which case the full deduction is allowed.[128]

¶ 721   Employer-Provided Child Care Credit

Effective for tax years beginning after 2001, Congress has instituted a credit for employer-provided child care. The credit rate is 25 percent of qualified child care expenditures and 10 percent of qualified child care resource and referral expenditures.[129] However, the total credit claimed for a tax year cannot exceed $150,000.[130]

"Qualified child care expenditures" are any amounts paid or incurred to acquire, construct, rehabilitate, or expand qualified child care facilities, the cost of which would be depreciable or amortizable, and which does not constitute part of a personal residence of the taxpayer or an employee. Also included are operating costs as well as contracts with a qualified care facility to proved child care services to employees.[131]

"Qualified child care resource and referral expenditures" are expenses paid or incurred by the employer under a contract to provide child care resource and referral services to the employees. These expenditures cannot discriminate in favor of highly paid employees (as defined by Code Sec. 414(q)).[132]

"Qualified child care facilities" must meet all applicable laws and regulations of the local and state government in which they are located. Generally, its principal use must be to provide child care assistance. However, the principal use test does not apply if the child care facility is located in the principal residence of the operator of the facility.[133] In addition, for a facility to qualify for the credit, three requirements must be met:[134]

1. The facility must be open to enrollment of employees of the taxpayer during the taxable year;

2. If the child care facility is the principal business of the taxpayer, at least 30 percent of the children cared for must be dependents of employees of the taxpayer; and

3. The use of the facility cannot discriminate in favor of highly paid employees (as defined by Code Sec. 414(q)).

---

[128] Economic Growth and Tax Relief Reconciliation Act of 2001, Act Sec. 619(a), adding Code Sec. 45E(e).

[129] Economic Growth and Tax Relief Reconciliation Act of 2001, Act Sec. 205A, adding Code Sec. 45F(a).

[130] Economic Growth and Tax Relief Reconciliation Act of 2001, Act Sec. 205A, adding Code Sec. 45F(b).

[131] Economic Growth and Tax Relief Reconciliation Act of 2001, Act Sec. 205A, adding Code Sec. 45F(c)(1).

[132] Economic Growth and Tax Relief Reconciliation Act of 2001, Act Sec. 205A, adding Code Sec. 45F(c)(3).

[133] Economic Growth and Tax Relief Reconciliation Act of 2001, Act Sec. 205A, adding Code Sec. 45F(c)(2)(A).

[134] Economic Growth and Tax Relief Reconciliation Act of 2001, Act Sec. 205A, adding Code Sec. 45F(c)(2)(B).

The act prevents a double benefit. An expenditure that would otherwise be deductible cannot be deducted if the credit is taken. If the expenditure would be capitalized, the basis is reduced by the credit.[135]

Recapture of the Credit

The credit must be recaptured if there is a recapture event within the first 10 years of taking the credit. A "recapture event" results if either:[136]

- The employer ceases to operate the facility as a qualified child care facility; or

- There is a change of ownership. However, there is no recapture if the acquirer agrees to "step into the shoes" of the seller, i.e., agrees to recapture the credit should the buyer later have a recapture event.

The recapture percentage is a sliding scale beginning at 100 percent for recaptures in the first three years and decreasing to 10 percent by years nine and ten.[137] The carryback or carryover of unused business credits must be adjusted to reflect a recapture. The act also provides that other credits cannot be used to offset a recapture.[138]

Tax Tips and Pitfalls

Generally, nontaxable fringe benefits are very attractive to employees. This provision, by granting tax incentives to small businesses to provide child care, should be of benefit to both employers and employees. However, the harsh recapture rules may make it inadvisable for an employer who expects to sell his or her business to set up a child care facility.

¶ 723   Investment Credit

The investment tax credit was first enacted in 1962. During the next decade the credit had an uncertain future. It was suspended and then reinstated during the Johnson administration, only to be repealed by the Tax Reform Act of 1969. Two years later the credit was restored by the Revenue Act of 1971. Various tax acts since 1971 have modified (mostly liberalized) the credit. The Tax Reduction Act of 1975 increased the credit from 7 percent to 10 percent. The Revenue Act of 1978 increased the amount of tax against which investment credit can be offset. The Economic Recovery Tax Act of 1981, in conjunction with ACRS depreciation, shortened the life years necessary to get the full credit. The Tax Equity and Fiscal Responsibility Act of 1982 reduced the amount of tax that investment credit could be offset against and also provided for a basis reduction

---

[135] Economic Growth and Tax Relief Reconciliation Act of 2001, Act Sec. 205A, adding Code Sec. 45F(f).

[136] Economic Growth and Tax Relief Reconciliation Act of 2001, Act Sec. 205A, adding Code Sec. 45F(d)(3).

[137] Economic Growth and Tax Relief Reconciliation Act of 2001, Act Sec. 205A, adding Code Sec. 45F(d)(2).

[138] Economic Growth and Tax Relief Reconciliation Act of 2001, Act Sec. 205A, adding Code Sec. 45F(d)(4).

for one-half of the credit taken (thus taking us partly back to 1962 law). Finally, the Tax Reform Act of 1986 retroactively repealed the credit generally for assets placed into service after 1985. As currently structured, the investment credit is the sum of:[139]

- The rehabilitation credit;

- The energy credit; and

- The reforestation credit.

¶ 725   Rehabilitation Credit

A credit is allowed for the cost of substantially rehabilitating certain buildings. To qualify, the building must either be a certified historic structure (not used for personal purposes) or an industrial or commercial building originally placed into service before 1936.[140] A "substantial rehabilitation" is defined as an expenditure during a 24-month period ending with or within the tax year that exceeds the greater of:[141]

- The adjusted basis of the building; or

- $5,000.

Except for certified historical structures, in order to qualify for the credit, the building must be largely retained. Three structural tests must be met for this purpose:[142]

1.   50 percent or more of the existing external walls must be retained in place as external walls;

2.   75 percent or more of the existing external walls must be retained in place as internal or external walls; and

3.   75 percent or more of the existing internal structural framework must be retained in place.

The area of existing external walls includes windows and doors, non-supporting elements (e.g., a curtain) as well as a single wall shared with an adjacent building.[143] "Retained in place" means that the supporting elements are retained rather than replaced. However, supporting elements may be reinforced, existing doors and windows may be replaced or eliminated, and the wall may be disassembled as long as the same supporting elements are retained.[144] The basis of the building must be reduced by the amount of the credit taken.[145]

The amount of the credit is 20 percent of qualified rehabilitation expenditures of certified historic structures, and 10 percent for industrial or commercial buildings first placed into service before 1936.[146]

---

[139] Code Sec. 46.
[140] Code Sec. 47(a), and (c)(1) and (2).
[141] Code Sec. 47(c)(1)(C).
[142] Code Sec. 47(c)(1)(A)(iii).

[143] Reg. § 1.48-12(b)(3).
[144] *Id.*
[145] Code Sec. 50(c)(1).
[146] Code Sec. 47(a) and (c)(1).

A "qualified rehabilitation expenditure" must be properly chargeable to a capital account and must be depreciable. Included are amounts incurred for architectural and engineering fees, site survey fees, legal expenses, insurance premiums, development fees, and other capitalizable construction-related costs.[147]

Qualified rehabilitation expenditures do not include the following expenditures:[148]

- Expenditures which are not depreciated under straight-line;

- The cost of acquiring the building or land;

- Any expenditure in connection with the enlargement of a building (not including an increase in floor space due to interior remodeling); or

- Any expenditures attributable to a certified structure unless the rehabilitation is certified. Generally, the building must either be listed in the National Register or be located in a registered historic district and certified by the Secretary of Interior as being of historic significance to the district.[149]

.01 Reporting Requirements

Generally, a copy of the final certification of completed work by the Secretary of Interior must be attached to Form 3468.[150]

However, if the certificate has not been issued by filing time, a copy of the first page of the Historic Preservation Certification Application—Part 2—Description of Rehabilitation (NPS Form 10-168a) with an indication that it has been received by the Department of the Interior or its designate may be attached to Form 3468. In that event, the final certification must be submitted with the next return filed.

.02 Recapture

The credit must be recaptured if there is an early disposition (within five years) of the property. Recapture can also occur if the Department of the Interior revokes or invalidates a certification of rehabilitation.[151]

¶ 727 Business Energy Investment Credit

An additional credit, over and beyond the 10 percent investment credit, was allowed for acquisitions or constructions of "business energy property." As originally enacted in 1978, "business energy property" was broadly defined to include many alternative energy sources. However, Congress has gradually phased out these credits. The remaining available

---

[147] Reg. § 1.48-12(c)(2).
[148] Reg. § 1.48-12(c)(7).
[149] Code Sec. 47(c)(2)(C).

[150] Reg. § 1.48-12(d)(7).

[151] Code Sec. 50(a)(1); Reg. § 1.48-11(d)(3).

credit is 10 percent of "energy property."[152] "Energy property" is any property which is:[153]

- Equipment which uses solar energy to generate energy; or

- Equipment used to produce, distribute, or use geothermal energy.

The property must have been constructed, reconstructed, or erected by the taxpayer, or, if acquired, the taxpayer must be the original user of the property.[154]

The credit does not apply to that portion of the basis that which is attributable to qualified rehabilitation expenditures.[155]

The depreciable basis must be reduced by one-half of the credit.[156]

.01 Reporting Requirements

The credit is claimed on Part I of Form 3468, "Investment Credit." If the property ceases to be energy property, recapture is computed on Form 4255, "Recapture of Investment Credit."

¶729   Reforestation Credit

The reforestation credit is 10 percent of the portion of the amortizable basis of any qualified timber property which was acquired during the tax year and which is eligible for amortization under Code Sec. 194.[157]

¶731   Work Opportunity Credit

A work opportunity credit is available for certain workers beginning work before January 1, 2002.[158] The credit rate is generally 35 percent of the first $6,000 of wages for the first 12 months of employment; however, for qualified summer youth employees the base is only $3,000.[159] As was true of the old jobs credit, the work opportunity credit reduces the allowable deduction for wages.[160]

.01 Definition of Targeted Groups

Their are fewer targeted groups in the work opportunity credit than in the old jobs credit. The following are members of targeted groups:

- A qualified TANF recipient;

- A qualified veteran;

- A qualified ex-felon;

- A high-risk youth;

---

[152] Code Sec. 48(a)(1) and (2).
[153] Code Sec. 48(a)(3).
[154] Code Sec. 48(a)(3)(B).
[155] Code Sec. 48(a)(2)(B).
[156] Code Sec. 50(c)(3).
[157] Code Sec. 48(b)(1).
[158] Code Sec. 51(c)(4).
[159] Code Sec. 51(a), (b), and (d)(7).
[160] Code Sec. 280C(a).

- A vocational rehabilitation referral;

- A qualified summer youth employee;

- A qualified food stamp recipient;

- A qualified SSI recipient.[161]

No credit is allowed with respect to an employee unless the employee has performed at least 120 hours of service for the employer.[162]

¶ 733   Welfare-to-Work Credit

The welfare-to-work credit provides an incentive to hire workers who are on welfare. The credit is 35 percent of the first $10,000 of qualified wages paid to an employee in the first year of employment, plus 50 percent of the first $10,0000 of qualified wages paid in the second year of employment.[163] Therefore, the maximum credit for the two-year period is $8,500. Qualified wages are wages paid to employees who are long-term family assistance recipients.[164] In general, long-term recipients are individuals who have been receiving assistance under a public aid program for at least an 18-month period ending on the hiring date.[165] An employer may not take both the welfare-to-work credit and the work opportunity credit for the same employee.[166] The wage deduction is reduced by the welfare-to-work credit.[167] The credit is scheduled to expire for employees hired after December 31, 2001.[168]

¶ 735   Credit for Prior Year Minimum Tax

Because of timing differences such as the depreciation deduction, the alternative minimum tax may be greater than the regular tax in one year, but less than the regular tax in later years. Therefore, there is allowed as a credit against the regular tax liability an amount equal to the minimum tax credit. This credit is discussed in Chapter 3.

¶ 737   Foreign Tax Credit

Domestic corporations (as well as citizens) are generally allowed a credit for any income, war profits, and excess profits taxes paid or accrued during their tax year to either a foreign country or to any possession of the United States.[169] Members of partnerships or beneficiaries of estates or trusts may claim their proportionate share of foreign taxes paid by the partnership, etc.[170] The credit is allowed in lieu of a deduction.

---

[161] Code Sec. 51(d).

[162] Code Sec. 51(i)(3).

[163] Code Sec. 51A(a) and (b)(4).

[164] Code Sec. 51A(b)(1).

[165] Code Sec. 51A(c).

[166] Code Sec. 51A(e).

[167] Code Secs. 280C(a) and 51(d)(2).

[168] Code Sec. 51A(f).

[169] Code Sec. 901(b)(1).

[170] Code Sec. 901(b)(5).

.01 Limitation on the Credit

The credit cannot exceed the portion of U.S. tax attributable to the taxpayer's taxable income from sources outside the United States.[171] For this purpose, in the case of a corporation, the taxable income outside the United States does not include income which is subject to the tax credit for taxable income from Puerto Rico and the Virgin Islands.[172]

> **Example 7-6.** Global Co., Inc., had a taxable income of $1,000,000 in 2001, and a U.S. tax liability before credits of $340,000. $200,000 of taxable income was generated in Sweden, and a corporate tax of $95,000 was paid to Sweden. Of the foreign taxes of $95,000 paid, only $68,000 (($200,000/$1,000,000) × $340,000) may be taken as a credit.

If because of the limitation, the full amount of foreign taxes paid cannot be taken as a credit, the excess taxes may be carried back two years and forward five years, and taken as a credit to the extent that the limitation in the carryback or carryforward year exceeds the foreign taxes paid.[173]

> **Example 7-7.** Assume the same facts as in the previous example and that in 1999 the corporation paid foreign tax of $70,000 but the limitation was $117,000. The excess foreign tax paid in 2001 of $27,000 ($95,000 − $68,000) can be carried back and applied in full as a credit to 1999 taxes.

The limitation and carryback and carryover must be applied to several categories of income.[174]

Foreign losses must be recaptured in later years. The recapture is accomplished by requiring the taxpayer in a succeeding year to treat as income from the United States (thus decreasing the foreign tax credit limitation) the lesser of[175]

- The unused loss of the prior year; or

- 50 percent of the taxable income from foreign sources (or a larger percent as the taxpayer may choose).

> **Example 7-8.** In 2000 Worldwide Movers, Inc., had a loss from foreign sources of $500,000. In 2001 the company had total taxable income of $2,500,000, of which $200,000 was from foreign sources. U.S. tax before credits was $850,000; foreign tax was $63,000. For purposes of the limitation, the $200,000 of income from abroad must be reduced by $100,000. Thus only $34,000 (($100,000/$2,500,000) × $850,000) of the $63,000 foreign tax credit may be used.

---

[171] Code Sec. 904(a).
[172] Code Sec. 904(b)(4).
[173] Code Sec. 904(c).

[174] Code Sec. 904(d); Reg. § 1.904-4.

[175] Code Sec. 904(f).

.02 *Other Restrictions on the Credit*

Since many foreign taxes on oil and gas are in substance more like royalties, the Internal Revenue Code imposes a limit on foreign taxes on mineral income. The foreign tax must be reduced by the amount by which the amount of such taxes or (if smaller) the U.S. tax on the foreign income, computed without regard to percentage depletion, exceeds the U.S. tax on such income.[176]

Payments for oil or gas are not considered taxes if the taxpayer has no economic interest in the oil or gas and the purchase or sale price differs from the fair market value of the oil or gas.[177]

The credit may not be taken on foreign taxes paid to a country which the United States does not recognize, or has severed relations with, or if the Secretary of State has designated the nation as a country which repeatedly supports international terrorism.[178]

¶ 739   Clinical Testing Expenses for Certain Drugs

A credit is allowed for 50 percent of qualified clinical testing expenses for the year.[179] "Qualified clinical testing expenses" are research expenses which would qualify under Code Sec. 41 (for the research credit) if the phrase "clinical testing" was substituted for the term "qualified research." Also, 100 percent of contract research expenses, rather than 65 percent, is eligible for the credit.[180] To the extent that the expenditures are funded by any external source (e.g., a grant, contract, or otherwise), they are not eligible for the credit.[181]

For this purpose, "clinical testing" is any human clinical testing which is carried out under an exemption for a rare disease or condition (Section 505(i) of the Federal Food, Drug, and Cosmetic Act). The testing must also occur after the drug is designated as being for a rare disease or condition and before the drug is approved for use.[182] A rare disease or condition is one which either affects less than 200,000 people in the United States or for which there is no reasonable expectation that the development costs can be recovered from U.S. sales.[183]

A credit cannot be taken under both Code Secs. 45C and 41. In that event, the credit under Code Sec. 41 is reduced. However, qualified clinical testing expenses which also qualify as research expenses are included in base year computations for Code Sec. 41 purposes.[184]

The credit may not be used to offset the alternative minimum tax. It is limited to the excess of the regular tax (reduced by nonrefundable personal credits and Subpart B credits) over the tentative minimum tax for the year

---

[176] Code Sec. 901(e).
[177] Code Sec. 901(f).
[178] Code Sec. 901(j).
[179] Code Sec. 45C(a).
[180] Code Sec. 45C(b)(1).

[181] *Id.*
[182] Code Sec. 45C(b)(2).
[183] Code Sec. 45C(d)(1).
[184] Code Sec. 45C(c).

or, if greater, 25 percent of so much of regular tax (reduced by nonrefundable personal credits and Subpart B credits) exceeds $25,000.[185]

.01 Reporting Requirements

The credit is elected by filing Form 8820, "Orphan Drug Credit."

¶ 741   Credit for Producing Fuel from a Nonconventional Source

A credit of $3.00 per barrel-of-oil equivalent of qualified fuels produced and sold is allowed.[186] "Qualified fuels" includes:[187]

- Oil produced from shale and tar sands;

- Gas produced from geopressured brine, Devonian shale, coal seams, or a tight formation, or biomass; and

- Liquid, gaseous, or solid synthetic fuels produced from coal (including lignite), including such fuels when used as fuelstocks.

The purpose of the credit is to stimulate production of fuel from nonconventional sources. If the wellhead price exceeds $23.50 (adjusted for inflation), the credit is reduced.[188] The credit is reduced for grants, tax-exempt bonds, subsidized energy financing, and the energy credit.[189]

The credit is available only for production in the United States or U.S. possessions.[190]

---

185 Code Sec. 38(c)(1).
186 Code Sec. 29(a).
187 Code Sec. 29(c)(1).

188 Code Sec. 29(b)(1).
189 Code Sec. 29(b)(3) and (4).
190 Code Sec. 29(d)(1).

Chapter 8

Cost Recoveries

¶ 801   Introduction

Some capital expenditures have an indefinite life and thus their cost cannot be recovered until the item is sold, exchanged, or otherwise disposed. However, *most* capital expenditures do have a limited life. In other words, they will wear out, become obsolete, or, in the case of intangibles, their legal or contractual life will expire, or, in the case of natural resources, the asset will become exhausted through its consumption. Cost recoveries for these three types of assets (i.e., depreciation, amortization, and depletion, are discussed in this chapter).

¶ 803   Depreciation

The depreciation deduction is available only for property used in a trade or business, or property held for the production of income.[1] The deduction does not apply to inventories, land, or natural resources.[2] Personal use assets, such as the taxpayer's residence, automobile, furniture, and clothing, are not depreciable.[3] Assets that are used partly for business, such as an automobile, are subject to depreciation on the business portion.

.01   Basis of Depreciable Property

The basis for depreciation for pre-ACRS property is the adjusted basis for determining gain on a sale.[4] The depreciable basis is not always the basis to use in computing gain/loss on the sale of property. There are two important exceptions.

In the case of gift property, the depreciable basis is the donor's basis; however, if the gift property is later sold by the donee at a loss and if fair market value at the date of the gift was less than donor's basis, the depreciation taken would be deducted from the fair market value at the time of the gift to get the adjusted basis for loss purposes.

For property converted from personal use to business use, the depreciable basis is the lesser of adjusted basis at the time of conversion or fair market value at the time of conversion.[5] Note that neither exception is particularly applicable to partnerships or corporations.

.02   Apportioning Basis Between Land and Buildings

Buildings are depreciable while land is not depreciable. Therefore, when a lump-sum price is paid, the costs must be allocated between land and buildings. Further, the basis for depreciation cannot exceed an amount

---

[1] Code Sec. 167(a).
[2] Reg. § 1.167(a)-2.
[3] Id.

[4] Code Sec. 167(c).
[5] Reg. § 1.167(g)-1.

which bears the same proportion to the lump sum as the value of the depreciable property at the time of acquisition bears to the value of the entire property at that time.[6] A reasonable method of apportionment would be to use the ratio of land to buildings as shown on the property tax statement.

> **Example 8-1.** Loud Chimes Co. purchased 10 acres of land which had an office building on it. The company paid $240,000 for the property. The previous year's property tax appraisal listed the value of the land at $20,000 and the office building at $180,000. Loud Chimes Co. valued the office building at $216,000 ($180,000/$200,000) × ($240,000) and the land at $24,000.

¶ 805 Accelerated Cost Recovery System

The accelerated cost recovery system (ACRS) stems from the Economic Recovery Tax Act of 1981 (ERTA). The purpose of ACRS is to stimulate investment in plant and equipment. To achieve this objective, ACRS provides for much shorter recovery periods than did prior law. In most cases, these recovery periods have little relationship to the actual service lives. The Tax Reform Act of 1986 (TRA '86) significantly modified ACRS with respect to both lives and rates. Hence, assets placed into service after 1986 are subject to the modified accelerated cost recovery system (MACRS). However, pre-1987 law (ACRS) will be discussed first.

.01 Applicability of ACRS

ACRS did not apply to assets placed into service before 1981; for these assets, the pre-ACRS rules continued to apply (see the discussion later in this chapter). In addition, the following kinds of property were not eligible for ACRS:

1. Property that the owner makes an election to depreciate using units-of-production or any similar method that is not based on the time held.[7]

2. Intangible property.[8]

3. Property acquired after 1980 in certain nonrecognition transactions where the basis of the property is determined by reference to the basis of the exchanged property to the transferor or distributor and the exchanged property was placed in service by the transferor or distributor before 1981.[9]

The purpose of this restriction is to prevent taxpayers from swapping like-kind property merely to get the ACRS deduction.

---

[6] Reg. § 1.167(a)-5.
[7] Code Sec. 168(e)(2) (prior to amendment by TRA '86).
[8] Code Sec. 168(c) (prior to amendment by TRA '86).

[9] Code Sec. 168(e)(4)(C) (prior to amendment by TRA '86).

Example 8-2. In 1983, the Garza-Hart partnership and Hobbs swapped trucks. Both of the trucks were purchased before 1981. Even though both taxpayers have an "acquisition" after 1980, ACRS depreciation would not be permitted since the basis of Garza-Hart's "new" truck would be determined by the basis of its "old" truck. The same would be true for Hobbs.

4. Property (both personal and real) acquired after 1980 from relatives who owned or used the item during 1980.[10]

"Relatives" are defined as:[11]

a. Brothers and sisters, spouses, ancestors, and lineal descendants;

b. An individual and a corporation if the individual owns directly or indirectly over 10 percent of the value of the outstanding stock;

c. Certain "brother-sister" corporations;

d. Certain relationships between trusts and the grantor beneficiary, corporation or another trust;

e. Certain S corporations and other S corporations, C corporations, or partnerships;

f. A person and a tax-exempt organization which the person or the person's family controls;

g. A partnership and a partner if the partner owns directly or indirectly over 10 percent of the partnership or certain "brother-sister" partnerships.

Example 8-3. Good Grocers, Inc., purchased refrigeration equipment from a brother-sister corporation in 1983 for $18,000. The brother-sister corporation had purchased the equipment in 1980. Good Grocers, Inc., must depreciate the equipment under pre-ACRS rules.

5. Property that has been "churned."[12] Since the ACRS deductions are more substantial than under pre-ACRS rules, there is an incentive to transfer the ostensible ownership of property in order to create the ACRS deduction. Hence the need for the anti-churning rules as detailed below. "Churned" Code Sec. 1245 property acquired after 1980 that is not eligible for ACRS includes:

a. Property that was owned or used at any time during 1980 by the taxpayer or a related person;

---

[10] Code Sec. 168(e)(4)(D) (prior to amendment by TRA '86).

[11] Code Secs. 168(e)(4)(D) (prior to amendment by TRA '86), 267(b), and 707(b)(1).

[12] Code Sec. 168(e)(4) (prior to amendment by TRA '86).

b. Property that is acquired from a person who owned such property at any time during 1980, and, as part of the transaction, the user of such property does not change;

c. Property that the taxpayer leases to a person (or a person related to such person) who owned or used such property at any time in 1980; or

d. Property that is acquired in a transaction as part of which the user of such property does not change and the property is not recovery property in the hands of the person from which the property is acquired by reason of requirements (b) or (c) above.[13]

Example 8-4. The Spencer and McGuire partnership purchased a computer from Black in 1983 and immediately leased it back to Black. Black had purchased the computer in 1980 and had used it up to the date of the sale to Spencer and McGuire. Spencer and McGuire *may not* use ACRS.

Example 8-5. Briggs Inc. rented an automobile from Smith Chevrolet in 1980. In 1981, the company purchased the automobile. Briggs Inc. *may not* use ACRS.

"Churned" Code Sec. 1250 property (that was not eligible for ACRS) includes:

a. Property that was owned by the taxpayer or by a related person at any time during 1980;

b. Property that the taxpayer leases to a person (or a person related to such a person) who owned such property in 1980; or

c. Property that is acquired in an exchange described in Code Sec. 1031, 1033, 1038, or 1039 (repealed by OBRA 1990) to the extent that the basis of such property includes an amount representing the adjusted basis of other property owned by the taxpayer or a related person in 1980.[14]

The preceding code sections pertain to exchanges that are essentially nontaxable. To the extent that cash boot is a part of the exchange, that part will qualify for ACRS.

Anti-churning rules do not apply to property acquired by death or property acquired by gift. In both cases, there will be a new MACRS or ACRS depreciation period.[15]

Example 8-6. Fleming Company's office building, which was built in 1979, was destroyed by fire in 1983. The adjusted basis of the

---

[13] Code Sec. 168(e)(4)(A) (prior to amendment by TRA '86).

[14] Code Sec. 168(e)(4)(B) (prior to amendment by TRA '86).

[15] Code Secs. 168(f)(4) (prior to amendment by TRA '86), 168(f)(5)(A), and 168(i)(7)(D) (before it was repealed by TMRA '88).

building was $81,000, and the company received $128,000 in insurance proceeds. The corporation spent $157,000 to replace the property and elected to defer the gain under Code Sec. 1033. The basis of its new building was $110,000 ($157,000 − $47,000 of postponed gain). Of that basis, $81,000 was not eligible for ACRS and the remaining $29,000 was eligible.

6.   Automobiles, if the straight-line mileage rate had been previously used.[16]

Example 8-7. Donnelly and Sons purchased an automobile in 1982 and used the standard 20¢ (for the first 15,000 miles of use) and 11¢ (for excess miles) mileage rate to determine business expenses. In 1983, the company switched to the actual expense method. In computing depreciation expense, it *may not* use ACRS but rather must use the actual life of the auto as a means for depreciation.

.02 Limitation on Mixed-Use Assets

The eligibility of mixed-use (part business, part personal) assets for ACRS was made more stringent by TRA '84. Unless "listed property" is used for business purposes over 50 percent of the time, it must have been depreciated by the use of straight-line methods.[17] The required depreciable life-years were:[18]

ACRS Life	Required Depreciable Life Years (Effective for Items Placed into Service After June 18, 1984)
3-year personal property	5 years
5-year personal property	12 years
10-year personal property	25 years
real property	40 years

"Listed property" was defined as:

• Any passenger automobile;

• Any other property used for transportation;

• Any property of a type generally used for purposes of entertainment, recreation, or amusement;

• Any computer or peripheral equipment (except that used exclusively at a business establishment); and

• Other property that the IRS may specify in the regulations.[19]

As noted above, taxpayers are barred from taking either ACRS depreciation or investment tax credit in the year in which the property is placed

---

[16] Rev. Proc. 82-61, 1982-2 CB 849.
[17] Code Sec. 280F(b) (prior to amendment by TRA '86).
[18] Code Secs. 280F(b)(4)(B) (prior to amendment by TRA '86) and 312(k)(3) (prior to amendment by TRA '86).
[19] Code Sec. 280F(d)(4) (prior to amendment by TRA '86).

in service unless it is used more than 50 percent for business purposes. If, in a later year, the property fails to meet the 50 percent business use test, the ACRS and investment credit previously claimed are subject to recapture in this later tax year. The ACRS recapture is equal to the difference between the ACRS deductions and the deductions that would have resulted by using the straight-line method. Further, the depreciation thereafter must be computed by using the straight-line method. In computing this straight-line depreciation, the basis of the property is increased by the ACRS recapture and the investment credit recapture.

.03 Recovery Periods of ACRS Personal Property—Prescribed Method

Rather than computing depreciation by applying some depreciation method to the adjusted basis of property, ACRS involves applying a statutory percentage to property which was divided into four recovery periods. The table for all personal property acquired after 1980 and before 1985, except 15-year public utility property, is reproduced below:

The applicable percentage for the class of property is: *

If the recovery year is:	3-year	5-year	10-year
1	25	15	8
2	38	22	14
3	37	21	12
4		21	10
5		21	10
6			10
7			9
8			9
9			9
10			9

---

* Code Sec. 168(b)(1)(A) (prior to amendment by TRA '86).

The above table incorporates the half-year convention [20] (one-half year's depreciation is taken for the year that the asset is placed into service) and a rate that is 150 percent of declining balance. Unlike the pre-ACRS declining methods, however, there is no nondepreciable tail, i.e., the entire cost is recovered. Also, salvage value need not be deducted.

Example 8-9. Cano Brothers purchased in February 1981 a pickup truck costing $9,000. Cano's depreciation deduction for 1981 is $9,000 × .25 = $2,250. In 1982, Cano deducts $9,000 × .38, or $3,420. In 1983, the partnership would deduct $9,000 × .37, or $3,330. The

---

[20] Code Sec. 168(b)(3)(B)(iii) (prior to amendment by TRA '86).

yearly deductions would have been identical if Cano had purchased the pickup in November 1981.

No deduction is permitted for the year of disposition.

Example 8-10. Assume the same facts as in the previous example, except that Cano Brothers sold the pickup in December 1983. No deduction would be permitted in 1983; hence, the basis at the time of sale would be $3,330.

.04 *"Luxury Automobiles" and Certain Other Personal Property*

Congress wished to tax benefits associated with the use of very expensive automobiles believing that ". . . the extra expense of a luxury automobile operates as a tax-free personal emolument."[21] To accomplish this objective, Congress in 1984 and in 1985 made several changes in the way in which automobiles are depreciated. The rules are different for business automobiles than for mixed-use automobiles. (For a discussion of leased automobiles, see such headings under the discussion of MACRS later in this chapter.)

Passenger automobiles were defined as any four-wheeled vehicle:[22]

- Which is manufactured primarily for use on public streets, roads, and highways; and

- Which is rated at 6,000 pounds gross vehicle weight or less.

However, passenger autos did not include:[23]

- Any ambulance or hearse used directly in a trade or business; or

- Any vehicle used by the taxpayer directly in the trade or business of transporting people or property for compensation.

.05 *Automobiles Used Primarily for Business*

The basic three-year write-off was left unchanged for autos used more than half for business. However, a yearly limit was placed on depreciation. Depreciation for autos placed into service after June 18, 1984, and before April 3, 1985, is limited to $4,000 the first year, and $6,000 in each of the next two years.[24] For autos placed into service after April 2, 1985, and before 1987, the ceilings are $3,200 the first year and $4,800 for subsequent years.[25] The above amounts are reduced by the percentage used for personal use.

The remaining cost may be written off in the fourth and succeeding years, except that depreciation can never exceed $4,800 per year, or $6,000, depending on when purchased.

---

[21] Committee on Ways and Means, Rept. No. 98-432, p. 1387.
[22] Code Sec. 280F(d)(5) (prior to amendment by TRA '86).
[23] Id.

[24] Code Sec. 280F(a) (prior to revision by P.L. 99-44).

[25] Code Sec. 280F(a) (prior to revision by TRA '86).

Example 8-11. Mountain-Top Ranch, Inc. purchased in June 1985 two autos used 100 percent for business purposes. Cost of auto A was $12,000 and cost of auto B was $25,000. Allowed depreciation is as follows:

Year	Auto A	Auto B
1985	$3,000	$3,200
1986	4,560	4,800
1987	4,440	4,800
1988	—	4,800
1989	—	4,800
1990	—	2,600

.06 Automobiles Used Primarily for Personal Purposes

As previously mentioned, automobiles not used mostly for business are not eligible for the three-year write-off. Instead, the autos must be depreciated on a straight-line basis over five years. This is without regard to salvage value and assumes the use of the half-year convention. These autos are also not eligible for investment credit or the $5,000 expense allowance deduction (for 1982 and 1983).

Example 8-12. Assume the same facts as those in Example 8-11, except that auto A is used only 40 percent for business purposes. Allowed depreciation is as follows:

Year	Auto A
1985	$480 ($12,000 × .20 × 1/2 × .40)
1986	960
1987	960
1988	960
1989	960
1990	480

In meeting the over 50 percent business use requirement, use for nonbusiness activity that results in income production cannot be counted. However, once the 50 percent requirement is met, the nonbusiness activity can be counted in determining ACRS depreciation and investment credit.

Example 8-13. Assume the same facts as those in Example 8-11, except that the business, personal, and nonbusiness income production is as follows:

	Business	Personal Income	Nonbusiness Production*
Auto A	60	25	15
Auto B	30	45	25

* This activity, for example, could constitute use of the auto to examine land rented to others (rental income purposes).

Auto A would be eligible for both ACRS and investment credit to the extent of 85 percent of its cost. However, auto B flunks the over 50 percent business use test; hence, the 55 percent of its cost that is subject to depreciation must be depreciated over five years, and no investment credit may be taken.

.07 Other Personal Property

Many of the provisions applicable to autos also apply to certain personal property that is used less than half for business purposes. Covered property, called "listed property," includes:[26]

- Other property used for transportation;

- Property of a type generally used for entertainment, recreation, or amusement;

- Any computer or peripheral equipment; and

- Other property (to be specified in the regulations).

This property has no direct depreciation cap, as do autos. However, if used less than half for business purposes, investment credit is not allowed and depreciation must be computed at straight-line rates over longer recovery periods than under ACRS. The recordkeeping requirements previously mentioned are also applicable.

.08 Personal Property—Alternate Method

The combination under ACRS of shortened lives and accelerated depreciation rates resulted in a very rapid write-off. Taxpayers wishing a more graduated cost write-off could use the alternate method cost recovery. This method incorporated straight-line depreciation along with longer recovery periods. The alternate recovery lives are shown below:

Class Life	Elective Recovery Periods[*]
3-year property	3, 5, or 12 years
5-year property	5, 12, or 25 years
10-year property	10, 25, or 35 years

---

[*] Code Sec. 168(b)(3) (prior to amendment by TRA '86).

This "alternate method" retained the essential characteristics of ACRS. Salvage value could be ignored, the half-year convention was required, and no depreciation was allowed in the year of sale.[27] A taxpayer must select a single recovery period for each class of property placed into service that tax year.[28] A different recovery period could be picked for property placed in service in succeeding tax years.

Example 8-14. Nugent, Inc. purchased in 1984 two autos having a three-year class life and four items of equipment having a five-year class life. It could not use a three-year life for one auto and another life for the other. However, it could use a five-year life for both autos and

---

[26] Code Sec. 280F(d).
[27] Code Sec. 168(b)(3) (prior to amendment by TRA '86).

[28] Code Sec. 168(b)(3) (prior to amendment by TRA '86).

then use the ACRS five-year life, the five-year straight-line life, or the 12- or 25-year straight-line lives for the equipment. Also, any assets that Nugent, Inc. purchased in 1985 would be eligible for any of the elective recovery periods.

.09 Real Property—Prescribed Method

The ACRS tables for all realty except low-income housing and public utility property are presented below. Life years for realty are as follows:

Date Acquired	Life Years	Convention
Prior to 3-16-84	15	whole month
After 3-16-84 and before 6-23-84	18	whole month
After 6-22-84 and before 5-9-85	18	mid-month
After 5-8-85 and before 1-1-87	19	mid-month

Table I*
ACRS Cost Recovery—Real Estate Placed into Service
Prior to March 16, 1984

(Use the Column for the Month Placed into Service)

If the Recovery Year Is	1	2	3	4	5	6	7	8	9	10	11	12
1	12	11	10	9	8	7	6	5	4	3	2	1
2	10	10	11	11	11	11	11	11	11	1	11	12
3	9	9	9	9	10	10	10	10	10	10	10	10
4	8	8	8	8	8	8	9	9	9	9	9	9
5	7	7	7	7	7	7	8	8	8	8	8	8
6	6	6	6	6	7	7	7	7	7	7	7	7
7	6	6	6	6	6	6	6	6	6	6	6	6
8	6	6	6	6	6	6	5	6	6	6	6	6
9	6	6	6	6	5	6	5	5	5	6	6	6
10	5	6	5	6	5	5	5	5	5	5	6	5
11	5	5	5	5	5	5	5	5	5	5	5	5
12	5	5	5	5	5	5	5	5	5	5	5	5
13	5	5	5	5	5	5	5	5	5	5	5	5
14	5	5	5	5	5	5	5	5	5	5	5	5
15	5	5	5	5	5	5	5	5	5	5	5	5
16	—	—	1	1	2	2	3	3	4	4	4	5

* Prop. Reg. § 1.168-2(b)(2).

Table II[*]
ACRS Cost Recovery—Real Estate Placed into Service
After March 15 and Before June 23, 1984

(Use the Column for the Month Placed into Service)

If the Recovery Year Is	1	2	3	4	5	6	7	8	9	10	11	12
1	10	9	8	7	6	6	5	4	3	2	2	1
2	9	9	9	9	9	9	9	9	9	10	10	10
3	8	8	8	8	8	8	8	8	9	9	9	9
4	7	7	7	7	7	7	8	8	8	8	8	8
5	6	7	7	7	7	7	7	7	7	7	7	7
6	6	6	6	6	6	6	6	6	6	6	6	6
7	5	5	5	5	6	6	6	6	6	6	6	6
8	5	5	5	5	5	5	5	5	5	5	5	5
9	5	5	5	5	5	5	5	5	5	5	5	5
10	5	5	5	5	5	5	5	5	5	5	5	5
11	5	5	5	5	5	5	5	5	5	5	5	5
12	5	5	5	5	5	5	5	5	5	5	5	5
13	4	4	4	5	5	4	4	5	4	4	4	4
14	4	4	4	4	4	4	4	4	4	4	4	4
15	4	4	4	4	4	4	4	4	4	4	4	4
16	4	4	4	4	4	4	4	4	4	4	4	4
17	4	4	4	4	4	4	4	4	4	4	4	4
18	4	4	4	4	4	4	4	4	4	4	4	4
19	—	—	1	1	1	2	2	2	3	3	3	4

[*] IRS Notice 84-16, 1984-2 CB 475.

Table III[*]
ACRS Cost Recovery—Real Estate Placed into Service After June 22, 1984 and Before May 9, 1985

(Use the Column for the Month Placed into Service)

If the Recovery Year Is	1	2	3	4	5	6	7	8	9	10	11	12
1	9	9	8	7	6	5	4	4	3	2	1	.4
2	9	9	9	9	9	9	9	9	9	10	10	10.0
3	8	8	8	8	8	8	8	8	9	9	9	9.0
4	7	7	7	7	7	8	8	8	8	8	8	8.0
5	7	7	7	7	7	7	7	7	7	7	7	7.0
6	6	6	6	6	6	6	6	6	6	6	6	6.0
7	5	5	5	5	6	6	6	6	6	6	6	6.0
8	5	5	5	5	5	5	5	5	5	5	5	5.0
9	5	5	5	5	5	5	5	5	5	5	5	5.0
10	5	5	5	5	5	5	5	5	5	5	5	5.0
11	5	5	5	5	5	5	5	5	5	5	5	5.0
12	5	5	5	5	5	5	5	5	5	5	5	5.0
13	4	4	4	5	4	4	5	4	4	4	5	5.0
14	4	4	4	4	4	4	4	4	4	4	4	4.0
15	4	4	4	4	4	4	4	4	4	4	4	4.0
16	4	4	4	4	4	4	4	4	4	4	4	4.0
17	4	4	4	4	4	4	4	4	4	4	4	4.0
18	4	3	4	4	4	4	4	4	4	4	4	4.0
19	–	1	1	1	2	2	2	3	3	3	3	3.6

[*] IRS Notice 84-16, 1984-2 CB 475.

Table IV*
ACRS Cost Recovery—Real Estate Placed into Service
After May 8, 1985 and Before January 1, 1987

(Use the Column for the Month Placed into Service)

If the Recovery Year Is	1	2	3	4	5	6	7	8	9	10	11	12
1	8.8	8.1	7.3	6.5	5.8	5.0	4.2	3.5	2.7	1.9	1.1	0.4
2	8.4	8.5	8.5	8.6	8.7	8.8	8.8	8.9	9.0	9.0	9.1	9.2
3	7.6	7.7	7.7	7.8	7.9	7.9	8.0	8.1	8.1	8.2	8.3	8.3
4	6.9	7.0	7.0	7.1	7.1	7.2	7.3	7.3	7.4	7.4	7.5	7.6
5	6.3	6.3	6.4	6.4	6.5	6.5	6.6	6.6	6.7	6.8	6.8	6.9
6	5.7	5.7	5.8	5.9	5.9	5.9	6.0	6.0	6.1	6.1	6.2	6.2
7	5.2	5.2	5.3	5.3	5.3	5.4	5.4	5.5	5.5	5.6	5.6	5.6
8	4.7	4.7	4.8	4.8	4.8	4.9	4.9	5.0	5.0	5.1	5.1	5.1
9	4.2	4.3	4.3	4.4	4.4	4.5	4.5	4.5	4.5	4.6	4.6	4.7
10	4.2	4.2	4.2	4.2	4.2	4.2	4.2	4.2	4.2	4.2	4.2	4.2
11	4.2	4.2	4.2	4.2	4.2	4.2	4.2	4.2	4.2	4.2	4.2	4.2
12	4.2	4.2	4.2	4.2	4.2	4.2	4.2	4.2	4.2	4.2	4.2	4.2
13	4.2	4.2	4.2	4.2	4.2	4.2	4.2	4.2	4.2	4.2	4.2	4.2
14	4.2	4.2	4.2	4.2	4.2	4.2	4.2	4.2	4.2	4.2	4.2	4.2
15	4.2	4.2	4.2	4.2	4.2	4.2	4.2	4.2	4.2	4.2	4.2	4.2
16	4.2	4.2	4.2	4.2	4.2	4.2	4.2	4.2	4.2	4.2	4.2	4.2
17	4.2	4.2	4.2	4.2	4.2	4.2	4.2	4.2	4.2	4.2	4.2	4.2
18	4.2	4.2	4.2	4.2	4.2	4.2	4.2	4.2	4.2	4.2	4.2	4.2
19	4.2	4.2	4.2	4.2	4.2	4.2	4.2	4.2	4.2	4.2	4.2	4.2
20	0.2	0.5	0.9	1.2	1.6	1.9	2.3	2.6	3.0	3.3	3.7	4.0

* Rev. Proc. 86-14, 1986-1 CB 542.

Table V*
Real Property Placed into Service
After June 22, 1984 and Before May 9, 1985
For Which Alternate ACRS Method
Over an 18-Year Period Is Elected

If the Recovery Year Is	1-2	3-4	5-7	8-9	10-11	12
1	5	4	3	2	1	0.2
2-10	6	6	6	6	6	6
11	5	5	5	5	5	5.8
12-18	5	5	5	5	5	5
19	1	2	3	4	5	5

* IRS Notice 84-16, 1984-2 CB 475.

Table VI*
Real Property Placed into Service
After March 15, 1984 and Before June 23, 1984
For Which Alternate ACRS Method
Over an 18-Year Period Is Elected

If the Recovery Year Is	1	2-3	4-5	6-7	8-9	10-11	12
1	6	5	4	3	2	1	0.5
2-10	6	6	6	6	6	6	6
11	5	5	5	5	5	5	5.5
12-18	5	5	5	5	5	5	5
19	—	1	2	3	4	5	5

* IRS Notice 84-16, 1984-2 CB 475.

Table VII*
Real Property Placed into Service
After May 8, 1985 and Before January 1, 1987
For Which Alternate ACRS Method Over
a 19-Year Period Is Elected

If the Recovery Year Is	1	2	3	4	5	6	7	8	9	10	11	12
1	5.0	4.6	4.2	3.7	3.3	2.9	2.4	2.0	1.5	1.1	0.7	0.2
2-13	5.3	5.3	5.3	5.3	5.3	5.3	5.3	5.3	5.3	5.3	5.3	5.3
14-19	5.2	5.2	5.2	5.2	5.2	5.2	5.2	5.2	5.2	5.2	5.2	5.2
20	0.2	0.6	1.0	1.5	1.9	2.3	2.8	3.2	3.7	4.1	4.5	5.0

* IRS Notice 84-16, 1984-2 CB 475.

Table VIII*
Real Property Placed into Service
After June 22, 1984 and Before May 9, 1985
For Which Alternate ACRS Method Over
a 35-Year Period Is Elected

If the Recovery Year Is	1-2	3-6	7-10	11	12
1	3	2	1	0.4	0.1
2-30	3	3	3	3	3
31	2	2	2	2.6	2.9
32-35	2	2	2	2	2
36	—	1	2	2	2

* IRS Notice 84-16, 1984-2 CB 475.

¶ 805.09

Table IX[*]
Real Property Placed into Service
After March 15, 1984 and Before June 23, 1984
For Which Alternate ACRS Method Over
a 35-Year Period Is Elected

If the Recovery Year Is	1-2	3-6	7-12
1	3	2	1
2-30	3	3	3
31-35	2	2	2
36	—	1	2

[*] Table II, IRS Publication 534 (Rev. Nov. 1995),
"Depreciating Property Placed in Service Before 1987."

Table X[*]
Real Property Placed into Service
After May 8, 1985 and Before January 1, 1987
For Which Alternate ACRS Method Over
a 35-Year Period Is Elected

If the Recovery Year Is	1	2	3	4	5	6	7	8	9	10	11	12
1	2.7	2.5	2.3	2.0	1.8	1.5	1.3	1.1	0.8	0.6	0.4	0.1
2-20	2.9	2.9	2.9	2.9	2.9	2.9	2.9	2.9	2.9	2.9	2.9	2.9
21-35	2.8	2.8	2.8	2.8	2.8	2.8	2.8	2.8	2.8	2.8	2.8	2.8
36	0.2	0.4	0.6	0.9	1.1	1.4	1.6	1.8	2.1	2.3	2.5	2.8

[*] Rev. Proc. 86-14, 1986-1 CB 542.

Table XI[*]
Real Property Placed into Service
After June 22, 1984 and Before May 9, 1985
For Which Alternate ACRS Method Over
a 45-Year Period Is Elected

If the Recovery Year Is	1	2	3	4	5	6	7	8	9	10	11	12
1	2.1	1.9	1.8	1.6	1.4	1.2	1.0	0.8	0.6	0.5	0.3	0.1
2-11	2.3	2.3	2.3	2.3	2.3	2.3	2.3	2.3	2.3	2.3	2.3	2.3
12-45	2.2	2.2	2.2	2.2	2.2	2.2	2.2	2.2	2.2	2.2	2.2	2.2
46	0.1	0.3	0.4	0.6	0.8	1.0	1.2	1.4	1.6	1.7	1.9	2.1

[*] IRS Notice 84-16, 1984-2 CB 475.

¶ 805.09

Table XII*
Real Property Placed into Service
After May 8, 1985 and Before January 1, 1987
For Which Alternate ACRS Method Over
a 45-Year Period Is Elected

If the Recovery Year Is	1	2	3	4	5	6	7	8	9	10	11	12
1	2.3	2.0	1.9	1.7	1.5	1.3	1.2	0.9	0.7	0.6	0.4	0.2
2-11	2.3	2.3	2.3	2.3	2.3	2.3	2.3	2.3	2.3	2.3	2.3	2.3
12-45	2.2	2.2	2.2	2.2	2.2	2.2	2.2	2.2	2.2	2.2	2.2	2.2
46	0.1	0.3	0.4	0.6	0.8	1.0	1.2	1.4	1.6	1.7	1.9	2.1

* Rev. Proc. 86-14, 1986-1 CB 542.

ACRS for real property is different in several respects than for personalty. The accelerated rate is 175 percent of straight-line; it is 150 percent for personal property. Also, instead of the half year convention, depreciation for real property is taken according to the number of months used. In the tables for realty acquired before June 23, 1984, the asset is considered to be placed into service on the first day of the month in which it was acquired, while in the tables of realty acquired after June 22, 1984, the asset is considered placed into service on the 15th day of the month in which it was acquired.[29]

Example 8-15. Wind River Trucking, Inc., a fiscal year corporation, purchased real property for $90,000 on April 2, 1984. Its fiscal year end is October 31. Since April is the sixth month of its tax year, the ACRS deduction would be $90,000 × .06, or $5,400. For the fiscal year ending (FYE) October 31, 1985, the deduction would be $90,000 × .09, or $8,100.

If the asset is sold or otherwise disposed of before the end of the tax year, depreciation may be taken for the number of months held.[30]

Example 8-16. Assume the same facts as in the preceding example and that the property is sold in February 1986. The deduction for FYE 10-31-86 would be $90,000 × .08 × 4/12 = $2,400.

.10 Component Depreciation

Prior to the advent of ACRS, taxpayers often used component depreciation for buildings, depreciating such parts as wiring, plumbing, etc., over much shorter lives than the shell of the building. ACRS generally forbids component depreciation, with two exceptions:[31]

[29] Code Sec. 168(b)(2) (prior to amendment by TRA '86).
[30] Code Sec. 168(d)(2) (prior to amendment by TRA '86).

[31] Code Sec. 168(f)(1) (prior to amendment by TRA '86).

¶ 805.10

1.   Substantial improvements are treated as separate buildings. "Substantial improvements" are improvements made within a 24-month period if the improvements are at least 25 percent of the adjusted basis of the building as of the first day of the 24-month period "Substantial Improvements" do not include improvements made within three years after the building was placed in service.

2.   For buildings placed into service before 1981, for components of the building placed into service after December 31, 1980, the deduction for components is computed in the same manner as it is with respect to the first component placed into service after December 31, 1980. For buildings placed into service before March 16, 1984, for components of the building placed into service after March 15, 1984, the deduction for components is computed in the same manner as it is with respect to the first component placed into service after March 15, 1984.

.11 Real Property—Alternate Method

The taxpayer could select an alternate method for realty. The alternate years are as follows:[32]

ACRS Lives	Alternate Lives
15	15, 35, or 45
18	18, 35, or 45
19	19, 35, or 45

As with personal property, straight-line depreciation is used. In all other respects the rules are the same as they are for the prescribed method for real estate. The election to use the alternate method is made on a property-by-property basis.[33]

Example 8-17. Sandberg and Sons, a calendar year partnership, acquired on May 3, 1985, real property costing $90,000. The partnership elected to use a 45-year alternate life. The deduction for 1985 (from Table XI) is $90,000 × .014 = $1,260.

.12 Real Property—Improvements

The cost recovery used for improvements to real property depends on when the original property was placed into service and whether or not the improvements are "substantial."

Where a taxpayer makes a substantial improvement to a building, it is treated as a separate building rather than as one or more components. Thus, the taxpayer may use the regular ACRS deduction for the substantial improvement or it may elect the straight-line ACRS deduction over the regular or a longer recovery period, regardless of the ACRS method or

---

[32] Code Sec. 168(b)(3) (prior to amendment by TRA '86).   [33] Id.

recovery period that is used for the rest of the building. An improvement is a substantial improvement if (1) the amounts added to the capital account of the building over a two-year period are at least 25 percent of the adjusted basis of the building (disregarding depreciation and amortization adjustments) as of the first day of that period, and (2) the improvement is made at least three years after the building was placed into service.[34]

There are *transitional rules* (discussed in ¶ 805.10) that generally *allow* the *first component* placed into service after 1980, if the building was placed into service after the inception of ACRS but before one of the two revised ACRS tables went into effect, *to be treated as a separate building* even if it is not a substantial improvement.

> **Example 8-18.** Parker, Inc. constructed an office building in 1980. In January 1984, it added a wing to the office. The office is being depreciated (using pre-ACRS rules) over a period of 25 years. The wing would be depreciated using the ACRS tables for 15-year property or, if the corporation elects, a 15-, 35-, or 45-year period using the straight-line method.

> **Example 8-19.** Assume the same facts as in the previous example, except that the wing was added in April 1985. The wing would be depreciated using the ACRS tables for 18-year property or with the straight-line election.

> **Example 8-20.** Frye Brothers purchased a machine shed for $25,000 in 1981. In August 1985, Frye rewired the shed at a cost of $3,500. In January 1986, it replaced the roof at a cost of $4,000. These would be considered substantial improvements and would be depreciated separately from the machine shed.

.13 Classes of Recovery Property Defined

The term "recovery property" was defined as depreciable tangible property either used in a trade or business or held for the production of income.[35] Recovery property was divided into different classes: 3-year property, 5-year property, 10-year property, 15-year, 18-year, and 19-year real property, and 15-year public utility property. Only the first four will be considered here:

1.   3-year property—This is Code Sec. 1245 property with either a present class life of four years or less or property that is used in connection with research and experimentation.

2.   5-year property—Included herein is Code Sec. 1245 property that does not fit the 3-year or 10-year class (and is not 15-year public utility property).

---

[34] Code Sec. 168(f)(1)(C) (prior to amendment by TRA '86).

[35] Code Sec. 168(c)(1) (prior to amendment by TRA '86).

3. 10-year property—In addition to certain public utility property (not covered in this book), this includes certain Code Sec. 1250 class property with a present class life of 12.5 years or less.

4. 15-year, 18-year, and 19-year real property—This means Code Sec. 1250 class property with a present class life of over 12.5 years.[36]

Examples of ACRS Class Lives[*]

3-year property	5-year property	10-year property	15-year, 18-year, and 19-year property
Automobiles	Heavy-duty trucks	Manufactured houses	Code Sec. 1250 class property with a class life of more than 12.5 years.
Light trucks	Computers	Mobile homes	
Tractor units for use over the road	Copiers	Theme-park structures	
Race horses (if over 2 years old when placed into service)	Office furniture and fixtures	Railroad tank cars	
Other horses (if over 12 years old when placed into service)	Single purpose livestock facilities	Certain public utility property	
Machinery or equipment used in connection with research and experimentation	Single purpose horticultural facilities	Other Code Sec. 1250 class property with a class life of 12.5 years or less.	
	Petroleum storage facilities		
	Airplanes		
	Buses		
Other Code Sec. 1245 class property with a present class life of four years or less.	Trailers		
	Construction equipment		
	Most machinery.		

[*] Code Sec. 168(c)(2) (prior to amendment by TRA '86); Rev. Proc. 83-35, 1983-1 CB 745.

¶ 807 MACRS

As previously mentioned, TRA '86 made significant changes in depreciation lives and methods. The modified accelerated cost recovery system (MACRS) is effective generally for acquisitions after December 31, 1986. Minor modifications were made to MACRS in the Technical and Miscellaneous Revenue Act of 1988 (TAMRA).

[36] Code Sec. 168(c)(2) (prior to amendment by TRA '86).

.01 MACRS Personal Property

Personal property under MACRS falls into one of six classes: 3-year, 5-year, 7-year, 10-year, 15-year, and 20-year property.[37] The depreciation rate is 200 percent of straight-line except for 15-year property, 20-year property, and property used in a farming business, for which the rate is 150 percent of straight-line.[38] The tables switch to the straight-line method during the first year that it yields a greater deduction.[39]

If the taxpayer has a short tax year, the use of the tables is not permitted for the short year and all later years.[40]

The half-year convention under MACRS works differently than under ACRS. Under MACRS, one-half year depreciation is allowed in the year of disposition.[41]

Example 8-21. Wyatt Electric, Inc. purchased in February 1999 property with a five-year recovery period costing $12,000. The corporation sold the equipment in May 2001. Depreciation deductions are:

Year		Deduction
1999	$12,000 × .20	$2,400
2000	$12,000 × .32	3,840
2001	$12,000 × .192 × ½	1,152

Because the half-year convention could be abused by taxpayers making asset acquisitions during the last few days of their tax year, MACRS contains a mid-quarter convention. Taxpayers are subject to the mid-quarter convention if more than 40 percent of the personal property acquired during the tax year is placed into service during the fourth quarter. In that event, a mid-quarter convention must be used for *all* of the personal property placed into service that year.[42]

Example 8-22. The Moore and Moore partnership purchased office equipment costing $60,000 in May 2000 and factory equipment for $50,000 in November 2000. Both are seven-year properties. Since over 40 percent of the purchases were in the last quarter of the year, the mid-quarter convention must be used. Depreciation in 2000 is as follows:

Office equipment:	$60,000 × .1785 =	$10,710
Factory equipment:	$50,000 × .0357 =	1,785
Total		$12,495

---

[37] Code Sec. 168(c).

[38] Code Sec. 168(b).

[39] *Id.*

[40] Rev. Proc. 89-15, 1989-1 CB 816. The procedure contains rules for prorating the depreciation in such instance.

[41] Code Sec. 168(d)(4)(A).

[42] Code Sec. 168(d)(3).

Tax Tips and Pitfalls

The mid-quarter convention makes the *timing* of equipment purchases exceedingly important. For example, a business that placed into service $120,000 of equipment that is seven-year property on August 1, 2000, and another $90,000 on September 28, 2000, would have a 2000 deduction of $30,009 ($210,000 × .1429). However, if the last purchase did not occur until October 1, 2000, the deduction would be only $16,065, computed as follows:

August 1 purchase	($120,000 × .1071) =	$12,852
October 1 purchase	($ 90,000 × .0357) =	3,213
Total		$16,065

On the other hand, in certain circumstances, use of the mid-quarter convention could result in a *larger* deduction. For example, assume the same facts as above except that the $120,000 of equipment was purchased on January 2. If the $90,000 of equipment was purchased on September 28, the deduction would be $29,000 as computed above. However, if the $90,000 purchase was delayed until October 1, the deduction would jump to $33,213, computed as follows:

January 2 purchase	($120,000 × .2500) =	$30,000
October 1 purchase	($ 90,000 × .0357) =	3,213
Total		$33,213

Careful planning of equipment purchases is very important if achieving tax savings is one of the motives in purchasing the items.

.02 Automobiles and Other Listed Property

The limitations on ACRS deductions for automobiles instituted in the Deficit Reduction Act of 1984 (discussed previously) were strengthened by the Tax Reform Act of 1986. The ceiling for the sum of the depreciation deduction and the expense election for automobiles placed into service in 2001 (the limit is indexed for inflation) is:[43]

Year	Limit
1	$3,060
2	4,900
3	2,950
Succeeding years	1,775

For electric automobiles, the corresponding amounts are $9,280, $14,800, $8,850, and $5,325.

---

[43] Code Sec. 280F(a)(2); Rev. Proc. 2001-19, 2001-9 IRB 732.

As was true under ACRS, if the automobile is not used more than 50 percent for business during the year placed into service, the Code Sec. 179 deduction is not allowed, and depreciation must be taken at straight-line rates over the alternate depreciation system (ADS) life.[44]

Example 8-23. Jim Robocken purchased an auto for $18,000 in 2000. He used the auto on business 30 percent of the time in 2000. His depreciation rate the first year would be for five-year property, a rate of 10 percent. Therefore, his depreciation would be $18,000 × .30 × .10 = $540.

If usage in a subsequent year drops below 50 percent, then excess depreciation for all preceding years must be recaptured, i.e., included in income for such tax year. Also depreciation for such tax year and any subsequent tax years must be computed under straight-line rates.[45]

Example 8-24. Scott Higgenbottom purchased an auto in 1999 for $18,000. He used the auto 60 percent for business purposes in 1999 and 55 percent in 2000, but in 2001 his business use dropped to 45 percent. His recapture is as follows:

Year		Amount Taken	Amount Allowed	Recapture
1999	$ 3,060 × .60	$1,836		
	$18,000 × .60 × .10		$1,080	$ 756
2000	$ 5,000 × .55	2,750		
	$18,000 × .55 × .20		1,980	770
Total		$4,361	$3,060	$1,526

.03 Record Keeping for Listed Property

Taxpayers will not be allowed deductions for the use of any listed property unless substantiated by adequate records. Elements to be proved with respect to any listed property are:[46]

- The amount of each separate expenditure with respect to an item of listed property, such as the cost of acquisition, the cost of capital improvements, lease payments, the cost of maintenance and repairs, or other expenditures;

- The amount of each business/investment use, based on the appropriate measure, i.e., mileage for autos and time for other listed property, and the total use of the listed property for the tax period;

[44] Code Sec. 280F(b) and (d)(1).
[45] Code Sec. 280F(b)(2).
[46] Temp. Reg. § 1.274-5T(b)(6).

- The date of the expenditure or use; and

- The business or investment purpose for the use.

A taxpayer must prove each element of an expenditure or use. Written evidence has much more probative value than oral evidence alone.[47] Although contemporaneous logs are not required, the closer to contemporaneous, the more credible the evidence.

To meet the adequate records requirement, taxpayers must maintain an account book, diary, log, expense statement, trip sheet, or similar records.[48]

.04 Leased Automobiles and Other Listed Property

Congress recognized that one way to obtain a higher deduction for the use of luxury automobiles would be to lease the auto. Therefore, Code Sec. 280F(c) was enacted. This section does not apply to automobiles leased or held for leasing by a person regularly engaged in the business of leasing.[49] Leases of under 30 days are also not covered in this section. The nature of the taxpayer's business in its entirety is to be taken into account in determining whether the taxpayer is regularly engaged in the business of leasing. Occasional or incidental leasing activity, e.g., leasing only one automobile in a year, is insufficient. An employer who charges employees for the personal use of their automobiles is not regularly engaged in the business of leasing.[50]

The impact of leasing an automobile is that the full leasing expense may be deducted, but an inclusion in gross income is required. The purpose of the inclusion in gross income is to effectively limit the deduction to that allowed for owned automobiles. The inclusion amount for automobiles first leased in 2001 is in Table 3 of Rev. Proc. 2001-19. A portion of the table is reproduced below.

Fair market value		Tax year of lease				
Greater than	But not greater than	1st	2nd	3rd	4th	5th & Later
$17,500	$ 18,000	$ 20	$ 44	$ 64	$ 77	$ 89
20,000	20,500	40	89	131	156	181
45,000	46,000	247	540	802	961	1,108
95,000	100,000	671	1,472	2,182	2,617	3,020

The amount to be included in income is determined by selecting the dollar amount from the proper column (the year in which the automobile is

---

[47] Temp. Reg. § 1.274-5T(c).
[48] *Id.*

[49] Code Sec. 280F(c).
[50] Temp. Reg. § 1.280F-5T(c).

first used under the lease). That amount is then prorated for the number of days of the lease term included in the taxable year and is then multiplied by the business/investment use for the taxable year.[51]

> **Example 8-25.** On January 17, 1999, John Gibbons leased (for four years) and placed into service a passenger automobile with a fair market value of $45,250 on the first day of the lease term. The car was used 75 percent of the time for business and 25 percent for personal purposes. Assuming the car continues to be used 75 percent for business purposes, the inclusion amounts are as follows:

Tax Year	Dollar Amount	Proration	Business Use	Inclusion
1999	$ 196	349/365	75%	$141
2000	426	365/365	75%	320
2001	633	365/365	75%	475
2002	759	365/365	75%	569
2003	759	16/365	75%	33

.05 Other Leased Listed Property

For listed property (other than autos) leased after June 18, 1984, the lessee must include a certain amount in gross income for the first tax year in which the property is not used predominantly in a qualified business use.[52] The inclusion amount for property leased after 1986 is the sum of:

1. The fair market value of the property; times

2. The business/investment use for the first tax year in which the business use percentage is 50 percent or less; times

3. The applicable percentage from Table XIII (see below),

    plus

1. The fair market value of the property; times

2. The average of the business/investment use for all tax years (in which the property is leased) that precede the first tax year in which the business use percentage is 50 percent or less; times

3. The applicable percentage from Table XIV (see following).[53]

---

[51] Reg. § 1.280F-7(a)(2).
[52] Reg. § 1.280F-7(b)(1).

[53] Reg. § 1.280F-7(b)(2).

Table XIII
First Tax Year During Lease in Which
Business Use Percentage Is 50% or Less

Type of Property	1	2	3	4	5	6	7	8	9	10	11	12 or later
Recovery period under 7 years under alternate MACRS ..	2.1	-7.2	-19.8	-20.1	-12.4	-12.4	-12.4	-12.4	-12.4	-12.4	-12.4	-12.4
Recovery period 7-10 years under alternate MACRS ..	3.9	-3.8	-17.7	-25.1	-27.8	-27.2	-27.1	-27.6	-23.7	-14.7	-14.7	-14.7
Recovery period over 10 years under alternate MACRS ..	6.6	-1.6	-16.9	-25.6	-29.9	-31.1	-32.8	-35.1	-33.3	-26.7	-19.7	-12.2

Table XIV
First Tax Year During Lease in Which
Business Use Percentage Is 50% or Less

Type of Property	1	2	3	4	5	6	7	8	9	10	11	12 & Later
Recovery period under 7 years under alternate MACRS	0.0	10.0	22.0	21.2	12.7	12.7	12.7	12.7	12.7	12.7	12.7	12.7
Recovery period 7-10 years under alternate MACRS	0.0	9.3	23.8	31.3	33.8	32.7	31.6	30.5	25.0	15.0	15.0	15.0
Recovery period over 10 years under alternate MACRS	0.0	10.1	26.3	35.4	39.6	40.2	40.8	41.4	37.5	29.2	20.8	12.5

Example 8-26.[54] On February 1, 1999, Larry House, a calendar year taxpayer, leased and placed into service a computer with a fair market value of $3,000. The lease is for a period of three years. House's qualified business use of the property is 80 percent in 1999, 40 percent

---

[54] Reg. § 1.280F-7(b)(3).

in 2000, and 35 percent in 2001. House must add an inclusion amount to gross income in 2000, the first tax year in which he does not use the computer more than 50 percent for business. Since 2000 is the second year of the lease, and since the computer has a five-year recovery period under both MACRS and the alternate MACRS method, the applicable percentage from Table XIII is − 7.2 percent and the applicable percentage from Table XIV is 10 percent. House's inclusion amount is $154, which is the sum of $-86 ($3,000 × .40 × − .072) and $240 ($3,000 × .80 × .10).

The fair market value is the value on the first day of the lease term. If the capitalized cost of an item of listed property is specified in the lease terms, the lessee must treat that amount as the fair market value.[55]

If the lease term begins within nine months before the closing of the taxpayer's year, the property is not predominantly used in a qualified business use during that portion of the tax year, and the lease term continues into the lessee's subsequent tax year, then the inclusion amount is added to gross income in the lessee's subsequent tax year. The amount is determined by taking into account the average of the business/investment use for both tax years and the applicable percentage for the tax year in which the lease term begins (or, in the case of a passenger automobile with a fair market value greater than $16,500, the appropriate dollar amount for the tax year in which the lease begins).[56]

If the lease term is less than one year, the amount which must be added to gross income is an amount that bears the same ratio to the additional inclusion amount as the number of lease days in the year bears to 365.[57]

The inclusion amount cannot exceed the sum of the deductible amounts of rent allocable to the lessee's tax year in which the inclusion amount must be included in gross income.[58]

Example 8-27. On August 1, 1999, Julie Dale, a calendar year taxpayer, leased and placed into service an item of listed property that is five-year property, with a fair market value of $10,000. The property has a recovery period of five years under the alternate MACRS method. The lease is for five years. Dale's qualified business use of the property is 50 percent in 1999 and 90 percent in 2000. Dale pays rent of $3,600 for 2000 of which $3,240 is deductible. Dale must include $147 in gross income in 2000. The applicable percentage from Table XIII is 2.1 percent; the applicable percentage from Table XIV is 0

---

[55] Reg. § 1.280F-7(b)(2).
[56] Temp. Reg. § 1.280F-5T(g)(1).

[57] Temp. Reg. § 1.280F-5T(g)(2).
[58] Temp. Reg. § 1.280F-5T(g)(3).

percent. Therefore, the inclusion is equal to $10,000 \times 70\% \times 2.1\% =$ $147.

Example 8-28. On October 1, 2000, John Joyce, a calendar year taxpayer, leased and placed into service an item of listed property that is three-year property, with a fair market value of $15,000. The property has a recovery period of five years under the alternate MACRS method. The lease term is for 6 months (ending on March 31, 2001) during which Joyce will use the property 45 percent in business. Joyce must include $71.07 in gross income in 2000. The applicable percentage from Table XIII is 2.1 percent; the applicable percentage from Table XIV is 0 percent. Therefore, the inclusion is equal to $15,000 \times 45\% \times 2.1\% \times 182/365 = $70.68.

.06 Employer-Provided Autos

If employees use employer-provided autos for personal purposes, problems may be created for the employer. Since some of the usage is for personal purposes, the employer may not depreciate the entire cost of the automobile unless any of the following conditions are met:[59]

- The use is directly connected to the business of the taxpayer (in that case there *is* no personal usage); or

- The use is reported by the taxpayer as income to the employee; or

- The employee pays a fair rent for the personal use. Qualified business use does not include the use of property by a person who owns more than five percent of the business.[60] Therefore, depreciation must be based only on the business usage, regardless of whether the employee reports the amount as income or pays rent.

In determining the amount to be included in income, the regulations for Code Sec. 61 allow valuation to be determined under general valuation rules or under three special valuation rules, which are used under certain circumstances for certain commonly used fringe benefits.[61] Under general valuation rules, the value is determined by reference to the cost of leasing a comparable vehicle on the same or comparable terms in the geographic area in which the vehicle is available for use.[62]

One of the special valuation methods is an Annual Lease Valuation Table (see following).

---

[59] Temp. Reg. § 1.280F-6T(d)(3)(iv).
[60] Temp. Reg. § 1.280F-6T(d)(2)(ii).

[61] Reg. § 1.61-21(b)(4).
[62] *Id.*

Table XV
Annual Lease Value Table[*]

FMV of Auto	Annual Lease Value	FMV of Auto	Annual Lease Value
$ 0–999	$ 600	22,000–22,999	6,100
1,000–1,999	850	23,000–23,999	6,350
2,000–2,999	1,100	24,000–24,999	6,600
3,000–3,999	1,350	25,000–25,999	6,850
4,000–4,999	1,600	26,000–27,999	7,250
5,000–5,999	1,850	28,000–29,999	7,750
6,000–6,999	2,100	30,000–31,999	8,250
7,000–7,999	2,350	32,000–33,999	8,750
8,000–8,999	2,600	34,000–35,999	9,250
9,000–9,999	2,850	36,000–37,999	9,750
10,000–10,999	3,100	38,000–39,999	10,250
11,000–11,999	3,350	40,000–41,999	10,750
12,000–12,999	3,600	42,000–43,999	11,250
13,000–13,999	3,850	44,000–45,999	11,750
14,000–14,999	4,100	46,000–47,999	12,250
15,000–15,999	4,350	48,000–49,999	12,750
16,000–16,999	4,600	50,000–51,999	13,250
17,000–17,999	4,850	52,000–53,999	13,750
18,000–18,999	5,100	54,000–55,999	14,250
19,000–19,999	5,350	56,000–57,999	14,750
20,000–20,999	5,600	58,000–59,999	15,250
21,000–21,999	5,850		

[*] Reg. § 1.61-21(d)(2)(iii).

The annual lease value for automobiles having a fair market value of over $59,999 = (.25 × FMV of auto + 500).[63]

The above table is based on a four-year lease term. Generally, the table is again used for each subsequent four-year period by recalculating the fair market value as of the start of the fifth year.[64]

The annual lease value in the table above does not include the value of any fuel furnished by the employer; such fuel may be valued at fair market value or at 5.5 cents per mile.[65]

A taxpayer may also use a second special valuation method, the *vehicle cents per mile valuation rate*. If this method is used, the value of the personal use is the standard mileage rate[66] (e.g., 34.5 cents/mile in 2001).

---

[63] *Id.*
[64] Reg. § 1.61-21(d)(2)(iv).

[65] Reg. § 1.61-21(d)(3)(ii)(B).
[66] Reg. § 1.61-21(e)(1)(i).

Example 8-29. In 2001, Allen Bouvier had the total use of an automobile furnished by his employer. During the year, he put a total of 30,000 miles on the car, 18,000 for personal use and 12,000 for business use. The value of the personal use of the auto is $6,210 (18,000 × .345).

The above mileage rule can be used only if the auto is driven at least 10,000 miles during the year, and it is used primarily by employees.[67]

The mileage rate *does* include fuel. If fuel is not furnished by the employer, the mileage rate may be reduced by 5.5 cents per mile.[68]

A third special rule may be used if the only personal use to which the employee puts the auto is for commuting. In that event, the employee may value the commuting at $1.50 per vehicle per one-way commute (e.g., home to work or work to home).[69]

.07 Recovery Period of Personal Property

Following are descriptions of the six personal property classes under MACRS:

3-year property. This class includes property with a class life of four years or less.[70] Examples include:[71]

- Over-the-road tractor units;

- Race horses over two years old when placed into service;

- Other horses over twelve years old when placed into service;

- Breeding hogs;

- Special handling devices for manufacturing food and beverages (e.g., returnable pallets);

- Assets used in the manufacture of plastic products and the molding of primary plastics for the trade; and

- Special tools for the manufacturing of glass products, fabricated metal products (e.g., dies, jigs, molds), and motor vehicles (e.g., dies, jigs, molds).

5-year property. This class includes property with a class life of more than four years, but less than 10 years.[72] Examples include: taxis, buses, heavy general-purpose trucks (actual unloaded weight of 13,000 pounds or more), automobiles, light-duty trucks (actual unloaded weight of under

---

[67] Reg. § 1.61-21(e)(1)(ii).
[68] Reg. § 1.61-21(e)(3).
[69] Reg. § 1.61-21(f).
[70] Code Sec. 168(e)(1).

[71] Code Sec. 168(e)(3)(A); Rev. Proc. 87-56, 1987-2 CB 674.

[72] Code Sec. 168(e)(1).

13,000 pounds), computers and peripheral equipment, office equipment (typewriters, copiers, calculators, etc.), property used in connection with research and experimentation, airplanes not used for commercial or contract-carrying purposes, helicopters, trailers, and trailer-mounted containers, dairy or breeding cattle, breeding goats and sheep, assets used for offshore drilling, and for drilling oil and gas wells, assets used in the manufacture of: knitted goods; yarn, thread and woven fabric; textured yarns; apparel; cutting of timber; construction; sawing of dimensional stock from logs; chemicals; primary nonferrous metals (special tools); electronic components; semiconductors; ship and boat building (special tools); assets used in motor transport of passengers and freight, assets used in radio and television broadcasting (except transmitting towers); and computer-based telephone switching equipment.[73]

7-year property. This class includes property with a class life of 10 or more years but less than 16 years.[74] Examples include railroad cars and locomotives, most agricultural equipment, office furniture and fixtures, much manufacturing equipment, and property that does not have a class life.[75]

10-year property. This class includes property with a class life of at least 16 years, but less than 20 years.[76] Examples include vessels, barges, tugs, many assets used to manufacture food, certain assets used to manufacture and repair boats, and single-purpose agricultural and horticultural structures.[77]

15-year property. This class includes property with a class life of at least 20 years, but less than 25 years.[78] Examples include roads, shrubbery, wharves, municipal treatment plants, pipeline transportation assets, and assets used in the manufacture of cement.[79]

20-year property. This class includes property with a class life of 25 years or more.[80] Examples include certain farm buildings, certain railroad structures, municipal sewers, and telephone central office buildings.[81]

Following is the MACRS table for personal property assuming that the half-year convention is applicable:

---

[73] Code Sec. 168(e)(3)(B); Rev. Proc. 87-56, 1987-2 CB 674.

[74] Code Sec. 168(e)(1).

[75] Code Sec. 168(e)(3)(C); Rev. Proc. 87-56, 1987-2 CB 674.

[76] Code Sec. 168(e)(1).

[77] Code Sec. 168(e)(3)(D); Rev. Proc. 87-56, 1987-2 CB 674.

[78] Code Sec. 168(e)(1).

[79] Rev. Proc. 87-56, 1987-2 CB 674.

[80] Code Sec. 168(e)(1).

[81] Rev. Proc. 87-56, 1987-2 CB 674.

Table XV[*]
MACRS Depreciation Using the Half-Year Convention

Recovery Year	3-year	5-year	7-year	10-year	15-year	20-year
1	33.33	20.00	14.29	10.00	5.00	3.750
2	44.45	32.00	24.49	18.00	9.50	7.219
3	14.81	19.20	17.49	14.40	8.55	6.677
4	7.41	11.52	12.49	11.52	7.70	6.177
5		11.52	8.93	9.22	6.93	5.713
6		5.76	8.92	7.37	6.23	5.285
7			8.93	6.55	5.90	4.888
8			4.46	6.55	5.90	4.522
9				6.56	5.91	4.462
10				6.55	5.90	4.461
11				3.28	5.91	4.462
12					5.90	4.461
13					5.91	4.462
14					5.90	4.461
15					5.91	4.462
16					2.95	4.461
17						4.462
18						4.461
19						4.462
20						4.461
21						2.231

[*] Rev. Proc. 87-57, 1987-2 CB 687.

.08 MACRS Real Property

Congress saved the most dramatic change in ACRS for real property. Effective generally for assets placed into service after 1986, the recovery period went from 19 years, 175 percent of straight-line, to 31.5 years (27.5 years for residential rental property) at straight-line rates.[82] Nonresidential real property placed into service on or after May 13, 1993, must be recovered over 39 years.[83] As under ACRS, the mid-month convention is used.[84] The rates for residential rental and commercial rental are shown in the tables following.[85]

---

[82] Code Sec. 168(b) and (c) (prior to amendment by P.L. 103-66).

[83] Act Sec. 13151(a), Revenue Reconciliation Act of 1993, amending Code Sec. 168(c).

[84] Code Sec. 168(d).

[85] Rev. Proc. 87-57, 1987-2 CB 687.

Table XVI
MACRS Depreciation—27 1/2 Year Residential Rental
Month Placed into Service

Recovery Year	1	2	3	4	5	6
1	3.485	3.182	2.879	2.576	2.273	1.970
2	3.636	3.636	3.636	3.636	3.636	3.636
3	3.636	3.636	3.636	3.636	3.636	3.636
4	3.636	3.636	3.636	3.636	3.636	3.636
5	3.636	3.636	3.636	3.636	3.636	3.636
6	3.636	3.636	3.636	3.636	3.636	3.636
7	3.636	3.636	3.636	3.636	3.636	3.636
8	3.636	3.636	3.636	3.636	3.636	3.636
9	3.636	3.636	3.636	3.636	3.636	3.636
10	3.637	3.637	3.637	3.637	3.637	3.637
11	3.636	3.636	3.636	3.636	3.636	3.636
12	3.637	3.637	3.637	3.637	3.637	3.637
13	3.636	3.636	3.636	3.636	3.636	3.636
14	3.637	3.637	3.637	3.637	3.637	3.637
15	3.636	3.636	3.636	3.636	3.636	3.636

Month Placed into Service

Recovery Year	7	8	9	10	11	12
1	1.667	1.364	1.061	0.758	0.455	0.152
2	3.636	3.636	3.636	3.636	3.636	3.636
3	3.636	3.636	3.636	3.636	3.636	3.636
4	3.636	3.636	3.636	3.636	3.636	3.636
5	3.636	3.636	3.636	3.636	3.636	3.636
6	3.636	3.636	3.636	3.636	3.636	3.636
7	3.636	3.636	3.636	3.636	3.636	3.636
8	3.636	3.636	3.636	3.636	3.636	3.636
9	3.636	3.636	3.636	3.636	3.636	3.636
10	3.636	3.636	3.636	3.636	3.636	3.636
11	3.637	3.637	3.637	3.637	3.637	3.637
12	3.636	3.636	3.636	3.636	3.636	3.636
13	3.637	3.637	3.637	3.637	3.637	3.637
14	3.636	3.636	3.636	3.636	3.636	3.636
15	3.637	3.637	3.637	3.637	3.637	3.637

Month Placed into Service

Recovery Year	1	2	3	4	5	6
16	3.637	3.637	3.637	3.637	3.637	3.637
17	3.636	3.636	3.636	3.636	3.636	3.636
18	3.637	3.637	3.637	3.637	3.637	3.637
19	3.636	3.636	3.636	3.636	3.636	3.636
20	3.637	3.637	3.637	3.637	3.637	3.637
21	3.636	3.636	3.636	3.636	3.636	3.636
22	3.637	3.637	3.637	3.637	3.637	3.637
23	3.636	3.636	3.636	3.636	3.636	3.636
24	3.637	3.637	3.637	3.637	3.637	3.637
25	3.636	3.636	3.636	3.636	3.636	3.636
26	3.637	3.637	3.637	3.637	3.637	3.637
27	3.636	3.636	3.636	3.636	3.636	3.636
28	1.970	2.273	2.576	2.879	3.182	3.485
29	—	—	—	—	—	—

Month Placed into Service

Recovery Year	7	8	9	10	11	12
16	3.636	3.636	3.636	3.636	3.636	3.636
17	3.637	3.637	3.637	3.637	3.637	3.637
18	3.636	3.636	3.636	3.636	3.636	3.636
19	3.637	3.637	3.637	3.637	3.637	3.637
20	3.636	3.636	3.636	3.636	3.636	3.636
21	3.637	3.637	3.637	3.637	3.637	3.637
22	3.636	3.636	3.636	3.636	3.636	3.636
23	3.637	3.637	3.637	3.637	3.637	3.637
24	3.636	3.636	3.636	3.636	3.636	3.636
25	3.637	3.637	3.637	3.637	3.637	3.637
26	3.636	3.636	3.636	3.636	3.636	3.636
27	3.637	3.637	3.637	3.637	3.637	3.637
28	3.636	3.636	3.636	3.636	3.636	3.636
29	0.152	0.455	0.758	1.061	1.364	1.667

Table XVII
MACRS Depreciation—31 1/2 Year Commercial Rental
Month Placed into Service

Recovery Year	1	2	3	4	5	6
1	3.042	2.778	2.513	2.249	1.984	1.720
2	3.175	3.175	3.175	3.175	3.175	3.175
3	3.175	3.175	3.175	3.175	3.175	3.175
4	3.175	3.175	3.175	3.175	3.175	3.175
5	3.175	3.175	3.175	3.175	3.175	3.175
6	3.175	3.175	3.175	3.175	3.175	3.175
7	3.175	3.175	3.175	3.175	3.175	3.175
8	3.175	3.174	3.175	3.174	3.175	3.174
9	3.174	3.175	3.174	3.175	3.174	3.175
10	3.175	3.174	3.175	3.174	3.175	3.174
11	3.174	3.175	3.174	3.175	3.174	3.175
12	3.175	3.174	3.175	3.174	3.175	3.174
13	3.174	3.175	3.174	3.175	3.174	3.175
14	3.175	3.174	3.175	3.174	3.175	3.174
15	3.174	3.175	3.174	3.175	3.174	3.175
16	3.175	3.174	3.175	3.174	3.175	3.174
17	3.174	3.175	3.174	3.175	3.174	3.175
18	3.175	3.174	3.175	3.174	3.175	3.174
19	3.174	3.175	3.174	3.175	3.174	3.175
20	3.175	3.174	3.175	3.174	3.175	3.174
21	3.174	3.175	3.174	3.175	3.174	3.175
22	3.175	3.174	3.175	3.174	3.175	3.174
23	3.174	3.175	3.174	3.175	3.174	3.175
24	3.175	3.174	3.175	3.174	3.175	3.174
25	3.174	3.175	3.174	3.175	3.174	3.175
26	3.175	3.174	3.175	3.174	3.175	3.174
27	3.174	3.175	3.174	3.175	3.174	3.175
28	3.175	3.174	3.175	3.174	3.175	3.174
29	3.174	3.175	3.174	3.175	3.174	3.175
30	3.175	3.174	3.175	3.174	3.175	3.174
31	3.174	3.175	3.174	3.175	3.174	3.175
32	1.720	1.984	2.249	2.513	2.778	3.042
33	—	—	—	—	—	—

Month Placed into Service

Recovery Year	7	8	9	10	11	12
1	1.455	1.190	0.926	0.661	0.397	0.132
2	3.175	3.175	3.175	3.175	3.175	3.175
3	3.175	3.175	3.175	3.175	3.175	3.175
4	3.175	3.175	3.175	3.175	3.175	3.175
5	3.175	3.175	3.175	3.175	3.175	3.175
6	3.175	3.175	3.175	3.175	3.175	3.175
7	3.175	3.175	3.175	3.175	3.175	3.175
8	3.175	3.175	3.175	3.175	3.175	3.175
9	3.174	3.175	3.174	3.175	3.174	3.175
10	3.175	3.174	3.175	3.174	3.175	3.174
11	3.174	3.175	3.174	3.175	3.174	3.175
12	3.175	3.174	3.175	3.174	3.175	3.174
13	3.174	3.175	3.174	3.175	3.174	3.175
14	3.175	3.174	3.175	3.174	3.175	3.174
15	3.174	3.175	3.174	3.175	3.174	3.175
16	3.175	3.174	3.175	3.174	3.175	3.174
17	3.174	3.175	3.174	3.175	3.174	3.175
18	3.175	3.174	3.175	3.174	3.175	3.174
19	3.174	3.175	3.174	3.175	3.174	3.175
20	3.175	3.174	3.175	3.174	3.175	3.174
21	3.174	3.175	3.174	3.175	3.174	3.175
22	3.175	3.174	3.175	3.174	3.175	3.174
23	3.174	3.175	3.174	3.175	3.174	3.175
24	3.175	3.174	3.175	3.174	3.175	3.174
25	3.174	3.175	3.174	3.175	3.174	3.175
26	3.175	3.174	3.175	3.174	3.175	3.174
27	3.174	3.175	3.174	3.175	3.174	3.175
28	3.175	3.174	3.175	3.174	3.175	3.174
29	3.174	3.175	3.174	3.175	3.174	3.175
30	3.175	3.174	3.175	3.174	3.175	3.174
31	3.174	3.175	3.174	3.175	3.174	3.175
32	3.175	3.174	3.175	3.174	3.175	3.174
33	0.132	0.397	0.661	0.926	1.190	1.455

Table XVIII
MACRS Depreciation—39 year Commercial
Month Placed into Service

Recovery Year	1	2	3	4	5	6
1	2.461	2.247	2.033	1.819	1.605	1.391
2-39	2.564	2.564	2.564	2.564	2.564	2.564
40	0.107	0.321	0.535	0.749	0.963	1.177

	7	8	9	10	11	12
1	1.177	0.963	0.749	0.535	0.321	0.107
2-39	2.564	2.564	2.564	2.564	2.564	2.5654
40	1.391	1.605	1.819	2.033	2.247	2.461

Example 8-30. Benton Co. purchased an apartment building for $250,000 on August 2, 2000. The value of the land was estimated to be $40,000. The $210,000 allocated to the building is depreciated, using Table XVI, over 27 and one-half years in total. Depreciation the first year (2000) would be $210,000 × .01364 = $2,864.

Example 8-31. Assume the same facts as in the previous example and that Benton Co. sold the property on March 10, 2003. Depreciation during the year of sale would be $210,000 × .03636 × 2.5/12 = $1,591. Note that one-half month's depreciation is allowed in the month of sale.

¶ 809   Code Sec. 179 Election

An election to expense (rather than capitalize and depreciate) certain property is available. Eligible property is tangible depreciable property which is Code Sec. 1245 property which is purchased for use in the active conduct of a trade or business.[86] The term "purchased" does not include acquisitions from relatives. The term "relatives" is generally as defined by Code Secs. 267 and 707(b). However, family members for this purpose include only spouses, ancestors, and lineal descendants.[87] Also not eligible are purchases by one member of a controlled group from another member of the same controlled group.[88] Basis of the property cannot have been determined by reference to the adjusted basis in the hands of the person from whom the property was acquired (e.g., gifts), nor can the property be inherited property.[89] If property is acquired in a nontaxable exchange, only the portion of the adjusted basis composed of boot is eligible for the expense election.[90]

The dollar amount which may be expressed in a tax year may not exceed $24,000 (for 2001 or 2002).[91] The dollar limitation is $25,000 for 2003 and thereafter.[92] The dollar limitation is reduced dollar for dollar by

---

[86] Code Sec. 179(d).
[87] Id.
[88] Id.
[89] Id.

[90] Id.
[91] Code Sec. 179(b)(1).
[92] Act Sec. 1111(a), Small Business Job Protection Act, amending Code Sec. 179(b)(1).

the amount by which the eligible property placed into service in a tax year exceeds $200,000.[93]

> **Example 8-32.** Grey Harbor Marina Co. placed into service $204,000 of tangible personal property in 2001. The maximum expense allowance is $20,000 ($24,000 − ($204,000 − $200,000)).

Also, the expense election, as determined under the two limitations previously mentioned, cannot exceed the taxable income from all of a taxpayer's trades or businesses computed without regard to the expense election.[94] Any amount not deductible because of the taxable limitations may be carried forward to future years. However, the deduction in any tax year cannot exceed the limitation in effect for that year.[95]

The election may be made simply by filling out Part I of Form 4562. Once made, the election is irrevocable.[96]

The expense allowance reduces the basis for both depreciation and gain or loss purposes.

> **Example 8-33.** In 2001, the McCoy-Barton partnership purchased light trucks costing $79,000. It took an expense election of $24,000 on the trucks. Depreciable basis would be $55,000 ($79,000 − $24,000). Depreciation in 2001 (see Table XV) would be $55,000 × .20 = $11,000. The total deduction would be $35,000 ($24,000 + $11,000).

If Code Sec. 179 property is no longer used predominantly for trade or business purposes, any expense allowance taken must be recaptured.[97] The amount recaptured is the difference between the amount expensed and the depreciation that would have been allowable had the Code Sec. 179 expense allowance not been elected.[98]

> **Example 8-34.** River Valley Extermination Co. purchased a van for $20,000 in 1995. On January 1, 1997, the van was converted from business to income-producing property use. The $17,500 expense election was elected in 1995. River Valley Co. must recapture (include in income) in 1997 $8,400. The MACRS deduction in 1995 and 1996 had the expense allowance not been elected would have been $3,500 ($17,500 × .20), and $5,600 ($17,500 × .32) greater. Therefore, the amount to be recaptured is $17,500 − $3,500 − $5,600 = $8,400.

Tax Tips and Pitfalls

The total deduction is maximized if the expense election is taken on property with the longest recovery period. For example, using the expense election on seven-year as opposed to five-year property will increase depreciation the first year for equipment acquired in 1997 by $1,028 ($18,000 × (.2000 − .1429)), and the second year by $1,352 ($18,000 × (.3200 − .2449)).

---

[93] Code Sec. 179(b)(2).
[94] Code Sec. 179(b)(3).
[95] Code Sec. 179(b)(3)(B).

[96] Code Sec. 179(c)(2).
[97] Code Sec. 179(d)(10).
[98] Reg. § 1.179-1(e)(1).

¶ 811   Straight-Line Election

Although most of the recovery period for personal property incorporates a rate of 200 percent of straight-line, the taxpayer may elect to use straight-line depreciation for one or more classes of property.[99] If the election is made, it is applicable to all property in that class placed into service that year.[100] A table incorporating the straight-line election is shown below:

Table XIX
Depreciation Rates Using Straight-Line and the
Half-Year Convention*
Property Class

Recovery Year	3-year	5-year	7-year	10-year	15-year	20-year
1	16.67	10.00	7.14	5.00	3.33	2.50
2	33.33	20.00	14.29	10.00	6.67	5.00
3	33.33	20.00	14.29	10.00	6.67	5.00
4	16.67	20.00	14.28	10.00	6.67	5.00
5		20.00	14.29	10.00	6.67	5.00
6		10.00	14.28	10.00	6.67	5.00
7			14.29	10.00	6.67	5.00
8			7.14	10.00	6.66	5.00
9				10.00	6.67	5.00
10				10.00	6.66	5.00
11				5.00	6.67	5.00
12					6.66	5.00
13					6.67	5.00
14					6.66	5.00
15					6.67	5.00
16					3.33	5.00
17						5.00
18						5.00
19						5.00
20						5.00
21						2.50

* Rev. Proc. 87-57, 1987-2 CB 687.

¶ 813   Alternative Depreciation System

The Tax Reform Act of 1986 provided an alternative depreciation system (ADS) that is elective in some instances and mandatory in other cases. ADS must be used in the case of:[101]

---

[99] Code Sec. 168(b)(5).   [101] Code Sec. 168(g).
[100] *Id.*

- Any tangible property which during the tax year is used predominantly outside the United States;

- Tax-exempt property; and

- Tax-exempt bond financed property.

An exception applies (i.e., MACRS is allowed) for certain high technology equipment leased to tax-exempt entities for five years or less.[102] If the lease term exceeds five years, this equipment should be depreciated using straight-line over five years.[103] High technology equipment includes such items as computers and peripheral equipment, high technology telephone station equipment, and high technology medical equipment, e.g., CAT scanners.[104]

ADS also must be used for AMT purposes[105] and for earnings and profits purposes.[106] If a taxpayer elects ADS for depreciable tangible personal property, the election applies to all of the property in that class placed into service in the tax year. However, the election is made separately for each item of *real* property.[107]

The ADS recovery periods are as follows:[108]

Property	Recovery Period
Personal property with no class life	12 years
Nonresidential real and residential rental property ...	40 years
Code Sec. 1245 property that is real property with no class life	40 years
Automobiles and light-duty trucks	5 years
Computers and peripheral equipment	5 years
Single-purpose agricultural and horticultural structures...................................	15 years
Most other property	class life

¶ 815   General Asset Accounts

Many businesses have large numbers of capital assets which have little individual value, e.g., railroad ties, beer kegs, and so on. Accounting for the separate depreciation and disposition of these items would be tedious. Fortunately, a taxpayer is allowed to group the assets together and depreciate them as a whole. However, when these assets are disposed of, all proceeds realized are included in income as ordinary income.[109]

Example 8-35. Four Stars Brewery purchased 5,000 kegs at a cost of $20 each in 1997. In 2001, the company sold 500 of the kegs for $7,500. The entire proceeds are ordinary income in 2001, but depreciation will continue to be taken on all 5,000 kegs.

---

[102] Code Sec. 168(h)(3).
[103] Code Secs. 168(h)(3) and (g)(3)(C).
[104] Code Sec. 168(i)(2).
[105] Code Sec. 56(g)(4)(A).

[106] Code Sec. 312(k)(3)(A).
[107] Code Sec. 168(g)(7).
[108] Code Sec. 168(g)(2) and (3).
[109] Code Sec. 168(i)(4).

¶ 817   Pre-ACRS Rules for Depreciation

Property that was either placed into service before 1981 or property that is ineligible for ACRS for various reasons is subject to the rules that existed before the Economic Recovery Tax Act of 1981 (ERTA). The relevant factors in determining depreciation are the depreciable life, the salvage value, and the method used.

.01   Depreciable Life

For property placed into service after December 31, 1970 and before 1981, or property that does not qualify for ACRS, two options are available. A taxpayer may elect the ADR system or use the actual useful life.

.02   Actual Useful Life

This is the period that the asset is expected to be useful to the taxpayer in the taxpayer's trade or business or in the production of income.[110] The taxpayer's experience with like property is a prime factor in determining useful life.[111] Criteria to be considered include:

- Wear and tear and decay or decline from natural causes;

- Technological developments;

- Climatic and other local conditions; and

- The taxpayer's policy as to repairs, replacement, and renewals.[112]

If the taxpayer lacks sufficient experience to establish useful lives, industry norms may be used.[113]

.03   ADR System

The key element of the asset depreciation range (ADR) system is that a range of depreciable lives (low end, midpoint, and upper end) is established for each class of assets. If a taxpayer used the range of depreciable lives provided in the ADR system, the IRS would not challenge the depreciation deduction. Alternatively, a taxpayer could apply the facts and circumstances known to justify a different life.[114]

.04   Salvage Value

"Salvage value" is the net realizable value (sales price less selling expenses) that the taxpayer could expect to receive from a sale of the asset once the asset is retired from service. If the taxpayer retires assets from service while they are still in good condition, the salvage value may constitute a substantial portion of the asset's cost. On the other hand, salvage value may be no more than junk value if the asset is largely used up.[115]

---

[110] Reg. § 1.167(a)-1(b).
[111] Id.
[112] Id.

[113] Id.
[114] Reg. § 1.167-11.
[115] Reg. § 1.167(a)-1(c)(1).

As previously mentioned, salvage value is disregarded if ACRS is applicable. For non-ACRS property, salvage value may be ignored for personal property up to 10 percent of the asset's cost, provided that the asset has at least a three-year life. Livestock is not eligible for this reduction.[116]

> **Example 8-36.** Millworks, Inc., purchased in 1983 a truck as well as office furniture. The truck cost $14,000 and Millworks, Inc., estimated salvage value to be $3,000; the respective amounts for the office furniture were $6,000 and $500. Since all items were purchased from a 20 percent stockholder, and the stockholder had placed them into service before 1981, ACRS is not available. The depreciable cost of the truck is $14,000 − ($3,000 − $1,400), or $12,400. However, the depreciable cost of the office furniture is $6,000 − ($500 − $500) = $6,000.

Under the ADR option, salvage value is not deducted to arrive at depreciable cost, but the asset cannot be depreciated below salvage value (reduced by 10 percent of the asset's cost if applicable).[117]

¶ 819   Pre-ACRS Depreciation Methods

The use of depreciation methods which incorporate rapid write-offs (accelerated methods) is not permitted for certain assets.[118] Subject to that constraint, however, any reasonable and consistently applied method may be used.[119] The Internal Revenue Code does specify four methods:

1. The straight-line method;

2. The double declining balance (or any rate less than double declining balance) method;

3. The sum of the years-digits method; and

4. Other consistent methods.[120]

.01 Straight-Line Method

Under this method, the depreciable cost (adjusted basis − salvage value) is divided by the remaining useful life to arrive at the annual depreciation.

> **Example 8-37.** In January 1984, Reuter Co. exchanged a hoist for a used cutting machine. Since the hoist was purchased in 1980, ACRS is not permitted for the cutting machine. The adjusted basis of the cutting machine is $8,000, salvage value is $1,200, and a four-year life is estimated. Depreciation per year would be ($8,000 − ($1,200 − $800)) divided by 4, or $1,900.

---

[116] Reg. § 1.167(f)-1(b)(1).
[117] Reg. § 1.167(a)-11(d)(1)(i)(iv).
[118] See the discussion of each depreciation method for details.

[119] Code Sec. 167(b) (prior to being striken by OBRA 1990); Reg. § 1.167(b)-0.

[120] *Id.*

.02 Declining Balance Method

This method entails applying a percentage rate to a continually declining balance, such balance being the original adjusted basis less depreciation taken in previous years.[121] The maximum percentage rate permitted for different asset types is as follows:[122]

Type of Asset	Permitted	Maximum Percentage of Straight Line Permitted
Assets with a useful life of under three years.	No	N.A.
New tangible personal property.	Yes	200%
Used tangible personal property.	Yes	150%
New residential rental property.	Yes	200%
Used residential rental property.	Yes	125%
Other Section 1250 property.	Yes	150%

These rates are generally applicable to property acquired after July 24, 1969, which is *not* ACRS or MACRS property. Different rules apply in some cases to property acquired before that date.

Example 8-38. Assume the same facts as in Example 8-37, except that Reuter Co. chooses the declining balance method. Depreciation for the four years is computed as follows.

Year	Cost	Prior Depr.	Depr. Cost	Life Yrs.	%	Current Depr.
1984	8,000	—	8,000	4	37.5	$3,000
1985	8,000	3,000	5,000	4	37.5	1,875
1986	8,000	4,875	3,125	4	37.5	1,172
1987	8,000	6,047	1,953	4	37.5	732

In this example, the nondepreciable tail is $1,221 (the basis at the end of 1987). This is greater than the $400 of salvage that had to be taken into account; however, if the salvage value had been higher, say $1,300, depreciation for the last year would have been reduced from $732 to $653. This is true because the undepreciated cost at the end of the asset's useful life cannot be less than the salvage value.[123]

.03 Sum of the Years-Digits Method

This is also an accelerated method, but, unlike the declining balance method, there is no residual basis left over other than the salvage value. Sum of the Years-Digits (S-Y-D) method can only be used where double declining balance is permissible. The key to S-Y-D is that a changing (and declining) fraction is applied each year to the cost of the asset. The numerator of this fraction is the number of years of remaining useful life. The denominator is the sum of all of the digits of the asset's useful life.[124]

---

[121] Reg. § 1.167(b)-2.
[122] Code Sec. 167(c) and (j).
[123] Reg. § 1.167(b)-2(a).
[124] Reg. § 1.167(b)-3(a)(1).

Example 8-39. Assume the same facts as in Example 8-37, except that the cutting machine is new and that S-Y-D is used. Depreciation for the four years would be as follows:

Year	Cost	Salvage Value	Depr. Cost	Prior Depr.	Life Yrs.	Fraction	Current Depr.
1984	8,000	400	7,600	—	4	4/10	3,040
1985	8,000	400	7,600	3,040	4	3/10	2,280
1986	8,000	400	7,600	5,320	4	2/10	1,520
1987	8,000	400	7,600	6,840	4	1/10	760

¶ 821   Reduction of Basis

The adjusted basis of an asset is reduced by the greater of depreciation allowed or allowable.[125] If a taxpayer fails to deduct depreciation in a given year, the taxpayer may not increase the deduction in later years.[126] Rather, the basis of the asset will be reduced as if the taxpayer *had* taken the depreciation.[127]

However, Rev. Proc. 99-49 provides an automatic method change procedure that generally applies when the taxpayer took too little on depreciation or amortization on an asset that the taxpayer owns at the beginning of the year. The company is able to catch up on any missed depreciation in the current year.

Example 8-40. Crane Co. placed an asset into service on January 2, 1995. The asset cost $15,000, had a 5-year life and no salvage value. The company chose straight-line depreciation. It took a full year's depreciation in 1995; however, it forgot to take depreciation on the item in 1996. Despite this, basis in the asset at the end of 1996 would have been $15,000 − $6,000, or $9,000.

On the other hand, if too much depreciation is taken, basis is reduced by the amount allowed (the amount taken); but to the extent that the amount allowed exceeds the amount allowable, the excess depreciation will reduce basis only to the extent that a tax benefit is gained from taking the extra depreciation.

¶ 823   Amortization

The cost of certain intangible assets is recovered through amortization. Section 197, effective for acquisitions after August 10, 1993, made major changes in amortization rules. Prior to the passage of Section 197, much uncertainty existed as to the amortizable life and as to the eligibility for amortization.

Section 197 intangibles are amortized over 15 years. They include: goodwill, going-concern value, covenants not to compete, customer lists and

---

[125] Reg. § 1.1016-3(a)(1).
[126] Reg. § 1.167(a)-10(a).

[127] Reg. § 1.1016-3(a)(1).

subscription lists, know-how, customer-based intangibles, licenses and permits, franchises, trademarks, and trade names.

Old Rules for Intangibles and Intangibles Not Covered by Code Sec. 197

The cost of intangible assets with limited, determinable lives was recovered through amortization. Amortizable assets included certain bond discounts or premiums, patents, copyrights, leasehold improvements, covenants not to compete, trademarks, and trade name expenditures. Amortizable assets (some tangible) which could have been written off over an artificially short period of time included child care facility costs, experimental expenditures, low-income housing, organization costs, partnership organization fees, pollution control facilities, reforestation expenditures and business start-up costs. Although there are several permissible depreciation methods, only straight-line amortization is allowed.

.01 Leasehold Improvements

Leasehold improvements are not covered by Code Sec. 197. Leasehold improvements made in lieu of rent are deductible as rent expense and thus are not subject to amortization.[128] However, other leasehold improvements are treated as capital expenditures and must be depreciated over their MACRS life, regardless of the lease term.[129]

> **Example 8-41.** In 2001, Inman Co. constructed a factory building on land that the company had leased for 50 years. Since the MACRS recovery period is 39 years, that is the recovery period. If the lease period were only 30 years, the building would still be depreciated over 39 years with the remaining basis written off when the lease ended.

.02 Reforestation Expenditures—Election to Amortize

Reforestation expenditures are not covered by Code Sec. 197. Taxpayers must capitalize costs of forestation or reforestation. Normally, these costs are then subject to depletion as the trees are cut or sold. However, a limited amount of these expenditures may be instead amortized over an 84-month period, provided it is incurred for qualified timber property.

Reforestation expenditures are defined as direct costs incurred in connection with forestation or reforestation by planting or by artificial or natural seeding. This includes costs included in the site preparation, cost of seeds or seedlings, and the cost of labor and tools (including depreciation of equipment) used in planting or seeding.[130]

Qualified timber property is property located in the United States which will contain trees in significant commercial quantities. The size of the woodlot must be at least one acre. Qualified timber property does not include shelter belts or ornamental trees such as Christmas trees.[131]

---

[128] *Journal-Trib. Publishing Co. v. Commr.*, CA-8, 54-2 USTC ¶ 9630, 216 F2d 138.
[129] Code Sec. 168(i)(8).

[130] Code Sec. 194(c)(3).

[131] Reg. § 1.194-3(a).

The maximum amount of basis that may be amortized during a tax year is $10,000 ($5,000 if the taxpayer is married filing separately). The law does not provide for a carryback or carryforward of expenditures exceeding $10,000.[132] The half-year convention is required; hence, six months of amortization is taken the first year and six months the eighth year.[133]

> **Example 8-42.** Jeff Hale, a calendar year taxpayer, incurred $2,520 of reforestation expenses in February and another $3,360 in October of 2001. His amortization deduction for 2001 would be $5,880/84 × 6, or $420.

The election is made by deducting the proper amount of amortization on the return and by attaching a statement that states the amount of the expenditures, the nature of the expenditures, the date incurred, the type of timber being grown, and the purpose for which it is being grown.[134]

If the property is disposed of within 10 years of the year of creation of the expenditure, part or all of the gain, as provided in Code Sec. 1245, may be recaptured.[135]

.03 Pollution Control Facilities

Amortization of pollution control facilities is not covered by Code Sec. 197. Certified pollution control facilities may be amortized over a period of 60 months at the election of the taxpayer.[136] The term "certified pollution control facility" is any treatment facility used in connection with property in operation before January 1, 1976, to abate or control water or atmospheric pollution or contamination.[137] The facilities must be certified by both state and federal authorities and must not significantly increase the output or capacity, extend the useful life, or reduce the total operating costs of the property or alter the nature of the production process or facility.[138]

If the useful life exceeds 15 years, the portion of the cost eligible for amortization equals a fraction, the numerator of which is 15 and the denominator of which is the useful life.[139]

> **Example 8-43.** Black Smoke, Inc., spent $300,000 on pollution control facilities having a useful life of 20 years. Only $225,000 ($300,000 × 15/20) is eligible for amortization. The remaining basis of $75,000 must be depreciated.

.04 Research and Experimental Costs

Code Sec. 197 does not apply to research and experimental costs. Research and experimental expenditures which are capitalizable, but which are not the cost of depreciable property, may, at the election of the taxpayer, be amortized over a 60-month period, beginning with the month

---

[132] Reg. § 1.194-2(b).
[133] Reg. § 1.194-1(b).
[134] Reg. § 1.194-4(a).
[135] Reg. § 1.194-1(c).

[136] Code Sec. 169(a).
[137] Code Sec. 169(d).
[138] Id.
[139] Code Sec. 169(f)(2); Reg. § 1.169-3(d).

in which benefits are first realized.[140] The other alternatives are to currently expense the items (generally preferable), or to capitalize the items and leave them untouched until sale or abandonment (usually the worst alternative).

The term "research or experimental expenditures" means research and development costs in the experimental or laboratory sense. Included are generally all costs incident to the development of an experimental or pilot model, a plant process, a product, a formula, an invention, or similar property, and the improvement of already existing property.[141] The term includes the costs of obtaining a patent, but the costs of acquiring another's patent, model, production or process are not included. Also not included are expenditures for the ordinary testing or inspection of materials or products for quality control, efficiency surveys, management studies, or advertising.[142]

If the taxpayer decides to amortize (rather than expense or capitalize), annual depreciation on buildings and equipment used in the research and experimental work is amortized over the 60-month period.

> **Example 8-44.** Fools Are Us Co. developed and introduced into the market a low-calorie sweetener. Research and experimental costs were as follows:

Salaries of researchers	$ 70,000
Costs of obtaining a patent	18,000
Laboratory supplies	12,000
Depreciation on lab building	30,000
Depreciation on lab equipment	15,000
Total	$145,000

> If Fools Are Us Co. elects to amortize the expenditures, the $145,000 would be amortized over a 60-month period beginning with the month the sweetener is put to use.

¶ 825   Depletion

Depletion is the cost recovery method permitted for wasting assets, i.e., assets that are used up through the extraction process.

.01 Eligibility for Depletion

Only taxpayers who have an "economic interest" in mineral deposits or standing timber are entitled to the depletion deduction. The question as to what is an economic interest has been a much litigated issue. This is understandable since the regulations state that an economic interest exists where two conditions are fulfilled:

1.   The taxpayer has acquired by investment any interest in mineral in place or standing timber; and

---

[140] Code Sec. 174(b).
[141] Reg. § 1.174-2(a).
[142] *Id.*

2.	The taxpayer has secured, by any form of legal relationship, income derived from the extraction of the mineral or severance of the timber, to which the taxpayer must look for a return of capital.[143]

The mere possession of an economic or pecuniary advantage derived from production does not necessarily meet the second condition. For example, a contract entitling someone to purchase or process the product upon production or entitling that person to compensation for extracting or cutting does not convey an economic interest.[144]

.02 Leases

The deduction for depletion is to be equitably apportioned between the lessor and the lessee.[145] However, if the lease is in substance merely an employment contract, the lessee may not be entitled to any depletion. Generally, the lessee must derive its income from a share of production rather than, say, from a flat fee, or a fee per unit of item extracted.[146] Legal title to the item being extracted, while not definitive, would help in establishing the right to depletion.[147] The regulations provide little guidance; hence, this is also a frequently litigated area.

.03 Working Interest

A working interest is one where the owner of the interest has the responsibility of running the mineral or timber extraction process, i.e., oversees the operation, pays the expenses, and receives the income from the sale of the products. The owner of a fractional interest need not actually participate in the day-to-day operations, so long as it pays its fractional share of all expenses including drilling and development costs.

.04 Royalty Interest

When a land owner leases a mineral interest, the lease normally provides that the owner is to receive a certain fraction of the output of the lease. For oil and gas wells, the fraction traditionally was 1/8; however, in recent years it has been higher, often 5/32, sometimes more. The royalty owner's share comes out of gross revenue or gross production; expenses are normally not deducted except for state severance taxes. Overriding royalties occur when the lessee (the operator) sells a fraction of the gross revenue or net income of his or her interest.

.05 Mineral Production Payments

The term "production payment" is defined as the right to a specified share of the production from minerals in place or the right to proceeds from the production. This right must have an expected economic life less than

---

[143] Reg. § 1.611-1(b).
[144] Id.
[145] Reg. § 1.611-1(c)(2).
[146] Anderson v. Helvering, 40-1 USTC ¶ 9479, 310 US 404 (1940).

[147] Paragron Jewel Coal Co. v. Commr., 65-1 USTC ¶ 9379, 380 US 624 (1965).

the economic life of the minerals in place.[148] Three types of production payments are commonly used:

1.   *Carved-out production payments.* This type of payment occurs when the owner of a mineral property sells (or carves out) part of the future production. This is treated as a loan to the seller of the production payment. Hence, the buyer (creditor) has no economic interest in the property, and the depletion deduction is retained by the seller. Since the transaction is treated as a loan, the seller has no income at the time the production payment is created. When the mineral is produced, all income, including that going to the buyer, is taxed to the seller, and is eligible for the depletion deduction. When payments are made to the buyer, they are treated as a return of capital and are thus nontaxable. Any payments in excess of cost, as well as any interest income, would be taxable.[149]

2.   *Retained production payments.* These occur when the owner of a mineral interest sells the working interest but retains a production payment. The results are similar to the preceding case. The retained payment is treated as a purchase money loan. Thus, it becomes part of the seller's (land owner) proceeds and a part of the buyer's (operator of the working interest) basis. Payments made to the seller are taxed as income to the buyer and are eligible for depletion.[150]

3.   *Retained production payment on lease.* If a production payment is retained by the lessor in a leasing transaction, the amounts paid are treated as a bonus payable in installments. Thus, the lessee would include in income the payments going to the lessor. The lessee would also capitalize these payments (including interest) and would recover these costs through depletion. The lessor would include the amounts in income as received; they would be eligible for the depletion deduction.[151]

Example 8-45. In 2000, Chris Brinkman carves out a production payment of $500,000 plus interest in favor of Eric Hickman. The payments are to come out of 25 percent of the first oil produced from the property. In 2001, Brinkman produces and sells $300,000 of oil. He pays Hickman $75,000 plus interest of $60,000. Brinkman would include the full $300,000 in income. He would deduct $60,000 of interest as well as depletion and other expenses from gross income. Hickman would report only $60,000 of income and the amount would not be subject to depletion.

---

[148] Reg. § 1.636-3(a)(1).

[149] Reg. § 1.636-1(a).

[150] Code Sec. 636(b).

[151] Code Sec. 636(c); Reg. § 1.636-2.

Example 8-46. Lisa Smathers sells a mineral interest for $300,000 plus a $200,000 production payment payable out of the mineral interest. The $200,000 is treated as a purchase money loan; hence, the total sales price is $500,000.

Example 8-47. In 2000, Pat Lorris leased mineral property to Midwest Oil, Inc., receiving a one-eighth royalty interest plus a production payment of $200,000 plus interest. In 2001, Midwest Oil, Inc., paid Lorris, in addition to the royalty payment, $25,000 of production payment plus interest of $20,000. Lorris has ordinary income of $45,000 subject to depletion, and Midwest Oil, Inc., has an increased basis in the property of $45,000 which would be subject to depletion.

.06 Computing Depletion—The Cost Method

A taxpayer is entitled to take the greater of depletion computed using the cost method or the percentage method. The cost method is applicable in all cases; percentage depletion is not applicable in certain instances. The adjusted basis for determining gain on the sale is the amount subject to depletion.[152]

.07 Computing Cost Depletion

Cost depletion is determined by multiplying the number of units sold by a fraction, the numerator of which is the adjusted basis of the property, and the denominator of which is the number of units of mineral remaining at the end of the year to be recovered (including units recovered but not sold) plus the number of units sold within the taxable year.[153]

Example 8-48. Valley Oil, Inc., owned oil wells with an adjusted basis of $600,000, and estimated recoverable oil of 50,000 barrels. In 2000, it produced 8,500 barrels from the property and sold 8,000 barrels. The depletion deduction is $600,000/50,000 $\times$ 8,000 = $96,000.

If the original estimate of remaining units turns out to be incorrect, the change is made prospectively and for future years, i.e., depletion taken in previous years is not revised.[154]

Example 8-49. Assume the same facts as in the previous example except that in 2001 it is discovered that there are 50,400 barrels remaining instead of 42,000. The remaining adjusted basis is $504,000 ($600,000 − $96,000 of depletion taken in 2000). Hence, if 9,000 barrels are sold in 2001, the depletion deduction would be $504,000/50,400 $\times$ 9,000, or $90,000.

.08 Bonuses and Advance Royalty Payments

When bonuses and advance royalties are received, cost depletion is allowed against the income. The depletion deduction is computed by multi-

---

[152] Code Sec. 612.
[153] Reg. § 1.611-2(a).

[154] Reg. § 1.611-2(c).

plying the adjusted basis for depletion by a fraction, the numerator of which is the bonus, and the denominator of which is the bonus plus the expected royalties.[155]

> **Example 8-50.** In 2000, Kevin Pimroy leased mineral property for a one-eighth royalty and a bonus of $8,000. The total expected royalties are estimated at $72,000. The adjusted basis of the property is $30,000. Cost depletion would be ($8,000/($72,000 + $8,000)) × $30,000 = $3,000.

If bonuses or advanced royalties are received, but the minerals or timber are not extracted, the depletion taken in prior years must be restored and such amount must be taken into income during the year in which the lease terminates or the property is abandoned.[156]

> **Example 8-51.** Assume the same facts as in the preceding example and that the lease expires in 2001 without any production having taken place. Pimroy would have to take into income the $3,000 of depletion in 2001 and the basis of the property would go back up from $27,000 to $30,000.

.09 Computing Depletion—The Percentage Method

As opposed to cost depletion, which involves writing off the adjusted basis of the property as the mineral is sold, percentage depletion is based on the gross income from the property, i.e., a certain percentage of gross income is taken. Hence, percentage depletion is allowable even if the adjusted basis of the property has been reduced to zero. Percentage depletion generally is limited to 50 percent of the taxable income from the property before the depletion deduction, but the percentage is 100 percent in the case of oil and gas properties.[157]

> **Example 8-52.** Steve Wiggins had an adjusted basis in mineral property at the end of 2001 before the depletion deduction of $15,000. Cost depletion for 2001 would be $11,000; percentage depletion would be $19,000. Wiggins can deduct the percentage depletion of $19,000, even though it exceeds his adjusted basis. The adjusted basis will be reduced to zero, but not below zero.

.10 Property Eligible for Percentage Depletion

In the table below, a sample of minerals eligible for percentage depletion, along with the applicable rates, is shown.[158]

---

[155] Reg. § 1.612-3(a)(1).

[156] Reg. § 1.612-3(a)(2).

[157] Code Sec. 613(a).

[158] Code Sec. 613(b).

Type of Mineral	Rate
Oil and gas wells	Not permitted except for limited production of independent producers and royalty owners and for certain production from domestic gas wells. See the following section.
Gravel and sand	5 percent
Clay	5, 7½, 14, or 22 percent, depending on the use to which it is put and whether or not the deposit is in the U.S.
Coal, asbestos (if from a deposit outside the U.S.)	10 percent
Rock asphalt	14 percent
From deposits in the U.S., gold, silver, copper and iron ore	15 percent
Sulfur, uranium and, if from deposits in the U.S., bauxite, lead, nickel, and zinc	22 percent
Timber, soil, sod, turf	Not allowable.

The foregoing is only a small portion of minerals eligible for percentage depletion. Code Sec. 613(b) and Reg. § 1.613-2 provide the exhaustive list.

.11 Oil and Gas Wells

Generally, oil and gas wells are not eligible for percentage depletion.[159] There are two important exceptions to this rule.

1. *Certain domestic gas wells.* Depletion is allowable on these wells if the natural gas is sold under a fixed contract existing on February 1, 1975. The allowable rate is 22 percent, subject to the 50 percent of taxable income limitation. If the natural gas is produced from geopressured brine drilled after September 30, 1978 and before January 1, 1984, the rate is 10 percent of gross income.[160]

2. *Independent producers and royalty owners.* A discussion of eligible independent producers is outside the scope of this book. Royalty owners may take percentage depletion on only the first 1,000 barrels of oil produced each day (6,000,000 cubic feet in the case of gas). The applicable percentage is 15 percent for years starting after December 31, 1983.[161] The depletion deduction is subject to the general limitation applicable to percentage depletion of 100 percent of the taxable income before the depletion deduction. For oil and gas wells there is a separate

---

[159] Code Sec. 613(d).
[160] Code Sec. 613A(b).

[161] Code Sec. 613A(c).

limitation; the deduction may not exceed 65 percent of the taxpayer's taxable income computed without regard to:

a. Depletion;

b. Any net operating loss carryback; and

c. Any capital loss carryback.[162]

Example 8-53. Valerie Knap had in 2001 gross income from royalties from oil wells of $80,000; taxable income from the oil property before the depletion deduction was $60,000, and total taxable income was $100,000. Assume percentage depletion would be ($80,000 × .15), or $12,000. The taxable income limitation from oil would be $60,000 and the taxable income limitation overall would be $65,000 ($100,000 × .65). Since neither of the limitations apply, the deduction would be $12,000.

Example 8-54. Assume the same facts as in Example 8-53, except that the taxable income from the oil property was only $11,500. Percentage depletion would be limited to $11,500.

Example 8-55. Assume the same facts as in Example 8-53, except that total taxable income was only $10,000. Since the maximum percentage depletion that may be taken is $6,500 ($10,000 × .65), cost depletion will be taken since it is greater ($8,000).

.12 Aggregating Royalty Interests

There exists criteria for aggregating working interests; however, those are outside the scope of this book. This section deals with aggregating nonoperating (royalty) interests. If a taxpayer owns two or more separate nonoperating mineral interests in either a single tract of land or in two or more adjacent tracts or parcels of land, the taxpayer may request permission from the IRS to treat those interests as one property. Permission will not be given if a principal purpose is tax avoidance. If the combination of mineral interests would result in a substantial reduction in tax, such constitutes evidence that avoidance of tax is a principal purpose.[163]

The term "adjacent" does not mean that the properties must have common boundaries, but merely that they be in reasonably close proximity to each other, depending on the circumstances of each case.[164]

.13 Depletion of Timber

Cost depletion is the only method permitted for timber. Depletion of timber occurs when the timber is cut. However, the taxpayer may wait to compute depletion until the quantity of timber cut is first accurately measured in the process of exploitation. Depletion is computed by multiplying the units of timber cut during the year by a fraction, the numerator of which is the adjusted basis of the timber at the beginning of the year plus

---

[162] Code Sec. 613A(d).
[163] Reg. § 1.614-5(d).

[164] *Id.*

¶ 825.12

the cost of timber acquired during the year plus capitalizable items, and the denominator of which is the units of timber on hand at the beginning of the year plus the number of units acquired during the year and plus or minus the number of units added or subtracted in order to correct the estimate of units.[165]

Example 8-56. Fred Stevens, a taxpayer, cut 20,000 board feet of timber. At the beginning of the year, the adjusted basis of the property was $25,000, and the estimated board feet remaining was $100,000. During the year, he acquired another 50,000 board feet and capitalized an additional $5,000 of expenditures subject to depletion. Depletion for the current year would be (($25,000 + $5,000)/ ($100,000 + 50,000)) × 20,000, or $4,000.

[165] Reg. § 1.611-3.

Chapter 9

Gains and Losses

¶ 901   Introduction

The purpose of determining the basis of property is to establish the amount of the property that can be recovered tax-free. Receipts that constitute a return of capital are nontaxable. Therefore, the basis of the property is significant to the taxpayer in determining the portion of the proceeds that is taxable.

Later, we shall discuss adjustments that are made to the original basis of property in order to arrive at its *adjusted basis*. First, we consider the basis that is determined by the fair market value of the property and basis that is determined with reference to other property or to other individuals, i.e., a *substituted* basis.

¶ 903   Fair Market Value as a Basis—Purchased Property

Property acquired by purchase has a basis equal to its purchase price.[1] If the transaction is between unrelated taxpayers, this purchase price is presumptive evidence of fair market value. Exceptions to this rule include property purchased from related parties who sold it at a loss, bargain purchases, and wash sales.

.01   *Property Purchased from Related Parties*

The basis of property acquired from a relative who sold the property at a loss is cost to the transferee. The seller is not allowed to deduct the loss.[2] However, if the property is later sold by the transferee at a gain, the disallowed loss on the original sale may be offset against the gain.[3]

Example 9-1. Snomish Valley Sales Co. sold equipment to Sam Hicks, a majority shareholder, for $12,000. The adjusted basis at the time of sale was $15,000. The $3,000 loss is disallowed to the corporation; the basis to Hicks is $12,000. Assume that Hicks sells the equipment to a nonrelated party when its adjusted basis is $11,000. If the sales price exceeds $14,000, the basis of the equipment would be $14,000 (adjusted basis at the time of sale plus the $3,000 disallowed loss of the corporation). If the sales price is less than $11,000, the basis would be $11,000 (disallowed losses cannot be used to increase subsequent losses). Finally, if the sales price is between $11,000 and $14,000, there is no gain or loss since as much of the original disallowed

---

[1] Code Sec. 1012; Reg. § 1.1012-1(a).
[2] Code Sec. 267(a).
[3] Code Sec. 267(d).

loss as necessary could be used to offset the gain, but it could not be used to *create* a loss.

Note that the depreciable basis to Hicks is his cost of $12,000.

Code Sec. 267 lists 12 types of "related parties." The most frequently encountered in a business context are:[4]

1. Members of a family. Family members for this purpose include spouses, brothers and sisters, ancestors, and lineal descendants.[5]

2. An individual and a corporation, if the individual owns (directly or indirectly) more than 50 percent of the value of the stock.

3. Brother-sister corporations (see Chapter 3 for details on brother-sister corporations).

4. A fiduciary of a trust and a corporation more than 50 percent in value of which is owned, directly or indirectly, by or for the trust or a person who is a grantor of the trust.

5. A corporation and a partnership if the same persons control both entities. Control is present when the same persons own:

   a. More than 50 percent in value of the outstanding stock of the corporation, and

   b. More than 50 percent of the capital interest, or the profits interest, in the partnership.

6. Two S corporations if the same persons own more than 50 percent in value of the outstanding stock of each corporation.

7. An S corporation and a C corporation, if the same persons own more than 50 percent in value of each corporation.

8. Except in the case of a sale or exchange in satisfaction of a pecuniary bequest, an executor of an estate and a beneficiary of the estate.

Stock owned directly or indirectly by or for a corporation, partnership, estate, or trust is considered owned proportionately by or for its shareholders, partners, or beneficiaries.[6] Stock owned, directly or indirectly, by an individual stockholder's family is considered owned by the individual, as is stock owned by a partner.[7]

Example 9-2. Dana Smith owns 30 percent of Salina Ford Co. and 60 percent of Newton Mercury, Inc. Newton Mercury, Inc. owns 55 percent of Salina Ford Co. Under attribution rules, Smith owns 30 percent directly and 33 percent (.60 × .55) indirectly of Salina Ford Co. for a total of 63 percent. Since this is more than 50 percent, any

---

[4] Code Sec. 267(b).
[5] Code Sec. 267(c)(4).

[6] Code Sec. 267(c)(1).
[7] Code Sec. 267(c)(2) and (3).

transactions between Smith and Salina Ford Co. will be subject to the loss disallowance rule.

Stock considered owned by an individual solely because of the family or partner attribution rules is not attributed a second time to make another the constructive owner of the stock.[8]

Example 9-3. Ray Morton owns 20 percent of Hilltop Co., while his son owns 25 percent, and his son's wife owns 12 percent. The son owns a total of 57 percent (25 percent directly and 32 percent indirectly). However, only the son's direct ownership is attributed to the father; hence the father owns only 45 percent (daughter-in laws are not relatives for this purpose). Similarly, the daughter-in law constructively owns only the 25 percent owned by her husband. Her total ownership is only 37 percent.

.02 Bargain Purchases

If there is a "bargain purchase," cost to the purchaser is less than fair market value. However, basis to the purchaser will be fair market value, and the difference between fair market value and basis will in some cases constitute income to the buyer. For example, if the buyer is an employee of the seller, the difference is included in gross income.[9] If the buyer is a stockholder of the seller, the difference may be treated as a constructive dividend.[10]

Example 9-4. Arvada Appliances sells a stove to Jake Cole, an employee, for $400 although its value is $600. Cole has gross income of $200 and the stove has a basis to him of $600.

Example 9-5. L&M Farms sells 10 acres of land to Marina Turner, a stockholder, for $7,000. Its value is $9,500. Turner, unless she could establish that the transaction was at arm's length, has a constructive dividend of $2,500 and a basis in the land of $9,500.

.03 Wash Sales

The loss from a wash sale is disallowed, but the disallowed loss is added to the basis of the new stock or security purchased. A "wash sale" is considered to occur when stock or securities is sold at a loss and substantially identical stock is acquired within 30 days before or after the sale.[11] However, the wash sale provisions do not apply to noncorporate taxpayers disposing of stock or securities in connection with their trade or business or to dispositions made by corporate dealers if made in the ordinary course of business as a dealer.[12] The entering into of a contract or purchase option within plus or minus a 30-day period is considered to be an acquisition.[13]

---

[8] Code Sec. 267(c)(5).
[9] Reg. § 1.61-2(d)(2).
[10] Reg. § 1.301-1(j).

[11] Code Sec. 1091(a).
[12] Reg. § 1.1091-1(a).
[13] Reg. § 1.1091-1(f).

Example 9-6. Laura Eaton sold 100 shares of Hawkins Corp. stock at a loss of $800 on December 20. On January 15 of the next year, she purchased 100 shares of the same stock for $3,000. Her basis in the new stock is $3,800.

Tax Tips and Pitfalls

There are several ways to avoid the wash sale provision. One strategy, obviously, is to wait more than 30 days before or after the sale to replace the security. Another is to replace the security with stock in a company in the same industry (which presumably will react similarly to the original stock).

¶ 905   Fair Market Value as a Basis—Inherited Property

The basis of inherited property is generally its fair market value at the date of death.[14] However, there are several exceptions. If the estate elects the alternate valuation date, the basis will be its fair market value on the alternate valuation date, generally six months after the date of death.[15] If the alternate valuation date is used and the property is distributed before the valuation date, basis will be fair market value at the date of distribution. If the special use valuation under Code Sec. 2032A is elected, basis is the value included in the estate.[16] If an election is made to reduce the estate by the conservation easement exclusion of Code Sec. 2031(c), the basis is basis in the hands of the decedent.[17] Also, if property is distributed in lieu of a specific bequest of money, the basis of the property is the estate's adjusted basis in the property, adjusted for any gain or loss recognized by the estate on the distribution.[18] If the decedent acquired by gift appreciated property within one year of death, and if the donor inherits the property back from the decedent, basis is *not* stepped up to fair market value but instead is the adjusted basis in the hands of the decedent immediately before death.[19] The purpose of this law is to prevent death-bed gifts to the decedent in order to achieve a step-up in basis.

If property is transferred to satisfy a specific bequest of money, such transfer is considered to be a sale or exchange. Therefore, gain or loss is recognized by the transferor to the extent of the difference between the fair market value of the property at the date of the exchange and the estate tax value. The person acquiring the property receives a basis equal to the fair market value as of the date of the transfer.[20]

Because the repeal of the estate tax is under current law scheduled to reappear in 2011, basis of inherited property for deaths after December 31, 2010 will, if there are no further law changes, revert back to fair market value.

---

[14] Code Sec. 1014(a).
[15] Code Sec. 1014(a)(2).
[16] Code Sec. 1014(a)(3).
[17] Code Sec. 1014(a)(4).

[18] Code Sec. 643(e).
[19] Code Sec. 1014(e).
[20] Reg. § 1.1014-4(a)(3).

For the year 2010, property transferred at death will have a carryover basis (see the discussion below). However, if a specific bequest of money is satisfied with a transfer of property, gain will be recognized only to the extent that the fair market value at the date of the transfer exceeds the fair market value at death.[21] A similar rule will apply when a trustee distributes property to satisfy a specific pecuniary bequest to the beneficiary of the trust.[22] The basis of the property to the person receiving it will be equal to the basis of the property immediately before the exchange increased by any gain recognized to the estate or trust.[23]

> **Example 9-7.** The will of Elder Dee who died in 2010 provided for a pecuniary bequest to his daughter Cider of $50,000. The bequest was satisfied with property worth $50,000 at the date of transfer. The property had a basis in the hands of Elder of $30,000 and was worth $42,000 at the date of death. The estate must recognize a gain of $8,000, and Cider's basis is $38,000 ($30,000 + $8,000).

Finally, property which represents "income in respect of a decedent" is income that the decedent had earned and had the right to collect, but which was not included in income on the decedent's final return due to the decedent's method of accounting.[24] Examples include accrued income of cash basis taxpayers and receivables which are being reported under the installment method. The basis of this property is basis in the hands of the decedent.

> **Example 9-8.** Dennis Mize died on July 9, 2000, holding bonds purchased for $180,000, but worth $200,000 as of the date of death. The alternate valuation date is not elected. Basis to his son (the inheritor) is $200,000.

> **Example 9-9.** Assume the same facts as in Example 9-8 except that the alternate valuation date was elected by the executor, and the value as of January 9, 2001, was $192,000. Basis to the son is $192,000.

> **Example 9-10.** Assume the same facts as in Example 9-9 except that the bonds were sold by the son on October 10, 2000. Fair market value at that date was $194,000. Basis to the son is $194,000.

> **Example 9-11.** Assume the same facts as in Example 9-8, that Mize was a cash basis taxpayer and the bonds had interest accrued of $6,200 as of July 9. Basis of the accrued interest to the son is zero (the basis in the hands of the decedent).

---

[21] Economic Growth and Tax Relief Reconciliation Act of 2001, Act Sec. 542(d)(1), amending Code Sec. 1040(a).

[22] Economic Growth and Tax Relief Reconciliation Act of 2001, Act Sec. 542(d)(1), amending Code Sec. 1040(b).

[23] Economic Growth and Tax Relief Reconciliation Act of 2001, Act Sec. 542(d)(1), amending Code Sec. 1040(c).

[24] Code Sec. 691(a).

Example 9-12. Assume that at his death Mize also owned a store building used in his hardware business which had a fair market value of $600,000, but a use value under Code Sec. 2032A of only $350,000. Basis to the son is $350,000.

Example 9-13. Ten months before his death, Walter Bates was given by his son property with a basis to the son of $90,000. Bates left the property to his son in his will. Basis to the son is $90,000.

Partial Abolition of Stepped-up Basis Rules

Effective for decedents dying after December 31, 2009, the stepped-up basis rules are replaced with a modified carryover basis.[25] In general, property acquired from a decedent dying after December 31, 2009, is treated as being transferred by gift. The basis of the property to the heir is the lesser of the adjusted basis to the decedent or the fair market value as of the date of death.[26] However, the executor may elect to increase the carryover value.[27] In general, the basis increase is limited to $1,300,000.[28]

The basis increase of $1,300,000 is further increased by any capital loss carryovers and net operating loss carryovers that would have been carried over from the decedent's last tax year to a later tax year, had the decedent lived. It is also increased for any losses that would have been allowable under Code Sec. 165 if the property had been sold immediately before death for fair market value.[29] For "qualified spousal property" passing to a surviving spouse, the executor may elect an additional $3,000,000 increase.[30]

Example 9-14. Dan Dorney died in 2010. He owned at death stock in Colonel Mills Co. which had a basis of $1,000,000, but which was worth $6,000,000 at death. He left his entire estate to his wife. The executor may elect to increase the carryover basis of $1,000,000 by both $1,300,000 and $3,000,000. Thus, the basis to the spouse is $5,300,000.

Example 9-15. Assume the same facts as in the previous example except that Dorney left the stock to his daughter. If the executor elects, her basis is $1,000,000 plus $1,300,000, or $2,300,000.

"Qualified spousal property" is outright transfer property and qualified terminable interest property.[31] "Outright transfer property" does not include transfers where the lapse of time, the occurrence of an event or

---

[25] Economic Growth and Tax Relief Reconciliation Act of 2001, Act Sec. 541, adding Code Sec. 1014(f).

[26] Economic Growth and Tax Relief Reconciliation Act of 2001, Act Sec. 542(a), adding Code Sec. 1022(a).

[27] Economic Growth and Tax Relief Reconciliation Act of 2001, Act Sec. 542(a), adding Code Sec. 1022(d)(3).

[28] Economic Growth and Tax Relief Reconciliation Act of 2001, Act Sec. 542(a), adding Code Sec. 1022(b)(2).

[29] *Id.*

[30] Economic Growth and Tax Relief Reconciliation Act of 2001, Act Sec. 542(a), adding Code Sec. 1022(c).

[31] *Id.*

contingency, or the failure of an event or contingency to occur terminates the interest of the surviving spouse if:[32]

1. The following conditions are met:

   a. An interest in such property passes or has passed (for less than adequate consideration) from the decedent to any person other than the surviving spouse (or the estate of the surviving spouse), and

   b. By reason of such passing the person (or his or her heirs) may possess or enjoy any part of the property after termination or failure of the interest so passing to the surviving spouse, or

2. If such interest is to be acquired for the surviving spouse, by reason of directions of the decedent, by his or her executor or the trustee of a trust.

However, an interest passing to a surviving spouse that terminates if the spouse dies within six months of the decedent's death, or terminates because of the death of the spouse in a common disaster resulting in the decedent's death is not considered a terminal interest (and therefore qualifies for the $3,000,000 step-up in basis).[33]

If property was held jointly by the decedent with the surviving spouse and there are no other tenants, the decedent is considered to own 50 percent of the property, regardless of how the property was acquired or who furnished the consideration.[34] However, if there were tenants other than the surviving spouse, and the decedent gave consideration for the acquisition of the property, the decedent's ownership will be the fraction of the total consideration that he or she furnished.[35]

> **Example 9-16.** Rick Smithson and his brother purchased as joint tenants with right of survivorship property at a cost of $150,000, $100,000 of which was paid by Smithson. At Smithson's death, he is considered to own two-thirds of the value of the property.

If there were more than two joint tenants with right of survivorship and the property was acquired by gift, bequest, device, or inheritance, the decedent's share will be determined by state law. If not specified by state law, each tenant is deemed to have a fractional interest in the value of the property (determined by dividing the value of the property by the number of joint tenants with right of survivorship).[36]

If the property is owned by a revocable trust established by the decedent, the decedent is deemed to own the property (and therefore the

---

[32] *Id.*
[33] *Id.*
[34] Economic Growth and Tax Relief Reconciliation Act of 2001, Act Sec. 542(a), adding Code Sec. 1022(d).
[35] *Id.*
[36] *Id.*

property is eligible for the step-up in basis). However, holding a power of appointment over the property is not deemed to give the decedent ownership over the property.[37] Property which is the surviving spouse's one-half share of community property held by the decedent and the surviving spouse is treated as acquired from the decedent if at least one-half of the whole of the community interest in such property is treated as owned and acquired from the decedent without regard to this rule.[38]

Property acquired within three years of death by the decedent either by gift or by a lifetime transfer for less than adequate and full consideration is generally not eligible for the basis step-up. However, if the property is acquired from the decedent's spouse during that time period, the property is eligible for the basis step-up unless the spouse acquired the property in the three-year time period by gift or by *inter vivos* transfer for less than adequate and full consideration.[39]

Tax Tips and Pitfalls

Even though the alternate valuation date may lower the taxable estate, it should not always be used. It *cannot* be used if the estate will not be subject to the federal estate tax; it should not be used if the marginal estate tax rate is low, or if the heir plans to sell the property in the near future. The reason is that the heir will have a lower basis (hence, a higher capital gains tax) if the lower of the two amounts is used to value the gross estate. However, if the marginal estate tax rate is fairly high, or if the heir does not contemplate a near-term sale, the alternate valuation date, if lower, should be used. Although death-bed gifts to the decedent are not effective if the property is willed back to the donor, there is nothing to preclude the decedent from willing the property to a relative of the donor.

Example 9-17. Assume the same facts as in Example 9-13 except that Bates left the property to his granddaughter. Her basis would be $200,000 (fair market value at death).

¶ 907 A Substituted Basis—Nontaxable Exchanges

The rationale supporting the nontaxability of an exchange is that the taxpayer has merely exchanged one asset for another, the differences of which are more formal than substantial.[40] "The underlying assumption of these exceptions is that the new property is substantially a continuation of the old investment still unliquidated. . . ."[41]

There are 14 basic categories of nontaxable exchanges:

1.   A transfer to a corporation controlled by the transferor[s];

2.   Transfers of property to a partnership;

---

[37] *Id.*
[38] *Id.*
[39] *Id.*

[40] Reg. § 1.1002-1(c) (prior to repeal of Code Sec. 1002 by TRA '76).
[41] *Id.*

3. A transfer of property between spouses or incident to a divorce;

4. An exchange of securities for securities of the same corporation;

5. An exchange of "like-kind" property;

6. Exchanges of various insurance policies;

7. Exchanges of stock and property in corporate reorganizations;

8. Certain exchanges of U.S. obligations;

9. Certain reacquisitions of real property;

10. Transfers of certain farm and other real property;

11. Sales of stock to employee stock ownership plans or certain cooperatives;

12. Involuntary conversions;

13. Rollover of publicly traded securities gains into specialized small business investment companies;

14. Rollover of gain from qualified small business stock to another qualified small business stock.

.01 *Transfers to a Corporation Controlled by the Transferors*

As is discussed in detail in Chapter 3, generally no gain or loss is recognized if property is transferred to a corporation by one or more persons solely in exchange for stock in such corporation if immediately after the exchange the transferors "control" the corporation.[42] Recall that "control" means that the transferors own at least 80 percent of the total combined voting power of all classes of stock entitled to vote and at least 80 percent of the total number of shares of all other classes of stock of the corporation.[43] Since the exchange is nontaxable, the basis of the contributed property is carried over to the corporation, and the transferor's basis in the stock received is the basis of the property transferred, increased and decreased by:[44]

Decreased by:

- The fair market value of any other property (except money) received by the taxpayer,

- The amount of any money received by the taxpayer, and

- The amount of loss to the taxpayer which was recognized on such exchange.

---

[42] Code Sec. 351(a).
[43] Code Sec. 368(c).

[44] Code Sec. 358(a)(1).

Increased by:

- The amount which was treated as a dividend, and

- The amount of gain to the taxpayer which was recognized on such exchange (not including any portion of such gain which was treated as a dividend).

However, any basis increase by reason of the transfer of excess liabilities shall not result in a basis in excess of the property's fair market value.[45] The purpose of Code Sec. 351 is to permit a business to change its form of entity without suffering tax consequences.

.02   Transfers of Property to a Partnership

The same purpose is present in allowing partners to transfer property to a partnership generally without immediate tax consequences.[46] Basis of property in the hands of the partner generally carries over to the partner. See Chapter 2 for details.

.03   Transfer of Property Between Spouses or Incident to Divorce

In line with Congress's intent to not tax interspousal transfers, Code Sec. 1041 exempts from gain or loss recognition transfers of property between spouses.[47] Also generally exempted are transfers to former spouses incident to divorce.[48] Transfers of property are incident to divorce if the transfer either occurs within one year after the date the marriage ends or is related to the cessation of the marriage.[49] Generally, transfers of property are considered incident to cessation of the marriage if the transfer is pursuant to a divorce or separation instrument and the transfer occurs within six years after the date on which the marriage ceases.[50] Basis of the property is a carryover basis.[51]

.04   Exchange of Securities for Securities of the Same Corporation

No gain or loss is recognized if common stock in a corporation is exchanged solely for common stock or if preferred stock is exchanged solely for preferred stock of the same corporation.[52] However, nonqualified preferred stock is treated as property rather than stock for this purpose.[53] The fact that one stock is voting stock and the other is not does not make the transaction taxable.[54] The transaction might also qualify under Code Sec. 368(a)(1)(E) as a recapitalization.[55] If the exchange is not wholly in kind, the rules for nontaxable exchanges where boot is involved would apply.[56]

.05   Exchange of Like-Kind Property

Gain or loss need not be recognized when property that is held for productive use in a trade or business or if held for investment is traded for

---

[45] Code Sec. 358(h).
[46] Code Sec. 721.
[47] Code Sec. 1041(a).
[48] Id.
[49] Code Sec. 1041(c).
[50] Temp. Reg. § 1.1041-1T, Q&A 7.

[51] Code Sec. 1041(b).
[52] Code Sec. 1036(a).
[53] Code Sec. 1036(b).
[54] Reg. § 1.1036-1(a).
[55] Id.
[56] Code Sec. 1031(b) and (d); Reg. § 1.1036-1(b).

like-kind property.[57] (This treatment is not elective.) The grade or quality of the property is not important, but rather the nature or character of the property determines if it is like-kind property.[58] Some key considerations are:

1. The property must *not* be inventory, stocks, bonds, notes, partnership interests, certificates of trust or beneficial interests, or chooses in action.[59]

2. Personal property must be exchanged for personal property and real property for real property in order to be nontaxable.

3. For exchanges of depreciable tangible personal property to qualify, the personal property must belong to the same General Asset Class or Product Class.[60] The general business asset classes are as originally specified in Revenue Procedure 87-56 (subject to updates by Revenue Procedures and/or rulings).

Example 9-18. Jones & Sons exchanged an old computer for a new computer, a fax machine for office furniture, and other office equipment for an old building. The first exchange would be nontaxable. The second exchange is taxable because fax machines and office furniture do not fall in the same general business asset class. The third exchange involves personal property for real property and would also be taxable.

4. Property held for personal use does not qualify for nonrecognition.

5. An exchange of livestock of different sexes does not qualify for nonrecognition.[61]

6. With respect to realty, the definition of like-kind property is quite broad. Hence the exchanges of improved property for unimproved property, a farm for a rental duplex, investment property for business property, are all nontaxable.

Like-Kind Exchanges Where the Replacement Property Is Identified After the Exchange

Often an exchange will be structured such that the replacement property is not named at the time of the exchange. Prior to the Deficit Reduction Act of 1984, a like-kind exchange did not have to be completed within any particular time period to qualify for tax-free treatment. In apparent response to a court case that allowed a five-year period in which to complete the exchange,[62] Congress amended Code Sec. 1031 to be more

---

[57] Code Sec. 1031(a).
[58] Reg. § 1.031(a)-1(b).
[59] Code Sec. 1031(a)(2).
[60] Reg. § 1.1031(a)-2(b).

[61] Code Sec. 1031(e).

[62] *Starker v. U.S.*, 79-2 USTC ¶ 9541, 602 F.2d 1341 (9th Cir., 1979).

restrictive. Effective for transfers after July 18, 1984, the party seeking nontaxable status must receive the property the earlier of:[63]

1.   180 days after the date of transfer of the relinquished property, or

2.   The due date (determined with regard to extensions) for the transferor's return for the taxable year of the exchange.

In addition to the above requirement, the replacement property must be identified as such by the 45th day after the transfer of the relinquished property.[64]

Basis Rules

The general rule for basis determination in a nontaxable exchange is that the basis of the old property carries over to the basis of the new property.[65]

> **Example 9-19.** Sanders, Inc., exchanged investment land with a basis of $200,000 for an apartment building worth $500,000. The basis of the apartment building to the corporation is $200,000.

If cash boot or other property (non-like-kind) is received in connection with the exchange, the exchange may be partially taxable. Losses are not recognized; however, gains are recognized to the extent of the lesser of the total gain or the cash boot received.[66]

> **Example 9-20.** The Jenkins-Beneley partnership exchanged a copier with a basis of $6,000 for an older copier worth $3,000. It also received $500 in cash. Since the exchange resulted in a realized loss, none is recognized.

> **Example 9-21.** Assume the same facts as in Example 9-20, except that the copier received is worth $5,800. A gain of $300 would be recognized.

> **Example 9-22.** Assume the same facts as in Example 9-20, except that the copier received is worth $6,200. The total gain is $700; however, the gain is recognized only to the extent to the $500 cash boot received. A liability that the taxpayer is relieved of is considered the equivalent of cash boot received.[67]

> **Example 9-23.** As in Example 9-19, Sanders, Inc., exchanged investment land with a basis of $200,000 for an apartment building worth $500,000. Assume that the land is encumbered by a $70,000 mortgage which the other party assumes. The total gain would be $370,000; the gain recognized for tax purposes would be $70,000. If cash boot is paid in an otherwise nontaxable exchange, no gain or loss

---

[63] Code Sec. 1031(a)(3)(B).
[64] Code Sec. 1031(a)(3)(A).
[65] Code Sec. 1031(d).

[66] Code Sec. 1031(b) and (c).

[67] Code Sec. 1031(d).

is recognized. However, if non-like-kind property is paid, gain or loss on it will be recognized.

Example 9-24. The ABC Co. exchanged land with a basis of $90,000 plus a used truck with a basis of $16,000 and a value of $11,000 for a plant site worth $150,000. The ABC Co. actually has a realized gain of $44,000 ($150,000 − ($90,000 + $16,000)). However, since the truck is non-like-kind property, a loss of $5,000 ($16,000 − $11,000) will be recognized for tax purposes.

Basis of Property Exchanged Where Cash or Other Property Is Received or Paid

The starting point is still basis of the property exchanged. The basis is increased by cash boot and non-like-kind property given and recognized gain, and the basis is decreased by cash boot and non-like property received, and also decreased by any recognized loss.[68]

Example 9-25. Refer to Example 9-24. The basis of the plant site is basis of the land ($90,000) plus basis of the other property ($16,000) less the loss ($5,000) on the exchange, or the total basis is $101,000.

Tax Tips and Pitfalls

The provisions of Code Sec. 1031 give a taxpayer who is ready to retire an opportunity to convert low cash yield property to higher yield property without incurring the capital gains tax. For example, a farmer who is ready to retire might exchange farm land for an apartment building. Exchanges which convert high yield to low yielding property could also be helpful in avoiding or minimizing the accumulated earnings tax or the personal holding company tax.

.06 *Exchanges of Various Insurance Policies*

Code Sec. 1035 provides for the nonrecognition of gain or loss on the exchange of:[69]

- A life insurance policy for either another life insurance policy or for an endowment or annuity contract.

- An endowment contract for another endowment contract so long as payments begin at a date no later than payments would have begun under the contract exchanged.

- An endowment contract for an annuity contract.

- An annuity contract for an annuity contract.

.07 *Exchanges of Stock and Property in Corporate Reorganizations*

These exchanges are covered in some detail in Chapter 12.

---

[68] Code Sec. 1031(d); Reg. § 1.1031(d)-1(b) and (e).

[69] Code Sec. 1035(a).

.08   Certain Exchanges of U.S. Obligations

Code Sec. 1037 permits nonrecognition of gains or losses when U.S. obligations are exchanged for other U.S. obligations, as provided by regulations. Although there have been two law changes since the regulations on Code Sec. 1037 were issued, the thrust of the law and the regulations (presumably not changed) is to make nontaxable such exchanges as Series EE bonds for Series HH bonds as well as exchanges of treasury notes and other obligations. If the obligation exchanged was issued at discount, such amount must be recognized as ordinary income when the second obligation matures or is sold.[70]

> **Example 9-26.** Ricardo Jiminez held Series EE bonds which cost him $6,500 but have a face value of $9,600. He has not reported the annual increment in value. He exchanges the EE bonds plus $400 in cash for Series HH bonds paying 8 percent semiannually and maturing in 10 years. Reporting of the $3,100 on the EE bonds income on the discount of $3,100 may be deferred until the Series HH bonds are sold or mature.

.09   Certain Reacquisitions of Real Property

This section applies only when the seller of realty owns debt secured by the realty and reacquires the property in partial or full satisfaction of the debt (foreclosures because of nonpayment).[71] Realized gain on the repossession need be recognized only to the extent that money and the fair market value of other property received prior to the acquisition exceeds the amount of gain previously reported.[72] The amount of gain recognized from the preceding computation is limited to the gain on the original sale less the sum of the amount of gains previously reported and the amount of any property or money paid by the seller in connection with the repossession.[73]

Nonrecognition generally does not apply to a reacquisition of real property where the seller pays consideration in addition to discharging the purchaser's debt if the reacquisition and payment of additional consideration was not provided for in the original contract, and if the purchaser has not defaulted in his or her obligations under the contract or such a default is not imminent.[74]

> **Example 9-27.** The Norgel Company sold land on installment to Lewis for $200,000, the terms being $50,000 down and $25,000 per year plus interest at 15 percent. The land had a basis to Norgel Company of $75,000. After collecting the down payment and three installments, the purchaser defaulted and Norgel Company accepted a voluntary reconveyance of the property in satisfaction of the debt. Norgel Company paid $2,000 in connection with the reacquisition.

---

[70] Code Sec. 1037(b).
[71] Code Sec. 1038(a).
[72] Code Sec. 1038(b)(1).

[73] Code Sec. 1038(b)(2).

[74] Code Sec. 1038(b)(2); Reg. § 1.1038-1(a)(3).

Fair market value of the property at the time of reacquisition was $225,000. Calculations of the gain is as follows:

Money received prior to the reacquisition	$125,000
less—Gain reported previously:	
($125,000 × (($200,000 − $75,000) /	
$200,000)	78,125
Maximum gain to be recognized:	$ 46,875
Calculations of limitation:	
Gain realized on original sale	
($200,000 − $75,000)	$125,000
less—Gains previously reported.............. ($78,125)	
less—Money paid in connection with	
reacquisition............................. (2,000)	80,125
Limitation on amount of gain	$ 44,875

The basis of reacquired real property is the basis of the debt (cost of sales percentage times the debt) increased by the gain on the reacquisition and the money and other property paid by the seller in connection with the reacquisition of the property.[75]

> **Example 9-28.** Assume the same facts as in Example 9-27. Basis of the reacquired land is basis of the debt ($75,000 × ($75,000 / $200,000)) = $28,125 plus the gain recognized of $44,875 plus the $2,000 paid to reacquire the property, for a total of $75,000.

.10 Transfer of Certain Farm, Etc., Real Property

If the executor of an estate having a farm or closely held business elects the special use valuation under Code Sec. 2032A, the value of the farm or closely held business for estate tax purposes and its basis for income tax purposes will be less than fair market value. What happens to the estate when it transfers the property to a qualified heir? Fortunately, Code Sec. 1040 provides that gain need be recognized only to the extent that on the date of the transfer, the fair market value exceeds the fair market value that would have been used for estate tax purposes had Code Sec. 2032A *not* been elected.[76]

> **Example 9-29.** Frank Farner died holding farm land that was worth $250,000 on the date of death, but which had a special use value of only $140,000. The executor elected special use valuation. The land was conveyed to Farner's son by which time the value had increased to $260,000. For income tax purposes, the estate would recognize a $10,000 gain.

---

[75] Code Sec. 1038(c); Reg. § 1.1038-1(g)(1).   [76] Code Sec. 1040(a).

Basis of the property to the qualified heir is the Code Sec. 2032A value plus any gain recognized by the estate.[77]

Example 9-30. Assume the same facts as in Example 9-29. The basis to the son is $140,000 + $10,000 = $150,000.

.11 Sales of Stock to Employee Stock Ownership Plans

Code Sec. 1042 allows the election of nonrecognition of gain on the sale of "qualified securities" in certain instances if the sale is to an employee stock ownership plan (ESOP) or to an eligible worker-owned cooperative.[78] In order to defer the gain, qualified replacement property must be purchased within the replacement period. The ESOP or co-op must own immediately after the sale (including the effect of stock options) at least 30 percent of either the number of shares of each class of stock or the total value of the stock.[79]

"Qualified securities" must have been issued by a domestic C corporation that has no stock traded on an established securities market (i.e., must not be publicly held) and the taxpayer must not have received the stock in a Code Sec. 401(a) distribution or a transfer to which Code Secs. 83, 422, or 423 applied.[80]

"Qualified replacement property" is any security issued by a domestic operating corporation (using over 50 percent of its assets in the active conduct of a business) which:[81]

- Did not in the preceding year have passive income in excess of 25 percent of its gross receipts, and

- Is not the corporation which issued the qualified securities which the security is replacing or a member of the same controlled group.

The "replacement period" begins three months before the date of the sale and ends 12 months later.[82]

The gain not recognized is merely deferred and must be recaptured on the sale or after disposition of the new securities (qualified replacement property). Deaths, gifts, and generally reorganizations do not trigger the recapture.[83]

.12 Involuntary Conversions

Involuntary conversions result when property is converted to cash or other property due to factors beyond the taxpayer's control. Those factors include casualties, theft, and condemnations, or the threat or imminence thereof.[84]

---

[77] Code Sec. 1040(c).
[78] Code Sec. 1042(a) and (b).
[79] Code Sec. 1042(b)(2).
[80] Code Sec. 1042(c)(1).

[81] Code Sec. 1042(c)(4).
[82] Code Sec. 1042(c)(3).
[83] Code Sec. 1042(e).
[84] Code Sec. 1033(a).

Recognition of Gains and Losses

Losses on involuntary conversions must be recognized when incurred, regardless of whether the property is replaced. However, gains may be deferred at the election of the taxpayer, provided that there is a timely replacement with qualified replacement property. If the cost of replacement is greater than or equal to the amount realized, no gain is recognized provided the election is made. If the amount realized exceeds the cost of replacement, the lesser of the realized gain or the excess of the amount realized over the replacement cost would be the recognized gain.[85]

Example 9-31. Denton Manufacturing Company's factory was destroyed by fire. Its basis in the factory was $2,000,000. The corporation received $3,500,000 in insurance and spent $3,700,000 to build a new factory. The corporation makes a timely election to defer gain. Although the realized gain is $1,500,000, the corporation need not recognize any gain since the cost of replacement exceeded the proceeds. If instead Denton Manufacturing Company had spent only $3,100,000 on the new factory building, it would have recognized $400,000 of gain. Had the corporation spent only $1,200,000 on the new factory, it would have recognized the full $1,500,000 of gain.

What if the insurance policy covers more than one type of property? Both the courts and the IRS have ruled that the proceeds from an involuntary conversion need not be treated as a unit. The scenario covered in a revenue ruling was where the taxpayer had a fire insurance policy covering both the building and machinery. The insurance recovery resulted in a gain on the building and a loss on the machinery. The taxpayer was allowed nonrecognition treatment on the building.[86] On the other hand, the courts have allowed treatment of the destruction of several types of assets (e.g., buildings, machinery, and equipment) as a single conversion even though expenditures for the replacement of one type of asset are less than the insurance allowance.[87]

When Is There "Threat or Imminence of Condemnation?"

Property need not always be formally condemned in order to qualify for nonrecognition treatment. A newspaper report that a governmental unit has decided to acquire property for public use is considered a threat if the taxpayers get confirmation from the government.[88] However, a mere report by the media that property is being considered for condemnation is not regarded as a threat or imminence of a condemnation.[89]

Discussions with the governmental unit may also indicate a threat of condemnation. A statement made by the governmental unit during negotia-

---

[85] *Id.*
[86] Rev. Rul. 70-501, 1970-2 CB 163; also see *International Boiler Works Co.*, 3 BTA 283, Dec. 1108 (1926) (Acq.).

[87] See for example, *Massillon-Cleveland-Akron Sign Co.*, 15 TC 79, Dec. 17,783 (1950) (Acq.).
[88] Rev. Rul. 63-221, 1963-2 CB 322.
[89] Rev. Rul. 58-557, 1958-2 CB 402.

tions or discussions that the property would be condemned if necessary is considered a threat.[90]

It is possible for two taxpayers to obtain involuntary conversion treatment on the same piece of property. This could occur if the first taxpayer had grounds to believe that condemnation was imminent and sold it to a second taxpayer who had it condemned by the government.[91]

Definition of Replacement Property

In most cases, the rules governing qualified replacement property are more strict than for tax-free exchanges. Generally, replacement property must be similar or related in use or service to the converted property.[92] For owner-users, the replacement property must perform the same function.[93] For example, a copier is not functionally similar to a fax machine and would therefore not qualify as replacement property.

There are two important exceptions to the functional use test. The first exception applies to owner-investors (generally lessors of property). After losing a number of cases in several different appellate circuits, the IRS reconsidered its position, stating that it would direct its attention primarily to the similarity in the relationship of the services or uses to which the original and replacement properties have to the taxpayer (referred to as the taxpayer use test).[94] In effect, if rental realty was replaced with other realty that also produced rent incomes, the use to which the lessee put the property would be immaterial. There is also an exception for real property which has been condemned. Here, qualified replacement property need only meet the like-kind test of Code Sec. 1031.[95]

> **Example 9-32.** Akin-Girgis Inc.'s farm was condemned in order to build a lake. The corporation purchased an apartment building within the time period. The purchase would qualify as replacement property since under Code Sec. 1031 the farm and apartment building are "like-kind property" (they are held for productive use in trade or business or for investment).

In addition to buying the property, replacement can be made by buying control of a corporation that owns such property. Control for this purpose means owning at least 80 percent of the voting stock as well as at least 80 percent of all of the other classes of stock.[96]

If real property is condemned, and replacement is made by purchasing control in a corporation with similar property, that property must meet the functional use test, rather than the more liberal like-kind test.[97] Acquiring a corporation with similar assets and then doing an in-kind liquidation of

---

[90] *Dominguez Estate Co.*, 22 TCM 521, Dec. 26,075(M), TC Memo. 1963-112; *Carson Estate Co.*, 22 TCM 425, Dec. 26,038(M), TC Memo. 1963-90; Rev. Rul. 76-69, 1976-1 CB 219.
[91] Rev. Rul. 81-180, 1981-2 CB 161; Rev. Rul. 81-181, 1981-2 CB 162.

[92] Reg. § 1.1033(a)-1(a).
[93] Rev. Rul. 64-237, 1964-2 CB 319.
[94] *Id.*
[95] Reg. § 1.1033(g)-1(a).
[96] Code Sec. 1033(a)(2)(A) and (E).
[97] Code Sec. 1033(g)(2).

the corporation has been held by the IRS to meet the replacement requirement.[98]

Time Period for Replacement

From the end of the taxable year in which part or all of the taxpayer's gain is realized, the taxpayer has two years in which to make the replacement.[99] In the case of real property which has been condemned, the replacement period is extended to three years.[100] An extension of time to replace the property can be applied for with the IRS.[101] If reasonable cause is shown, the request for an extension of time could be made within a reasonable time after the expiration of the two- or three-year time periods.[102]

The replacement requirements are not met by efforts to expend the funds but rather by actual expenditures, however sincere are the efforts.[103] Similarly, the lack of available land for replacement purposes does not exempt the taxpayer from the replacement requirement within the specified time period.[104]

> **Example 9-33.** Michael Isom's office building was condemned in October 1999. On May 10, 2000, he received a condemnation award of an amount in excess of the basis. He has until December 31, 2003 to replace the property. If instead, the building had been destroyed by a tornado, Isom would have had only until December 31, 2002, to make the replacement.

Basis of Replacement Property

If the involuntary conversion results in a loss, it must all be recognized; therefore, the basis of replacement property is the cost of the property. If the involuntary conversion results in a gain and the taxpayer does not make an election to defer the gain, the same rule is applicable. However, if the taxpayer *does* elect to defer the gain, the basis of the replacement property will be its cost reduced by any *unrecognized* gain on the conversion.[105]

> **Example 9-34.** Consider again the facts in Example 9-31. In the first instance, none of the $1,500,000 realized gain was recognized. Therefore, the basis of the new factory would be $3,700,000 — $1,500,000 or $2,200,000. If Denton Manufacturing Company had spent only $3,100,000 and therefore had recognized $400,000 of the gain, basis in the replacement factory would be $3,100,000 — $1,100,000, or $2,000,000.

---

[98] Rev. Rul. 69-241, 1969-1 CB 200.
[99] Code Sec. 1033(a)(2)(B).
[100] Code Sec. 1033(g)(4).
[101] Reg. § 1.1033(a)-2(c)(3).
[102] *Id.*

[103] *Estate of Jacob Resler*, 17 TC 1085, Dec. 18,701 (1952).
[104] *Fullilove v. U.S.*, 4 USTC ¶ 1316, 71 F.2d 852 (5th Cir., 1934).
[105] Code Sec. 1033(b).

Reporting Requirements of Involuntary Conversions

If the taxpayer intends to replace the property, an election must be made in order to defer the gain. The election is made by recognizing only the gain that is required to be recognized (to the extent that the amount realized exceeds the replacement cost).[106] A statement must be submitted with the return for the year the gain was realized. This statement should include: the nature of the involuntary conversion, the realized gain, the cost of replacement property if acquired (or a statement of intention to replace the property if the replacement was not yet made), and an election to defer the gain.[107]

Severance Damages and Easements

A severance damage is paid to a taxpayer when part of the taxpayer's property is condemned and the rest of the property loses some value as a result. For example, if a farmer's land is bisected by a highway, the value of the remaining two parcels of land is decreased. The damages first offset any expenses involved; any remaining damages decrease the basis of the property. If the basis were reduced to zero, gain would be reported.[108]

The IRS has ruled that where severance damages are received as part of condemnation proceeds, nonrecognition treatment may be taken even if the severance damages are reinvested in property that is not similar to the condemned property.[109]

In most cases, granting an easement will not result in any immediate taxable gain; the proceeds, instead, reduce the basis of the property. However, if the amount received exceeds the taxpayer's basis, the excess must be recognized as gain.[110]

The IRS permits proceeds from an easement on business property granted under the threat of condemnation to be used to acquire property held for productive use or investment use.[111]

Use and Occupancy Insurance

The regulations provide that the proceeds of a use and occupancy insurance contract which insures against loss of net profits are not involuntary conversion proceeds, but instead are ordinary income.[112]

The Sixth Circuit Court has held that proceeds received for the loss of the destroyed premises were eligible for involuntary conversion. The policy provided for payment of a fixed sum limited by a formula based on profit. The Court found that there was a lack of correlation between loss of profits and recovery under the policy.[113] However, the IRS announced that it

---

[106] Reg. § 1.1033(a)-2(c)(2).
[107] *Id.*
[108] Rev. Rul. 68-37, 1968-1 CB 359.
[109] Rev. Rul. 83-49, 1983-1 CB 191.
[110] Rev. Rul. 70-510, 1970-2 CB 159.
[111] Rev. Rul. 72-549, 1978-2 CB 472.

[112] Reg. § 1.1033(a)-2(c)(8). Also see *Miller v. Hocking Glass Co.*, 35-2 USTC ¶ 9671, 80 F.2d 436 (6th Cir., 1935).

[113] *Shakertown Corp. v. Commr.*, 60-1 USTC ¶ 9422, 277 F.2d 625. (6th Cir., 1960).

would not follow *Shakertown Corp.*[114] Few court cases since have addressed a similar set of facts, but the Court of Claims implied that it might rule likewise with similar facts.[115]

Reporting Recognized Gains and Losses from Involuntary Conversions

As a general rule, gains and losses from involuntary conversions qualify for Code Sec. 1231 treatment. This includes conversions of properties used in a trade or business and capital assets that were used in a trade or business or held for over one year in connection with a transaction entered into for profit. However, a special rule applies to casualty or theft losses on depreciable business property and on the above capital assets. Gains and losses from these types of transactions must be separately grouped. If casualty gains exceed casualty losses, then the net gain is further grouped with other Code Sec. 1231 transactions to determine whether there is an overall Code Sec. 1231 gain or loss. However, if the above grouping results in a net loss, the transactions are not further grouped with Code Sec. 1231. They are, instead, excluded from Code Sec. 1231 and are treated as an ordinary loss. This initial grouping is done on Form 4684, Casualties and Thefts, and the gains are carried over to Form 4797. Gains and losses from condemnations are reported only on Form 4797. Examples of matching casualty gains and losses are contained in the discussion of Section 1231 assets.

Rollover of Publicly Traded Securities Gains into Specialized Small Business Investment Companies

Subchapter C corporations and individuals may elect to defer the recognition of a limited amount of capital gain on the sale of publicly traded securities if the taxpayers reinvest the sales proceeds within 60 days to purchase common stock or a partnership interest in a specialized small business investment company (SSBIC).[116] If the sales proceeds exceed the cost of the SSBIC common stock or partnership interest, gain must be recognized to such extent.[117]

The gain that is deferred reduces the basis, in the order acquired, for determining gain or loss of any common stock or partnership interest in any SSBIC which is purchased by the taxpayer in the 60-day period.[118]

Individuals may elect to defer gain for any taxable year to the extent of the lesser of:[119]

- $50,000, or

- $500,000, reduced by the amount of gain previously excluded under this provision.

---

[114] Rev. Rul. 73-477, 1973-2 CB 302.
[115] *Maryland Shipbuilding and Drydock Co. v. U.S.,* 69-1 USTC ¶ 9325, 409 F.2d 1363 (Ct.Cl. 1969).

[116] Code Sec. 1044(a).
[117] *Id.*
[118] Code Sec. 1044(d).
[119] Code Sec. 1044(b)(1).

Rollover limits for individuals married filing separately are $25,000 and $250,000 respectively.[120] On a joint return, the deferred gain is allocated equally between the spouses.[121]

C corporations may exclude for any taxable year the lesser of:[122]

- $250,000, or

- $1,000,000, reduced by the amount of gain previously excluded under this provision.

"Publicly traded securities" is defined as securities traded on an established securities market. A "specialized small business investment company" is any partnership or corporation licensed by the Small Business Investment Administration Act under Sec. 301(d) of the Small Business Investment Administration Act of 1958 as in effect on May 13, 1993.[123]

Rollover of Gain from Qualified Small Business Stock to Another Qualified Small Business Stock

Taxpayers other than corporations who sell qualified small business stock that is held for more than six months may elect to defer realized gain on the sale of such stock.[124] The taxpayer must reinvest in "qualified small business stock" in another corporation during the 60-day period beginning on the date of the sale. If the sales proceeds exceed the amount reinvested, gain must be recognized to such extent.[125]

"Qualified small business stock" is any stock in a C corporation which is originally issued after August 10, 1993, if the corporation at that date is a qualified small business and the stock is acquired by the taxpayer at its original issue in exchange for money or other property (not including stock) or as compensation for services (other than services provided as an underwriter of the stock).[126] In addition, the corporation must meet the active business requirement specified in Code Sec. 1202(e).[127]

A "qualified small business" is a C corporation that had aggregate gross assets on or after August 10, 1993, and before the issuance of no more than $50,000,000, and which has not more than $50,000 of aggregate gross assets immediately after the issuance, taking into account the amounts received in the issuance.[128] In determining the $50 million dollar limit, the adjusted basis of assets is used, except that assets contributed for stock are valued at fair market value at the time of contribution.[129]

For purposes of this provision, members of a parent-subsidiary controlled group are counted as one corporation. A "parent-subsidiary controlled group" is as defined in Code Sec. 1563(a)(1), except that "more than

---

[120] Code Sec. 1044(b)(3)(A).
[121] Code Sec. 1044(b)(3)(B).
[122] Code Sec. 1044(b)(2).
[123] Code Sec. 1044(c).
[124] Code Sec. 1045(a).

[125] *Id.*
[126] Code Sec. 1202(c)(1).
[127] Code Sec. 1202(c)(2).
[128] Code Sec. 1202(d)(1).
[129] Code Sec. 1202(d)(2).

50 percent" is substituted for "more than 80 percent," and Code Sec 1563(a)(4) does not apply.[130]

For purposes of determining whether the gain may be rolled over, the taxpayer's holding period is determined without regard to Code Sec. 1223, and only the first six months of the taxpayer's holding period for the stock shall be taken into account in applying the active business requirement of Code Sec. 1202(c)(2).[131]

¶ 909 Capital Gains and Losses

When capital assets are sold or exchanged, a capital gain or loss is achieved. The gain or loss may be either long-term or short-term, depending on how long the asset has been held.[132] If the asset was acquired after December 31, 1987, the required holding period for long-term treatment is one year plus one day. For assets acquired before January 1, 1988, but after June 22, 1984, the required holding period is six months plus one day.

> **Example 9-35.** Paul Welles purchased some securities on January 7, 2000. He sold the securities on January 7, 2001. The gain or loss is short-term since the property was held exactly one year.

.01 Definition of Capital Assets

The code defines capital assets in a negative sense, telling us what items are not capital assets. A list of noncapital assets includes:[133]

1. Property which is inventory or held for sale to customers by the taxpayer.

2. Depreciable property or land used in a trade or business.

3. Certain copyrights, compositions, and similar items. Self-created works of art, literature, music, letters and so on are not capital assets, and are also not capital assets to a transferee if basis is determined by reference to the basis in the hands of the transferor (e.g., a gift). If such assets are inherited, however, they have been treated as capital assets. Although inherited property of this sort will, after 2009, have a basis determined by reference to basis of the decedent, the Economic Growth and Tax Relief Reconciliation Act of 2001 states that such assets will continue to be capital assets.[134]

4. Accounts or notes receivable acquired in the ordinary course of doing business.

5. Certain U.S. government publications.

---

[130] Code Sec. 1202(d)(3).
[131] Code Sec. 1045(b)(4).
[132] Code Sec. 1222.
[133] Code Sec. 1221(a).

[134] Economic Growth and Tax Relief Reconciliation Act of 2001, Act Sec. 542(e)(2)(A), amending Code Sec. 1221(a)(3)(C).

6. Any commodities derivative financial instrument held by a commodities derivatives dealer, unless:

   a. It is established to the satisfaction of the Secretary that such instrument has no connection to the activities of such dealer as a dealer, and

   b. Such instrument is clearly identified in such dealer's records as being described in subparagraph (A) before the close of the day on which it was acquired, originated, or entered into (or such other time as the IRS may by regulations prescribe).

7. Any hedging transaction which is clearly identified as such before the close of the day on which it was acquired, originated, or entered into (or such other time as the Secretary may by regulations prescribe); or

8. Supplies of a type regularly used or consumed by the taxpayer in the ordinary course of business.

All other assets are capital assets. Included are assets held for investments such as securities or land, and personal use assets such as a boat, an automobile, or a personal residence. Note that most business assets, e.g., inventory, equipment, buildings, and land, are not capital assets.

The Supreme Court has held that a taxpayer's motivation in purchasing on asset is irrelevant to the question as to whether it falls within the broad definition of capital asset as provided in Code Sec. 1221.[135] In short, if an asset does not fit one of the eight exceptions listed above, it should qualify as a capital asset. Obviously the above discussion leaves open many questions. Following is a discussion of administrative and judicial rulings in the area of definition of capital assets.

The IRS has ruled that real estate acquired by a bank in either foreclosure proceedings or by voluntary conveyance in lieu of foreclosure is not a capital asset.[136]

Taxpayers have often sought to convert the ordinary income from service contracts to capital gains. Both the IRS and the courts have generally held that settlements of service contracts is ordinary income because the performance of the service, had it occurred, would have resulted in ordinary income.[137] Similarly, employment contracts have generally been found to create ordinary income, whether sold or settled pursuant to litigation.[138]

---

[135] *Arkansas Best Corp. v. Commr.*, 88-1 USTC ¶ 9210, 485 US 212, 108 SCt 971 (USSC, 1988).
[136] Rev. Rul. 74-159, 1974-1 CB 232.
[137] See for example *G.E. Alexander v. Commr.*, 34 TC 758, Dec. 24,293 (1960); Rev. Rul. 59-325, 1959-2 CB 185.

[138] See, for example *L. Hyatt v. Commr.*, 64-1 USTC ¶ 9139, 325 F.2d 715 (5th Cir., 1963) (cert. den.); *A.L. Parker v. Commr.*, 5 TC 1355, Dec. 14,909 (1945).

Goodwill *is* a capital asset. Separating goodwill from covenants not to compete and other intangible assets has long been a thorny problem. For example, goodwill must be separated from the value of noncompetition agreement. Generally the IRS and the courts will go along with whatever allocation is provided for in a sales contract, assuming an arm's length transaction. However, the allocation may be disregarded if the amount allocated to the covenant not to compete has no relationship to its time value.[139]

Effective for acquisitions after October 9, 1990, a buyer and seller who agree to the allocation of the sales price of a business are each bound by that agreement unless the IRS determines that the allocation is not appropriate.[140]

If a 10-percent owner transfers an interest and in connection with the transfer the transferor (or a related person) enters into an employment contract, covenant not to compete, or other agreement with the transferee, the transferor and transferee must furnish certain information to the IRS (to be specified by the IRS).[141]

.02 Mineral Rights as Capital Assets

Income from the granting of a mineral lease is ordinary income. On the other hand, the taxpayer may have capital gains if he or she sells the minerals in place. The test is whether or not the taxpayer has retained an economic interest in the mineral. If so, the payments are ordinary income. The Supreme Court has stated that an "economic interest" exists where: (1) the taxpayer has acquired by investment an interest in the mineral in place and (2) the taxpayer has to look to the extraction of the mineral for the return of his or her capital.[142] Capital gain treatment has been denied for removal of sand and gravel because under the terms of the contract, if no material had been received, the taxpayer would not have received any payment.[143] On the other hand, if payments are a fixed rate per unit, the sale has been treated by the courts as a capital gain, even though the total payments do depend on the number of units extracted, as long as the seller does not share in the profit or income derived by the extractor.[144]

.03 Damages from Loss of Income

Damages received in payment for loss of income have generally been treated by the courts as ordinary income, e.g., failure to complete a

---

[139] See, for example, *J.L. Schmitz v. Commr.*, 72-1 USTC ¶ 9333, 457 F.2d 1022 (9th Cir., 1972); *Servicemaster of Memphis, Inc., v. U.S.*, 74-2 USTC ¶ 9626 (W.D. Tenn., 1974).

[140] Revenue Reconciliation Act of 1990, P.L. 101-508, § 11323(a), amending Code Sec. 1060(a).

[141] Code Sec. 1060(e).

[142] *Palmer v. Bender*, 3 USTC ¶ 1026, 287 U.S. 551 (1933).

[143] *W.W. Oliver, Sr., v. U.S.*, 69-1 USTC ¶ 9302, 408 F.2d 769 (4th Cir., 1969); also see Rev. Rul. 69-466, 1969-2 CB 140.

[144] See, for example, *Cromwell Land and Mineral Corp. v. Commr.*, 57-1 USTC ¶ 9579, 242 F.2d 864 (5th Cir., 1957).

contract to purchase stock,[145] breach of agency contract damages,[146] and liquidated damage deposit foregone by the buyer for failure to perform.[147]

.04 Mortgage Foreclosures

In *Helvering v. Hammel,* the Supreme Court ruled that a foreclosure does constitute a sale. The definitive event establishing the sale is the actual foreclosure sale (since such sale establishes the value), rather than the foreclosure decree.[148] There need not be a formal foreclosure. A voluntary conveyance to a mortgage of real property held for investment by an individual taxpayer not personally liable for the mortgage is held by the IRS to result in a capital transaction.[149]

.05 Leasehold Cancellations and Distributorship Cancellations

Payments to the lessor for canceling or modifying a lease are held by the Supreme Court to be ordinary income, even though the amount received may be less than the present value of the unmatured rental payment.[150]

.06 Transfers of Franchises, Trademarks, and Tradenames

The transfer of a franchise, trademark, or tradename is *not* treated as a capital transaction if the transferor retains any significant power, right, or continuing interest with respect to the asset transferred.[151] The term "significant power, right, or continuing interest" includes, but is not limited to, the following rights:[152]

1. A right to disapprove any assignment of the transferred interest, or a part of the transferred interest;

2. A right to terminate the transferred interest at will;

3. A right to prescribe quality standards of products used or sold or of services furnished, and of the equipment and facilities used to promote such products or services;

4. A right to require that the transferee sell or advertise only products or services of the transferor;

5. A right to require that the transferee purchase substantially all of the transferee's supplies and equipment from the transferor; and

6. A right to payments contingent on the productivity, use, or disposition of the subject matter of the transferred interest, if the payments constitute a "substantial element."

---

[145] *M. Mittleman v. Commr.,* 73-2 USTC ¶ 9679, 464 F.2d 1393 (3rd. Cir., 1972).

[146] *R. Furrer v. Commr.,* 35 TCM 1525, Dec. 34,076(M), TC Memo. 1976-331.

[147] *M.A. Mechanic v. Commr.,* 19 TCM 667, Dec. 24,227(M), TC Memo. 1960-126.

[148] *Helvering v. Hammel,* 41-1 USTC ¶ 9169, 311 US 504, 61 SCt 368 (USSC, 1941).

[149] Rev. Rul. 78-164, 1978-1 CB 264.

[150] *Hort v. Commr.,* 41-1 USTC ¶ 9354, 313 US 28, 61 SCt 757 (USSC, 1941).

[151] Code Sec. 1253(a).

[152] Code Sec. 1253(b)(2).

Code Sec. 1253 does not apply to the transfer of a professional sports franchise.[153] However, it does apply to franchises to operate sporting enterprises as a trade or business (e.g., a bowling alley).

Code Sec. 1253 also describes how the franchisee must treat the expenditures.

.07 Stock and Securities

A dealer in stock, e.g., a securities firm, has ordinary income from its purchases and sales. However, a trader's securities (as opposed to a dealer's securities) constitute capital assets. Therefore, sales results in capital gains or losses.[154]

Can stock in another corporation be an ordinary income asset (and thus eligible for ordinary loss deductions) if the motive in purchasing the stock is a business motive (e.g., to protect one's supply sources)? In *Corn Products Refining Co. v. Commr.*, the Supreme Court, in holding that the definition of capital assets does not include hedging transactions, stated that "the definition of a capital asset must be narrowly applied and its exclusions interpreted broadly."[155] Relying on this decision, some courts applied the business motive test to determine whether or not stock was a capital asset.[156]

However, in *Arkansas Best Corporation*, the Supreme Court held that the taxpayer's motivation in purchasing an asset is irrelevant to the question of whether it falls within the broad definition of capital assets, and that the judicial application of *Corn Products* was an unwarranted expansion of *Corn Products*.[157] The Supreme Court held that this decision was not inconsistent with *Corn Products*, stating that *Corn Products* applied only to commodity hedges, although a plethora of cases unrelated to commodity futures had cited *Corn Products*. In *Arkansas Best*, the Supreme Court opted for a broad definition of capital assets as opposed to its definition in *Corn Products* and considered the exclusions from capital assets to be exhaustive rather than illustrative.

One impact of *Arkansas Best* is to make more difficult the taking of ordinary loss deductions, since having a business purpose for acquiring an asset does not necessarily make it a noncapital asset.[158]

---

[153] Code Sec. 1253(e).

[154] *George R. Kemon*, 16 TC 1026, Dec. 18,271 (1951).

[155] *Corn Products Refining Co. v. Commr.*, 55-2 USTC ¶ 9746, 350 US 46, 76 SCt 20 (USSC, 1955).

[156] See, for example, *Schlumberger Technology Corp. v. U.S.*, 71-1 USTC ¶ 9473, 443 F.2d 1115 (5th Cir., 1971); *Electrical Fittings Corp. v. Commr.*, 33 TC 1026, Dec. 24,085 (1960); *Booth Newspapers, Inc., v. U.S.*, 62-2 USTC ¶ 9530, 303 F2d 916 (Ct. Cl., 1962).

[157] *Arkansas Best Corporation v. Commr.*, 88-1 USTC ¶ 9210, 485 US 212, 108 S.Ct. 971 (USSC 1988).

[158] See, e.g., *C.H. Butcher, Jr.*, 89-1 USTC ¶ 9356 (E.D. Tenn. 1989), and *Olson v. Commr.*, 58 TCM 393, Dec. 46,095(M), TC Memo. 1989-564 (1989), (Stock held in financial institutions held to be capital assets); *Azur Nut Company*, 94 TC 455, Dec. 46,470 (1990), (Loss on sale of house not ordinary because not used in business).

.08   Worthless Securities

If a stock or bond becomes totally worthless during the tax year, the security is deemed to have been sold for nothing on the last day of such tax year.[159] "Securities" for this purpose are defined as stock, stock options and rights, and bonds, notes, and certificates, etc., with interest coupons or in registered form.[160] Whether the loss is a capital loss or ordinary loss depends on whether the stock is a capital asset in the hands of the taxpayer.

Example 9-36. Ryan Company owns 5 percent of Gibson Company, purchased on February 4, 2000 at a cost of $200,000. On January 5, 2001 the stock is worthless. The loss is deemed to have occurred on December 31, 2001. Thus Ryan Company has a long-term capital loss (the holding period is considered to run from February 5, 2000 through December 31, 2001).

If a parent company has a loss on worthless securities of holdings in a subsidiary, the loss is an ordinary loss.[161] For this purpose, the parent company must own directly at least 80 percent of the subsidiary's voting stock and at least 80 percent of all classes of nonvoting stock except for nonvoting, nonparticipating preferred stock.[162]

Code Sec. 1244 stock that becomes worthless is entitled to Code Sec. 1244 treatment (e.g., ordinary loss deduction up to the specified limit).[163]

Tax Tips and Pitfalls

If the security has even a nominal value, it is not considered worthless and therefore no loss deduction is available. In that instance it may be possible to sell the security for the nominal value to establish a realized loss on the sale or exchange of the asset.

.09   Retirement, Sale, or Exchange of Debt Instruments

Generally, the retirement of a debt instrument is considered to be an exchange of the instrument and thus will result in capital gain or loss if acquired at other than face value.[164]

Gain realized on the sale or exchange of a debt instrument is ordinary or capital, depending on the character in the hands of the holder. However, a portion of the income will be ordinary if there was an intention to call the debt instrument before maturity or if the debt instrument is a short-term obligation issued at a discount.[165] A "short-term obligation" is any debt which has a fixed maturity date not more than one year from the date of issue.[166] The term of the debt instrument includes either the issue date or the maturity date, but not both dates.[167] However, the income will not be

---

[159] Code Sec. 165(g)(1).
[160] Code Sec. 165(g)(2).
[161] Reg. § 1.165-5(d).
[162] *Id.*
[163] Reg. § 1.1244(a)-1.

[164] Code Sec. 1271(a).
[165] Code Sec. 1271(a)(2)(B).
[166] Code Sec. 1271(a)(3) and (4).
[167] Reg. § 1.1272-1(f).

ordinary (will be capital gain or loss) if the security is tax exempt or if the purchaser paid a premium when purchased.[168]

Example 9-37. On January 1, 2001, Veronica Fry purchases at original issue for cash of $9,100 a one-year Treasury bill with a maturity value of $10,000. On August 1, 2001, Fry sells the bill to Amy Wesson for $9,825. Of the total gain of $725, $523 is ordinary, computed as follows:

Total discount	$ 900
Fraction of total discount earned by Fry (212/365) = ...	0.5808
Ratable discount (900 × 0.5808) = ...	$ 523
Capital gain = $9825 − ($9100 + $523) = ...	$ 202
Ordinary income = ...	$ 523
Total = ...	$ 725

If the debt is original issue discount debt, a portion of the discount, depending on when the debt was issued, may have already been taken into income (See Chapter 5 for a detailed discussion of OID), and thus would not be eligible for capital gain treatment.

Example 9-38. On November 1, 2001, Stan Boyd, a calendar year taxpayer, purchases at original issue discount for cash of $86,235.17 Nugget Corporation's 15-year bond, maturing on October 31, 2011 at a stated redemption price of $100,000. Assume that the bond is a capital asset in Boyd's hands. The bond provides for semiannual payments of interest at 10 percent. The bond has $13,764.83 of original discount (stated redemption price at maturity, $100,000, less issue price, $86,235.17). There is no intention to call the bond before maturity. On November 1, 2004, Boyd sells the bond to Melissa Chong, a calendar year taxpayer, for cash of $90,000. Boyd has included $1214.48 of OID in gross income and has increased his basis by that amount to $87,449.65. Boyd has realized a gain of $2550.35 (amount realized, $90,000, less adjusted basis, $87,449.65). Since there was no intention to call the bond before maturity, all of Boyd's gain, $2550.35, is capital gain.

¶ 911   Options

The tax implications of the granting, exercising, selling, or letting lapse of an option vary according to whether the taxpayer is the grantor (seller) of the option or is the grantee (purchaser) of the option.

An option is a capital asset in the hands of the grantee if the underlying asset (e.g., stock, land, etc.) is a capital asset.[169] Failure to exercise an option is considered to be a sale for a zero sales price on the date of expiration.[170]

---

[168] Code Sec. 1271(a)(2)(B).
[169] Code Sec. 1234(a); Reg. § 1.1234-1(a).

[170] Reg. § 1.1234-1(b).

Grantors of options generally receive ordinary income on the lapse of the options.[171] However, important exceptions exist for options granted by dealers in stock, securities, commodities, or commodity futures. Lapse of these options results in short-term capital gain treatment.[172]

> **Example 9-39.** Fawcett Investments grants a call option to Ben Marron on 100 shares of common stock it owns, receiving $1,500 from the purchaser. The option lapses, and Fawcett Investments has $1,500 of short-term capital gain.

If the option is exercised, the grantor adds the option price to the proceeds to determine gain or loss on the sale. The grantee adds the amount paid for the option to the option price to determine basis.

> **Example 9-40.** Assume the same facts as in Example 9-39 and that Fawcett Investments had purchased the shares two years ago for $9,600 and that the option price was $10,000. Fawcett Investments has a long-term capital gain of $10,000 + $1,500 − $9,600 = $1,900. Marron has a basis in his stock of $10,000 + $1,500 = $11,500.

¶ 913   Subdivided Realty

Generally, when subdivided real estate is sold, the taxpayer has ordinary income. However, a taxpayer other than a C corporation may get capital transaction treatment on the sale if these conditions are met:[173]

1.   The taxpayer did not previously hold the real estate and does not hold any other real property, primarily for sale to customers.

2.   No "substantial" improvements have been made to the property by either the taxpayer or by a relative (as defined in Code Sec. 267(c)(4)), by a corporation controlled by the taxpayer, an S corporation that included the taxpayer as a shareholder, a partnership that included the taxpayer as a partner, a lessee (but only if the improvement constitutes income to the taxpayer), or a governmental unit (but only if the improvement constitutes an addition to basis for the taxpayer). Considered "substantial" are shopping centers, other commercial or residential buildings, and the installation of hard surface roads, or utilities such as sewers, water, gas, or electric lines. Not considered substantial are such activities as surveying, filling, draining, leveling, and clearing and constructing minimum all-weather access roads.[174] In no case will the improvements be considered substantial if the value of the property is not in-

---

[171] Reg. § 1.1234-1(b).
[172] Code Sec. 1234(b).

[173] Code Sec. 1237(a).
[174] Reg. § 1.1237-1(c)(4).

creased by more than 10 percent.[175] If the taxpayer has held the property for 10 years, even major improvements will not be considered substantial if all of the tests described below are met:[176]

    a. The improvement consists of the building or installation of water, sewer, or drainage facilities or roads, including hard surface roads, curbs and gutters.

    b. The district director is satisfied that without the improvements, the lot sold would not have brought the prevailing local price for building sites.

    c. The taxpayer elects neither to adjust the basis of the lots sold for the cost of the improvement, nor to deduct the cost as an expense (i.e., the costs will neither be deductible nor capitalizable).

3.   The real property, unless acquired by inheritance or devise, has been held by the taxpayer for five years.

.01 Computation of Capital Gain on Subdivided Realty

Gain from the sale of the lots is capital gain until the tax year in which the sixth lot is sold.[177] Two or more contiguous lots sold to a single buyer in a single sale are counted as only one lot.[178] During the year in which the sixth lot is sold and subsequent years, five percent of the sales price must be treated as ordinary income.[179] All selling expenses (e.g., realtor's commissions, attorney fees, etc.) may be used to reduce the ordinary income. To the extent that selling expenses exceed that ordinary gain, they reduce the amount realized on the sale or exchange.[180]

    Example 9-41. Mayhew and Sons, a partnership, subdivides land into 12 lots. The first year after subdividing, the partnership sold four lots, the second year, six lots, and the remaining two lots the third tax year. The cost of each lot was $5,000. The sales price was $20,000 per lot. Selling expenses amounted to $800 per lot. The results are as follows:

---

[175] Reg. § 1.1237-1(c)(3)(ii).
[176] Code Sec. 1237(b)(3); Reg. § 1.1237-1(c)(5)(i).
[177] Code Sec. 1237(b)(1).
[178] Code Sec. 1237(c).
[179] Code Sec. 1237(b)(1).
[180] Code Sec. 1237(b)(2).

	1st Year	2nd Year	3rd Year
Sales	$80,000	$120,000	$40,000
less—selling expenses	$ 3,200	—	—
Amount realized	$76,800	$120,000	$40,000
less—Basis	$20,000	$ 30,000	$10,000
	$56,800	$ 90,000	$30,000
Ordinary income	-0-	$ 6,000	$ 2,000
less—selling expenses	-0-	$ 4,800	$ 1,600
Ordinary income taxed	-0-	$ 1,200	$ 400
Capital gains	$56,800	$ 88,800	$29,600

¶ 915   Tax Rates

For sales of long-term capital assets after May 6, 1997, the maximum capital gains rate, depending on the type of asset sold, the date sold, holding period, and the taxpayer's tax bracket, can be 8 percent, 10 percent, 15 percent, 18 percent, 20 percent, 25 percent, or 28 percent. The maximum rate is generally 20 percent; however, the maximum rate is 10 percent for taxpayers in the 15 percent bracket.[181] For tax years beginning after December 31, 2000, the 20 percent and 10 percent rates are reduced to 18 and 8 percent for assets that have been held by the taxpayer for more than five years.

Two categories of assets are subject to higher tax rates. Gain on the sale of collectibles held for more than 12 months is taxed at a maximum rate of 28 percent. Unrecaptured Code Sec. 1250 gain is taxed at a maximum rate of 25 percent.

¶ 917   Reporting Capital Gains and Losses

The ordering procedure for capital gains and losses is as follows:[182]

1.   Segregate all capital gains and losses into those that are short-term and those that are subject to the 8, 10, 15, 20, 25, and 28 percent rates.

2.   Net the short-term gains and losses to obtain either a net short-term capital gain or a net short-term capital loss.

3.   Any short-term capital loss is then applied first to reduce 28 percent gains, then 25 percent gains, then 20 percent gains.

---

[181] Code Sec. 1(h).   [182] Code Sec. 1222; Reg. § 1.1222-1.

4. A net loss from the 28 percent group first reduces gains from the 25 percent group and then from the 20 percent group.

5. A net loss from the 20 percent group first reduces gains from the 28 percent group and then from the 25 percent group.

¶ 919 Reporting on Net Capital Losses

As with net gains, the first step is to separate the capital losses into short-term and long-term losses. Individuals may deduct capital losses only to the extent of $3,000 per year ($1,500 for married filing separately).[183] Short-term capital losses are deducted before long-term capital losses. C corporations, as was noted in Chapter 3, may deduct losses from sales or exchanges of capital assets only to the extent of gains from such sales or exchanges.[184] Capital losses of S corporations pass through to their shareholders, who are then subject to the above limits.

Capital losses for individuals in excess of $3,000 may be carried forward to future years.[185]

Tax Tips and Pitfalls

Because the maximum rate for most long-term capital gains is currently 20 percent, there are several general rules about combining capital gains and losses that may minimize taxes.

1. If possible, let long-term capital gains stand alone, so as to maximize the amount eligible for the preferential treatment. If any property is sold to offset long-term gains, it may be preferable to sell long-term capital loss property rather than short-term capital loss property. Selling long-term capital loss property would preserve any short-term capital losses which could offset short-term capital gains. If long-term capital gains are later realized, they would stand alone and thus qualify for the favorable rates afforded long-term capital gains.

2. If possible, offset short-term capital gains against existing short-term capital losses, rather than offsetting long-term capital gains. This is so because the preferential treatment will then be lost.

Example 9-42. Near the end of the tax year, Barbara Rucker has $6,000 of short-term capital losses. She has two batches of stock, each of which would result in a $5,000 gain if sold. One batch has been held for 5 months, the other has been held 21 months. The tax results for the current year are identical regardless of which batch is sold. However, for the next tax year, it would be ideal to have a long-term

---

[183] Code Sec. 1211(b).
[184] Code Sec. 1211(a).

[185] Code Sec. 1212(b).

capital gain. Hence, the 5-month stock should be sold during the current year and the 21-month stock held.

3. If possible, offset short-term capital gains against existing long-term capital losses rather than offsetting long-term capital gains. The reasoning is similar to (2). In this instance, offsetting *some* kind of gains is critical, if only a partial deduction is allowed for net losses.

4. If possible, offset long-term capital losses against existing short-term capital gains. Here the reasoning is similar to (3) but offsetting some kind of loss is critical because the short-term capital gains standing alone will be taxed at ordinary income rates.

To reiterate, the above strategies are important *only* if preferential treatment for long-term capital gains is applicable to the individual taxpayer, i.e., his or her marginal rate is above the maximum capital gains tax rate.

¶ 921 Code Sec. 1231 Assets

As previously mentioned, depreciable property used in a trade or business does not qualify as capital assets. However, these assets may qualify for long-term capital-gains treatment under Code Sec. 1231.[186] Code Sec. 1231 property includes:[187]

- Depreciable business property and business real property;

- Timber, coal, and iron ore to which Code Sec. 631 applies;

- Unharvested crops;

- Livestock if held for breeding, draft, dairy, or sporting purposes (poultry, fish, and reptiles are not included); and

- Casualty and theft conversions of business property or property held for the production of income in certain circumstances (see the discussion later in this chapter).

Inventory and property held primarily for sale do not qualify as depreciable business property or business real property. Neither do copyrights, literary compositions, musical compositions, artistic compositions, letters, or memoranda if held by the taxpayer whose personal efforts created the property, or in the case of letters or memoranda, if held by the taxpayer for whom such property was prepared. U.S. government publications received from the U.S. government, other than by purchase at the price at which they are offered for sale to the public, are also not Code Sec. 1231 assets.

---

[186] Code Sec. 1231(a)(1).   [187] Code Sec. 1231(b); Reg. § 1.1231-1(a).

"Used in the trade or business" means devoted to the trade or business. Hence it includes all such property, whether actually in use during the taxable year or not, until it is shown to have been withdrawn from business purposes.[188] It includes property purchased with a view to its future use in the business even though that purpose is later thwarted by circumstances beyond its control.[189] The Tax Court apparently will not recharacterize property merely because it has not been used in the business for a number of years. For example, in *Carter-Colton Cigar Co.,* the land had been purchased with the objective of building a warehouse but was sold 17 years later with the building never having been built.[190] However, if the property is acquired with the *intent* to *begin* a business but it is never actually begun, the issue is more murky. In a divided opinion, the Seventh Circuit upheld the Tax Court's decision that in such an instance the property is a capital asset.[191]

In order to qualify for Section 1231 treatment, assets generally must be held more than 12 months. For livestock, the holding period is 12 months or more except for cattle and horses which must be held at least 24 months.[192]

> **Example 9-43.** The Minotte-Yen partnership purchased land used in its business for $60,000 and held it for only 10 months before selling it for $80,000. The $20,000 gain is not eligible for Section 1231 treatment; therefore it is ordinary income.

.01 Cutting of Timber

If a taxpayer owns timber or a contract to cut timber, and if held for over one year, an election can be made to treat the cutting of the timber as a Code Sec. 1231 sale or exchange.[193] Once an election is made, it is binding for all subsequent taxable years, unless the Commissioner permits a revocation of the election.[194] The difference between the fair market value of the property as of the first day of the taxable year in which the property is cut and the adjusted basis for depletion will be Section 1231 gain.[195] When the cut timber is subsequently sold, there will be ordinary income or loss equal to the difference between the sales price and the fair market value of the timber on the first day of the year that the timber was cut.[196]

> **Example 9-44.** Murray Bros., Inc., bought a farm in 2000 and allocated $20,000 to the basis of the timber on it. In April 2000, the timber was cut. At that time, the timber had a fair market value of $42,000; on January 1, 2000, the timber was worth $39,000. After making an election to treat the cutting of the timber as a 1231

[188] *Kittredge v. Commr.,* 88 F.2d 632, 37-1 USTC ¶ 9165 (2nd Cir., 1937).
[189] See *Carter-Colton Cigar Co.,* 9 TC 219, Dec. 15,972 (1947).
[190] *Id.*
[191] *Richard E. Beck v. Commr.,* 50-1 USTC ¶ 9165, 179 F.2d 688 (7th Cir. 1950), aff'g 8 TCM 126, Dec. 16,833(M) (1949).

[192] Code Sec. 1231(b)(3).
[193] Reg. § 1.631-1(a)(1).
[194] Reg. § 1.631-1(a)(3).
[195] Reg. § 1.631-1(d)(1).
[196] Reg. § 1.631-1(e)(1).

exchange, the corporation sold the timber in 2001 for $41,000. The corporation would report a Code Sec. 1231 gain in 2000 of $19,000 ($39,000 − $20,000), and ordinary income in 2001 of $2,000 ($41,000 − $39,000).

The definition of "timber" includes Christmas trees which are more than six years old and which are severed from their roots rather than sold in a live state.[197]

.02 Royalties from Timber, Coal, or Iron Ore

If an owner of timber, coal, or iron ore deposits disposes of these assets, has held the asset for over one year before the disposal, and retains an economic interest in the item, then the difference between the amount realized and the adjusted basis for depletion is considered to be a Code Sec. 1231 gain or loss. The date of disposal is considered to be the date that the item is cut or mined.[198] However, if payment is made to the owner before the timber is cut, the owner may elect to treat the date of such payments as the date of disposal.[199] The election is made by attaching a statement to the return for the year in which the payment is received.[200] Payments received in advance of cutting timber are given Code Sec. 1231 treatment if the amounts are to be applied as payment for timber subsequently cut.[201] However, if the right to cut timber under the contract expires, terminates, or is abandoned before the timber that has been paid for is cut, payments received in advance must be treated as ordinary income. Amended returns must be filed if necessary.[202]

In the case of coal or iron ore, Code Sec. 1231 treatment is not available to co-adventurers, partners, or principals in the mining operation. This treatment is also denied if the coal or iron ore is sold or exchanged to a "relative" as defined in Code Secs. 267 and 707(b), or to a person owned or controlled directly or indirectly by the same interests owning or controlling the person disposing of the coal or iron ore.[203]

.03 Unharvested Crops Sold with Land

The sale of unharvested crops is eligible for Code Sec. 1231 treatment if:[204]

- The land was used in the taxpayer's business and held more than one year;

- The crop and the land are sold or exchanged (or compulsorily or involuntarily converted) at the same time and to the same person; and

- The taxpayer does not retain any right or option to reacquire the land (other than a right customarily incident to a mortgage or other security transaction).

---

[197] Reg. § 1.631-1(b)(2).
[198] Code Sec. 631(b) and (c).
[199] Code Sec. 631(b).
[200] Reg. § 1.631-2(c)(1).

[201] Reg. § 1.631-2(d)(1).
[202] Reg. § 1.631-2(d)(2).
[203] Code Sec. 631(c).
[204] Reg. § 1.1231-1(c) and (f).

The costs of raising the unharvested crops for the year of sale and previous years are not deductible, but rather must be capitalized and thus decrease the gain. If the expenses have been deducted in a previous year, an amended return must be filed.[205] Sale of growing crops with a leasehold does not qualify for Code Sec. 1231 treatment.[206]

Tax Tips and Pitfalls

Generally it will pay to sell the unharvested crop with the land, rather than harvesting it first, since the taxpayer is converting ordinary income into 1231 gains. It is also possible to exchange unharvested crops along with the land for "like-kind" property and have the exchange subject to the nonrecognition provision of Code Sec. 1031.[207]

.04 Livestock as 1231 Transactions

Livestock held by the taxpayer for draft, breeding, dairy, or sporting purposes is eligible for Code Sec. 1231 treatment if held long enough. The holding period for cattle and horses is 24 months; for other livestock, it is 12 months.[208] Included in the definition of livestock are cattle, hogs, horses, mules, donkeys, sheep, goats, fur-bearing animals, and other mammals.[209] Birds such as chickens or turkeys, frogs, fish, and reptiles do not qualify.[210]

The purpose for holding livestock is generally shown by the taxpayer's actual or intended use of the animal.[211] If used for one of the qualified purposes, the animal may qualify for Code Sec. 1231 treatment even if held for ultimate sale to customers.[212]

Example 9-45. A taxpayer in the business of raising hogs for slaughter customarily breeds sows to obtain a single litter to be raised by her for sale, and sells these brood sows after obtaining the litter. They are considered as held for breeding purposes even though they are held for sale to customers in the ordinary course of business.[213]

If the intent exists to use the livestock for a qualified purpose, actual use is not required.[214] Good record keeping is essential to establish that the intent was to use the livestock for a qualified purpose; otherwise the IRS will apply the use test. Livestock to be used for breeding or dairy purposes ideally should be selected at an early age, identified with a permanent identification mark, and kept separate from the livestock held for sale.[215]

On the other hand, merely breeding livestock and then selling them does not necessarily qualify them for Code Sec. 1231 treatment. A taxpayer

---

[205] Reg. § 1.268-1.
[206] *Bidart Brothers*, 59-1 USTC, ¶ 9193, 262 F.2d 607 (9th Cir., 1959).
[207] Rev. Rul. 59-229, 1959-2 CB 180.
[208] Code Sec. 1231(b)(3).
[209] Reg. § 1.1231-2(a)(3).
[210] *Id.*

[211] Reg. § 1.1231-2(b)(1).
[212] *Id.*
[213] Reg. § 1.1231-2(b)(2), Example 3.
[214] *B.B. Carter v. Commr.*, 58-2 USTC ¶ 9668, 257 F.2d 595 (5th Cir., 1958).
[215] *Estate of Smith v. Commr.*, 23 TC 690, Dec. 20,828 (1955).

may have more than one purpose for holding livestock, but the primary purpose must be one of the qualified purposes.[216]

When a farmer culls out his or her breeding herd, the sales qualify for Code Sec. 1231 treatment.[217] Death from disease is treated as an involuntary conversion but not as a casualty loss because the "suddenness" test is not met.[218] However, death due to a natural occurrence, such as lightening, would qualify as a casualty loss.

Although animals such as poultry, fish, frogs, and reptiles are not considered livestock, they may still qualify as Code Sec. 1231 assets if used in the taxpayer's trade or business and held for over one year.

.05 Rental Realty

Is a single piece of residential rental property a Code Sec. 1231 asset (considered used in a trade or business) or is it a capital asset (held for investment purposes)? The courts are not in total agreement. The Tax Court has repeatedly held that renting even a single unit constitutes use in a trade or business.[219] Similar conclusions were reached by the Sixth Circuit and the Second Circuit in *Gilford,* and in *Fackler,* although the rationale appeared based on the fact that the landlord was actively involved in management of the property.[220]

On the other hand, in the Second Circuit, a district court in *Grier* ruled that a single rental property was not used in a trade or business because the "activities, although of long duration, were minimal in nature."[221] Other courts in the Second Circuit have followed the decision.[222] Even the Tax Court conceded that it was ". . . not prepared to conclude that, in every case, the ownership and management of such properties (single rental units) would, *as a matter of law,* constitute a trade or business . . ."[223]

What if contractors, builders, developers, etc., construct houses originally for sale, but decide to rent them due to a slow housing market? The courts have consistently ruled that these assets are ordinary income property.[224] The Tax Court ruled that even though rented for 11 years, the original intent (to resell) made the assets ordinary income assets rather than capital assets.[225]

---

[216] *R.B. Gotfredson v. U.S.,* 62-2 USTC ¶ 9516, 303 F.2d 464 (6th Cir., 1962).

[217] *Richard Pfister v. U.S.,* 52-1 USTC ¶ 9276, 102 F. Supp. 640 (DC S.D. 1952).

[218] Rev. Rul. 61-216, 1961-2 CB 134.

[219] See, for example, *Leland Hazard v. Commr.,* 7 TC 372 (1946) Dec. 15,273; *Quincy A. Shaw McKeen v. Commr.,* 6 TC 757 (1946) Dec. 15,083; *Fegan v. Commr.,* 71 TC 791, Dec. 35,880 (1979).

[220] *John Fackler v. Commr.,* 43-1 USTC ¶ 9270, 133 F.2d 509, (6th Cir., 1943); *Almy Gilford v. Commr.,* 53-1 USTC ¶ 9201, 201 F.2d 735 (2nd Cir., 1953).

[221] *Grier, et. al. v. U.S.,* 54-1 USTC ¶ 9268, 120 F. Supp. 395 (DC Comr., 1954) (aff'g per curiam, 55-1 USTC ¶ 9184, 218 F.2d 603 (2nd Cir., 1955)).

[222] See *Union National Bank of Troy v. U.S.,* 61-2 USTC ¶ 9561, 195 FSupp 382 (DC N.D. NY, 1961), rev'd 61-1 USTC ¶ 9232.

[223] *Curphey v. Commr.,* 73 TC 766, Dec. 36,753 (1980).

[224] See, for example, *Walter G. Morley v. Commr.,* 8 TC 904, Dec. 15,752 (1947); *Marion A. Blake v. Kavanagh,* 53-1 USTC ¶ 9128, 107 F. Supp. 179 (DC S.D. Mich., 1952).

[225] *Neils Schultz v. Commr.,* 44 BTA 146, Dec. 11,754 (1941).

If the motives for holding property appear to be mixed, i.e., either to rent or sale, or if the frequency of sales is great, the courts tend to treat the houses as ordinary income property.[226]

.06 Rental Personal Property

Whether or not the sale of rental personal property yields Code Sec. 1231 gains and losses often depends on interpretation of the phrase "primarily held for sale." The term has usually been interpreted to mean "essential" or "substantial" rather than "principal or chief."[227] Thus, for example, a taxpayer who was in the business of leasing and selling electric, water, beer, and food coolers, sold only about two percent of the items. Nonetheless, a district court held that the profits from their sale were taxable at ordinary income rates.[228] Although the Supreme Court in *Malat v. Riddel* defined "primarily" as "of first importance" or "principally,"[229] later court cases have continued to reject Code Sec. 1231 treatment for property which has been both leased and sold, rejecting a literal interpretation of "primarily" in the context of dual enterprises, i.e., those conducting both rental and sales of the same goods.[230]

.07 Autos

The primary disputes about Code Sec. 1231 treatment for automobiles concern the treatment of: (1) demonstrator automobiles and other autos used in the business of auto dealers and (2) autos held by leasing companies.

The IRS has ruled, and the Tax Court followed, that auto dealers are presumed to have acquired all of their vehicles for sale in the ordinary course of business. To overcome this presumption, it must be shown that the autos were actually devoted to use in the dealer's business and that the dealer looks to consumption through use of the vehicle in the ordinary course of business operations to recover the dealer's cost. A temporary withdrawal of an auto from inventory does not qualify it for use in the trade or business.[231]

Leasing companies that acquire automobiles at wholesale prices or at fleet discounts and then lease them for periods of substantially shorter duration than their normal useful life generally will not have Code Sec. 1231 gains. However, if the leasing company sells the vehicles only to dealers, wholesalers, or jobbers at wholesale prices that do not contemplate a dealer's profit and the leasing company does not maintain facilities for the retail sale of motor vehicles, Code Sec. 1231 treatment will apply.[232]

---

[226] See, for example, *Pacific Homes, Inc. v. U.S.,* 56-1 USTC ¶ 9307, 230 F.2d 755 (9th Cir., 1956) (aff'g 55-1 USTC ¶ 9280, 129 F. Supp. 796 (N.D. Calif., 1955)).

[227] *Rollingwood Corp. v. Commr.,* 51-2 USTC ¶ 9374, 190 F.2d 263 (9th Cir., 1951).

[228] *S.E.C. Corporation v. U.S.,* 56-1 USTC ¶ 9364, 140 F. Supp. 717 (SD NY, 1956) (aff'd per curium, 57-1 USTC ¶ 9433, 241 F.2d 416 (2nd Cir., 1957)) (cert. den., 354 US 909).

[229] *Malat v. Riddell,* 66-1 USTC ¶ 9317, 383 US 569, 86 SCt 1030 (USSC, 1966).

[230] See *International Shoe Machine Corp. v. U.S.,* 74-1 USTC ¶ 9200, 491 F.2d 157 (1st Cir., 1974) (cert. den., 419 US 834).

[231] Rev. Rul. 75-538, 1975-2 CB 34; *Luhring Motor Co., Inc.,* 42 TC 732, Dec. 26,887 (1964).

[232] Rev. Rul. 75-544, 1975-2 CB 343.

.08   Involuntary Conversions

Involuntary conversions for this purpose means the conversion of property into money or other property as a result of complete or partial destruction, theft or seizure, an exercise of the power of requisition or condemnation, or the threat or imminence of condemnation. Losses from the events described above are involuntary conversions whether or not anything is received (e.g., an uninsured theft loss).[233] If the taxpayer elects under Code Sec. 1033 not to have the gain recognized, it is of course not a Code Sec. 1231 gain.

When land held for sale to customers is condemned, or there is a threat of condemnation, and the owners abandon the idea of selling to customers, does the change of purpose convert the asset to a Code Sec. 1231 asset? Although early Tax Court cases and other court cases went for the taxpayer, the Tax Court and the Ninth and Third Circuits have ruled that the condemnation factor does not change the intent to hold the property for sale.[234] On the other side, the Fifth Circuit upheld an early Tax Court decision which treated the property as no longer being held for sale to customers (thus being Code Sec. 1231 or capital assets).[235] A district court case in the Sixth Circuit held for the taxpayer, though in this case the property had not been developed at the time of condemnation, i.e., the land was still in a raw state.[236]

.09   Leaseholds

The characteristics of a leasehold depend on the type of property leased (i.e., personal property, buildings, land), the use to which the property is put (i.e., trade or business, investment, or personal), and the length of the lease (i.e., limited or perpetual). A leasehold of property used in a trade or business (other than the trade or business of selling leases) is Code Sec. 1231 property.[237] If the property is personal property, it is subject to the recapture rules under Code Sec. 1245; if a building, it is subject to Code Sec. 1250 recapture. A perpetual lease is not depreciable (since the life is not limited). Therefore, it is treated as real estate used in a trade or business.

.10   Miscellaneous Definitions—Code Sec. 1231 Assets

Whether the sale of water rights is a sale of property used in a trade or business or ordinary income depends on whether an economic interest in the water is retained by the taxpayer. If so, the payments will likely be treated as ordinary income.[238] However, if all of the rights are transferred, the gain

---

[233] Reg. § 1.1231-1(e).

[234] See, *W.B. Daugherty v. Commr.*, 78 TC 623, Dec. 38,943 (1982); *McManus v. Commr.*, 78-2 USTC ¶ 9748, 583 F.2d 443 (9th Cir., 1978); *Juleo, Inc.*, 73-2 USTC ¶ 9529, 483 F.2d 47 (3rd Cir., 1973) (cert. den., 414 US 1103).

[235] *Ridgewood Land Co., Inc. v. Commr.*, 73-1 USTC ¶ 9308, 477 F2d 135 (5th Cir. 1973).

[236] *Hart B. Morrison, et. al. v. U.S.*, 79-2 USTC ¶ 9587, 449 F. Supp. 663 (DC N.D. Ohio, 1979).

[237] Rev. Rul. 72-85, 1972-1 CB 234.

[238] See Rev. Rul. 70-204, 1970-1 CB 173; *Earl Vest v. Commr.*, 73-2 USTC ¶ 9513, 481 F.2d 238 (5th Cir., 1973).

or loss should be Code Sec. 1231 (or capital gain or loss if not used in a trade or business). The reservation of a *de minimis* water right should not create a problem.[239]

Assignment of oil payment rights until a fixed sum is collected or for a period of time shorter than the seller's interest in the oil is considered to be an assignment of income and thus ordinary income rather than Code Sec. 1231 gains.[240]

Deposits forfeited on returnable containers, cables, and the like are considered to result in Code Sec. 1231 gains.[241]

Standard football and baseball contracts are Code Sec. 1231 assets. Since the contracts are depreciable, they are also subject to Code Sec. 1245 recapture rules.[242]

.11   Reporting of Code Sec. 1231 Gains and Losses

The taxpayer in a sense has the best of both worlds with respect to Code Sec. 1231 transactions. The Code Sec. 1231 gains and losses are matched; if there are net gains they are taxed as long-term capital gains, while if there are net losses they are deductible as ordinary losses.

Example 9-46. Bates Co., Inc., sold land held for two years at a $22,000 gain and sold a machine held for three years at a $6,000 loss. The Code Sec. 1231 gains exceed the losses by $16,000, hence they are taken to Schedule D and reported with the rest of the long-term capital gains.

Example 9-47. Assume the same facts as the previous example except that the land was sold at only a $4,000 gain. The Code Sec. 1231 transactions produce a net loss of $2,000 which is deducted as an ordinary loss (Code Sec. 1231 losses can even create net operating losses).

Even if the netting process results in net gains, taxpayers are required to report as ordinary income Code Sec. 1231 gains to the extent of Code Sec. 1231 losses during the five most recent tax years preceding the gains.[243] The five-year period begins with tax years ending after 1981.[244]

Example 9-48. Sweetbrier Co. had the following Code Sec. 1231 gains and losses:

---

[239] See Rev. Rul. 73-341, 1973-2 CB 306; *D.C. Day v. Commr.*, 54 TC 1417, Dec. 30,210 (1970) (Acq.).

[240] *Commr. v. P.G. Lake, Inc.*, 58-1 USTC ¶ 9428, 356 US 260 (USSC, 1958).

[241] Rev. Rul. 75-34, 1975-1 CB 271.

[242] Rev. Rul. 71-137, 1971-1 CB 104; Rev. Rul. 67-380, 1967-2 CB 291.

[243] Code Sec. 1231(c).

[244] *Id.*

Tax Year	Code Sec. 1231 Gains (Losses)
1994	6,000
1995	(4,000)
1996	(15,000)
1997	(12,000)
1998	(19,000)
1999	20,000
2000	(10,000)
2001	42,000

In 1999, the $20,000 of Code Sec. 1231 gains would be reported as ordinary income, since the five preceding years had 1231 losses aggregating $44,000. The $10,000 of losses in 2000 would be deducted as ordinary losses. Thus going into 2001, the five most recent preceding years have unabsorbed losses of $36,000 ($15,000 of unabsorbed losses in 1996, $12,000 in 1997, $19,000 in 1998, and $10,000 in 2000, minus absorbed losses of $20,000 from 1999). Of the $42,000 in Code Sec. 1231 gains in 2001, $36,000 would be reported as ordinary income and only $6,000 would get long-term capital gain treatment.

.12 Detailed Procedure for Computing 1231 Gains and Losses

The first step in the netting procedure is to net all casualty and theft gains and losses from property used in a trade or business or property held for the production of income.[245] If net gains result, the casualty gains are included with other Code Sec. 1231 transactions. If net losses result, all of the items are excluded from Code Sec. 1231 treatment.[246] Instead, the items must be separated. The gains are ordinary income. Losses from business casualties are deducted for AGI; losses from property held for the production of income are deducted from AGI.[247]

The second step is to add any net casualty gains to other Code Sec. 1231 transactions. If net gains result, they are Code Sec. 1231 gains and will receive long-term capital gain treatment except to the extent of nonrecaptured losses (see preceding discussion). If net losses result again, the items must be separated. All gains are ordinary income. Losses from business casualties are deducted for AGI; losses from property held for the production of income are deducted from AGI.

Condemnations of business property and property held for the production of income are automatically Code Sec. 1231 items, and are *not* included with casualty gains and losses. Condemnation gains of personal use property are capital gains; condemnation losses of personal use property are not deductible. Casualty gains and losses on personal use property are netted

---

[245] Casualty gains and losses on personal use assets are not included here.

[246] Code Sec. 1231(a)(4)(C).

[247] At the partnership and S Corporations level, such losses flow through to the partners/shareholders, retaining the same characteristics. At the C Corporation level, all losses are deductible to arrive at taxable income.

separately. Net gains receive capital gain treatment; net losses are deducted from adjusted gross income after subtracting 10 percent of AGI.

Example 9-49. In 2001, Valley Falls Mfg. Co. had land used in its business condemned at a loss of $7,000. It also sold an office building at an $18,000 loss, land used in the business at a $40,000 gain, and had a $2,800 gain from insurance proceeds on the destruction of a business auto and a $1,900 loss from the destruction of a truck used in the business. All assets had been held more than 12 months. The corporation has no unrecaptured Code Sec. 1231 losses. Since business casualty gains exceed losses by $900, the net gains are Code Sec. 1231 gains. Thus, its Code Sec. 1231 gains and losses are:

	Gains	Losses
Net business casualty gains	$ 900	
Condemnation loss		$ 7,000
Loss on sale of building		$18,000
Gain on sale of land	$40,000	
	$40,900	$25,000
	$25,000	
Net Section 1231 gains (LTCG)	$15,900	

Example 9-50. Assume the same facts as in the preceding example except that the loss on the truck was $4,900, and the gain on the sale of land was only $20,000. Business casualty losses exceed gains by $2,100. Hence, both the gain and the loss are ordinary. The Code Sec. 1231 gains and losses are:

	Gains	Losses
Condemnation loss		$ 7,000
Loss on sale of building		$18,000
Gain on sale of land	$20,000	
	$20,000	$25,000
		$20,000
Net Section 1231 losses (ordinary)		$ 5,000

¶ 923   Depreciation Recapture Provisions

The various depreciation recapture provisions were enacted to prevent taxpayers from trading a depreciation deduction one year for Code Sec. 1231 gains in later years. Since the depreciation deduction reduces income on a dollar-for-dollar basis and Code Sec. 1231 gains are taxed at favorable rates, this would be a very advantageous tradeoff for high-income taxpayers. There are three sections to be considered here: Code Sec. 1245, Code Sec. 1250, and Code Sec. 1252. Although the computations differ, all three sections result in the recapture of all or part of depreciation or other deductions as ordinary income in the event that the property is sold at a gain. None of the recapture provisions apply to loss transactions. All of the gains are reported on Form 4797.

¶ 925   Code Sec. 1245 Transactions

If Code Sec. 1245 property is sold or otherwise "disposed of," gain to the extent of depreciation taken (including the Code Sec. 179 expense allowance) for tax years beginning after December 31, 1962, is reportable as ordinary income.[248] Note that the provision does not apply to losses. For property placed into service after 1990 for which the energy or reforestation credit was taken, the bases of property must be reduced by the amount of the credit. The basis adjustment is considered to be depreciation and is therefore subject to depreciation recapture.[249]

Normally, the entire gain on Code Sec. 1245 property will be taxed as ordinary income; however, if the sales price exceeds the basis before depreciation is deducted (the original basis if no adjustments other than depreciation have been made), then some of the gain will be Code Sec. 1231 gain.

Example 9-51. Reilly Brothers purchased for $40,000 a truck in 1999. The partnership used the truck for two years, taking depreciation of $16,000, and then sold it in 2001 for $35,000. The gain is $11,000 ($35,000 − ($40,000 − $16,000)). Since the gain is less than depreciation taken since December 31, 1961, all of it is taxed as ordinary income.

Example 9-52. Assume the same facts as in Example 9-51, except that the truck is sold for $45,000. Of the total gain of $21,000 ($45,000 − ($40,000 − $16,000)), $16,000 is taxed as ordinary income, while the remaining $5,000 gain is a Code Sec. 1231 gain.

.01   Definition of Code Sec. 1245 Property

Code Sec. 1245 property is defined as depreciable property used in a trade or business or held for the production of income, that is either:[250]

1.   Personal property, whether tangible or intangible;

2.   Other tangible property (not including buildings or their structural components) if used as an integral part of production, manufacturing, or extraction, or as an integral part of furnishing transportation, communications, electrical energy, gas, water, or sewage disposal services;

3.   Research or storage facilities (not including buildings or their structural components) if used in connection with the activities described in (2) above;

4.   Elevators and escalators, if placed into service before 1987;

---

[248] Code Sec. 1245(a)(1).
[249] Code Sec. 50(c)(4).

[250] Code Sec. 1245(a)(3); Reg. § 1.1245-3.

5. Single-purpose agricultural or horticultural structures;

6. Storage facilities (not including buildings or their structural components) used in connection with the distribution of petroleum products;

7. Any railroad grading or tunnel bore;

8. Leaseholds of Section 1245 property;

9. Real property subject to rapid depreciation or amortization including:

    a. Pollution control facilities;

    b. The expense election under Code Sec. 179;

    c. Railroad grading and tunnel bores (pre-1987);

    d. Child care and facilities (pre-November 5, 1990);

    e. Expenditures to remove architectural and transportation barriers to the handicapped and elderly;

    f. Deductions for tertiary injectants in oil and gas wells;

    g. Amortization of reforestation expenditures;

10. Livestock subject to depreciation; and

11. Nonresidential real estate acquired after 1980 and before 1987, provided that the accelerated cost recovery method is used.[251]

Property need not be subject to depreciation in the hands of the taxpayer to be Code Sec. 1245 property if the taxpayer's basis for the property is determined in part by the basis in the hands of a taxpayer who took depreciation on the property.[252]

> **Example 9-53.** Matt Haines has a computer which he used in his business. After two years, he withdrew the computer from the business and gave it to his daughter. The computer is Code Sec. 1245 property in the hands of the daughter.

In addition, even though property at the time of disposition is no longer used as it was in the past, the property is considered Code Sec. 1245 property.[253]

Note that intangible property is Code Sec. 1245 property, provided that it is amortizable. Thus, leaseholds of Code Sec. 1245 property, and Code Sec. 197 intangibles such as patents, copyrights, goodwill, going concern value, franchises, trademarks, and trade names, for example, constitute Code Sec. 1245 property. Special rules exist with respect to

---

[251] Code Sec. 1245(a)(5) (prior to amendment by Act. Sec. 201(d)(11)(D) of TRA '86).

[252] Reg. § 1.1245-3(a)(3).
[253] *Id.*

recapture of depreciation of sports franchises and professional athlete contracts.[254]

.02 Dispositions Subject to Recapture

Not all dispositions trigger depreciation recapture. A transfer at death generally does not require recapture and the recapture is not transferred to the transferee.[255] However, the regulations define "transfer at death" as a transfer of property that has a basis determined under Code Sec. 1014(a) (which provides a basis equal to fair market value).[256] Therefore, if fair market value at death cannot be used, the recapture potential *will* pass to the heir. For example, a transfer to the heir of appreciated property which had been given to the decedent within 12 months of death will result in the transfer of the recapture potential to the heir. Receipt of income in respect of a decedent will trigger the recapture.

.03 Gifts

Gifts also do not trigger the recapture, but the recapture potential *does* pass to the donee.[257] A charitable gift also does not trigger the recapture; however, the fair market value of appreciated property must be reduced by the recapture amount in determining the amount of the contribution.[258] If the transfer is part gift and part sale, depreciation recapture must be recognized to the extent of any gain recognized.[259]

.04 Tax-Free Transactions

Certain tax-free transactions in which the basis of the property in the hands of the transferee is determined by reference to its basis in the hands of the transferor triggers recapture only to the extent of any gain recognized; however, the recapture potential passes to the property received. The transactions are:[260]

Type of Transaction	Relevant Code Section
1. Liquidation of a subsidiary	332
2. Transfers to a controlled corporation	351
3. Certain corporate reorganizations	361
4. Transfers in exchange for a partnership interest	721
5. Certain distributions of a partnership	731

.05 Like-Kind Exchanges and Involuntary Conversions

If part or all of the realized gain on a like-kind exchange or involuntary conversion is not recognized, the amount of depreciation recaptured is limited to the sum of:[261]

---

[254] Code Sec. 1245(a)(4).
[255] Code Sec. 1245(b)(2).
[256] Reg. § 1.1245-4(b)(1).
[257] Code Sec. 1245(b)(1); Reg. § 1.1245-4(a).
[258] Code Sec. 170(e).
[259] Reg. § 1.1245-4(a)(3).
[260] Code Sec. 1245(b)(3); Reg. § 1.1245-4(c).
[261] Reg. § 1.1245-4(d)(1).

- The recognized gain, plus

- The fair market value of non-Code Sec. 1245 property acquired which is qualifying property under Code Secs. 1031 or 1032.

Example 9-54. Vasilou, Inc. exchanges a computer worth $30,000 for a smaller computer worth $16,000 and $14,000 in cash. The computer traded had a basis of $12,000 and $16,000 of depreciation had been taken. The realized gain would be $18,000, $14,000 of which is recognized. All of the recognized gain would be Code Sec. 1245 gain. The remaining $2,000 of depreciation potential would pass to the new computer.

Example 9-55. Reeve Brothers has Code Sec. 1245 property with an adjusted basis of $100,000 and $17,000 of depreciation recapture potential. The property is destroyed by fire and the partnership receives $118,000 of insurance proceeds. The company used $102,000 to buy qualified replacement property and $10,000 to acquire stock in a corporation owning similar property. The amount of gain recognized under Code Sec. 1033 (without regard to Code Sec. 1245) is $6,000. However, to that must be added the $10,000 of stock purchased (since it is not Code Sec. 1245 property). Thus, the total ordinary income to be recognized is $16,000, while $1,000 of depreciation recapture potential would pass to the new Code Sec. 1245 property.

.06 Installment Sales

All depreciation recapture is recognized as gain during the year of disposition of an installment sale, regardless of the amount that is actually received in the year of sale.[262] The recapture income is subtracted from the gross profit before the gross profit ratio is computed.

Example 9-56. Red Mountain, Inc., sold Code Sec. 1245 property for $100,000, the terms being $25,000 down and $15,000 per year plus interest at 9 percent for five years. Adjusted basis of the property was $65,000; depreciation recapture amount is $20,000. The total gain is $35,000; $20,000 of which must be reported immediately. The remaining gain of $15,000 is divided by the $100,000 contract price to obtain a gross profit percentage of 15 percent. An additional $3,750 ($25,000 × 0.15) would be reported in the year of sale; the remaining amount would be reported as the installments are collected.

.07 Allocation of Sales Price

If a number of assets are sold, it is in the interest of the seller to allocate a large portion of the sales price to nondepreciable assets, so that depreciation recapture is minimized. Even though the contract allocates the sales price among the individual assets, the burden of proof to show that

---

[262] Code Sec. 453(i).

the allocation is reasonable rests on the taxpayer.[263] The Tax Court indicated that if the parties to the contract have adverse interest (e.g., where the purchaser would wish a high allocation to depreciable assets), it is more likely that the allocation is reasonable.[264] The Tax Court also admonished both the IRS and the taxpayer that issues of valuation are "more properly suited for the give and take of the settlement process than adjudication.[265] The Sixth Circuit, however, stated that sanctioning a taxpayer for seeking a judicial determining of the case ". . . would directly contradict fair market value standards and our conceptions of justice."[266]

¶ 927   Code Sec. 1250 Transactions

Code Sec. 1250 applies to depreciable real property (buildings and their structural components) except for the various structures that, as mentioned previously, are considered Code Sec. 1245 property.[267] If the Code Sec. 1250 property is held for one year or less, there will be ordinary income to the extent of all depreciation taken. If held for over one year, the portion of depreciation recaptured depends on whether the property is MACRS property, ACRS property, pre-ACRS commercial or industrial property, or pre-ACRS residential rental property. In any case, the act only applies to depreciation taken since December 31, 1963.

.01 *Pre-ACRS Commercial or Industrial Property*

The amount to be recaptured is an applicable percentage of the lesser of the recognized gain or the excess depreciation taken.[268] "Excess" depreciation is the difference between whatever accelerated method is used and the straight-line method.[269] The applicable percentage depends on when the property was purchased and what kind of property it is. For commercial or industrial property, the percentage is 100 percent for depreciation after 1969.[270] For depreciation from January 1, 1964, to December 31, 1969, the percentage was 100 percent less one percentage point for each full month that the property was held over 20 months.[271] This percentage is zero for property sold in 1980 or later since a holding period of 10 years reduces the percentage to zero.

Example 9-57. Swenson and Daughters purchased a building for $40,000 on January 2, 1975. It had a 25-year life and an estimated salvage value of $2,000. The partnership sold the building on January 3, 1996, for $45,000. The double-declining balance depreciation was used, and a total of $33,060 of depreciation was taken. The total gain is $38,060 ($45,000 − ($40,000 − $33,060)). The portion of the gain that is Code Sec. 1250 is computed as follows:

---

[263] *Buffalo Tool and Die Manufacturing Co. Inc., v. Commr.*, 74 TC 441, Dec. 36,977 (1980).

[264] *Id.*

[265] *Id.*

[266] *Est. of Kaplin v. Commr.*, 85-1 USTC ¶ 9127, 748 F.2d 1109 (6th Cir., 1984) (rev'g and rem'g 44 TCM 660 (1984)).

[267] Code Sec. 1250(c).

[268] Code Sec. 1250(a).

[269] Code Sec. 1250(b)(1).

[270] Code Sec. 1250(a)(2)(B)(v).

[271] Code Sec. 1250(a)(3)(B).

	Double-declining Balance	Straight Line	Excess
Depreciation taken:	$33,060	$31,920	$ 1,140
Total gain			$38,060
Excess depreciation taken after 1969			$ 1,140
Lessor of the two			$ 1,140
Applicable percentage			100%
Code Sec. 1250 gain			$ 1,140
Code Sec. 1231 gain			$36,920

.02 Pre-ACRS Residential Rental Property

The applicable percentage for residential rental property, property the rent from which is at least 80 percent gross receipts from dwelling units, is as follows:

Post 1975 depreciation—100 percent[272]

1970-1975 depreciation—100 percent until property held 100 months, declines 1 percent per month thereafter until at 200 months the applicable percentage is zero.[273] This percentage is zero for property sold after August 31, 1992.

1964-1969 depreciation—100 percent until property held 20 months, declines 1 percent per month thereafter until at 120 months the applicable percentage is zero.[274] As previously mentioned, for property sold in 1980 or later, the percentage is zero.

Example 9-58. Assume the same facts as in the previous example except that the property is a rental duplex.

	Double-declining Balance	Straight Line	Excess
1976-1995	$30,660	$30,400	260
1975	$ 2,400	$ 1,520	$ 880
	$33,060	$31,920	$ 1,140
Total gain			$38,060
Excess depreciation taken since 1976			260
Lessor of the two			260
Code Sec. 1250 gain			260
Code Sec. 1231 gain			$37,800

---

[272] Code Sec. 1250(a)(1)(B)(v).
[273] Code Sec. 1250(a)(2)(B)(iii).

[274] Code Sec. 1250(a)(3)(B).

.03   ACRS Property—Commercial or Industrial Real Property

The recapture rules are more harsh for ACRS property. For property placed into service during the ACRS years, if the accelerated ACRS method is used, all depreciation taken, not just the excess over straight-line, will be ordinary income to the extent of any gain on the sale and the property is classified as Code Sec. 1245 property.[275] But if the straight-line method was elected, all gain will be Code Sec. 1231 gain.

> **Example 9-59.** Doug Erickson constructed a general purpose building and placed it into service on June 3, 1986. The building cost $300,000 and was depreciated over a 19-year ACRS life. On March 4, 1996, Erickson sold the building for $360,000. Since depreciation to the date of sale would be $184,050, the total gain would be $244,050, i.e., ($360,000 − ($300,000 − $184,050)). The Code Sec. 1245 gain (ordinary income) would be $184,050 (to the extent of all depreciation taken), and the remaining $60,000 gain would be Code Sec. 1231 gain.

> **Example 9-60.** Assume the same facts as in the previous example except that Erickson elects the optional straight-line method and selects a 19-year life. The depreciation taken would be $167,700, the total gain would be $227,700, i.e., ($360,000 − ($300,000 − $167,700)) and the entire gain would be Code Sec. 1231 gain.

As is true for Code Sec. 1245 property, effective for dispositions made after June 6, 1984 (unless pursuant to a contract which was binding on or before March 22, 1984), the entire portion of the gain attributable to depreciation recapture must be reported in the year of sale *whether or not* any installment is collected.[276] The remaining gain *is* recognized using the installment method.[277]

.04   ACRS Property—Residential

The rules for ACRS residential property are similar to those for pre-ACRS property. Only the excess of the ACRS deduction over the straight-line method need be recaptured as ordinary income.[278]

> **Example 9-61.** Mills and Sons purchased a triplex on June 3, 1986, for $300,000. The partnership depreciated it over a 19-year ACRS life. It was sold on March 4, 1996. Total depreciation would be $184,050; straight-line depreciation would have been $167,700. Assuming a sales price of $360,000, the total gain would be $244,050. The Code Sec. 1250 gain would be $16,350 (i.e., $184,050 − $167,700), and the remaining $227,700 of gain would be Code Sec. 1231 gain.

Special rules exist for property which is substantially improved. The following will be treated as separate elements:[279]

---

[275] Code Sec. 1245(a)(1).
[276] Code Sec. 453(i).
[277] *Id.*

[278] Code Sec. 1250(a)(1).
[279] Code Sec. 1250(f)(3); Reg. § 1.1250-5(c).

1. *Separate improvements.* A "separate improvement" is an addition to capital account that qualifies as an improvement under the one-year test and satisfies the 36-month test.[280] An addition to capital account satisfies the one-year test only if the sum of all additions to the capital account of the property for the taxable year exceeds the greater of:[281]

   a. $2,000; or

   b. One percent of the unadjusted basis of the property, determined as of the beginning (1) of such taxable year, or (2) of the holding period, whichever is the later.

   The 36-month test is met if during the 36-month period ending on the last day of any taxable year the sum of the improvements satisfying the one-year test exceeds the greatest of:[282]

   i. 25 percent of the adjusted basis of the property;

   ii. 10 percent of the unadjusted basis of the property determined as in (1)(b) above; or

   iii. $5,000.

2. *Units.* If before completion of Code Sec. 1250 property, one or more units are placed into service, each such unit is treated as an element.

3. *Remaining property.* The remaining property after items (1) and (2) is treated as are elements.

4. *Special elements.* If a like-kind exchange or involuntary conversion gives rise to an addition to the capital account and it is not a separate improvement, then it is considered a special element.

5. *Low-income housing elements.* In certain instances the replacement of a qualified housing project after an approved disposition may result in separate elements being established.

.05 MACRS Realty

Since realty subject to MACRS (acquired after 1986) must be depreciated using straight-line depreciation, there is no Code Sec. 1250 recapture.[283]

---

[280] Code Sec. 1250(f)(4); Reg. § 1.1250-5(d)(1).
[281] Code Sec. 1250(f)(4)(B); Reg. § 1.1250-5(d)(3).
[282] Code Sec. 1250(f)(4)(A); Reg. 1.1250-5(d)(4).

[283] However, corporations selling depreciable realty must recapture some depreciation under Section 291. See Chapter 3 for details.

¶ 929   Recapture of Low-Income Housing Amortization

Acquisition and rehabilitation of low-income housing is subject to more rapid depreciation and amortization than for other realty. Sale of this property is also subject to Code Sec. 1250 recapture, but the recapture rates are slightly different.

Qualified low-income housing projects (those with mortgages insured under the National Housing Act or financed by direct loan or tax abatement under similar state or local laws and which are limited with respect to rate of return and maximum rental charges) are subject to recapture of 100 percent of the excess post 1975 depreciation less one percentage point for each full month the property was held in excess of 100 months.[284] The rule also applies to dwelling units held for rental to families eligible for subsidies, for depreciation of rehabilitation expenditures of low-income housing, and property with respect to which a loan is made or insured under Title V of the Housing Act of 1949.[285]

¶ 931   Code Sec. 1254 Recaptures

When oil, gas, geothermal or other mineral property is disposed of, ordinary income is recaptured to the lesser of:

1.   The amount of the Code Sec. 1254 costs, or

2.   The amount, if any, by which the amount realized on the sale, exchange, or involuntary conversion, or the fair market value of the property on any other disposition, exceeds the adjusted basis of the property.[286]

The term "Code Sec. 1254 costs" means:

a.   The total expenditures that have been deducted by the taxpayer or any person under Code Sec. 263, 616, or 617 with respect to such property and that, but for the deduction, would have been included in the adjusted basis of the property or in the adjusted basis of certain depreciable property associated with the property; and

b.   The deductions for depletion under Section 611 that reduced the adjusted basis of the property.[287]

Generally, if a portion (other than an undivided interest) of the property is disposed of, the Code Sec. 1254 costs applicable to the entire property must be recaptured (to the extent of the gain). If such amount is more than the gain, the remaining amount remains subject to recapture. However, in the case of a transfer which is not immediately subject to recapture (e.g., a gift), or in the case of the transfer of an undivided

---

[284] Code Sec. 1250(a)(1)(B)(i).
[285] Code Sec. 1250(a)(1)(B)(ii)-(iv).
[286] Reg. § 1.1254-1(a).

[287] Reg. § 1.1254-1(b). The above definition is for property placed into service after December 31, 1986.

interest, then only a proportionate part of the Section 1254 costs is assigned to the portion transferred.[288]

The rules regarding dispositions requiring recapture are similar to those governing Code Sec. 1245.[289]

¶ 933   Code Sec. 1255 Recaptures

Certain items excluded from gross income under Code Sec. 126 must be recaptured if Code Sec. 126 property is disposed of within 20 years after the date the excluded payments were received.[290] These items involve payments received under:[291]

- The rural clean water program;

- The rural abandoned mine program;

- The water bank program;

- The emergency conservation measures program;

- The agricultural conservation program;

- The great plains conservation program;

- The resources conservation and development program;

- The forestry incentives program;

- Certain small watershed programs; and

- Programs of a state, U.S. possession or subdivision, or D.C. under which payments are made to individuals primarily for the purpose of conserving soil, protecting or restoring the environment, improving forests, or providing a habitat for wildlife.

The payments must have been certified by the Secretary of Agriculture as primarily for the purpose of conservation.[292]

The amount to be recaptured is the lesser of:[293]

- The applicable percentage of the total payments received which were excluded from gross income; or

- The amount realized (if the property is sold, exchanged, or involuntarily converted), or the fair market value of Section 126 property (in the case of any other disposition), over the adjusted basis.

The "applicable percentage" is 100 percent if disposed of less than 10 years after the date of receipt of the last payment which has been certified by the Secretary of Agriculture. The applicable percentage is reduced by 10

---

[288] Reg. § 1.1254-1(c).
[289] Code Sec. 1254(b)(1); Reg. § 1.1254-1(b)(3).
[290] Code Sec. 1255(a).

[291] Code Sec. 126(a).
[292] Code Sec. 126(b)(1).
[293] Code Sec. 1255(a).

percent for each year or partial year held in excess of 10 years.[294] If only a portion of Section 126 property is disposed of, the aggregate of excludable amounts with respect of the entire property is allocated to each portion in proportion to the fair market value of each at the time of the disposition.[295] The term "disposition" has the same meaning as in Reg. § 1.1245-1(a)(3).[296]

¶ 935   Code Sec. 1252 Recaptures

This section requires the recapture of deductions for soil and water conservation expenditures (as provided by Code Sec. 175) and land clearing costs (as provided by Code Sec. 182 prior to its repeal by TRA '86).[297] The recapture applies to the extent that these deductions were taken after December 31, 1969. In no event can the recapture exceed the realized gain.[298] The percentages of the deductions recaptured decreases as the holding period increases. If the land is disposed of within five years after the date it was acquired, the applicable percentage is 100 percent. The percentage decreases 20 percent for each year thereafter until a farmer has the land for in excess of 10 years, at which time there is no recapture.[299]

> **Example 9-62.** On January 10, 1997, Joyce Griffin sold for $150,000 land that she had purchased January 3, 1990 for $100,000. Griffin had deducted $40,000 of soil conservation expenditures during that time period. Since the property is disposed of during the eighth year after it was acquired, the applicable percentage is 40%. Thus, $16,000 would have to be recaptured as ordinary income.

The amount of recapture is determined separately for each parcel of farm land in accordance with the regulations for Code Sec. 1245. If the recapture cannot be separated among the parcels, relative fair market values are used as an allocation basis.[300] The rules regarding dispositions requiring recapture are similar to those governing Code Sec. 1245.[301]

---

[294] Code Sec. 1255(a)(3); Temp. Reg. § 16A.1255-1(a)(4). Left unanswered is the percentage to be recaptured for property held for exactly 10 years.

[295] Reg. § 16.1255-1(a)(5).

[296] Temp. Reg. § 16A.1255-1(a)(3)(iii).

[297] Code Sec. 1252(a)(1).

[298] *Id.*

[299] Code Sec. 1252(a)(3); Reg. § 1.1252-1(a)(3)(iv).

[300] Reg. § 1.1252-1(a)(4).

[301] Code Sec. 1252(b); Reg. § 1.1252-2.

Chapter 10

Deferred Compensation

¶ 1001 Introduction

Small business owners who commit to providing a retirement plan for themselves and their employees have a variety of plans from which to choose. Code Secs. 401 (pension profit-sharing, stock bonus plans, Keogh plans, and other qualified deferred arrangements), 408 (individual retirement arrangements, including simplified employee pensions (SEPs)), and 402 and 83 (nonqualified deferred compensation plans) provide, what is to a small businessman, a rather bewildering array of alternatives.

The Tax Reform Act of 1986 (TRA '86) made significant changes to previous legislative actions on retirement plans. The dust has now settled somewhat from TRA '86, i.e., pertinent regulations and rulings either are currently or have been promulgated, and enough time has passed to obtain perspective about the very pervasive impact of TRA '86.

The purpose of this chapter is to review the various types of retirement plans available to small businesses, and to consider some tax planning implications of the various alternatives.

¶ 1003 Requirements of Qualified Plans

Code Sec. 401 defines qualified pension, profit-sharing, and stock bonus plans. Plans that are "qualified" have two distinct advantages: employer contributions are not currently taxed to the employee but are deductible to the employer, and the plan itself is exempt from taxation (therefore the earnings are not taxed until made available to the employee).

The major requirements generally required in order to qualify a plan are: minimum coverage rules, minimum participation rules, minimum vesting rules, distribution requirements, and funding requirements. In addition, a special set of rules exists for top-heavy plans (these plans are discussed in the section following the discussion of minimum vesting rules).

.01 Minimum Coverage

The coverage specifications of qualified plans must not discriminate in favor of highly compensated employees.[1] An employee will be considered highly compensated if the employee:[2]

- Was a five percent owner at any time during the current or preceding year; or

---

[1] Code Sec. 401(a).   [2] Code Sec. 414(q).

¶ 1003.01

- Had compensation from the employer in excess of $85,000 (effective January 1, 2001) during the preceding year (indexed for inflation) and, if the employer elects, was in the top-paid group (i.e., the top 20 percent of employees by compensation) of the employer.

Plans are considered nondiscriminatory if:[3]

- 70 percent or more of all employees who are not highly compensated employees benefit from the plan and the percentage of nonhighly compensated employees who benefit is at least 70 percent of the percentage of highly compensated employees who benefit (the ratio percentage test); or

- The plan benefits such employees as qualify under a classification found by the IRS not to discriminate in favor of highly compensated employees and the average benefit percentage for nonhighly compensated employees is at least 70 percent of the average benefit percentage for highly compensated employees (average benefits test).

If the above coverage rules are not met, the highly compensated employees are taxed on the value of their vested accrued benefits that is attributable to employer contributions as well as on any income earned from the contributions. However, nonhighly paid employees are not taxed on the contributions or earnings of the trust, i.e., the plan is in effect "qualified" with respect to them.[4]

.02 Minimum Participation

In order for the plan to qualify, minimum participation rules must also be met. For minimum participation to be achieved, the plan must benefit the lesser of 50 employees or at least 40 percent of all employees.[5] "Eligibility" requirements govern the conditions that an employee must meet in order to participate in the plan. Generally, an employee must be eligible to join upon attaining the age of 21 or after the completion of one year of service, whichever is later.[6] However, the one year of service may be extended to two years of service if the participant's rights are immediately nonforfeitable upon joining the plan.[7]

"Service" is generally defined as a 12-month period during which the employee has at least 1,000 hours of service.[8] Exceptions exist for seasonal industries and maritime industries.[9] Breaks-in-service can be quite costly to the employee. If an employee has not completed the required two years under the two-year 100 percent vesting plan, and then has a one-year or

---

[3] Code Sec. 410(b); Reg. § 1.410(b)-2(b).
[4] Code Sec. 402(b)(4).
[5] Code Sec. 401(a)(26).
[6] Code Sec. 410(a)(1)(A).

[7] Code Sec. 410(a)(1)(B).
[8] Code Sec. 410(a)(3).
[9] *Id.*

more break-in-service, the service prior to the break is lost and the employee must start over.[10]

.03 Minimum Vesting Rules

"Vesting" occurs when the employee's rights to the employer contributions are nonforfeitable, even if he or she should resign or be fired. One of the following vesting schedules must be met:[11]

- The employee must have a nonforfeitable right to 100 percent of the accrued benefit derived from employer contributions after five years of service, or

- The employee must be fully vested after seven years of service and must be partially vested before then, under the following vesting schedule:

Years of Service	Percentage
3	20
4	40
5	60
6	80

Effective for contributions for plan years beginning after 2001, participants have a speeded up minimum vesting schedule for employer's matching contributions. Either the employee must be fully vested after three years of service, or the vesting schedule must be as follows:[12]

Years of Service	Nonforfeitable Percentage
2	20
3	40
4	60
5	80
6	100

The time frame for earlier vesting is different for plans that are maintained pursuant to a collective bargaining agreement.[13]

.04 Top-Heavy Plans

"Top-heavy plans" are essentially plans that provide disproportionate benefits to certain key employees. Because the benefits are not proportionate, top-heavy plans must meet more strict rules. A plan is considered top heavy with respect to any plan year:[14]

---

[10] Code Sec. 410(a)(5)(B).

[11] Code Sec. 411(a).

[12] Economic Growth and Tax Relief Reconciliation Act of 2001, Act Sec. 633(a)(2), adding Code Sec. 411(a)(12).

[13] See Economic Growth and Tax Relief Reconciliation Act of 2001, Act Sec. 633(c)(2).

[14] Code Sec. 416(g)(1).

- *For a defined benefit plan.* If the present value of the cumulative accrued benefits under the plan for key employees exceeds 60 percent of the present value of the cumulative accrued benefits for all employees.

- *For a defined contribution plan.* If the total of the accounts of the key employees under the plan exceeds 60 percent of the total of the accounts of all employees under the plan.

Effective for years beginning after 2001, for purposes of determining the present value of the cumulative accrued benefits or the amount of the account of an employee, such present value or amount is increased by the aggregate distributions made with respect to the employee under the plan during the one-year period ending on the determination date. This rule applies to distributions under a terminated plan which if it had not been terminated would have been required to be included in an aggregation group. However, if the distribution is made for other than separation of service, death, or disability, the five-year look-back remains in effect.[15]

The five-year look-back has also been reduced to one year for former employees. In determining the minimum accrued benefit, if the former employee has not performed services for the employer during any time in the one-year period ending on the determination date, such accrued benefit is not taken into account.[16]

Effective for years beginning after 2001, a new safe harbor rule for 401(k) plans is in effect. A plan will not be top heavy if it consists solely of a cash or deferred arrangement under 401(k) and matching contributions of Code Sec. 401(m)(11) are met.[17]

For either type of plan, the test is applied each year on the "determination date," which is the last day of the preceding plan year (last day of the current year for new plans).[18] "Key employees" are defined as employees who at any time during the plan year or any of the four preceding plan years are:[19]

1. An officer with an annual compensation in excess of 150 percent of the current dollar contribution limit for defined benefit plans; or

2. One of the ten employees who owns the largest interest in the employer, provided that annual compensation is in excess of $35,000; or

---

[15] Economic Growth and Tax Relief Reconciliation Act of 2001, Act Sec. 613(c)(1), amending Code Sec. 416(g)(3).

[16] Economic Growth and Tax Relief Reconciliation Act of 2001, Act Sec. 613(c)(2), amending Code Sec. 416(g)(4)(E).

[17] Economic Growth and Tax Relief Reconciliation Act of 2001, Act Sec. 613(d), adding Code Sec. 416(g)(4)(H).

[18] Code Sec. 416(g)(4)(C).

[19] Code Sec. 416(i)(1).

3.   A five percent owner of the employer; or

4.   A one percent owner of the employer who also has annual compensation of over $150,000.

New Simplified Top-Heavy Rules

Effective for tax years beginning after 2001, the top-heavy rules have been simplified. The four-year look-back to determine whether an employee is a key employee is eliminated. An officer is not considered a key employee unless he or she earns more than $130,000. And, the 10 largest stock-owning employees are no longer automatically considered key employees.[20]

Additional Requirements of Top-Heavy Plans

Top-heavy plans must meet stricter vesting requirements and stricter minimum benefits than other plans. The additional requirements are as follows:[21]

1.   *Vesting.* Employees must be either 100 percent vested after three years of service or 20 percent vested after two years of service, with an additional 20 percent vesting per year until six years of service (100 percent vested at that point).

2.   *Minimum benefits—Defined Benefit Plans.* Nonkey employees must receive a minimum accrued benefit. The accrued benefit must be at least equal to the applicable percentage of the participant's average compensation for the highest five years of compensation. The "applicable percentage" is the lesser of

a. 2 percent times the number of years of service with the employer, or

b. 20 percent.

Effective for years beginning after 2001, any year in which a plan is "frozen" is not considered a year of service. A plan is "frozen" for a year when no key employee or former key employee derives benefits under the plan.[22]

3.   *Minimum benefits—Defined Contribution Plans.* Nonkey employees must receive an employer contribution of at least 3 percent of annual compensation.

For defined contribution plans, employer matching contributions will now be taken into account in determining whether the minimum benefit requirement is satisfied. Any reduction in benefits that occurs because the employer may take matching contributions into account will not be a violation of the contingent benefit rule of Code 401(k)(4)(A).[23]

---

[20] Economic Growth and Tax Relief Reconciliation Act of 2001, Act Sec. 613(a)(1), amending Code Sec. 416(i)(1)(A).
[21] Code Sec. 416(b) and (c).
[22] Economic Growth and Tax Relief Reconciliation Act of 2001, Act Sec. 613(e), amending Code Sec. 416(c)(1)(C).

[23] Economic Growth and Tax Relief Reconciliation Act of 2001, Act Sec. 613(b), amending Code Sec. 416(c)(2)(A).

.05 Limitation on Benefits from Qualified Defined Benefit Plans; Limitation on Contributions to Defined Contribution Plans

The annual benefit payable to an employee under a defined benefit plan in the year 2001 is the lesser of $140,000, or 100 percent of the employee's average compensation for the three highest years of employment.[24] For the year 2002, the limit is increased to $160,000, and it is indexed for inflation.[25] The limitation is increased actuarially if the employee retires after age 65; the limitation is decreased actuarially if the employee retires before age 62.[26]

The annual contribution to a defined contribution plan cannot exceed the lesser of $35,000 (for 2001) or 25 percent of the participant's compensation.[27] Effective for tax years beginning after 2001, the contribution limit is the lesser of the increased base amount of $40,000, or 100 percent of compensation, and is to be indexed for inflation.[28]

.06 Distribution Requirements

Minimum distribution requirements apply to qualified employer-sponsored plans and traditional IRAs. Distributions must begin at least by the "required beginning date," which is generally April 1 of the calendar year following the later of:[29]

- The calendar year in which the employee became 70 and one-half years of age, or

- The calendar year in which the employee retires.

After the required beginning date is reached, annual or more frequent distributions (starting no later than the applicable April 1 and continuing no later than each subsequent December 31) must be made in minimum amounts. The minimum amount for a defined contribution plan is computed by dividing the balance in the account as of December 31 of the previous year by the applicable distribution period for someone the employee's age (determined from the table in Prop. Reg. § 1.401(a)(9)-5, Q&A 4).[30] The minimum distribution is recomputed each year, using the updated December 31 balance and the new life expectancy. The penalties for failure to make the minimum required distributions are discussed later in this chapter.

New Optional Treatment of Elective Deferrals

Effective for tax years beginning after 2005, employers having 401(k) plans and 403(b) plans can incorporate a qualified Roth contribution

---

[24] Code Sec. 415(b)(1).
[25] Economic Growth and Tax Relief Reconciliation Act of 2001, Act Sec. 611(a)(1)(A), amending Code Sec. 415(b)(1).
[26] Code Sec. 415(b)(2)(C) and (D), as amended by Act Sec. 611(a) of the Economic Growth and Tax Relief Reconciliation Act of 2001.

[27] Code Sec. 415(c)(1).
[28] Economic Growth and Tax Relief Reconciliation Act of 2001, Act Sec. 611(b)(1), amending Code Sec. 415(c)(1)(A).
[29] Act Sec. 1404(a), Small Business Job Protection Act, amending Code Sec. 401(a)(9)(C).
[30] Prop. Reg. § 1.401(a)(9)-5, Q&A 1.

program.[31] Employees may make a designated Roth contribution under this program.[32] Just as with a Roth IRA, these contributions are not excludable from income, but qualified distributions are not taxable.[33] A contribution is considered from a "qualified Roth contribution program" when an employee elects to make a designated Roth contribution.[34] A "designated Roth contribution" is an elective employee contribution that an employee is otherwise eligible to defer.[35] For a distribution from a Roth contribution program to qualify for exclusion from income, it must not be made within the five-year period beginning with the first tax year for which the participant makes a designated Roth contribution.[36] In addition, the distribution must either:[37]

- Be made on or after reaching age 59 and one-half, or

- Be made after the death of the participant, or

- Be attributable to disability of the participant.

Note that distributions to first-time homebuyers from qualified Roth contribution programs are taxable and would also be subject to the 10 percent penalty.

.07 Funding Requirements

The funding of a retirement plan involves the contribution of money or property to a trust to provide for the eventual payment of benefits. Failure to properly fund a retirement plan may subject the employer to interest, an excise tax, or possible civil action.

The actual funding requirements depend on the type of plan. Stock bonus plans and profit-sharing plans are not subject to funding requirements.[38] Defined contribution plans are not subject to funding requirements so long as the amount funded equals the contribution formula. However, defined benefit plans are subject to a rather complicated set of minimum funding requirements. Essentially, the so-called "normal cost" must be fully funded as well as a certain portion of past service costs and other retroactively applied benefits.[39]

For the year 2001 the full-funding limit is the excess (if any) of:[40]

1. The lesser of:

    a. The accrued liability under the plan, including normal costs, or

---

[31] Economic Growth and Tax Relief Reconciliation Act of 2001, Act Sec. 617(a), adding Code Sec. 402A(a).

[32] Id.

[33] Economic Growth and Tax Relief Reconciliation Act of 2001, Act Sec. 617(a), adding Code Secs. 402A(a)(1) and 402A(d)(1).

[34] Economic Growth and Tax Relief Reconciliation Act of 2001, Act Sec. 617(a), adding Code Sec. 402A(b)(1).

[35] Economic Growth and Tax Relief Reconciliation Act of 2001, Act Sec. 617(a), adding Code Sec. 402A(c)(1).

[36] Economic Growth and Tax Relief Reconciliation Act of 2001, Act Sec. 617(a), adding Code Sec. 402A(d)(1).

[37] Economic Growth and Tax Relief Reconciliation Act of 2001, Act Sec. 617(a), adding Code Sec. 402A(d)(2)(A).

[38] Code Sec. 412(h).

[39] See Code Sec. 412 for details.

[40] Code Sec. 412(c)(7).

      b. 160 percent (applicable percentage) of the plan's current liability, over

2.   The value of the plan's assets.

The applicable percentage is raised to 165 percent in 2002 and 170 percent in 2003, but is repealed for 2004.[41]

¶ 1005 Profit-Sharing Plans and Stock Bonus Plans

The purpose of a profit-sharing plan is to permit employees to defer compensation through their participation in the profits earned by the company.[42] Payments may be made from either current or accumulated profits. Payments are made from the employer to the designated trustee of the plan. A profit-sharing plan must provide a definite, predetermined formula for allocating the share of profits contributed by the employer, and for distributing the funds accumulated under the plan.[43] Allocations are often made based on salary; it is also typical to give some weight to years of service. There are no minimum funding standards for profit-sharing plans; however, "recurring and substantial contributions" must be made for the plan to qualify.[44]

The treatment of forfeitures is given more flexibility in a profit-sharing plan than under a defined benefit plan. Forfeitures may be used to decrease the employer's contribution, or, more typically, they may be allocated to the remaining employees.

Distributions from the plan must be made after a fixed number of years, the attainment of a certain age, or because of a layoff, illness, disability, retirement, death, or severance of employment.[45]

Employees may make voluntary contributions to the plan. The plan may also provide for a choice between receiving an amount in cash (taxed currently as compensation) or having it contributed to the profit-sharing plan (deferring tax).

.01   Advantages of Profit-Sharing Plans

The main advantage of a profit-sharing plan is the flexibility afforded the employer contributions. Since there is no requirement to contribute a fixed amount, contributions may be reduced or eliminated in loss or low-profit years. From the viewpoint of the employee, forfeiture allocations can provide a substantial benefit to an employee who remains with the company over a long term, especially if there is high turnover.

---

[41] Economic Growth and Tax Relief Reconciliation Act of 2001, Act Sec. 651(a), amending Code Sec. 412(c)(7).

[42] Reg. § 1.401-1(b)(1)(ii).

[43] *Id.*

[44] Reg. § 1.401-1(b)(2).

[45] Reg. § 1.401-1(b)(1)(ii).

.02 Stock Bonus Plans

A stock bonus plan is similar to a profit-sharing plan except that the *contributions* are not necessarily dependent on profits (though they could be) and the *benefits* are distributable in stock of the employer company.[46]

¶ 1007 Employee Stock Ownership Plans

An employee stock ownership plan (ESOP) is a defined contribution plan that qualifies for exemption from tax under Code Sec. 401(a), is designed to invest primarily in employer securities, and meets certain other requirements discussed below.[47]

- The plan must provide for the yearly allocation of all securities transferred to the trust or purchased by the trust substantially in proportion to employee compensation except that compensation in excess of $100,000 is disregarded.[48]

- The employee must have nonforfeitable rights.[49]

- Generally, no employer security may be distributed from the trust until the end of 84 months after the month that the security was allocated to the account. Certain exceptions exist due to death, disability, separation from service, etc.[50]

- Certain other requirements must be met.[51]

.01 Advantages of an ESOP

ESOPs can be very advantageous to both employers and employees for these reasons:

1. The employer may contribute its own stock and take a deduction based on the fair market value of the stock at the time of contribution. Since the corporation incurs no out of pocket cost in contributing its own stock, a tax deduction is created without any outward cash flow.

2. The corporation may take a deduction for certain dividends paid to the ESOP on shares held by it.[52] Generally, to be deductible, the dividends must either be distributed to the employee participants or must be used to make payments on loans used by the ESOP to buy the employer securities. For securities acquired by the ESOP after August 4, 1989, the dividends paid by the corporation are deductible only if the dividends are on stock acquired by the loan.[53]

Effective for tax years beginning after 2001, a C corporation may deduct, at the election of the plan participants or their beneficiaries,

---

[46] Reg. § 1.401-1(b)(1)(iii).
[47] Code Sec. 409(a).
[48] Code Sec. 409(b).
[49] Code Sec. 409(c).

[50] Code Sec. 409(d).
[51] See Code Sec. 409(e)-(h) and (o).
[52] Code Sec. 404(k).
[53] *Id.*

dividends paid to an ESOP that are reinvested in the employer's stock.[54] However, the IRS may disallow the deduction if determined that the dividend constitutes in substance an avoidance or evasion of taxation.[55]

Tax Tips and Pitfalls

This new provision should increase the appeal of ESOP plans for closely held corporations. In effect, the corporation receives a tax deduction without any net cash outflow to the extent that the dividends are reinvested in stock in the company. However, it is worrisome for Congress to disallow a deduction that is undertaken in a tax avoidance motive. Tax avoidance, as opposed to tax evasion, constitutes legally arranging one's financial transactions so as to minimize tax. As the estimable Judge Learned Hand said, "Anyone may so arrange his affairs that his taxes shall be as low as possible; he is not bound to choose that pattern which will best pay the Treasury; there is not even a patriotic duty to increase one's taxes."[56]

3. Shareholders may sell stock to an ESOP and under certain circumstances defer the gain on the sale of the stock if qualified replacement property (generally, any security issued by a domestic operating corporation *except* for securities of the company whose stock is being sold) is acquired within a certain time period.[57]

¶ 1009   Deferred Arrangements—401(k) Plans

A 401(k) plan is a qualified cash or deferred compensation arrangement included in a profit-sharing or stock bonus plan.[58]

Participants in 401(k) plans may choose either to receive compensation in the form of cash or to defer receipt of compensation. Two options exist with respect to this type of plan: (1) the employer may make annual contributions in the form of a bonus; or (2) more commonly, the arrangement may involve a salary reduction. In either case, the employee in effect agrees to defer a portion of his or her compensation and to have it contributed to the plan by the employer.

Elective second-option contributions are generally attributed entirely to the employer. In either option (1) the amount of deferred compensation under the plan is not currently taxed as income to the employee, and (2) the employer receives a deduction for the same amount. For this to be true, the employer and employee must have entered into a salary reduction agreement and the employer must have adopted a 401(k) plan prior to the deferral of compensation.[59]

---

[54] Economic Growth and Tax Relief Reconciliation Act of 2001, Act Sec. 662(a), amending Code Sec. 404(k)(2)(A).

[55] Economic Growth and Tax Relief Reconciliation Act of 2001, Act Sec. 662(b), amending Code Sec. 404(k)(5)(A).

[56] *Helvering v. Gregory*, 69 F2d 809, Dec. ¶ 9180, (2nd Cir. 1934).

[57] Code Sec. 1042.

[58] Code Sec. 401(k)(1).

[59] Reg. § 1.401(k)-1(a)(2).

While contributions are not subject to income taxation, they are subject to FICA taxes.[60]

.01 Annual Limits

The Tax Reform Act of 1986 originally established a limit of $7,000 on the amount of the elective contribution to the employee's account under all qualified cash or deferred arrangements. The total contribution limit (elective deferral plus additional contributions made by the employer) is limited to the lesser of a participant's compensation or $40,000, and is reduced by contributions to other qualified plans.[61] The original $7,000 limit is adjusted annually for inflation. The limit is adjusted at the same time as are the benefits from defined benefit plans.[62] The limit effective for 2001 is $10,500.

For tax years beginning after 2001, the dollar limit on elective deferrals is increased as follows:[63]

Year	Dollar Limit
2002	$11,000
2003	12,000
2004	13,000
2005	14,000
2006 & later	15,000

Effective for contributions in tax years beginning after 2001, additional catch-up contributions are allowed for individuals who are age 50 or older by the end of the tax year. The catch-up contributions are the lesser of the "applicable dollar amount" or the employee's compensation reduced by other elective deferrals. The applicable dollar amount is:[64]

Year	Applicable Dollar Amount
2002	$1,000
2003	2,000
2004	3,000
2005	4,000
2006 or thereafter	5,000

All 401(k) plans in which an individual participates are aggregated in applying the limits. Excess contributions not withdrawn according to the time limits are subject to a 10 percent excise tax.

---

[60] Code Sec. 3121(v).

[61] See Code Sec. 415(c)(1), as amended by Act Secs. 611(b)(1) and 632(a)(1) of the Economic Growth and Tax Relief Reconciliation Act of 2001, for the limitation on defined contribution plans, and Code Sec. 401(k)(1) for the integration of 401(k) plans with other qualified plans.

[62] Code Sec. 402(g)(4).

[63] Economic Growth and Tax Relief Reconciliation Act of 2001, Act Sec. 611(d)(1), amending Code Sec. 402(g)(1).

[64] Economic Growth and Tax Relief Reconciliation Act of 2001, Act Sec. 631(a), adding Code Sec. 414(v).

.02 Advantages of 401(k) Plans

Code Sec. 401(k) plans give maximum flexibility to employees in that they have the option each year to decide (within the annual limits) between current cash payments and provision for old age. While certain other plans also have some flexibility, qualified money payment or defined benefit plans are much more rigid with respect to the trade-off between current and deferred compensation.

.03 Participation Rules

401(k) plans are subject to the general participation standards of Code Sec. 410, i.e., participation cannot be excluded beyond the later of one year of service with the employer or attainment of age 21.[65] However, participation may be postponed for an additional year if under the plan the employee's accrued benefit is fully vested after two years of service.[66]

.04 Special Nondiscrimination Test

The flexibility inherent in a 401(k) plan makes it especially vulnerable to discrimination toward higher-paid employees (who are in less need of current earnings and are thus able to defer a much greater percentage of their salary). Therefore, 401(k) plans must meet a special annual nondiscrimination test. In essence, the test compares the percentage of elective deferrals to wages of highly compensated employees with the percentage of elective deferrals to wages of nonhighly compensated employees.[67] Alternatively, for tax years beginning after 1996, 401(k) plans can adopt a SIMPLE plan to meet the nondiscrimination tests.[68]

.05 Distribution Restrictions

Once money has been deferred under a 401(k) plan, there are numerous restrictions on the participant's ability to recover the funds. Historically, distributions of deferred compensation amounts could be made only in the event of the participant's retirement, death, disability, hardship, or separation from service.[69] TAMRA '88 established some additional circumstances under which distributions are permitted without penalty. Termination of a plan without establishment or maintenance of a successor defined contribution plan now qualifies for distribution treatment.[70]

Prior to the Economic Growth and Tax Relief Reconciliation Act of 2001, the merger or consolidation, or liquidation of an employer did not constitute separation from service if the employee continued on the same job (the "same desk" rule). Effective for distributions after 2001, the same desk rule is eliminated. Thus, following a merger, consolidation, or liquida-

---

[65] Code Sec. 410(a)(1)(A).
[66] Code Sec. 410(a)(1)(B).
[67] Code Sec. 401(k)(3).

[68] Code Sec. 401(k)(11).
[69] Code Sec. 401(k)(2)(B).
[70] Code Sec. 401(k)(10)(A).

tion, employees may receive a lump sum distribution from 401(k) plans without penalty.[71]

Distributions for hardship may be made only from contributions, not from plan earnings.[72] In addition, only salary reduction contributions, not matching employer contributions, are eligible for hardship distributions. "Hardship" is defined as an immediate and heavy financial need of the employee.[73] The distribution will qualify as a hardship distribution only to the extent that the need is not reasonably satisfied from other resources of the employee.[74] Examples mentioned in the regulations include: medical expenses, purchase of a principal residence for the employee, and payment of tuition for the next 12 months for the employee or his or her dependents.[75] An excise tax of 10 percent is imposed on premature distributions. Loans from 401(k) plans are subject to provisions applicable to loans by qualified plans.

¶ 1011 Keogh Plans

Keogh plans stem from the Self-Employed Individuals Tax Retirement Act of 1962. Until the passage of the Tax Equity and Fiscal Responsibility Act of 1982 (TEFRA), Keogh plans were subject to much different rules than were qualified employee plans. These differences were considerably narrowed by TEFRA, with the result being that Keogh plans have the same deduction limits as qualified plans.

.01 Types of Keogh Plans

As with qualified employee plans, Keogh plans may be one of two types: defined benefit plans or defined contribution plans. Since defined benefit plans can be somewhat costly for small businesses, defined contribution plans are more common. In turn, defined contribution plans may be constituted as either profit-sharing plans (where the defined contribution is based on earnings) or money purchase plans (where the defined contribution is a set percentage of eligible employees' compensation or the owner's earned income from the sole proprietorship).

.02 Definitions Applicable to Keogh Plans

Self-Employed Individuals

The "self-employed" are individuals who have earned income from self-employment, generally as defined in Code Sec. 1402(a).[76]

---

[71] Economic Growth and Tax Relief Reconciliation Act of 2001, Act Sec. 646(a)(1), amending Code Sec. 401(k)(2)(B)(i)(I).

[72] Code Sec. 401(k)(2)(B)(i)(IV).

[73] Reg. § 1.401(k)-1(d)(2).

[74] Reg. § 1.401(k)-1(d)(2)(iii)(B).

[75] Reg. § 1.401(k)-1(d)(2)(iv).

[76] Code Sec. 401(c)(2)(A). Net earnings from self-employment under Code Sec. 1402 includes income from a trade or business, as well as a distributive share of partnership trade or business profits, but excludes passive income such as interest or dividends.

Owner-Employers

An "owner-employer" is any employee who owns the entire interest in an unincorporated trade or business or, in the case of a partnership, is a partner who owns more than 10 percent of the capital interest or profits interest in the partnership.[77]

Earned Income

For tax years beginning after 1989, "earned income" is defined as the net earnings from self-employment, except that the computation:[78]

- May include income from a trade or business *only* if personal services of the taxpayer are a material income-producing factor;

- May not include exempt income or expenses attributable thereto;

- Is computed *with* regard to the deduction for contributions to a pension, etc., plan (as allowed by Code Sec. 404);

- Is computed *with* regard to the deduction for one-half of self-employment taxes (as provided by Code Sec. 164(f)); and

- Reflects certain other adjustments outside the scope this book.

.03 Contribution and Deduction Limits

The Tax Equity and Fiscal Responsibility Act of 1982 generally brought the contribution and deduction limits for Keoghs in line with those for qualified employee plans. Prior to the Economic Growth and Tax Relief Reconciliation Act of 2001, the limit on contributions and deductions to a money purchase Keogh made by the proprietor on behalf of *employees* was the lesser of 25 percent of net compensation or $35,000 (for 2001).[79] The contribution limit on the contribution made by the proprietor on *his or her behalf* was also limited to 25 percent; however, the contribution itself must have been deducted before the 25 percent limit was applied.[80] Hence, the effective limit was 20 percent before the deduction.

> **Example 10-1.** Angela Smith's income from self-employment was $50,000 in 2001. Her maximum allowable Keogh contribution is $10,000 ($50,000 × .20). Taxable earnings *after* deducting the contribution are $40,000, and the contribution of $10,000 is 25 percent of $40,000.

Effective for years beginning after 2001, the contribution to a Keogh is limited to the lesser of $40,000 or 100 percent of compensation.[81]

---

[77] Code Sec. 401(c)(3); Reg. § 1.401-10(d).
[78] Code Sec. 401(c)(2)(A).
[79] Code Sec. 415(c)(1).
[80] Code Sec. 401(c)(2)(A)(v).

[81] Economic Growth and Tax Relief Reconciliation Act of 2001, Act Sec. 611(b)(1), amending Code Sec. 415(c)(1).

Profit-sharing Keogh plans are subject to the same limit on contributions as are the money purchase plans; however, the *deduction* allowable to the proprietor is subject to a much lower limit. Prior to the Tax Relief Reconciliation Act of 2001, the limit was the greater of 15 percent of net compensation of the employee, or the amount the employer was required to contribute to the trust under Code Sec. 401(k)(11).[82] Again, however, the limit was applied *after* the deduction. Hence, the effective rate limit for Keogh profit-sharing plans was 13.04 percent. Effective for years beginning after 2001, the limit for stock bonus or profit-sharing plans is raised to the greater of 25 percent of the compensation of the employee, or the amount the employer was required to contribute to the trust under Code Sec. 401(k)(11).[83]

Tax Tips and Pitfalls

Many small employers prefer stock bonus or profit-sharing plans because of the flexibility accorded contributions. This law change should encourage even more employers to establish such plans.

Excess contributions to a profit-sharing Keogh may be carried forward indefinitely; however, the deduction in succeeding years can never exceed the 25 percent (or 20 percent) limit.[84]

.04 *How Keogh Contributions Are Deducted*

Contributions to Keogh plans made by proprietors on behalf of both their employees and themselves are taken as a business deduction for adjusted gross income purposes. However, for net operating loss deduction purposes, the portion of the total contributions that is made on behalf of the proprietor is treated as a nonbusiness deduction.[85]

.05 *Qualifying the Keogh Plan*

The procedures for qualifying a Keogh plan differ according to whether the proprietor joins a prototype (master) plan. If a master plan is joined, the organization offering the plan (bank, insurance company, brokerage firm, etc.) should already have received approval from the IRS. In that event, the proprietor will be furnished a plan number and notification that the plan is qualified.

If a self-employed individual wishes to qualify his or her own plan, it is desirable (though not required) to submit the plan for advance approval by the IRS. Forms 5300 (defined benefit), 5301 (defined contribution), and 5303 (collectively bargained) should be used to request the determination letter. The relevant form is filed with the district director.

---

[82] Code Sec. 404(a)(3)(A)(i).

[83] Economic Growth and Tax Relief Reconciliation Act of 2001, Act Sec. 616(a)(1)(A), amending Code Sec. 404(a)(3)(A)(i)(I).

[84] Code Sec. 404(a)(3)(A)(ii).

[85] Code Sec. 172(d)(4)(D). Since the contributions are treated as non-business deductions, they are deductible only to the extent of non-business income.

¶ 1013   Traditional IRAs

Congress first established IRAs in 1974. At first, the scope of eligible employees was quite limited, no deduction for contributions being available to employees who were covered by employer plans, self-employed plans, or tax-sheltered annuities.[86] However, coverage was widened by ERTA to include employees who are covered by other plans.[87]

.01   Contribution and Deduction Limits

Taxpayers generally may contribute to an IRA the lesser of $2,000 or their earned compensation.[88] For this purpose, "compensation" is as defined by Code Sec. 401(c)(2), i.e., it is defined as "earned income."[89] An exception to the general rule exists for married couples where only one spouse has earned income. For years after 1996, nonworking spouses can contribute up to $2,000 per year to a deductible IRA.[90] However, the total contribution for both spouses cannot exceed the combined compensation for both spouses.

New Contribution Limits

Effective in 2002, the contribution limits for IRA contributions will be raised. The deductible amount for the years 2002 through 2004 is $3,000. The limit increases to $4,000 for the years 2005 through 2007, and to $5,000 for 2008 and beyond.[91] After 2008, the limit is to be adjusted for inflation.[92]

The new law also provides for additional "catch-up" contributions for taxpayers who are age 50 or older by the end of the taxable year. The additional contribution allowed is $500 for the years 2002 through 2005 and $1,000 for the years 2006 and thereafter.[93]

Tax Tips and Pitfalls

Residents of community property states are treated the same as residents of common-law states for this purpose in that, for IRA contribution purposes, earned income is *not* considered community property income.[94]

Taxpayers are not necessarily allowed to deduct all that may be contributed to an IRA. The deduction limitations put into place by TRA '86 are more stringent than the contribution limits. The deduction may be less than the amount contributed if both of the following are true:[95]

- The individual is an "active participant" in an employer-sponsored plan; and

---

[86] Code Sec. 219(b)(2), prior to amendment by ERTA '81.

[87] Code Sec. 219(b).

[88] Code Sec. 219(b)(1).

[89] Code Sec. 219(f)(1).

[90] Act Sec. 1247, Small Business Job Protection Act, amending Code Sec. 219(c).

[91] Economic Growth and Tax Relief Reconciliation Act of 2001, Act Sec. 601(a)(2), adding Code Sec. 219(b)(5).

[92] *Id.*

[93] *Id.*

[94] Code Sec. 219(f)(2).

[95] Code Sec. 219(g).

- Adjusted gross income exceeds the "applicable amount."

"Active participants" are taxpayers who belong to:[96]

- A qualified pension, profit-sharing, or stock bonus plan; or

- A tax-sheltered annuity; or

- A simplified employee trust (SEP) (see discussion below);

- SIMPLE retirement account; or

- A trust described in Code Sec. 501(c)(18).

An employee who belongs to a plan is considered an active participant even if his or her rights are not vested as of the end of the current tax year.[97]

The "applicable amount" is a base AGI level of $53,000 in 2001 ($54,000 in 2002; $60,000 in 2003; $65,000 in 2004; $70,000 in 2005; $75,000 in 2006; and $80,000 in 2007 or thereafter) for taxpayers filing jointly, and $33,000 in 2001 ($34,000 in 2002; $40,000 in 2003; $45,000 in 2004; and $50,000 in 2005 or thereafter) for all other taxpayers, except those married filing separately, for whom it is generally zero.[98] However, husbands and wives who lived apart the entire year and who file separately are considered not married for this purpose.[99]

In the event that both of the above tests are met (applicable amount and participation in an employer-sponsored plan), the portion of the contribution that may be *deducted* is determined by multiplying the contribution limit by a fraction whose numerator is the difference between the taxpayer's adjusted gross income and the applicable dollar amount and whose denominator is $10,000 ($20,000 in the case of joint returns for taxable years after 2006).

> **Example 10-2.** Phil Nostrum and his wife file a joint return. Both are employed, but only Nostrum is covered by an employer-sponsored plan. Their 2001 AGI is $54,000. The maximum deduction for Nostrum in 2001 is $2,000 − ($2,000 × ($54,000 − $53,000)/ $10,000) = $1,800.

> **Example 10-3.** Beth Higgins is single with an AGI of $240,000. She is not covered by an employer-sponsored plan. She may deduct up to $2,000 of contributions to an IRA.

A special rule applies to spouses who are not active participants. In that event, their applicable dollar amount is $150,000 and the denominator of the phaseout fraction is $10,000.[100]

---

[96] Code Sec. 219(g)(5).
[97] *Id.*
[98] Code Sec. 219(g)(3).

[99] Code Sec. 219(g)(4).

[100] Code Sec. 219(g)(7).

New Deemed IRAs Under Employee Plans

Effective for plan years beginning after 2002, qualified plans may allow employees to make voluntary contributions to accounts which, if they meet the requirements for traditional IRAs, will be treated as IRAs rather than qualified plans. In addition, the establishment of a deemed IRA program will not jeopardize the employer's qualified plan.[101]

New Tax Credit for Elective Deferrals and IRA Contributions

Effective for tax years beginning after 2001, low- and moderate-income taxpayers are allowed a credit for the first $2,000 of qualified retirement savings contributions made during the tax year.[102] The credit rate, a decreasing scale as AGI increases, is as follows:[103]

AGI

Joint Return		Head of Household		Other		%
Over	Not Over	Over	Not Over	Over	Not Over	
$ 0	$30,000	$ 0	$22,500	$ 0	$15,000	50
30,000	32,500	22,500	24,375	15,000	16,250	20
32,500	50,000	24,375	37,500	16,250	25,000	10
50,000	—	37,500	—	25,000	—	0

A "qualified retirement savings contribution" is the sum of:[104]

- IRA contributions (including Roth IRAs) made by the individual;

- Elective deferrals under Code Sec. 402(g)(3);

- Elective deferrals of compensation under Code Sec. 457(b);

- Voluntary contributions to any qualified retirement plan as defined by Code Sec. 4974(c).

Not all taxpayers are eligible for the credit. A taxpayer must be 18 by the close of the taxable year and must not be a full-time student (as defined in Code Sec. 151(c)(4)) or a dependent of another taxpayer.[105]

The contribution amount that is eligible for the credit is reduced (but not below zero) by distributions during the testing period from:[106]

---

[101] Economic Growth and Tax Relief Reconciliation Act of 2001, Act Sec. 602(a), amending Code Sec. 408(q).

[102] Economic Growth and Tax Relief Reconciliation Act of 2001, Act Sec. 618(a), adding Code Sec. 25B(a).

[103] Economic Growth and Tax Relief Reconciliation Act of 2001, Act Sec. 618(a), adding Code Sec. 25B(b).

[104] Economic Growth and Tax Relief Reconciliation Act of 2001, Act Sec. 618(a), adding Code Sec. 25B(d)(1).

[105] Economic Growth and Tax Relief Reconciliation Act of 2001, Act Sec. 618(a), adding Code Sec. 25B(c).

[106] Economic Growth and Tax Relief Reconciliation Act of 2001, Act Sec. 618(a), adding Code Sec. 25B(d)(2)(A).

- Any distribution from either a qualified plan (defined in Code Sec. 4974(c)), or from an eligible deferred compensation plan (defined in Code Sec. 457(b)) that is includible in gross income;

- Distributions from Roth IRAs except for qualified rollover contributions.

The "testing period" for a given tax year is the period which includes the current year, the two preceding years, and the period after the current year that is before the due date (including extensions) for filing the return for the tax year.[107]

Adjusted gross income for this purpose is computed before the foreign income exclusion of Code Sec. 911 and before the foreign possession income exclusions of Code Sec. 931 and Code Sec. 933.[108] The credit is a nonrefundable credit and cannot exceed the excess of the regular tax liability plus the alternate minimum tax over the sum of all other credits allowed except for adoption expenses and the foreign tax credit.[109]

Tax Tips and Pitfalls

Low- and moderate-income taxpayers are often dissuaded from contributing to 401(k)s and IRAs due to an inability to fund the contributions. This credit should be of considerable help. However, two cautions are in order. Because of the phaseout levels, taxpayers who are close to certain AGI levels should consider deferring income or increasing business deductions so as to maximize the credit. For example, a married couple filing jointly with AGI income of $30,000 would lose as much as $600 of credit if AGI should exceed $30,000 by even $1. Thus, the marginal rate of taxation on income above the phaseout levels will be extremely high. The new credit will also reduce the attractiveness of taking distributions from IRAs for first-time home purchases, medical expenses, or for education. The distribution will reduce the credit for the taxable year and also perhaps for the following two tax years.

.02 Nondeductible Contributions to an IRA

Designated nondeductible contributions may be made to an IRA. The amount designated as nondeductible is limited to the total amount contributed, not to exceed $2,000 each, less the amount that is deductible.[110]

Example 10-4. Assume the same facts as in Example 10-2, except that Nostrum contributes the maximum $2,000. The amount that may be designated as nondeductible is $2,000 − $1,800 = $200.

---

[107] Economic Growth and Tax Relief Reconciliation Act of 2001, Act Sec. 618(a), adding Code Sec. 25B(d)(2)(B).

[108] Economic Growth and Tax Relief Reconciliation Act of 2001, Act Sec. 618(a), adding Code Sec. 25B(e).

[109] Economic Growth and Tax Relief Reconciliation Act of 2001, Act Sec. 618(a), adding Code Sec. 25B(g)[(h)].

[110] Code Sec. 408(o).

Since the nondeductible contribution is an *after-tax* contribution, the taxpayer will have a tax basis in the nondeductible part of the contribution, and if a distribution is made from the IRA, part of the distribution will be nontaxable. The reporting requirements for either of these events (making nondeductible contributions or taking partly nontaxable distributions) are met by filing Form 8606 with Form 1040. Distributions are treated *pro rata* from both the pre-tax and after-tax contributions.

.03   Rollovers to and from an IRA

Amounts withdrawn from an IRA are not treated as distributions (the transactions are given tax-free treatment) if they are rolled over into another IRA within 60 days after the distribution.[111] In that case, the new IRA would succeed to the tax basis (if any) of the old IRA. Effective for distributions after 2001, the IRS may waive the 60-day requirement where the failure to waive would be against equity or good conscience, including casualty, disaster, or other event beyond the reasonable control of the individual.[112] However, only one rollover per 12-month period is permitted.[113]

> **Example 10-5.** Marcus Kim withdrew $25,000 from his S&L IRA on April 5 and rolled it into a mutual fund on June 1. Dissatisfied with the mutual fund performance, he withdrew the balance from it (it had dropped to $23,500) on January 10 of the next year and rolled it into a bond fund at a brokerage firm. The second rollover is treated as a taxable distribution.

Rollovers are also generally permitted *into* an IRA from qualified employer-sponsored plans such as a pension plan, profit-sharing plan, or tax-sheltered annuity.[114] Prior to the Tax Relief Reconciliation Act of 2001, it was not possible to roll over an IRA into a qualified retirement plan. However, effective for distributions after 2001, an eligible rollover distribution from an IRA may be made into a qualified employer plan, 403(b) plan, or a Code Sec. 457 deferred compensation plan.[115] An "eligible rollover contribution" is generally the amount of distribution from an IRA that would be includible in income if distributed instead of rolled over.[116] Nondeductible after-tax contributions made to an IRA are ineligible for rollover to a qualified plan.

Effective for distributions after 2001, the surviving spouse of a deceased participant may make a tax-free rollover from the IRA to another

---

[111] Code Sec. 408(d)(3)(A).

[112] Economic Growth and Tax Relief Reconciliation Act of 2001, Act Sec. 644(b), amending Code Sec. 408(d)(3).

[113] Code Sec. 408(d)(3)(B).

[114] Code Sec. 402(c).

[115] Economic Growth and Tax Relief Reconciliation Act of 2001, Act Sec. 642(a), amending Code Sec. 408(d)(3)(A)(ii).

[116] Economic Growth and Tax Relief Reconciliation Act of 2001, Act Sec. 642(a), amending Code Sec. 408(d)(3)(A)(ii).

IRA, a qualified plan, a 403(b) plan, or to a Code Sec. 457 governmental plan.[117]

If the proceeds are transferred directly to the new IRA, it is not considered a rollover. For it to be treated as a direct transfer, the check should be made out to the institution as trustee for the individual. Employers are required to withhold 20 percent of lump-sum distributions unless the transfer is made directly to an IRA or other qualified plan.[118]

.04 Distributions from an IRA

As previously mentioned, distributions from IRAs that contain nondeductible contributions are treated as both a return of basis (nontaxable) and a return of untaxed funds (taxed at ordinary income rates). Distributions received before the age of 59 and one-half may be subject to a 10 percent premature distribution penalty (this applies only to the portion of the distribution that is included in income).[119] However, the 10 percent penalty does not apply to the following distributions:[120]

- Made on or after the employee becomes age 59 and one-half,

- Made to a beneficiary (or to the estate of the employee) on or after the death of the employee,

- Attributable to the employee being disabled,

- Those part of a series of substantially equal periodic payments,

- Payment of medical expenses in excess of 7.5 percent of adjusted gross income,

- In certain instances, payment of health insurance premiums after separation from employment,

- Payments for qualified higher education expenses,

- Distributions for first-time homebuyers.

(Also, see ¶ 1027, "Penalties for Inadequate, Early, or Excessive Distributions.")

Although distributions *before* 59 and one-half are generally too early and thus subject to a penalty, distributions not made until *after* a certain age are also subject to a penalty. Generally, distributions must begin by no later than April 1 following the year in which the IRA owner becomes 70 and one-half.[121] An excess accumulation penalty also can apply if distributions are insufficient. A complicated set of rules exists to determine if distributions are sufficient.[122]

---

[117] Economic Growth and Tax Relief Reconciliation Act of 2001, Act Sec. 642(a), amending Code Sec. 408(d)(3).
[118] Code Sec. 3405(c).
[119] Code Sec. 72(t).
[120] Code Sec. 72(t)(2).
[121] Code Secs. 408(a)(6) and (b)(3), and 401(a)(9)(C).
[122] Code Secs. 408(a)(6) and (b)(3), and 401(a)(9).

Proposed regulations issued in January 2001 provide simplified minimum distribution rules (MRDs). The regulations provide a single table that recipients can use to calculate their yearly MRDs. The table eliminates the need to elect recalculation of life expectancy, determine a designated beneficiary by the required beginning date, or satisfy a separate incidental death benefit rule.

The proposed regulations reduce MRDs for most IRA holders. Although MRDs will be calculated without regard to the beneficiary's age, the regulations continue to permit a longer payout period if the beneficiary is a spouse more than 10 years younger than the employee.[123]

Tax Tips and Pitfalls

Even for those taxpayers who cannot *deduct* IRA contributions, the ability to *make* contributions constitutes a very important tax planning device. "The tax deferral element of nondeductible contributions can be considered equivalent to a direct investment in tax-exempt securities. The IRA, if invested in a mutual fund, or self-directed brokerage account, may return far more than would tax-exempt securities. Also, the repeal of the 60 percent capital gains deduction leaves the IRA as one vehicle for selling appreciated stock and other securities without having to pay any tax on the capital gains.

¶ 1015   Roth IRAs

Roth IRAs (named after the former senator from Delaware) are "back-loaded IRAs," i.e., contributions are nondeductible, but all distributions from the IRA, providing that time requirements are met, are nontaxable.[124] The maximum contribution to a Roth in 2001 was $2,000. Effective in 2002, the contribution limits for IRA contributions will be raised. The deductible amounts for the years 2002 through 2004 are $3,000. The limit increases to $4,000 for the years 2005 through 2007, and to $5,000 for 2008 and beyond.[125] After 2008, the limit is to be adjusted for inflation.[126]

The new law also provides for additional "catch-up" contributions for taxpayers who are age 50 or older by the end of the of the taxable year. The additional contribution allowed is $500 for the years 2002 through 2005 and $1,000 for the years 2006 and thereafter.[127]

However, the modified adjusted gross income (MAGI) phaseout limitations are higher than for traditional IRAs. For Roths, the phaseouts are from $150,000 and $160,000 for taxpayers filing jointly, and $95,000 to $110,000 for all other taxpayers except married filing separately.[128]

---

[123] Prop. Reg. § § 1.408-8 and 1.401(a)(9)-5.
[124] Code Sec. 408A.
[125] Code Sec. 408A(c)(2); Economic Growth and Tax Relief Reconciliation Act of 2001, Act Sec. 601(a)(2), adding Code Sec. 219(b)(5).

[126] *Id.*
[127] *Id.*
[128] Code Sec. 408A(c).

.01 Distributions from Roths

Qualified distributions from Roth IRAs are tax-free. In order to qualify, the distribution may not be made before the end of the five-tax-year period beginning with the first tax year in which a contribution was made to the Roth IRA.[129] The distribution must also be made for one of the following reasons:[130]

- Made on or after the individual reaches age 59 and one-half,

- Made on or after the individual's death,

- Is attributable to the individual being disabled,

- Is a distribution for a first-time homebuyer (the maximum distribution is $10,000).

Tax Tips and Pitfalls

The ordering of distributions from Roths is very favorable to taxpayers.[131] First the distributions are deemed to come from contributions (and are therefore nontaxable). Only after all contributions are withdrawn are the distributions taxable (if the distributions are not qualified) and subject to the 10 percent penalty.

Example 10-6. Bob Hanks contributed $2,000 to a Roth IRA in both 1999 and 2000. In the year 2001 he withdrew the entire balance in the IRA (now $6,800) in a nonqualifying distribution. The first $4,000 is nontaxable. The remaining $2,800 is taxable and also subject to the 10 percent penalty.

.02 Converting Traditional IRAs to Roths

Taxpayer's whose AGI is not more than $100,000 may roll a traditional IRA into a Roth IRA.[132] The rollover is includible in the taxpayer's income, but is not subject to the 10 percent penalty.[133]

Tax Tips and Pitfalls

All taxpayers who have AGI not exceeding $100,000 should consider converting their traditional IRAs. A wonderful feature of the Roth IRA is that it is not subject to required distributions as long as the individual is alive. Thus, a Roth IRA affords tremendous build-up of tax-free income. If a taxpayer expects his or her tax rate at retirement to be considerably less than his or her current rate, conversion may not be desirable. But in most other cases it will be advantageous to convert. Caution: the taxpayer must have sufficient funds outside the IRA to pay the income tax on the conversion. Using a portion of the IRA to pay the tax would cause the conversion to be subject to the 10 percent penalty.

---

[129] Code Sec. 408A(d)(2)(B).
[130] Code Sec. 408A(d)(2)(A).
[131] Code Sec. 408A(d)(4).

[132] Code Sec. 408A(c)(3)(B).

[133] Code Sec. 408A(d)(3).

As discussed previously, effective for years after 2005, the Tax Relief Reconciliation Act of 2001 permits participants in 401(k) and 403(b) plans to incorporate a "qualified Roth contribution program" whereby they may designate elective deferrals to be after-tax Roth contributions. Rollovers of these amounts will qualify as a tax-free "qualified rollover contribution" to a Roth IRA.

.03 Nondeductible Tax-Free IRAs

TRA '97 allows individuals to make contributions to IRAs where the contribution is nondeductible but the income accumulates tax-free.[134] This IRA option is referred to as Roth IRAs. The contribution limitation is $2,000 including any other deductible and nondeductible IRAs. The maximum contribution that can be made to a Roth IRA is phased out for individuals with AGI between $95,000 and $110,000 and for joint filers with AGI between $150,000 and $160,000.

¶ 1017 Simplified Employee Pensions (SEPs)

When Congress, in the Small Business Job Protection Act, created the SIMPLE retirement plan (see the discussion below), it also repealed elective deferrals by an employee under SEPs.[135] However, SEPs established before January 1, 1997, can continue to receive contributions under present-law rules, and new employees hired after December 31, 1996, can participate in the SEP.[136]

Simplified employee pensions (SEPs) are individual retirement plans established by the employer/proprietor for the benefit of the proprietor and employees of the proprietor.

.01 Coverage, Participation, and Vesting Requirements

A special set of participation rules exists for SEPs. Generally, the participation requirements for a SEP are met for a given year *only* if contributions are made for all employees who meet all of the criteria shown below:[137]

- The employee has attained age 21;

- The employee has performed services in at least three out of the last five immediately preceding years; and

- The employee has received at least $450 (for 2001) in compensation from the employer during the year.

For SEPs, as well as other qualified plans, a substantial exception exists to the participation rules. Not required to be covered are employees who are members of a labor union, provided that the union is both the

---

[134] Act Sec. 302, Taxpayer Relief Act of 1997 (P.L. 105-34); adding Code Sec. 408A.
[135] Senate Finance Committee Rept., Small Business Job Protection Act, June 24, 1996.

[136] *Id.*
[137] Code Sec. 408(k)(2).

bargaining agent and that retirement benefits were the "subject of good faith bargaining."[138]

.02 Contribution and Deduction Limits

The *contribution* limits for employees for 2001 were the lesser of 25 percent of compensation or $35,000.[139] For tax years after 2001, the contribution limits are increased to the lesser of $40,000 or 100 percent of compensation.[140] The amount *deductible* to the employer is subject to an annual limit of 15 percent of compensation (up to $170,000 in 2001) paid to the covered employees during the calendar year ending with or within the tax year (or during the tax year if the SEP has the same tax year as the employer).[141] For tax years beginning after 2001, the percentage is raised from 15 to 25 percent, and the limit is raised to $200,000.[142] Excess contributions may be carried over to succeeding tax years and deducted in order of time, subject, however, to the yearly 25 percent limit.[143] Some employers may maintain a qualified plan in addition to the SEP. In that event, deductions taken for contributions to the SEP reduce the amount otherwise allowable to the qualified plan.[144]

Certain nondiscrimination rules apply to contributions to SEPs. Generally, contributions may not discriminate in favor of highly compensated employees (see the previous discussion of highly compensated employees as defined for qualified plans). However, a special rule exists for SEPs when testing for discrimination. Employer contributions must bear a uniform relationship to compensation of the employees; only the first $170,000 (in 2001) of compensation per employee is taken into account for this purpose).[145] Effective for years beginning after 2001, this limit is raised to $200,000.[146]

The top-heavy rules discussed previously also apply to SEPs. The minimum benefits requirements of top-heavy plans are applied by treating SEPs as defined contribution plans.[147]

.03 Distributions from SEPs

SEPs are treated identically to traditional IRAs with respect to distributions, i.e., distributions result in ordinary income to the taxpayer.

Tax Tips and Pitfalls

SEPs have the advantage of simplicity; accounting and record-keeping costs should be minimal for SEPs, especially if either a model SEP or a prototype SEP is selected. The primary drawback from the

---

[138] Code Secs. 408(k)(2) and 410(b)(3)(A).
[139] Code Sec. 408(j).
[140] Economic Growth and Tax Relief Reconciliation Act of 2001, Act Sec. 601(b)(4), amending Code Sec. 408(j).
[141] Code Sec. 404(h)(1)(C).
[142] Economic Growth and Tax Relief Reconciliation Act of 2001, Act Sec. 611(c), amending Code Sec. 408(k); Act Sec. 616(a), amending Code Sec. 404(h)(1)(C).

[143] *Id.*
[144] Code Sec. 404(h)(2).
[145] Code Sec. 408(k)(3)(C).
[146] Economic Growth and Tax Relief Reconciliation Act of 2001, Act Sec. 611(c), amending Code Sec. 408(k)(3)(C).
[147] Code Sec. 416(i)(6).

standpoint of the employer is that the coverage requirements are more strict than for qualified plans, i.e. even temporary employees must be covered, and allocations must be made to employees who die or leave the firm during the year.

¶ 1019 SIMPLE Retirement Plans

Effective for 1997 and later, employers with 100 or fewer employees who received at least $5,000 in compensation during the preceding year may adopt a simplified retirement plan, called the Savings Incentive Match Plan for Employees (SIMPLE plan).[148] SIMPLE plans may not be adopted if the employer already has a qualified plan in effect.

A key advantage of SIMPLE plans is that they are not subject to the nondiscrimination rules of qualified plans, but have separate participation requirements (discussed below).

The contributions may take the form of an IRA plan or as a 401(k) plan. Contributions to a SIMPLE IRA account are limited to employee elective contributions and required employer matching contributions or nonelective contributions. An employee could make elective contributions of up to $6,500 per year in 2001. For tax years beginning in 2002 the limits are increased as follows:[149]

Year	Limit
2002	$ 7,000
2003	8,000
2004	9,000
2005 or after	10,000

Effective for contributions in tax years beginning after 2001, additional catch-up contributions are allowed for individuals who are age 50 or older by the end of the tax year. The catch-up contributions are the lesser of the "applicable dollar amount" or the employee's compensation reduced by other elective deferrals. The applicable dollar amount is:[150]

Year	Applicable Dollar Amount
2002	$ 500
2003	1,000
2004	1,500
2005	2,000
2006 or thereafter	2,500

The amount that employees may contribute is required to be expressed as a percentage of compensation.[151] The employer is required to make a

---

[148] Act Sec. 1421, Small Business Job Protection Act, adding Code Sec. 408(p).

[149] Economic Growth and Tax Relief Reconciliation Act of 2001, Act Sec. 611(f), amending Code Sec. 408(p)(2)(E)(i).

[150] Economic Growth and Tax Relief Reconciliation Act of 2001, Act Sec. 631(a), adding Code Sec. 414(v).

[151] Code Sec. 408(p)(2)(A)(ii).

matching contribution equal to the amount the employee contributes.[152] Alternatively, the employer can elect to make nonelective contributions of two percent of compensation for each employee who is eligible to participate and who has at least $5,000 of compensation for the year.[153]

The participation requirements are met if all employees are eligible who:[154]

- Received at least $5,000 in compensation from the employer during any two preceding years; and

- Are reasonably expected to receive at least $5,000 in compensation during the year.

Contributions to SIMPLE accounts must be fully vested (nonforfeitable) immediately.[155]

Distributions from a SIMPLE IRA are treated like a traditional IRA if the employee has participated in the plan for two years, and can therefore be rolled over into a traditional IRA, a qualified plan, a 403(b) plan, and a Code 457 deferred compensation plan as well as into another SIMPLE plan. However, if the employee has participated in the plan for less than two years, a distribution may be rolled over only to another SIMPLE plan.[156]

¶ 1021 Nonqualified Plans

Nonqualified plans usually take on of two forms: deferred compensation plans or restricted property plans. In both, the purpose is to defer taxation to the employee and to create, ultimately, a deduction to the employer.

.01 Deferred Compensation Plans

The specific purpose of a deferred compensation plan is to provide resources for key employees without their being taxed currently on those resources. Since the plan is nonqualified, it need not meet antidiscrimination or minimum benefits rules. Hence, the plan can be limited to key executives, if desired. A typical scenario would be an employment contract which called for, in addition to yearly salary and benefits, the payment of a lump sum or a certain amount per year at the end of a term of service, or at retirement. If (as is almost always true) the employee is on the cash basis method of accounting, deferred compensation plans will not be taxed until received, provided that the following two tax doctrines applicable to cash basis taxpayers are avoided:[157]

---

[152] Code Sec. 408(p)(2)(A)(iii).
[153] Code Sec. 408(p)(2)(B).
[154] Code Sec. 408(p)(4).
[155] Code Sec. 408(p)(3).

[156] Economic Growth and Tax Relief Reconciliation Act of 2001, Act Sec. 642(b), amending Code Sec. 408(d)(3)(G).
[157] For further discussion of these doctrines, see Chapter 5.

1. *Cash equivalency doctrine.* Even if the employee has not actually received a payment in cash or property, "notes or other evidences of indebtedness received in payment for services constitute income in the amount of their fair market value at the time of transfer."[158]

2. *Constructive receipt.* If the employee has power over disposition and control of the asset (the deferred compensation), the fact that payment is delayed is irrelevant; i.e., the compensation will be taxed when constructively received.

.02 Funded Nonqualified Plans

Funded nonqualified plans are included in the income of the employee for the tax year in which the contribution is made if the contribution is *substantially vested* at that time.[159] If, on the other hand, there is a *substantial risk of forfeiture,* the contribution is not taxed until the forfeiture is lifted. A "substantial risk of forfeiture" exists where rights in property transferred are conditioned, directly or indirectly, upon the future performance (or refraining from performance) of substantial services by any person, or the occurrence of a condition related to a purpose of the transfer, and the possibility of forfeiture is substantial if the condition is not satisfied.[160]

The *amount* included in the income of the employee is the beneficial interest in the net fair market value of all trust assets on the date of substantial vesting of all or some of the employee's interest in the trust.[161]

The term "funded" does not necessarily entail contributions put into a trust, though the term "trust" most often appears in the regulations. A custodial account or escrow account could be established, or payments could be made into an annuity for the benefit of the employee. Note that the cash equivalency doctrine and constructive receipt apply in determining whether the plan is funded.

.03 Unfunded Deferred Compensation Plans

Recipients of unfunded deferred compensation plans in essence have only the written contract or agreement which promises future payment as evidence of the intent to pay the compensation. The employer cannot sign a note payable to the employee; this constitutes funding under the cash equivalency rule.

Unfunded plans are not taxed to the employee until payment is made to the employee. The employer also receives a deduction at that time. Although the plan cannot be funded, the employer could: record the deferred liability on the books; appropriate retained earnings for that purpose; and even set up a special bank account out of which to pay the compensation. None of these actions would cause the plan to be funded per se.

---

[158] Reg. § 1.61-2(d)(4).
[159] Reg. § 1.402(b)-1(a)(1).

[160] Reg. § 1.83-3(c)(1).
[161] Reg. § 1.402(b)-1(b)(2).

Tax Tips and Pitfalls

Deferred compensation plans which are forfeitable not only achieve income deferral for the employee, but they can provide motivational factors for the employee to continue in employment with the firm as well as to achieve certain predetermined management goals, e.g., increases in revenue or earnings per share. Since forfeitable plans can be funded, this can remove anxiety and uncertainty on the part of the employee. On the other hand, unfunded plans need not have any restrictions or forfeitures in order to defer taxation of the compensation.

However, should the company later experience financial difficulties, the employee may not collect any of the deferred compensation.

¶ 1023   Restricted Property Plans

Code Sec. 83 covers restricted property plans, including restricted stock of the employer. The general rule provided in Code Sec. 83 is that the fair market value of the property is included in the gross income of the employee during the first tax year in which the rights of the employee are transferable or are not subject to a substantial risk of forfeiture.[162]

However, for an individual who performs services, an election may be made to include in gross income, for the tax year in which the restricted property is transferred, the excess of the fair market value of the property over the cost (if any) of the property.[163] If this election is selected, and the property is later forfeited, *no* deduction is permitted.

Tax Tips and Pitfalls

The decision to make this election should not be undertaken lightly. The reward for making this election is, perhaps, reduced recognizable income. This would be true if the property appreciates rapidly after the transfer, but before the restrictions are lifted, *and* if the individual has no plans to sell the property. The risks are twofold: (1) the income must be reported early; hence, unless the property rapidly appreciates, the time value of money works against the taxpayer; and (2) if the property is forfeited, the taxpayer has reported taxable income without receiving anything of value.

.01   Substantial Risk of Forfeiture and Transferability

A substantial risk of forfeiture exists if the person's rights to full enjoyment of the property depend on the future performance of substantial services.[164] As is pointed out in the regulations, whether a risk of forfeiture

---

[162] Code Sec. 83(a).
[163] Code Sec. 83(b).

[164] Code Sec. 83(c)(1).

is substantial is very much a question of fact. The regulations indicate that a requirement to return property if a person is discharged for cause is *not* a substantial risk of forfeiture, nor normally would be accepting a job with a competing firm. A covenant not to compete may or may not constitute a substantial risk of forfeiture.[165]

Property is considered "transferable" if the employee performing the service or receiving the property can sell, assign, or pledge his or her interest in the property to any other person, and the other person is not required to relinquish the property or its value in the event the substantial risk of forfeiture materializes.[166]

¶ 1025   Taxation of Benefits

Taxpayers receiving distributions from qualified plans (including Keoghs) have essentially three choices:

1. They can take the distribution in the form of an installment payment over a fixed term of years or over their and their beneficiaries' life expectancies;

2. They can take a lump-sum distribution; or

3. They can roll over the distribution.

The tax implications of each of these alternatives is discussed below.

.01   *Installment Payment Distribution (Annuities)*

Distributions made in installments are subject to annuity rules specified in Code Secs. 402(a) and 403(a). In turn, Code Secs. 402(a) and 403(a) provide that Code Sec. 72 (relating to annuities) is to be applied in taxing annuity payouts. The actual mechanics of determining the taxable portion of an employee annuity depend on whether the plan is noncontributory or contributory. If the plan is noncontributory, the employee has no investment in the contract; therefore all payments are taxable in the year received, i.e., there is no cost recovery to be excluded. However, if the plan is a contributory plan and the employee contributions were previously subject to tax, the employee has an investment in the contract equal to those after-tax contributions.

Congress, in the Small Business Job Protection Act, provided for a simplified method of determining the excludable portion (recovery of cost) of an annuity distribution from a qualified annuity or tax-sheltered annuity. The portion of each annuity payment that may be excluded as a return of cost is generally equal to the employee's investment in the contract as of the annuity starting date, divided by the number of anticipated monthly payments.[167] The number of anticipated monthly payments is dependent

---

[165] Reg. § 1.83-3(c)(2).
[166] Reg. § 1.83-3(d).

[167] Act Sec. 1403(a), Small Business Job Protection Act, amending Code Sec. 72(d)(1)(B).

on the age of the employee at the annuity starting date. The table is shown below:[168]

Age of Annuitant on the Annuity Starting Date	Number of Anticipated Payments
Not more than 55	360
56-60	310
61-65	260
66-70	210
More than 70	160

Example 10-7. Peter Dixon began drawing a $1,000 per month annuity at age 59. His contributions to the plan (his tax cost) amounted to $93,000. The nontaxable portion of the annuity is $93,000 divided by 310, or $300 per month. Therefore, $700 per month is taxable.

A simplified rule also applies to benefits based on the life of more than one annuitant. A chart uses the combined age of the annuitants to determine the recovery period.[169]

The investment in the contract for this purpose is determined without regard to the adjustment made for a refund feature.[170]

If in connection with the beginning of annuity payments, a lump-sum payment is received, the lump-sum payment is taxed under the rules of Code Sec. 72(e) (discussed below) as if received before the annuity starting date, and the investment in the contract is reduced by the amount of the payment.[171]

The simplified rule does not apply where the primary annuitant is 75 or older on the annuity starting date, unless there are fewer than five years of guaranteed payments under the annuity.[172] The table shown above is based on monthly payments. If the payments are not made on a monthly basis, appropriate adjustments are to be made to take into account the period on the basis of which the payments are made.[173]

.02 Lump-Sum Distributions

Distributions in a lump sum, to the extent in excess of the employee's investment in the contract, are subject to tax entirely in the year of receipt. To alleviate the harsh effects of income bunching resulting from a lump-sum distribution, the Code contained two separate income averaging rules for qualifying lump-sum distributions. Both have been repealed. However,

---

[168] Id.

[169] Act Sec. 1075(a), Taxpayer Relief Act of 1997 (P.L. 105-34), adding Code Sec. 72(d)(1)(B)(iv).

[170] Act Sec. 1403(a), Small Business Job Protection Act, amending Code Sec. 72(d)(1)(C).

[171] Act Sec. 1403(a), Small Business Job Protection Act, amending Code Sec. 72(d)(1)(D).

[172] Act Sec. 1403(a), Small Business Job Protection Act, amending Code Sec. 72(d)(1)(E).

[173] Act Sec. 1403(a), Small Business Job Protection Act, amending Code Sec. 72(d)(1)(F).

an extremely long-lasting transitional rule will make the 10-year averaging rule available to retirees for a number of years.

.03 Ten-Year Averaging

The 10-year averaging provision may be used only by employees who were born before January 1, 1936. Given the normal retirement age of 65, this provision would, unless modified by subsequent law changes, be applicable to taxpayers until the year 2001. In addition, since lump-sum distributions can be received by taxpayers who are well past 65, the outer limit of this transitional rule is even farther away. The 10-year averaging provision is applicable to the ordinary income portion of the lump-sum distribution.[174] The "ordinary income portion" is the total taxable distribution less the amount qualifying for long-term capital gains treatment (the portion of the taxable proceeds attributable to pre-1974 service).[175] However, an employee may elect to treat the entire taxable proceeds as ordinary income.[176] The trade-off is between the lower marginal tax rate effected by averaging versus the preferential treatment afforded long-term capital gains. Even though TRA '86 abolished preferential treatment for long-term capital gains, under this transitional rule, the taxpayer pays only a 20 percent rate on the long-term capital gains portion.

The mechanics of the 10-year averaging rule are outside the scope of this book.[177] Note that to be eligible for the 10-year averaging, the distribution must be made because of death or disability of the employee, separation from service, or attainment of age 59 and one-half.[178]

.04 Five-Year Averaging

The five-year averaging for lump-sum distributions was repealed, effective for tax years beginning after December 31, 1999.[179]

.05 Rollovers of Distributions

Lump-sum distributions from qualified pension or profit-sharing plans, among others, may be rolled over tax-free into IRAs, or into another qualified plan. The distribution must be transferred within 60 days into the IRA or other plan. Note that if the employee plans to use the IRA only as a transitional location of funds until it can be rolled into another qualified plan (e.g., with a new employer's plan), the IRA must contain only the rollover amount (i.e., an existing IRA cannot be used). A rollover is not the same as is a direct transfer to another qualified plan or a direct transfer to another IRA. Employers must withhold 20 percent of lump-sum distribution rollovers, but are not required to withhold for direct transfers.[180]

---

[174] Code Sec. 402(e)(1)(A) (prior to amendment by TRA '86).

[175] Code Sec. 402(e)(4)(E).

[176] Code Sec. 402(e)(4)(L).

[177] See Code Sec. 402(e) and accompanying regulations for details.

[178] Code Sec. 402(e)(4).

[179] Act Sec. 1401, Small Business Job Protection Act, striking Code Sec. 402(c)(10).

[180] Code Sec. 3405(c).

Therefore, in most situations, it is much better to have the check made out to the new plan rather than to the individual.

> **Example 10-8.** Sheila Jackson has $50,000 in a qualified plan. She receives a distribution of $50,000 less the 20 percent withheld, i.e., $50,000 less $10,000, or $40,000. She later rolls the money into an IRA. To make the rollover nontaxable, she will have to rollover $50,000, even though she received only $40,000. When she files her income tax return, she can get a refund of the $10,000. However, in the meantime, the IRS has use of her money. If she had instructed the qualified plan administrator to make a direct transfer, the $10,000 would not have been withheld.

Effective for distributions after 2001, employees may roll over the entire amount of any qualified distributions received from a qualified plan into another qualified plan or IRA, including the portion of the distribution that constitutes after-tax contributions.[181] If after-tax contributions are rolled over into a qualified plan, the plan must separately account for the contributions and related earnings.[182]

¶ 1027 Penalties for Inadequate, Early, or Excessive Distributions

Recall from the previous discussion that minimum distributions must be made after the attainment of a certain age of the employee. If the amount distributed is less than the required minimum, an excise tax of 50 percent of the deficiency is imposed on the payee.[183] This required minimum applies not only to qualified plans but to SEPs and individual IRAs as well.[184] The excise tax may be waived by the IRS if the shortfall was due to reasonable error and reasonable steps are being taken to remedy the shortfall.[185]

There is also an excise tax imposed on *early* distributions. The tax is 10 percent of the portion of the amount which is included in gross income.[186] This early distribution tax applies to the same types of retirement plans as does the tax on minimum distributions discussed above. Exceptions to the application of the excise tax exist for distributions:[187]

- Made on or after the employee becomes age 59 and one-half,

- Made to a beneficiary (or to the estate of the employee) on or after the death of the employee,

- Attributable to the employee being disabled,

- Are part of a series of substantially equal payments,

---

[181] Economic Growth and Tax Relief Reconciliation Act of 2001, Act Sec. 675(a)(2)(A), amending Code Sec. 401(a)(31); Act Sec. 643(a), amending Code Sec. 402(c)(2).
[182] *Id.*

[183] Code Sec. 4974(a).
[184] Code Sec. 4974(c).
[185] Code Sec. 4974(d).
[186] Code Sec. 72(t)(1).
[187] Code Sec. 72(t)(2)(A) and (B).

- Made to an employee after separation from service after attaining age 55,

- Payment of medical expenses in excess of 7.5 percent of adjusted gross income,

- Payment made pursuant to a QDRO,

- In certain instances, payment of health insurance premiums after separation from employment.

Chapter 11

Penalty Taxes

¶ 1101 Introduction

The Internal Revenue Code contains two penalty taxes to which corporations are subject: the accumulated earnings tax and the personal holding company tax. The purpose of both of these taxes is to discourage certain types of corporate behavior which have as their motivation the minimization of tax.

¶ 1103 Accumulated Earnings Tax

The accumulated earnings tax is applicable to every corporation (except those specifically excluded) that is formed or availed of for the purpose of avoiding the income tax with respect to either its shareholders or the shareholders of any corporation, by permitting earnings and profits (E&P) to accumulate instead of being divided or distributed.[1] The motive for accumulating earnings rather than distributing dividends is obvious, to avoid a double tax.

> **Example 11-1.** Assume that Ross Gibson, the 100 percent shareholder in Change, Inc., is in the 28 percent tax bracket, and assume that the corporate rate is 34 percent. Both Gibson and Change, Inc. can earn 15 percent on investments. The corporation has pre-tax income of $100,000. If Change, Inc. pays out all of its after-tax income in dividends, only $66,000 ($100,000 − ($100,000 × .34)) will be distributed to Gibson. After he pays a tax of $18,480 ($66,000 × .28), only $47,520 would be left to invest. At the end of one year, Gibson's after-tax investment would have grown to only $47,520 + ($47,520 × (.15 − (.28 × .15))) = $52,652. If the corporation accumulated the funds instead, after-tax investment at the end of one year would be $66,000 + ($66,000 × (.15 − (.34 × .15))) = $72,534.

The accumulated earnings tax does not apply to personal holding companies, foreign personal holding companies, corporations exempt from tax, and passive investment companies.[2] Although generally applied only to closely held companies, the accumulated earnings tax is determined without regard to the number of shareholders.[3] Thus, publicly held corporations are at least theoretically subject to the tax.[4] For the most part, however, stock ownership in publicly held corporations is so widely distributed as to make

---

[1] Code Sec. 532(a).
[2] Code Sec. 532(b).
[3] Code Sec. 532(c).
[4] For a rare instance in which the accumulated earnings tax *was* imposed on a publicly held corpo-

ration, see *Trico Products v. Commr.*, 43-2 USTC ¶ 9540, 137 F.2d 424 (2nd. Cir., 1943).

it unlikely that one individual or small group of individuals could impose a restrictive dividend policy with the intent of avoiding tax. S corporations, though not specifically excluded, are also very unlikely to be subjected to the accumulated earnings tax. S corporation shareholders pay individual income taxes on their share of taxable income, whether or not distributed. Hence, the motive of tax avoidance in accumulating earnings is not present.

.01 Accumulated Earnings Credit

The accumulated earnings tax is not imposed until a safe harbor threshold is exceeded. The safe harbor threshold is generally $250,000 of accumulated E&P, but is limited to $150,000 of accumulated E&P for corporations whose principal function is the performance of services in the fields of health, law, engineering, architecture, accounting, actuarial science, performing arts, or consulting.[5] This safe harbor threshold forms part of the accumulated earnings credit. Specifically, the accumulated earnings credit is the greater of:[6]

- The portion of E&P for the tax year retained for the reasonable needs of the business less net capital gains net of the capital gains tax; or

- $250,000 (or $150,000 for service concerns) less accumulated E&P as of the close of the preceding year.

Example 11-2. Cumulate, Inc., a retailer, had accumulated E&P of $128,000 as of January 1, 2001. For the tax year 2001, it had current E&P of $320,000, $140,000 of which was retained for reasonable business needs. The accumulated earnings credit is the greater of:

- $140,000; or

- $250,000 − $128,000 = $122,000.

Thus, the credit is $140,000.

Example 11-3. Assume the same facts as in Example 11-2, except that only $60,000 of E&P can be justified as being retained for reasonable business needs. The accumulated earnings credit is equal to the minimum of $122,000.

Example 11-4. Assume the same facts as in Example 11-2, except that the corporation is a law firm, and that only $15,000 of current E&P is retained for reasonable business needs. The accumulated earnings credit is the greater of:

- $15,000; or

- $150,000 − $128,000 = $22,000.

Thus, the credit is $22,000.

---

[5] Code Sec. 535(c)(2).   [6] Code Sec. 535(c).

Although called a credit, the item is more analogous to an exemption deduction. It is deducted from adjusted taxable income along with dividends paid to arrive at the tax base, i.e., accumulated taxable income.

.02 Dividends-Paid Deduction

As mentioned above, another deduction allowed from adjusted taxable income to arrive at accumulated taxable income is the dividends-paid deduction.[7] The dividends-paid deduction consists of three types of dividends paid: dividends paid during the tax year, dividends paid within two and one-half months after the close of the tax year, and "consent" dividends.[8]

To qualify for the dividends-paid deduction, the distribution must meet the requirements of Code Sec. 316, i.e., be either from current or accumulated earnings and profits.[9] No deduction is allowed for preferential dividends, i.e., the distribution must be *pro rata* either within or between classes of stock unless one class of stock is entitled to a preference.[10] The existence of a preference prohibits the dividends-paid deduction even if the preference was authorized by all of the shareholders or if it is entirely taxed as a dividend.[11]

Tax Tips and Pitfalls

Constructive dividends created by stockholder-corporation transactions can be especially disadvantageous if the corporation is subject to the accumulated earnings tax. For example, if the salary paid to the president/majority shareholder is deemed excessive, not only would constructive dividend treatment disallow the salary expense deduction to the corporation but, since the constructive dividend is not *pro rata*, a dividends-paid deduction would not be allowed either.

Dividends paid in property are deductible for this purpose only to the extent of the adjusted basis of the property, despite the fact that for other purposes the fair market value is the relevant value.[12]

Distributions in full or partial liquidation, including a stock redemption under Code Sec. 302, qualify for the dividends-paid deduction.[13] Generally, the portion of the distribution which is properly chargeable to E&P is treated as a dividend for purposes of the dividends-paid deduction.[14] The portion that is chargeable to E&P is determined by deducting from the distribution the part allocable to the capital account. The part allocable to the capital account is that stock's par or stated value plus its share of paid-in capital.[15]

---

[7] Code Sec. 535(a).
[8] Code Secs. 561(a) and 563(a).
[9] Code Sec. 562(a). This requirement is almost certainly met, however, if the company is being subjected to the accumulated earnings tax.
[10] Code Sec. 562(c).

[11] Reg. § 1.562-2(a).
[12] Reg. § 1.562-1(a).
[13] Code Sec. 562(b); Reg. § 1.562-1(b).
[14] Code Sec. 562(b)(1)(A).
[15] Reg. § 1.562-1(b)(1)(ii).

A special rule exists for complete liquidations occurring within 24 months after the adoption of a plan of liquidation. In that event, a dividends-paid deduction is allowed up to the current E&P for each tax year in which distributions are made.[16]

> **Example 11-5.** On March 7, 1999, Country Bakery Co. adopted a complete plan of liquidation. At that time, it had a $500,000 deficit in accumulated E&P. It made liquidating distributions on November 1, 1999, June 30, 2000, and February 10, 2001, of $300,000, $400,000, and $250,000, respectively. It had current E&P of $75,000 in 1999, $50,000 in 2000, and $16,000 for the partial year in 2001. The corporation, for accumulated earnings purposes, will be allowed a dividends-paid deduction for 1999, 2000, and 2001 of $75,000, $50,000, and $16,000 respectively.

Nontaxable stock dividends are represented on the books of the corporation by debiting retained earnings and crediting a paid-in capital account. However, for accumulated earnings purposes, nontaxable stock dividends do not qualify for the dividends-paid deduction.[17]

Dividends paid within two and one-half months of the close of the tax year are considered as paid during such tax year; hence they are thrown back to that tax year.[18] The dividends are thrown back even if the recipients become shareholders after the close of the tax year.[19]

The corporation can effectively remove itself from being subject to the accumulated earnings tax by paying a sufficient amount of dividends. If the corporation lacks the cash to pay dividends, the shareholders may consent to being taxed on a certain amount of dividends.[20] A consent dividend is considered to be distributed in cash to the shareholders, who then contribute the cash to the corporation. These hypothetical transactions are considered to take place on the last day of the tax year.[21] The corporation records a consent dividend by debiting retained earnings and crediting paid-in capital. The stockholders have dividend income but also have an increased basis in the stock.[22]

The consent form (Form 972) must be filed by the due date of the corporate return for which the dividends-paid deduction is claimed. It must be signed by every person who owned consent stock on the last day of the corporation's tax year. In the consent, the shareholder must agree to include in gross income for his or her tax year in which or with which the tax year of the corporation ends, the amount of the consent dividend.[23] "Consent stock" consists only of common stock and participating preferred stock.[24]

---

[16] *Id.*
[17] Rev. Rul. 65-68, 1965-1 CB 246.
[18] Code Sec. 563.
[19] Rev. Rul. 68-409, 1968-2 CB 252.
[20] Code Sec. 565(a).

[21] Code Sec. 565(c).
[22] Reg. § 1.565-1(c).
[23] Reg. § 1.565-1(b)(1).
[24] Reg. § 1.565-6(a).

.03 Computing the Accumulated Earnings Tax

The starting point for computing the accumulated earnings tax is the taxable income of the corporation. Taxable income is then subject to a number of adjustments to get to what is often called adjusted taxable income. The purpose of these adjustments is to arrive at an amount which represents the corporation's dividend-paying capacity. The next step is to deduct dividends paid and the accumulated earnings credit to arrive at accumulated taxable income. The tax is 39.6 percent of the accumulated taxable income.[25]

The deductions to arrive at adjusted taxable income are as follows:[26]

- Corporate income tax accrued, but not including the accumulated earnings tax or the personal holding company tax;

- Charitable contributions not deductible because of the 10 percent limit;

- Net capital losses incurred during the year, reduced by the lesser of the nonrecaptured capital gains deductions or the accumulated E&P as of the close of the preceding tax year (the "nonrecaptured capital gains deduction" is the excess of the aggregate net capital gains less the tax attributable to those gains for all prior tax years starting after July 18, 1984, and less previously recaptured capital gains deductions);

- Any net capital gains less the taxes attributable to the gain and less net capital losses from prior years ("net capital gain" is the excess of net long-term capital gains over net short-term capital losses);[27]

- Any net capital loss for the prior taxable year; it is treated as a short-term capital loss.

Additions to taxable income are as follows:

- The dividends-received deduction;

- The net operating loss deduction; and

- Capital loss carryovers and carrybacks.

---

[25] Code Sec. 531.
[26] Code Sec. 535(b).

[27] Code Sec. 1222(11).

Example 11-6. The taxable income of Jubilee Co. for 2000 was as follows:

Gross profit	$610,000
Dividend income	40,000
Total income	$650,000
Operating expenses	290,000
Contributions ($40,000 before limitation)	36,000
Taxable income before special deductions	324,000
Dividends-received deduction	28,000
Taxable income	296,000
Tax	$ 98,690

Jubilee Co. began the year with $205,000 in accumulated earnings and profits. Current E&P for 2000 was $415,000, $30,000 of which is reasonably accumulated. In addition to the above items, Jubilee Co. had a net capital loss in 2000 of $15,000. Dividends paid were as follows:

2-1-00	$10,000
5-10-00	10,000
8-2-00	10,000
11-5-00	10,000
2-3-01	12,000

Computation of the accumulated earnings tax is as follows:

Taxable income		$296,000
Add—dividends-received deduction		28,000
		$324,000
Less—federal income tax	$98,690	
excess contributions	4,000	
net capital loss	15,000	117,690
Adjusted taxable income		$206,310
Less—dividends paid	$42,000	
accumulated earnings credit	45,000	87,000
Accumulated taxable income		$119,310
Accumulated earnings tax @ .396		$47,247

.04 Interpretation of Tax Avoidance

As previously mentioned, the accumulated earnings tax is imposed on corporations formed or availed for the purpose of tax avoidance. The issue as to what constitutes evidence of purpose to avoid tax is a thorny issue indeed. The regulations provide limited guidance, stating that the following will be considered:[28]

---

[28] Reg. § 1.533-1(a)(2).

- Dealings between the corporation and its shareholders, e.g., loans to the shareholders of the use of corporate funds for the personal benefit of the shareholders;

- Investment by the corporation of undistributed earnings in assets having no reasonable connection with the business of the corporation; and

- The extent to which the corporation has paid dividends.

Does the tax avoidance purpose need to be the dominant reason for retention of earnings? A conflict among the circuit courts of appeal over the degree of purpose necessary for the application of the accumulated earnings tax was resolved by the Supreme Court in *Donruss* when the Court said that adopting ". . . a test that requires that tax avoidance purpose need be dominant, impelling or controlling . . . would exacerbate the problems that Congress was trying to avoid."[29]

The courts have placed considerable weight on whether or not the stockholders are in high personal tax brackets and whether their need for dividends would be strong. In *Simons-Eastern Co.* (case favorable to the corporation), the court noted that none of the stockholders were in a high personal tax bracket and that their personal need for extra income was strong.[30] If the shareholders are in a high tax bracket, the presumption of a tax avoidance purpose is strengthened. In *Golconda Mining Corp.*, the personal avoidance of $26,000 in income tax by a public corporation's dominant shareholder (who was also a CPA and thus presumed knowledgeable about the tax savings potential) was considered to constitute tax avoidance.[31] On the other hand, in *Salley*, even though the shareholders would have incurred additional income taxes of $127,611 if all of the after-tax income had been paid in dividends, a district court held that the shareholder's honest intent was to expand the business of the corporation.[32]

A corporation is not automatically subject to the accumulated earnings tax merely because it is shown to have been formed or availed for tax avoidance purposes. The IRS must also show that the taxpayers accumulated earnings beyond the reasonable needs of the business.[33]

.05 Burden of Proof

In any proceeding before the Tax Court involving a notice of deficiency based in whole or in part on the allegation that E&P accumulated beyond the reasonable needs of the business, the burden of proof shifts to the IRS if either:[34]

---

[29] *U.S. v. The Donruss Company,* 69-1 USTC ¶ 9167, 393 US 297 (1969).
[30] *Simons-Eastern Co. v. U.S.,* 73-1 USTC ¶ 9279, 354 FSupp 1003 (DC N.D. Ga. 1972).
[31] *Golconda Mining Corp.,* 58 TC 139, Dec. 31,355 (1972).

[32] *J.W. Salley, Inc. v. U.S.,* 76-2 USTC ¶ 9739 (WD La., 1976).
[33] *James Realty Co. v. U.S.,* 59-2 USTC ¶ 9660, 176 FSupp 306 (Minn., 1959).
[34] Code Sec. 534(a).

- Notification has not been sent to the taxpayer via certified or registered mail informing the taxpayer that the proposed notice of deficiency includes the accumulated earnings tax; or

- The taxpayer has submitted a statement to the IRS.

The statement by the taxpayer must provide the facts on which the taxpayer relies to establish that part or all of the E&P has not been permitted to accumulate beyond the reasonable needs of the business.[35] Generally, the taxpayer's statement must be sent within 60 days after the IRS has mailed notification of the deficiency.[36] The burden of proof shifts to the IRS only with respect to the relevant ground or grounds set forth in the taxpayer's statement, and then only if the grounds are supported by sufficient facts.[37]

The fact that a corporation is a mere holding company or investment company is *prima facie* evidence of the purpose to avoid the income tax.[38] Thus, the burden of proof shifting provided for in Code Sec. 534 would not be applicable.[39] The regulations define a holding company as one which has practically no activities except holding property and collecting the income or investing the income.[40] An investment company is a company whose activities include, or consist substantially of, buying and selling stocks, securities, real estate, or other investment property, so that the income is derived not only from the investment yield but also from profits from market fluctuations.[41] In *Dahlem Foundation, Inc.,* the Tax Court held that a corporation whose activities included managing two shopping centers, an apartment building, and other properties was not a "mere holding company." The court reiterated an earlier opinion in which it stated that being primarily a holding company is not the same as being a "mere holding company."[42]

The courts have tended to interpret rather strictly the requirement that for the burden of proof to shift to the IRS, the statement must be supported by sufficient facts. For example, in *Capital Sales, Inc.,* the Tax Court ruled that a timely filed statement by the corporation which listed grounds for retaining earnings as: (1) the need to improve the financial condition to meet the requirement of its principal supplier, (2) the need to expand its product line, (3) the need to increase investment and inventory, and (4) the need to keep large cash amounts on hand to carry large accounts receivable was not sufficient because it set forth no specific facts.[43] Also, in *Herzog Miniature Lamp Works,* the taxpayer's statement was considered too broad and general in scope so as to shift the burden to

---

[35] Code Sec. 534(c).

[36] Reg. § 1.534-2(d)(2).

[37] Reg. § 1.534-2(a)(2).

[38] Code Sec. 533(b).

[39] *Rhomber Co. Inc. v. Commr.,* 67-2 USTC ¶ 9743, 386 F.2d 510 (2nd Cir., 1967).

[40] Reg. § 1.533-1(c).

[41] *Id.*

[42] *Dahlem Foundation, Inc.,* 54 TC 1566, Dec. 30,272 (1970).

[43] *Capital Sales, Inc.,* 71 TC 416, Dec. 35,600 (1978).

the IRS.[44] In *Shaw-Walker Co.,* the taxpayer submitted a lengthy statement that listed five grounds for accumulating earnings. The Sixth Circuit rejected the last four for burden of proof purposes, but ruled that the first ground was sufficient to shift the burden of proof to the IRS.[45] The fifth ground for accumulating earnings was a statement that explained at some length its working capital needs. The Second Circuit allowed the burden of proof to shift to the IRS by submission of a statement which stated that its plants were in constant danger of being washed away and also that expansion of business and replacement of equipment required the accumulation.[46]

¶ 1105 Accumulated Earnings—Reasonable Needs of the Business

The tax avoidance purpose and burden of proof issues not withstanding, the vast majority of accumulated earnings cases rest on whether or not the earnings have been unreasonably accumulated. To state that the reasonable needs issue is complex and has resulted in a plethora of confusing and sometimes contradictory court cases is to understate the matter.

The starting point for examining the reasonable needs issue is the regulations. Reasonable needs of the business include the reasonable anticipated needs.[47] In order to justify an accumulation for reasonably anticipated needs, the corporation must have an indication that the future needs of the business require such accumulation, and the corporation must have specific, definite, and feasible plans to use the accumulation.[48] The accumulation need not be used immediately and the plans need not be consummated within a short period after the tax year if the accumulation will be used in a reasonable time.[49] On the other hand, where the future plans are vague or uncertain, or where the execution of a plan is postponed indefinitely, the accumulation will be considered unreasonable.[50] The need for accumulation is to be considered as of the close of the taxable year, and subsequent events are not to be used to indicate unreasonable accumulations if the accumulation seemed reasonable at the time. However, subsequent events may be used to determine whether the taxpayer actually intended to follow through on plans.[51]

> **Example 11-7.** In anticipation of a strike in the steel industry, Fabricators, Inc., a steel fabrication company, stockpiled inventory. Even though the strike did not materialize, the accumulation would likely be considered reasonable.

> **Example 11-8.** Each year, for a five-year period, a corporation appropriated $200,000 for construction of a building. However, at the

---

[44] *Herzog Miniature Lamp Works v. Commr.,* 73-2 USTC ¶ 9593, 481 F.2d 857 (2nd. Cir., 1973).
[45] *Shaw-Walker Co. v. Commr.,* 68-1 USTC ¶ 9211, 390 F.2d 205 (6th Cir., 1968).
[46] *Oyster Shell Products Corp., Inc. v. Commr.,* 63-1 USTC ¶ 9283, 313 F.2d 449 (2nd Cir., 1963).

[47] Reg. § 1.537-1(a).
[48] Reg. § 1.537-1(b)(1).
[49] *Id.*
[50] *Id.*
[51] Reg. § 1.537-1(b)(2).

end of five years, the company had made no progress and had not even acquired a site. The accumulation would likely be considered unreasonable.

Reasonable grounds for accumulating earnings include:[52]

- To provide for bona fide expansion of business or replacement of plant;

- To acquire a business enterprise through purchasing stock or assets;

- To provide for the retirement of bona fide debt that was created in connection with the trade or business;

- To provide the necessary working capital for the business, e.g., for purchasing or producing inventory;

- To provide for investments or loans to suppliers or customers if necessary in order to maintain business.

Other reasonable needs listed in the regulations include:

- Stock redemptions from an estate;[53] and

- Product liability loss reserves.[54]

.01 Expansion of Business or Replacement of Plant

The grounds for retaining earnings include replacing worn-out or outdated equipment as well as purchasing or constructing assets. The business judgment of the corporate officers ostensibly carries great weight, and the courts have stated that Code Sec. 531 does not empower a court to substitute its judgment for that of the corporate officers.[55]

Although accumulating earnings for reasonably anticipated needs is permissible, mere vague plans to use the funds are generally not acceptable. In *Oklahoma Press Publishing Co.*, for example, the taxpayer had been considering a new building off and on for a period of 15 years without any material progress being made toward construction. The Tenth Circuit denied reasonable needs.[56]

Similarly in *I.A. Dress Co.*, the alleged reason for accumulation of E&P was the taxpayer's plan to buy the building. But the taxpayer had no option to buy and had no reason to know whether or when it could come to terms with the owner.[57]

---

[52] Reg. § 1.537-2(b).

[53] Code Sec. 537(a); Reg. § 1.537-1(c)(1).

[54] Code Sec. 537(b)(4).

[55] See, for example, *Thompson Engineering Co., Inc. v. Commr.*, 85-1 USTC ¶ 9126, 751 F.2d 191, rev'g. 80 TC 672, Dec. 40,024 (6th Cir., 1985).

[56] *Oklahoma Press Publishing Co.*, 71-1 USTC ¶ 9218, 437 F.2d 1275 (10th Cir., 1971).

[57] *I.A. Dress Co. v. U.S.*, 60-1 USTC ¶ 9204, 273 F.2d 543 (2nd Cir., 1960).

The lack of specific plans is often detrimental to the taxpayer. In *Bahan Textile Machinery Co., Inc.,* the Fourth Circuit stated with some asperity that "it is no excuse to say, as Taxpayer does, that the alleged future plans lacked specificity because it was a small, informally conducted corporation."[58] The corporation in this case also was not helped by the presence of large loans to relatives of the president.

Documenting the expansion plans is very important, but is not always required by the courts. In *WDAY, Inc.,* a district court stated, "although no mention was made in the corporate minutes . . ., the management of WDAY was making definite and specific plans to alleviate its ever increasing space problem."[59]

Documentation of the anticipated cost of replacing plant and equipment is especially important. Depreciation expense reduces accumulated earnings and profits, and to the extent that the depreciation charge is adequate, any additional reserve for depreciation would constitute double counting. This was succinctly stated in *Smoot Sand & Gravel*: "It is only when rehabilitation plans involve replacement of old equipment with equipment costing more than the original, or when additional equipment is required, that appropriation of surplus is justified."[60]

As is stated in the regulations, the need for accumulation is considered as of the end of the taxable year. In *Sterling Distributors, Inc.,* the Fifth Circuit stated that the fact that expansion plans were abandoned after the illness of the manager/shareholder did not make the accumulation unreasonable.[61]

.02 Acquisition of a Business Enterprise

How much latitude does a corporation have in acquiring unrelated businesses, i.e., will the acquisition of a totally unrelated business enable the corporation to avoid the accumulated earnings tax? The regulations appear to be relatively liberal in this respect, stating, "The business of a corporation is not merely that which it has previously carried on but includes, in general, any line of business which it may undertake."[62] The regulations do contain the cautionary statement that the business of one corporation does not include the business of another corporation if the other corporation is a personal holding company, an investment company, or a corporation not engaged in the active conduct of a trade or business.[63]

A number of court cases have validated the reasonableness of expanding the current business via acquisitions. In *Freedom Newspapers, Inc.,* the retention of earnings for acquiring interests in other newspapers

---

[58] *Bahan Textile Machinery Co., Inc.,* 72-1 USTC ¶9184, 453 F.2d 1100 (4th Cir., 1972).
[59] *WDAY, Inc., v. U.S.,* 80-2 USTC ¶9772 (DC ND, 1980).
[60] *Smoot Sand & Gravel v. Commr.,* 60-1 USTC ¶9241, 274 F.2d 495 (4th Cir., 1960).

[61] *Sterling Distributors, Inc. v. U.S.,* 63-1 USTC ¶9288, 313 F.2d 803 (5th Cir., 1963).

[62] Reg. § 1.537-3(a).

[63] Reg. § 1.537-3(b).

was deemed reasonable.[64] In *Lane Drug Co.,* the use of funds to build a retail drug chain was considered reasonable.[65]

With respect to acquiring unrelated businesses, there have been fewer court cases and the issue is less clear. Using funds to acquire investment property will be considered an unreasonable accumulation.[66] Working interests in oil or gas wells, though considered business income rather than royalty income for regular income tax purposes, may or may not be considered for accumulated earnings tax purposes to be merely investments (depending on the magnitude of the interests and whether or not the owner has direct operating management responsibilities).[67]

.03   Retirement of Debt

The regulations state that accumulating funds to retire bona fide debt constitutes reasonable grounds. If the debt is held by outsiders, there should be no problem with accumulating earnings to retire the debt. However, if the debt is held by a majority stockholder, the grounds are not quite as solid. For example, in *Smoot Sand & Gravel,* the Fifth Circuit rejected the accumulation of earnings to retire bonds held by the sole shareholder, noting that it was difficult to perceive any justification for creating a reserve for bond indebtedness when the payments could be postponed indefinitely at the discretion of the sole shareholder.[68]

.04   Investments or Loans to Suppliers or Customers

The regulations provided for the accumulation of earnings to provide for investments or loans to suppliers "if necessary in order to maintain the business of the corporation."[69] Accumulations made in order to satisfy the business need of a brother or sister corporation cannot generally be considered as accumulations to meet business needs.[70] What does the term "necessary in order to maintain business" mean? In *Factories Investment Corp.,* the Second Circuit implied that the standard might be as strict as survivability of the customer or supplier.[71] However, the Tax Court imposed a less stringent standard in at least one case.[72]

.05   Contingencies, Including Product Liability Losses

In order to justify the accumulation of earnings for contingencies, the contingency should be both specific and have a reasonable likelihood of occurrence. The more vague the contingency, the less likely that the courts will be sympathetic. In *Cheyenne Newspapers, Inc.,* the taxpayer's assertions that a six-month operating reserve was necessary for strikes, major

---

[64] *Freedom Newspapers, Inc.,* 24 TCM 1327, Dec. 27,559(M) (1965).

[65] *Lane Drug Co.,* 3 TCM 394, Dec. 13,895(M) (1944).

[66] See, for example, *R.I. Smith, Inc.,* 61-2 USTC ¶ 9562, 292 F.2d 470 (9th Cir., 1961).

[67] *Cataphote Corp. of Mississippi,* CtCl, 76-1 USTC ¶ 9406, 535 F.2d 1225 (1976).

[68] *Smoot Sand & Gravel v. Commr.,* 60-1 USTC ¶ 9241, 274 F.2d 495 (4th Cir., 1960).

[69] Reg. § 1.537-2(b)(5).

[70] See *Factories Investment Corp. v. Commr.,* 64-1 USTC ¶ 9306, 328 F.2d 781 (2nd. Cir., 1964); *Chaney & Hope, Inc. v. Commr.,* 80 TC 263, Dec. 39,843 (1983).

[71] *Factories Investment Corp. v. Commr.,* 64-1 USTC ¶ 9306, 328 F.2d 781 (2nd. Cir., 1964).

[72] See *Farmers and Merchants Investment Co.,* 29 TCM 705, Dec. 30,190(M) (1970).

breakdowns, paper shortages, and so on were not considered reasonable or realistic contingencies.[73] The intrinsically hazardous nature of the business may aid in justifying the retention of earnings. District Courts in *Matter of John S. Barnes, Inc.*, and *WDAY, Inc.*, ruled respectively that a citrus fruit business was hazardous and that a radio station in an agricultural area made a reasonable decision to accumulate reserves during a peak economic cycle (a strong grain market).[74] A bakery that carried its own collision insurance (*Hardin Bakeries, Inc.*), a title company that was self-insured for all escrow losses (*Inter-County Title Co.*), and a company which maintained a reserve for flood damages where its offices were subject to annual floods (*Magic Mart*) were all considered to have reasonably accumulated earnings.[75] The Tax Court has also upheld the taxpayers' positions in several cases where the corporation faced pending or potential litigation.[76]

The regulations provide some guidance with respect to product liability loss reserves. Factors to be considered include the taxpayer's previous product liability experience, the extent of the taxpayer's coverage by commercial product liability insurance, the income tax consequences of the taxpayer's ability to deduct product liability losses and related expenses, and the taxpayer's potential future liability due to defective products in light of the taxpayer's plans to expand the production of products currently being manufactured.[77] The corporation must use discounted present value in taking into account the present value of the potential future liability.[78]

Only reserves for products that have been manufactured, leased, or sold shall be considered reasonable. For example, accumulations with respect to a development stage product are not reasonable accumulations.[79]

.06 Stock Redemptions from an Estate

Accumulating earnings to redeem stock from a decedent's estate is a reasonable purpose. The maximum to be accumulated for this purpose is the maximum that can qualify for Code Sec. 303 purposes, i.e., the sum of federal and state death taxes and funeral and administrative expenses.[80]

If the decedent has two or more corporations which would qualify for redemption treatment, reasonably accumulated earnings would, unless the particular facts and circumstances indicate otherwise, be the maximum redemption under Code Sec. 303 times the ratio of fair market value of the corporation divided by the fair market value of all stocks included in the gross estate which are eligible for redemption treatment.[81]

---

[73] *Cheyene Newspapers, Inc. v. Commr.*, 74-1 USTC ¶ 9294, 494 F.2d 429 (10th Cir., 1974).

[74] See *Matter of John S. Barnes, Inc.*, 53-2 USTC ¶ 9470 (DC S.D. Fla. 1953); *WDAY, Inc. v. U.S.*, 80-2 USTC ¶ 9772 (DC ND, 1980).

[75] See *Hardin's Bakeries, Inc.*, 67-1 USTC ¶ 9253, 293 FSupp 1129 (S.D. Miss., 1967); *Inter-County Title Co.*, 75-2 USTC ¶ 9845, (E.D. Calif., 1975); *Magic Mart*, 51 TC 775, Dec. 29,456 (1969).

[76] See, for example, *J.E. Casey*, 16 TCM 1024, Dec. 22,689(M) (1957); *M. Eden*, 53 TCM 195, Dec. 43,721(M) (1987).

[77] Reg. § 1.537-1(f)(2).

[78] *Id.*

[79] Reg. § 1.537-1(f)(3).

[80] Reg. § 1.537-1(c)(1).

[81] Reg. § 1.537-1(c)(3).

Example 11-9. Hernandez, Inc., has been accumulating $200,000 of earnings to redeem the stock owned by Jay Hernandez, who owns 40 percent of the corporation. Upon the death of Jay, his gross estate amounted to $1,200,000, consisting of the following assets:

	Value	Percentage of Stock Owned
Hernandez, Inc.	$500,000	40
Jay Finance, Inc.	200,000	25
Centervale, Inc.	250,000	15
Other assets...................	250,000	
Total	$1,200,000	

Federal estate taxes, state inheritance taxes, and funeral and administrative expenses amount to $140,000. The decedent's stock in Hernandez, Inc., and Jay Finance, Inc., are eligible for Code Sec. 303 treatment, but the stock in Centervale, Inc., is not. Hence, only $100,000 ($500,000/($500,000 + $200,000) × $140,000) of the $200,000 of accumulated earnings could be justified for stock redemption purposes.

Tax Tips and Pitfalls

If the IRS should interpret these regulations strictly, the result would be to create much confusion about the *amount* of earnings that the corporation could reasonably accumulate for stock redemption purposes. For example, the amount originally considered reasonable for this purpose could be decreased because of such outside events as the stockholder acquiring stock in another corporation, rapid growth in the shareholder's nonstock assets (thus causing the 35 percent requirement to be "flunked"), or a decrease in federal estate tax rates. Thus, planning is very difficult with respect to accumulations for stock redemptions.

.07 *Working Capital Requirements*

The issue of how much working capital a company needed to conduct its business operations was one that the courts wrestled with for many years. Finally, the Tax Court, in two cases, came up with a formula to compute the necessary working capital of corporations.[82] The method is now known as the *Bardahl* formula; it incorporates the working capital needed for one operating cycle. The concept of the operating cycle is that the company must use, purchase, or produce inventory, sell the inventory, collect the receivables, and pay creditors. The original *Bardahl* formula consisted of the inventory cycle plus the accounts receivable cycle. A later Tax Court decision incorporated an accounts payable cycle as well, which is

---

[82] *Bardahl Mfg. Corp.,* 24 TCM 1030, Dec. 27,494(M) (1965); *Bardahl International Corp.,* 25 TCM 935, Dec. 28,064(M) (1966).

subtracted from the first two cycles.[83] The accounts payable cycle has since been applied by many courts.[84]

The three cycles are incorporated as follows:

Inventory cycle = $\dfrac{\text{Average inventory}}{\text{Cost of goods sold}}$

plus:

Accounts receivable cycle = $\dfrac{\text{Average accounts receivable}}{\text{Sales}}$

minus:

Accounts payable cycle = $\dfrac{\text{Average accounts payable}}{\text{Purchases}}$

The sum of these three cycles equals the operating cycle (a decimal), which is then multiplied by the sum of cost of goods sold and operating expenses for the taxable year. Noncash charges such as depreciation are not included. The product of the expenses listed above and the computed decimal gives an estimate of working capital needs.

Example 11-10. The 2001 income statement and comparative balance sheets as of December 31, 2000 and 2001 for Bob's Cyclery are shown below:

Income Statement

Sales		$800,000
Cost of sales:		
Beginning inventory	$ 50,000	
Purchases	440,000	
Ending inventory	(40,000)	
Cost of sales		450,000
Gross profit		$350,000
Expenses:		
Selling and general	$ 45,000	
Depreciation	120,000	
Income taxes	50,000	
Total expenses		215,000
Net income		$135,000

---

[83] *Kingsbury Investments, Inc.*, 28 TCM 1082, Dec. 29,768(M) (1969).

[84] See *C.E. Hooper, Inc. v. United States*, CtCl, 76-1 USTC ¶9185, 539 F.2d 1276 (1976); *W.L. Mead, Inc.*, 34 TCM 924, Dec. 33,301(M) (1975).

Balance Sheet

Assets		2000		2001
Cash	$	25,000	$	50,000
Accounts receivable		100,000		120,000
Inventory		50,000		40,000
Property, plant, & equipment		900,000		1,000,000
Total assets	$	1,075,000	$	1,210,000
Liabilities and capital				
Accounts and notes payable	$	70,000	$	60,000
Other current liabilities		5,000		8,000
Long-term debt		250,000		225,000
Common stock		125,000		125,000
Paid-in capital		75,000		75,000
Other retained earnings		550,000		717,000
Total	$	1,075,000	$	1,210,000

The operating cycles are as follows:

Inventory cycle = (($50,000 + 40,000)/2)/$450,000 = .1000

plus:

Receivable cycle = (($100,000 + 120,000)/2)/$800,000 = .1375

minus:

Accounts payable cycle = (($70,000 + 60,000)/2)/$440,000 = .1477

Total operating cycle = .0898

The operating expenses consist of the cost of goods sold of $450,000, selling and general expenses of $45,000, and income taxes of $12,500 (assumes that four quarterly payments of income taxes are paid), for a total of $507,500. Thus, working capital needs amount to $45,574 ($507,500 × .0898). Since actual working capital is much greater ($142,000), other needs would have to be justified to avoid the accumulated earnings tax.

Adjustments of the Bardahl *Formula*

The operating cycles computed previously were based on average receivables and average inventory. However, in a seasonal business (e.g., a toy retailer), peak receivables and peak inventory might greatly exceed the average dollar amounts. The use of averages would then tend to understate the operating cycle. Use of peak amounts has been permitted in a number of cases.[85] Its use will obviously help the taxpayer.

---

[85] See *Magic Mart, Inc.,* 51 TC 775, Dec. 29,456 (1969); *Walton Mill, Inc.,* 31 TCM 75, Dec. 31,236(M) (1972); *Grob, Inc. v. U.S.,* 83-1 USTC ¶ 9401, 565 FSupp 391 (E.D. Wisc., 1983); *Alma* *Piston Co. v. Commr.,* 78-2 USTC ¶ 9591, 579 F2d 1000 (6th Cir., 1978) aff'g 35 TCM 464, Dec. 33,753(M) (1976).

Example 11-11. Assume the same facts as in the previous example, except that the company carries an inventory of bicycles in the spring and early summer of $75,000 and its receivables run as high as $150,000 during the summer. Calculation of the operating cycle using peak receivables and inventory would be as follows:

Inventory cycle = $75,000 / $450,000 =	.1667
Plus:	
Receivable cycle = $150,000 / $800,000 =	.1875
Minus:	
Accounts payable cycle (as before) =	− .1477
Total operating cycle	.2065

Therefore, when multiplied by the $507,500 of operating expenses, working capital needs of $104,799 can be justified.

The accounts payable cycle was unchanged in the example above. However, if the peak accounts payable were also to be significantly higher (very likely in a seasonal business), the IRS will insist that it also be used.

If a company does not have a significant accounts payable period, the accounts payable cycle may not have to be incorporated into the operating cycle. In *J.H. Rutter Rex Mfg. Co., Inc.*, the Fifth Circuit allowed a clothing manufacturing corporation to use the *Bardahl* formula without a credit cycle modification where evidence indicated that a significant percentage of its bills were paid within seven days.[86] In *Central Motor Co.*, the Tenth Circuit stated, "We are persuaded that the evidence was insufficient to justify submission to the jury of the credit cycle theory" (a general 30-day reference to credit from suppliers with no evidence of the actual turnover of payables).[87]

Tax Tips and Pitfalls

Corporations that feel vulnerable to the accumulated earnings tax might do well to reduce their average accounts payable, since doing so would reduce the credit cycle which in turn would increase the operating cycle decimal. On the other hand, a *larger* receivable balance would increase the operating cycle decimal. Reducing the discount for paying within 10 days might be helpful for accumulated earnings purposes since the accounts receivable cycle might thereby be increased.

Bardahl *Formula for Service Concerns*

Service concerns do not have inventory in the same sense that retailers, wholesalers, and manufacturing companies have inventory. However,

---

[86] *J.H. Rutter Rex Mfg. Co., Inc. v. Commr.*, 88-2 USTC ¶ 9499, 853 F.2d 1275 (5th Cir., 1988).

[87] *Central Motor Co. v. U.S.*, 78-2 USTC ¶ 9608, 583 F.2d 470 (10th Cir., 1978).

service concerns often expend considerable resources for salaries and other costs before the completion and billing of the service. For example, an accounting firm might have several audits in process which will not be billed until the audit report is delivered. This "work-in-process" is not carried on the balance sheet as inventory, but obviously requires much working capital.[88]

The courts have recognized the particular working capital needs of service companies. In *Simons-Eastern Co.,* a U.S. District Court, in evaluating the corporation (an engineering consulting company), stated, "The strength of the business and really its only asset is brainpower in the form of highly educated skilled technicians. . . . Assuming a decline in business . . ., it would be foolhardy to have an abrupt reduction in force by discharging those highly paid specialists . . . the court concludes that for a professional service company with no inventory of saleable goods, the accumulation of reserves for one full operating cycle . . . plus 60 days of professional payroll constitutes a reasonable operating reserve."[89]

The Court of Claims in *C.E. Hooper, Inc.,* said of a company that measured radio audiences: "Although plaintiff did not have inventories in the conventional sense, the time required for production of its report prior to billing may fairly be compared to the production of inventory. . . On the basis of these facts it is concluded that plaintiff's average production cycle . . . was approximately 30 days."[90]

Tax Tips and Pitfalls

It is apparent that many service concerns such as software developers would have a much longer inventory equivalency cycle than the 60 days allowed in *Simons-Eastern Co.* If a company feels vulnerable to the accumulated earnings tax or is already disputing the matter with the IRS, it should engage an accountant to conduct a detailed study of its inventory equivalency cycle.

¶ 1107 Personal Holding Company Tax

Congress began imposing the personal holding company (PHC) tax in 1934, at a time when the corporate tax rate was considerably below the highest individual income tax rate. Before the tax was enacted, corporations could be used to shelter passive income, i.e., income from interest, dividends, rents, or royalties. Also, professional athletes and entertainment personalities could incorporate and have the corporation sign contracts for the services. Thus, the corporation would be taxed on the personal service income of the individual.

---

[88] For a good discussion of the application of the *Bardahl* formula to service concerns, see Jerome S. Horvitz and Annette Hebble, "The Effect of the Section 531 Penalty on Accumulations of Earnings and Profits after TRA '86," *Journal of Corporate Taxation,* No. 3, 236 (1987).

[89] *Simons-Eastern Co. v. U.S.,* 73-1 USTC ¶ 9279, 354 FSupp 1003 (N.D. Ga., 1972).

[90] *C.E. Hooper, Inc. v. U.S.,* CtCl, 76-2 USTC ¶ 9538, 539 F.2d 1276 (1976).

Two tests must be "passed" in order for a company to be designated as a personal holding company. For planning purposes, a corporation seeks to "flunk" either of the tests. The two tests are:[91]

1. At any time in the last half of the tax year, more than 50 percent in value of the outstanding stock is owned, directly or indirectly, by or for five or fewer individuals; and

2. At least 60 percent of its adjusted gross income for the tax year is personal holding company income.

Note that although for accumulated earnings and profits purposes intent is very important, for PHC purposes, the tests are very objective.

Certain corporations are exempt from PHC status. They are:[92]

- Tax-exempt companies;

- Banks and savings and loan associations;

- Life insurance companies;

- Surety companies;

- Foreign personal holding companies;

- Certain lending or finance companies;

- Certain foreign corporations;

- Certain small business investment companies;

- Certain companies in bankruptcy; and

- Certain passive foreign investment companies.

.01 Stockholder Ownership Test

The corporation always meets the stockholder ownership test if it has fewer than 10 shareholders. The stock ownership attribution rules are provided in Code Sec. 544.[93]

- Stock owned, directly or indirectly, by or for a corporation, partnership, estate, or trust is considered owned proportionately by the shareholder, partner, or beneficiary.

- Stock owned, directly or indirectly, by an individual's "family" or an individual's partner, is considered owned by the individual. For this purpose, "family" includes spouse, ancestors, lineal descendants, and brothers and sisters.

- If an individual has stock options, they are considered to have been exercised for this purpose.

---

[91] Code Sec. 542(a).
[92] Code Sec. 542(c).
[93] Code Sec. 544(a).

- Generally, convertible securities are considered for this purpose to have been converted subject to the exception that if some of the convertible securities are convertible only after a later date than in the case of others, the class with the earlier conversion date may be included, although the others are not considered.[94]

Example 11-12. The stock of Gordon's Groceries, Inc. is owned by the following stockholders:

Name	Shares
Valley Foods, Inc. (Allen Leedy owns 40% of Valley Foods, Inc.)	200
Estate of Gordon Leedy (Allen Leedy has a one-half beneficial interest in the estate)	150
Allen Leedy	100
Allen Leedy, Junior (Allen's son)	50
Paul Kruse (unrelated to Allen)	125
Sam Smith (Paul's brother-in-law)	75
Katrinda Kruse (Paul's daughter)	50
Unrelated individuals (five, each owning 50 shares)	250
Total	1,000

The five individuals owning the most stock are:

Allen Leedy $((200 \times .40) + (150 \times .50) + 100 + 50)$	305
Paul Kruse $(125 + 50)$	175
Sam Smith	75
Unrelated individual #1	50
Unrelated individual #2	50
Total	655

Thus, the stock ownership of PHC status is met.

.02 Adjusted Ordinary Gross Income Test

To apply the second test, it is necessary to know the definitions of ordinary gross income, adjusted ordinary gross income, and personal holding company income. "Ordinary gross income," hereafter OGI, is defined as gross income except for all gains from the sale or disposition of capital assets and Code Sec. 1231 gains.[95] "Gross income" is generally as defined in Code Sec. 61 (receipts less returns of capital and less excluded items).[96] However, in the case of transactions in stocks, securities, and commodities, gross income for PHC purposes includes only the excess of gains over losses from the transactions.[97]

---

[94] Code Sec. 544(b).
[95] Code Sec. 543(b)(1).
[96] Reg. § 1.542-2.
[97] *Id.*

Example 11-13. Glenn Jewelers Co. had sales of inventory of $250,000 and cost of sales of $110,000. The company also had rent income of $75,000, a gain on the sale of stock A of $20,000, and a loss on stock B of $28,000. Gross income consists of the gross profit of $140,000 plus the $75,000 of rent income, a total of $215,000.

"Adjusted ordinary gross income" (AOGI) equals OGI less these adjustments:[98]

1. *Rents*—from the gross income from rents subtract:

    a. Depreciation and amortization of property (other than tangible personal property which is not customarily retained by any one lessee for more than three years);

    b. Property taxes;

    c. Interest expense; and

    d. Rent expense.

The above deductions cannot exceed the gross income from rents.

2. *Mineral royalties, etc.*—from the gross income from royalties subtract:

    a. Depreciation, amortization, and depletion;

    b. Property and severance taxes;

    c. Interest expense; and

    d. Rent expense.

The above deductions attributable to royalties cannot exceed the gross income from royalties and the deductions attributable to working interests cannot exceed the gross income from working interests.

3. *Interest*—received on a direct obligation of the United States held for sale to customers in the ordinary course of business by a regular dealer.

4. *Interest*—on a condemnation award, a judgment, and a tax refund.

5. *Lease income*—of tangible personal property manufactured or produced by the taxpayer. Permissible deductions are the four listed above for rent income. Again, the amounts subtracted cannot exceed gross income.

---

[98] Code Sec. 543(b)(2).

Example 11-14. In 2001, Affluent Co. had the following income and expenses:

Income

Rental income	$300,000
Dividends	60,000
Long-term capital gains—sale of stock	25,000
Total	$385,000

Expenses

Depreciation—rental property	$ 12,000
Interest—rental property	30,000
Taxes—rental property	5,000
Repairs—rental property	7,000
Miscellaneous—rental property	3,000
Officer's salaries	40,000
Income taxes	105,000
Dividends received deduction	28,000
Total	$230,000
Net income	$155,000

Gross income would amount to $385,000;
OGI is $385,000 − $25,000 = $360,000.
AOGI = $360,000 − $12,000 − $30,000 − $5,000 = $313,000.

.03 Personal Holding Company Income

Personal holding company income (PHCI) is the portion of AOGI which consists of:[99]

1. *Dividends, interest, royalties, and annuities.* This does not include mineral, oil, or gas royalties or copyright royalties. Also not included are software royalties or certain interest received by a stockbroker or dealer.

2. *Adjusted income from rents.* This term is defined as gross income from rents[100] minus the amounts permitted to be deducted from rents to get to AOGI (discussed previously). However, rent does not have to be included in PHCI if two tests are met:

    a. The adjusted income from rents is at least 50 percent of AOGI; and

    b. Dividends paid (including consent dividends) are at least equal to the excess of nonrent PHCI over 10 percent of OGI.

3. *Mineral, oil, and gas royalties.* However, these royalties do not have to be included in PHCI if:

    a. The adjusted income is 50 percent or more of AOGI; and

---

[99] Code Sec. 543(a).
[100] Code Sec. 543(b)(3). The Second Circuit has held that for this purpose, rent income does not include crop sharing arrangements. See *Webster Corp.*, 57-1 USTC ¶ 9341, 240 F.2d 164 (2nd Cir., 1957).

b. Nonroyalty PHCI is not more that 10 percent of OGI; and

c. The trade or business deductions allowed under Code Sec. 162 (other than compensation for personal services rendered by the stockholders of the corporation and deductions which are specifically allowed under sections other than Code Sec. 162) are at least equal to 15 percent of OGI.

4. *Copyright royalties.* However, copyright royalties are not included if:

a. The royalties (not including royalties created by shareholders) are 50 percent or more of OGI; and

b. PHCI (not including copyright royalties, except for royalties created by shareholders owning more than 10 percent of the total outstanding capital stock of the corporation, and also not including dividends from any corporation in which the taxpayer owns at least 50 percent of all classes of stock) does not exceed 10 percent of OGI; and

c. The trade or business deductions allowed under Code Sec. 162 that are allocable to such royalties (other than compensation for personal expenses rendered by the stockholders of the corporation, deductions for royalties paid or accrued, and deductions which are specifically allowed under sections other than Code Sec. 162) are at least equal to 25 percent of the amount by which the OGI exceeds the sum of the royalties paid or accrued and the amounts allowable as depreciation deductions with respect to copyright royalties.

PHCI does not include income from active business computer software royalties.[101] "Active business computer software royalties" are royalties received during the tax year in connection with the licensing of computer hardware provided that these tests are met:[102]

a. The royalties must be received by a company engaged in the active conduct of the trade or business of developing, manufacturing, or producing computer software. The royalties must be attributable to computer software which is developed, manufactured, or produced by the corporation or its predecessor in connection with the trade or business of software or is directly related to such business.

b. The royalties must comprise at least 50 percent of the OGI of the corporation.

c. The deductions allowed under Code Sec. 162 (trade or business expenses), Code Sec. 174 (research and experimental

---

[101] Code Sec. 543(a). [102] Code Sec. 543(d).

expenses), and Code Sec. 195 (start-up expenditures) must either:

  i. Be at least 25 percent of OGI; or

  ii. The average of such deductions for the five-year period before the tax year must be at least 25 percent of average OGI for that period.

d. Dividends paid must equal or exceed the amount by which personal holding company income (computed without regard to active business computer software royalties and certain income interest) exceeds 10 percent of OGI.

5. *Produced film rents.* However, these are not included if the rents are at least 50 percent of OGI. "Produced film rents" are defined as payments received with respect to an interest in a film to the extent that the interest was acquired before substantial completion of the film. Note that if the film was acquired *after* its substantial completion, it would be a copyright royalty as defined in (4) above.

6. *Use of corporate property by shareholders.* The objective of this provision was to penalize corporations by designating as PHCI rental income received by corporations for the use by shareholders of such personal-use items as apartments, yachts, airplanes, luxury automobiles, and so on. However, its applicability is not limited to personal use property. Corporations which lease tangible property to stockholders who own at least 25 percent of the value of the stock (including constructive ownership under attribution rules) must include the rent in PHCI if the company's PHCI (computed without regard to this income or other rent and without regard to certain income from the use of intangible property) exceeds 10 percent of OGI.

7. *Personal service contracts.* This provision was designed to prevent athletes and entertainers from sheltering their compensation in corporations. Contracts are considered personal service contracts if some person other than the corporation has the right to designate the individual who is to perform the services, or if the individual who is to perform the services is designated (by name or description), and the individual at any time during the year owned (including constructive ownership under attribution rules), at least 25 percent of the value of the stock of the corporation.

Although in theory many service companies (e.g., law, medical, accounting, engineering, and so on) could be subject to the PHC tax, a number of court cases and revenue rulings have provided some comfort to service corporations. In a 1971 revenue ruling, the IRS ruled that an incorporated broker on a stock exchange floor was not subject to the PHC tax because the contracts that the corporation would enter into would not designate the owner and the services could be performed by any broker. Therefore, the personal services "are not unique and could be substituted."[103]

What if the services are such that only one person in the corporation can perform the personal service? The IRS ruled that a one-professional personal service corporation was not a PHC merely because there is the expectation that a particular physician will perform the service. If there is a contract between the patient and the physician which provides that the physician will personally perform the service without right of substitution, such income would be PHC income. PHC income could also result if the physician's services are so unique as to preclude substitution of another physician.[104] A very similar conclusion was reached with respect to a solely owned CPA professional service corporation.[105] The IRS even ruled that income earned from musical and arrangement services furnished to clients by a solely owned corporation would not be considered income from personal service contracts as long as there was no contract providing that the owner would personally perform the service.[106] It should be noted that the IRS has ruled that oral contracts as well as written contracts with the individual rather than the corporation, constitute PHC income.[107]

8. *Income from estates and trusts.* Corporations that are beneficiaries of estates and trusts and report income from these entities have PHC income.

Example 11-15. Assume the same facts as in Example 11-14 and that the Affluent Co. paid no dividends during the year. Adjusted gross income from rents is $300,000 − $12,000 − $30,000 − $5,000 = $253,000. Since the adjusted gross income from rents ($253,000) is 80.8 percent of the AOGI of $313,000, the 50 percent test is met. However, since no dividends were paid, the second test is not met, and the rent income must be included as PHCI. Therefore, the dividends of $60,000 and the adjusted rents of $253,000 all must be counted as PHCI. Hence, PHCI equals 100 percent of AOGI and one of the tests for PHC status is met. If the stock ownership test is met, the company will be a PHC.

Example 11-16. Assume the same facts as in Example 11-14, except that $25,000 was paid in dividends during the year. The excess of nonrent PHCI over 10 percent of OGI is $24,000 ($60,000 − ($360,000 × .10)). Since dividends paid were at least that much, both of the rental income tests are met and the rent income is not a part of

---

[103] Rev. Rul. 71-372, 1971-2 CB 241.
[104] Rev. Rul. 75-67, 1975-1 CB 169.
[105] Rev. Rul. 75-250, 1975-1 CB 172.

[106] Rev. Rul. 75-249, 1975-1 CB 171.

[107] Rev. Rul. 69-299, 1969-1 CB 165.

PHCI. Hence, PHCI consists only of the dividend income of $60,000, and since $60,000 is less than 60 percent of AOGI ($60,000/$313,000 equals only 19.2 percent), the corporation is *not* a PHC, regardless of the stock ownership test.

Example 11-17. Oil Everywhere, Inc. had the following items of income and expenses for the tax year 2001:

Income
Dividends	$75,000
Interest	85,000
Oil and gas royalties	250,000
Long-term capital gains	100,000
Total	$510,000

Expenses
Depletion	$24,000	
Property taxes	6,000	
Severance taxes	4,000	
Officer's salaries	40,000	
Office salaries	25,000	
Miscellaneous general expenses	12,000	
Dividends received deduction	52,500	
Income taxes	98,000	
Total		$261,500
Net income		$248,500

Adjusted income from royalties is $250,000 − $24,000 − $6,000 − $4,000 = $216,000. Gross income is $510,000. OGI is $510,000 − $100,000 = $410,000. AOGI is $410,000 − $24,000 − $6,000 − $4,000 = $376,000. The first test is met since adjusted income from oil and gas royalties ($216,000) is at least 50 percent of AOGI ($376,000). However, nonroyalty PHCI ($75,000 + $85,000) is more than 10 percent of OGI. Hence, the royalty income will have to be counted as PHCI. It is immaterial in this case whether the Code Sec. 162 business expenses are at least equal to 15 percent of AOGI. However, the trade or business expenses of $37,000 ($25,000 + $12,000) are less than 15 percent of the AOGI of $376,000. Therefore, only the second test was not met. Since all of the AOGI is PHCI, the 60 percent test is met. Whether or not Oil Everywhere, Inc., is a PHC will depend on the stock ownership characteristics of the company.

.04 Computing the PHC Tax

The PHC tax is the product of the highest rate of tax imposed on unmarried individuals and the undistributed PHC income. The amount of "undistributed PHC income" is arrived at by deducting dividends paid from adjusted taxable income. In turn, the figure "adjusted taxable income" is taxable income plus or minus these adjustments:[108]

1. Deduct federal income taxes, not including the accumulated earnings tax or the PHC tax.

2. Deduct charitable contributions (without the 10 percent limit). However, the maximum limits applicable to individuals (50 percent, 30 percent, and 20 percent, depending on the type of property sold and type of charity) apply to the corporation for this purpose.

3. Add the dividends-received deduction.

4. Add the net operating loss deduction (but the NOL from the preceding year computed without the dividends-received deduction is allowed).

5. Deduct the net capital gains (excess of long-term capital gains over short-term capital losses) reduced by the income tax attributable to the gains.

6. Add the sum of the deductions under Code Sec. 162 (trade or business expenses) and Code Sec. 167 (depreciation) allocable to the operation and maintenance of property owned and operated by the corporation, but only in an amount equal to the rent income generated by property unless it can be established:

   a. That the rent or other compensation received was the highest obtainable, or if none was received, that none was obtainable;

   b. That the property was held in the course of a business carried on bona fide for profit; and

   c. Either that there was reasonable expectation that the operation of the property would result in a profit, or that the property was necessary to the conduct of the business.

The burden of proof rests on the corporation to sustain the deductions claimed for trade or business expenses and depreciation.[109] If the deductions in item (6) are claimed on a PHC return, the company must attach a statement setting forth:[110]

- A description of the property;

- The cost or other basis to the corporation and the nature and value of the consideration paid for the property;

---

[108] Code Sec. 545(b).
[109] Reg. § 1.545-2(h)(2).
[110] *Id.*

- The name and address of the person from whom the property was acquired and the date the property was acquired;

- The name and address of the person to whom the property is leased or rented, or the person permitted to use the property, and the number of shares of stock, if any, held by such person and the members of his or her family;

- The nature and gross amount of the rent or other compensation received for the use of, or the right to use, the property during the taxable year and for each of the five preceding years and the amount of the expenses incurred with respect to, and the depreciation sustained on, the property for such years;

- Evidence that the rent or other compensation was the highest obtainable or, if none was received, a statement of the reasons thereof;

- A copy of the lease agreement;.

- The purpose for which the property was received;

- The business, carried on by the corporation, with respect to which the property was held and the gross income, expenses, and taxable income derived from the conduct of such business for the taxable year and for each of the five preceding years;

- A statement of any reasons which existed for expectation that the operation of the property would be profitable, or a statement of the necessity for the use of the property in the business of the corporation, and the reasons why the property was acquired; and

- Any other information pertinent to the taxpayer's claim.

.05 Dividends-Paid Deduction

From adjusted taxable income, dividends paid are deducted to arrive at the tax base, undistributed personal holding company income.[111] The dividends-paid deduction is similar to but not identical to the dividends-paid deduction for accumulated earnings tax purposes. There are five basic types of dividends paid for PHC purposes:

1. Dividends paid during the taxable year.[112]

2. Consent dividends.[113]

---

[111] Code Sec. 545(a).
[112] Code Sec. 561(a)(1).

[113] See the discussion under Accumulated Earnings Tax.

3. Dividends paid within two and one-half months after the end of the taxable year. The rules are similar to those for the accumulated earnings tax except that in the case of the PHC, the throwback to the previous year is elective rather than mandatory.[114] Also, the amount allowed to be thrown back is the lesser of:[115]

   a. The undistributed PHC income for the taxable year computed without regard to this deduction, or

   b. 20 percent of the dividends paid during the taxable year (computed without regard to dividends paid after the close of the year).

4. Dividend carryovers.[116] For each of the two preceding taxable years, adjusted taxable income is computed (whether or not the corporation was a PHC in those years) and compared with dividends paid:[117]

   a. If in both years the dividends paid exceed the adjusted taxable income, the carryover is the sum of the two excess amounts.

   b. If there are excess dividends in the second preceding year, but excess adjusted taxable income in the first preceding year, the dividend carryover is the excess from the second year reduced by the excess income of the first year.

   c. If there are excess dividends in the first preceding year but excess adjusted taxable income in the second preceding year, the carryover is the excess dividends of the first preceding year.

Example 11-18. The Higgins Investment Company had adjusted taxable income in 2000 of $100,000 and dividends paid of $150,000. For 2001 its adjusted taxable income was $200,000 and its dividends paid was $170,000. The dividends carryover from 2000 of $50,000 is reduced by the $30,000 excess taxable income in 2001. Thus the dividend carryover to 2002 is $20,000.

Example 11-19. Assume the same facts as in the preceding example, except that in 2000 there was $30,000 of excess taxable income and in 2001 excess dividends were $50,000. The dividends carryover to 2002 is $50,000.

---

[114] Code Sec. 563(b).
[115] *Id.*

[116] Code Sec. 561(a)(3).
[117] Reg. § 1.564-1(a).

5. Deficiency dividends. Even after the liability for the PHC tax has been determined, the corporation has one last shot at avoiding the tax (but not the interest or penalties) by paying a dividend.[118] This "deficiency dividend" must be paid within 90 days after the "determination" of the PHC tax.[119] The term "determination" means either that a decision or judgment of a relevant court has become final, or a closing agreement has been signed, or an agreement between the IRS and the taxpayer relating to the PHC tax has been signed.[120]

Tax Tips and Pitfalls

The filing of a Schedule PH and payment of the PHC tax apparently precludes the taxpayer from using deficiency dividends. The IRS has so held in several rulings.[121] One writer has suggested that corporations subject to the PHC tax wishing to use deficiency dividends report on Schedule PH the undistributed personal holding company income but not state the tax and request the IRS to make a determination of the PHC tax and enter into an agreement under Section 547(c)(3).[122]

There are several important caveats to be noted about the dividends-paid deduction for PHC purposes. Like the dividends-paid deduction for accumulated earnings purposes, the distribution must be *pro rata*.[123] One major difference between dividends for accumulated earnings tax purposes and for PHC purposes is that for PHC purposes, dividends do not have to be from earnings and profits, they must merely not be in excess of undistributed personal holding company income.[124]

Example 11-20. Reddy Co. has been determined to be a personal holding company. Its taxable income for the year 2000 is as follows:

Sales	$ 390,000
Cost of sales	170,000
Gross profit	$ 220,000
Dividend income	300,000
Interest income	500,000
Total income	$1,020,000

---

[118] Code Sec. 547(a).

[119] Code Sec. 547(d).

[120] Code Sec. 547(c).

[121] See IRS Letter Rulings 8213068, 8230004, and 8223007.

[122] See Julian H. Baumann, Jr., "Deficiency Dividends and other Solutions to Avoiding Personal Holding Company Tax," *The Journal of Taxation,* Vol. 59, No. 4, pp. 202-205, October 1983.

[123] Code Sec. 562(c).

[124] Code Sec. 316(b)(2).

Expenses

Compensation of officers	$ 70,000
Salaries and wages	120,000
Taxes	45,000
Contributions (total was $70,000).....	46,000
Other deductions	325,000
Total	606,000

Taxable income before special deductions	$ 414,000
Dividends received deduction	210,000
Net operating loss deduction (from 1994)	(60,000)
Taxable income..............................	$ 144,000
Federal income tax	$ 39,410

The company paid $50,000 of dividends in 2000 and an additional $20,000 on January 30, 2001, which it threw back to 2000 to the maximum extent possible. Computation of the PHC tax is as follows:

Taxable income.............................		$ 144,000
Add: Dividends received deduction........	$210,000	
NOL	60,000	270,000
		$ 414,000
Less: Federal income tax	$ 39,410	
Excess contributions	24,000	63,410
Adjusted taxable income......................		$ 350,590
Less: Dividends paid-2000..............	$ 50,000	
Dividends thrown back to 2000 (limited to $50,000 × .20)	10,000	60,000
Undistributed personal holding company		$ 290,590
PHC tax at 39.6 percent......................		$ 115,074

The total federal tax would be $154,484 ($39,410 + 115,074). This represents a rather hefty tax rate of 107 percent of the taxable income of $144,000!

Tax Tips and Pitfalls

Note that the PHC tax requires the filing of a return (Schedule 1120 PH). Failure to file a timely return can lead to interest and penalties being imposed on the corporation. While payment of a deficiency dividend can reduce or eliminate the tax itself, the interest and penalties alone could be very costly. Thus, a premium is placed on the avoidance of PHC status.

Although wider stock ownership (having five or fewer stockholders own not more than 50 percent of the stock) is the easiest way to avoid PHC status, in many closely held corporations this tactic will not be practical. Hence, reducing PHC income below 60 percent of AOGI is often the only alternative. Possible ways of accomplishing this objective are as follows:

1. Convert taxable bond interest into exempt bond interest by purchasing state or local bonds.

2. Reduce dividend income by investing in lower yield common stocks, thus substituting capital gains for dividend income (capital gains are not included in OGI).

3. If possible get adjusted income from rents above 50 percent of AOGI by:

    a. Accepting prepaid rent income.

    b. Using straight-line depreciation over alternate lives rather than the statutory MACRS lives and rates.

4. Use a strategy similar to (3) above for oil and gas royalties.

5. Avoid leasing property to shareholders who own 25 percent or more of the stock.

6. For personal service companies, avoid contracts which specify an individual, rather than the corporation, is to perform the services. If this is not possible, consider an entity other than a C corporation.

7. If possible, acquire motion film rights *before* the film is substantially completed.

Given the harshness of the PHC tax, advance planning can prevent some unhappy results.

Chapter 12

Corporate Reorganizations

¶ 1201   Introduction

Change is a fact of life in a capitalistic society. At the corporate level, change is often reflected in combinations, acquisitions, divisions, restructurings, recapitalizations, and other forms of reorganizations. While usually thought of by the layperson as transactions involving only large corporations (e.g., the merger of Time-Warner and Turner Broadcastings), reorganization tax law is equally applicable to small, closely held corporations.

Many reorganizations are completely nontaxable, generally reflecting the wishes of the involved parties to not create a taxable event. The rationale behind treating reorganizations as tax-free is that the new enterprise or corporation is substantially a continuation of the old enterprise or corporation. Though the realization concept technically may have been met, i.e., there may have been an exchange with an outsider, the stockholder has a continuity of interest in the corporation, the assets, or the business such that there is not an appreciable change in the form of assets that he or she possessed. The situation is analogous, and the tax results similar to, a nontaxable exchange. In both cases, the taxpayer is left with property similar to that which the taxpayer gave up and the taxpayer has no cash from the transaction from which to pay income tax. Thus, tax law permits the gain or loss to be deferred and the basis of the new property reflects the deferred gain or loss. Though the basic concept of reorganizations is very simple, unfortunately the tax law governing reorganizations is immensely complicated.

¶ 1203   Tax-Free Reorganizations in Brief

Code Sec. 368 provides literally an alphabet soup of reorganizations, running the gamut of A through G (subparagraphs of Code Sec. 368). The various types of tax-free reorganizations are:[1]

Type A—a statutory merger or consolidation;

Type B—the acquisition by one corporation, in exchange solely for all or part of its voting stock (or in exchange for all or a part of the voting stock of a corporation which is in control of the acquiring corporation), of stock in another corporation if, immediately after the acquisition, the acquiring corporation has control of such other corporation (whether or not such acquiring corporation had control immediately before the acquisition);

---

[1] Code Sec. 368(a).

Type C—the acquisition by one corporation, in exchange solely for all or a part of its voting stock (or in exchange solely for all or a part of the voting stock of a corporation which is in control of the acquiring corporation), of substantially all of the properties of another corporation (in determining whether the exchange is solely for stock, the assumption by the acquiring corporation of a liability of the other, or the fact that property acquired is subject to a liability, shall be disregarded);

Type D—a transfer by a corporation of all or a part of its assets to another corporation if immediately after the transfer the transferor, or one or more of its shareholders (including persons who were shareholders immediately before the transfer), or any combination thereof, is in control of the corporation to which the assets are transferred; but only if, in pursuance of the plan, stock or securities of the corporation to which the assets are transferred are distributed in a transaction which qualifies under Code Secs. 354, 355, or 356;

Type E—a recapitalization;

Type F—a mere change in the identity, form, or place of organization, however effected; or

Type G—a transfer by a corporation of all or part of its assets to another corporation in a Title 11 or similar case; but only if, in pursuance of the plan, stock or securities of the corporation to which the assets are transferred are distributed in a transaction which qualifies under Code Secs. 354, 355, or 356.

.01   Type A Reorganizations

Type A reorganizations are either statutory mergers or consolidations. In order to qualify as type A, the transaction must be effected pursuant to the corporate laws of the United States, a state or territory, or the District of Columbia.[2] A merger comes about when one company absorbs the other so that the acquiring company is the only survivor.

> **Example 12-1.** Hilltopper, Inc., acquires all of the assets and liabilities of Round Mound Co. in exchange for Hilltopper, Inc., stock. The Hilltopper, Inc., stock is then distributed in a liquidating distribution to the Round Mound Co. shareholders. Hilltopper, Inc., is the only surviving entity.

A consolidation occurs when two corporations unite to form an entirely new corporation.

> **Example 12-2.** Perrino, Inc., and Yesson Co. each transfer their corporate assets and liabilities to a new corporation, Perrino & Yesson, in exchange for stock in Perrino & Yesson. The stock is then distrib-

---

[2] Reg. § 1.368-2(b)(1).

uted in a liquidating dividend to the shareholders of Perrino, Inc., and Yesson Co. Perrino & Yesson is the only surviving entity.

Although severe restrictions are placed on the form of consideration given by the acquiring corporation in a type B, C, or D reorganization, no restrictions per se are placed on a type A reorganization. Thus, consideration given could include cash and property as well as voting common stock. (**Caution:** Read the sections discussing the tax effects of boot and securities and the section discussing the continuity of interest doctrine.)

Since a type A reorganization must qualify under state law, the stockholders must approve the merger or consolidation. In many states, 75 percent of the target corporation stockholders must approve a merger or consolidation, and minority shareholders may have to be placated.

Using a Subsidiary in a Type A Reorganization

In a type A reorganization, the acquiring corporation winds up with the liabilities of the target corporation(s). In addition, depending on the state, anywhere from a majority to 75 percent of the shareholders in the acquiring corporation may be required to approve a merger. Both of these problems may be eliminated by using a subsidiary to effect a merger. Since the parent company owns at least 80 percent of the stock in the subsidiary, approval by the stockholders of the subsidiary is not a problem. Also, since the *subsidiary* will acquire the liabilities of the acquired company, the parent company's assets generally will be shielded from the impact of any contingent liabilities that the acquired company may have.

Whose stock should be given, the stock of the parent company or the stock of the subsidiary? It is possible to give only stock of the subsidiary, and if the acquired company is small in relation to the subsidiary, this strategy may be feasible. Often, however, this plan would not be practical since control of the subsidiary might pass from the parent company to the new stockholders. Fortunately, stock of the parent company can be given (however, in this case no stock of the subsidiary could be given) and the tax-free status of the type A reorganization is retained.[3]

> **Example 12-3.** Mills Fabrics has a 100 percent owned subsidiary, Mills Wollens Co. The subsidiary transfers stock of Mills Fabrics to Soft Cotton Co. in exchange for its assets under state law. Soft Cotton Co. then distributes the stock of Mills Fabrics in a liquidating dividend. After the merger, the assets and liabilities of Soft Cotton Co. are held by Mills Wollens Co., the subsidiary of Mills Fabrics.

It is also possible to use the subsidiary to effect a reverse merger, i.e., where the target corporation merges the subsidiary into it and the subsidiary is then liquidated. Two requirements for a reverse merger must be met:[4]

---

[3] Code Sec. 368(a)(2)(D).   [4] Code Sec. 368(a)(2)(E).

1.   After the transaction, the surviving corporation must hold sub-
     stantially all of its properties and the properties of the merged
     corporation (other than stock of the controlling corporation)
     that are distributed in the transaction; and

2.   The former shareholders of the surviving corporation must have
     exchanged, for an amount of voting stock of the controlling
     corporation, sufficient stock in the surviving corporation to
     constitute control. ("Control" for this purpose means the owner-
     ship of stock possessing 80 percent or more of voting power and
     80 percent or more of all other classes of stock.[5])

   Example 12-4. Zippo Bank Holding Co. owns a subsidiary,
Valley State Bank, and wishes to acquire Mountain Top Bank, which is
located in another state. State law prohibits Valley State Bank from
having an out-of-state branch; however, there is no such restriction in
the state in which Mountain Top Bank is located. Therefore, Valley
State is merged into Mountain Top Bank. The shareholders of Mountain Top Bank receive voting stock in Zippo Bank Holding Co. in
exchange for their stock in Mountain Top Bank. After the reverse
merger, Valley State Bank is out of existence, and its assets are now
held by Mountain Top Bank, which is now a subsidiary of Zippo Bank
Holding Co.

.02   Type B Reorganizations

   Type B reorganizations are stock-for-stock swaps, with the end result
being that the target company is a subsidiary of the parent company. The
two key requirements of a type B are that only voting stock may be used by
the acquiring company, and that the acquiring company after the stock
swap must own at least 80 percent of the voting stock and at least 80
percent of all other classes of stock.

   The first requirement is very strict, i.e., no cash, securities, or even
nonvoting stock may be used as consideration. In the case of fractional
shares, application of this provision would be awkward. Fortunately, the
IRS has ruled that the acquiring corporation in a type B reorganization can
issue cash in lieu of fractional shares if it is not bargained for but is merely
a mechanical rounding off of the fractions.[6]

   If the acquiring corporation exchanges its debentures for debentures of
the acquired corporation, such exchange does not disqualify an otherwise
qualifying type B reorganization.[7] Where the acquiring corporation issues
stock for both stock and debentures of the acquired corporation, the stock-
for-debentures swap does not disqualify the reorganization from type B
status. The stock-for-debenture swap is considered part of the reorganiza-

---

[5] Code Sec. 368(c).
[6] Rev. Rul. 66-365, 1966-2 CB 116.

[7] Rev. Rul. 98-10, 1998-1 CB 643.

tion, and, therefore, the debenture holders are not required to recognize gain or loss on the exchange.[8]

The second requirement warrants some amplification. Control does not have to be achieved by the *particular* acquisition so long as *after* the acquisition the total shares owned equals or exceeds 80 percent.

> **Example 12-5.** Hytrain Electronics Co. exchanges 30 percent of its voting stock for 100 percent of all classes of stock of Jayhawk Stereo. Stockholders did not have the option to receive cash or property in lieu of the stock. This acquisition would qualify as a type B reorganization. Afterward, both corporations would remain in existence, but Jayhawk Stereo would be a subsidiary of Hytrain Electronics Co.

> **Example 12-6.** Assume the same facts as in Example 12-5, except that four years ago Hytrain Electronics Co. had purchased for cash 80 percent of Jayhawk Stereo and in the current year acquired the additional 20 percent in a stock swap. The stock swap qualifies as a type B reorganization.

> **Example 12-7.** Assume the same facts as in Example 12-5, except that four years ago Hytrain Electronics had purchased for cash 40 percent of Jayhawk Stereo and in the current year acquired an additional 40 percent in a stock swap. The stock swap qualifies as a type B reorganization.

If a cash purchase is followed shortly thereafter by a stock swap (e.g., within a 12-month period), the IRS might aggregate the transactions in applying the solely stock-for-stock requirement. In that event, the requirements for a type B reorganization would not be met.

> **Example 12-8.** Assume the same facts as in Example 12-5, except that in January of the current year Hytrain Electronics purchased for cash 40 percent of Jayhawk Stereo and in March acquired an additional 40 percent in a stock swap. The IRS will likely aggregate the two transactions, thus causing the transaction to fail the type B requirements.

The regulations state that a tax-free acquisition is permitted in a single transaction or in a series of transactions so long as they take place over a relatively short period, such as 12 months.[9]

The acquiring corporation may not wish to acquire all of the assets of the target corporation. The IRS has ruled that a company may, prior to being acquired, spin off part of its assets to another corporation.[10]

---

[8] *Id.*
[9] Reg. § 1.368-2(c).

[10] Rev. Rul. 70-434, 1970-2 CB 83.

Tax Tips and Pitfalls

The restrictions on the type of consideration given, i.e., voting stock only, often make a type B reorganization less attractive to the shareholders of the acquired corporation, since many stockholders may prefer to have the option to receive cash, or may wish to have at least part of the consideration in cash. However, from the standpoint of the acquiring corporation, the type B reorganization has two attractive features:

1. It is relatively informal; generally acquired corporation stockholder approval will not be needed; and

2. The acquiring corporation's assets could not be taken to satisfy contingent or off-the-book liabilities of the acquired corporation (since it remains a separate entity).

.03 Type C Reorganizations

A type C reorganization is a stock-for-assets swap, i.e., the acquiring corporation exchanges its stock for assets of the target corporation. There are essentially four criteria necessary to qualify for type C status.

1. The acquiring corporation must acquire "substantially all" of the assets of the target company.[11] Although the term "substantially all" is defined in neither the Code nor the regulations, the IRS has stated that in order to receive an advance ruling on a type C reorganization, at least 90 percent of the fair market value of the net assets (assets − liabilities), and at least 70 percent of the gross value of the assets must be acquired from the target corporation.[12]

   Example 12-9. Uptown Bottlers, Inc., issued voting stock in exchange for assets held by Softdrink, Inc., having a fair market value of $500,000. Immediately before the acquisition, Softdrink, Inc., had assets with a fair market value of $700,000 and had $150,000 of liabilities. Both the 70 percent test and the 90 percent test are met since $500,000 exceeds 70 percent of $700,000 and also exceeds 90 percent of $550,000 ($700,000 − $150,000).

2. At least 80 percent of the consideration given by the acquiring corporation must be in the form of voting stock.[13] Liabilities assumed are not counted as cash boot given if only voting stock is given. However, if property other than voting stock is given, liabilities assumed must be counted in determining the 20 percent requirement.

---

[11] Code Sec. 368(a)(1)(C).
[12] Rev. Proc. 77-37, 1977-2 CB 568.

[13] Code Sec. 368(a)(2)(B).

Example 12-10. Assume the same facts as in Example 12-9, except that Uptown Bottlers, Inc., issued $350,000 of voting stock for $500,000 of assets which were subject to $150,000 of liabilities. The liabilities are 30 percent of the total consideration; however, since the only other consideration given was voting stock, the 80 percent test is met.

Example 12-11. Assume the same facts as in Example 12-10, except that $300,000 of voting stock and $50,000 of cash are transferred, and $150,000 of liabilities are assumed. In this instance, the liabilities must be counted; hence, less than 80 percent of the consideration ($300,000 divided by ($300,000 + $50,000 + $150,000) = only 60 percent) given was voting stock. Hence, the reorganization does not qualify as a type C.

Example 12-12. Assume the same facts as in Example 12-10, except that the $500,000 of assets received were subject to liabilities of only $80,000. Voting stock of $400,000 and cash of $20,000 were given. In this case, the 80 percent test is just met ($400,000 = .8($400,000 + $80,000 + $20,000)).

3. The acquired corporation must distribute the stock, securities, and other properties it receives, as well as its other property (i.e., it must liquidate).[14] However, the IRS is empowered to waive this requirement.[15]

4. If the transaction qualifies as both a type C and a type D reorganization, it is to be treated as a type D reorganization.[16]

Another aspect of a type C reorganization is that a corporation may transfer part or all of the assets to a corporation controlled by the acquiring corporation.[17]

Example 12-13. Assume the same facts as in Example 12-9, except that Uptown Bottlers, Inc., creates a new subsidiary, Suburban Bottling Co., and transfers all of the assets of Softdrink, Inc., to it. Assuming the other requirements are met, the reorganization would qualify as a type C reorganization.

Example 12-14. Uncle Mick's Co., a restaurant, has a subsidiary, Uncle Mick's West Co. In exchange for voting stock of the parent company, Quick Tacos, Inc., transferred substantially all of its assets to the subsidiary. Assuming that the other requirements are met, the reorganization would qualify as a type C reorganization.

Where a corporation sold 50 percent of its historic assets for cash and then immediately afterwards transferred to an acquiring corporation all of

---

14 Code Sec. 368(a)(2)(G).
15 *Id.*

16 Code Sec. 368(a)(2)(A).
17 Code Sec. 368(a)(2)(C).

its assets (including cash from the sale) for voting stock, the IRS ruled that the reorganization qualified as a type C.[18]

Tax Tips and Pitfalls

A type C reorganization is more informal than a type A, is somewhat more flexible with respect to consideration than a type B, and has the advantage over both types A and B in that no hidden liabilities will be present in a type C. On the other hand, it is somewhat more formal than a type B, because the stockholders of the target corporation will have to approve the reorganization. A type C is often called an informal type A, since the end results are very similar.

.04 Type D Reorganizations

A type D reorganization is an assets-for-stock swap. It can either take the form of an *acquisitive* reorganization or a *divisive* reorganization. A discussion of these two forms of a type D reorganization follows.

Acquisitive Type D Reorganizations

In an acquisitive type D reorganization, the three requirements are:[19]

1. The corporation to which the assets are transferred must acquire "substantially all" of the assets (as used in this context, "substantially all" does not necessarily have the same meaning as it does for advance ruling purposes in a type C);

2. The asset transferor must distribute the stock, securities, and other property received as well as any other property owned, pursuant to the plan of reorganization (in effect, the transferor corporation in an acquisitive type D cannot retain any assets, though it is not required to liquidate per se); and

3. The transferor corporation and/or one or more of its shareholders must obtain control of the transferee corporation ("control" is at least 80 percent of the stock).

Example 12-15. Big Sky Ranching Co. wishes to acquire Circle OB Ranch, Inc. However, Circle OB Ranch, Inc., holds grazing rights on National Forest Land from the Department of the Interior, which are nontransferable. Therefore, Big Sky Ranching Co. transfers all of its assets to Circle OB Ranch, Inc., in exchange for 75 percent of its stock. Big Sky then distributes the stock in Circle OB to its shareholders and liquidates. Afterward, the surviving corporation is Circle OB Ranch, Inc. However, the stockholders of Big Sky are in control. Thus, in effect, Big Sky, though it loses its existence, is the acquiring corporation.

---

[18] Rev. Rul. 88-48, 1988-1 CB 117.   [19] Code Secs. 368(a)(1)(D) and 354(b).

Divisive Type D Reorganizations

A divisive reorganization results in the separation or division of a corporation into two or more corporations. Divisive D reorganizations consist of three types: spin-offs, split-offs, and split-ups. While more often thought of in the context of large, publicly held corporations, divisive reorganizations can be an effective tool for closely held corporations as well.

Example 12-16. Jerry Mason and his brother Milton own a corporation with two sporting goods stores, Jock Brothers, Inc. Jerry wishes to expand into other cities while Milton is more conservative. They transfer the assets of one store to a newly formed corporation, Westtown Sporting Goods, Inc., in exchange for all of its stock. Jock Brothers, Inc., then distributed the stock to Milton in exchange for all of Milton's stock in Jock Brothers, Inc. This should qualify as a split-off.

Example 12-17. Chou Lang and his two children own all of the stock in Ag Bio Tech Co., a corporation which produces both pesticides and growth hormones. It is felt that the growth hormone business will grow much faster, and be more profitable, in the years ahead. Therefore, for estate planning purposes, Chou would like to see the hormone business owned by his children. They effect a reorganization similar to that in Example 12-16. The result is that, in a tax-free transaction, the children have acquired the business, which will rapidly appreciate in value.

To qualify, a divisive reorganization must meet the requirements of Code Sec. 355. There are four requirements to be met:[20]

1. The distributing corporation must distribute at least 80 percent of the stock of the new corporation to its shareholders.

2. Both the distributing corporation and the new corporation must be engaged in the active conduct of a trade or business which has been conducted for at least five years prior to the distribution, and the business *must not* have been acquired in a taxable transaction within the last five years.

3. Only stock or securities of the new corporation may be distributed to the shareholders. If other property is distributed, it is considered to be boot and gain must be recognized (see ¶ 1207.03, "Tax Impact on the Shareholders").

4. The transaction must not have been used principally as a device to distribute E&P of the distributing corporation.

---

[20] Code Sec. 355(a). See Chapter 14 for a more detailed discussion of Code Sec. 355.

The question as to what is "active conduct of a trade or business" naturally arises. The regulations offer some guidance in this area, stating that a corporation will be treated as engaged in a trade or business "if a specific group of activities are being carried on by the corporation for the purpose of earning income or profit, and the activities included in such group include every operation that forms a part of, or a step in, the process of earning income or profit." Such group of activities ordinarily must include the collection of income and the payment of expenses.[21] The active conduct of a business does not include:[22]

- The holding of stock, securities, land, or other property for investment purposes; or

- The ownership and operation (including leasing) of real or personal property used in a trade or business unless the owner provides significant services with respect to the operation and management of the property.

The regulations provide several examples of the application of the "active conduct of a business" rules. Examples which *do not* constitute the active conduct of a business include:[23]

- A manufacturer spinning off its investment securities into a new corporation;

- A corporation with rental income spinning off vacant land into a new corporation;

- The spin-off of unexploited mineral rights from a ranching operation; and

- A bank spinning off a two-story building, half of which it operates.

Examples which *do* constitute the active conduct of a business include:[24]

- A bank spinning off an 11 story building, only one story of which it occupies;

- Spin-off of a suburban clothing store from a downtown store where the warehouse will continue to serve both stores and will be retained by the downtown store;

- Spin-off of a coal mine from a steel company; and

- Spin-off of a research department which will then continue research on a combined basis with several corporations, including the distributing corporation.

---

[21] Reg. § 1.355-3(b)(2)(ii).
[22] Reg. § 1.355-3(b)(2)(iv).
[23] Reg. § 1.355-3(c).
[24] *Id.*

¶ 1203.04

The performance of management services as a general contractor has been held to be a trade or business.[25] The IRS has also ruled that no matter how large the portfolio or the amount of activity, the management of an investment portfolio is not an active trade or business.[26]

The division of a business into two or more businesses has been held to be a nontaxable type D reorganization.[27]

.05 Type E Reorganizations (Recapitalizations)

The Code contains no definition of what is meant by the term "type E reorganization," and the regulations provide amplification only by examples. The regulations provide five examples of tax-free recapitalizations:[28]

1. An exchange by the corporation of its preferred stock for bonds held by bondholders;

2. A corporation exchanges no par value common stock in exchange for 25 percent of its preferred stock, which it then cancels;

3. A corporation issues preferred stock, previously authorized but unissued, for outstanding common stock;

4. A corporation exchanges a new issue of common stock in exchange for preferred stock; and

5. An exchange is made of a corporation's outstanding preferred stock with dividends in arrears for other stock of the corporation.

"Continuity of interest" (see the discussion in ¶ 1205.01) is not a requirement for a type E reorganization.[29]

A conversion of common into preferred of equal value or conversion of preferred to common of equal value will qualify as a type E if done under a specific provision in the certificate of incorporation, if it is to accomplish a corporate purpose.[30]

A transaction may qualify as a type E reorganization even though individuals have taxable income resulting from the transaction. In *Microdot,* a corporation's issuance of debentures for approximately 10 percent of its outstanding common stock was ruled to be a type E recapitalization even though Code Sec. 354(a)(2)(B) resulted in taxable income for the shareholders.[31]

[25] Rev. Rul. 73-237, 1973-1 CB 184.
[26] Rev. Rul. 66-204, 1966-2 CB 113.
[27] See, for example, *E.P. Coady v. Commr.,* 33 TC 771, Dec. 24,024, aff'd CA-6, 61-1 USTC ¶ 9415, 289 F.2d 490; *W.W. Marett v. U.S.,* 63-2 USTC ¶ 9806, 325 F.2d 28 (5th Cir., 1963); Rev. Rul. 75-160, 1975-1 CB 112.

[28] Reg. § 1.368-2(e).

[29] Rev. Rul. 82-34, 1982-1 CB 59.

[30] Rev. Rul. 77-238, 1977-2 CB 115.

[31] *Microdot, Inc. v. U.S.,* 84-1 USTC ¶ 9262, 728 F.2d 593 (2nd Cir., 1984).

.06 Type F Reorganizations

A type F reorganization is a mere change in the identity, form, or place of organization of one corporation, however effected.[32] For transactions occurring before September 1, 1982, more than one corporation could be involved in a type F reorganization. However, generally for transactions occurring after August 31, 1982, only one corporation may be involved. Prior to the 1982 law change, the reincorporation of a corporation into another was considered a type F reorganization. Since one corporation is defined as one operating company, reincorporation should continue to get type F status.

> **Example 12-18.** Colorado Electronics Co. moved to New Mexico and reincorporated as New Mexico Electronics, Inc. Even though two corporations are involved, only one operating company is involved. Hence, it would qualify as a type F reorganization.

Overlap of Type F with Other Types of Reorganizations

Prior to September 1, 1982, a transaction might have qualified as several other types of reorganizations in addition to type F. The IRS ruled that if a type F also qualified as a type A, C, or D, that the type F would predominate.[33] This was important because if designated as a type F, the same tax year would continue and all of the tax attributes would also continue. However, since passage of the one corporation rule, it is difficult to envision many situations where a type A, C, or D reorganization could qualify as a type F.[34] One commentator has noted that fusion of an operating subsidiary with its passive holding company parent might still qualify as a type F (i.e., there might be only one operating company involved).[35]

Since a type F changes little in substance, the tax year remains unchanged, and net operating losses and other tax attributes are unaffected. Also, Code Sec. 1244 designation is unaffected.[36] Since there is no change in stockholders, the IRS has ruled that an S corporation election also remains intact.[37]

¶ 1205 Judicial Doctrines

The courts have applied various precepts which have become prerequisites to the achievement of a tax-free reorganization. These judicial doctrines (some have also been codified) include:

- Continuity of interest;

---

[32] Code Sec. 368(a)(1)(F).
[33] Rev. Rul. 57-276, 1957-1 CB 126; also see *Dunlap & Associates v. Commr.*, 47 TC 542, Dec. 28,354 (1967).
[34] In Rev. Rul. 87-66, 1987-2 CB 168, the IRS ruled that a reorganization wherein a foreign corporation reincorporated in the U.S., qualified as both a type D and a type F.

[35] Boris I. Bittker and James E. Eustice, *Federal Income Taxation of Corporations and Shareholders,* Warren, Gorham, and Lamont, 1987, p. 14-100.
[36] Reg. § 1.1244(d)-3(d)(1).
[37] Rev. Rul. 64-250, 1964-2 CB 333.

- Continuity of business enterprise;

- Sound business purpose;

- The step-transaction doctrine; and

- A plan of reorganization.

.01 Continuity of Interest

Reorganizations are granted tax-free treatment based on the premise that the stockholders' positions are essentially unchanged, i.e., they remain equity owners in the new entity. The continuity of interest doctrine was originally created by judicial fiat in *Cortland*.[38] Continuity of interest requires that in substance a substantial part of the value of the proprietary interests in the target corporation be preserved in the reorganization.[39]

Thus, complying with the continuity of interest doctrine is very important; failure to comply creates a taxable sale instead of a reorganization. In deciding whether continuity of interest has been accomplished, the relevant questions to be answered are:

1. What kind of stock must be issued to the stockholders in order for them to retain a proprietary interest?

2. How much of the consideration must be in stock?

3. How long must the former owners retain an interest in the new entity?

The answers to questions (1) and (2) are easy in the case of a type B, C, or D reorganization, since the Code specifies limitations on the type of consideration which may be given. Recall, for example, that in a C reorganization at least 80 percent of the consideration given must be voting stock. Further, since as previously mentioned, continuity of interest need not be present in a type E reorganization, only a type A reorganization is affected by the first two aspects of the continuity of interest requirement.

The courts have held that nonvoting preferred stock meets the continuity of interest requirement because, "The right of management is only one of the powers incident to ownership and that power may be waived or delegated."[40]

As to how much of the consideration need be in stock, the IRS has indicated that at least 50 percent of the consideration must be in the form of voting stock of the target corporation.[41] However, *each* shareholder need

---

[38] *Cortland Speciality Co. v. Commr.*, 3 USTC ¶ 980, 60 F.2d 937 (2nd Cir., 1932).
[39] Reg. § 1.368-2(e)(1).
[40] See, for example, *Rosensteel v. Commr.*, 46 BTA 1184, Dec. 12,534 (1942), aff'd (CA-3) 134 F.2d 334, 43-1 USTC ¶ 9351.

[41] Reg. § 1.368-1(e)(6), Example 1. However, courts have allowed less than 50% to be in stock. See, e.g., *John A. Nelson Co. v. Helvering*, 36-1 USTC ¶ 9019, 296 US 374, 56 SCt 273 (USSC 1935).

not receive 50 percent of his or her compensation in stock. The continuity of interest doctrine need only be satisfied in the aggregate.[42]

> **Example 12-19.** Rick Towns and Kate Grant are 70 percent and 30 percent owners of Blue Ridge Bottlers, Inc. Desiring to be part of a larger enterprise, the company is merged into Southeast Distributors Co. Towns receives voting stock in Southeast Distributors Co. for his stock; Grant receives cash. The continuity of interest doctrine would be satisfied by this form of consideration.

An obvious way to get around the consideration requirement would be to have the corporation redeem some stock before the reorganization. However, any stock which is redeemed or disposed of before or after the reorganization is included in determining the 50 percent requirement.[43]

> **Example 12-20.** Assume the same facts as in Example 12-19, except that before the merger the corporation redeemed all of the stock held by Grant, and Southeast Distributors Co. then issued 50 percent stock and 50 percent cash to Towns. Since 65 percent of the consideration given (30% + .5 (70%)) was in cash, the merger would not meet the continuity of interest rule. The matter would have to be litigated for Grant and Towns to have any chance of satisfaction.

As to how long the former owners must retain an interest, the IRS has ruled, in a now obsolete revenue ruling, that five years of unrestricted rights of ownership is long enough.[44] However, if nontax reasons motivate the sale and it is not part of the overall plan, the continuity of interest may be met in a shorter time period. For example, in *Penrod,* unhappy stockholders sold over 90 percent of the stock that they received only eight months after the mergers, but the Tax Court ruled that continuity of interest was met.[45]

.02 Continuity of Business Enterprise

In order to have a reorganization in substance as well as in form, the business activity of the acquired company must be continued. Continuity of business enterprise is met by the acquiring company either continuing the acquired corporation's historic business or by using a significant portion of the acquired company's historic business assets in a business.[46] The rationale is "to ensure that reorganizations are limited to readjustments of continuing interests in property under modified corporate form. . . ."[47] On the other hand, the receipt of a new ownership interest in an entity that retains none of the business attributes of the shareholder's former corporation is more closely akin to a sale or liquidation than to a mere adjustment in the form of ownership.[48]

---

[42] Rev. Rul. 66-224, 1966-2 CB 114.
[43] Reg. § 1.368-1(e)(1)(ii) and (e)(6).
[44] Rev. Rul. 66-23, 1966-1 CB 67.
[45] *Penrod v. Commr.,* 88 TC 1415, Dec. 43,941 (1987).

[46] Reg. § 1.368-1(d)(1).
[47] *Id.*
[48] *Honbarrier, et ux. v. Commr.,* 115 TC 300, Dec. 54,070 (2000).

Generally, a corporation's "historic business" is the business it has conducted most recently. If the company has more than one line of business, not all need be continued, but only a significant line of business.[49]

A corporation's "historic business assets" are the assets used in its historic business, including stock and securities and intangible operating assets such as goodwill, patents, and trademarks, whether or not they have a tax basis.[50]

> **Example 12-21.** Simtemp, Inc., manufactures both auto parts and computers, each business being of about equal value. After merger into Octock Co., the auto parts business was sold, but the computer business continued. Continuity of business enterprise is achieved.

> **Example 12-22.** Tatum Corp. manufactures farm machinery and Perez Inc. operates a lumber mill. Tatum merges into Perez. Perez disposes of Tatum's assets immediately after the merger as part of the plan of reorganization. Perez does not continue Tatum's farm machinery business. Continuity of business enterprise is lacking.[51]

The IRS has ruled that the acquired corporation's business must be continued rather than the acquiring corporation's business.[52]

The Tax Court has held that there was no continuity of business enterprise where the transferee corporation had a preconceived plan to sell all of the assets of the transferor corporation, and where only a small part of the transferor corporation's assets had, in fact, been transferred.[53]

Can the continuity of business enterprise be met if the acquired corporation is insolvent? The Sixth Circuit, in overruling the Tax Court, said that insolvency was not a factor so long as there were assets left in the business which were sufficiently valuable to make the continuation of the business, albeit in a changed manner, worthwhile.[54]

.03 Sound Business Purpose

The sound business purpose doctrine stems from the landmark case of *Gregory v. Helvering*. In that case, the taxpayer devised a sophisticated scheme to avoid dividend treatment on a transaction. Mrs. Gregory owned all of the stock of a corporation which in turn owned 1,000 shares of stock in another corporation. Mrs. Gregory wished to have the stock herself so that she could sell it. Having the corporation distribute the stock to her would have resulted in dividend treatment. Therefore, she organized a new corporation to which the 1,000 shares of stock were transferred. Stock in the new corporation was transferred to Mrs. Gregory, thus meeting the requirements for a spin-off. Six days after the new corporation was formed, it was liquidated, and its only asset, the 1,000 shares of stock, was distributed to Mrs. Gregory, who immediately sold it. Although the transactions met the

---

[49] Reg. § 1.368-1(d)(2).
[50] Reg. § 1.368-1(d)(3).
[51] Reg. § 1.368-1(d)(5), Example 5.
[52] Rev. Rul. 81-25, 1981-1 CB 132.

[53] *Standard Realization Co. v. Commr.*, 10 TC 708, Dec. 16,361 (1948).
[54] *Laure v. Commr.*, 81-2 USTC ¶ 9517, 653 F.2d 253 (6th Cir., 1981).

letter if not the spirit of the law, the Supreme Court held that the reorganization had no business or corporate purpose, but was instead, "a mere device which put on the form of a corporate reorganization as a disguise for concealing its real character."[55]

In the context of reorganizations, sound business purpose means that in addition to literal compliance with Code Sec. 368, the reorganization must have a legitimate business purpose. This doctrine is also reflected in the regulations. The regulations state, "Such transaction (plan of reorganization) and such acts must be an ordinary and necessary incident of the conduct of the enterprise and must provide for a continuation of the enterprise. A scheme, which involves an abrupt departure from normal reorganization procedure in connection with a transaction on which the imposition of tax is imminent, such as a mere device that puts on the form of a corporate reorganization as a disguise for concealing its real character, and the object and accomplishment of which is the consummation of a preconceived plan having no business purpose or corporate purpose, is not a plan of reorganization."[56]

Merely because the transaction reduces taxes does not mean that there is an absence of a business purpose. The Tax Court has repeatedly ruled that if the transaction has a business purpose, the result of tax minimization does not render the business purpose ineffective.[57]

Examples of motives which constitute a sound business purpose include:

- A high technology business is separated from another business upon the recommendation of an underwriter;[58]

- A highly unprofitable regulated business is separated from a more profitable business in order to help justify a rate increase;[59]

- A serious dispute creates a situation where the parties are so antagonistic that the normal operations of the business are affected;[60]

- The conversion of common to preferred to avoid the expense of redeeming the stock, conversion of preferred to common to simplify the capital structure, and where the motive was to reduce potential estate taxes;[61] and

- A recapitalization to eliminate preferred stock arrearages.[62]

---

[55] *Gregory v. Helvering*, 35-1 USTC ¶ 9043, 293 US 465, 55 S.Ct. 266 (USSC, 1935). This perhaps most famous of all tax cases has had an impact far beyond the tax status of reorganizations. The case formed the basis for the concept of substance over form, i.e., the idea that the essence of a transaction will be examined to determine its true impact, and also the related concept of a "sham transaction," i.e., a transaction without a business purpose.
[56] Reg. § 1.368-1(c).

[57] See, for example, *Munroe v. Commr.*, 39 BTA 685, Dec. 10,653 (1939); and *Ardbern Co. Ltd. v. Commr.*, 41 BTA 910, Dec. 11,072 (1940).
[58] Rev. Rul. 82-130, 1982-2 CB 83.
[59] Rev. Rul. 82-131, 1982-2 CB 83.
[60] Rev. Rul. 69-460, 1969-2 CB 51.
[61] Rev. Rul. 77-238, 1977-2 CB 115; Letter Ruling 8035014.
[62] *Kaufman v. Commr.*, 55 TC 1046, Dec. 30,689 (1971).

Examples of motives which *did not* constitute a sound business purpose include:

- A merger where the real purpose was to take advantage of a predecessor's NOL carryforward;[63] and

- A taxpayer contributed stock options to a new corporation which dissolved after a second corporation was formed and the taxpayer received the exercised stock in liquidation.[64]

Although the lack of a business purpose can be used by the IRS to deny tax-free reorganization status, a taxpayer who prefers the transaction to be *taxable* apparently may not use the lack of a sound business purpose to treat the transaction as taxable. The Tax Court, in *Golden Nugget,* in rejecting the taxpayer's argument that the transaction was not a reorganization because it lacked a sound business purpose, said, "Petitioner has cited no case in which the doctrine has been successfully asserted by a *taxpayer* seeking to avoid the consequences of *its own* transaction . . . and we question whether the doctrine can be so employed."[65]

.04 The Step Transaction Doctrine

If a series of steps are so related so as to constitute in substance a single transaction, the courts will apply the step transaction doctrine, i.e., they will disregard the effect of the individual steps, but instead will compare the results before the steps with the results after the steps. In an early Supreme Court case, the Court ruled that "transitory phases of an arrangement frequently are disregarded under these sections of the revenue acts where they add nothing of substance to the complete affair."[66]

Example 12-23. Monarch Ski Resorts Co. wished to acquire approximately 60 percent of the assets of Wolf Creek Resorts Co. Since 60 percent is not enough to effect a type C reorganization, 40 percent of the assets are distributed in a complete redemption to a stockholder of Wolf Creek. Monarch then issued voting stock for the remaining assets of Wolf Creek which distributed the stock to its remaining stockholders and then dissolved. If the steps are viewed separately, the result would be a Code Sec. 302(b)(3) redemption and a type C reorganization. If the two steps are viewed as one, however, not enough assets were transferred to qualify as a type C reorganization. This is likely how the courts would rule.

The Supreme Court has stated, "It would be wholly inconsistent . . . to hold that the essential character of a transaction, and its tax impact, should

[63] *Wortham Machinery Co. v. Commr.,* 75-2 USTC ¶ 9665, 521 F.2d 160 (10th Cir., 1975).

[64] *Franklin v. Commr.,* 34 BTA 927, Dec. 9462 (1936).

[65] *Golden Nugget, Inc. v. Commr.,* 83 TC 28, Dec. 41,345 (1984).

[66] *Helvering v. Alabama Asphaltic Limestone Co.,* 42-1 USTC ¶ 9245, 315 US 179, 62 SCt 540 (USSC, 1942).

remain not only undeterminable but unfixed for an indefinite and unlimited period in the future, awaiting events that might or might not happen. This requirement that the character of a transaction be determinable does not mean that the entire divestiture must necessarily occur within a single tax year. It does, however, mean that if one transaction is to be characterized as a 'first step' there must be a binding commitment to take the later steps."[67]

The existence of an overall plan does not in itself result in the application of the step transaction doctrine. The Tax Court has said, "Whether invoked as a result of 'the binding commitment,' 'interdependence,' or 'end result' tests, the doctrine combines a series of individually meaningless steps into a single transaction."[68]

The IRS has applied the step transaction doctrine especially vigorously to type D reorganizations. It ruled that a spin-off of one of a corporation's two businesses followed by a transfer of the new company's stock to another corporation for its voting stock was not a type D and a type B reorganization, as the taxpayer would wish, but instead was a taxable sale.[69] Note that if the step transaction is applied in these circumstances, a type B reorganization would not result because control of the original corporation was not obtained.

.05 A Plan of Reorganization

Code Sec. 368 contains no reference to a plan of reorganization. However, Code Sec. 361, which provides authority for nonrecognition of gains and losses arising from reorganization, refers to "in pursuance of the plan of reorganization."[70] Further, the regulations for Code Sec. 368 do discuss the term, stating that a "plan of reorganization has reference to a consummated transaction specifically defined as a reorganization under Code Sec. 368(a)." The term is not be construed as broadening the definition of "reorganization" as set forth in Code Sec. 368(a), but is taken as limiting the nonrecognition of gain or loss to such exchanges or distributions as are directly a part of the transaction specifically described as a reorganization in Code Sec. 368(a). Moreover, the transaction, or series of transactions, embraced in a plan of reorganization must not only come within the specific language of Code Sec. 368(a), but the readjustments involved in the exchanges or distributions effected in the consummation thereof must be undertaken for reasons germane to the continuation of the business of a corporation that is a party to the reorganization.[71]

The records to be kept and the information filing requirements are as follows:[72]

---

[67] *Commr. v. Gordon*, 68-1 USTC ¶ 9383, 391 US 83, 88 SCt 1517 (USSC, 1968).
[68] *Esmark v. Commr.*, 90 TC 171, Dec. 44,548 (1988).

[69] Rev. Rul. 54-96, 1954-1 CB 111.
[70] Code Sec. 361(a).
[71] Reg. § 1.368-2(g).
[72] Reg. § 1.368-3.

1. The plan of reorganization must be adopted by all corporations involved and must appear on the official records of the corporation. All corporations involved must file with their tax returns a statement disclosing all pertinent facts, including:

    a. A copy of the plan of reorganization along with a statement executed under penalties of perjury showing the purposes and the details of all relevant transactions.

    b. A complete statement of the cost or other basis of all property transferred incident to the plan.

    c. A statement of the amount of stock or securities or other property or money received, including a statement of all distributions made. The amount is to be the fair market value at the date of the exchange.

    d. A statement of the amount and nature of any liabilities assumed and the amount and nature of any liabilities to which any property acquired is subject.

2. Each noncorporate taxpayer who receives stock, securities, or other property or money in a tax-free reorganization must file a statement with his or her income tax return which discloses all pertinent facts, including:

    a. A statement of the cost or other basis of the stock or securities transferred in the exchange.

    b. A statement in full of the amount of stock or securities and other property or money received from the exchange, including any liabilities assumed and any liabilities to which property received is subject. The amount of each kind of stock or securities and other property (other than liabilities assumed) received is to be the fair market value at the date of the exchange.

3. Permanent records in substantial form are to be kept by every taxpayer in the reorganization showing the cost or other basis of the transferred property and the amount of stock or securities and other property received (including any liabilities assumed on the exchange, or any liabilities to which any of the properties received were subject), in order to facilitate the determination of gain or loss from a subsequent disposition of such stock or securities and other property received from the exchange.

¶ 1207 Tax Impact of Reorganizations

Those involved in tax planning need to know what the immediate and long-term impacts of reorganizations are on the affected parties, i.e., the acquiring and acquired corporations, and the shareholders. The various rules governing carryover of tax attributes are discussed subsequently.

.01 Tax Impact on the Acquiring Corporation

Tax consequences, in general, to the acquiring corporation are provided by Code Sec. 1032, which states that no gain or loss is recognized to a corporation on the receipt of money or other property in exchange for its stock.[73] However, if the acquiring corporation also transfers other property, it must recognize gain or loss on that property. Note that the acquiring company can transfer property only in an A or C reorganization.

> **Example 12-24.** Red Lakes Marina Co. transferred voting stock worth $450,000 and a building worth $50,000 in exchange for all of the assets of Lake Leisure, Inc. The building had a basis of $75,000. Red Lakes Marina would recognize a $25,000 loss on the transfer of the property.

The basis to the acquiring corporation is a carryover basis, i.e., it is the basis in the hand of the acquired corporation increased by any gain recognized by the *acquired* corporation.[74] However, gain recognized to the transferor as a result of the assumption of a liability in excess of basis cannot increase the basis of the property to the corporation above the fair market value of the property.[75]

> **Example 12-25.** Assume the same facts as in Example 12-24 and that the assets of Lake Leisure, Inc. have a basis of $325,000 but are worth $500,000. Basis to Red Lakes Marina is the carryover basis of $325,000.

.02 Tax Impact on the Acquired Corporation

No gain or loss is recognized to the target corporation when it exchanges property for stock and securities.[76] However, if other property is received by the acquired corporation, the rules are as follows:[77]

- Losses are never recognized; and

- Gains are not recognized if the property is distributed to the shareholders. If the corporation does not distribute the property, gain is recognized, but only to the extent of the sum of the fair market value of the property and money received that is not distributed.

> **Example 12-26.** Grey Wolf Theatres transferred all of its assets worth $1,500,000 and having a basis of $1,100,000 to Elegant Theatres Co. in exchange for $1,000,000 of voting stock and $500,000 of 15-year bonds. Grey Wolf Theatres does not recognize any gain as a result of the transaction.

> **Example 12-27.** Assume the same facts as in Example 12-26, except that the consideration is $1,000,000 of voting stock and

---

[73] Code Sec. 1032(a).
[74] Code Sec. 362(b).
[75] Code Sec. 362(d).

[76] Code Sec. 361(a).
[77] Code Sec. 361(b).

$500,000 of cash and that Grey Wolf transfers all of the consideration received to its shareholders. Despite the receipt of cash, Grey Wolf does not recognize any gain.

> **Example 12-28.** Assume the same facts as in Example 12-27, except that Grey Wolf retains the $500,000 of cash. Of the total realized gain of $400,000 ($1,000,000 + $500,000 − $1,100,000), all $400,000 would have to be recognized.

Relief of the acquired corporation's liabilities generally does not create a tax problem. The relief of a liability is not treated as boot unless the principal purpose of the transaction was tax avoidance.[78]

> **Example 12-29.** Decade 22 Realty transferred assets with a basis of $2,000,000, a fair market value of $3,000,000, and subject to a mortgage of $600,000 for voting stock worth $2,400,000. The transaction was not motivated by tax avoidance motives. The relief of the mortgage is not treated as boot; hence, there is no gain to be recognized.

The relief of a mortgage in excess of the basis of property transferred is a problem in reorganizations only if it is a type D reorganization. In that event, the excess of the mortgage over the basis must be recognized as a gain.[79]

A liquidating distribution in connection with a reorganization generally does not create taxable income for the liquidating corporation. In a type C reorganization or an acquisitive D reorganization, the target corporation must liquidate. Most of the liquidation proceeds necessarily have to be stock, securities, and property from the acquiring corporation. The basis of this property to the target corporation would be fair market value as of the date of distribution to the target corporation. Hence, there should be little if any gain to be recognized. Losses are not recognized on the distribution of property acquired in a reorganization.[80]

> **Example 12-30.** Assume the same facts as in Example 12-26, except that Grey Wolf retained inventory with a basis of $100,000 and a fair market value of $120,000. Also assume that the consideration received from Elegant Theatres Co. was $1,000,000 of voting stock and $500,000 of stock in New Films, Inc., having a basis of $320,000. Elegant Theatres (the acquiring corporation) would have to recognize a gain of $180,000 on the acquisition. When Grey Wolf distributes the inventory and stock to its shareholders, no gain would be recognized on the distribution of the stock (assuming the value remained at $500,000). However, Grey Wolf would recognize a gain on the inventory.

---

[78] Code Sec. 357(a) and (b).
[79] Code Sec. 357(c).

[80] Code Sec. 361(c)(1).

.03 Tax Impact on the Shareholders

The tax impact on shareholders is covered in Code Secs. 354, 355, 356, 357, and 358. No gain or loss is recognized if stock or securities are exchanged *solely* for stock or securities in the acquiring corporation or other party (e.g., a parent) to the reorganization.[81]

> **Example 12-31.** Assume the same facts as in Example 12-26, except that Grey Wolf receives only voting stock worth $1,500,000 from Elegant Theatres and that it transfers in liquidation the voting stock to Greer Grey, its sole shareholder. Greer's basis in the stock she surrendered was $600,000. Although Greer has a realized gain of $900,000, none is recognized.

The nontaxability status does not apply if the principal amount of any securities received exceeds the principal amount of securities surrendered.[82]

> **Example 12-32.** Assume the same facts as in Example 12-26 and that Grey Wolf Theatres transfers in liquidation the voting stock and the bonds which were worth $400,000 (and whose principal amount was $500,000) to Greer Grey, its sole shareholder. Greer surrenders stock with a basis of $400,000 and a bond whose principal amount was $200,000. The excess principal amount received is $300,000. Thus, the boot received is $300,000/$500,000 × $400,000, or $240,000.

The receipt of "boot," i.e., property other than stock or securities, in a reorganization causes gain (but not loss) to be recognized to the shareholders.[83] The gain cannot exceed the boot received.[84] For this purpose, non-qualified preferred stock is not treated as stock or securities, but rather as "other property."[85]

> **Example 12-33.** Assume the same facts as in Example 12-30 and that the $1,000,000 of voting stock, inventory worth $120,000, and $500,000 of New Films, Inc., stock was transferred to Greer Grey in exchange for her stock having a basis to her of $600,000. Her realized gain, is $1,020,000 ($1,000,000 + $120,000 + $500,000 − $600,000). Her recognized gain, however, would be limited to the boot of $620,000.

If the exchange has the effect of a distribution of a dividend, then the gain recognized is treated as a dividend to the extent of each shareholder's ratable share of E&P. Any remaining gain is treated as a gain from the exchange of property.[86]

Basis to the shareholders of the stock and securities received is essentially carried over from the basis of the stock and securities exchanged. However, the basis is decreased by:[87]

---

[81] Code Sec. 354(a)(1).
[82] Code Sec. 354(a)(2).
[83] Code Sec. 356(a) and (c).
[84] Code Sec. 356(a).

[85] Code Sec. 356(e).
[86] Code Sec. 356(a)(2).
[87] Code Sec. 358(a)(1)(A).

- The fair market value of property (not money) received;

- Money received; and

- Any losses recognized on the exchange.

Basis is increased by:[88]

- Any amount treated as a dividend; and

- Any nondividend gain recognized on the exchange.

The above calculation yields only the total basis of the stock and securities. If more than one class of stock is received, or if both stock and securities are received, basis is allocated in proportion to the fair market value of the stock and securities received.[89]

Example 12-34.[90] C, an individual, owns stock of corporation Y with a basis of $5,000 and owns a security issued by Corporation Y in the principal amount of $5,000 with a basis of $5,000. In a transaction to which Code Sec. 354 is applicable, C exchanges the stock of Corporation Y for stock of Corporation Z with a value of $6,000, and he exchanges the security of Corporation Y for stock of Corporation Z worth $1,500 and a security of Corporation Z in the principal amount of $4,500 worth $4,500. No gain is recognized to C on either exchange. The basis of the stock of Corporation Z received for the stock of Corporation Y is $5,000. The basis of the stock and security of Corporation Z received in exchange for the security of Corporation Y are $1,250 and $3,750, respectively.

Example 12-35. D, an individual, owns stock in Corporation M with a basis of $15,000, worth $40,000, and owns a security issued by Corporation M in the principal amount of $5,000 with a basis of $4,000. In a transaction qualifying under Code Sec. 356 (so far as such section relates to Code Sec. 355), D exchanges the security of Corporation M for a security of Corporation O (a controlled corporation) in the principal amount of $5,000, worth $5,000, and exchanges one-half of his stock of Corporation M for stock of Corporation O, worth $15,000, and a security of Corporation O in the principal amount of $5,000, worth $5,000. All of the stock and securities of Corporation O are distributed pursuant to the transaction. D realized a gain of $12,500 on the exchange of the stock of Corporation M for the stock and security of Corporation O, of which $5,000 is recognized. D also realized a gain of $1,000 on the exchange of a security of Corporation M for a security of Corporation O, none of which is recognized. The basis of his stock of Corporation M held before the transaction is allocated 20/35ths to the stock of Corporation M held after the transaction and 15/35ths to the stock of Corporation O. The basis of

---

[88] Code Sec. 358(a)(1)(B).
[89] Reg. § 1.358-2(a)(2) and (3).

[90] Examples 12-34 and 12-35 are taken from Reg. § 1.358-2.

¶ 1207.03

the security of Corporation O received in exchange for his security of Corporation M is $4,000, the basis of the security of Corporation M exchanged. The basis of the security of Corporation O received with respect to D's stock of Corporation M is $5,000, its fair market value.

¶ 1209 Carryforward of Tax Attributes

Code Sec. 381 covers carryovers of tax attributes for most reorganizations. Specifically, Code Sec. 381 applies to Code Sec. 332 (liquidations of subsidiaries) and, under Code Sec. 368, types A, C, nondivisive D, F, and G reorganizations.[91]

.01 Carryovers of Net Operating Losses

There are several limitations applicable to net operating carryovers from reorganized companies.

1. The tax year to which the NOL carryover is first carried is the first tax year ending after the distribution, i.e., the acquiring company cannot apply the transferor's NOL to a carryback year.[92]

    Example 12-36. Orange Ball Moving Co. was merged into Hercules Van Lines, Inc., on May 3, 2001. Hercules Van Lines, Inc., is on a March 31 fiscal year. At the time of liquidation, Orange Ball Moving Co. had an NOL carryover of $200,000. The earliest year that Hercules can use the NOL carryover is the year beginning on April 1, 2001 and ending on March 31, 2002.

2. The portion of the NOL carryover which may be used by the acquiring company in the first year is limited to the portion of the taxable income of the acquirer times the number of days in the tax year after the distribution over the total days in the tax year.[93]

    Example 12-37. Assume the same facts as in Example 12-36 and that Hercules has taxable income of $182,500 for the year ending March 31, 2002. The NOL deduction for the year ending March 31, 2002 is limited to $182,500 × 332/365, or $166,000. The remaining NOL of $34,000 is carried over to the next tax year.

3. NOLs generated after the distribution cannot be carried back to tax years of the transferor corporation.[94] The purpose of this restriction is to prevent unprofitable companies from acquiring a profitable corporation so as to carryback losses and obtain refunds of taxes paid in previous years by the profitable corporation.

---

[91] Code Sec. 381(a).
[92] Code Sec. 381(c)(1)(A).

[93] Code Sec. 381(c)(1)(B).
[94] Code Sec. 381(b)(3).

Example 12-38. Profit, Inc., has generated taxable income of $1,000,000 for each of the last three years. It is merged into Poor Co. Poor Co. has a NOL of $2,000,000 the first year after liquidation of the subsidiary. The $2,000,000 loss cannot be carried back to a previous year of Profit, Inc.

4. NOL carryforwards are limited where there has been an ownership change.[95] If there has been an ownership change (described below), the yearly limitation equals the value of the old loss corporation multiplied by the long-term tax-exempt rate.[96] The "value of the old loss corporation" is generally the value of the stock immediately before the ownership change.[97] The "long-term tax-exempt rate" is the highest of the adjusted federal long-term rates in effect for any month in the three-month period ending with the calendar month in which the change occurs and is published monthly by the IRS.[98]

Example 12-39. Assume that there has been an ownership change in connection with a reorganization and that the acquired corporation has a NOL carryover of $200,000 and a value of $500,000. Also, assume a long-term tax-exempt rate of seven percent. The maximum amount of carryover which may be used in a year is $500,000 × .07, or $35,000.

Ownership changes in the context of a reorganization occur if immediately after any "owner shift involving a 5 percent shareholder," or equity structure shift, the percentage of the stock of the loss corporation owned by one or more 5 percent shareholders has increased by more than 50 percentage points over the lowest percentage of stock owned by the shareholder or shareholders during the testing period.[99] The testing period is the three-year period ending on the day of any owner shift involving a 5 percent shareholder or equity structure shift.[100] An "owner shift involving a 5 percent shareholder" occurs whenever there is any change in stock ownership and the change affected the percentage of stock owned by any person who was a 5 percent owner either before or after the change.[101] After all 5 percent shareholders are identified, those shareholders whose percentage ownership has increased are aggregated and compared with the aggregate of each shareholder's lowest percentage interest during the testing period. If the total increase exceeds 50 percentage points, the Code Sec. 382 limitations will apply. All stock owned by less than five percent shareholders is treated as a single 5 percent shareholder.[102] The term "equity structure shift" means any reorganization (but not a type D or G reorganization, unless the requirements of Code Sec. 354(b)(1) are met, or a type F reorganization).[103]

---

[95] Code Sec. 382(a).
[96] Code Sec. 382(b)(1).
[97] Code Sec. 382(e).
[98] Code Sec. 382(f).
[99] Code Sec. 382(g)(1).

[100] Code Sec. 382(i).
[101] Code Sec. 382(g)(2).
[102] Code Sec. 382(g)(4)(A).
[103] Code Sec. 382(g)(3)(A).

5. If there has been an ownership change and the continuity of business requirement is not met, the NOL carryover will be totally disallowed.[104] To meet the "continuity of business requirement," the parent corporation must continue the business enterprise for at least two years after the liquidation, or continue to use a significant portion of the subsidiary's assets in a business.[105]

6. There is a built-in gains limitation.[106] Code Sec. 384 closes a loophole that is not addressed by Code Sec. 381 or 382. Without Code Sec. 384, it would be possible for an unprofitable company to, after a type A, C, or D reorganization, sell off the transferor corporation's appreciated assets and offset its NOL against the resulting gains. Code Sec. 384, however, provides generally that in a reorganization, income for any recognition period tax year (to the extent that it is attributable to recognized built-in gains) may not be offset by pre-acquisition loss of the acquiring company.[107] However, if the acquiring company has met the 80 percent stock ownership requirement at all times during the five-year period ending on the date of acquisition (or the period in which the subsidiary has been in existence, if shorter), then the built-in gains limitation does not apply.[108]

.02 Capital Loss Carryovers

The Code Sec. 381 limitations applicable to net operating loss carryovers also apply to capital loss carryovers.[109]

.03 Earnings and Profits

In general, the E&P of the transferor corporation is considered to have been received by the acquiring company as of the close of the date of distribution.[110] However, a deficit in the E&P of the transferor company may only be used to offset E&P accumulated after the transfer.[111] E&P for the acquiring company during the year of reorganization is prorated daily to determine the amount accumulated after the liquidation.[112]

.04 Business Credit Carryovers

Generally, any business credits, e.g., the investment tax credit, the targeted jobs credit, etc., may be carried forward, subject to certain limitations during the year of reorganization.[113]

.05 Accounting Methods

The acquiring corporation must use the method of accounting used by the transferor corporation on the date of transfer unless different methods

---

[104] Code Sec. 382(c).
[105] Reg. § 1.368-1(d)(1).
[106] Code Sec. 384.
[107] Code Sec. 384(a).
[108] Code Sec. 384(b).

[109] Code Sec. 381(c)(3).
[110] Code Sec. 381(c)(2)(A).
[111] Code Sec. 381(c)(2)(B).
[112] *Id.*
[113] Code Sec. 381(c)(24)-(26).

were used by several distributor or transferor corporations or by a distributor or transferor corporation and the acquiring corporation. If different methods were used, the acquiring corporation must use the method or combination of methods as follows:[114]

- If the business of the transferor corporation is continued by the acquiring corporation as a separate and distinct business, the method of accounting used by the transferor corporation must be continued, unless permission to change accounting methods is obtained from the IRS.[115]

- If the businesses are integrated into one business, a change of accounting method to the principal method is required.[116] The "principal method" is the accounting method used by the business with a majority of both the adjusted bases of the assets and the gross receipts for the most recent 12 consecutive months ending on or prior to the date of distribution.[117] If one business has more assets, but the other has more gross receipts, the corporation must request the IRS to determine the accounting method.[118]

---

[114] Code Sec. 381(c)(4); Reg. § 1.381(c)(4)-1(a).
[115] Reg. § 1.381(c)(4)-1(b)(2).
[116] Reg. § 1.381(c)(4)-1(b)(3).

[117] Reg. § 1.381(c)(4)-1(c)(2).

[118] *Id.*

Chapter 13

Partnership Sales, Distributions, and Liquidations

¶ 1301 Introduction

The differing concepts governing partnership taxation, i.e., the entity concept and the conduit rule, also guide partnership sales and liquidations. Under the entity concept, we would expect a partnership interest to be an indistinguishable interest in a mass of assets which would be considered a capital interest. And, in fact, a partnership interest is a capital asset.[1] However, under the conduit rule, we would expect unrealized ordinary income existing at the partnership level to pass through to the selling or liquidating partner. And, in fact, to the extent that a partnership has "751 assets," a sale or liquidation will result in ordinary income.

¶ 1303 Sale of a Partnership Interest

The proceeds from the sale of a partnership include, in addition to cash and fair market value of property, any partnership liabilities of which the partner is relieved.[2] Recall from Chapter 2 that the adjusted basis of a partnership interest includes a share of liabilities.

Example 13-1. Assume that a 50 percent partner has a $40,000 basis in a partnership whose only asset is land worth $150,000. The partnership then borrows $50,000 and immediately thereafter the partner sells her interest for $75,000 cash. The gain on the sale would be computed as follows:

Amount realized		
Cash		$ 75,000
Liabilities relieved of		25,000
Total		$100,000
Basis		
Original basis	$40,000	
Share of liabilities	25,000	65,000
Total gain		$ 35,000

The result would be the same as if the partnership had never borrowed the money, i.e., the gain then would have been $75,000 − 40,000 = $35,000.

---

[1] Code Sec. 741.

[2] Code Sec. 1001(b); Reg. § 1.001-2(a)(1).

Tax Tips and Pitfalls

Relief of debt is considered to be cash received during the year of sale. Thus, the presence of partnership debt increases the down payment and results in more gain being recognized during the year of sale if the installment method is used.

Example 13-2. Refer to Example 13-1 and assume that the partnership interest is sold on installment with $25,000 cash received as a down payment and $25,000 plus interest received in each of the next two tax years. The gross profit ratio would be $35,000/100,000 = 35 percent. Cash deemed received during the year of sale would equal $25,000 plus $25,000 of debt relief or a total of $50,000. Therefore, $17,500 of gain ($50,000 × .35) would be reported during the year of sale and an additional $8,750 for each of the next two years. If the money had not been borrowed, the gross profit percentage would be $35,000/75,000 = 46.667 percent. Each year $11,667 ($25,000 × .4667) would be reported. The existence of partnership debt accelerated the reporting of gains reported on the installment method.

The sale of a fiscal year partnership can, if sold at the wrong time, result in almost two years of income being reported in one year. Assume a January 31 FYE partnership that has $180,000 of income for the year ended January 31, 2000, and $192,000 for the year ended January 31, 2001. On December 15, 2000, Jeremy Shaw sells his 25 percent interest. On Shaw's calendar year 2000 return, he would report $45,000 of partnership income from the partnership year ending January 31, 2000, and $41,688 ($192,000 × .25 × 317/365) for the partial year 2000, or a total of $86,688. A sale in January 2001 would remove the problem of bunching.

¶ 1305 Section 751 Assets

The general rule that a partnership interest is a capital asset is not followed to the extent that the partnership has Section 751 assets. When a partnership interest is sold or exchanged, Section 751 assets are defined as:[3]

- Unrealized receivables; or

- Inventory items of the partnership.

"Unrealized receivables" includes, to the extent not previously includible in income under the method of accounting used by the partnership, any rights (contractual or otherwise) to payment for:[4]

- Goods delivered (or to be delivered) which are not capital assets; or

- Services rendered (or to be rendered).

---

[3] Code Sec. 751(a).   [4] Code Sec. 751(c).

Included in this definition are receivables of a cash basis taxpayer (which have a zero basis) and the deferred gross profit included in installment receivables.

In addition to receivables, the term includes:[5]

1. Recapture of mining exploration expenditures under Code Sec. 617;

2. Stock in a DISC as described in Code Sec. 992;

3. Recapture of depreciation on personal property under Code Sec. 1245;

4. Stock in certain foreign corporations as described in Code Sec. 1248;

5. Recapture of depreciation on real property under Code Sec. 1250;

6. Recapture of potential gain from farm recapture property as defined in Code Sec. 1251 (in effect before TRA '84);

7. Recapture of soil and water conservation expenditures on farm land under Code Sec. 1252;

8. Potential gain from franchises, trademarks, or trade names referred to in Code Sec. 1253(a);

9. Certain oil, gas, or geothermal property as described in Code Sec. 1254; and

10. The ordinary income element of market discount bonds as defined in Code Sec. 1278.

According to the regulations, unrealized receivables includes rights to payment for work or goods begun but incomplete at the time of sale or distribution.[6] The potential Code Sec. 1245 and 1250 gain is the amount which would result if the property were sold at fair market value.[7] Any arm's-length agreement between the buyer and seller or between the partnership and distributed partner will generally fix the fair market value.[8]

The term "inventory items of the partnership" is very broad. It includes, in addition to inventory, unrealized receivables and all other assets which, if sold, would result in ordinary income.[9] The only assets excluded are Section 1231 assets and capital assets.

In the case of distributions, inventory is considered a Section 751 asset only if it is substantially appreciated.[10] The items are considered "substan-

[5] *Id.*
[6] Reg. § 1.751-1(c)(1).
[7] Reg. § 1.751-1(c)(4).
[8] Reg. § 1.751-1(c)(3).
[9] Code Sec. 751(d)(2).
[10] Code Sec. 751(b)(1)(A).

tially appreciated" when the fair market value exceeds 120 percent of the adjusted basis of the property.[11] If inventory is acquired for the principal purpose of avoiding the 120 percent test, it is excluded in applying the 120 percent test.[12]

The term "substantially appreciated inventory" applies to the aggregate of all partnership inventory, rather than specific inventory items or specific groups. Therefore, the distribution of specific inventory items which are not appreciated in value is still considered to be a distribution of substantially appreciated inventory if the inventory as a whole is substantially appreciated. On the other hand, if the inventory as a whole is not substantially appreciated, a distribution of a specific inventory item which is appreciated would not constitute a distribution of substantially appreciated inventory.[13]

Inventory must be substantially appreciated only for distributions after August 5, 1997.[14] Inventory, whether or not substantially appreciated, will be classified as Section 751 property with respect to a sale or exchange of a partnership interest.

Example 13-3. The balance sheet of the DEF Partnership is as follows:

	Basis	FMV
Cash	$ 40,000	$ 40,000
Accounts Receivable	60,000	60,000
Inventory	90,000	160,000
Equipment	75,000	65,000
Total	$265,000	$325,000
Liabilities	$ 85,000	$ 85,000
Dinger, Capital	60,000	80,000
Enger, Capital	60,000	80,000
Farley, Capital	60,000	80,000
Total	$265,000	$325,000

In this case there are no unrealized receivables. The test to check for substantially appreciated inventory is as follows:

	Basis	FMV
Accounts Receivable	$ 60,000	$ 60,000
Inventory	90,000	160,000
Total	$150,000	$220,000

---

[11] Code Sec. 751(b)(3)(A).
[12] Code Sec. 751(b)(3)(B).
[13] Reg. § 1.751-1(d)(1).

[14] Act Sec. 1062, Taxpayer Relief Act of 1997 (P.L. 105-34), amending Code Secs. 751(a), (b) and (d).

The fair market value of the inventory exceeds basis by more than 20 percent ($220,000 is greater than $150,000 × 120 percent). Thus, the inventory is considered substantially appreciated, for this purpose. After August 5, 1997, inventory is substantially appreciated for sale or exchange purposes whether or not the 120 percent threshold is met.

.01 Determining the Characteristic of Gains/Losses if Code Sec. 751 Assets Are Present

If Section 751 assets are present when a partnership interest is sold, the proportionate share of the Section 751 gain is determined and reported by the partner as ordinary income. The remaining gain or loss will be a capital loss.

Example 13-4. Assume the same facts as in Example 13-3 and that Dinger sells his one-third interest to Gingham for $80,000 cash. Dinger's total realized gain is:

Amount realized		
Cash	$80,000	
Relief of debt ($85,000 × 1/3)	28,333	$108,333
Basis ($60,000 + 28,333)		88,333
Total gain realized		$ 20,000

The gain is broken down into:	
Ordinary income ($220,000 − 150,000) × 1/3	$ 23,333
Capital loss ($20,000 − 23,333)	$ (3,333)

If Code Sec. 751 assets are present, ordinary income results even if the transaction results in a total loss.

Example 13-5. Assume the same facts as in Example 13-4, except that the sale is for $55,000 cash. The total realized loss is:

Amount Realized		
Cash	$55,000	
Relief of debt ($85,000 × 1/3)	28,333	$ 83,333
Basis ($60,000 + 28,333)		88,333
Total realized loss		$ (5,000)

The loss breakdown would be as follows:	
Ordinary income ($220,000 − 150,000) × 1/3	23,333
Capital loss	$(28,333)

.02 Information Required with Return

A partner who sells or exchanges an interest in a partnership that has any Section 751 property must submit with his or her income tax return for the year sold a statement which describes the following:[15]

- Date of the sale or exchange;

- The amount of any gain or loss attributable to the Section 751 property; and

- The amount of any gain or loss attributable to capital gain or loss on the sale of the partnership interest.

Tax Tips and Pitfalls

The presence of Section 751 assets is undesirable if capital gains are sought (e.g., the taxpayer already has realized capital losses). Little can be done with unrealized receivables. However, recall that inventory must meet two tests to be considered substantially appreciated. Since zero basis receivables increase the probability of the inventory being substantially appreciated, collecting the receivables before selling a partnership interest may be helpful. Selling some of the inventory that is most appreciated may also help decrease the total appreciation below 20 percent.

¶ 1307 Cash Liquidations

When a partnership makes payments in complete liquidation of a partner's interest, Code Sec. 736 comes into play. The payments may be made due to the death of the partner, the reaching of retirement age, or simply a desire to terminate an interest in the partnership. In any case, payments made are allocated between payments made for the interest in the partnership (Section 736(b)) and other payments (Section 736(a)).[16] Payments under Section 736(a) are considered to be either:[17]

- A distributive share of partnership income if the amount of the payment is determined with regard to the income of the partnership; or

- A guaranteed payment if the amount is determined without regard to the income of the partnership.

If considered a distributive share of income, the amount reduces taxable income for the remaining partners. If deemed a guaranteed payment, the payments are deducted by the partnership to arrive at ordinary taxable income. In any case, Code Sec. 736(a) payments reduce the taxable profits of the partnership. A guaranteed payment to a partner is always

---

[15] Reg. § 1.751-1(a)(3).
[16] Code Sec. 736.

[17] Code Sec. 736(a).

taxed as ordinary income; a distributive share of income is taxed subject to the conduit rules applicable to partnerships (i.e., the retiring partner would report his or her share of capital gains, charitable contributions, etc.).

The definition of Code Sec. 736(a) payments depends on whether the partnership is a service partnership. Effective for partners dying or retiring on or after January 5, 1993, partnerships that are not service partnerships do not include any payments for property under Code Sec. 736(a), even if the property consists of unrealized receivables or goodwill.[18] However, unrealized receivables and goodwill remain Code Sec. 736(a) payments for service partnerships if:[19]

- Capital is not a material income-producing factor for the partnership; and

- The retiring or deceased partner was a general partner in the partnership.

Even service partnerships will no longer be able to deduct depreciation recapture as payments under Code Sec. 736(a). Although depreciation recapture is considered an unrealized receivable for purposes of Code Sec. 751, for purposes of Code Sec. 736, unrealized receivables include only income from the sale of ordinary income property (i.e., inventory) or from the provision of services which, under the accounting method of the business, have not been reported.[20]

Payments under Code Sec. 736(b) are entitled to capital gain treatment except for the portion that is considered to be for substantially appreciated inventory.[21]

> **Example 13-6.** Wayne Madison, a 20 percent partner in the Jefferson, Madison, & Monroe partnership, a retailing business, retired from the partnership for a cash payment of $20,000. The balance sheet is shown below:

Assets	Basis	FMV
Cash	$12,000	$ 12,000
Accounts receivable	4,000	4,000
Inventory	8,000	18,000
Equipment	12,000	19,000
Land	24,000	48,000
Goodwill	-0-	9,000
Total	$60,000	$110,000

---

[18] Act Sec. 13262(a), Revenue Reconciliation Act of 1993, amending Code Sec. 736(b).
[19] *Id.*

[20] Code Sec. 751(c).
[21] Code Sec. 736(b)(1).

Liabilities and Capital

Liabilities	$10,000	$ 10,000
Jefferson, Capital	20,000	40,000
Madison, Capital	10,000	20,000
Monroe, Capital	20,000	40,000
Total	$60,000	$110,000

The total realized gain is $10,000, computed as follows:

Amount realized

Cash		$ 20,000
Liabilities relieved of		2,000
		$ 22,000

Basis

Capital Account	$10,000	
Share of liabilities	2,000	12,000
Total gain		$ 10,000

In this example, all of the payments are property payments (Code Sec. 736(b) payments). The inventory and the equipment are Code Sec. 751 assets. Therefore, Madison's ordinary income is 20 percent of the appreciation in those assets, or 20 percent of $17,000, or $3,400. The remaining $6,600 of gain is a capital gain.

Example 13-7. Assume the same facts as in Example 13-6 except that the partnership is a service concern where capital is not a material income-producing factor, and the balance sheet is as follows:

Assets	Basis	FMV
Cash.................................	$24,000	$ 24,000
Accounts receivable	-0-	10,000
Equipment	12,000	19,000
Land	24,000	48,000
Goodwill	-0-	9,000
Total	$60,000	$110,000

Liabilities and Capital

Liabilities	$10,000	$ 10,000
Jefferson, Capital.........................	20,000	40,000
Madison, Capital	10,000	20,000
Monroe, Capital	20,000	40,000
Total..............................	$60,000	$110,000

Madison's share of the zero basis receivables constitutes a Code Sec. 736(a) payment. Therefore, the breakdown of the payments is as follows:

	Ordinary	Capital	Total
736(a) payments	$2,000	-0-	$ 2,000
736(b) payments	1,400	6,600	8,000
	$3,400	$6,600	$10,000

The partnership has a deduction for the $2,000 of Code Sec. 736(a) payments, but cannot deduct the ordinary income portion of the Code Sec. 736(b) payments.

¶ 1309 Installment Payments to the Retiring Partner

It is very common for retiring partners to be paid in installments. In that event, the payments must be allocated between Code Sec. 736(a) payments and Code Sec. 736(b) payments.

The allocation may be made in any manner to which the retiring partner and the remaining partners agree, so long as the total allocation to Code Sec. 736(b) payments does not exceed the fair market value of such property.[22]

Example 13-8. Assume the same facts as in Example 13-7, except that the $20,000 is to be paid in four yearly installments of $5,000 each, and that the first $18,000 is to be considered paid for Madison's interest in partnership property. The tax status of the payments is as follows:

---

[22] Reg. § 1.736-1(b)(5)(iii).

Year		Return of Capital	Capital Gains	Ordinary Income
1	12,000/20,000 × 7,000	$ 4,200		
	8,000/20,000 × 7,000 × 6,600/8,000 ...		$2,310	
	8,000/20,000 × 7,000 × 1,400/8,000 ...			$ 490
2	12,000/20,000 × 5,000	3,000		
	8,000/20,000 × 5,000 × 6,600/8,000 ...		1,650	
	8,000/20,000 × 5,000 × 1,400/8,000 ...			350
3	12,000/20,000 × 5,000	3,000		
	8,000/20,000 × 5,000 × 6,600/8,000 ...		1,650	
	8,000/20,000 × 5,000 × 1,400/8,000 ...			350
4	12,000 × 20,000 × 3,000...............	1,800		
	8,000 × 20,000 × 3,000 × 6,600/8,000 .		990	
	8,000 × 20,000 × 3,000 × 1,400/8,000 .			210
	736(a) payments......................			2,000
		$12,000	$6,600	$3,400

The partnership would have a $2,000 deduction in year four.

If there is no agreement as to the timing of the payment entered into, a *pro rata* portion of each payment is treated as being a distribution under Code Sec. 736(b), bearing the same ratio as the total fixed payments under Code Sec. 736(b) bear to the total fixed payments to be received.[23] If the total amount received in any year is less than required, the Code Sec. 736(b) payments are reduced first. Payments in later years are considered a payment of the deficient Code Sec.736(a) payments.[24]

Example 13-9. Assume the same facts as in Example 13-8 except that the partners do not enter into any agreement about allocating the payments. The allocation is as follows:

Year	Total	Return of Capital 54.545%	Capital Gains 30.000%	Ordinary Income 15.455%
1	$7,000	$ 3,818	$2,100	$1,082
2	5,000	2,727	1,500	773
3	5,000	2,728	1,500	772
4	5,000	2,727	1,500	773
Total	$22,000	$12,000	$6,600	$3,400

---

[23] Reg. § 1.736-1(b)(5)(i).   [24] *Id.*

Tax Tips and Pitfalls

It will be to the advantage of the partners to have the payments designated first as Code Sec. 736(a) payments, since an immediate deduction is thereby attained. Generally, the withdrawing partner would have the opposite motivation, but if the partner is retiring and will be in a lower tax bracket than usual, the impact may not be great. In any case, the matter could be a subject of negotiation between the partners.

¶ 1311 Contingent Payments

If a retiring partner receives payments which are not fixed in amount (e.g., a percent of net income), the return of capital method is used, i.e., first, the payments are a return of capital, second, a capital gain, and third, ordinary income.[25]

Example 13-10. Assume the same facts as in Example 13-8 except that Madison is to receive one-third of the profits for six years. The results are as follows:

Year	Net Profit	Return of Capital	Capital Gains	Ordinary Income	Total
1	$10,500	$ 3,500	$ —	$ —	$ 3,500
2	12,000	4,000	—	—	4,000
3	13,500	4,500	—	—	4,500
4	12,000	—	4,000	—	4,000
5	19,500	—	2,600	3,900	6,500
6	22,500	—	—	7,500	7,500
	$90,000	$12,000	$6,600	$11,400	$30,000

¶ 1313 Property Distributions

A property distribution can be proportionate, i.e., a partner receives his or her share of both Code Sec. 751 and non-Code Sec. 751 assets. Alternatively, it could be disproportionate, i.e., a partner receives either more or less than his or her share of Code Sec. 751 assets.

.01 Proportionate Distributions

A proportionate liquidating distribution does not result in ordinary income at the time of distribution. Only in limited instances will gain or loss be recognized. Gain is recognized only when cash received exceeds the basis of the partner's interest. Losses are recognized only if the only assets distributed to the partner are cash, unrealized receivables, and inventory, and the basis of those assets in the hands of the partnership is less than the basis of the partnership interest.

---

[25] Reg. § 1.736-1(b)(5)(ii).

The basis of property received in a liquidating distribution is equal to the adjusted basis of the partner's interest in the partnership reduced by money received.[26] The basis is allocated as follows:[27]

1. First to any unrealized receivables and inventory to the extent of the adjusted basis to the partnership, or if the basis to be allocated is less than the sum of their bases, it is allocated in proportion to the bases; and

2. Any remaining basis is allocated to other assets in proportion to their adjusted bases to the partnership, and then, to the extent of any increase or decrease in basis is required in order to have the adjusted bases of such other distributed properties equal such remaining basis, in the manner provided for allocating increases or decreases as shown below.

3. Increases are allocated:

    a. First to properties with unrealized appreciation in proportion to their respective amounts of unrealized appreciation before such increase (but only to the extent of each property's unrealized appreciation), and

    b. Then, to the extent such increase is not allocated under the rules in (a) above, in proportion to their respective fair market values.

4. Decreases are allocated:

    a. First to properties with unrealized depreciation in proportion to their respective amounts of unrealized depreciation before such decrease (but only to the extent of each property's unrealized depreciation), and

    b. Then, to the extent such decrease is not allocated under (a) above, in proportion to their respective adjusted bases (as adjusted under (a) above).

Example 13-11. Evan Brown received a liquidating distribution from the Brown, Jones, Smith partnership. Prior to the distribution, the balance sheet was as follows:

Assets	Basis	FMV
Cash	$30,000	$ 30,000
Inventory	21,000	45,000
Equipment	27,000	24,000
Land	18,000	42,000
Total	$96,000	$141,000

---

[26] Code Sec. 732(b).   [27] Code Sec. 732(c).

¶ 1313.01

Liabilities and Capital

Brown, Capital	$32,000	$ 47,000
Jones, Capital	32,000	47,000
Smith, Capital	32,000	47,000
Total	$96,000	$141,000

Brown received his *pro rata* share of all the assets. The basis he has to assign to the assets received equals $32,000 − $10,000 cash received, or $22,000. It must be first assigned to the inventory to the extent of $7,000. The remaining $15,000 is allocated between the equipment and the land. The equipment is allocated $27,000/$27,000 + $18,000 × $15,000 = $9,000. The land is allocated $18,000/$27,000 + $18,000 × $15,000 = $6,000. There is no gain or loss on the liquidation.

Example 13-12. The Green-White-Blue partnership's balance sheet immediately prior to a proportionate liquidating distribution to White is as follows:

Assets	*Basis*	*FMV*
Cash................................	$ 90,000	$ 90,000
Inventory	15,000	42,000
Equipment	51,000	48,000
Building...........................	48,000	240,000
Total	$204,000	$420,000

Liabilities and Capital

Green, Capital	$ 90,000	$140,000
White,Capital	25,000	140,000
Blue, Capital	89,000	140,000
Total	$204,000	$420,000

White's realized gain is $140,000 − $25,000 = $115,000. He must recognize gain equal to the excess of the cash over the adjusted basis of his partnership interest ($30,000 − $25,000) = $5,000. The basis of the equipment and building is zero.

Example 13-13. Assume the same facts as in Example 13-12, except that the balance sheet was as follows:

Assets	*Basis*	*FMV*
Cash................................	$90,000	$ 90,000
Unrealized receivables	-0-	-0-
Inventory	-0-	72,000
Total	$90,000	$162,000

Liabilities and Capital

Green, Capital	$24,000	$ 54,000
White, Capital	42,000	54,000
Blue, Capital..........................	24,000	54,000
Total	$90,000	$162,000

After deducting the $30,000 cash received, White would have $12,000 of basis to apply to the unrealized receivables and inventory. However, since they have a zero basis in the hands of the partnership, and since unrealized receivables and inventory cannot be assigned a *higher* basis than in the hands of the partnership, White has a $12,000 loss.

.02 *Disproportionate Liquidating Distributions*

The rules governing disproportionate distribution are among the more complicated provisions of partnership taxation.[28]

To the extent that the partner has received either more or less than his or her share of Code Sec. 751 assets, there has been a deemed sale of both Code Sec. 751 and non-Code Sec. 751 assets. In determining the character of the gain or loss, i.e., whether it is capital or ordinary, look at the type of asset given up. The rules are as follows:

	Partner	*Partnership*
Partner receives more than his or her share of non-751 assets	Has "sold" part or all 751 assets; hence, gain is ordinary.	Has "sold" part or all of non-751 assets; hence, gain or loss is capital or 1231.
Partner receives less than his or her share of non-751 assets	Has "sold" part or all of non-751 assets; hence, gain or loss is capital.	Has "sold" part or all of 751 assets; hence, gain is ordinary.

Example 13-14. Alan Snyder decided to withdraw from the Furillo-Hodges-Snyder partnership. Immediately prior to the liquidating distribution, the balance sheet was as follows:

Assets	*Basis*	*FMV*
Cash....................................	$ 12,000	$ 12,000
Inventory	30,000	50,000
Equipment	66,000	59,000
Building (straight-line dep.).............	33,000	50,000
Total	$141,000	$171,000

[28] For a good basic coverage of this topic, see Martin and Jones, "Tax Consequences of a Partnership Distribution." *The Tax Adviser,* February, 1989, pp.112-121.

Liabilities and Capital

Liabilities	$ 21,000	$ 21,000
Furillo, Capital.............................	40,000	50,000
Hodges, Capital	40,000	50,000
Snyder, Capital............................	40,000	50,000
Total.....................................	$141,000	$171,000

Snyder is given the building in full satisfaction of his partnership interest. Snyder's share of each of the assets, and the amount he received, is as follows:

	Share of FMV	Share of Basis	Amount Received
Cash	$ 4,000	$ 4,000	$ 7,000[*]
Inventory	16,667	10,000	-0-
Equipment	19,667	22,000	-0-
Building	16,666	11,000	50,000
	$57,000	$47,000	$57,000

[*] Snyder is deemed to have received cash to the extent of the liability relief.

Snyder's realized gain (loss) is:

Amount realized	
Liability relief	$ 7,000
FMV of building	50,000
	$57,000
Basis (40,000 + 7,000)	47,000
Realized gain	$10,000

Snyder received an extra $3,000 of cash and $33,334 ($50,000 − $16,666) of building, but $19,667 was for his share of equipment, hence, the *extra* amount of non-Code Sec. 751 assets received was ($3,000 + $33,334 − $19,667) = $16,667. To receive the extra non-Code Sec. 751 assets, he gave up inventory with a basis to him of $10,000. Hence, his recognized gain is $6,667. Since he is deemed to have sold inventory, his gain is ordinary income. Snyder's basis in the building is equal to his one-third interest in the equipment and the building ($22,000 + $11,000) less the extra cash received ($3,000) plus the price he is deemed to have paid for the portion he is considered to have purchased from the partnership ($16,667). Thus, his basis is $46,667. Another way to determine the basis in the building is to start with the basis of his partnership interest of $47,000, deduct the cash of $7,000 received and his $10,000 share of the basis of the inventory and add the deemed purchase price of the inventory of $16,667. Again, the answer is $46,667. Note also that if he immediately sold the building for its fair market value (FMV) of $50,000, he would report a gain of $3,333. This plus the recognized gain of $6,667 on the distribution equals $10,000. The $10,000 represents his share of the total net appreciation of the partnership assets.

The partnership's share of each of the assets, and the amount retained, is as follows:

	Share of FMV	Share of Basis	Amount Received
Cash	$ 8,000	$ 8,000	$ 5,000
Inventory	33,333	20,000	50,000
Equipment	39,333	44,000	59,000
Building	33,334	22,000	-0-
	$114,000	$94,000	$114,000

The partnership received an extra share of inventory of $16,667 and an extra share of equipment of $19,667. It received $3,000 less cash and $33,334 less of building. Since the cash, equipment, and building are all non-Code Sec. 751 assets, more of one type of these assets for another does not render the distribution disproportionate. However, the extra inventory received is disproportionate. Of the partnership's $33,334 share of building, $16,667 was sold to obtain inventory worth $16,667. The cost of the building sold is $16,667/$33,334 × $22,000 = $11,000. Thus, the gain to the partnership is $16,667 − $11,000 = $5,667. Since the property being given up is 1231 property (the building), the gain is Code Sec. 1231. Basis of inventory is the partnership's original share of basis of $20,000 plus the deemed purchase price of $16,667, or a total of $36,667. Note that if the partnership then sold the inventory for its fair market value of $50,000, it would have ordinary income of $13,333. Since the partner recognizes ordinary income of $6,667, the total recognized would be $20,000.

Absent a Code Sec. 754 election (discussed later), the basis of the equipment to the partnership is unchanged at $66,000.

Example 13-15. Assume the same facts as in Example 13-14 except that Snyder receives the inventory in complete liquidation of his interest. Snyder's share of the assets, and the amount he received, is now as follows:

	Share of FMV	Share of Basis	Amount Received
Cash	$ 4,000	$ 4,000	$ 7,000
Inventory	16,667	10,000	50,000
Equipment	19,667	22,000	-0-
Building	16,666	11,000	-0-
	$57,000	$47,000	$57,000

Snyder received an extra $3,000 of cash and $33,333 ($50,000 − $16,667) of inventory. To get the extra $36,333 of cash and inventory, he gave up equipment and building with a basis of $33,000. Hence, he recognizes a Code Sec. 1231 gain of $3,333. Note that this is one-third of the potential Code Sec. 1231 gain of the partnership immediately before the liquidation. Snyder's basis in the inventory is his share of the partnership basis of $10,000 plus the fair market value of the assets he used to "purchase" the partnership's share ($19,667 + $16,666 − $3,000), a total of $43,333. Note that if he immediately sold the inventory for its fair market value of $50,000, he would have ordinary income of $6,667. This is his one-third share of the appreciation on the partnership's balance sheet immediately before payment of his liquidating interest.

The partnership's share of each of the assets, and the amount retained, is as follows:

	Share of FMV	Share of Basis	Amount Received
Cash	$ 8,000	$ 8,000	$ 5,000
Inventory	33,333	20,000	-0-
Equipment	39,333	44,000	59,000
Building	33,334	22,000	50,000
	$114,000	$ 94,000	$114,000

The partnership received an extra share of equipment ($19,667) and building ($16,666), but gave up cash of $3,000 and inventory worth $33,333. Thus, the partnership is deemed to have sold inventory for $33,333 which has a basis of $20,000. Thus, it has ordinary income of $13,333. To get the extra equipment and building, the partnership paid cash and inventory worth $36,333. Thus, the basis of the equipment is $44,000 + $19,667 = $63,667, and the basis of the building is $22,000 + 16,666 = $38,666.

.03 Exception to Code Sec. 751(b)

Code Sec. 751(b) does not apply to the distribution of a portion of property which the partner had originally contributed to a partner.[29]

.04 Statement Required by Partnership

A partnership which makes a disproportionate distribution of property to a partner must submit with its return for the year of distribution a statement.[30] The statement must show the computation of any income or loss to the partnership. The distributee partner must furnish the information discussed earlier in this chapter under sales of a partnership interest.

¶ 1315 Elective Basis Adjustments

The desirability of making basis adjustments stems from situations in which the inside basis and the outside basis of a partner will differ.

Example 13-16. Before the purchase of Rob Akin's interest by Tony Dunn, the balance sheet of A-B-C partnership was as follows:

Assets	Basis	FMV
Cash	$ 30,000	$ 30,000
Inventory	42,000	75,000
Equipment	54,000	45,000
Building	45,000	120,000
	$171,000	$270,000

Dunn paid $90,000 cash for Akin's one-third interest. Dunn's outside basis (basis in the partnership) is $90,000. However, his inside basis is only $57,000. Absent an election, Dunn would have to report his share of income from selling, for example, the inventory. To remove this inequity, Code Sec. 754 permits the partnership to file an election to adjust the basis of partnership property.[31] The mechanics of the adjustment are provided for in Code Sec. 743 in the event of a sale of a partnership interest, and in Code Sec. 734 in the case of a property distribution.[32]

The election is made by filing a written statement with the partnership return for the taxable year in which a distribution or transfer occurs. The statement should contain:[33]

- The name and address of the partnership making the election;

- A signature by one of the partners; and

- A declaration that the partnership makes the election under Code Sec. 734 or 743, whichever is applicable.

---

[29] Code Sec. 751(b)(2)(A); Reg. § 1.751-1(b)(4).
[30] Reg. § 1.751-1(b)(5).
[31] Code Sec. 754.

[32] Id.

[33] Reg. § 1.754-1(b)(1).

If the election has been previously made, and has not been revoked, no new election is required.[34]

The election may be revoked only with approval of the IRS.[35] A revocation request should be filed by 30 days after the close of the partnership tax year for which the revocation takes effect. Examples of situations which may be considered an adequate reason for approval include:[36]

- A change in the nature of a partnership business;

- A substantial increase in the assets of the partnership;

- A change in the character of partnership assets; and

- An increased frequency of retirement, or shifts of partnership interests.

If the purpose of the revocation is to avoid a step-down in the basis of partnership assets, the revocation will not be approved.[37]

.01 Code Sec. 743 Adjustments

If a partnership interest is sold or exchanged or if the partner dies, and the election under Code Sec. 754 is in effect, basis is adjusted as follows:[38]

- The adjusted basis of partnership property is increased by the excess of the partnership basis to the transferee (the outside basis) over his or her proportionate share of the adjusted basis of partnership property (the inside basis); or

- The adjusted basis of property is decreased by the excess of the transferee's proportionate share of the adjusted basis of property (his or her inside basis) over the basis of his or her partnership interest (his or her outside basis).

The adjustment is applicable only to the transferee partner (the buyer).

Example 13-17. Assume the same facts as in Example 13-16 except that a Code Sec. 754 election was in effect. The basis of the partnership assets would be increased by $33,000 (the excess of the $90,000 outside basis over the $57,000 inside basis).

The basis adjustment is apportioned to the partnership in accordance with rules under Code Sec. 755.[39] The amount of the basis adjustment allocated to ordinary income property is the total amount that would be allocated to the transferee from the sale of all ordinary income property in a hypothetical transaction. The amount for the basis adjustment to capital gain property is equal to the total basis adjustment less the amount that is

---

[34] Id.
[35] Reg. § 1.754-1(c).
[36] Id.

[37] Id.
[38] Code Sec. 743(b).
[39] Code Sec. 743(c).

allocated to ordinary income property. However, in no event may the decrease in basis allocated to capital gain property exceed the partnership's basis in the capital gain property.[40] In the event that a decrease in basis allocated to capital gain property would otherwise exceed the partnership's basis in capital gain property, the excess must be applied to reduce the basis of ordinary income property.[41]

The amount of the basis adjustment to each item of property within the class of ordinary income property is equal to the amount of income, gain, or loss that would be allocated to the transferee from the hypothetical sale of the item minus the product of any decrease to the basis of ordinary income property required because the decrease in basis of capital gain property exceeds its basis multiplied by a fraction, the numerator of which is the fair market value of the item of property and the denominator of which is the total fair market value of all of the partnership's items of ordinary income property.[42]

The amount of the basis adjustment to each item of property within the class of capital gain property is equal to the amount of income, gain, or loss that would be allocated to the transferee in a hypothetical sale of the capital gain assets minus the product of (1) the total amount of gain or loss that would be allocated to the transferee from the hypothetical sale of all items of capital gain property, minus the positive basis adjustment to all items of capital gain property or plus the amount of the negative basis adjustment to capital gain property, multiplied by (2) a fraction, the numerator of which is the fair market value of the item of property and the denominator of which is the fair market value of all the partnership's items of capital gain property.[43]

Example 13-18.[44] Claire Abbot and Lauren Baker form an equal partnership. Abbot contributes $50,000 and asset 1, a nondepreciable capital asset with a fair market value of $50,000 and an adjusted basis of $25,000. Baker contributes $100,000 cash. The partnership uses the cash to purchase assets 2, 3, and 4. After a year, Abbot sells her interest to Tracy Crank for $120,000. At the time of the transfer, Abbot's share of the partnership's basis in partnership assets is $75,000. Therefore, Crank receives a $45,000 basis adjustment.

Immediately after the transfer of the partnership interest to Crank, the adjusted basis and FMV of the partnership assets are as follows:

---

[40] Reg. § 1.755-1(b)(2)(i).
[41] *Id.*
[42] Reg. § 1.755-1(b)(3)(i).

[43] Reg. § 1.755-1(b)(3)(ii).

[44] Adapted from Reg. § 1.755-1(b)(2)(ii), Example 1.

	Assets	
	Adjusted Basis	*Market Value*
Capital Gain Property		
Asset 1	$ 25,000	$ 75,000
Asset 2	100,000	117,500
Ordinary Income Property		
Asset 3	40,000	45,000
Asset 4	10,000	2,500

If the partnership were to sell all of its assets in a fully taxable transaction at FMV immediately after the transfer of the partnership interest to Crank, the total capital gain that would be allocated to Crank would be equal to $46,250 ($25,000 Code Sec. 704(c) built-in gain from asset 1, plus 50 percent of the $42,500 appreciation in capital gain property). Crank would also be allocated a $1,250 ordinary loss from the sale of the ordinary income property. The basis adjustment allocated to ordinary income property is negative $1,250. The basis adjustment allocated to capital gain property equals $46,250 (the amount of the basis adjustment, $45,000 less the negative $1,250 amount of loss allocated to Crank from the hypothetical sale of the ordinary income property).

If the basis of a partnership's recovery property is increased as a result of the transfer of a partnership interest, then the increased portion of the basis is taken into account as if it were newly purchased recovery property placed in service when the transfer occurs.[45]

A transferee that acquires, by sale or exchange, an interest in a partnership with an election under section 754 in effect for the taxable year of the transfer, must notify the partnership, in writing, within 30 days of the sale or exchange. The written notice to the partnership must be signed under penalties of perjury and must include the names and addresses of the transferee and (if ascertainable) of the transferor, the taxpayer identification numbers of the transferee and (if ascertainable) of the transferor, the relationship (if any) between the transferee and the transferor, the date of the transfer, the amount of any liabilities assumed or taken subject to by the transferee, and the amount of any money, the fair market value of any other property delivered or to be delivered for the transferred interest in the partnership, and any other information necessary for the partnership to compute the transferee's basis.[46]

.02 Code Sec. 734 Adjustments

If property is distributed to a partner while a Code Sec. 754 election is in effect, the adjusted basis of property is increased by:[47]

---

[45] Reg. § 1.743-1(j)(4)(i)(B)(1).
[46] Reg. § 1.743-1(k)(2)(i).

[47] Code Sec. 734(b)(1).

- The amount of any gain recognized by the partner under Code Sec. 731(a)(1) with respect to the distribution; and

- In the case of distributed property to which Code Sec. 732(a)(2) or (b) applies, the excess of the adjusted basis of the distributed property in the hands of the partnership immediately before the distribution over the basis to which the distributee can assign to it.

The adjusted basis of property is decreased by:[48]

- The amount of any loss recognized to the distributed partner with respect to the distribution under Code Sec. 731(a)(2); and

- In the case of distributed property to which Code Sec. 732(b) applies, the excess of the basis to which the distributee can assign the property over the basis in the hands of the partnership immediately before the distribution.

Example 13-19. Immediately before a liquidating distribution to Art Nassar from the REN partnership, the balance sheet was as follows:

	Basis	FMV
Cash	$ 90,000	$ 90,000
Inventory	45,000	60,000
Equipment	45,000	40,000
Building	33,000	80,000
	$213,000	$270,000
Rodriguez, Capital	$ 71,000	$ 90,000
Ewing, Capital	71,000	90,000
Nassar, Capital	71,000	90,000
	$213,000	$270,000

The partnership paid $90,000 cash to Nassar. His gain was $90,000 − $71,000 = $19,000. The basis of the partnership may be increased by $19,000 provided that a Code Sec. 754 adjustment is in effect. The inventory would be increased by $15,000/$57,000 × $19,000 = $5,000. The equipment and the building would be increased by $42,000/$57,000 × $19,000 = $14,000.

Example 13-20. Assume the same facts as in Example 13-19, except that Nassar receives a distribution of $30,000 cash, $20,000 of inventory, and $40,000 of equipment. Since the distribution is proportionate as between Code Sec. 751 and non-Code Sec. 751 assets, and Nassar received less cash than his basis, he has no gain on the

---

[48] Code Sec. 734(b)(2).

liquidation. He would assign to the inventory a *pro rata* share of the inventory basis in the hands of the partnership of $20,000/$60,000 × $45,000, = $15,000. The basis to be assigned to the equipment would be the remaining outside basis of $71,000 − $30,000 cash − $15,000 inventory = $26,000. Since that basis is $19,000 less than the basis of the equipment in the hands of the partnership, the partnership could increase the basis of the remaining assets by $19,000. Since there was no decrease in the basis assigned by the recipient partner to ordinary income assets, all of the Code Sec. 734 adjustment goes to the Code Sec. 1231 and capital assets on the partnership books, in this case the building. Thus, the basis of the building would be $33,000 + $19,000 = $52,000.

Example 13-21. The balance sheet of the J-K-L partnership immediately before a liquidating distribution was paid to Richard Lamb was as follows:

Assets	Basis	FMV
Cash..........................	$ 28,000	$ 28,000
Inventory	25,000	20,000
Equipment	40,000	22,000
Building......................	60,000	70,000
	$153,000	$140,000

Liabilities and Capital	Basis	FMV
Jarrell, Capital	$ 61,200	$ 56,000
Kamen, Capital	61,200	56,000
Lamb, Capital	30,600	28,000
	$153,000	$140,000

Lamb received $28,000 cash in full payment of his interest. He has a $2,600 loss. If a Code Sec. 754 election was in effect, the $2,600 would be allocated as follows:

	Decrease in FMV		Basis Adjustment
Inventory	$ 5,000	$ 5,000	$ − 1,000
Equipment	18,000		− 1,600
Building	(10,000)	8,000	-0-
		$13,000	$ − 2,600

Example 13-22. Assume the same facts as in Example 13-21 except that Lamb receives $6,000 in cash plus the equipment for his interest. Lamb could assign a basis to the equipment equal to his basis of $30,600 less the cash of $6,000, or $24,600. Since this is a higher basis than it had in the hand of the partnership, the $2,600 decrease

would be allocated entirely to the inventory since it is the only remaining asset that has declined in value.

Tax Tips and Pitfalls

Since it is more likely than not that partnership assets will appreciate rather than decline in value, it is generally advisable to elect a Code Sec. 754 adjustment the first time that a partnership interest is sold or liquidated at a gain. On the other hand, if there is little or no benefit from the election, the partnership can wait. Failure to make the election at the first opportunity does not keep the partnership from making an election at a later time.

¶ 1317 Reporting Requirements of Code Sec. 751 Sales or Distributions

The reporting requirements of partners to the IRS was previously discussed. The selling partner also is required to notify the partnership, and the partnership is not required to file a report until receiving information from the partner.[49] The partnership must be notified in writing by the earlier of 30 days of the exchange or January 15 following the calendar year of the exchange.[50] The written notification must include the following:[51]

- The names and addresses of the transferor and the transferee;

- The taxpayer identification number of the transferor and, if known, the number of the transferee; and

- The date of the exchange.

The partnership, upon receiving notice of an exchange from the transfer, must file Form 8308 with the IRS, the transferor, and the transferee.[52] Required information includes:[53]

- Names, addresses, and taxpayer identification numbers of the transferor, the transferee, and the partnership;

- The date of the exchange; and

- Other information required by Form 8308 (including the fair value and the basis of Code Sec. 751 assets sold).

¶ 1319 Partnership Mergers and Divisions

A partnership is considered to be terminated only if either no part of the business is carried on by any of its partners, or if 50 percent or more of the total interest in partnership profits and capital is sold or exchanged within a 12-month period.[54] The death of one partner in a 2-member partnership does not terminate the partnership if the estate or other successor in interest of the deceased partner continues to share in the

---

[49] Code Sec. 6050K(c).
[50] Reg. § 1.6050K-1(d).
[51] *Id.*

[52] Reg. § 1.6050K-1(c).
[53] Reg. § 1.6050K-1(b).
[54] Code Sec. 708(b)(1).

profits or losses of the partnership business.[55] The sale of a 30-percent interest in partnership capital and a 60-percent interest in partnership profits is not the sale or exchange of 50 percent or more of the total interest in partnership capital and profits.[56]

In the case of the merger or consolidation of two or more partnerships, the new partnership is considered to be the continuation of any of the merging partnership whose members own an interest of more than 50 percent of the capital and profits of the new partnership.[57]

There are two forms of partnership mergers. Under the assets-over form, the merged or consolidated partnership that is considered terminated contributes all of its assets and liabilities to the resulting partnership in exchange for an interest in the resulting partnership, and immediately thereafter, the terminated partnership distributes interests in the resulting partnership to its partners in liquidation of the terminated partnership.[58]

In an assets-up form, the partnership distributes all of its assets to its partners (in a manner that causes the partners to be treated, under the laws of the applicable jurisdiction, as the owners of such assets) in liquidation of the partners' interests in the terminated partnership, and immediately thereafter, the partners in the terminated partnership contribute the distributed assets to the resulting partnership in exchange for interests in the resulting partnership.[59]

If a partnership is divided into two or more partnerships, the resulting partnership, if any, that retains an interest of more than 50 percent of the capital and profits is considered a continuation of the prior partnership.[60] If the members of none of the resulting partnerships owned an interest of more than 50 percent in the capital and profits of the prior partnership, none of the resulting partnerships will be considered a continuation of the prior partnership, and the prior partnership will be considered to have terminated.[61]

The resulting partnership that is treated as the divided partnership files a return for the taxable year of the partnership that has been divided and retains the employer identification number (EIN) of the prior partnership. The return includes the names, addresses, and EINs of all resulting partnerships that are regarded as continuing. The return should also state that the partnership is a continuation of the prior partnership and should set forth separately the respective distributive shares of the partners for the periods prior to and including the date of the division and subsequent to the date of division. All other resulting partnerships that are regarded as continuing and new partnerships should file separate returns for the taxable

---

55 Reg. § 1.708-1(b)(1)(i).
56 Reg. § 1.708-1(b)(2).
57 Code Sec. 708(b)(2)(A).
58 Reg. § 1.708-1(c)(3)(i).

59 Reg. § 1.708-1(c)(3)(ii).
60 Code Sec. 708(b)(2)(B).
61 Reg. § 1.708-1(d)(1).

year beginning on the day after the date of the division with new EINs for each partnership. The return for a resulting partnership that is regarded as continuing and that is not the divided partnership should include the name, address, and EIN of the prior partnership.[62]

---

[62] Reg. § 1.708-1(d)(2)(i).

Chapter 14

Corporate Distributions and Redemptions

¶ 1401 Introduction

The taxation of distributions from C corporations is somewhat involved. Among the many issues are such questions as:

- What is included in earnings and profits?

- Are the distributions from earnings and profits, or are they a return of capital of the shareholder?

- How are earnings and profits allocated over different distributions?

- What is the impact on the corporations and shareholders of distributing property?

- What is the impact of distributing stock dividends and stock rights?

- Are stock redemptions treated as dividends or as a sale?

- What is the impact of a "preferred stock bailout?"

- What is the tax result of having a "collapsible corporation?"

- What is the tax impact of liquidating a subsidiary?

These and other issues will be addressed in this chapter.

¶ 1403 Distributions vs. Dividends

The Code does not explicitly define a distribution. However, from the overall information contained in Code Secs. 301-307 and the regulations, a distribution may be considered as a payment from a corporation to a shareholder of cash, property, or stock or other securities absent consideration given by the shareholder. In other words, it is a one-way exchange. A dividend, however, is a distribution from either current or accumulated earnings and profits.[1] Therefore, distributions in excess of current and accumulated earnings and profits are not dividends but instead:[2]

- Reduce the adjusted basis of the stock; and

- Are treated as a gain from the sale of property.

---

[1] Code Sec. 316(a).   [2] Code Sec. 301(c).

Example 14-1. Brad Wyeth is the 100 percent owner of a corporation. His adjusted basis in the stock is $80,000. The corporation has earnings and profits of $50,000, but distributed $150,000 to Wyeth. His tax results are:

- A taxable dividend of $50,000;

- A nontaxable return of capital of $80,000 reducing the basis to zero; and

- A $20,000 capital gain.

¶ 1405   Earnings and Profits

The Code does not completely define the term "earnings and profits" (E&P). A conceptual definition of E&P that has evolved through legislative and judicial decisions is that E&P represents economic income, i.e., the amount that could be distributed without reducing the contributed capital of the corporation.[3] Therefore, the purpose of the various adjustments to taxable income provided for in Code Sec. 312 and the regulations is to arrive at the ability of the corporation to pay dividends. A list of the most common adjustments to taxable income to arrive at current E&P is as follows:

	Add to Taxable Income	Deduct from Taxable Income
Tax-exempt income	X	
Expenses attributable to tax-exempt income		X
Proceeds of life insurance—corporation is the beneficiary	X	
Premiums paid on life insurance policy—corporation is the beneficiary		X
Charitable contributions carried over from previous years	X	
Charitable contributions in excess of the 10 percent limitation		X
Net capital loss carryover from previous years	X	
Net capital losses—current year		X
Net operating loss carryover from previous years	X	

---

[3] Senate Finance Report No. 98-169, Vol. 1, p. 198, April 2, 1984.[4] Code Sec. 316(a).[5] Reg. § 1.316-2(b).

	Add to Taxable Income	Deduct from Taxable Income
Dividends-received deduction	X	
Deferred gain on installment sales ...	X	
Federal income tax refunds.........	X	
Federal income tax		X
Excess of percentage depletion over cost depletion..................	X	
Excess of accelerated depreciation over straight-line	X	
Excess of ACRS or MACRS depreciation for tangible property over ADS depreciation	X	
Amortization of organization and circulation expenditures	X	
Excess of percentage of completion over completed-contract method ..	X	
Excess of LIFO cost of sales over FIFO cost of sales	X	
Recoveries of expenses previously deducted to the extent not included in income because of the tax benefit rule	X	
Excess of deductions for construction period interest and taxes over what would have been amortized	X	
80 percent of the deduction under Section 179 for the current year ...	X	
20 percent of the deduction under Section 179 taken during the four previous years		X
Nondeductible expenses		X
Losses between related parties under Section 167		X
Gains on sale of depreciable or depletable property to the extent that depreciation allowed for regular income tax purposes exceeds that allowed for E&P		X
Foreign taxes, if taken as a credit on the tax return		X

Example 14-2. For the calendar year 2001 the G-Nee Corporation had taxable income of $55,000, determined as follows:

Sales	$300,000
Cost of sales	175,000
Gross profit	$125,000
Dividend income	40,000
Total income	$165,000

Expenses

Selling and office expenses	$22,000	
Depreciation expense	30,000	
Net operating loss deduction	30,000	
Dividends-received deduction	28,000	
Total expenses		110,000
Taxable income		$ 55,000
Tax		$ 8,750

Additional information is as follows:

- Depreciation was taken under ACRS. Straight-line depreciation under ADS would have been $18,000.

- Municipal bond interest totaled $8,000.

- The corporation paid $2,000 life insurance premiums on policies it owned on corporate officers.

- Fines and penalties amounted to $500.

Earnings and profits are as follows:

Taxable income		$ 55,000
Add: Dividends-received deduction	$28,000	
Net operating loss deduction	30,000	
Excess depreciation	12,000	
Municipal bond interest	8,000	78,000
		133,000
Less: Federal income tax	$ 8,750	
Life insurance premiums	2,000	
Fines and penalties	500	11,250
Current earnings and profits		$121,750

.01 Allocation of E&P

Distributions are considered to come first from current E&P and then, to the extent necessary, from accumulated E&P.[4] If distributions exceed the total of current and accumulated E&P, current E&P is allocated *pro rata* over all of the distributions; however, accumulated E&P is allocated on a FIFO basis.[5]

Example 14-3. The MLM Corporation was 100 percent owned by Mary McCoy at the start of the year. Her basis in the stock was $70,000. It made two distributions during the year, one on April 10 of $120,000 and a second distribution on October 5 of $80,000. Current E&P amounted to $90,000; accumulated E&P was $60,000. On July 1 of the current year, she sold her stock to Bryan Slivka for $400,000. The tax results are as follows:

Date	Amount of Dist.	Portion from Current E&P	Portion from Accum. E&P	Taxable Dividend Amount
April 10	$120,000	$54,000	$60,000	$114,000
October 5	80,000	36,000	-0-	36,000
Total	$200,000	$90,000	$60,000	$150,000

Thus, of the $120,000 distribution received by McCoy, $114,000 is taxed as a dividend; the remaining $6,000 is nontaxable but reduces her basis to $64,000. Thus, her gain on the sale is $400,000 − $64,000 = $336,000. Of the $80,000 distribution received by Slivka on October 5, only $36,000 is taxable; the remaining $44,000 is nontaxable but reduces his basis down to $356,000.

If there is a positive balance in accumulated E&P, but a current deficit, the books are deemed to be "closed" as of the day before the distribution date, and the two amounts are netted together, unless the actual deficit up to the date of distribution can be established.

Example 14-4. The Daisy Wheel Corporation had a current deficit of $91,250 in 2001. It began the year with accumulated E&P of $100,000. It made one distribution on May 5 of $50,000, and a second distribution of $30,000 on November 5. The results are as follows:

May 5 distribution

Accumulated E&P—start of year	$100,000
Less: *Pro rata* share of current deficit	(31,000)
($91,250 × 124/365)	
Deemed E&P before distribution	$69,000
Distribution (completely taxed as a dividend)	$50,000

empty footnote   empty footnote

November 5 distribution

Accumulated E&P—start of year	$100,000
Less: *Pro rata* share of current deficit	77,000
($91,250 × 308/365)	
Deemed E&P before distribution	23,000
Less: May 5 distribution	50,000
Deemed E&P before November 5 distribution	($27,000)
Distribution (return of capital up to stock basis)	$30,000

If there is a deficit in accumulated E&P, but a positive current E&P, the deficit is not taken into account as long as current E&P is sufficient to cover the distributions.

Example 14-5. Implacable, Inc. made one distribution of $20,000 during the year. It began the year with a deficit of $30,000, but had current E&P of $24,000. The distribution is fully taxed as a dividend.

Example 14-6. Assume the same facts as in Example 14-5, except that the distribution is $27,000. The dividend part of the distribution is $24,000; $3,000 is a return of capital lowering the shareholder's basis.

Tax Tips and Pitfalls

Advance planning can in some instances reduce the amount of distributions that are taxed as dividends. For example, assume that a company has only a modest amount in accumulated earnings and profits, and wishes to make a substantial distribution during the current tax year. Further assume that the company prepares quarterly financial statements and expects a net operating loss during the first quarter but expects to have a profit for the year as a whole. The company could effect a distribution immediately after the first quarter, and because the actual loss could be deemed closed to accumulated E&P, the amount taxed as a dividend would be less than if the distribution were made during the last quarter of the year.

If the corporation has an accumulated deficit but current E&P, the timing of distributions can have a substantial effect on the tax status of the distributions.

Example 14-7. Assume that a calendar year corporation begins the year 2000 with an accumulated deficit of $200,000, but expects to have current E&P of $75,000 for both 2000 and 2001. The stockholders desire a total of $120,000 in distributions on or around December 31, 2000. The corporation could: (a) distribute $120,000 on December 31, 2000, (b) distribute $60,000 on December 31, 2000, and another $60,000 on January 1, 2001, or (c) distribute $120,000 on January 1,

2001. If the first alternative is selected, the taxpayers have $75,000 of dividend income in 2000 and the corporation begins 2001 with a deficit in accumulated E&P of $200,000 (accumulated deficits cannot be *increased* by distributions). Assuming no other distributions in 2001, the deficit at the end of 2001 would be $125,000 ($200,000 − $75,000). If the second alternative is selected, the taxpayers would have $60,000 of dividend income in both 2000 and 2001, and the corporation would begin 2001 with an accumulated deficit of $185,000 ($200,000 − ($75,000 − $60,000)). Assuming no other distributions in 2001, the deficit at the end of 2001 would be $170,000 ($185,000 − ($75,000 − $60,000)). If the third alternative is selected, the stockholders would have $75,000 of dividend income in 2001. The accumulated deficit at the start of 2001 would be $125,000 ($200,000 − $75,000). Assuming no other distributions in 2001, the accumulated deficit at the end of 2001 would be $125,000 ($125,000 − ($75,000 − $75,000)). The second alternative would be far worse for the taxpayers than alternatives one and three. The taxpayers would, due to the deferral of the tax liability, probably prefer alternative three.

¶ 1407   Property Distributions

Distributions in the form of property have an impact on the distributing corporation as well as on the shareholders. The effect on shareholders will be discussed first.

.01   *Impact on Shareholders*

The amount of a property distribution is equal to the sum of the fair market value of the property plus any money received.[6] If liabilities are either assumed by the stockholder, or if the property is subject to a liability, such amount will reduce the amount of the distribution, but not below zero.[7] As would be expected, the basis of the property is its fair market value.[8]

> **Example 14-8.** River Valley, Inc., distributed property worth $60,000 to its sole shareholder. The property had an adjusted basis of $25,000, and was subject to a mortgage of $42,000. The taxable dividend (assuming sufficient E&P) is $60,000 − $42,000 = $18,000. The basis to the shareholder is $60,000.

.02   *Impact on the Distributing Corporation*

Losses resulting from the distribution of property with a basis exceeding fair market value are *not* recognized to the distributing corporation.[9] However, gains resulting from the distribution of appreciated property must be recognized.[10] If any property distributed is subject to a liability,

---

[6] Code Sec. 301(b)(1).
[7] Code Sec. 301(b)(2).
[8] Code Sec. 301(d).

[9] Code Sec. 311(a).

[10] Code Sec. 311(b)(1).

the fair market value of the property is treated as being at least equal to the amount of the liability.[11]

> **Example 14-9.** Dark Days, Inc., distributed a building worth $150,000 but encumbered by a $70,000 mortgage. The basis of the building was $62,000. The corporation recognizes a gain of $150,000 − $62,000 = $88,000. The stockholders have a taxable dividend of $150,000 − $70,000 = $80,000. The stockholders' basis in the building is $150,000.

> **Example 14-10.** Assume the same facts as in Example 14-9 except that the building is worth only $65,000. The value is deemed to be equal to the mortgage; hence, the corporation has a gain of $8,000 ($70,000 − $62,000). The stockholders have a taxable dividend of $70,000 and a basis in the building of $70,000.

.03 Impact on the Corporation's E&P

The E&P of the corporation is increased by the excess of the fair market value of the property over the adjusted basis.[12] However, E&P is decreased by the distribution of the property. If the property has decreased in value, E&P is decreased by the adjusted basis of the property.[13] However, if the property is appreciated, E&P is decreased by the fair market value of the property.[14]

> **Example 14-11.** The Sunnyvale Co., distributed land worth $200,000 to its sole shareholder. Its adjusted basis was $260,000. E&P is decreased by $260,000.

> **Example 14-12.** Assume the same facts as in Example 14-11, except that the land is worth $400,000. The company would *increase* E&P by $140,000 (the gain recognized) and would *decrease* E&P by $400,000 (the fair market value of the property). Note that the *net* decrease is equal to the adjusted basis of the property.

If property subject to a liability is distributed, the corporation's resources actually increase to the extent of the debt relief. Therefore, the mortgage relief reduces the decrease to E&P.[15]

> **Example 14-13.** Rockscreen Company distributed an office building to its sole shareholder. The building was worth $250,000, had an adjusted basis of $100,000, and a mortgage of $70,000. The impact on E&P is as follows:

---

[11] Code Sec. 311(b)(2).

[12] Code Sec. 312(b). This rule is logical since the appreciation must be reported as a taxable gain, and gains increase E&P.

[13] Code Sec. 312(a)(3).

[14] Code Sec. 312(b)(2).

[15] Code Sec. 312(c).

E&P is decreased by:

FMV of property	$250,000	
Less: Mortgage	70,000	$180,000

E&P is increased by:

Gain recognized	150,000
Net decrease in E&P	$ 30,000

Example 14-14. Assume the same facts as in Example 14-13, except that the mortgage is $275,000. The impact on E&P is as follows:

E&P is decreased by:

FMV (deemed to be equal to mortgage) on property	$275,000	
Less: Mortgage	275,000	-0-

E&P is increased by:

Gain recognized	$175,000
Net increase in E&P	$175,000

Note that when the debt that the corporation distributes exceeds the fair market value of the property, the corporation will experience a net increase in E&P.

Tax Tips and Pitfalls

Generally, it is not wise to distribute property to shareholders if the property is worth less than basis. The loss is not deductible to the corporation, and because the shareholder picks up basis equal to fair market value, the shareholder will not be able to deduct the loss either. A better strategy would be for the corporation to sell the asset, deduct the loss, and distribute the cash to the shareholders.

¶ 1409 Distribution of Stock Dividends and Rights

Generally, the distribution of stock dividends and stock rights has no gross income implications for either the distributing corporation or the shareholders.[16] The rationale for this rule is that the relative interest of each shareholder remains unchanged, and the corporation does not lose resources when it distributes its own stock. There are, however, several exceptions to the nontaxability rule. Distribution of the corporation's stock is taxed to the shareholder if:[17]

1.   Distributions are in lieu of "money" (the stockholder has the election of receiving either stock or property (including cash)).

---

[16] Code Sec. 305(a).   [17] Code Sec. 305(b).

The distribution will then be taxable regardless of the fact that:[18]

a. The stockholder actually receives only stock;

b. The election may not be exercisable until after the declaration of the distribution;

c. The distribution will be made in stock unless the stockholder specifically requests cash;

d. The election is provided in the declaration of the distribution or in the corporate charter or arises from the circumstances of the distribution; or

e. Only some of the stockholders have the election.

2.   The distribution is disproportionate. A distribution (or series of distributions) is considered disproportionate if some shareholders receive money or other property and other shareholders receive stock (and thus increase their proportionate share).[19] For disproportionate distributions to occur, it is not necessary that there be a plan to increase the interests of some shareholders. For example, a quarterly stock dividend to class A common stock and an annual cash dividend to class B common would be considered disproportionate.[20]

Both elements of the disproportionality condition need not even occur in the form of a distribution. For example, if a corporation makes a distribution of stock to its shareholders and pursuant to a prearranged plan redeems part of the stock of the shareholders who want cash, the original distribution will be considered disproportionate.[21]

A distribution will not be considered disproportionate if more than 36 months pass between the distribution and an increase in the proportionate interest of other shareholders.[22]

3.   The distribution is such that some shareholders receive common stock while other shareholders receive preferred stock. For example, if a corporation has both class A and class B common, and declares a class A stock dividend on the class A common and a preferred stock dividend on the class B common, both dividends are taxable.[23]

4.   The distribution is on preferred stock, except for an increase in the conversion ratio of convertible preferred that is changed to reflect a stock dividend or stock split on the common stock to which the preferred is convertible. For this purpose "preferred stock" is stock which has certain limited rights and privileges

---

[18] Reg. § 1.305-2(a).
[19] Reg. § 1.305-3(a).
[20] Reg. § 1.305-3(b)(2).

[21] Reg. § 1.305-3(b)(3).
[22] Reg. § 1.305-3(b)(4).
[23] Reg. § 1.305-4(b).

(usually dividend and liquidation priorities) but does not participate in corporate growth to any significant extent.[24] Among facts to be considered in determining whether the stock is to be treated as preferred are the prior and anticipated earnings per share, cash dividends per share, book value per share, the extent of preference and of participation of each class, and any other facts which indicate whether or not the stock has a real and meaningful probability of participating in the earnings and growth of the corporation.[25]

A redemption premium which is more than a *de minimis* amount (as determined under the principles of Code Sec. 1273(a)(3)) may be deemed to be a distribution on preferred.[26]

5. The distribution is of convertible preferred stock unless it is established to the satisfaction of the IRS that the distribution will not be disproportionate.

The distribution of convertible preferred is likely to be disproportionate when both of these conditions exist:[27]

a. The conversion right must be exercised within a relatively short period of time; and

b. It may be anticipated that some shareholders will exercise their rights and others will not.

The distribution is unlikely to be considered disproportionate if the conversion right may be exercised over many years and the dividend rate is consistent with market conditions at the time of distribution of the stock.[28]

.01 Adjustment in Conversion Ratio

The mere existence of convertible preferred stock or bonds can make the issuance of a stock dividend disproportionate and thus taxable, since the stock dividend would in effect worsen the value of the conversion and thus make the dividend disproportionate with respect to the convertible securities. This can be avoided only by making a full adjustment in the conversion ratio or conversion price.[29] An example of a full adjustment formula is one where the conversion price in effect at the opening of business on the day following the dividend record date is reduced by multiplying such conversion price by a fraction, the numerator of which is the number of shares of common stock outstanding at the close of business on the record date, and the denominator of which is the sum of such shares so outstanding and the number of shares constituting the stock dividend.[30]

Example 14-15. Growers, Inc., had 200 shares of common stock outstanding as well as debentures convertible into common stock at a

---

24 Reg. § 1.305-5(a).
25 *Id.*
26 Reg. § 1.305-5(b)(1).
27 Reg. § 1.305-6(a)(2).

28 *Id.*
29 Reg. § 1.305-3(d)(1)(i).
30 Reg. § 1.305-3(d)(1)(ii).

conversion price of $2.50. A 10 percent stock dividend was declared on the common stock and the conversion price was adjusted as described above. The new conversion price is:

$$\frac{200}{220} \times 2.50 = \$2.27$$

.02 Basis and Income Implications of Nontaxable Stock Dividends

Obviously, there is no immediate income to the shareholder upon the *receipt* of a nontaxable dividend. Determination of the basis of the stock dividend depends on whether the stock dividend is identical to the old stock. If it is identical to the old stock, basis is reallocated simply by dividing the new number of shares into the adjusted basis of the old stock.[31]

Example 14-16. In 2000, Ken Harton purchased 200 shares of stock at a cost of $10,000. On October 1, 2001, he received a nontaxable stock dividend of 5 percent (10 shares). His new per-share basis is $10,000/210 = $47.619.

If the stock is *not* identical (e.g., a preferred dividend on common), basis is allocated between the old and new stock according to their respective share of the total fair market value.[32]

Example 14-17. Assume the same facts as in Example 14-16, except that the 10 shares of stock received are preferred, the value of the old stock is $15,000, and the value of the preferred is $2,000. The amount allocated to the common is $10,000 × 15,000/17,000 = $8,824, or $44.12 per share. The amount allocated to the preferred is $10,000 × 2,000/17,000 = $1,176, or $117.65 per share.

The holding period of a nontaxable dividend goes back to the date that the old stock was acquired.[33]

A nontaxable stock dividend results in a book (accounting) reduction in retained earnings and an increase in paid-in capital. However, for tax purposes, a nontaxable stock dividend has no effect on E&P.[34]

.03 Basis and Income Implications of Taxable Stock Dividends

If a stock dividend is taxable, the amount taxable, the amount which reduces E&P of the distributing corporation, and the basis to the shareholder is fair market value at the date of distribution.[35] The holding period begins on the date of receipt.

Example 14-18. Assume the same facts as in Example 14-16, except that the stock dividend is taxable and the fair market value of the stock on the distribution date was $75 per share. Harton has a

---

[31] Reg. § 1.307-1.
[32] Id.
[33] Code Sec. 1223(5).

[34] Code Sec. 312(d)(1).
[35] Reg. § 1.305-1(b).

taxable dividend of $750 ($75 × 10) and a basis in his stock of $750. The holding period of the new stock begins on October 1, 2001.

.04 Stock Rights

A stock right gives the holder the option, within a specified time period, of purchasing the stock for less than the fair market value of the stock at the time of issuance of the right. The criteria for determining taxability of a stock right are the same as for a stock dividend. Hence, taxable stock rights will not be discussed. However, the basic rules for nontaxable stock rights are somewhat different from those for stock dividends, and warrant further discussion.

If the fair market value of the rights at the time of distribution is less than 15 percent of the fair market value of the old stock, the basis of the rights is zero unless the stockholder elects to allocate basis.[36] However, if the fair market value is 15 percent or more, allocation must be made.

Example 14-19. Sheri Takimoto is the owner of 100 shares of stock in Healthful Eating Co. Healthful Eating Co. issues 100 nontaxable rights to Takimoto. Four rights allow Takimoto to purchase 1 share of stock for $40 per share. The stock cost Takimoto $20 per share, and at the distribution date each right was selling for $3 per share and the stock was selling for $50 per share. The fair market value of the rights ($300) is only six percent of the value of the stock ($5,000), hence no basis is allocated to the rights in the absence of an election.

Example 14-20. Assume the same facts as Example 14-19 except that Takimoto received 400 rights. Since the value of the rights ($1,200) is at least 15 percent of the value of the stock, basis must be allocated to the rights.

$$\text{Basis of the rights is} \quad \frac{\$1,200}{\$5,000 + \$1,200} \times \$2,000 = \$\ 387.10$$

$$\text{Basis of the old stock is} \quad \frac{\$5,000}{\$5,000 + \$1,200} \times \$2,000 = \$1,612.90$$

If nontaxable stock rights are sold, the date basis goes back to is when the stock was acquired. However, if the rights are exercised, the date basis becomes the date of exercise. If the rights lapse, no loss is allowed, and the basis of the old stock is restored.

The election to allocate basis must be in the form of a statement attached to the shareholder's return for the year in which the rights are received.[37] Once made, the election is irrevocable for those rights.[38]

---

[36] Code Sec. 307(b).
[37] Reg. § 1.307-2.

[38] *Id.*

.05 Constructive Dividends

Distributions do not need to be formally declared as dividends in order to be treated as such. Instead, if the transaction provides an economic benefit to the shareholders, it may be treated as a dividend in substance, i.e., a "constructive dividend" to the shareholders.[39] Constructive dividends represent a major bone of contention between the IRS and closely held corporations. Types of constructive dividends to be discussed in greater detail include:

- Fees paid to stockholders who guarantee loans;

- Payments to family members of shareholders;

- Excessive rentals paid to shareholders;

- "Gifts" to shareholders or relatives;

- Improvements made to property of shareholders;

- Personal use of corporate property;

- Insurance benefits;

- Thinly capitalized corporations;

- Sale of property to the corporation;

- Personal expenses paid by the corporation;

- Bargain purchases;

- Assumption of stockholders liability;

- Withdrawals by the shareholders; and

- Excessive compensation paid to shareholder-employees.

Fees Paid to Stockholders Who Guarantee Loans

If it is customary in the industry for stockholders to guarantee loans. If the loan guarantees are necessary in order to conduct business, and if the payments are based on the loans guaranteed rather than the amount of stock owned, the corporation may receive a deduction for the fees.[40] On the other hand, where payments were in proportion to stock ownership,[41] or where the shareholders had previously guaranteed loans without taking a fee,[42] constructive dividends resulted.

Payments to Shareholders' Families

Payments to family members of a stockholder, unless accompanied by a corresponding level of services or property provided to a corporation, will

---

[39] *Loftin & Woodward Inc. v. U.S.*, 78-2 USTC ¶ 9645, 577 F.2d 1206 (5th Cir. 1978).
[40] *Tulia Feedlot, Inc.*, Ct. Cls., 83-2 USTC ¶ 9516.

[41] *Olton Feed Yard, Inc.*, 79-1 USTC ¶ 9299, 592 F.2d 272 (5th Cir. 1979).

[42] IRS Letter Rulings 8610009 and 8610010.

almost certainly be deemed a constructive dividend. Thus, where there was determined to be excessive compensation,[43] a lease entered into without a business purpose,[44] or payments made to the widow of a brother,[45] constructive dividends resulted.

Excess Rentals Paid to Shareholders

Rent paid to shareholders in excess of the fair market value will be treated as constructive dividends. In one case, for example, the corporation paid a fixed rental (which alone was a fair rental) plus 40 percent of net income before taxes.[46]

"Gifts" to Shareholders or Relatives

It is difficult for a corporation's payment to stockholders or relatives to be categorized as a gift. For example, where a close-knit family corporation made payments which were not intended as gifts and no compensation was due, the payments were considered constructive dividends.[47] However, in *Bankston* the court held that a payment to a widow was excludable from her income as a gift. The corporation passed a resolution stating that the payment was made in recognition of services rendered by the deceased. The court said that Congress did not intend to exclude the right of a corporation to make a gift merely because the recipient was a shareholder.[48] In a similar case, but one in which the two principal shareholders had made a prior oral agreement that their surviving spouses would be paid, the court nonetheless held that the payments were gifts.[49]

Improvements to Property of Shareholders

If a corporation leases property from a shareholder and makes improvements in excess of what would be normal for a lessee to make, given the type and value of property and the length of the lease, the excess could be treated as a constructive dividend. In *Jaeger,* a case which involved fraud in its other aspects, the principal shareholder leased a building on a year-to-year basis to the corporation for $500 per month. The corporation paid taxes and insurance and also paid over $16,000 to correct the foundation and to add a second floor. The court found that a constructive dividend resulted.[50] The short-term lease was obviously a very negative factor in this case. However, in *Bardes* the corporations leased two parcels of land from a shareholder for 12 years and erected buildings having a useful life of 40 years. The Tax Court held that the transactions had economic substance

---

[43] *H.L. Snyder,* 47 TCM 355, Dec. 40,611(M) (1983).

[44] *58th Street Plaza Theatre, Inc. et al. v. Commr.,* 52-1 USTC ¶ 9248, 195 F.2d 724 (2nd Cir. 1952).

[45] *P.B. Hardin,* 72-1 USTC ¶ 9464, 461 F.2d 865 (5th Cir. 1972).

[46] *Sunnyside Beverages, Inc.,* DC N.D. Ind. 71-2 USTC ¶ 9752 (1971).

[47] *Jordano's, Inc.,* 68-1 USTC ¶ 9409, 396 F.2d 829 (9th Cir. 1968).

[48] *E.A. Bankston,* 58-1 USTC ¶ 9495, 254 F.2d 641 (6th Cir., 1958).

[49] *Allinger,* 60-1 USTC ¶ 9312, 275 F.2d 421 (6th Cir., 1960).

[50] *Jaeger Motor Car Co.,* 60-2 USTC ¶ 9793, 284 F.2d 127 (7th Cir. 1960).

and that no part of the value of the improvements were dividends.[51] However, the IRS did not acquiesce.[52]

Personal Use of Corporate Property

If a shareholder uses corporate property for personal purposes, a constructive dividend results. If the property is owned by the corporation, the fair rental is the amount of the constructive dividend. The IRS has routinely won many decisions in this area. The Tax Court considers most of these cases to be so uneventful that they have been issued in memo decisions. The cases usually have involved residences, automobiles, boats, and food and lodging.[53]

Insurance Benefits

If a corporation is the owner of the policy on the life of the stockholder and is also the beneficiary, i.e., the stockholder is only the insured, no constructive dividend should result. Constructive dividend scenarios result when:

- The stockholder is the owner of the policy and the corporation pays the premiums; or

- The corporation is the owner but the stockholder or a relative is the beneficiary.

In the first instance, the Tax Court has held that payments of the premiums by the corporation will constitute dividend income.[54] In the second instance, in *Ducros,* a stockholder in a closely held corporation applied for an insurance policy on his life and pursuant to a pre-arranged plan transferred ownership to the corporation who named several stockholders as beneficiaries. The court held that the amounts received were not constructive dividends but were instead excludable from income as life insurance proceeds.[55] However, the IRS did not acquiesce.[56]

On the other hand, where the corporation purchases life insurance on the lives of its stockholders with the proceeds to be used to purchase the stock of the stockholder, even though the stockholder has the right to designate a beneficiary, if such right of the beneficiary to receive the proceeds is conditional upon the transfer of the corporate stock to the corporation, no constructive dividend results.[57]

---

[51] *Bardes, Oliver L.* 37 TC 1134, Dec. 25,416 (1962).

[52] 1964-1 CB 6.

[53] See, for example, *Lang Chevrolet Co.,* 26 TCM 1054, Dec. 28,648(M) (1967); *Ray R. Tanner,* 45 TCM 1419, Dec. 40,071(M) (1983); *T.E. Brock Jr.,* 44 TCM 128, Dec. 39,108(M) (1982); *L.E. Peterson,* 24 TCM 1383, Dec. 28,098(M) (1966); *Parker Tree Farms,* 46 TCM 493, Dec. 40,217(M) (1983).

[54] *B. Schwartz,* 22 TCM 1786, Dec. 26,447(M) (1963).

[55] *Ducros v. Commr.,* 59-2 USTC ¶ 9785, 272 F.2d 49 (6th Cir. 1959).

[56] Rev. Rul. 61-134, 1961-2 CB 250.

[57] Rev. Rul. 59-184, 1959-1 CB 65, in which the IRS agreed to follow *Henry E. Prunier et al. v. Commr.,* 57-2 USTC ¶ 10,015 248 F.2d 818 (1st Cir. 1957).

Thinly Capitalized Corporations

Stockholders in a closely held corporation have a great incentive to hold most of their equity in the form of long-term debt rather than stockholders' equity. This is so because the corporation can deduct interest payments but not dividends. Thus, if the corporation is "thinly capitalized," i.e., has a high debt to equity ratio, the IRS may assert that some or all of the debt is really equity and that the interest payments are constructive dividends. This has been a frequently litigated issue. Although a high debt to equity ratio is obviously not a favorable factor to the taxpayer, more important negative factors appear to be debt held in proportion to stock holdings, lack of a reasonable prospect of repayment, and lack of a reasonable chance of repayment. In *Creston,* for example, the notes were held in direct proportion to their stock interests. That, along with a debt-equity ratio of 205 to 1 was sufficient rationale for the Tax Court to treat the debt as equity.[58] In *Du Gro Frozen Foods* the corporation made about as poor a case as was possible. The court was troubled by: a capital insufficiency (a debt-equity ratio of 20.5 to 1); lack of creditor's safeguards; identity of note holders and stockholders (there was a direct proportion); unobserved maturity dates; and insignificant interest payments. Repayment of the advances then, was dividend income to the shareholder.[59] Lack of a business purpose was a critical factor in *Rialto Realty.* The corporation reorganized by exchanging preferred stock for bonds to, according to the corporate minutes, "effect a substantial saving in corporate taxes." The court said that there was no apparent business reason for the reorganization except for the tax savings.[60]

On the other hand, where the stock holdings and debt holdings are disproportionate and there is a reasonable likelihood of repayment, the corporation may prevail. For example, the designation of debt was held up by the court even though the debt to equity ratio was 26 to 1, because there was a sharply disproportionate ratio of ownership between stock and bonds.[61] In another case won by the taxpayer, the taxpayer held only a small minority interest, the advances were not in proportion to the share holdings, and there was a reasonable chance of repayment.[62]

Sale of Property to the Corporation

A sale of property by a stockholder to the corporation need not result in a constructive dividend if the sale is for the fair market value.[63] However, if the sale is for more than the fair market value, constructive

---

[58] *Creston Corp.,* 40 TC 932, Dec. 26,294 (1963).

[59] *Du Gro Frozen Foods, Inc.,* DC Northern Georgia, 73-1 USTC ¶ 9164, aff'd by curiam by CA-5, 73-2 USTC ¶ 9573, 481 F.2d 1271.

[60] *Rialto Realty Co., Inc. v. U.S.,* 73-2 USTC ¶ 9791, 366 FSupp 253 (DC E.D. Pa. 1973).

[61] *Lansall Co. v. U.S.,* DC S.D. NY, 81-1 USTC ¶ 9418, 512 F. Supp. 1178 (1981).

[62] *Adelson v. U.S.,* 84-2 USTC ¶ 9599, 737 F.2d 1569 (Fed. Cir. 1984).

[63] See, for example, *Jolly's Motor Livery Co.,* 16 TCM 1048, Dec. 22,698(M) (1957).

dividends will result even if the sale is not directly to the shareholder, but instead to another entity controlled by the corporation.[64]

Personal Expenses Paid by the Corporation

Personal expenses of the stockholder paid by the corporation and/or reimbursed expenditures of the stockholder/employee which cannot be substantiated will be treated as constructive dividends. Taxpayers have consistently lost these kinds of cases.

In *Cummins Diesel,* a business deduction was denied a corporation for expenses of having a registered nurse accompany its employee/stockholder (who was ill) on a combined business and pleasure trip even though she performed minor secretarial duties.[65] In *Whitfield* the travel expenses of the wife of an employee/stockholder were denied even though she helped entertain and sometimes made appointments for him.[66] In *Ma-Tran Corp.* amounts paid in excess of vouchers for travel expenses, reimbursements for local meals, and an apartment rental were all treated as constructive dividends because the corporation could not substantiate a business purpose.[67]

Expenditures which benefit both the corporation and the shareholder need not necessarily be disallowed. In *Martin v. Machiz,* the court held that a payment to a brokerage firm to aid in finding a buyer for the majority stockholder's stock was not a constructive dividend since the corporation benefited from having an orderly succession. The fact that the expense was not deductible to the corporation did not necessarily make it a personal expense of the stockholders.[68]

In 1993, Congress placed tough restrictions on travel expense deductions of spouses, relatives, or others (presumably aimed at significant others), unless:[69]

- The spouse, dependent, or other individual is an employee of the taxpayer;

- The travel of the spouse, dependent, or other individual is for a bona fide business purpose; and

- The expenses would otherwise be deductible by the spouse, dependent, or other individual.

Bargain Purchases from the Corporation

An early Supreme Court case set the parameters for sales by a corporation being treated as constructive dividends. The Court said that "while a sale of corporate assets to stockholders is, in a literal sense, a

---

[64] *A.A. Emmerson,* 44 TC 86, Dec. 27,352 (1965).
[65] *Cummins Diesel Sales of Oregon, Inc.,* 63-2 USTC ¶ 9641, 321 F.2d 503 (9th Cir. 1963).
[66] *Alabama-Georgia Syrup Co. v. Commr.,* 36 TC 747, Dec. 24,957 (1961).

[67] *Ma-Tran Corp. v. Commr.,* 70 TC 158, Dec. 35,134 (1978).
[68] *Martin v. Machiz* (DC Maryland), 66-1 USTC ¶ 9338, 251 F. Supp. 381 (1966).
[69] Code Sec. 274(m)(3).

distribution of its property, such a transaction does not necessarily fall within the statutory definition of a dividend. For a sale to stockholders may not result in any diminution of its net worth and in that case cannot result in any distribution of its profits. On the other hand, such a sale, if for substantially less than the value of the property sold, may be as effective a means of distributing profits among stockholders as the formal declaration of a dividend." It must be true that ". . . the transaction is in purpose or effect used as an implement for the distribution of corporate earnings to stockholders."[70]

In applying these principles, the courts have not necessarily required a sale for substantially less than fair market value. In *Nelson* the taxpayer purchased machines for a 100 percent markup over cost, but the sale to unrelated purchases later that year for greater prices indicated a bargain purchase which was treated as a constructive dividend.[71] Book value cannot be used as a surrogate for fair market value. In *Lacy* the corporation sold a building at its book value of $33,000 to a shareholder. However, the fair market value was considerably more ($133,000), and the difference was treated as a constructive dividend.[72] In *Honigman* the corporation sold to a minority shareholder a hotel for a substantial amount ($661,280), but less than the capitalized value of the earnings ($830,000). The excess was treated as a constructive dividend.[73] On the other hand, in *Rodman,* a stockholder purchased stock in a subsidiary corporation from the parent company for the same amount that the parent company had paid five years ago. The Tax Court ruled that, since the subsidiary had a low rate of profit on sales and its net income had declined, the amount paid was not a bargain purchase.[74]

Assumption of Shareholder's Liability

Unless directly a part of a Code Sec. 351 transaction, the assumption of a shareholder's debt will generally result in a constructive dividend. In a U.S. District Court case, a jury found that the payment made by a corporation to the estranged wife of a principal stockholder was a constructive dividend. The corporation had claimed that the payment was an ordinary and necessary business expense because it was made to protect the company's business reputation (there was a threatened suit against the stockholder for assault).[75]

In *Wolf,* a rather complicated set of transactions resulted in a newly formed corporation assuming a partnership obligation (the partnership was

[70] *Palmer v. Commr.,* 37-2 USTC ¶ 9532, 302 US 63, 58 S Ct. 67 (1937).
[71] *R.T. Nelson,* 85-2 USTC ¶ 9504, 767 F.2d 667 (10th Cir. 1985).
[72] *W. Lacy,* 65-1 USTC ¶ 9205, 341 F.2d 54 (10th Cir., 1965).
[73] *Honigman,* 55 TC 1067, Dec. 30,691 (1971), aff'd, 72-2 USTC ¶ 9613, 466 F.2d 69 (6th Cir., 1972).

[74] *Rodman v. Commr.,* 57 TC 113, Dec. 31,039 (1971).
[75] *Mobile Beverage Co. v. Patterson* (DC N.D. Ala.), 60-1 USTC ¶ 9403.

a shareholder). The corporation claimed the transaction was nontaxable under Code Sec. 351. However, the court ruled that applying the step transaction made it apparent that the transaction was a constructive dividend.[76]

In *Ackerson,* however, the taxpayer prevailed. A corporation was formed to purchase the stock of an existing corporation. Most of the purchase price was obtained from a $100,000 note of the new corporation. The IRS claimed that since the stockholders had guaranteed the loan, the payments on it were constructive dividends. The court held for the taxpayer, reasoning that all of the criteria for a legitimate loan were met.[77]

Withdrawals

A number of factors govern whether or not withdrawals made by shareholders should be treated as dividends. In a U.S. District Court case, the judge, in his instructions to the jury said, "In determining whether the withdrawals involved in this case or any part of them were loans or taxable dividends . . . you should give consideration to the following. First, whether the amount of the withdrawals were charged to the account of the stockholder and were carried on the records of the corporation as accounts receivable. Second, whether the withdrawals were secured by the stockholder's note or otherwise, or whether interest was paid by him thereon. Third, whether the withdrawals are regarded as an indebtedness by both the stockholders and the corporation . . . . Fourth, whether any interest is paid by the stockholder or is charged by the corporation. Fifth, whether the corporation had sufficient surplus [accumulated earnings and profits] to cover the withdrawals at the time such withdrawals were made. Sixth, whether the stockholder intended to make repayment with interest at the time he made the withdrawal."[78]

In *Turner* a slightly different set of criteria was set forth. "The subjective statement of intention to repay the borrower is merely one item of evidence regarding actual intention to repay, and other evidence of actual intention to repay includes, but is not limited to, the observance of corporate formalities with regard to documentation of the loan, the treatment of the loan upon the books and records of the corporation, the existence of promissory notes, whether the loans are *pro rata* with respect to the shareholdings in the corporation, the size of the advances, ability to repay the loans, and actual efforts of repayment of the loans."[79]

Early court cases appeared to place considerable weight on whether or not the corporation treated the withdrawals as loans on their books.[80]

---

[76] *W.F. Wolf Jr.,* 66-1 USTC ¶ 9316, 357 F.2d 483 (9th Cir. 1966).
[77] *Ackerson v. US* (DC W.D. Ky.) 67-2 USTC ¶ 9686, 277 F. Supp. 475 (1967).
[78] *Adams et al. v. Glenn* (DC W.D. Ky.), 50-2 USTC ¶ 9447 (1950).
[79] *Turner vs. U.S.* (DC Wy.), 85-1 USTC ¶ 9440 (1985).

[80] See, for example, *Shaken,* 21 TC 785, Dec. 20,176 (1954) and *Bush, Irving T.,* 45 BTA 609, Dec. 12,152 (1941). However, an opposite view was given in *Christopher,* 2 USTC ¶ 841, 55 F.2d 527 (D.C. Circuit 1931).

However, more recent court cases have given that criterion little weight. For example, in *Williams* the subjective intent to repay was outweighed by the withdrawals over a long period of years, the accumulation of an impressive earned surplus, nonpayment when the taxpayer had the ability to pay, the failure to execute notes until the tax problems became acute, and the circumstances surrounding repayment (the shareholders had learned that their returns could be audited).[81] In *Dolese* notes were given, interest was paid and some payments were made on principal. However, the loan balance was very high compared to the stockholders income and there was an "excessive and continuous diversion of corporate funds into the controlling shareholder's pocket."[82] The lack of an apparent ceiling on advances was also a factor in *Alterman,* as were other factors such as the lack of a repayment schedule and no fixed date of maturity.[83]

Below market loans from a corporation to a shareholder require the imputation of interest generally for all demand loans and all term loans entered into after June 6, 1984.[84] An exception exists for corporate-shareholder loans, the aggregate outstanding amount of which does not exceed $10,000 unless the principal purpose is the avoidance of tax.[85] A "below market loan" is any demand loan where the interest rate is less than the applicable federal rate or a term loan where the amount loaned exceeds the present value (determined by using a discount rate equal to the applicable federal rate).[86]

In a below market loan, the shareholder is deemed to have received a distribution from the corporation which he or she then pays back in the form of interest. Thus, the corporation has interest income and a dividend paid (assuming earnings and profits), while the stockholder has dividend income and investment interest expense.[87]

> **Example 14-21.** On July 1, 2001, Village Design Co. makes a $200,000 interest-free term loan for three years to shareholder Terri Crowe. The applicable federal rate is 6.27 percent, compounded semi-annually. The present value of this payment is $166,186, determined as follows:

$$\$166{,}186 \quad = \quad \frac{\$200{,}000}{(1 + (.0627/2))^6}$$

> The discount of $33,814 ($200,000 − $166,186) is treated as a distribution of property paid to Crowe on July 1, 2001, and the same amount is treated as original issue discount (see Code Secs. 163 and 1272).[88] Crowe would use the constant yield method to determine her interest expense deduction as provided by Code Sec. 1272(a).

---

[81] *C.F. Williams v. Commr.,* 80-2 USTC ¶ 9550, 627 F.2d 1032 (10th Cir. 1980).

[82] *R. Dolese,* 79-2 USTC ¶ 9540, 605 F.2d 1146 (10th Cir. 1979), cert. denied, 100 S Ct. 1648.

[83] *Alterman Foods, Inc. v. U.S.,* 75-1 USTC ¶ 9151, 505 F.2d 873 (Fifth Cir. 1975).

[84] Act Sec. 172(a), TRA-84, adding Code Sec. 7872.

[85] Code Sec. 7872(c).

[86] Code Sec. 7872(e) and (f).

[87] The investment interest expense would be subject to the limitations imposed by Code Sec. 163(d).

[88] Prop. Reg. § 1.7872-14.

The "applicable federal rate" for a term loan is the applicable rate under Code Sec. 1274(d) as of the loan date, compounded semiannually. The applicable federal rate for demand loans is the short-term rate in effect under Code Sec. 1274(d) for the period for which the interest is being determined, compounded semiannually.[89]

Both the lender and the borrower have reporting requirements with respect to below market interest. The borrower must attach a statement to his or her return for any year in which he or she either has imputed dividend income or claims a deduction for interest expense. The statement must contain:[90]

- An explanation that it relates to an amount taxable or deductible under Section 7872;

- The name, address, and taxpayer ID of the lender;

- The amount of imputed interest expense and the amount of income imputed to the lender; and

- The mathematical assumptions used (see Reg. § 1.7872-13) for computing the amounts.

The lender must attach a statement which contains essentially the same information from the perspective of the lender.[91]

Tax Tips and Pitfalls

Loans to shareholders is a treacherous issue in federal taxation. Steps to take which would reduce the possibility of the loans being treated as constructive dividends include:

- Loans for a fixed term, rather than an indefinite open account;

- Sporadic and irregular advances, rather than continuously;

- Advance totals not so large as to call into question the ability to repay;

- Provision for interest and provision for repayment;

- Carried on the books of the corporation as loans;

- Signed notes, ideally with collateral; and

- Loan balances which are disproportionate to shareholdings.

Excessive Compensation

Of all the forms that excessive compensation may take, excessive compensation to stockholder/employees is doubtless the most common and the most often litigated. Over the many years of court cases, the courts

---

[89] Code Sec. 7872(f).
[90] Prop. Reg. § 1.7872-11(g)(2).
[91] Prop. Reg. § 1.7872-11(g)(1).

have attempted to set forth criteria to determine the reasonableness of compensation. In an oft-cited case, the Sixth Circuit in *Mayson* said that "... such factors include the employee's qualifications; the nature, extent and scope of the employee's work, the size and complexities of the business; a comparison of salaries paid with the gross income and the net income; the prevailing general economic conditions; comparison of salaries with distributions to stockholders; the prevailing rates of compensation for comparable positions in comparable concerns; the salary policy of the taxpayer as to all employees; and in case of small corporations with a limited number of officers the amount of compensation paid to the particular employee in previous years."[92]

In a more recent case, the Ninth Circuit described five broad categories of factors:[93]

1.   Role of the employee in the company;

2.   External comparison (salaries paid by similar companies for similar services);

3.   Character and size of company;

4.   Conflict of interest (a relationship between the company and the employee which might permit the company to disguise nondeductible distributions as salaries); and

5.   Internal consistency (evidence of a long-standing, formally structured, consistently applied compensation plan).

Another noteworthy feature of *Elliot* is the court's rejection of the "automatic dividend" rule which carried the presumption that a portion of even reasonable compensation is a constructive dividend if the company is profitable but has never paid a dividend.[94] However, in an earlier case the Tenth Circuit, in ruling against the taxpayer, said that "the nonpayment of a dividend in conjunction with a contingent compensation scheme for a controlling shareholder has frequently been recognized as an indication that unreasonable and excessive compensation has been paid."[95]

The courts have operationalized various specific criteria. For example, in *Giles Industries* the Court of Claims said that if the reasonableness of a salary is determined in prior years, salaries for later years must be adjusted for inflation (the court used the CPI) as well as for changes in their duties.[96] In *Levenson & Klein, Inc.* the Tax Court said that not only the hours worked, but the quality of service as represented by such factors as experience and expertise was important. The court placed more value on

---

[92] *Mayson Manufacturing Co. v. Commr.*, 49-2 USTC ¶ 9467, 178 F.2d 115 (6th Cir. 1949).
[93] *Elliotts, Inc. v. Commr.*, 83-2 USTC ¶ 9610, 716 F.2d 1241 (9th Cir. 1983).
[94] *Id.*; For the "automatic dividend" rule see *Charles McCandless Tile Serv. v. U.S.*, 70-1 USTC ¶ 9284 422 F.2d 1336 (Ct. Cl. 1970).

[95] *Pepsi-Cola Bottling Co. of Salina, Inc.*, 76-1 USTC ¶ 9107, 528 F.2d 176 (10th Cir. 1976).
[96] *Giles Industries v. U.S.*, 81-1 USTC ¶ 9444, 650 F.2d 274 (Ct. Cl. 1981).

one hour of an executive's time who had over 50 years of experience than on that of an executive with 27 years of expertise. The court also disregarded the lack of board of directors approval of the salary, noting that "closely held corporations, as is well known, often act informally."[97]

Tax Tips and Pitfalls

Compensation is less likely to be disallowed as excessive if:

- The board of directors fixes the compensation and notes the reasons for paying the compensation (e.g., expertise);

- The compensation arrangement is formally structured and consistently applied;

- The compensation is in line with the employee's duties and pay rates for employees in comparably sized companies in the same industry (industry data can be very helpful in justifying the pay); and

- Pay above the norm can be justified by reference to high profit levels, hours worked, nature of duties, and so on.

¶ 1411   Stock Redemptions

Stock is considered to be redeemed by a corporation if the corporation acquires its stock from a shareholder in exchange for cash or property, regardless of whether the stock is actually canceled or retired, or merely held as treasury stock.[98]

Redemptions will either be treated as an exchange (and thus qualify for capital gains treatment) or be treated as a dividend. Exchange treatment is generally a much more favorable alternative to the stockholder. If considered an exchange, not only are the gains subject to capital gains tax rates which are likely to be lower than the taxpayer's marginal income tax rate, but the stock basis reduces the gain. However, if the stockholder has a net operating loss, dividend treatment may enable the corporation to get rid of all or part of its earnings and profits at no cost to the taxpayer.

There are four instances in which redemptions from a living taxpayer are treated as exchanges rather than as dividends:[99]

1.   The redemption is not equivalent to a dividend;

2.   The redemption is substantially disproportionate;

3.   The redemption completely terminates the shareholder's interest; or

4.   The redemption is from a noncorporate shareholder in partial liquidation of the corporation.

---

[97] *Levenson & Klein, Inc.,* 67 TC 694, Dec. 34,221 (1977).

[98] Code Sec. 317(b).

[99] Code Sec. 302(b).

.01 Redemptions Not Equivalent to a Dividend

This criterion is by far the most vague and subjective of the four. The regulations shed little light on the application of this criterion. The regulations do state that the existence or lack of E&P does not affect the status of the redemption, i.e., a redemption could be treated as a distribution even if there was no E&P.[100] The question as to whether a redemption is not essentially equivalent to a dividend depends on the facts and circumstances of each case.[101]

In *Davis,* the Supreme Court said that for a redemption to be treated as an exchange, there must be a meaningful reduction of the shareholder's proportionate interest.[102] The IRS has ruled that if an individual shareholder does not experience a meaningful reduction of his or her interest, the redemption is treated as a distribution to him or her even if other stockholders' interests are meaningfully reduced.[103]

Should the attribution rules be applied in determining whether a meaningful reduction has occurred when there is family hostility? The courts are divided on this issue. In *Robin Haft Trust* the First Circuit said that family discord might tend to negate the presumption that taxpayers would exert continuing control over the corporation despite the redemption.[104] However, the Fifth Circuit in *David Metzer Trust* held that even though the redemption was due to family hostility, attribution rules had to be applied to determine if there was a meaningful reduction of the taxpayer's interest.[105]

Can there be a meaningful reduction if the shareholder still owns a majority interest afterward? Two of the circuit courts and the IRS disagree. The IRS said that a redemption of stock that reduced the ownership from 90 percent to 60 percent was *not* a meaningful reduction because the day-to-day operation of the corporation was still under his control.[106]

However, both the Eighth Circuit and the Sixth Circuit have ruled that where ownership is reduced below the level required for liquidation, merger, or consolidation (two-thirds ownership in both of the states involved), a meaningful reduction in voting power occurred.[107]

If a redemption is one of a series of redemptions under a plan that would as a whole meaningfully reduce the shareholder's interest, it will be

---

[100] Reg. § 1.302-2(a). However, note that if the corporation has *no* E&P, the distribution will be treated as a return of capital up to basis.

[101] Reg. § 1.302-(b).

[102] *U.S. v. Davis,* 70-1 USTC ¶ 9289, 397 US 301 (1970).

[103] Rev. Rul. 81-289, 1981-2 CB 82.

[104] *Robin Haft Trust,* 75-1 USTC ¶ 9209, 510 F.2d 43 (1st Cir. 1975) vacating and remanding, 61 TC 398 (1973).

[105] *David Metzger Trust,* 82-2 USTC ¶ 9718, 693 F.2d 459 (5th Cir. 1982). Also see Rev. Rul. 80-26, 1980-1 CB 67.

[106] Rev. Rul. 78-401, 1978-2 CB 127.

[107] See, *William F. Wright,* 73-2 USTC ¶ 9583, 482 F.2d 600 (8th Cir. 1973) and *Patterson Trust v. U.S.,* 84-1 USTC ¶ 9315, 729 F.2d 1089 (6th Cir. 1984).

given exchange treatment even though it alone does not meaningfully reduce the shareholder's interest.[108]

Tax Tips and Pitfalls

Relying on Code Sec. 302(b)(1) to get exchange treatment is a risky strategy. Regardless of the business purpose or family hostility, a redemption that leaves the stockholder owning indirectly over two-thirds of the stock is unlikely to receive redemption treatment. Stock ownership afterward of over 50 percent but less than two-thirds will be challenged by the IRS and would have to be resolved in court. The taxpayer has a stronger case if ownership afterward is under 50 percent, or exactly 50 percent (if another stockholder owns the other 50 percent). Nonetheless, it is *far* better, if possible, to meet the mechanical tests of Code Sec. 302(b)(2).

.02 Substantially Disproportionate Redemptions

In contrast to the first instance of exchange treatment, which is quite subjective, the substantially disproportionate test is a mechanical test. This test is met if:[109]

- Immediately after the redemption the shareholder owns less than 50 percent of the total combined voting power of all classes of stock which can vote;

- The percentage of voting stock owned immediately after the redemption is less than 80 percent of the percentage owned immediately before the redemption; and

- The percentage of common stock owned immediately after the redemption is less than 80 percent of the percentage owned immediately before the redemption.

.03 Constructive Ownership Rules

In applying these tests the constructive ownership rules of Code Sec. 318(a) apply.[110] An individual is considered to own stock by or for:[111]

- The taxpayer's spouse (unless legally separated);

- The taxpayer's children (including legally adopted children), grandchildren, and parents;

- Partnerships as owned proportionately by its partners;

- Trusts, generally in proportion to the actuarial interest of the beneficiaries; and

---

[108] See *Blanche S. Benjamin*, 66 TC 1084, Dec. 34,044 (1976) and *Mary G. Roebling*, 77 TC 30, Dec. 38,039 (1981).

[109] Code Sec. 302(b)(2).
[110] Code Sec. 302(c)(1).
[111] Code Sec. 318(a).

- Corporations, as owned proportionately by the shareholder, but only if the shareholder owns (directly or indirectly) 50 percent or more in value of the stock.

Entities also are considered to own stock that their owners own. Partnerships and estates own stock that partners or beneficiaries own, directly or indirectly.[112] Trusts are considered to own stock that beneficiaries own, unless the beneficiary's interest is a remote contingent interest. A "remote contingent interest" exists if, under the maximum exercise of discretion by the trustee in favor of the beneficiary, the value of the interest, computed actuarially, is five percent or less of the value of the trust property.[113] Corporations own the stock that their shareholders own only if the shareholder owns, directly or indirectly, 50 percent or more of the stock.[114] S corporations are considered to be partnerships for this purpose. If any person has an option to buy stock, such stock is considered to be owned.[115]

Example 14-22. Don Juette, his wife, his son, and his grandson each own 25 shares of the 100 shares outstanding in Convenient Hardware, Inc. Juette, his wife, and his son each are considered to own all 100 shares of Convenient Hardware, Inc. The grandson, however, only owns 75 shares (grandparents are not relatives for this purpose).

Example 14-23. Tara Blue owns 40 percent of a partnership. The partnership owns 30 percent of Tea Corporation. Blue owns 60 percent of Tea Corporation. Under the attribution rules, Blue owns 72 percent of Tea Corporation; the partnership owns 90 percent.

Example 14-24. Jim Black and Dean Redd, unrelated individuals, each own 25 percent of the Weimer Corporation. They also own 60 percent and 30 percent, respectively, of the Luther Corporation, which owns 20 percent of the Weimer Corporation stock. Stock owned, under the attribution rules, in Weimer Corporation is:

Black (25% + .60 (20%))	=	37%
Redd	=	25%
Luther Corporation (20% + 25%)	=	45%

Examples of meeting, or failing, the 80 percent and the 50 percent test are shown below.

Example 14-25. White, Red, Blue, and Green each own 25 shares out of the 100 shares outstanding of the Multi-Color Corporation. The corporation redeemed six shares of Red's stock. Before the redemption, Red owned 25 out of 100 shares (25%). After the redemption, he owns 19 out of 94 shares (20.21%). Since 20.21/25 = 80.85%, the 80 percent test is failed (Red's ownership percentage is over 80 percent of what it

---

was before the redemption), and the redemption will be treated as a dividend.

> **Example 14-26.** Henry Medrano owns 40 shares out of the 100 shares outstanding of Woodwork Co. His daughter owns another 35 shares and his brother the remaining 25 shares. The corporation redeems 38 of his shares. Before the redemption he owned 75/100 shares or 75 percent. After the redemption he owned 37 (2 + 35) out of 62 shares, or 59.68 percent. Although 59.68/75 = 79.57%, which meets the 80 percent test, the redemption is treated as a dividend because the 50 percent test is not met (he directly or indirectly owns 59.68 percent afterward).

> **Example 14-27.** Alan, Bates, Cairns, and Dinwitty, all unrelated, each own 25 percent of ABCD Co. The corporation redeems 10 shares of Cairns and eight shares of Dinwitty. Cairns afterward owns 15 out of 82 shares, or 18.29 percent. Since his ownership percentage (18.29/25) is only 73.16 percent of his previous ownership percentage, he may treat the redemption as an exchange. However, Dinwitty's ownership percentage afterward is 17/82, or 20.73 percent. Since 20.73/25 = 83 percent, Dinwitty treats the redemption as a dividend.

.04 Redemptions Which Completely Terminate a Shareholder's Interest

Redemptions in complete liquidation of a shareholder's interest are treated as exchanges.[116] One would expect that attribution rules would make it very difficult for stockholders in family corporations to completely terminate their interest. Fortunately, the family attribution rules do not apply to complete terminations provided that these conditions are met:[117]

- Immediately after the distribution the former stockholder must have no interest other than as a creditor, i.e., he or she must not be an officer, director, or employee.

- The former stockholder must not acquire any stock within 10 years of the date of distribution unless by bequest or inheritance.

- The former stockholder must file an agreement to notify the IRS of any acquisition within the 10-year period. The agreement must be in duplicate, must be signed by the former stockholder, and must be attached to the first return to which the redemption applies.[118] If the former stockholder acquires stock (other than by bequest or inheritance) within the 10-year period, the statute of limitations is extended and the IRS could recategorize the redemption as a dividend.[119]

---

[116] Code Sec. 302(b)(3).
[117] Code Sec. 302(c)(2).
[118] Reg. § 1.302-4(a).
[119] Code Sec. 302(c)(2)(A).

In order to prevent excessive manipulation of the family attribution rules, the family ownership rules are *not* waived if the former stockholder:[120]

- Acquired the stock from a family member within the 10 years preceding the redemption, or

- A family member acquired stock from the former stockholder within the 10-year period preceding the redemption, unless that family member's stock is also redeemed.

The above two rules do not apply if the acquisition or disposition by the former stockholder did not have tax avoidance as a principal purpose.[121]

Recall that the only interest that the former stockholder can have is that of creditor. Certain items called "debt" may be considered proprietary instead if the "debt" is subordinate to the general creditors or if the debt repayment or interest rate is dependent on the level of corporate earnings.[122]

Entities (partnerships, estates, trusts, or corporations) may waive the attribution rules only if all of their stock and all of the stock of the individual whose ownership is attributed to the entity are redeemed.[123] All persons must also agree to be jointly and severally liable for any deficiency resulting from the redemption.[124]

Example 14-28. Russell Mason owns 40 percent of a corporation and his two sons each own 30 percent. Mason wishes to move to a retirement village in Florida. The corporation redeems all of his stock. Although the redemption does not qualify as a disproportionate distribution, it is considered to be in complete liquidation of Mason's interest and thus receives exchange treatment.

.05 Redemptions in Partial Liquidation of the Corporation

Distributions qualifying as partial liquidations must either:[125]

1. Be not essentially equivalent to a dividend (determined at the corporate level, not at the shareholder level); or

2. Be pursuant to the termination of an active business.

The first criterion is, as was true of Code Sec. 302(b)(1), quite subjective. The regulations state that if the distribution results from a genuine contraction of the corporate business, the distribution will not be equivalent to a dividend.[126] In *Imler*, a fire destroyed the top two floors of a business, and faced with a costly rebuilding, the corporation decided instead to distribute the insurance proceeds to shareholders in redemption of about

[120] Code Sec. 302(c)(2)(B).
[121] Code Sec. 302(c)(2).
[122] Reg. § 1.302-4(d).
[123] Code Sec. 302(c)(2)(C).
[124] *Id.*
[125] Code Sec. 302(e)(1).
[126] Reg. § 1.346-1(a)(2).

one-half of the stock. Because of the shortage of space and other factors, the company discontinued its main business. The Tax Court ruled that there was a bona fide contraction of business operations and consequent reduction in capital need.[127] On the other hand, the distribution of funds attributable to a reserve for an expansion program which has been abandoned does not qualify as a partial liquidation.[128]

The second criterion involves more objective requirements. The requirements are as follows:[129]

- The distribution must be attributable to the distributing corporation's ceasing to conduct, or consists of the assets of, a "qualified trade or business," and

- Immediately after the distribution, the distributing corporation must be actively engaged in a "qualified trade or business."

A "qualified trade or business" is one that was actively conducted during the entire five-year period ending on the date of the redemption and which was *not* acquired by the corporation during that period in a fully or partly taxable transaction.[130]

Example 14-29. The Klean-Rug Corporation was formed in 1990 and was successful in its rug cleaning business. In 1997 it added a mail service business in a nontaxable Code Sec. 351 transfer. The mail service business was started in 1994. In 2001 increased competition made the rug-cleaning business less profitable, and the assets were sold and the proceeds distributed to the shareholders in return for 15 percent of their stock. The redemption would qualify as a partial liquidation because: (1) the business being disposed of was actively conducted during the five-year period and was not acquired in a taxable transaction during that period (it was owned throughout the period), and (2) the business retained was operated (by somebody) during the five-year period and was not acquired in a taxable transaction during the five-year period.

Example 14-30. Assume the same facts as in the previous example, except that the mail service business was purchased during 1997. The redemption does not qualify as a partial liquidation because the business being continued was acquired in a taxable transaction during the five-year period.

Example 14-31. The Four Star Movie Theatre, in operation since 1960, acquired in 1996 in a taxable transaction, assets to form a video business. In 2001, after two video chains moved to town, it distributed the video business in kind to its shareholders. The redemption does *not* qualify as a partial liquidation since the business being terminated

---

[127] *Joseph W. Imler v. Commr.*, 11 TC 836, Dec. 16,691 (1948).
[128] Reg. § 1.346-1(a)(2).

[129] Code Sec. 302(e)(2).

[130] Code Sec. 302(e)(3).

was not conducted for five years; it was also acquired in a taxable transaction during that period (either item would have disqualified it as a partial liquidation).

.06 Redemptions to Pay Death Taxes

The estate of a decedent having as its primary asset an interest in a closely held corporation is likely to not be very liquid. Often the corporation has more cash than does the decedent. To help mitigate this liquidity problem, Congress has enacted several helpful laws, one of which is Code Sec. 303. If a corporation redeems stock which is included in the gross estate of a decedent, the redemption will be treated as a sale or exchange to the extent that the redemption does not exceed the sum of:[131]

- The estate and inheritance taxes (both federal and state) imposed; and

- Funeral and administration expenses.

In order to qualify, the corporate stock must form a substantial part of the adjusted gross estate. Specifically, the value of the corporate stock must exceed 35 percent of the adjusted gross estate (the excess of the gross estate over deductions allowed for funeral and administration expenses, claims against the estate, unpaid mortgages, taxes, and casualty and theft losses).[132]

Example 14-32. Jeff Mizer died in 2001. He had a gross estate of $3,000,000 including $1,200,000 worth of Mizer, Inc., stock. Funeral and administration expenses were $100,000, debts were $500,000, and federal and state death taxes $200,000. The corporation redeemed $300,000 of stock from Mizer's estate. The value of the stock is in excess of 35 percent of the adjusted gross estate ($1,200,000/($3,000,000 − $100,000 − $500,000 − $200,000)) = 55 percent. Also, the amount redeemed does not exceed the funeral and administration expenses and the death taxes. Hence, the redemption qualifies as an exchange.

If stock in two or more corporations form a part of the gross estate, they are treated as one corporation in meeting the 35 percent requirement, provided that 20 percent or more in value of the outstanding stock is included in the gross estate.[133]

Example 14-33. K. Bucket died in 2001. His gross estate of $1,000,000 included $200,000 of KB Inc. stock and $100,000 of Bucket Co. stock. The ownership percentages were 30 percent and 25 percent, respectively. His adjusted gross estate was $800,000. Stock was redeemed in the amount of $25,000 from each corporation to pay death taxes. Since the value of stock owned in each corporation is at least 20

---

[131] Code Sec. 303(a).
[132] Code Sec. 303(b)(2)(A).
[133] Code Sec. 303(b)(2)(B).

percent, their stock may be combined for the 35 percent test. Since the combined value of the stock equals 37.5 percent of the adjusted gross estate, the 35 percent test is also met. Therefore, the redemption qualifies for exchange treatment.

Example 14-34. Assume the same facts as in Example 14-33, except that only 15 percent of the value of Bucket Co. is owned and the value of the stock owned is still $100,000. Since the value of the Bucket stock is under 20 percent, it cannot be counted in meeting the 35 percent test. This would then cause the stock owned in KB Inc. to flunk the 35 percent test, and both redemptions would be treated as dividends.

Example 14-35. Assume the same facts as in Example 14-33, except that the KB stock is worth $295,000 and Bucket's ownership percentage is only 18 percent. The KB stock qualifies by itself for exchange treatment since it represents over 35 percent of the adjusted gross estate. However, the Bucket Co. stock does not qualify by itself and cannot be combined with the KB stock for purposes of the 35 percent rule. Hence, redemption of the KB stock qualifies for exchange treatment, but the Bucket Co. stock redemption will be a dividend.

The distribution must occur after the date of death and generally within 90 days after the expiration of the statute of limitations for assessment of the estate tax.[134] If a petition is before the Tax Court, the time period is extended to 60 days after the decision of the Tax Court becomes final.[135] The Tax Court case must be bona fide, and not merely one which is initiated solely for the purpose of extending the time period.[136] If an election has been made under Code Sec. 6166 to extend the time of payment of the tax, the time period is extended to the time allowed for the installment payments.[137]

The exchange of stock held in the decedent's estate for new stock will not preclude redemption of the new stock from getting exchange treatment so long as the exchange of old for new was nontaxable under Code Sec. 368 (a nontaxable reorganization), Code Sec. 355 (a devisive reorganization), Code Sec. 1036 (an exchange of stock for stock of the same corporation), or Code Sec. 305(a) (a stock dividend).[138]

Example 14-36. A.C. Litvak owned 100 shares of stock in Sunly Co. at the time of his death. His estate received a 20 percent nontaxable dividend. Later, all 120 shares were redeemed. Assuming that all of the other requirements are met, all 120 shares redeemed qualify for exchange treatment.

---

[134] Code Sec. 303(b)(1)(A).
[135] Code Sec. 303(b)(1)(B).
[136] Reg. § 1.303-2(e).

[137] Code Sec. 303(b)(1)(C).
[138] Reg. § 1.303-2(d).

Code Sec. 303 will apply most frequently when stock is redeemed from the executor of the estate. However, it is also applicable to redemptions of the decedent's stock now held by heirs, a surviving joint tenant, surviving spouse, transferee of a trust created by the decedent, or the donee where the stock was transferred in contemplation of death.[139]

If the amount redeemed exceeds the sum of the funeral and administration expenses and the death taxes, and there is more than one redemption, the distribution eligible for Code Sec. 303 treatment will be in the order in which the distributions occur.[140]

> **Example 14-37.** Assume the same facts as in Example 14-32, except that in the first year of administration $250,000 of stock was redeemed and in the second year another $150,000 was redeemed. The first distribution would qualify for exchange treatment. Of the second distribution of $150,000, $50,000 would qualify under Code Sec. 303; the tax treatment of the remaining $100,000 would be determined under other provisions of the code.

Tax Tips and Pitfalls

Code Sec. 303 can be very beneficial to estates and the heirs. Since the income tax basis is revalued at death to fair market value, the redemption value should be very close to the income tax basis and, therefore, little gain or loss should result. Assuming the 35 percent test is met, it is easy to qualify for Code Sec. 303. The distribution does not have to be disproportionate, and attribution rules do not apply. On the other hand, if the total desired redemption exceeds the sum of the funeral and administrative expenses and the death taxes, the excess, while not eligible for Code Sec. 303, could be eligible under Code Sec. 302.

> **Example 14-38.** Assume the same facts as in Example 14-32, except that the stock worth $1,200,000 represents 60 percent of the company's stock and that the other 40 percent is held by people not related to the estate. Further assume that $800,000 of stock is redeemed. Although only $300,000 of redeemed stock is eligible under Section 303, the remainder would qualify under Code Sec. 302(b)(2) since the total redemption is disproportionate (the ownership of $33\frac{1}{3}$ percent afterward is less than 80 percent of the 60 percent ownership beforehand).

.07 Effect of Redemption on the Redeeming Corporation

The corporation must recognize gains, but not losses, if property is distributed in redemption of stock.[141] This is so whether the stockholder treats the redemption as an exchange or as a dividend. If the property is

---

[139] Reg. § 1.303-2(f).
[140] Reg. § 1.303-2(g).

[141] Code Sec. 311(b).

subject to a liability, the fair market value of the property is considered to be of at least equal to the amount of the liability.

> **Example 14-39.** Johnson, Inc., is distributing property worth $40,000 to a shareholder in redemption of part of his stock. The property has a basis to the corporation of $16,000 and has a $45,000 mortgage against it. The fair market value is deemed to be $45,000; hence, the corporation must recognize a $29,000 gain on the redemption.

Earnings and profits (E&P) is also impacted by redemption distributions. E&P must be increased by any gain recognized on the redemption. E&P must be decreased because of the distribution, whether it is treated by stockholders as dividends or as exchanges. However, the rules for determining the *amount* of the reduction differ. If the redemption is treated as a dividend, E&P is reduced by the greater of the adjusted basis or the fair market value of the property distributed. If the property is subject to a liability, the E&P reduction is decreased by the amount of the liability. The above rules are the same as for property dividends, discussed previously in the chapter.

If the redemption is treated as an exchange, the maximum reduction in E&P is the ratable share of earnings and profits attributable to the stock so redeemed.[142]

> **Example 14-40.** Ripley Motors redeemed during the year all 30 shares owned by Nicholas Rip. Total shares outstanding before the redemption were 100. E&P before the redemption was $200,000. Rip received $65,000 for the stock redeemed. The reduction in E&P is $200,000 × .30 = $60,000.

> **Example 14-41.** Assume the same facts as in Example 14-40, except that the redemption price was $55,000. The reduction in E&P is the lesser of $60,000 (the *pro rata* share of E&P) or the redemption price of $55,000.

.08 Redemptions by Related Corporations

The purchase of stock by a related corporation is not literally a redemption, yet results similar to a redemption might, in the absence of Code Sec. 304 occur.

> **Example 14-42.** Robert Pryor owns 100 percent of both Bob's Autos Inc. and Pryor Motors Co. Robert sold 20 percent of his stock in Bob's Autos Inc. to Pryor Motors Co. Although not literally a redemption, the effect would be the same since Robert would have extracted cash from the corporation without losing control over the corporation.

---

[142] Code Sec. 312(n)(7).

Code Sec. 304 generally prevents exchange treatment on stock redeemed by related corporations. In the case of brother-sister corporations, if one or more persons are in "control" of each of two corporations, and in return for "property," one of the corporations acquires stock in the other corporation from the person (persons) in control, then the transaction is treated as a distribution in redemption of the stock of the acquiring corporation.[143] "Control" for this purpose means the ownership of at least 50 percent of the total combined voting power of all classes of stock entitled to vote, or 50 percent or more of the total value of all classes of stock.[144] The attribution rules of Code Sec. 318 apply, except that the 50 percent ownership in a corporation requirement is dropped to five percent.[145]

Example 14-43. Dave Limbird owned 10 percent of Fruity Corporation and 47 percent of Chewey Corporation. In turn, Fruity Corporation owned 40 percent of Chewey Corporation. Limbird's total ownership of Chewey is 47% + .10 (40%) = 51%. Thus, he has control for Code Sec. 304 purposes.

"Property" is defined as money, securities, and any other property, not including stock in the corporation making the distribution.[146]

If the redemption is through brother-sister corporations, the property given is treated as a redemption of the acquiring corporation. The stockholder is deemed to have contributed stock in the issuing corporation to the acquiring corporation in exchange for the acquiring corporation's stock. Then the stockholder is considered to have given stock of the acquiring corporation to the acquiring corporation in exchange for property (the deemed redemption).[147]

Example 14-44. Assume the same facts as in Example 14-42, and that the stock had a basis to Robert Pryor of $16,000 and the sales price was $25,000. Robert is considered to have contributed $16,000 of stock in Bob's Autos Inc. to Pryor Motors Co. Robert is then deemed to have turned in the Pryor Motors Co. stock for $25,000 in cash in a stock redemption. Since none of the exchange provisions of Code Sec. 302 apply, the $25,000 is a dividend, assuming adequate E&P.

If treated as a distribution, first the E&P of the acquiring company are used, then, if necessary, the E&P of the issuing company are used.[148] Basis of the stock in the hands of the acquiring corporation is carried over from the stockholder.[149]

Example 14-45. Assume the same facts as in Example 14-44, and that Bob's Autos Inc. has E&P of $38,000 and Pryor Motors Co. has E&P of $20,000. The dividend first comes out of Pryor Motors Co. (the acquiring company), and the remaining $5,000 is considered to come

---

[143] Code Sec. 304(a)(1).
[144] Code Sec. 304(c)(1).
[145] Code Sec. 304(c)(3).
[146] Code Sec. 317(a).

[147] Code Sec. 304(a)(1).
[148] Code Sec. 304(b)(2).
[149] Reg. § 1.304-2(c) (Example 1).

from the E&P of Bob's Autos Inc. The basis of Robert's stock in Pryor Motors Co. is increased by $16,000 (the basis of the stock in Bob's Autos Inc. which was redeemed). The basis of the stock in Bob's Autos Inc. owned by Pryor Motors Co. is $16,000 (its basis in the hands of Robert).

It would be possible, of course, for the redemption to qualify for exchange treatment under one of the Code Sec. 302 provisions. In that event, gain to the shareholder is the sales price less the basis of the basis of stock redeemed. The basis of the remaining stock in the issuing company is unchanged and the total basis of the stock of the acquiring remains the same. The basis of the stock to the acquiring corporation is the amount paid.

> **Example 14-46.** Assume the same facts as in Example 14-45, except that Robert owns 55 percent of both corporations before the redemption and that 30 percent of the stock in Bob's Autos Inc. is redeemed. Robert's ownership afterward would be 25% + .55 (30) = 41.5%. Since 41.5 percent is under 50 percent and less than 80 percent of 55 percent, the redemption would be disproportionate. Hence, Robert would have a capital gain of $9,000 ($25,000 − 16,000), and Pryor Motors Co. would have a $25,000 basis in its stock in Bob's Autos Inc.

A redemption can also be effected by a subsidiary. If an individual's stock in the parent company is redeemed by a subsidiary, the redemption is treated as being by the parent company.[150] A parent-subsidiary relationship exists in this context if the parent owns 50 percent of the subsidiary.[151] Even though the redemption is considered to be effected by the parent company, the dividend is deemed to come first from the E&P of the subsidiary and from the E&P of the parent only after E&P of the subsidiary is reduced to zero. The stock of the shareholder in the parent company will retain the same total basis, but the basis per share will increase.[152]

> **Example 14-47.** Sam's Super Inc. owns 70 percent of Valley Markets Co. Sam owns 30 out of the 100 shares outstanding of Sam's Super Inc. His basis is $60,000 in the shares. Sam sold five shares to the subsidiary, Valley Markets Co. for $17,000. Since the redemption is not disproportionate, Sam has a dividend of $17,000. His total basis in Sam's Super Inc. stock remains at $60,000; however, the per-share basis is now $2,400 ($60,000/25). Valley Markets will reduce its E&P by $17,000.

If one of the provisions of Code Sec. 302 is met, and the redemption thereby qualifies for exchange treatment, the rules are the same as for those

---

[150] Code Sec. 304(a)(2).
[151] Reg. § 1.304-3(a).

[152] *Id.*

brother-sister corporation redemptions which qualify for exchange treatment.

Tax Tips and Pitfalls

Because of the proportionate rule governing entity-to-owner attribution, redemption through brother-sister may qualify as disproportionate, yet leave the shareholder in effective control over both corporations. For example, if a shareholder owns 70 percent of corporation A and 60 percent of corporation B and all other shareholders are unrelated, a redemption of 60 percent of the stock in corporation A by corporation B would leave direct ownership of 10 percent and indirect ownership of 36 percent (60 × .60). Thus, the redemption would be disproportionate, yet the stockholder still effectively controls 70 percent of corporation A.

.09 Preferred Stock Bailouts

Prior to 1954 taxpayers in closely held corporations successfully used preferred stock to get money out of a corporation without the double tax penalty of dividend treatment. This result was achieved in a three-step transaction. First, the company would issue a nontaxable preferred stock dividend on common. A portion of the basis of the common stock would then be properly allocated to the preferred stock. The second step would be to sell the preferred stock to a third party. Since the holding period of the preferred dates back to the date of acquisition of the common, the gain would generally be a long-term capital gain. The third and final step was to have the corporation redeem the preferred stock at a premium from the third party. Since the redemption would result in a complete termination of the third party's interest, Code Sec. 302(b)(3) would apply and the redemption would receive exchange treatment. The result of all three transactions would be a cash transfer to the stockholders partly tax-free (to the extent of basis allocated) and partly at capital gains rates. This rather complicated set of transactions was upheld by the Sixth Circuit.[153] Congress, in response, enacted Code Sec. 306. This Code section provides generally that if a stockholder sells or otherwise disposes of "Section 306 stock," ordinary income would result, whether the stock is sold or redeemed. If the stock is sold to a third party, ordinary income is recognized to the extent that the fair market value of the stock sold, on the date distributed to the shareholder, would have been a dividend to the shareholder had the distributing corporation distributed cash instead of stock.[154]

Example 14-48. On September 30, 2000, Valley Software Co. distributed 100 shares of preferred stock as a dividend on its common to the two equal shareholders, Babcock and Wilson. On that date the preferred stock had a value of $30,000. E&P as of December 31, 2000,

---

[153] *Chamberlin v. Commr.*, 53-2 USTC ¶ 9576, 207 F.2d 462 (6th Cir. 1953), cert den. 347 US 918.

[154] Code Sec. 306(a)(1).

was $60,000. The 50 shares distributed to Wilson had an allocated basis to him of $1,500, but were worth $15,000 when issued. Wilson sold the 50 shares of preferred on May 4, 2001, for $18,000. Of the proceeds of $18,000, $15,000 will be treated as ordinary income (the fair market value of the stock at the distribution since the *pro rata* share of E&P exceeds $15,000), and $1,500 ($18,000 − $15,000 − $1,500) will be treated as a capital gain.

Example 14-49. Assume the same facts as in Example 14-48, except that the stock is sold for $15,300. Of this amount, $15,000 will be treated as ordinary income. No loss deduction is permitted and the unabsorbed basis of $1,200 ($1,500 − $300) is added back to the basis of the common stock.

Example 14-50. Assume the same facts as in Example 14-48, except that the E&P on December 31, 2000, is only $18,000. Ordinary income will be $9,000 (half the E&P), and capital gain will equal $7,500, ($18,000 − $9,000 − $1,500).

Even though the ordinary income is determined by reference to the E&P, the corporation does *not* reduce E&P.

If the corporation redeems the Section 306 stock, the transaction is treated as a property distribution. Thus, the redemption will be a dividend to the extent of E&P existing at the time of the redemption. Any amount in excess of that is treated as a return of capital until basis is exhausted, and then would be a capital gain.

Example 14-51. Assume the same facts as in Example 14-50, except that the stock is redeemed on May 4, 2001, instead of sold, and that E&P by that date has grown to $21,000. The redemption is taxed totally as a dividend since the E&P exceeds the $15,000 distribution.

"Section 306 stock" is defined as stock that is not common stock and that either:[155]

- Is distributed to the seller as a nontaxable stock dividend;

- Is received in a tax-free reorganization or separation; or

- Has a basis which is determined by reference to the basis (in the hands of the shareholder or another person) of Section 306 stock.

Certain transactions are granted specific exceptions to Section 306 designation. They are:[156]

1. Complete termination of a shareholder's interest by sale to a nonrelated party (as defined in the attribution rules in Section 318);

2. Complete termination of a shareholder's interest by either:

---

[155] Code Sec. 306(c).   [156] Code Sec. 306(b).

      a. A redemption qualifying under Code Sec. 302(b)(3), or

      b. A partial liquidation qualifying under Code Sec. 302(b)(4);

3.   A redemption under complete liquidation as provided in Code Secs. 331-346;

4.   Any transaction where gain or loss is not recognized, e.g., a nontaxable exchange or a gift; and

5.   A transaction not in pursuance of a plan which had as a principal purpose the avoidance of federal income tax. Cited as examples are isolated dispositions of Section 306 stock by minority stockholders and the sale by a shareholder of all of his or her voting common stock before the disposition of the Section 306 stock.[157]

.10 Distribution of Stock and Securities of a Controlled Corporation

Code Sec. 355 applies to divisive reorganizations, i.e., where an existing corporation is divided into two or more corporations. The three types of divisive reorganizations are called spin-offs, split-offs, and split-ups. In a spin-off some or all of the shareholders of the parent company are distributed stock in the subsidiary. The shareholders are not required to surrender any stock in the parent company.

    Example 14-52. Plains Retailers, Inc., owns both a supermarket and a large drugstore, a subsidiary named Plains Sundries. Wishing to concentrate on the grocery business, the company distributed all of the stock in Plains Sundries to its shareholders in a transaction which met all of the requirements of Code Sec. 355. The distribution is a spin-off. Had not all of the Code Sec. 355 requirements been met, the transaction would have been a dividend to the shareholders.

    A split-off is similar to a spin-off except that the shareholders receiving stock in the subsidiary are required to surrender all or part of their stock in the parent company.

    Example 14-53. Hawk Motors, Inc., owns 100 percent of the stock of Blue Finch Autos. Brothers Robert and Jim each own 100 shares of stock in Hawk Motors, Inc., all of the outstanding stock. Robert wishes to embark on an ambitious expansion plan while Jim is more conservative. The brothers agree that the best solution is to have Hawk Motors, Inc., distribute all of the stock in Blue Finch Autos to Jim in return for all of Jim's stock in Hawk Motors, Inc. If all of the provisions of Code Sec. 355 are met, the transaction will be a split-off. Otherwise, the transaction would be treated as a stock redemption.

---

[157] Reg. § 1.306-2(b)(3).

A split-up occurs when a parent company distributes the stock of two or more subsidiaries in complete liquidations of the parent company.

Example 14-54. Thompson T-V Co. owns two stores, one in Denver and one in Boulder, Colorado. Two subsidiary companies, Thomden Co. and Thombould Co. were created and all assets transferred to them in exchange for stock in the subsidiaries. The parent company then distributed stock in the subsidiary in exchange for its stock. The parent company was then liquidated. This transaction would be a split-up.

.11 Code Sec. 355 Requirements

The following requirements must be met in order to qualify for Code Sec. 355 treatment:[158]

First, the distributing company must control the subsidiaries whose stock it is distributing. "Control" for this purpose is the ownership of at least 80 percent of the voting stock and at least 80 percent of all other classes of stock.[159]

Second, the distributing company must distribute to the shareholders sufficient stock so that the shareholders "control" (as defined above) the corporation.

Third, the "active business requirement" must be met. This requirement is met if either:[160]

- The distributing corporation and the controlled corporations are engaged immediately after the distribution in the active conduct of a trade or business; or

- Immediately before the distribution, the distributing corporation had no assets other than stock or securities in the controlled corporations and each of the controlled corporations is engaged immediately after the distribution in the active conduct of a trade or business.

A corporation is considered to be in an active trade or business if the business has been actively conducted during the five-year period ending on the date of distribution, and it was not acquired in a taxable transaction during the five-year period ending on the date of distribution.

The active business requirement has been troublesome for some taxpayers, especially where the corporation's activity is leasing or investment in securities. The courts have not been unified in this matter. In *Rafferty* the First Circuit held that the leasing of real estate to a parent company is not the active conduct of a business.[161] However, the Sixth Circuit held that

---

[158] Code Sec. 355(a)(1).
[159] Code Sec. 368(c).
[160] Code Sec. 355(b).

[161] *J.V. Rafferty*, 72-1 USTC ¶9101, 452 F.2d 767 (1st Cir. 1972) cert. denied, 408 US 922.

net leases (all expenses paid by the tenants) which three subsidiaries entered into with their parent company qualified as the active conduct of a trade or business. In this opinion the Sixth Circuit questioned the validity of former Reg. § 1.355-1(c)(3).[162]

The regulations state that the corporation is required itself to perform active and substantial management and operational functions.[163] The regulations deny active business treatment to, among other activities:

- The holding of investment securities; and

- The ownership and operation (including leasing) of real or personal property used in a trade or business unless the owner performs significant services with respect to the operation and management of the property.[164]

On the other hand, a rental activity where the landlord rents the building to various tenants, manages the building, negotiates leases, seeks new tenants, and repairs and maintains the building would meet the active business requirement.[165] In various rulings the IRS has ruled that:

- The development of mineral properties which had produced no income was not an active trade or business;[166]

- A farm corporation which leased the land to a tenant and provided advice to the tenants, who planted, cultivated, and harvested and sold the crop using their own equipment and supplies was not an active business; and[167]

- The management of an investment portfolio, no matter how large or active, is not an active business.[168]

Finally, the transaction must not be used principally as a device for the distribution of the earnings and profits of the parent company, the subsidiary, or both.

The determination of whether a transaction was used principally as a device is to be made from all of the facts and circumstances.[169] Factors indicating a device include:[170]

1. A distribution that is substantially *pro rata*;

2. A sale or exchange of the stock of either the distributing or controlled corporation shortly after the distribution (a sale or exchange which was agreed upon before the distribution is *substantial evidence* of device, while a sale or exchange which

---

[162] *E.W. King*, 72-1 USTC ¶ 9341, 458 F.2d 245 (6th Cir. 1972).
[163] Reg. § 1.355-3(b)(2)(iii).
[164] Reg. § 1.355-3(b)(2)(iv).
[165] *Id.*

[166] Rev. Rul. 57-492, 1957-2 CB 247.
[167] Rev. Rul. 86-126, 1986-2 CB 58.
[168] Rev. Rul. 66-204, 1966-2 CB 113.
[169] Reg. § 1.355-2(d)(1).
[170] Reg. § 1.355-2(d)(2).

was not agreed upon before the distribution is *evidence* of device); and

3.   The presence of certain assets, including:

   a.   Assets not used in a trade or business such as excess cash or other liquid assets, and

   b.   The business is a secondary business, i.e., has as its principal function the serving of the business the other corporation, e.g., a cattle feedlot serving a packing plant.

Factors generally not indicating a device include:[171]

1.   A corporate business purpose. Factors indicating a corporate business purpose include:

   a.   The importance of achieving the purpose to the success of the business;

   b.   The extent to which the transaction is prompted by a person not having a proprietary interest in either corporation, or by other outside factors beyond the control of the distributing corporation; and

   c.   The immediacy of the conditions prompting the transaction.

2.   The distributing corporation is publicly traded and widely held (no shareholder owning over five percent of any class of stock).

3.   Distribution of the stock of the controlled corporation to corporate shareholders who, if the transaction were treated as a dividend, would be entitled to the dividends-received deduction.

Even if one or more of the device factors are present, three distributions ordinarily do not present the potential for tax avoidance. They are:[172]

1.   Absence of earnings and profits;

2.   The distribution, in the absence of Code Sec. 355, would qualify as a redemption under Code Sec. 303(a); or

3.   The distribution, in the absence of Code Sec. 355, could qualify as a redemption under Code Sec. 302.

Generally, if the Code Sec. 355 requirements are met, the corporation distributing appreciated property to its shareholders need not recognize gain. However, an exception exists for stock that is distributed to a shareholder having at least a 50 percent interest in either the distributing corporation or the corporation whose stock is being distributed. Such distributions constitute disqualified distributions.[173] Tax on the distributing corporation could be avoided if it has purchased and owned the stock for

---

[171] Reg. § 1.355-2(d)(3).
[172] Reg. § 1.355-2(d)(5).

[173] Code Sec. 355(d)(2).

more than five years prior to the distribution.[174] If the five-year test is not met, gain must be recognized by the distributing corporation as if the property were sold to the distributee at its fair market value.[175]

Certain distributions, however, are not disqualified because the purposes of Code Sec. 355(d) are not violated. Distributions do not violate the purposes of Code Sec. 355(d) if the effect of the distribution is neither to increase the ownership of the disqualified person, nor to provide a purchased basis in any controlled stock to the disqualified person.[176]

A disqualified person is any person who, immediately after a distribution, holds disqualified stock in a distributing or controlled corporation that was acquired by purchase during the five-year period or received in a distribution during the five-year period and which constitutes a 50 percent or greater interest.[177]

.12 Determining Gain or Loss

If the various requirements of Code Sec. 355 are met, no gain or loss is recognized to the shareholder on the receipt of stock or securities. For this purpose, nonqualified preferred stock is treated as other property rather than as securities, except to the extent that it is permitted to be received under Code Sec. 355 without triggering gain.[178] However, if the principal value of the securities received exceeds the principal value of the securities surrendered (if any), the excess is treated as boot.[179] Boot also includes cash, property, and short-term notes.[180]

> **Example 14-55.** In a Code Sec. 355 transaction, Bradley Hansen received 200 shares of Diamond Co. stock and a $20,000, 15-year note. He surrendered a $18,000 bond as part of the transaction. The fair market value of the $20,000 note is $20,000. Hansen has boot of $2,000.

Code Sec. 356 provides the rules for treating boot in a Code Sec. 355 transaction. The gain, if any, is recognized, but only to the extent of the sum of the money and fair market value of the boot received.[181]

Losses are not recognized.[182] If the distribution has the effect of a dividend, it is treated as such to the extent of the shareholder's ratable share of the E&P of the distributing corporation.[183] Any amount in excess of the E&P is recognized as a capital gain.[184]

> **Example 14-56.** Smith and Wesson each own 50 out of the 100 shares outstanding of Re Volver, Inc. Re Volver, Inc., owns all 100 shares of Pistol Co. Re Volver distributes 50 shares of Pistol Co. to each shareholder plus $2,500 in cash.

---

[174] Code Sec. 355(d)(3).
[175] Code Sec. 355(c) and (d).
[176] Reg. § 1.355-6(b)(3)(i).
[177] Reg. § 1.355-6(b)(3)(ii).
[178] Code Sec. 356(e).
[179] Code Sec. 355(a)(3).

[180] Code Sec. 356.
[181] Code Sec. 356(a)(1).
[182] Code Sec. 356(c).
[183] Code Sec. 356(a)(2).
[184] Reg. § 1.356-1(b)(2).

No stock is surrendered by the individuals. This is a spin-off and the cash is taxed as a dividend to the extent of the E&P of Re Volver, Inc.

Example 14-57. Assume the same facts as in Example 14-56, except that each shareholder surrenders 10 shares of Re Volver, Inc. This is a split-off and the cash received is treated as a redemption and will be a dividend unless the requirements for exchange treatment under Code Sec. 302 are met.

.13 Basis of the Property Received

The basis of stock and securities received in a Code Sec. 355 transaction is a carryover basis (basis of the stock and securities exchanged), increased by any gain or dividend income recognized, and decreased by the fair market value of any boot received.[185] The basis of boot received is its fair market value.[186]

Example 14-58. C&J Plumbing Supplies distributed stock in its subsidiary, High Roofing Co., to its shareholders. For each share of stock surrendered in C&J Plumbing, the stockholders received one share of stock in High Roofing Co. worth $70, cash of $10, and other property worth $20. Carson exchanged one share of C&J Plumbing in which his basis was $68. His share of the E&P of C&J Plumbing was $7. The distribution had the effect of a dividend. Carson has a realized gain of ($70 + $10 + $20) − $68 = $32. Only $30 of gain is recognized (to the extent of the boot received). Of the $30 of gain, $7 is a dividend, and $23 is a capital gain. The basis of the stock in High Roofing Co. is $68 less the cash ($10) less the other property ($20) plus the recognized gain ($30). The basis of the other property is $20, its fair market value.

.14 Impact on the Distributing Corporation

If all of the requirements of Code Sec. 355 are met, the distribution of stock and securities does not result in recognized gain to the distributing corporation.[187] However, distributions of other property, if appreciated, result in taxable gains (losses are not recognized).[188]

Example 14-59. Assume the same facts as in Example 14-58 and that the other property has a basis to C&J Plumbing of $16. C&J would recognize a $4 gain on the distribution of the property.

The earnings and profits of the distributing corporation immediately before the transaction is allocated between the distributing corporation and the controlled corporation. If the controlled corporation is newly formed, the allocation is made in proportion to the fair market value of the business

---

[185] Code Sec. 358(a)(1).
[186] Code Sec. 358(a)(2).
[187] Code Sec. 355(c)(1).
[188] Code Sec. 355(c)(2).

retained by the distributing corporation and the business transferred to the controlled corporation.[189]

>   **Example 14-60.** Zucker Co. transferred $500,000 of assets to Yoohoo Inc., a newly formed company, in exchange for all of its stock, which it then transferred to its shareholders in a spin-off. After the spin-off, Zucker Co. has $1,000,000 of assets. E&P immediately before the spin-off was $450,000. Zucker Co. would reduce its E&P by $500,000/($1,000,000 + $500,000) × $450,000, or $150,000.

If the subsidiary was previously in existence, the reduction in E&P is the lesser of:[190]

- E&P of the distributing company times the portion of total assets owned by the subsidiary; or

- The net worth of the subsidiary (adjusted basis of the assets less liabilities).

>   **Example 14-61.** Assume the same facts as in Example 14-60, except that Yoohoo Inc. has previously been in existence and has assets worth $500,000 and a net worth of $125,000. The reduction in E&P of Zucker Co. is the lesser of:

- $500,000/($1,000,000 + $500,000) × $450,000 = $150,000; or

- $125,000.

If the E&P of the controlled corporation immediately before the transaction is less than the decrease in E&P of the parent company, the E&P of the controlled corporation is set equal to the decrease. However, if the E&P of the controlled corporation is greater than the decrease in E&P of the decrease of the parent company, the controlled corporation's E&P is left unchanged.[191]

>   **Example 14-62.** Assume the same facts as in Example 14-61 and that E&P of Yoohoo Inc. was $90,000. After the distribution, Yoohoo's E&P will be increased to $125,000.

>   **Example 14-63.** Assume the same facts as in Example 14-61 and that E&P of Yoohoo was $162,000. Yoohoo's E&P would remain at $162,000 after the distribution.

---

[189] Reg. § 1.312-10(a).
[190] Reg. § 1.312-10(b).

[191] Reg. § 1.312-10(b).

Chapter 15

Corporate Liquidations

¶ 1501 The Rationale for Liquidating a Corporation

There are many reasons why management and owners of a corporation may seek liquidation. The most common reason is a desire to end the business. The motive behind wanting to terminate the business might be a lack of profitability, an interest on the part of shareholders/officers to engage in a different line of work, or a desire to invest the capital in other investments or business activities. Other reasons for liquidating include:

1. *Accumulated earnings problems.*[1] Once a corporation accumulates $250,000 ($150,000 for certain service companies), it must justify the retention of all earnings. Failure to justify the accumulation of earnings can result in the IRS imposing the accumulated earnings tax, a tax which has relatively high rates and is imposed on top of the regular income tax. On the other hand, avoidance of the accumulated earnings tax by paying dividends may not be considered attractive either. Thus, the stockholders may see liquidation as the best alternative.

2. *Subjection to the personal holding company tax.* Corporations which have over 50 percent of the value of the outstanding stock owned by five or fewer individuals and which derive at least 60 percent of their income from passive sources may be subject to the personal holding company tax. Like the accumulated earnings tax, this tax is imposed in addition to the regular income tax.[2] The PHC tax may be avoided by undertaking such strategies as acquiring an active business or by paying sufficient dividends. However, the stockholders may view liquidation as preferable to PHC avoidance strategies.

3. *Stockholder quarrels.* It is not uncommon for stockholders of closely held corporations to have a falling out. If the conflict cannot be resolved, the choices often boil down to one party acquiring the stock of the other party, or an outright liquidation. If neither party wishes to buy the other out (e.g. because of advanced age or lack of financial resources), liquidation may be the most practical solution.

4. *Retirement of a shareholder.* If the majority shareholder is also active in managing a closely held corporation, his or her retire-

---

[1] See Chapter 11 for a discussion of the accumulated earnings tax.

[2] See Chapter 11 for a discussion of the personal holding company tax.

ment may lead to the liquidation of the corporation. This is especially likely if there are no relatives or employees wishing to continue the business in its present form.

5.   *Death of a shareholder.* Although death should not necessarily lead to liquidation of a corporation, there are several scenarios where liquidation might be desirable. If the estate is not sufficiently liquid to pay death taxes, and the corporation does not have the cash to redeem some of the decedent's shares, liquidation might be deemed the best way to achieve liquidity.[3] Again, if no one is capable or desirous of continuing the business, the executor and the heirs may decide to liquidate.

¶ 1503   Requirements for Liquidation Treatment

One requirement is that the liquidation not be in substance a reorganization. This most often arises in a liquidation-reincorporation scheme, i.e., where the corporation is liquidated and the assets are immediately transferred to a new corporation. Though a taxable transaction, this plan would result in a stepped-up basis in the assets to the successor corporation and might also eliminate any potential accumulated earnings tax problems.

The main weapon that the IRS employs against a liquidation-reincorporation is to treat the liquidation as a type D reorganization. If treated as a reorganization, there would be no step-up in basis of the assets and the distribution of any boot would be taxable.[4] Since there are three very specific requirements which must be met in order to qualify for a type D reorganization, one tactic in a liquidation-reincorporation scheme would be to deliberately avoid meeting one of the requirements. Often, however, the courts have treated liquidation-reincorporation events as type D reorganizations even if one or more requirements is not met. For example, one requirement of a type D is that the old corporation must transfer substantially all of its assets to the new corporation. However, in *Smothers,*[5] assets transferred amounted to only about 15 percent of net worth, but amounted to substantially all of the operating assets. The Fifth Circuit held that this transfer met the test of substantially all of the assets. One could argue that such a liberal interpretation amounts to the court engaging in legislating, or as a dissenting opinion put it, "loophole closing."

In *Rose,* the Ninth Circuit disregarded two other requirements of a type D reorganization, stating that in the case of identical ownership of stock in the new and old corporation, the requirement that stock of the new corporation be distributed to the shareholders of the old corporation was a mere formality.[6] As for the requirement that a type D have a formal plan

---

[3] Another strategy would be to pay the federal estate tax in installments under Code Sec. 6166.

[4] See Chapter 12 for a detailed discussion of reorganizations.

[5] *J.E. Smothers v. U.S.*, 81-1 USTC ¶ 9368, 642 F.2d 894 (5th Cir., 1981).

[6] *S.B. Rose*, 81-1 USTC ¶ 9271, 640 F.2d 1030 (9th Cir., 1981).

of reorganization, the court stated, "If what resulted was in fact a plan of reorganization, the chosen label is not dispositive."[7]

¶ 1505 Valuing Contingent Assets

When a stockholder receives the right to receive indefinite amounts of income arising from a contract or claim, the issue of valuation is difficult. Should a value be estimated, however crude? Or should the cost recovery method be used, i.e., defer all income until basis is recovered, and then recognize all income? The former is often referred to as an "open transaction," where the amount of income is held open until actually collected, while the latter is called a "closed transaction" since the asset is assigned an immediate value and amounts in excess of basis are recognized immediately. In a closed transaction, if amounts collected are more or less than the initial valuation, additional income or deductions would result.

As might be expected, the IRS takes a narrow view of the issue, stating that "only in rare and extraordinary cases will property be considered to have no fair market value."[8] Examples cited in the revenue ruling of rare and extraordinary cases include greatly disturbed and uncertain conditions in an oil field, a certain contingent reversionary interest, and uncertainty regarding whether the Mexican government would make payments for land.[9]

On the other hand, the revenue ruling listed many cases in which contracts to receive indefinite amounts of income have been valued for tax purposes, including certain motion picture contract rights, royalties from producing oil wells, and patent rights which were dependent on future earnings.[10]

¶ 1507 Impact on the Corporation

The Tax Reform Act of 1986 repealed the *General Utilities* doctrine, the concept that a liquidating or nonliquidating distribution should not result in gain or loss to the distributing corporation.[11] Hence, gains and losses are recognized as if the corporation had sold the property to the distributee at its fair market value.[12]

> **Example 15-1.** Turminate Co. as part of a complete liquidation distributed land with a basis of $120,000 and a fair market value of $200,000 to a shareholder. The company must recognize a gain of $80,000.

If the property distributed is subject to a liability or if the shareholder assumes a liability, the fair market value of the property is deemed to be at least equal to the amount of the liability.[13]

---

[7] *Id.*
[8] Rev. Rul. 58-402, 1958-2 CB 15.
[9] *Id.*
[10] *Id.*

[11] *General Utilities Co. v. Helvering*, 36-1 USTC ¶ 9012, 296 US 200, 56 S.Ct. 185 (USSC, 1935).
[12] Code Sec. 336(a).
[13] Code Sec. 336(b).

Example 15-2. Assume the same facts as in Example 15-1, except that the shareholder assumes a mortgage of $300,000 on the land. The deemed fair market value is $300,000 and the corporation must recognize a gain of $180,000.

Although losses generally are recognized, losses may not be recognized if the property is distributed to a "related person" and the distribution is either:[14]

- Not *pro rata*; or

- The property is "disqualified property."

"Related persons" are defined in Code Sec. 267. Relevant relationships include:[15]

1.   An individual and a corporation more than 50 percent in value of the outstanding stock of which is owned, directly or indirectly, by or for such individual;

2.   Two corporations which are members of the same controlled group;

3.   A fiduciary of a trust and a corporation more than 50 percent in value of the outstanding stock of which is owned, directly or indirectly, by or for the trust or by or for a person who is a grantor of the trust;

4.   A corporation and a partnership if the same persons own:

     a.   More than 50 percent in value of the outstanding stock of the corporation, and

     b.   More than 50 percent of the capital interest, or the profits interest, in the partnership;

5.   An S corporation and another S corporation if the same persons own more than 50 percent in value of the outstanding stock of each corporation; or

6.   An S corporation and a C corporation, if the same persons own more than 50 percent in value of the outstanding stock of each corporation.

Example 15-3. Shortly before liquidation of Hoss, Inc., a shareholder contributed obsolete inventory with a basis of $75,000 but a value of only $58,000. As part of a liquidation, Hoss, Inc., distributed the inventory to one of four equal shareholders. Since the distribution is not *pro rata*, no loss can be recognized.

---

[14] Code Sec. 336(d).   [15] Code Sec. 267.

The term "disqualified property" refers to any property which was acquired by the liquidating corporation in a Code Sec. 351 transaction (a tax-free contribution of property by shareholders), or as a contribution to capital, during the five-year period ending on the date of the distribution.[16] Also included is other property if its adjusted basis is determined (in whole or in part) by reference to the adjusted basis of property as discussed in the previous sentence.[17]

Example 15-4. In 1998, Timothy Jamison contributed property with a basis of $100,000 to a corporation in exchange for all of its stock in a transaction which qualified under Code Sec. 351. In 2001 the property was distributed to him as part of a liquidation distribution. Fair market value as of the distribution date was $86,000. Even though the distribution is *pro rata*, the loss is not recognized because the property was acquired within the last five years in a Code Sec. 351 transaction.

Example 15-5. Assume the same facts as in Example 15-4 and that the property is traded in 1999 in a nontaxable exchange for other property. If the other property is distributed in the liquidation and if it is worth less than basis, no loss would be recognized because its basis is determined in whole or in part to the property acquired in a Code Sec. 351 transfer within five years of the liquidation date.

Built-in losses are also not deductible if the property was acquired in a Code Sec. 351 transaction or as a contribution to capital, and the acquisition was part of a plan, the principal purpose of which was to recognize loss by the liquidating corporation with respect to such property in connection with the liquidation.[18] Again, any property whose adjusted basis is determined (in whole or in part) by reference to the adjusted property previously described is also included.[19] Any property acquired by the corporation within a two-year period prior to the date of the adoption of the plan of complete liquidation is presumed to be acquired with a tax-avoidance motive.[20]

The "built-in loss" is the excess of the adjusted basis of the property immediately after acquisition over its fair market value.[21] Any loss in excess of the built-in loss is deductible.

Example 15-6. Claude Simpson, an 80 percent owner of Farmers Co., contributed land to Farmers Co. in 2000. The land had a basis to Simpson of $150,000 but was worth only $120,000 at the time of contribution. In 2001, the corporation liquidates and distributes the land to Megan Stone, a minority stockholder who is not related to Simpson. At the time of distribution, the land had fallen in value to $109,000. Since Stone is a minority shareholder, the loss prohibition on

---

[16] Code Sec. 336(d)(1)(B).
[17] *Id.*
[18] Code Sec. 336(d)(2).

[19] *Id.*
[20] Code Sec. 336(d)(2)(B)(ii).
[21] Code Sec. 336(d)(2)(A).

distributions to related parties does not apply. However, since the property was acquired in a Code Sec. 351 transaction within two years of liquidation, it is presumed to be acquired principally to recognize a loss. Therefore, of the total loss of $41,000 ($150,000 − 109,000), only $11,000 is deductible. The built-in loss of $30,000 is not deductible.

Exactly how the IRS will interpret the two-year presumption rule is unclear as regulations have not been issued as of this writing. The Conference Committee stated that it expected that only in rare and unusual cases would a contribution outside two years of liquidation be considered made principally for loss recognition purposes.[22] The committee stated that the presumed prohibited purpose for contributions of property two years from liquidation is to be disregarded unless there is no clear and substantial relationship between the contributed property and the conduct of the corporation's current or future business enterprises.[23] The committee gave the following example:

> **Example 15-7.** Pete Arcos, who owns Good Tool Corporation, is the operator of a widget business in New Jersey. The business operates exclusively in the northeastern region of the United States and has no plans for expansion. Arcos has unimproved real estate in New Mexico that has declined in value. On March 22, 2001, Arcos contributes such real estate to Good Tool Corp. and six months later a plan of complete liquidation is adopted. All of Good Tool's assets are sold to an unrelated party and the liquidation proceeds are distributed. Because Arcos contributed the property to Good Tool Corp. less than two years prior to the adoption of the plan of liquidation, it is presumed to have been contributed with a prohibited purpose. Moreover, because there is no clear and substantial relationship between the contributed property and the conduct of Good Tool's business, any loss arising from the disposition of the New Mexico real estate would not be allowed.[24]

The Conference Committee also expected that the forthcoming regulations would permit the allowance of any resulting loss from the disposition of any of the assets of a trade or business (or a line of business) contributed to a corporation. The committee believed that disallowing such a loss would be inappropriate if there is a meaningful relationship between the contribution and the utilization of the asset.[25] The committee also expected that the loss disallowance would not apply to a corporation's acquisition of assets during the first two years of the existence.[26]

---

[22] Conference Committee Report No. 99-841, 99th Cong. 2nd session (September 18, 1986), p II-200.

[23] *Id.*, p.II-201.

[24] *Id.*

[25] *Id.*

[26] *Id.*

¶ 1509 Impact on the Stockholders

Liquidating distributions are treated by stockholders as being in full payment in exchange for their stock, i.e., they are given exchange treatment.[27] Since stock is generally a capital asset, gain or loss will be capital in nature. If the stock was acquired at different times, the gain or loss must be computed for each batch of stock.[28]

> **Example 15-8.** Barry Corbett acquired 100 shares of Sports, Inc. stock on April 5, 1974 for $10,000, and another 100 shares on June 2, 2000 for $22,000. On March 4, 2001 he received a liquidating distribution of $190 per share. He has a long-term capital gain of $9,000 and a short-term capital loss of $3,000.

If the corporation makes a series of liquidating distributions which cover more than one tax year, the shareholder uses the cost recovery method to report gains or losses, i.e., no gain is recognized until the cost of the stock is recovered, and then all subsequent distributions result in taxable gains. If basis is not fully recovered, i.e., there is an ultimate loss, the loss is not recognized until the final distribution is received.[29]

> **Example 15-9.** Sandy Gregory owns 200 shares in Greg Fashions, Inc., with a basis of $50,000. The company adopted a plan of liquidation in early 1999. Gregory received a $20,000 liquidating distribution in December 1999, another $35,000 in December 2000, and the final distribution in June 2001 of $17,000. She has no income in 1999, $5,000 in 2000 ($35,000 less the unrecovered cost of $30,000), and $17,000 of income in 2001.

> **Example 15-10.** Assume the same facts as in Example 15-9, except that the liquidating distributions are $10,000, $18,000, and $9,000, respectively. Gregory has no income in 1999 or 2000. In 2001, she has a capital loss of $13,000 ($50,000 − 10,000 − 18,000 − 9,000).

¶ 1511 Distribution of Installment Notes

It is not uncommon for liquidating corporations to sell property on the installment method and to then distribute the installment notes to the shareholders. Under the general rules provided in Code Sec. 331, receipt of the installment notes would constitute proceeds to the extent of their fair market value, and the stockholder would have immediate gain or loss recognition. This general rule would be unfavorable to shareholders since they would be required to pay tax in advance of collecting the notes. Relief treatment is provided for in Code Sec. 453. To qualify, the installment note must have been acquired via a sale or exchange by the corporation during the 12-month period beginning on the date a plan of liquidation is

---

[27] Code Sec. 331(a).
[28] Reg. § 1.331-1(e).

[29] Rev. Rul. 68-348, 1968-2 CB 141.

adopted.[30] The liquidation must also be completed during the same 12-month period.[31] The shareholder treats the receipt of the payments (not the receipt of the installment note itself) as the receipt of payment for the stock.[32]

If the requirements for installment treatment are met, basis of the shareholder's stock is allocated among the various assets received in proportion to their fair market values, including the installment notes. The basis allocated to the installment notes is then deducted from their value to arrive at the gross profit ratio, which is applied to each collection to determine the gain recognized.

Example 15-11. On January 10, 2000, Crafts Co., a cash basis corporation, adopted a plan of liquidation. On December 11, it completed the liquidation by distributing to Julie Xavier, its sole shareholder, the following assets:

	Face Value	Fair Market Value
Installment note A	$250,000	$250,000
Installment note B	400,000	400,000
Cash	NA	150,000
Land	NA	200,000

Installment note A was acquired from the sale of property in 1999. Installment note B resulted from the sale of a building in July 2000, and calls for the payment of $50,000 per year plus interest at 12 percent starting July 2001. Xavier has a basis in her stock of $400,000. Since installment note A resulted from a sale before the liquidation, gain must be recognized on it at the date of distribution. Therefore, 6/10 (($250,000 + 150,000 + 200,000)/1,000,000) of the stock basis must be allocated to installment note A, the cash, and the land, while the other 4/10 is allocated to installment note B. Therefore, the receipt of installment note A, the cash, and the land results in a capital gain recognized in 2000 of $600,000 − 240,000 = $360,000. The gross profit percentage on note B is 60 percent (($400,000 − 160,000)/400,000). Thus, in 2001, $30,000 ($50,000 × 60%) of capital gain will be recognized on the $50,000 collection.

Code Sec. 453 treatment does not apply to installment obligations resulting from the sale of inventory, unless it is a bulk sale, i.e., substantially all of the inventory is sold to one person in one transaction.[33]

Example 15-12. Morton County Sales, Inc., operates an auto dealership in one town and a farm implement business in another town. Pursuant to a plan of liquidation, the corporation sells all of the auto dealership inventory on installment, but sells the farm implement

---

[30] Code Sec. 453(h)(1)(A).
[31] *Id.*
[32] *Id.*
[33] Code Sec. 453(h)(1)(B).

inventory to three different dealers, one of those sales being on the installment basis. Distribution of the auto inventory installment notes would not result in gain recognition to the shareholders; however, receipt of the installment from the sale of part of the implement business *would* require immediate gain recognition.

Example 15-13. Plains State Lumber operates a chain of retail lumber yards and maintains a warehouse for inventory. The part of the inventory in the warehouse attributable to each share is indeterminable. Pursuant to a plan of liquidation adopted by the corporation, the assets of two stores, but not any of the inventory held in the warehouse, is sold on installment to one person in one transaction. All of the remaining assets are distributed to the shareholders. The sale of inventory to the one person will *not* qualify for the installment sales treatment to the shareholders.

Example 15-14. Assume the same facts as in Example 15-13, except that the part of the inventory in the warehouse which is attributable to the suburban store can be clearly determined, and both the inventory held in the two stores and that part of the inventory in the warehouse attributable to the two stores is sold on contract. Receipt of the installment notes would not result in gain recognition to the shareholders.

¶ 1513 Basis to the Shareholder

Since a complete liquidation is treated as an exchange by shareholders, the basis of property received in a liquidation is generally fair market value as of the date of the distribution.[34]

Example 15-15. Steven Blake received from B-C, Inc., in liquidation proceeds cash of $10,000 and a building worth $50,000. Blake's basis in his stock was $18,000. Blake has a capital gain of $42,000 ($10,000 + 50,000 − 18,000). His basis in the building is $50,000.

As previously noted, the basis of installment notes distributed to shareholders will, if gain is not recognized upon receipt, not be fair market value, but rather will be an allocated portion of the basis of the stock. Since there is a fresh basis, there is also a fresh holding period, i.e., the holding period starts with the date of distribution.[35]

¶ 1515 Liquidation of a Subsidiary

Although TRA '86 generally repealed the *General Utilities* doctrine, an important exception remains for the liquidation of a subsidiary. The rules for the liquidating corporation (the subsidiary) and the stockholders

---

[34] Code Sec. 334(a).
[35] Technical and Miscellaneous Revenue Act of 1988 (Act. Sec.1006(e)(12), repealing Code Sec.301(e)).

(the parent company and minority shareholders, if any) are described in the material following.

.01   Impact on the Parent Company

In general, no gain or loss is recognized to the parent company on the receipt of property distributed in complete liquidation of the subsidiary.[36] The basis of the property to the parent company is the same as it was in the hands of the subsidiary.[37]

> **Example 15-16.** Pleasant Valley Farms, a 100 percent owned subsidiary of Agra Business Co., distributed a building and farm land in complete liquidation under Code Sec. 332. The building had a value of $150,000 and a basis of $200,000; the land was worth $500,000, but had a basis of only $320,000. Agra Business Co. does not recognize gain or loss on the distribution, and takes a basis in the building of $200,000 and $320,000 in the land.

Two requirements must be met in order for tax-free treatment to apply:[38]

1.   As of the date of the adoption of the plan of liquidation and at all times until the receipt of the property, the parent company must meet the ownership requirements of Code Sec. 1504(a)(2) (must own at least 80 percent of the voting power and at least 80 percent of the total value of the stock (not including nonvoting, nonparticipating preferred[39])).

2.   Either:

   a.   The distribution is in complete cancellation or redemption of all of the parent company's stock, and the transfer of all of the property occurs within the tax year. In such case, the adoption by the shareholders of the resolution under which is authorized the distribution of all of the assets of such corporation in complete cancellation or redemption of all of its stock is considered the adoption of a plan of liquidation, even though no time is set for the completion of the transfer; or

   b.   The distribution is one of a series of distributions in complete cancellation or redemption of all of its stock in accordance with a plan of liquidation under which the transfer of all property is to be completed within three years of the close of the taxable year in which the first distribution is made.

> **Example 15-17.** Stars, Inc., distributed in 1998 property in the first of a series of distributions. The distribution must be completed by

---

[36] Code Sec. 332(a).
[37] Code Sec. 334(b)(1).

[38] Code Sec. 332(b).
[39] Code Sec. 1504(a)(4).

2001 to qualify as tax-free. If the transfer of property does not occur entirely within the taxable year, the IRS may at its option require the taxpayer to provide a bond or to waive the statute of limitations or both.[40]

Code Sec. 332 applies only if the recipient corporation receives at least partial payment for its stock. If the subsidiary corporation is insolvent, the parent company would have a loss on worthless securities.[41]

For the taxable year in which the liquidation occurs (every year if it is a series of distributions), the recipient (parent company) must file with its return the following information:[42]

- A certified copy of the plan for complete liquidation, and of the resolutions along with a statement under oath showing in detail all transactions incident to, or pursuant to, the plan.

- A list of all properties received, with the adjusted basis in the hands of the subsidiary and the fair market value on the date distributed.

- A statement of any debt owed by the subsidiary to the parent company existing both on the date of adoption of the plan of liquidation and on the date of the first distribution. If the debt was acquired for less than face value, its cost to the parent company must be shown.

- A statement which shows its ownership of all classes of stock in the subsidiary as of the adoption of the plan of liquidation and at all times up to and including the date of distribution. The statement should show for each class of stock the number of shares, percentage owned, voting power, adjusted basis, and the date purchased.

.02 Tax Attributes to the Parent Company

Normally, a distribution would trigger depreciation recapture. However, in a Code Sec. 332 liquidation, the subsidiary is not required to recapture depreciation.[43] The recapture potential, along with the property's basis, carries over to the parent. The holding period also carries over to the parent.[44]

The following tax attributes are carried over to the parent company:

1. *Net operating loss carryovers.* There are, however, several limitations and restrictions. They include:

    a. The tax year to which the NOL carryover is first carried is the first taxable year ending after the distribution, i.e., the

---

[40] Code Sec. 332(b).
[41] Reg. § 1.332-2(b).
[42] Reg. § 1.332-6(b).

[43] Code Secs. 1245(b)(3) and 1250(d)(3).

[44] Code Sec. 1223(2).

parent company cannot apply the subsidiary's NOL to a carryback year.[45]

Example 15-18. Sands Co. completed a liquidating distribution to Beach Co., its 100 percent owner on May 3, 2000. Beach Co. is on a March 31 fiscal year. At the time of liquidation, Sands Co. had a NOL carryover of $200,000. The earliest year that Beach Co. can use the NOL carryover is the year beginning on April 1, 2000 and ending on March 31, 2001.

    b. The portion of the NOL carryover which may be used by the parent company in the first year is limited to the portion of the taxable income of the parent times the number of days in the taxable year after the distribution over the total days in the taxable year.[46]

Example 15-19. Assume the same facts as in Example 15-18, and that Beach Co. has taxable income of $182,500 for the year ending March 31, 2001. The NOL deduction for the year ending March 31, 2001 is limited to $182,500 × 332/365 = $166,000. The remaining NOL of $34,000 is carried to the next tax year.

    c. NOLs generated after the distribution cannot be carried back to taxable years of the subsidiary.[47] The purpose of this restriction is to prevent unprofitable companies from acquiring or liquidating a profitable corporation so as to carry back losses and obtain refunds of taxes paid in previous years by the profitable corporation.

Example 15-20. Profit, Inc., has generated taxable income of $1,000,000 for each of the last three years. LL Co., its parent, liquidates the corporation under Code Sec. 332. The parent has an NOL of $2,000,000 the first year after liquidation of the subsidiary. The $2,000,000 loss *cannot* be carried back to a prior year of Profit, Inc.

    d. NOL carryforwards are limited where there has been an ownership change.[48] If there has been an ownership change (described below), the limitation equals the "value of the old loss corporation" multiplied by the "long-term tax exempt rate."[49] The "value of the old loss corporation" is generally the value of the stock immediately before the ownership change.[50] The "long-term tax exempt rate" is the highest of the adjusted federal long-term rates in effect for any month in the three-month period ending with the calendar month in which the change occurs and is published monthly by the IRS.[51]

---

[45] Code Sec. 381(c)(1)(A).
[46] Code Sec. 381(c)(1)(B).
[47] Code Sec. 381(b)(3).
[48] Code Sec. 382(a).

[49] Code Sec. 382(b).
[50] Code Sec. 382(e).
[51] Code Sec. 382(f)(1).

Example 15-21. Assume that there has been an ownership change in connection with a Code Sec. 332 liquidation, and that the subsidiary had an NOL carryover of $500,000. Also assume a long-term tax-exempt rate of seven percent. The maximum amount of carryover which may be used is $500,000 × .07 = $35,000.

Ownership changes in the context of a Code Sec. 332 liquidation occur if immediately after any "owner shift involving a five percent shareholder" the percentage of the stock owned by one or more five percent shareholders has increased by more than 50 percentage points over the lowest percentage of stock owned by the shareholder or shareholders during the testing period.[52] The testing period is the three-year period ending on the day of any owner shift involving a five percent shareholder.[53] An "owner shift involving a five percent shareholder" occurs whenever there is any change in stock ownership and the change affected the percentage of stock owned by any person who was a five percent owner either before or after the change.[54] After all five percent shareholders are identified, those shareholders whose percentage ownership has increased are aggregated and compared with the aggregate of each shareholder's lowest percentage interest during the testing period. If the total increase exceeds 50 percentage points, the Code Sec. 382 limitations will apply. All stock owned by less than five percent shareholders is treated as a single five percent shareholder.

e. If there has been an ownership change and the "continuity of business requirement" is not met, the NOL carryover will be totally disallowed.[55] To meet the "continuity of business requirement," the parent corporation must continue the business enterprise for at least two years after the liquidation, or continue to use a significant portion of the subsidiary's assets in a business.[56]

f. There is a "built-in gains limitation."[57] Code Sec. 384 closes a loophole that is not addressed by Code Secs. 381 or 382. Without Code Sec. 384 it would be possible for an unprofitable parent company to, after a Code Sec. 332 liquidation, sell off the subsidiary's appreciated assets and offset its NOL against the resulting gains. Code Sec. 384, however, provides generally that in a Code Sec. 332 liquidation, income for any recognition period taxable year (to the extent that it is attributable to recognized built-in gains) may not be offset by pre-liquidation loss carryforwards of the parent company.[58] However, if the parent company has met the 80 percent requirement at all times during the five-year period ending on the date of liquidation (or the period

---

[52] Code Sec. 382(g)(1).
[53] Code Sec. 382(i).
[54] Code Sec. 382(g)(2).
[55] Code Sec. 382(c).

[56] *Id.*
[57] Code Sec. 384.
[58] Code Sec. 384(a).

in which the subsidiary has been in existence, if shorter), then the built-in gains limitation does not apply.[59]

2.   *Capital loss carryovers.* All of the limitations applicable to net operating loss carryovers also apply to capital loss carryovers.

3.   *Earnings and profits.* In general the E&P of the subsidiary is considered to have been received by the parent company as of the close of the date of liquidation.[60] However, a deficit in the E&P of the subsidiary may only be used to offset E&P accumulated *after* the liquidation.[61] E&P for the parent company during the year of liquidation is pro-rated daily to determine the amount accumulated after the liquidation.

4.   *Business credit carryovers.* Generally any business credits, e.g., the work opportunity credit, may be carried forward, subject to certain limitations during the year of liquidation.[62]

.03 Impact on the Subsidiary

In general, no gain or loss is recognized to the subsidiary when it makes liquidating distributions to the parent company in a complete liquidation.[63] This tax-free treatment also applies when the subsidiary distributes property to the parent company in satisfaction of debt as part of a complete liquidation.[64]

Example 15-22. Beds Co. distributed to Linens Co., an 80 percent owner, property worth $17,000 in satisfaction of a $20,000 debt. Although Beds Co. has a realized gain of $3,000, none of the gain need be recognized.

Example 15-23. Assume the same facts as in Example 15-22, except that Linens Co. owns only 25 percent of Beds Co. The gain on the debt settlement is taxable to Beds Co.

.04 Distributions to Minority Shareholders

The general rules of Code Secs. 332 and 337 do not apply to distributions to minority shareholders. Instead, the subsidiary is governed by the rules of Code Sec. 336, which require gain or loss recognition on property distributed in complete liquidation.[65] However, in order to prevent the subsidiary from distributing all of its appreciated assets to the parent company and its loss assets to minority shareholders, the recognition of losses on distributions to minority shareholders is prohibited.[66] Meanwhile the minority shareholders, since they are not eligible for Code Sec. 332 treatment, must abide by the general rule of Code Sec. 331, which treats the receipt of property in a complete liquidation as an exchange.[67]

---

[59] Code Sec. 384(b).
[60] Code Sec. 381(c)(2)(A).
[61] Code Sec. 381(c)(2)(B).
[62] Code Sec. 381(c)(24)-(26).
[63] Code Sec. 337(a).

[64] Code Sec. 337(b)(1).
[65] Code Sec. 336(a).
[66] Code Sec. 336(d).
[67] Code Sec. 331(a).

Example 15-24. Cyclone Supply, Inc. has two shareholders, Cardinal Co., an 80 percent shareholder, and Joe Worthy, the owner of the remaining 20 percent. In a complete liquidation, Cyclone Supply distributed the following assets:

	To Cardinal Co.		To Joe Worthy	
	Basis	FMV	Basis	FMV
Inventory	$112,000	$160,000	$28,0000	$ 40,000
Equipment	80,000	90,000	—	—
Land	100,000	150,000	—	—
Building	—	—	100,000	60,000
Total	$292,000	$400,000	$128,000	$100,000

Cardinal Co. has a basis in its stock of $175,000; Worthy's stock cost $62,000. With respect to Cyclone Supply, Inc., the entire distribution to Cardinal Co. is tax-free. The gain on the distribution of the inventory to Joe Worthy must be recognized; the loss on the building cannot be recognized. Cardinal Co. has no gain or loss on the distribution and takes a basis in the property of $292,000. Worthy, however, has a capital gain of $38,000 ($100,000 − 62,000), and has a basis in its property of $100,000.[68]

¶ 1517 Code Sec. 338 Subsidiary Liquidations

Recall that in a Code Sec. 332 liquidation the subsidiary does not recognize gain or loss and the subsidiary's assets carries over to the parent company. However, an election can be made to treat the qualified stock purchase of stock of a subsidiary as a purchase of assets. The subsidiary is then treated as if it had engaged in two hypothetical transactions:[69]

1. Sold all of its assets at the close of the acquisition date at their fair market value; and

2. As a new corporation purchased all of its assets as of the day after the acquisition date.

A "qualified stock purchase" occurs when the parent company has acquired in any transaction or series of transactions within any 12-month period, at least 80 percent of both the voting power and the value of the stock (except nonvoting, nonparticipating, preferred stock).[70]

Example 15-25. Little Valley Co. has 1,000 shares of stock outstanding. On April 2, 2000 Big Valley acquires 100 shares of Little Valley Co. stock. It makes additional purchases of 500 shares on September 27, 2000 and 250 shares on June 10, 2001. Although the

---

[68] The reader will note that the potential loss of $40,000 on the building is totally lost, not being deducted by either the corporation or the minority shareholder. Depreciated property should not be distributed to minority shareholders.

[69] Code Sec. 338(a).
[70] Code Sec. 338(d)(3).

total percentage acquired is 85 percent, the highest percentage acquired during a 12-month period was only 75 percent; hence there was not a qualified stock purchase and a Code Sec. 338 election is not allowed.

Example 15-26. Assume the same facts as in Example 15-25, except that an additional 75 shares was acquired on August 18, 2001. The transactions fulfill the requirements for a qualified stock purchase even though the total transactions encompass more than a 12-month period.

Qualified stock purchases do not include acquisitions if:[71]

- The basis is not determined in whole or in part by the basis in the hands of the transferor;

- The stock is inherited from a decedent;

- The stock is acquired in a Code Sec. 351 exchange (the nontaxable transfer of property to a controlled corporation);

- The stock is acquired in a reorganization under Code Secs. 354, 355, or 356;

- The stock is acquired in a partly or totally nontaxable exchange; or

- The stock is acquired from a "relative" as defined in Code Sec. 318(a).

In order to be valid, the election generally must be made by the 15th day of the 9th month, beginning after the month in which the "acquisition date" occurs.[72] The "acquisition date" is the first day on which there is a qualified stock purchase.[73]

Example 15-27. Assume the same facts as in Example 15-26. The election time period does *not* start running in July 2001, even though 80 percent control was achieved in July. The time period begins in September 2001 (the month following the qualified purchase). Hence the last day for a Code Sec. 338 to be filed is May 15, 2002.

.01 A Deemed Election

In general, the parent company will be deemed to have made an election under Code Sec. 338 if during the consistency period, it acquires any asset of the subsidiary.[74] The "consistency period" consists of a three-year period which begins one year before the beginning of the 12-month acquisition period and ends one year after the acquisition date.[75] The IRS

---

[71] Code Sec. 338(h)(3).
[72] Code Sec. 338(g).
[73] Code Sec. 338(h)(2).

[74] Code Sec. 338(e).
[75] Code Sec. 338(h)(4)(A).

can extend the consistency period if it determines that a plan to make a qualified stock purchase was in effect.[76]

> **Example 15-28.** Assume the same facts as in Example 15-26 and that Big Valley Co. purchased on May 5, 2000 10 percent of the assets of Little Valley Co. The 12-month acquisition period ended on August 18, 2001 and hence began on August 19, 2000. One year prior to that would begin on August 19, 1999. Therefore, the consistency period would begin on August 19, 1999 and end on August 18, 2002. Since the asset purchase falls within that time period, a deemed election has occurred.

There are several exceptions to the deemed election rule. Acquisitions do not create a deemed election if:[77]

- The sale by the subsidiary is in the ordinary course of business.

- The basis of the property acquired by the parent is determined (wholly) by reference to the adjusted basis of such property in the hands of the subsidiary (e.g., a nontaxable exchange).

- The regulations provide for an exception.

Tax Tips and Pitfalls

The deemed election rules can present a pitfall to parent companies that have had transactions with subsidiaries. If the subsidiary has assets which have substantially appreciated, a deemed election would result in the unnecessary imposition of income tax to the subsidiary. Therefore, transactions with unconsolidated subsidiaries should be undertaken with caution. On the other hand, if a Code Sec. 338 election would be beneficial, the deemed election could effectively extend the time to make a Code Sec. 338 election.

> **Example 15-29.** Kelly Realty Co., an unconsolidated subsidiary of World Inc., has a substantial NOL carryover. Some years ago Kelly Realty Co. had purchased property for a future office site. Due to the growth of the city, the land has appreciated a great deal. World Inc. has plans to develop the land. Since World Inc. purchased 85 percent of Kelly Realty Co. 18 months ago, it is too late for a Code Sec. 338 election. However, by purchasing say $60,000 of equipment from Kelly Realty Co., World Inc. could create a deemed election. Although Kelly Realty Co. would have taxable income from the election, its NOL carryover would offset the income. Meanwhile, World Inc. would obtain a higher basis in the land than if a Code Sec. 332 liquidation had taken place.

---

[76] Code Sec. 338(h)(4)(B).   [77] Code Sec. 338(e).

.02 Effect of a Section 338 Election

As previously mentioned, in a Code Sec. 338 election the subsidiary is considered to have sold all of its assets at their fair market value as of the close of the acquisition date.[78]

The aggregate deemed sales price (ADSP) is the sum of:[79]

- The grossed-up amount realized on the sale to the purchasing corporation of the purchasing corporation's recently purchased target stock (as defined in section 338(b)(6)(A)); and

- The liabilities of old target.

ADSP is redetermined at such time and in such amount as an increase or decrease would be required, under general principles of tax law, for the elements of ADSP. For example, ADSP is redetermined because of an increase or decrease in the amount realized for recently purchased stock or because liabilities not originally taken into account in determining ADSP are subsequently taken into account.[80]

The basis in the assets of the subsidiary is determined from the deemed purchase price, which is the sum of:[81]

- The "grossed-up basis" of the parent company's "recently purchased stock," and

- The basis of the parent company's nonrecently purchased stock, adjusted for

- The liabilities of the subsidiary and other relevant items.

"Recently purchased stock" is any stock which is held on the acquisition date and which was acquired during the 12-month acquisition period.[82] Nonrecently purchased stock is stock that is held on the acquisition date but which was not acquired during the 12-month acquisition period.[83] The "grossed-up basis" is equal to the basis of the corporation's recently purchased stock, multiplied by a fraction the numerator of which is 100 percent minus the percentage of stock (by value) of the corporation's nonrecently purchased stock, and the denominator of which is the percentage (by value) of stock of the corporation's recently purchased stock.[84] Let the following symbols apply:

---

[78] Code Sec. 338(a)(1).
[79] Reg. § 1.338-4(b)(1).
[80] Reg. § 1.338-4(b)(2)(ii).
[81] Code Sec. 338(b).

[82] Code Sec. 338(b)(6)(A).
[83] Code Sec. 338(b)(6)(B).
[84] Code Sec. 338(b)(4).

$$\text{AGUB} = \text{adjusted grossed-up basis of the subsidiary's assets.}$$

AGUB = adjusted grossed-up basis of the subsidiary's assets.

GRP = the parent's grossed-up basis in the recently purchased stock of the subsidiary.

BNP = the parent's basis in nonrecently purchased stock.

L = the subsidiary's liabilities (including tax liabilities on the gain on the deemed sale).

Then AGUB = GRP + BNP + L

Example 15-30. On July 1, 2000, Myers Inc. purchased 80 out of the 100 shares of Ed Co. stock outstanding for $60,000. Previously (on June 1, 1995), Myers Inc. had purchased 10 shares for $5,000. As of July 1, 2000, Ed Co. had only one asset, land with an adjusted basis of $70,000, and a fair market value of $110,000, and has no liabilities other than a tax liability from a deemed sale of assets. Assume the tax liability from the Code Sec. 338 election is $11,200. Therefore:

$$\text{AGUB} = \$60,000 \times ((1.00 - .10) / .80) + 5,000 + 11,200$$
$$= \$67,500 + 5,000 + 11,200 = 83,700$$

Myers Inc. will have a basis in the land of $83,700.

The above example assumes that the parent did not wish to increase the basis of its nonrecently purchased stock. The parent may elect instead to recognize gain and therefore also receive an increase in basis of its nonrecently purchased stock. The basis will be equal to the grossed-up basis of the recently purchased stock multiplied by a fraction, the numerator of which is the percentage of stock (by value) which is nonrecently purchased, and the denominator of which is 100 percent minus the percentage of nonrecently purchased stock.[85]

Example 15-31. Assume the same facts as in Example 15-30 except that Myers Inc. elects to recognize gain on the nonrecently purchased stock. Therefore:

$$\text{AGUB} = \$60,000 \times ((1.00 - .10)/.8) + 60,000 \times (.10/(1.00 - .10)) + 11,200 = 67,500 + 6,667 + 11,200 = \$85,367.$$

Myers Inc. will have a basis in the land of $85,367. However, Myers Inc. will have a gain to report of $667 ($6,667 − 6,000) on its nonrecently purchased stock.

.03 Allocating the Basis of the Purchase Price Among the Assets

For basis allocation purposes, assets acquired on or after March 15, 2001 are divided into the following seven groups:[86]

1. *Class I assets.* Class I assets consist of cash, demand deposits, and similar accounts in depository institutions. The face value of these assets reduces the AGUB.

---

[85] Code Sec. 338(b)(3)(B).   [86] Reg. § 1.338-6(b).

2.   *Class II assets.* Class II assets are actively traded personal property within the meaning of Code Sec. 1092(d)(1) and Reg. § 1.1092(d)-1 (determined without regard to Code Sec. 1092(d)(3)). In addition, Class II assets include certificates of deposit and foreign currency, even if they are not actively traded personal property. Class II assets do not include stock of target affiliates, whether or not of a class that is actively traded, other than actively traded stock described in Code Sec. 1504(a)(4). Examples of Class II assets include U.S. government securities and publicly traded stock.

3.   *Class III assets.* Class III assets are assets that the taxpayer marks to market at least annually for federal income tax purposes and debt instruments (including accounts receivable). However, Class III assets do not include:

   a.   Debt instruments issued by persons related at the beginning of the day following the acquisition date to the target under Code Secs. 267(b) or 707;

   b.   Contingent debt instruments subject to Reg. §§ 1.1275-4 or 1.483-4, or Code Sec. 988, unless the instrument is subject to the noncontingent bond method of Reg. § 1.1275-4(b) or is described in Reg. § 1.988-2(b)(2)(i)(B)(2); and

   c.   Debt instruments convertible into the stock of the issuer or other property.

4.   *Class IV assets.* Class IV assets are stock in trade of the taxpayer or other property of a kind that would properly be included in the inventory of taxpayer if on hand at the close of the taxable year, or property held by the taxpayer primarily for sale to customers in the ordinary course of its trade or business.

5.   *Class V assets.* Class V assets are all assets other than Class I, II, III, IV, VI, and VII assets.

6.   *Class VI assets.* Class VI assets are all Code Sec. 197 intangibles, as defined in Code Sec. 197, except goodwill and going concern value.

7.   *Class VII assets.* Class VII assets are goodwill and going concern value (whether or not the goodwill or going concern value qualifies as a section 197 intangible).

Allocation of AGUB. AGUB (reduced by the amount of Class I assets) is allocated among assets in proportion to their fair market value.[87] The basis allocated to an asset (other than Class VII assets) may not exceed the

---

[87] Reg. § 1.338-6(b)(2)(i).

fair market value of that asset at the beginning of the day after the acquisition.[88]

Another limitation provides that the AGUB allocated to an asset is subject to the same limitations as if the asset were acquired from an unrelated person in a sale or exchange.[89]

A special rule also applies to the allocation of basis when the purchasing corporation has nonrecently purchased stock and it has *not* elected to recognize a gain on the nonrecently purchased stock.[90] This special rule applies if the "hypothetical purchase price" exceeds the AGUB.[91] The "hypothetical purchase price" is the AGUB that would result if a gain recognition election were made.

Subject to the limitations in Reg. § 1.338-6(c)(1) and (2) of this section, the portion of AGUB (after reduction by the amount of Class I assets) to be allocated to each Class II, III, IV, V, VI, and VII asset of target held at the beginning of the day after the acquisition date is determined by multiplying:

1. The amount that would be allocated to such asset under the general rules of this section were AGUB equal to the hypothetical purchase price; by

2. A fraction, the numerator of which is actual AGUB (after reduction by the amount of Class I assets) and the denominator of which is the hypothetical purchase price (after reduction by the amount of Class I assets).[92]

Example 15-32. On March 30, 2000 Dad, Inc. purchased 100 percent of the stock of Sub. Co. at a cost of $200,000. The basis and fair market value of Sub. Co.'s assets as of the beginning of March 31 were as follows:

	Basis	FMV
Cash	$ 5,000	$ 5,000
Accounts receivable	40,000	45,000
Inventory	65,000	100,000
Equipment	50,000	60,000
Building	48,000	75,000
Land	6,000	15,000
Total	$214,000	$300,000

Sub. Co. has liabilities of $120,000. Assume an income tax rate of 25 percent. AGUB = $200,000 + 120,000 + .25(300,000 − 214,000) = $341,500. The basis is allocated to the Class I and Class III, IV and

---

[88] Reg. § 1.338-6(c).
[89] *Id.*
[90] *Id.*

[91] *Id.*
[92] Reg. § 1.338-6(c)(3).

V assets (there are no Class II or VI assets) up to their fair market value of $300,000. The remaining basis of $41,500 is allocated to goodwill (a Class VII asset).

Example 15-33. Assume the same facts as in Example 15-32, except that Dad, Inc., paid only $108,500 for the stock. AGUB = $108,500 + 120,000 + .25 (300,000 − 214,000) = $250,000. Basis of $5,000 is allocated to the cash. Basis allocated to the Class III, IV and V assets is as follows:

Accounts receivable....	$ 45,000/295,000 × 245,000 =	$ 37,373
Inventory............	100,000/295,000 × 245,000 =	83,051
Equipment...........	60,000/295,000 × 245,000 =	49,830
Building	75,000/295,000 × 245,000 =	62,288
Land................	15,000/295,000 × 245,000 =	12,458
Total		$245,000

Example 15-34. Assume the same facts as in Example 15-32, except that 25 percent of the stock was purchased by Dad, Inc., for $36,000, and the purchase on March 30, 2000, of the other 75 percent was for $150,000. Dad, Inc., does *not* elect to recognize gain on the nonrecently purchased stock.

GRP	= $150,000 × (1 − .25)/.75		= $150,000.
AGUB	= $150,000 + 36,000 + 120,000 +		
	.25 (300,000 − 214,000)		= $327,500.

The hypothetical purchase price is:

Grossed-up basis of recently purchased stock under Reg. § 1.338-4(c) ($150,000/.75)	=	$200,000
Liabilities (.25 (300,000 − 214,000)) + 120,000	=	141,500
Total		$341,500

Since the hypothetical purchase price exceeds AGUB, and no gain recognition is made, AGUB must be allocated. A basis of $5,000 is allocated to the cash. This leaves $322,500 to be allocated among the Class III, IV and V assets (there are no Class II and Class VI assets). The fair market value of the Class III, IV, V and VII assets is deemed to be the hypothetical purchase price less the fair market value of the Class I assets. Hence the fair market value of the Class VII assets is $341,500 − 300,000 = $41,500. Allocation of basis to the assets is as follows:

Accounts receivable	$ 45,000/336,500 × 322,500 =	$ 43,128
Inventory	100,000/336,500 × 322,500 =	95,840
Equipment	60,000/336,500 × 322,500 =	57,503
Building	75,000/336,500 × 322,500 =	71,880
Land	15,000/336,500 × 322,500 =	14,375
Goodwill	41,500/336,500 × 322,500 =	39,774
Total		$322,500

.04 Subsequent Adjustments to Adjusted Grossed-Up Basis

The calculations of AGUB, complicated though they are, are not always final. AGUB and ADSP must be redetermined at such time and in such amount as an increase or decrease would be required, under general principles of tax law, with respect to an element of AGUB.[93] When ADSP or AGUB is redetermined, a new allocation of ADSP or AGUB is made by allocating the redetermined ADSP or AGUB under the rules of Reg. § 1.338-6.[94]

.05 Code Sec. 338(h)(10) Election

Members of an affiliated group may do an alternative of the Code Sec. 338 election. The Code Sec. 338(h)(10) election allows the target corporation to recognize gain or loss as if it had sold all of its assets in a single transaction. The parent of the target corporation does not recognize gain on the stock sale. Thus, the double tax is avoided.

.06 Return Requirements

Unless the target corporation is part of a consolidated return, any deemed sale gain is reported on the final return of old target filed for old target's taxable year that ends at the close of the acquisition date.[95]

.07 Pros and Cons of a Code Sec. 338 Election

The Tax Reform Act of 1986 (requiring gain recognition to the target corporation) has greatly lessened the attractiveness of a Code Sec. 338 liquidation. While a Code Sec. 338 election will step-up the basis of the target company's assets, the cost, a tax on the appreciation in value, will generally not be acceptable. However, if the target corporation has NOL carryovers that would absorb the gain from the deemed sale, a 338 election may be appropriate, since an increase in asset basis would be achieved without any tax liability.

Example 15-35. On June 30, 2000, Diamond Inc. acquired 100 percent of the stock of Coal, Inc. If a Code Sec. 338 election is effected, the deemed sale will produce a taxable gain of $500,000. However, Coal, Inc., has a NOL carryover of $600,000. Almost all of Coal, Inc.'s, assets are in inventory and depreciable property with three years of

---

[93] Reg. § 1.338-7(a).
[94] Reg. § 1.338-7(b).

[95] Reg. § 1.338-10(a).

remaining life. The Code Sec. 338 election would cost no tax and would result in increased cost write-offs of $500,000 over a two-year period.

Another scenario in which a Code Sec. 338 election would be attractive would be where the parent has a lower basis in the stock than the subsidiary has as a basis in its assets. In that event, a Code Sec. 338 election would result in a tax loss which could be carried back to the subsidiary's three prior tax years.[96]

Example 15-36. Red Co. has a basis in its assets of $1,000,000. It has made a total profit of $600,000 in the three years preceding the current tax year. Blue Co. in the current year acquires 100 percent of Red Co. for $750,000. Use of the Code Sec. 338 election would result in a deemed sales price of $750,000. Hence, Red Co. would have a $250,000 loss to carryback the two previous years.

¶ 1519 Collapsible Corporations

A gain from the sale of exchange of stock of a collapsible corporation, or a distribution in complete or partial liquidation of a "collapsible corporation" is considered to be ordinary income rather than capital gains.[97] Thus the collapsible corporation rules prevent stockholders from obtaining capital gains treatment from the liquidation of their interest in a corporation that has not yet realized income that would be, if realized, ordinary income to the corporation. A "collapsible corporation" is defined as a corporation formed or availed of principally for the manufacture, construction, production, or purchase of "Section 341 assets" with the view of either liquidating the corporation or having the shareholders sell the stock, before the corporation has realized two-thirds of the taxable income to be derived from the property.[98] Property is considered to have been manufactured, purchased, constructed, or produced by the corporation if it either actually manufactured, etc., the property, or if the basis is determined in whole or in part by reference to the cost of property manufactured, etc., by the corporation or the cost of such property in the hands of a person who manufactured, etc., the property.[99]

Example 15-37. Doug Jenson constructed Code Sec. 341 property and shortly afterward contributed the property to a corporation in a Code Sec. 351 transaction. The property is Code Sec. 341 property to the corporation.

Example 15-38. Con-struct, Inc., produced Code Sec. 341 property and then exchanged the property for property of E-Quoir Co., a nonrelated corporation, in an exchange which was nontaxable to E-Quoir Co. The property will be Code Sec. 341 property to E-Quoir Co.

---

[96] However, to the extent that the losses are capital losses, they could only be carried to years in which capital gains are present.

[97] Code Sec. 341(a).
[98] Code Sec. 341(b)(1).
[99] Code Sec. 341(b)(2); Reg. § 1.341-2(a)(5).

"Code Sec. 341 assets" are defined as property held less than three years which is either:[100]

- Inventory;

- Property held by the corporation primarily for sale to customers in the ordinary course of business;

- Unrealized fees or receivables except for receivables from the sale of non-Code Sec. 341 assets; or

- Code Sec. 1231 property (the 12-month holding period need not be met) except for Code Sec. 1231 property which is used to produce or sell Code Sec. 341 assets.

Code Sec. 341 contains an important rebuttable presumption. A corporation is presumed to be a collapsible corporation if the fair market value of its Code Sec. 341 assets is both 50 percent or more of the fair market value of its total assets (not including cash, obligations which are capital assets in the hands of the corporation, and stock owned in another corporation), and is 120 percent or more of the adjusted basis of the Code Sec. 341 assets.[101]

Example 15-39. D-Vel, Inc. has the following assets (all held for less than three years):

	Basis	FMV
Cash	$ 50,000	$ 50,000
Investment in Haven Co.	100,000	400,000
Inventory (houses)	180,000	300,000
Machinery & equipment	250,000	200,000
Land (raw)	50,000	60,000
Total	$630,000	$1,010,000

The inventory of houses and the raw land are Code Sec. 341 assets. The machinery and equipment, though Code Sec. 1231 assets, are *not* Code Sec. 341 assets since they are used to produce the houses. The fair market value of the Code Sec. 341 assets is $360,000. This is 156 percent of the adjusted basis; hence the 120 percent test is met. The fair market value of the Code Sec. 341 assets ($360,000) is also 64 percent of the value of all assets except the cash and the investment in Haven Co. Hence the 50 percent test is also met and the corporation is presumed to be collapsible.

.01 Limitations on the Application of Code Sec. 341

Code Sec. 341(d) contains three limitations on the applicability of the law. Only shareholders who own more than five percent of the value of the stock or who owned stock that was considered owned (by attribution rules) by another shareholder who owned more than five percent are subject to

---

[100] Code Sec. 341(b)(3).

[101] Code Sec. 341(c).

Code Sec. 341.[102] Attribution rules in this context are very wide sweeping. Stock owned by a corporation, partnership, estate, or trust is considered owned proportionately by its owners. Family relationships include brothers and sisters and their spouses, spouse, ancestors, and lineal descendants.[103]

> **Example 15-40.** Andrew Fair owns only two percent of Mountain Water Co. However, one year after construction was begun on a Code Sec. 341 asset and until six months before the liquidation of the corporation, an additional 15 percent was owned by Fair's brother's wife. Therefore, Fair is subject to the Code Sec. 341 rules.

Another limitation applies if at least 30 percent of the gain recognized during the taxable year is *not* attributable to Code Sec. 341 assets.[104] To determine if the 30 percent test is met, the assets must be separated into collapsible and noncollapsible groups, and the gain attributable to each class of property determined. Land and improvements, for this purpose, are treated as a single piece of property.[105]

> **Example 15-41.** On January 2, 2000, Roy Garcia formed the Valley Construction Co. by contributing cash of $500,000. Valley Construction Co. invested in two housing projects, one which was completed by June 30, 2001, and yielded a profit of $75,000, and the other of which was not sold as of October 15, 2001, the date that a liquidating distribution was made to Garcia. Garcia received $300,000 in cash, and houses with a value of $325,000. Garcia's total gain is $125,000 ($300,000 + 325,000 − 500,000). The gain attributable to noncollapsible property is $75,000 and the gain attributable to collapsible property is $50,000. Since the 30 percent is easily met, none of the gain is subject to Code Sec. 341.

The third limitation applies to that portion of the gain that is realized more than three years after the manufacture, etc., of the property.[106] If all of the property is manufactured, etc., more than three years before the date of realization of the gain, then *none* of the gain realized is subject to Code Sec. 341.[107]

.02 Code Sec. 341(e) Limitation on Collapsibility

Yet another exception to the collapsible corporation rules exists where most of the corporation's potential gain is capital gain rather than ordinary income. Specifically, a corporation will not be considered collapsible with respect to the sale or exchange of stock by a shareholder if at such time the sum of the following three items does not exceed 15 percent of the "net worth" of the corporation:[108]

---

[102] Code Sec. 341(d)(1).
[103] Reg. § 1.341-4(b).
[104] Code Sec. 341(d)(2).
[105] Rev. Rul. 68-476, 1968-2 CB 139.

[106] Code Sec. 341(d)(3).
[107] Reg. § 1.341-4(d).
[108] Code Sec. 341(e).

1. The net unrealized appreciation in "subsection (e) assets;" plus

2. If the shareholder owns more than five percent in value of the outstanding stock of the corporation, the net unrealized appreciation in assets which would be "subsection (e) assets" if the shareholder owned more than 20 percent in value of such stock; plus

3. If the shareholder owns more than 20 percent in value of the outstanding stock of the corporation and owns, or at any time during the preceding three-year period owned, more than 20 percent in value of the outstanding stock of any other corporation more than 70 percent in value of the assets of which are, or were at any time during which such shareholder owned during such three-year period more than 20 percent in value of the outstanding stock, assets similar or related in service or use to assets comprising more than 70 percent in value of the assets of the corporation, the net unrealized appreciation in assets of the corporation which would be "subsection (e) assets" if the determination whether the property, in the hands of the shareholder, would be property gain from the sale or exchange of which would be considered in whole or in part as ordinary income, were made:

   a. By treating any sale or exchange by the shareholder of stock in such other corporation within the preceding three-year period (but only if at the time of such sale or exchange the shareholder owned more than 20 percent in value of the outstanding stock in such other corporation) as a sale or exchange by such shareholder of his or her proportionate share of the assets of such other corporation, and

   b. By treating any liquidating sale or exchange of property by such other corporation within such three-year period (but only if at the time of such sale or exchange the shareholder owned more than 20 percent in value of the outstanding stock in such other corporation), as a sale or exchange by such shareholder of his or her proportionate share of the property sold or exchanged.

"Subsection (e) assets" are property held by any corporation that is:[109]

- Property (except Code Sec. 1231 property (determined without regard to the holding period requirement) used in the trade or business) which in the hands of a corporation is, or, in the hands of a more than 20 percent shareholder, would be, ordinary income property.

[109] Code Sec. 341(e)(5).

- Code Sec. 1231 property (determined without regard to the holding period requirement) used in a trade or business but only if the unrealized depreciation on all such property on which there is unrealized depreciation exceeds the unrealized depreciation on all such property on which there is unrealized appreciation.

- If there is net unrealized appreciation on all Code Sec.1231 property (determined without regard to the holding period requirement) used in a trade or business, such property which, in the hands of a shareholder who owns more than 20 percent in value of the outstanding stock of the corporation, would be ordinary income if sold (the depreciation recapture rules).

- Certain copyrights, literary, musical, or artistic compositions, or letters of memorandum created in whole or in part by the personal efforts of, or prepared or produced for, any individual who owns more than five percent of the value of the stock.

"Net worth" is defined for this purpose as the excess of the fair market value of the assets over its liabilities as of the date of distribution (amounts previously distributed are added to the fair market value of the assets for this purpose).[110]

.03 Code Sec. 341(f) Limitation

Another exception to collapsible corporation treatment is provided if the corporation consents to recognize gain when a "subsection (f) asset" is disposed of *at any time* by the corporation or in certain instances by a transferee corporation.[111] "Subsection (f) assets" are assets which are not capital assets and which are owned, or subject to an option to acquire, by the consenting corporation.[112]

Tax Tips and Pitfalls

As can be seen from the previous discussion, the collapsible corporation rules are extremely complicated. And the spread between the maximum capital gains rate and the current highest individual rate makes avoidance of these rules important. In any event, the easiest way to avoid collapsible corporation treatment is to hold assets for three years or more. Another strategy is to have the corporation sell enough Code Sec. 341 assets to bring their total below 50 percent of the total assets. The other exceptions are less desirable. The Code Sec. 341(e) exception is immensely complicated and the Code Sec. 341(f) exception imposes a burden on the consenting corporation.

---

[110] Code Sec. 341(e)(7).
[111] Code Sec. 341(f)(1)-(2).

[112] Code Sec. 341(f)(4)(A).

Chapter 16

Tax Planning

¶ 1601 Objectives of Tax Planning

The overall objective of tax planning is to structure one's financial transactions so as to maximize the taxpayer's *after-tax wealth*. This objective is rather specific and carries with it connotations which can be confused with other objectives. Hence, a discussion of what should *not* necessarily be objectives of tax planning follows:

1. *To minimize taxes.* Although in many instances, after-tax wealth is *maximized* by *minimizing* taxes, this is not always true.

    Example 16-1. In order to offset $25,000 of realized capital gains, Smith sells stock in December.to create $20,000 of capital losses. Two months later the stock sold in December has appreciated by $40,000.

2. *To achieve nontax objectives.* Although tax planning can sometimes achieve nontax objectives in many cases, it is unrealistic to expect these goals to be accomplished through tax planning.

    Example 16-2. Allan Harding is advised by his estate planner to begin a series of *inter vivos* transfers (gifts) to his children in order to minimize transfer taxes. However, Harding enjoys retaining power over his children through his ability to change his will. Tax planning will not necessarily help him achieve his nontax objective (control).

Although a limited amount of tax planning can be done in conjunction with filing the return, most tax planning must be done in advance of or concurrently with, transactions or events. This chapter focuses on basic income tax planning tactics and the income and estate planning aspects of disposal of a closely held business.

¶ 1603 Basic Income Tax Planning Tactics

If one may analogize income tax planning tactics to roads, there are at several primary roads leading to the destination. They are:

- Avoiding the recognition of income;

- Deferring tax by deferring income;

- Deferring tax by accelerating deductions;

- Selecting of the tax entity;

- Selecting of accounting methods;

- Selecting of the tax year;

- Converting ordinary income into capital gains;

- Smoothing year-to-year taxable income; and

- Lowering marginal tax rates by spreading income (family tax planning).

Each road will be discussed in some detail. Not all of these roads always lead in the same direction, i.e., two or more of the tactics may be at cross-purposes.

.01 Avoiding the Recognition of Income

If economic income can be structured or converted so as to avoid the *recognition* of income (i.e., having to report the item as income), the tax savings are obviously considerable. Ways in which to increase economic income and/or cash flow and still avoid income recognition include:

1. *Borrow money against appreciated assets.* With the exception of certain life insurance policies (discussed later in this chapter), the borrowing of money does not create a taxable event.

Example 16-3. Grace Brothers, Inc., wishes to redeem the stock of a retiring stockholder at a cost of $300,000. The corporation does not have that much surplus cash but does have many appreciated assets, among them an office building which cost only $200,000 and has a mortgage paid down to $60,000, but which appraises at $700,000. Borrowing the $300,000 by taking out a second mortgage against the office building would require much less cash than would funding the stock redemption out of an after-tax gain on the sale of assets.

Partnerships, individuals, estates, trusts, and S corporations are all subject to limitations on interest deductions if the funds are used to acquire property held for investment (C corporations are not subject to investment interest limitations).

2. *Invest in tax-exempt bonds.* Assume federal treasury securities with a 10-year maturity period are yielding 6 percent, while high-quality municipal bonds with a comparable maturity period are yielding 4.87 percent. A taxpayer in the 39.6 percent bracket in 2000 who invests in the federal treasury securities would have an after-tax yield of only 3.684 percent, considerably less than the municipal bonds. Of course, a taxpayer in a state that imposes state income taxes should also consider the fact that interest on federal securities is exempt from state income tax, and interest on municipal bond may also be exempt, depending on state law, if it was issued by a municipality in that state.

3. *Use life insurance policies.* Although premiums on life insurance policies are not deductible if the payer is the beneficiary, income avoidance recognition potential for life insurance policies is strong, since policy proceeds are generally excludable from income, and borrowings against the cash value of the policy are also generally free of income tax consequences.

Example 16-4. Heady Heating & Air, Inc., took out a $500,000 whole-life policy on James Heady, its president and majority stockholder. After paying net premiums of $120,000, the corporation collected the face amount upon the death of James. The entire $500,000 was free of income tax and was used to redeem stock from the estate of James Heady.

4. *Take compensation from the business in the form of fringe benefits.* The benefit of owner/employees receiving after-tax income cannot be overstated. Therefore, the use of employer-provided group term life insurance, health and accident policies, meals and lodging, child care facilities, educational assistance programs, no-cost fringes, qualified employee discounts, working condition fringes, cafeteria plans, and pension and profit-sharing plans (see Chapter 10 for a discussion of pension and profit-sharing plans) is strongly recommended. One could also consider providing athletic facilities to the employees. In addition, certain benefits that, in some circumstances might be taxable may, if carefully structured, be excludable under the *de minimis* rules for fringes. For example, meals provided at an employer-provided cafeteria may be excludable, provided that revenue from the facility equals or exceeds the "direct operating" costs (the cost of food and direct labor).[1] The regulations also state that occasional supper money or local transportation fare provided to an employee because of overtime qualifies as a fringe benefit. Similarly, personal use of a copying machine is *de minimis* if at least 85% of the use is business use.[2] However, such fringe benefits as an employer-provided automobile, a flight on an employer-provided aircraft, an employer-provided free or discounted commercial airline flight, an employer-provided vacation, certain employer-provided discounts, an employer-provided membership in social clubs and employer-provided tickets to entertainment or sporting events are taxable.[3]

5. *Plan with respect to security tax benefits.* Social Security tax recipients who have adjusted gross income above $32,000 ($25,000 if not filing jointly) may be subject to marginal income tax rates in effect 50 percent higher than the rate schedule. If

---

[1] Code Sec. 132(e)(8); Reg. § 1.132-7(a).
[2] Reg. § 1.132-6(e)(1).
[3] Reg. § 1.61-21(a).

adjusted gross income is above $44,000 ($34,000 if not filing jointly), the marginal income tax rates may be 85 percent higher than the rate schedule. This is so because an additional dollar of income may also require an additional 50 cents (or 85 cents) of Social Security benefits to be included in income. If a taxpayer is in this situation it may pay to replace high-yielding securities with low-yielding growth securities or with exempt state or local securities. In structuring transactions and events so as to avoid the recognition of income, one should always remember that there should be a "sound business purpose." To have the IRS disregard the event as a "sham transaction" is to have the basic tax planning purpose defeated.

6. *Exclude gain on sale of principal residence.*[4] Taxpayers may exclude up to $250,000 ($500,000 on a joint return) of the gain on the sale of a principal residence. The exclusion is allowed each time a taxpayer selling or exchanging a principal residence meets the eligibility requirements, but generally no more frequently than once every two years. Gain is recognized to the extent of any depreciation allowable with respect to the rental or business use of such principal residence after May 6, 1997. The exclusion replaces the principal residence rollover provision and the one-time $125,000 exclusion for taxpayers over 55.

To be eligible for the exclusion, a taxpayer must have owned the residence and occupied it as a principal residence for at least two of the five years prior to the sale or exchange. If a taxpayer acquired his or her current residence in a rollover transaction, periods of ownership and use of the prior residence is taken into account in determining ownership and use of the current residence.[5]

7. *Owner/employees acquire EE educational bonds.* Effective for bonds issued after December 31, 1989, an individual who is at least 24 at the time of issuance may exclude EE bonds interest if the proceeds are used to pay higher education costs (tuition and fees paid on behalf of the taxpayer, spouse, or dependent). The exemption is not available to high-income taxpayers; in 2001 the phaseout begins at an AGI (for married couples filing jointly) in excess of $83,650 and ends at $113,650. The comparable phase-out for single taxpayers in 2001 is $55,750 and $70,750.

---

[4] Code Sec. 121.
[5] For a discussion of residences as tax shelters, see Gary L. Maydew, and Robert D. Swanson, "Personal Residences Now Offer More Tax Shelter," *Practical Tax Strategies*, Vol. 62, no. 4 (1999).

.02 Defer Tax by Deferring Income

Deferring tax by deferring income has one definite and one possible benefit. The definite benefit arises from the time value of money concept, that a dollar paid in tax one or more years from now is worth less than a dollar paid in the current year.

> **Example 16-5.** A taxpayer in the 28 percent bracket is able to defer the recognition of $50,000 of income for three years. Assuming a 10 percent discount rate, the present value of the $14,000 to be paid in three years is only $10,518.

The other possible benefit is that the deferral may postpone recognition of income to years in which the recipient has a lower tax bracket, thus decreasing the effective tax rate.

> **Example 16-6.** Jeff Rosen, a taxpayer in the 36 percent bracket, has a deferred compensation agreement providing for the payment of $10,000 in the year following his retirement. If his marginal rate drops from 36 percent to 28 percent after retirement, he saves $800 in tax.

Following are ways to defer tax by deferring income.

1. *Use nontaxable exchanges.* As mentioned in Chapter 9, gain or loss need not be recognized when property held for productive use in a trade or business or if held for investment is traded for like-kind property. Since this definition of "like-kind" is very broad, many uses of nontaxable exchanges are possible.

> **Example 16-7.** Dixon Brothers are in need of a distribution center in the southern suburbs of the city. Fortunately, the owner of a suitable building is willing to trade the building for some highly appreciated vacant land that Dixon Brothers had been holding for possible plant expansion. The nontaxable exchange results in the deferral of gain on the vacant land until the distribution center is sold (which could be far into the future).

2. *Utilize involuntary conversion rules where applicable.* When involuntary conversion of assets occurs, taxpayers may have an unenviable combination of taxable income and an economic loss. This occurs when the insurance recovery is more than the basis but less than the fair market value. This set of circumstances makes the use of the elective deferral of gains on involuntary conversion especially important.

> **Example 16-8.** Wainright Inc.'s office building was destroyed by fire. The building had a basis of $70,000, but a fair market value of $200,000. The insurance recovery was $160,000. Absent an election to defer gain, the company would have a tax of $90,000 × .39 = $35,100 (assuming a 39 percent tax rate). Thus, the after-tax proceeds would be only $124,900. However, replacing the building at a cost of at least

$160,000 within the specified time period would postpone indefinitely the $35,100 of tax.

3.   *Consider use of the installment sales election.* The Work Incentive Improvement Act of 1999 repealed the installment method for accrual method taxpayers for sales or dispositions after December 16, 1999. However, the Installment Tax Correction Act of 2000 retroactively reinstated the method. The applicability of this election has been restricted by other recent tax acts. The installment method is generally not available for dealer dispositions or for personal property held as inventory. However, if personal property is not sold regularly on the installment plan, it is not considered a dealer disposition and is, therefore, still eligible for the installment sales treatment. Hence, the installment method is primarily available to nondealers (casual sales). If the total of all deferred payments at the end of a year exceeds $5 million, interest on the tax deferred may have to be paid. However, this rule does not apply to sales of personal use property and farm property, regardless of the amount deferred.[6] To summarize, the installment sales method for small businesses remains a very viable method for deferring gain on noninventory items.

4.   *Owner/employees utilize deferred compensation plans.* See Chapter 10 for a discussion of deferred compensation.

5.   *Owner/employees use Section 401(k) plans.* 401K plans are also discussed in Chapter 10. Many tax planners regard 401(k) plans as the single best discretionary way for employees to shelter income.

6.   *Taxpayers invest in Series EE bonds.* Given the combination of safety, exemption from state and local taxes, and deferral of income potential, Series EE bonds are often underrated as an investment. The ability to defer the interest income even longer if Series EE bonds are exchanged for Series HH bonds is an added advantage.

.03   Defer Tax by Accelerating Deductions

There are a number of expense acceleration tactics available at both the business and individual taxpayer level. A list of some of these tactics is as follows:

1.   *Use the Code Section 179 expense election.* The expense election is discussed in Chapter 8. The ability to expense up to $24,000 per year (for 2001) of depreciable tangible personal property,

---

[6] Code Sec. 453A.

increasing to $25,000 by the year 2003 saves considerable record-keeping costs as well as accelerating deductions.

2. *Minimize nonbusiness use of listed property so as to keep eligibility for MACRS lives and rates.* In order to qualify for MACRS lives and accelerated rates, business use of listed property (automobiles, entertainment property, recreation property, amusement property, computers or peripheral equipment, and cellular phones) must exceed 50 percent.

3. *Realize capital losses to offset previously realized capital gains.* Both businesses and owner/employees should, during the last quarter of their tax year, review their completed to-date capital and Code Sec. 1231 transactions, and if there are net gains, consider if any assets having a basis in excess of fair market value should be sold.

4. *Pre-pay expenses (if cash basis taxpayer).* Some limitations do exist on the deductibility of prepayments (see Chapter 6 for details). However, this remains an excellent method for cash basis taxpayers to defer tax.

5. *Accelerate the incurrence of expense (if accrual basis taxpayers).* Unfortunately, accrual basis taxpayers have much less flexibility with respect to expense acceleration than to cash basis taxpayers. However, expenses can be accelerated by incurring the expense at an earlier date. For example, before the end of the tax year an accrual business could take such steps as scheduling repair expenses, doing advertising campaigns, paying accrued bonuses to related taxpayers (assuming that this was agreeable to the related taxpayer), charging off partially worthless bad debts, and so on.

6. *Owner/employees can prepay deductible personal expenses.* Estimated state income taxes (typically the last installment is due in January) can be prepaid in December. Medical costs can be paid up and discretionary medical costs can be incurred and paid before the end of the year. Contributions (e.g., church tithes) can be prepaid. The entire year's property taxes can be paid before year end. Another tactic in conjunction with the prepayment of deductible personal expenses that is especially applicable to young owner/employees, who may not have a large amount of itemized deductions, is to *bunch* as much as possible of two or more years of itemized deductions into one tax year. The objective of bunching is to itemize for the year in which the deductions are bunched, and to take the standard deduction for the other year. In that way, the total two-year deduction can often be considerably increased.

¶ **1603.03**

.04 Selection of Tax Entities

In many cases, selection of the tax entity is not discretionary to the taxpayer, i.e., circumstances may dictate the use of a particular entity. There are also many nontax considerations when selecting an entity, e.g., limited or unlimited liability, ease of transfer, and so on. However, with respect to tax considerations, where the choice is between partnerships, S corporations, limited liability companies, or C corporations, certain observations may be made.

Partnerships

Partnerships have the advantage of a greater loss deduction flow though than S corporations, because partnership debt increases basis, while S corporation debt is available for loss absorption only if it is owed to the particular shareholder. There is no loss flow though from C corporations to shareholders. Partnerships also have more flexibility with respect to allocation of profits and losses. As long as the allocation has economic substance, profits may be allocated in a different ratio than the ratio of partnership capital. Losses may also be allocated in a different manner than profits, again subject to the economic substance constraint. Partnerships also are able to elect basis revision upon the sale or liquidation of a partner's interest. This can have the effect of a stepped-up basis in partnership assets for a new partner. There is no comparable election available for C or even S corporations, e.g., a new shareholder could pay $100,000 for stock whose share of basis of corporate assets is only $40,000.

A primary tax drawback to partnerships is the lack of fringe benefits available to the partner/employees. Since a partner is generally not treated as an employee for income tax purposes, fringe benefits such as group term life insurance are not available. The complexity of keeping track of the inside and outside bases of a partnership interest is another disadvantage of the partnership entity.

S Corporations

S corporations retain the characteristics (and certain advantages) of the corporate entity while achieving much of the conduit feature advantages of a partnership. Thus, the double tax is all but eliminated (built-in gains and excessive passive income can be subject to tax at the corporate level in some instances), net operating losses of new businesses can flow through to the shareholders giving immediate tax benefits, and, to the extent that shareholders are in lower tax brackets than the corporation, a tax savings will be achieved even over C corporations that are paying no dividends.

Another important advantage of S corporations as opposed to C corporations is that the basis of S corporation stock held by a shareholder floats up as the S corporation retains income. Thus, the seller of S corporation stock will likely have a much smaller capital gain than if it had been organized as a C corporation.

A major drawback of S corporations when compared to C corporations is the lack of fringe benefits available to over two percent shareholders. Depending on the business, the tax savings from fringes can swamp in importance any possible advantage from income tax rate differentials.

Example 16-9. Hickock Family, Inc., owns and operates a large cattle ranch. The corporation owns the ranch house and purchases all of the food for the family. The value of the meals and lodging is $12,000 per year. If the corporation elects S status, the tax savings from a $12,000 deduction will be lost; as a C corporation the meals and lodging would be deductible to the corporation and likely totally excludable to the shareholders.

An S corporation also may not be appropriate if the corporation needs to retain earnings for expansion, and the stockholders would have difficulty paying the tax on their share of earnings without a distribution.

S corporations are subject to several stringent restrictions which make them much less flexible than C corporations. There can be no preferred stock in an S corporation. Preferred stock is often used in closely held corporations as an estate planning device for, among other objectives, "freezing" the transfer taxes. The limitation on the number of shareholders, while not a serious problem for most small companies, can be a problem if the company wishes to use stock incentive plans to reward employees. The fact that S corporations cannot be members of an affiliated group (except, for years starting after 1996, as parents to C corporations or qualified subchapter S subsidiaries) can sometimes limit business expansion possibilities.

Corporations and partnerships cannot own stock in S corporations. This may act as a constraint on the raising of capital in some instances. However, S corporations can be partners in a partnership, and can also own stock in other corporations.

Limited Liability Companies

Limited liability companies are very attractive entities because they combine the strengths of the corporate and the partnership entities. Generally, an LLC will have the advantages and drawbacks of a partnership without the drawback of unlimited liability.

C Corporations

C corporations permit the payment of fringe benefits to shareholders. The *highest* marginal rate of C corporations (39 percent) is greater than the highest marginal rate of individuals. However, the generous rate for the first $50,000 of C corporation income often results in a lower effective tax rate for small C corporations than the marginal tax rate of its shareholders.

Of course this advantage will hold true only to the extent that earnings are retained in the business rather than paid out in dividends.

The drawbacks of C corporations as compared with S corporations are as follows:

- The double tax is a serious disadvantage if distributions in the form of dividends need to be made to shareholders.

- The absence of the flow through of losses to shareholders makes the C corporation disadvantageous for the first years of existence if losses are expected or even possible.

- If the retention of earnings cannot be justified, the accumulated earnings tax could be assessed.

- The marginal rates for C corporations with taxable income from $100,001 to $335,000 is a high 39 percent.

- Closely held C corporations and personal service C corporations are subject to passive loss limitations as well as most of the at-risk limitations. Therefore the C corporation entity has no advantage over S corporations or partnerships in this respect.

.05 Selection of Accounting Methods

A listing of all of the elective accounting methods is outside the scope of this discussion. Hence, the focus is on cash v. accrual v. hybrid, the installment sales method, LIFO inventory, MACRS depreciation rates and lives, and long-term construction.

Cash v. Accrual v. Hybrid

Where businesses have a choice (generally service concerns), the cash method is almost always superior to accrual or hybrid. Income deferral opportunities for cash basis businesses are considerable, since revenue is not taxed until actually or constructively received.

Example 16-10. Kirk Newberry, an attorney, selects the cash basis method for year 0, the year in which he opens his practice. His receivables at the end of his first year of practice were $20,000; the receivables grew as his practice increased so that by the end of year 40, his year of retirement, they amounted to $60,000. Assuming an average income tax rate over the years of 40 percent, and 10 percent interest, the present value in year 0 of one dollar of tax to be paid in year 40 on his receivables is only about two cents.

Opportunities for accelerating expense deductions are also much greater for cash basis businesses. Generally, expenditures for items that will be used up or will expire by the end of the year following the year of prepayment are deductible in the year incurred. (See Chapter 6 for details.)

The cash basis method is not without its drawbacks. In most instances the relationship between revenue deferrals and expense accelerations to cash inflows and outflows is direct, i.e., revenue deferrals carry the cost of delayed cash inflows, and expense prepayments require early cash outflows. Thus, tax planning through use of the cash method may be limited if cash flow needs are great.

Accrual Method

The accrual method affords far fewer tax planning opportunities than does the cash method. Some flexibility does exist with respect to the timing of billing of customers and the amount received on advance payments. For suggestions on the expenditures side, see the preceding discussion of expense accelerations.

Hybrid Method

Since the hybrid method entails the use of the cash basis method for nonsales revenue and expenses not related to cost of goods sold, it contains more flexibility than the accrual method, especially with respect to acceleration of expenses.

Installment Sales

See the discussion above under deferral of income.

LIFO Inventory Method

The LIFO inventory method is not without drawbacks, such as the financial statement conformity requirement and generally increased record-keeping costs. However, in times of even moderate inflation it is a tremendous tax saver since early acquired, low cost goods are not costed out, but are retained in inventory. However, if inventory is *reduced,* unusually high taxable income can result in the year of reduction, due to the low tax basis of the various LIFO inventory layers.

MACRS

See the discussion above under acceleration of deductions.

Long-Term Construction

Although Congress in the Revenue Reconciliation Act of 1989 restricted the use of the completed contract method, it may still be used by small businesses in a number of instances. The method is still available for:

1. "Home construction contracts" (any construction contract where 80 percent or more of the contract costs are for dwelling units of four or fewer units);

2. Construction contracts entered into by a taxpayer whose annual gross receipts for the three taxable years preceding the tax year are not more than $10,000,000; however, the contract must be

completed within the two-year period beginning on the contract commencement date.

A modification of the completed contract method, the "percentage of completion-capitalized-cost method" may be used for residential construction contracts that do not qualify as "home construction contracts" described in (1) above.

The completed contract method, if available for use, can defer income for as much as several years. Its use would generally be very advantageous to the taxpayer.

.06 Selection of the Tax Year

Certain entities are not granted very much latitude in selection of their tax year. Individuals are required to use a calendar year unless they keep a set of books, which few individuals do. Sole proprietors are required to use the same tax year for their business as they use for their individual income and expenses. Partnerships, S corporations, and personal service corporations are generally required to use a calendar year. Of the various exceptions to the calendar year requirement, the only exception that contains much of a tax advantage is the "natural business year" exception. If a partnership, S corporation, or personal service corporation has a seasonal business and qualifies under the natural business year exception, no deposit of tax need be made with the IRS. Hence, the deferral of income potential for owners of partnerships and S corporations will be present.

> **Example 16-11.** Sam's Ski Shop, Inc., an S corporation, has a natural business year-end of April 30. Sam, the sole shareholder, is on the calendar year. Sam has a permanent deferral of eight months of S corporation earnings.

C corporations, unless they are personal service corporations, may use any fiscal year they wish so long as it ends on the last day of a month or is a 52- to 53- week year. The first year cannot exceed 12 months. Since C corporations do not flow through income or losses, the deferral possibilities for fiscal years are rather minimal.

.07 Converting Ordinary Income into Capital Gains

Capital gains receive a tax advantage under current law. Capital assets held more than 12 months are taxed at 20 percent (10 percent for lower income taxpayers). Ordinary income is taxed at maximum rate of 38.6 percent (for 2002).

This discussion will take three forms: discussion of instances under current law in which capital gains *are* preferred over ordinary income, a discussion of *ways* in which to convert ordinary income into capital gains, and tax planning tactics assuming that preferential treatment to capital gains remains.

When Capital Gains Are Preferred

Under current law, long-term capital gains receive very preferential tax treatment. Most capital gains are taxed at a maximum rate of 20 percent for taxpayers in a 25 percent or higher bracket, and a maximum of only 10 percent for taxpayers in the 15 percent bracket; individuals with a marginal tax rate in excess of that benefit from long-term capital gains. Also, individuals are subject to a $3,000 yearly capital loss deduction, while C corporations cannot deduct net capital losses. Therefore, if a tax entity already has experienced a net capital loss for the year, the netting feature of capital gains makes them preferable to ordinary income.

Example 16-12. Spoon-feed, Inc., a corporation in the 39 percent bracket, has a net capital loss to date in 2001 of $30,000. It is contemplating signing a contract to sell a small branch building held for slightly less than one year. The sale would generate a gain of $32,000. Delaying the sale until the one-year holding period for Code Sec. 1231 property has been met would, assuming no other Code Sec. 1231 transactions, enable the full offset against the capital losses, saving $11,700 ($30,000 × .39).

Converting Ordinary Income into Capital Gains

There are several ways in which businesses or their employee/owners can convert ordinary income into capital gains. Many of these tactics have been discussed in various chapters of this book. Hence, they will be discussed here in summary form.

Code Sec. 1231 gains. Depreciable property used in a trade or business and real property used in a trade or business are potentially Code Sec. 1231 assets. The two keys to generating maximum Code Sec. 1231 treatment are to meet the holding period requirement and to avoid depreciation recapture. In most instances the holding period for Code Sec. 1231 assets is one day over a year.

Example 16-13. Deespose, Inc. purchased land for a plant site but soon thereafter changed circumstances dictated a sale of the land. Land prices were appreciating and they were able to sell for $250,000 land that had cost only $180,000 11 months earlier. The $70,000 gain would be ordinary income; holding the land an additional month would convert the ordinary income into Code Sec.1231 gains, which would, if there were no Code Sec. 1231 losses, become a long-term capital gain.

Avoiding depreciation recapture is not always an optimum strategy, since acceleration of expense deductions is usually sacrificed by avoiding the recapture. Unless preferential treatment for capital gains is increased over its current rate, this trade-off would not generally be advisable. Thus, this discussion assumes the existence of preferential treatment for capital gains.

¶ **1603.07**

To operationalize tax planning in this area, it is useful to divide depreciable assets into three groups: personal property, real property acquired before 1987, and real property acquired after 1986. Because of the harsh recapture rules of Code Sec. 1245, little or no Code Sec.1231 gain is likely to result on a sale or disposition of personal property. Little tax planning after-the-fact exists for real commercial property acquired before 1987. If the straight-line alternative was selected, *all* gain is Code Sec. 1231 gain; however, if ACRS rates were selected, *all* gain is ordinary income. The depreciation choice previously made for residential rental property acquired before 1987 will govern the tax planning available. If straight-line has been selected, *all* gain will be Code Sec. 1231. If ACRS rates were selected, only the excess of ACRS depreciation over straight-line will be ordinary income; the remaining gain will be Code Sec. 1231 gain. Here, a careful comparison of the accumulated and future depreciation under ACRS and straight-line rates can lead to effective tax planning. As the holding period approaches the latter point of the statutory life of the asset, excess depreciation will begin to diminish. Thus, the longer the asset is held, the less ordinary income and the more Code Sec. 1231 gains will be generated.

Real property acquired after 1986 is not subject to depreciation recapture, since the use of straight-line rates is mandatory. Thus tax-planning is minimized in this area. However, as previously mentioned, the most favorable tax rate on the depreciation recapture on buildings is 15 percent (for corporations).

The *cutting* of timber may, at the election of the taxpayer, be given Code Sec. 1231 treatment. This election would generally be advantageous unless sale of the timber is not contemplated until subsequent tax years. In that event, Code Sec. 1231 treatment would be achieved at the expense of accelerating income.

Subdivided realty. Noncorporate businesses may in certain instances receive capital gain treatment on the sale of all or part of subdivided realty. Essential requirements are for the business to not be a dealer in real estate, substantial improvements not have been made, and the property must generally have been held at least five years. Code Sec. 1237 and corresponding regulations should be seen for details.

Conversion opportunities for employee/owners. For corporate employee/shareholders, conversion opportunities involve converting ordinary income compensation to capital gains and extracting earnings from the corporation while avoiding the ordinary income treatment created by dividends. The first objective may be accomplished through the use of stock options. Incentive stock options are a good vehicle for this purpose, since if various holding period requirements are met,[7] the employee receives capital

---

[7] See Code Sec. 422.

gain treatment upon the sale. Of the several qualification requirements for incentive stock options, the one most restricting for closely held corporations is the requirement that employees owning more than 10 percent of the stock of the corporation immediately before the grant date are *not* eligible for incentive stock options unless the option price is at least 110 percent of the fair market value at the grant date *and* the option period does not run more than five years. Since attribution rules apply, these restrictions will apply in many instances to employees who are close relatives of stockholders.

Taking resources out of a corporation and receiving capital gain rather than ordinary dividend treatment entails fewer options than before the repeal of the *General Utilities* doctrine. If the corporation has a positive cash flow, but no earnings and profits, distributions will generally be treated as a nontaxable return of capital until basis is exhausted; the remainder will be capital gains.

Caution: Distributions in some instances could be subject to the "collapsible corporation" rules of Code Sec. 341 (see Chapter 14 for details). *Disproportionate* stock redemptions may also be used to extract resources and receive capital gain treatment (also see Chapter 14 for details). When owners are ready to dispose of the business, selling the stock (rather than liquidating the corporation or selling the assets), will generate capital gains. Since the sales price reflects earnings retained in the business, earnings are in effect extracted as capital gains.

.08 Tax Planning Tactics Assuming Preferential Treatment

There are several general rules of thumb concerning the optimal combination of capital gains and losses.

1.   If possible, let long-term gains stand alone, so as to maximize the amount subject to preferential treatment.

   Example 16-14. Assume a top marginal tax rate of 39.6 percent and a maximum capital gains rate of 20 percent. Stephanie Crowder has already sold securities resulting in a $3,000 long-term capital gain. She also has securities held for two months which toward the end of her tax year have a $3,000 paper loss. She could sell the loss securities this year or next, but plans on no additional dispositions. If she sells the loss securities in the current year, her net tax for both years is zero. However, if she waits until the next year to sell the loss securities, she pays tax of $600 in the current year, but has a tax savings of $1,188 in the next year, for a net tax savings of $588.

2.   If loss property is sold to offset capital gains, it is preferable for individuals and flow-through entities to sell long-term capital loss property over short-term loss property. The short-term capital loss could then be sold in the next year (before long-term holding period is met) and deducted first against short-term

capital gains. This increases the potential for losses not offsetting long-term capital gains.

Example 16-15. Near the end of his tax year, Mike Jenrod had $7,000 of long-term capital gains realized. An S corporation which he totally owns has two capital assets which it could sell, each asset would create an approximate $6,000 loss if sold. One asset has been held for 4 months; the other has been held for 22 months. If the assets are sold, the losses would flow through to him. Next year Jenrod expects both short-term capital gains and long-term capital gains in excess of $10,000. Jenrod's tax results for the current year would be just as favorable if the S corporation sells the stock held for 4 months as if it sold the stock held for 22 months (in either case the net gains subject to preferential treatment would be $1,000). However, by selling the stock held for 22 months this year, the loss on the sale of the 4-month stock early next year would first offset the expected short-term gains next year, leaving the long-term gains subject to a maximum tax rate of 20 percent.

3.   If possible, offset short-term capital gains against existing long-term capital losses, rather than using long-term capital gains to offset the long-term losses. This is to preserve the preferential treatment for long-term capital gains.

Example 16-16. Near the end of the current year, Cara Rutherford has already realized $8,000 of long-term capital losses. She has two batches of stock, each of which would result in a $7,000 gain if sold. One batch has been held for 5 months; the other has been held 21 months. Tax results for the current year are identical regardless of which batch is sold. However, for the next tax year, it would be ideal to be assured of a long-term gain without having to hold the stock for an additional period of time. Hence, the 5-month stock should be sold during the current year, and the 21-month stock held.

4.   If property is sold to create a $3,000 capital loss deduction, it is generally preferable to sell short-term capital loss property rather than long-term capital loss property. Then, if later in the year both short-term and long-term capital gains are realized, the capital loss offsets income taxed at ordinary rates (short-term capital gains) rather than offsetting income taxed at preferential rates (long-term capital gains).

5.   If possible, offset long-term capital losses against existing short-term capital gains. Here the reasoning is similar to Rule (3) but offsetting some kind of loss is critical because the short-term capital gains standing alone will be taxed at ordinary income rates.

¶ **1603.08**

.09 Smoothing Year-to-Year Taxable Income

The idea behind smoothing year-to-year taxable income is to, as much as possible, stay in the same tax bracket for each year, i.e., to equalize year-to-year marginal tax brackets.

> **Example 16-17.** Elena Barchas estimated up her taxable income at the end of 2000, and discovered that she was $10,000 below the 36 percent tax bracket. She expects to have sufficient income in 2001 to place her well into the 36 percent bracket. She has traditionally received in January of each year an $8,000 bonus from the C corporation of which she is the majority shareholder. Accelerating receipt of the bonus to 2000 would save $400 ($8,000 × (.36 − .31)) of federal income tax.

> The advantage of smoothing income is sometimes lessened or completely negated by the fact that it may work opposite another basic tax planning tactic previously discussed, that of deferring tax.

> **Example 16-18.** Assume the same facts as in the previous example and also that Barchas can invest money and earn a 12 percent return. Accelerating the income to 2000 would cost her $297.60 ($8,000 × .31 × .12) of return. This would significantly lessen the tax savings from smoothing.

> On the other hand, smoothing and deferral will sometimes work in the same direction, resulting in very impressive tax savings.

.10 Lowering Marginal Tax Rates by Spreading Income (Family Tax Planning)

Lowering marginal tax rates by spreading income among family members is only one of several objectives of family tax planning. Other objectives include providing for the education of children and decreasing transfer taxes (both estate and gift taxes).

Means of Shifting Income

Income may be shifted to lower-bracket family members by: paying salaries to family members; transferring interests in family businesses; by gifts, either outright gifts or through trusts or custodial arrangements; or via interest-free loans. Each of these income shifting means will be discussed, along with a discussion of the pros and cons of various types of gift property.

Paying salaries to dependent children is one of the more effective ways to shift income. If the payment is made for work done in a trade or business or for rental or other income-producing or investment activities, the payment is deductible, subject of course to the ordinary, necessary, and reasonable requirements. The income will be earned income to the child; thus the child can take the standard deduction against it. Any wages above the maximum standard deduction will be taxed at the child's rates (this is true even if the child is under 14). Another advantage of paying wages is that the wages may be used for the child's support without the income being taxed back to the parents. Care should be taken to ensure that the child does not spend so much for his or her support that the dependency deduction is lost to the parents. If the child is under 18, wages paid by a parent to a child are not subject to FICA taxes.[8] It is important to keep the wages at a reasonable rate and to maintain good records of time worked by the child.

Another income-shifting method is to transfer an interest in a family business to children. An interest in either a corporate or partnership entity would shift income. However, a transfer of a corporate interest is reasonably similar to other gifts; hence it will be discussed in conjunction with other gifts. Only the partnership entity will be discussed here.

A self-employed parent could form a partnership and give a portion of the partnership to the children. If the business performs personal services, it is generally not possible to spread income among family members via a partnership arrangement.[9] However, "a person shall be recognized as a partner . . . if he owns a capital interest in a partnership in which capital is a material income-producing factor, whether or not such interest was derived by purchase or gift from any other person."[10] Capital ordinarily is a material income-producing factor if the operations of the business necessitate substantial inventories or a substantial investment in plant, machinery, or other equipment.[11] A child's share of income from a partnership in which the child is a general partner is considered net earnings from self-employment (assuming that the partnership carried on a trade or business).[12] However, if the child was a limited partner, only guaranteed payments attributable to services performed would constitute net earnings from self-employment.[13] Since partnership income is earned income, the child will be taxed at his or her marginal rates instead of the parent's rates. One significant drawback, however, is that the income will be subject to self-employment tax, whereas wages paid to a child under 18 by a sole proprietor parent will not be subject to self-employment tax.[14] Since the effective self-employment tax rate in 2001 is .141 (after the deduction for one-half of self-employment taxes), the combination of the child's income tax rate and the self-employment tax might be higher than the parent's rates. Thus, a limited partnership may be advantageous unless it is considered desirable to build up the child's Social Security tax base.

Gifts to children may be made outright, in trust, or under the Uniform Gifts to Minors Act (UGMA) or Uniform Transfers to Minors Act (UTMA). Outright gifts have an advantage in that the income may be used for the

---

[8] Code Sec. 3121(b)(3).
[9] See, for example, *Lucas v. Earl*, 2 USTC ¶ 496, 281 US 111 (1930).
[10] Code Sec. 704(e)(1).
[11] Reg. § 1.704-1(e)(1)(iv).

[12] *Self-Employment Tax*, IRS Publication 533 (2000 Ed.), p. 7.
[13] *Id.*
[14] Code Sec. 3121(b)(3).

child's support without it being taxed to the parent. An obvious drawback is that the parent may lose control over the property. Also, depending on the type of property, the minor may be unable to dispose of the property. A gift under the UGMA or UTMA, however, enables the parent to exercise control as custodian. A drawback of a UGMA or UTMA gift, in addition to possible adverse estate tax complications, is that the income *cannot* be used to fulfill the legal obligation for support of the child (the income will then be taxed back to the parent). Depending on the state of residence, and the financial and educational attainments of the parents, a college education *may* even be construed as a legal support obligation for this purpose.[15] Some parents may also find the requirement that the property pass to the child at majority age (18 in many states) to be disadvantageous (perhaps not wishing so young an individual to have absolute control over the property).

Trusts have been a basic part of family tax planning for many years. Code Secs. 2503(b) and 2503(c) trusts, *Crummey* trusts, and *Clifford* trusts have been the most frequent trust vehicles used to achieve various income and transfer tax goals.[16] One commentator believes that TRA '86 income tax changes have made trusts largely ineffective in rendering significant income tax savings in family tax planning situations, but that estate planning and other purposes still make then attractive.[17]

Clifford trusts (often called 10-year trusts) were once among the most popular of trust vehicles for family tax planning purposes, since they allowed for the corpus to revert back to the grantor without the trust being taxed as a "grantor trust" (in a grantor trust, the trust entity is disregarded and the income is taxed back to the grantor). However, for transfers after March 1, 1986, *Clifford* trusts are taxed to the grantor unless the reversionary interest of the grantor is not in excess of five percent of the value of the trust corpus at the time of contribution of the property.[18] The value of a reversionary interest at the end of a term certain is a function of the number of years and an interest rate which is 120 percent of the applicable federal rate (APR) at the time the trust is established. Given the range of the APR in recent years, the required years in which the trust would have to run in order to get the reversionary interest below five percent could be anywhere from 25 to 40 years. Thus the trust period would have to run well past the time period for which *Clifford* trusts have normally been intended. More to the point, a reversionary interest of only five percent is so negligible as to almost completely take away the big advantage of a *Clifford* trust, which was the grantor getting the corpus back. Thus the *Clifford* trust is no longer very viable for spreading family income.

---

[15] See Blake, "Parent's Legal Obligation of Support After the *Braun* Decision," *Estates, Gifts and Trusts Journal,* Vol. 10, p. 154.

[16] For an excellent discussion of the role of trusts in family tax planning, see Hicks, Zoe M., "How to Make Transfers for the Benefit of Children," *The Practical Accountant,* Dec. 1989, pp. 33-50.

[17] *Id.*

[18] Code Sec. 673(a).

The two Code Sec. 2503 trusts (b) and (c) are referred to as such because of the desire of the grantor to avoid or minimize gift tax on the transfer to the trust. Section 2503 provides for an annual exclusion of $10,000 (in 2001) per year per donee (doubled if the donor is married and the spouse consents to gift-splitting).[19] A Code Sec. 2503(b) trust involves giving a life income interest to the minor child. The value of the income interest, if required to be distributed annually to the child, qualifies for the annual exclusion. The remainder interest, being a future interest, does not qualify for the annual exclusion.

> **Example 16-19.** Wally Burns placed $10,076 in a Code Sec. 2503(b) trust for his five-year-old child. The child has a lifetime interest in the trust. Assuming a required discount rate of 10.6 percent, the value of the remainder interest is .00755 × $10,076 = $76. The value of the income interest is therefore $10,000 ($10,076 − 76). Of the $10,076 gift, $10,000 would escape gift tax (assuming no other gifts in the current year), and $76 would be a taxable gift (however, the unified credit, if not previously used would offset any transfer tax due).

Code Sec. 2503(c) is applicable only if the donee of the trust is under 21 at the time of transfer of property to the trust. If the requirements of Code Sec. 2503(c) are met, the entire value of the property transferred into the trust qualifies as a present interest; thus all of the transfer is eligible for the annual exclusion. However, two strict requirements must be met:[20]

1. Both the corpus and the income *may* be expended for the benefit of the donee before age 21, i.e., the trust instrument must not prohibit such distributions before age 21, but must leave to the discretion of the trustee the amounts, if any, to be distributed.

2. To the extent not distributed, the amounts must either:

   a. Pass to the donee at the age of 21, or

   b. If the donee dies before age 21, the benefits must either be payable to his or her estate, or as the donee may appoint under a general power of appointment.

The Code Sec. 2503(b) trust is preferable over the 2503(c) trust in that the (b) trust can run past the age of 21 while the (c) trust must distribute all of the accumulated income and corpus at 21. On the other hand, the (c) trust has two advantages over the (b) trust, one of which relates to income tax, the other relating to the gift tax. Income does not have to be distributed annually in the (c) trust. If the child is under 14 (thus having unearned income in excess of $1,400 (in 2001) taxed at the parent's rates), this flexibility may be very important from an income tax standpoint, since

---

[19] Code Sec. 2503(b).

[20] Code Sec. 2503(c); Reg. § 25.2503-4.

the trust may have a lower marginal tax rate than does the parent. The other advantage that the (c) trust has over the (b) trust is that the entire gift is eligible for the annual exclusion.

A *Crummey* trust[21] tries to avoid the drawbacks of (b) and (c) trusts while retaining their advantages. The court in *Crummey* ruled that if the minor (or parent or guardian of the minor) has an annual right to demand property from the trust within a reasonable time period (e.g., 30 days), the annual exclusion was available to the extent of such demand rights. There are several compliance complexities involved with a *Crummey* trust. Although there are many instances in which a *Crummey* trust may be very advantageous,[22] the author believes that in most parent/child family tax planning situations of small families, a 2503(b) or 2503(c) trust will achieve satisfactory results. In deciding whether to use a trust as a means of shifting income among family members, the increased flexibility and possible income tax savings benefit of a trust must be balanced against the cost of setting up and maintaining the trust, including legal, accounting, and tax preparation fees.

Interest-Free Loans

Prior to TRA '84 there was considerable uncertainty about the income and gift tax effects of interest-free and below market loans. TRA '84 ended much of the uncertainty by providing imputation rules for many of these loans. With respect to gift loans, the foregone interest is treated as if the lender made a gift of the interest to the borrower and the borrower paid the interest back to the lender. Thus, the lender is considered to have made a gift, subject to the gift tax laws, and also must recognize the interest income. The borrower is considered to have received a gift and also has deductible interest expense (subject to the various limitations on the deduction of interest expense).[23] This required interest imputation not only removes the advantage of interest-free loans, but exacerbates the tax situation since the parent will have income, the child will presumably have income (from investing the loan proceeds), and the interest expense deemed paid by the child would in most cases be deductible only as an itemized deduction, and subject to the investment interest expense limitation at that. However, two exceptions to the interest imputation rule leave open some modest tax planning opportunities for interest-free loans. A *de minimis* exception applies to gift loans to individuals as long as income-producing assets are not purchased with the loan proceeds. The interest income and gift imputations do not apply to any day on which the total loans to the individual do not exceed $10,000.[24] The second exception limits the imputed interest income (but not the imputed gift) to the borrower's

---

[21] *Crummey*, 68-2 USTC ¶ 12,541, 397 F.2d 82 (9th Cir., 1968).

[22] For an excellent discussion of examples of uses of Crummey trusts, see Mark L. Vorsatz, "Trust with Beneficiary's Power of Withdrawal Adaptable for use in Many Family Situations," *Taxation for Accountants*, February, 1986, pp. 102-103.

[23] Code Sec. 7872(a)(1).

[24] Code Sec. 7872(c)(2).

"net investment income" (as defined in Code Sec. 163(d)(4)) for any day in which the total amount of loans does not exceed $100,000.[25] A further limitation applies where the borrower's net investment income is $1,000 or less; in that event the net investment income is assumed to be zero.[26] These limitations do not apply if one of the principal purposes is tax avoidance.[27] Proposed regulations here appear to interpret tax avoidance rather broadly as any loan in which a principal factor in making the below market loan is to reduce the federal income tax liability of either the borrower or lender or both.[28] Since the $10,000 exception applies even where tax avoidance is a principal factor, a modest tax advantage could be obtained from a $10,000 interest-free loan to children 14 or older.

Pros and Cons of Various Types of Gift Property to Children

Appropriate types of gift property to children depends on whether the child is 14. This is so because for a child under 14, unearned income in excess of $1,400 (in 2001) is taxed at the parent's rates. Children under 14 should generally be given property that has low *current* taxable income, but that has *deferred* income. Thus growth, low dividend-yielding stock is attractive, since the greatest part of the return, the capital gains, can be deferred and realized when the child is 14 or older. Series EE bonds can provide a total deferral of return until the child is 14. Market discount bonds (as opposed to original issue discount bonds) allow the holder the option of deferring the discount amortization (which creates taxable income) until the security matures or is disposed of. Gifts of stock in a closely held C corporation may be attractive since the dividend rate can be controlled by the parent/donors/corporate shareholders. Many other types of gift assets may be appropriate for children under 14.[29]

Children becoming 14 or older in the current tax year are not subject to tax at the parent's marginal rates. Since their marginal rates will usually be less than their parent's rates, a considerable amount of income-yielding assets can be given before the income tax savings potential is exhausted. These children should generally be given high-yielding assets. If they were previously given property which has appreciated or which has deferred income attached to it (e.g., Series EE bonds), it can now be sold with a minimum of tax. Dividend payments on closely held corporate stock could be increased. Parents may justifiably be reluctant to take full advantage of the income tax savings potential of gifts to children 14 or older, since to do so might require a transfer of assets in greater amount than they would deem advisable.

---

[25] Code Sec. 7872(d).
[26] *Id.*
[27] *Id.*
[28] Prop. Reg. § 1.7872-4(e).

[29] For a detailed lists of possible types of gift property, see Raabe and Bourcher, "Taxation of Unearned Income of Minor Dependents," *The Tax Adviser*, February, 1989, pp.74-80.

¶ 1605   Income and Estate Planning Implications of Disposal of a Closely Held Business

Here, "disposal" is intended in its broadest sense. Hence, sales, liquidations, gifts, and transfers at death will be examined. Gifts will be examined separately from other types of disposals. Sole proprietorships, partnerships, and corporations will each be examined.

.01   Disposal of a Sole Proprietorship

The disposal of a sole proprietorship for tax purposes is not considered the disposal of the business as a whole, but rather the disposition of all of the individual assets (both tangible and intangible), making up the business. If disposal is through a sale or taxable exchange to nonrelatives, the primary considerations are the advisability of the sale or exchange, and, assuming a sale or exchange is advisable, the timing and characteristics of income recognition. If the assets of the business have appreciated, advisability of the sale or exchange will hinge in part on the loss of the stepped-up basis feature of transfers at death.

> **Example 16-20.** Kevin Fletcher has a sole proprietorship with assets having a total basis of $300,000 but a fair market value of approximately $800,000. Having a terminal illness, he decides to sell his business. Ten months after the sale he dies. The income tax on the $500,000 of gain could have been avoided had he retained the business and allowed his heirs or his estate to sell the business.

On the other hand, nontax reasons may swamp in importance the stepped-up basis advantage of not selling.

> **Example 16-21.** Bob Crum has a sole proprietorship with assets having a total basis of $500,000, and a fair market value of $900,000. Crum is known to his customers as an extremely honest, efficient, and competent businessman. Of the total value of the business, approximately $300,000 is attributable to goodwill. He dies suddenly intestate. His estate drags on for some time and the business, rudderless without him, quickly deteriorates. By the time the administrator is able to sell it, the goodwill has evaporated, and the purchaser was even able to knock down the tangible assets to $550,000. Although a sale before death might have resulted in as much as $160,000 federal and state income tax, this is much less than the $350,000 loss in value of the business.

Assuming that a sale *is* advisable, the timing and recognition of income have tax planning implications. The sale or taxable exchange may generate a considerable amount of income tax. Regular income tax, but perhaps not the alternate minimum tax, can be minimized by selling on contract (see the discussion earlier in this chapter on installment sales). If an outright sale would push the seller into a high marginal income tax bracket, planning of an installment sale could have as an objective the reduction of marginal rates.

Changing the *characteristics* of income, if possible, is important as long-term capital gains are given preferential treatment. The characteristics of income from the sale of a sole proprietorship can be altered through the timing of the sale and through contract allocations. Timing of the sale involves ensuring that highly appreciated Code Sec. 1231 assets have met the required holding period so as to qualify for long-term capital gain treatment. Contract allocations of the sales price of the individual assets may be disregarded by the IRS if unrealistic. Both parties are required to sign Form 8594 (which details the allocation of the sales price).[30] Generally, it is to the seller's favor to allocate a maximum to such intangibles as goodwill, patents, leaseholds, franchises, trademarks, and trade names since capital gain treatment will usually result from such allocations. The value assigned to a covenant not to compete must be reported as ordinary income. High allocations to such ordinary income assets as receivables, inventory, and prepaid expenses should be avoided. With respect to fixed assets, land and buildings should carry a high value; however, high allocations to depreciable personal property such as equipment will result in ordinary income to the extent of potential depreciation recapture.

.02 Disposal of a Partnership Interest

The sale, taxable exchange, or liquidation of a partnership interest carries the same general issues as does the disposal of a sole proprietorship, i.e., advisability of the disposition and income characteristics. The issue of stepped-up basis versus a possible loss of value if transferred at death is likely weighted more heavily toward a transfer of a partnership interest than for a sole proprietorship, since a partnership will in most cases have management in addition to the decedent partner that is both competent and motivated to preserve the value of the business. In addition, the partnership may well have existing agreements to purchase the interest of a decedent which would have the effect of removing the forced sale aspect of some estate situations.

If the partnership interest is disposed of during the lifetime of the partner, some income characteristic flexibility will be possible. Recall from Chapter 13 that the general rule that a partnership interest is a capital asset is a rather weak rule due to the pervasive aspects of Code Sec. 751 (the partner's share of unrealized receivables and substantially appreciated inventory is treated as ordinary income property). To the extent that reasonable latitude in appraisal values is possible, one would want conservative values assigned to unrealized receivables and inventory. Partnership receivables should be carefully scrutinized for accounts where the likelihood of collection is questionable; inventory values should reflect slow-

---

[30] Code   Sec.1060(b);   Temp.   Reg.
§ 1.1060-1T(h)(2).

moving, obsolete or out of fashion, and physically deteriorated inventory. Many prepaid expenses will have a fair market value of less than book value. Since prepaid expenses usually must be counted as Code Sec. 751 assets, this lower fair market value should be reflected. On the other hand, since land and generally buildings will not be Code Sec. 751 assets, they should reflect full values.

If a partner takes a liquidating interest in the partnership, the *timing* of recognition of the income is affected by the type of property received. If the property received is proportionate with respect to Code Sec. 751 and non-Code Sec. 751 assets, generally there is no immediate income recognition. However, as soon as receivables are collected and/or inventory sold by the recipient partner, ordinary income is recognized. Given the short-term nature of receivables and inventory, deferral past the current tax year is probably not feasible. Also in many instances the partner will not wish to receive any receivables or inventory due to the difficulty of collecting and selling the items after disassociation from the partnership. If, as is true in many cases, the partner receives in liquidation a disproportionate amount of non-Code Sec. 751 assets (e.g., cash and a building), immediate recognition of ordinary income from his or her share of appreciated Code Sec. 751 assets is required. The appreciation in value of the partner's share of non-751 assets is deferred until or unless the assets are disposed.

If the partner takes a cash liquidating distribution from a partnership, some flexibility over the type of income (Code Sec. 736(a) or Code Sec. 736(b) payments) is possible. Even more flexibility is possible with respect to the timing of the reporting of ordinary income and capital gains.

.03 Disposal of an Interest in a Corporation

The advisability of selling a corporate interest before death is probably weighted somewhat more toward transferring at death than a partnership, since ease of transferability will be somewhat enhanced. However, the value of any closely held business, regardless of the entity, will be affected to some extent by the death of the principal owner/manager. If the focus is solely on the shareholder, the form of disposal (selling the stock, taking an in-kind liquidation, or having the corporation sell the assets) has no effect on the *characteristics* of income, i.e., in all three cases the shareholder will have capital gain. Such an analysis, however, ignores the double tax impact of disposal of a corporate interest. Selling the corporate stock will not generate the double tax; an in-kind liquidation or sale of the assets will generate the double tax if the entity is a C corporation. The double tax may also be a factor for S corporations if they were converted to S from C status after 1986. Of course, buyers may prefer to purchase the assets rather than the stock. If there will be a tax loss, and the stock is not Code Sec. 1244 stock, or if the loss exceeds the annual Code Sec. 1244 ordinary loss deduction limit, a sale of the assets at the corporate level may be preferable. Some flexibility with respect to the timing of the income is present.

Stock can be sold on piecemeal (probably only feasible if the sale is to a relative) or on an installment basis. Liquidating proceeds can be distributed in installments, thus taking advantage of the cost recovery benefit rule governing installment liquidating proceeds.

.04 Gifts of Interests in Closely Held Businesses

The advantages of effecting gifts of closely held businesses as opposed to taxable dispositions or transfers at death are several. A gift is not a taxable (for income tax purposes) disposition. In addition there are several other important advantages of gifts.

1. Income tax savings may be achieved if, as is often true, the donor is in a higher income tax bracket than the donee. If the property is appreciated and the ultimate objective is to sell the property, a transfer to a lower income tax bracket donee can result in less tax on the sale.

2. In most cases the basis for transfer tax purposes is frozen, as opposed to transfers at death, which are generally valued for transfer tax purposes at fair market value as of date of death.

    Code Sec. 2036(c), which prohibited estate freezes through the use of, among other devices, preferred stock recapitalizations, was repealed retroactively by the Revenue Reconciliation Act of 1990.[31] The repeal of this very unpopular law once again created opportunities to save transfer taxes through the use of preferred stock recapitalizations. However, very complicated valuation rules now apply to recapitalization freezes.[32] Therefore, tax practitioners must be cautious about implementing new recapitalization freezes.

    Example 16-22. Sam Software, the owner of HYTECH, Inc., owns stock currently worth $400,000. At the time of his death, four years later, the stock has increased in value to $1,500,000. A gift of the stock would (assuming the annual exclusion is already used up), create a taxable transfer for unified transfer tax purposes of $400,000; a transfer at death would create a taxable transfer for unified transfer tax purposes of $1,500,000.

3. Because taxable gifts are not "grossed up," and transfers at death *are* grossed up, the effective tax rate (though the tax is a unified rate schedule) is much lower than the tax on transfers at death.

---

[31] Revenue Reconciliation Act of 1990, P.L. 101-508, Act Sec. 11601, repealing Code Sec. 2036(c).

[32] Code Secs. 2701-2704.

4.　An annual exclusion of $10,000 (in 2001) per donee is allowed for gifts. This may be doubled if the donor is married and the spouse consents to split the gift.

On the other hand, gifts have some drawbacks when compared to transfers at death.

1.　The donee of a gift takes a basis for income tax purposes of a carryover basis. Recipients of property because of death generally receive a basis that is stepped up to fair market value. If the property is highly appreciated and the estate is sufficiently small to escape federal transfer taxes, this can be a very significant advantage.

Example 16-23. Jim Heithmeyer owns common stock in a closely held corporation having a basis of only $75,000, but a fair market value of $400,000. He has no other significant assets and has not previously used up his unified credit. Thus, a transfer, whether by gift or via death, will not be subject to federal transfer taxes. His only heir expects to sell the stock immediately after receiving it. Receiving the stock via a gift would, upon sale, generate a capital gain to the heir of $325,000. Selling after inheriting the property, would generate no additional gain (assuming the value remains at $400,000).

2.　If the transfer tax exceeds the unified credit, and thus tax is due, a taxable gift suffers the drawback of the time value of money, i.e., the gift tax is paid in the current period; the estate tax will not be paid until some time in the future upon the death of the donor/decedent.

Chapter 17

Taxation of International Transactions

¶ 1701 Introduction

The U.S. subjects its citizens, residents, and domestic corporations to tax on worldwide income. However, nonresident alien individuals and foreign corporations are generally taxed only on U.S. source income. Therefore, in considering taxation of international transactions, the source of income becomes very important.

¶ 1703 Sources Within the United States

.01 Interest

Generally, the source or location of the debtor determines whether interest income is U.S. source income.[1] Therefore, generally income from the U.S. government, the District of Columbia, and interest on debt issued by U.S. residents or domestic corporations is U.S. source income. However, an exception exists for interest paid by a resident alien individual or a domestic corporation if at least 80 percent of the individual's or corporation's gross income from all sources during the "testing period" is "active foreign business income."[2] The "testing period" is the three-year period ending with the close of the taxable year preceding the payment.[3] "Active foreign business income" is defined as gross income which is derived from sources outside the U.S., or, in the case of a corporation, is attributable to income so derived by a subsidiary of such corporation, and is attributable to the active conduct of a trade or business in a foreign country or U.S. possession.[4] Such companies are known as "80/20" companies.

There is also a bank deposit exception. Interest on deposits with a foreign branch of a domestic corporation or a domestic partnership if such branch is engaged in commercial banking is not U.S. source income.[5] In addition, there is an exception of interest on amounts paid by a foreign branch of a domestic corporation or of a domestic partnership on "deposits." For this purpose "deposits" are as defined by Code Sec. 871(i)(3).

Taxation of U.S. Source Interest

U.S. source interest income received by a nonresident alien individual or a foreign corporation generally is taxed at a 30 percent rate and is subject to withholding.[6] However, the tax does not apply to interest received by nonresident alien individuals and foreign corporations received

---

[1] Code Sec. 861(a)(1).
[2] Code Sec. 861(a)(1)(A) and (c)(1)(A).
[3] Code Sec. 861(c)(1)(C).

[4] Code Sec. 861(c)(1)(B)
[5] Code Sec. 861(a)(1)(B)(i).
[6] Code Secs. 871(a)(1)(A) and 881(a)(1).

from certain portfolio debt investments.[7] There is also an exemption for certain interest on bank deposits where the interest is not effectively connected with the conduct of a trade or business in the U.S.[8] Finally, an exemption exists for interest derived by a foreign central bank of issue from banker's acceptances.[9]

.02 Dividends

As is true of interest, generally the location of the payor of the dividend determines whether or not the income is U.S. source income.[10] There are three exceptions to this general rule (if any of the three exceptions are met, the dividends are not U.S. source income):[11]

1.   Dividends paid by a domestic corporation that has elected to claim the possession tax credit specified in Code Sec. 936.

2.   Dividends from a foreign corporation where less than 25 percent of the gross income from all sources for the three-year period ending with the close of its taxable year preceding the declaration of the dividends was effectively connected with the conduct of a trade or business within the U.S. However, if the 25 percent test is met, the portion of the dividend that is treated as U.S. source income is the dividend multiplied by a fraction, the numerator of which is the foreign corporation's gross income connected with a U.S. trade or business, and the denominator of which is the foreign corporation's gross income from all sources.

   Example 17-1. Forp Co., a foreign corporation, had $200 million in gross income from its U.S. business and $800 million gross income from its European operations. It paid $40 million in dividends during the year. None of the dividends that it paid are U.S. source income.

   Example 17-2. Assume the same facts as in Example 17-1 except that gross income from the U.S. was $300 million. Of the $40 million in dividends paid, $40 million × ($300 million/$1,100 million), or $10.91 million is U.S. source income.

3.   Dividends from DISCs or former DISCs are U.S. source income except to the extent that they are attributable to qualified export receipts described in Code Sec. 993(a)(1).

Taxation of U.S. Source Dividends

U.S. source dividends paid to nonresident alien individuals or to foreign corporations are generally subject to a 30 percent tax and are subject to withholding.[12] An exception exists for dividends received by

---

[7] Code Secs. 871(h) and 881(c).
[8] Code Secs. 871(i)(1) and (2)(A), and 881(d).
[9] Code Secs. 871(i)(1) and (2)(C), and 881(d).

[10] Code Sec. 861(a)(2).
[11] *Id.*
[12] Code Secs. 871(a)(1)(A) and 881(a)(1).

nonresident aliens or foreign corporations which are effectively connected with the conduct of a trade or business within the U.S.[13]

.03 Income Effectively Connected with a U.S. Trade or Business

The U.S. regular graduated income tax rates may apply to nonresident aliens or foreign corporations if the income from a trade or business is effectively connected to a trade or business within the U.S.[14] In determining whether gains, profits, income and certain other gains are effectively connected to a trade or business within the U.S., the principal tests to be applied are the asset-use test and the business-activities test.[15]

Asset-Use Test

The asset-use test determines whether the income, gain, or loss is derived from assets used in, or held for use in, the conduct of a trade or business within the U.S.[16] The asset-use test ordinarily applies in making a determination with respect to income, gain, or loss of a passive type where the trade or business activities as such do not give rise directly to the realization of the income, etc. However, even in the case of such income, etc., any activities of the trade or business which materially contribute to the realization of such income, gain, or loss shall also be taken into account as a factor in determining whether the income, etc. is effectively connected with the conduct of a trade or business in the U.S.[17]

Ordinarily, an asset is to be treated as used in, or held for use in, the conduct of a trade or business within the U.S. if the asset is:[18]

1. Held for the principal purpose of promoting in the present conduct of the trade or business in the U.S.;

2. Acquired and held in the ordinary course of the trade or business conducted in the U.S.; or

3. Otherwise held in a "direct relationship to the trade or business conducted in the U.S."

In determining whether an asset is held in a "direct relationship to the trade or business conducted in the U.S.," the principal consideration is whether the asset is needed in that trade or business. The asset must be held to meet the present needs of the trade or business rather than its anticipated future needs. An asset held to meet the operating expenses of the trade or business qualifies; however, an asset held for future diversification into a new trade or business, held for expansion of a trade or business outside the U.S., an asset held for future plant replacement, or an asset held for future business contingencies does not qualify.[19]

---

[13] Code Secs. 871(b)(1) and 882(a)(1).
[14] Code Secs. 871(b)(1) and 882(a)(1).
[15] Code Sec. 864(c)(2); Reg. § 1.864-4(c)(1).
[16] *Id.*

[17] Reg. § 1.864-4(c)(2)(i).
[18] Reg. § 1.864-4(c)(2)(ii).
[19] Reg. § 1.864-4(c)(2)(iv)(a).

An asset is presumed to be held in a direct relationship to the trade or business if:[20]

1.   It was acquired with funds generated by that trade or business;

2.   The income from the asset is retained or reinvested in that trade or business; and

3.   Personnel who are present in the U.S. and actively involved in the conduct of the trade or business exercise significant management and control over the investment of the asset.

Business-Activities Test

The business-activities test ordinarily applies in making a determination with respect to income, gain, or loss, even passive income, etc., if it arises directly from the active conduct of a trade or business in the U.S. This test is of primary significance, for example, where:[21]

1.   Dividends or interest are derived by a dealer in stock or securities;

2.   Gain or loss is derived from the sale or exchange of capital assets in the active conduct of a trade or business by an investment company;

3.   Royalties are derived in the active conduct of a business consisting of the licensing of patents or similar intangible property; or

4.   Service fees are derived in the active conduct of a servicing business.

Example 17-3.[22] Leeds, Ltd., a foreign corporation, is engaged in manufacturing in England. Leeds maintains a branch in the U.S. which acts as importer and distributor of the merchandise manufactured in England. The U.S. branch is required to hold a large cash balance at various times during the year, but at low cash need times it invests in U.S. stocks and receives dividend income. Because these investments are held to meet present needs of business conducted in the U.S., the dividend income is effectively connected with the conduct of business in the U.S.

Example 17-4.[23] Willhelm Distributors, a German corporation, has a branch in the U.S. which acts an importer and distributor of merchandise. By reason of the activities of that branch, Willhelm is engaged in business in the U.S. It also carries on a business in which it licenses patents to unrelated persons in the U.S. for use in the U.S. The businesses of the licenses in which these patents are used have no

---

[20] Reg. § 1.864-4(c)(2)(iv)(b).
[21] Reg. § 1.864-4(c)(3)(i).
[22] Adapted from Reg. § 1.864-4(c)(2)(v), Example 1.

[23] Adapted from Reg. § 1.864-4(c)(3)(ii), Example 2.

¶ 1703.03

direct relationship to the business carried on in Willhelm's branch in the U.S. However, the merchandise marketed by the branch is similar in type to that manufactured under its patents. The negotiations and other activities leading up to the consummation of theses licenses are conducted by employees of Willhelm who are not connected to the branch. Further, the U.S. branch does not otherwise participate in arranging for the licenses. Royalties for these licenses are not effectively connected for that year with the conduct of its business because the activities of the business are not a material factor in the realization of such income.

The 30 percent rate may be reduced by income tax treaties. (Table 1 in IRS Publication 515 lists the various treaty rates.) For example, the withholding rate for dividends paid by U.S. corporations to citizens of Germany is 15 percent; the withholding rate for dividends paid by a U.S. subsidiary to German corporations is 5 percent.[24]

.04 Rents and Royalties

Rentals or royalties from property located in the U.S. or from any interest in such property is U.S. source income.[25] Such items include rentals or royalties for the use of or for the privilege of using in the U.S. patents, copyrights, secret processes and formulas, goodwill, trademarks, trade brands, franchises, and other like property.[26]

.05 Sale of Purchased Inventory Property

If inventory is purchased outside the U.S., but is sold within the U.S., income derived from the sale is generally U.S. source income.[27] However, income from the sale of property within the U.S., but sold outside the U.S., is generally foreign source income.[28] A sale of inventory is generally considered consummated at the time when, and the place where, the rights, title, and interest of the seller are transferred to the buyer.[29] Where bare legal title is retained by the seller, the sale shall be deemed to have occurred at the time and place where beneficial ownership and the risk of loss passes to the buyer. However, the above rules are not applied if the primary purpose of the transaction is tax avoidance. All factors of the transaction are considered in such cases.[30]

¶ 1705 Source Rules for Deductions

From gross income from sources within the U.S., taxpayers are allowed deductions for expenses and losses that are properly apportioned or allocated to such income. In addition, taxpayers are allowed a ratable share of expenses and losses which cannot definitely be allocated to some item or class of gross income.[31]

---

[24] IRS Publication 515, Withholding of Tax on Nonresident Aliens and Foreign Corporations (Rev. February 2001).
[25] Code Sec. 861(a)(4).
[26] Id.

[27] Code Sec. 861(a)(6).
[28] Code Sec. 862(a)(6).
[29] Reg. § 1.861-7(c).
[30] Id.
[31] Code Sec. 861(b).

The regulations list 15 classes of income for this purpose:[32]

1.   Compensation for services,

2.   Gross income derived from businesses,

3.   Gains from dealings in property,

4.   Interest,

5.   Rents,

6.   Royalties,

7.   Dividends,

8.   Alimony and separate maintenance payments,

9.   Annuities,

10.   Income from life insurance and endowment contracts,

11.   Income from discharge of indebtedness,

12.   Distributive shares of partnership income,

13.   Pensions,

14.   Income in respect of a decedent, and

15.   Income from an interest in an estate or trust.

Allocation is accomplished by determining, for each deduction, the class of gross income to which the deduction is definitely related. Then the deduction is allocated to such class of gross income (without regard to the taxable year in which the income is received or accrued).[33] Some deductions are related to all gross income. Also, some deductions are treated as not definitely related to any gross income and are ratably apportioned to all gross income. These deductions include:[34]

- Certain interest expense,

- Real estate taxes on a personal residence or sales tax on items purchased for personal use,

- Medical expenses,

- Charitable contributions, and

- Alimony.

Deductions which are supportive in nature (e.g., overhead, general and administrative expenses, and supervisory expenses) may be allocated and apportioned along with the deductions to which they relate.[35] However, it is

---

[32] Reg. § 1.861-8(a)(3).
[33] Reg. § 1.861-8(b)(1).

[34] Reg. § 1.861-8(e)(9).
[35] Temp. Reg. § 1.861-8T(b)(3).

equally acceptable to attribute supportive deductions directly to activities or property which generate the gross income.[36]

To the extent that such expenses are not directly allocable to specific income-producing activities or property of the member of the affiliated group that incurred the expense, such expenses must be allocated and apportioned as if all members of the affiliated group were a single corporation.[37] Specifically, such expenses must be allocated to a class of gross income that takes into account gross income that is generated, has been generated, or could reasonably have been expected to have been generated by the member of the affiliated group. If the expenses related to the gross income of fewer than all members of an affiliated group, then those expenses must be apportioned as if those fewer members were a single corporation.[38]

Example 17-5.[39] Gold, Inc. owns all of the stock of both Copper Co. and Silver, Inc. All are domestic corporations. Gold, Inc. incurs general training program expenses of $100,000 in 2000. Employees of all three companies participated in the programs. In 2000, Gold, Inc. had U.S. source gross income of $200,000 and foreign source general limitation income of $200,000. Copper Co. had U.S. source gross income of $100,000 and foreign source general limitation income of $100,000. Silver, Inc. had U.S. source gross income of $300,000 and foreign source general limitation income of $100,000. The training expenses incurred by Gold, Inc. are not definitely related solely to specific income-producing activities or property of Gold, Inc. Therefore, it is allocable to all of the gross income, both foreign and domestic. The amount allocable to foreign source general limitation income is:

$$\$100,000 \times \frac{\$200,000 + \$100,000 + \$100,000}{\$400,000 + \$200,000 + \$400,000} = \$40,000$$

The amount allocable to U.S. source gross income is:

$$\$100,000 \times \frac{\$200,000 + \$100,000 + \$300,000}{\$400,000 + \$200,000 + \$400,000} = \$60,000$$

After a deduction has been allocated to a class of gross income that is included in a statutory and residual grouping, the deduction must be apportioned between the groups.[40] Therefore, for example, in determining the separate limitations on the foreign tax credit, the income within a separate limitation category constitutes a statutory grouping of income, and all other income not within that separate limitation category consti-

---

[36] *Id.*
[37] Temp. Reg. § 1.861-14T(e)(3).
[38] *Id.*

[39] Adapted from Temp. Reg. § 1.861-14T(J), Example 2.
[40] Temp. Reg. § 1.861-8T(c).

tutes the residual grouping.[41] The term "statutory grouping of gross income" is defined as the gross income from a specific source or activity which must first be determined in arriving at taxable income from a specific source or activity under an operative section.[42] "Residual grouping of gross income" is the income from other sources or activities.[43]

.01 Research and Development Expenses

The regulations governing the allocating and apportioning of research and development (R&D) incorporate the belief that "research and experimentation is an inherently speculative activity, that findings may contribute unexpected benefits, and that the gross income derived from successful research and experimentation must bear the cost of unsuccessful research and experimentation."[44] Expenditures for R&D ordinarily are considered deductions that are definitely related to all income reasonably connected with the relevant broad product category or categories of the taxpayer, and therefore allocable to all items of gross income as a class related to that product category.[45] Taxpayers are required to use the three digit standard industrial code (SIC) to determine the relevant product categories.[46] Once a taxpayer selects a product category, it must continue to use that product category unless it establishes to the IRS's satisfaction that a change is appropriate.[47]

Legally required R&D is allocated differently. If there is not a reasonable expectation that more than a *de minimis* gross income will be generated outside of a single geographic source, the R&D is allocated exclusively to the jurisdiction imposing the requirement.[48]

There are two permissible methods of apportionment of R&D that is not legally mandated R&D. If the sales method is used, an amount equal to 50 percent of the R&D is apportioned exclusively to the statutory grouping of gross income (or the residual grouping of gross income) arising from the geographic source where the R&D activities which account for more than 50 percent of the amount of such deduction were performed.[49] Under the optional gross income method, an amount equal to 25 percent of the R&D is apportioned exclusively to the statutory grouping of gross income (or the residual grouping of gross income) arising from the geographic source where the R&D activities which account for more than 50 percent of the amount of such deduction were performed.[50] A larger allocation can be made if the taxpayer can establish that the R&D will have a very limited or long delayed application outside the geographic source where it was performed.[51]

Under the sales-based apportionment method, the research expense remaining after the 50 percent exclusive apportionment is made is then

---

[41] *Id.*
[42] Reg. § 1.861-8(a)(4).
[43] *Id.*
[44] Reg. § 1.861-17(a)(1).
[45] *Id.*
[46] Reg. § 1.861-17(a)(2).

[47] *Id.*
[48] Reg. § 1.861-17(a)(4).
[49] Reg. § 1.861-17(b)(1)(i).
[50] Reg. § 1.861-17(b)(1)(ii).
[51] Reg. § 1.861-17(b)(2)(i).

apportioned between U.S. and foreign source income in the proportion that the sales from the product category that resulted in the income bears to the total sales from the product category.[52] For purposes of the apportionment, sales from the product category of a corporation controlled by the taxpayer are taken into account if the controlled corporation can reasonably expect to benefit, directly or indirectly, from the R&D.[53] A corporation can reasonably be expected to benefit from the R&D if the taxpayer can be expected to sell, license, or transfer intangible property to that corporation, either directly or indirectly.[54] When a taxpayer chooses either the sales method or the optional gross income method, such choice constitutes a binding election for subsequent years. The taxpayer is allowed to change methods without the IRS's consent after using one method for five years.[55]

Example 17-6.[56] Digs and Hattan, Inc. manufacturers and distributes small gasoline engines. D&H, Ltd., is a wholly owned foreign subsidiary. It also manufactures and sells the engines. During 2000, Digs and Hattan incurred research expenditures of $60,000 to patent a new gasoline engine. All of the research was done in the U.S. Domestic sales of the new engine totaled $500,000 in 2000, while sales by D&H, Ltd. of the engine were $300,000. In 2000, Digs and Hattan had gross income of $160,000, of which $140,000 was U.S. source income from sales of engines and $10,000 is foreign source royalties from D&H, Ltd., and $10,000 is U.S. source interest income. The apportionment is to be based on sales. Because more than 50 percent of the R&D was performed in the U.S., 50 percent of the $60,000 deduction, or $30,000, is apportioned exclusively to gross income from U.S. sources. Of the remaining $30,000, $11,250 ($30,000 × [$300,000/($300,000 + $500,000)]) is apportioned to the statutory grouping (sources within the foreign country). The amount apportioned to the residual grouping is $30,000 × [$500,000/($300,000 + $500,000)] = $18,750. The total amount apportioned to the residual grouping is $30,000 + $18,750 = $48,750.

Example 17-7.[57] Assume the same facts as Example 17-6 except that the apportionment is made using the optional gross income method. The exclusive apportionment to the residual grouping of gross income equals $60,000 × .25 = $15,000. The amount apportioned to the statutory grouping (sources within the foreign country) is $45,000 × [$10,000/($140,000 + $10,000)] = $3,000. The amount apportioned to the residual grouping is $45,000 × [$140,000/($140,000 + $10,000)] = $42,000. The total amount apportioned to the residual grouping is $15,000 + $42,000 = $57,000.

---

[52] Reg. § 1.861-17(c)(1).
[53] Reg. § 1.861-17(c)(3).
[54] Id.

[55] Reg. § 1.861-17(e).
[56] Adapted from Reg. § 1.861-17(h), Example 1.
[57] Id.

.02 Stewardship Expenses

"Stewardship expenses" are services undertaken for a corporation's own benefit as an investor in a related corporation. They generally represent a duplication of services which the related corporation has independently performed for itself.[58] The regulations list as an example a controlled corporation performing its own analysis of its borrowing needs and forwarding the report to the parent corporation which then performs its own review of the analysis without charge to the controlled corporation.[59] Deductions from stewardship expenses are considered definitely related and allocable to dividends received or to be received from the controlled corporation. On the other hand, if the parent corporation charges for the services on an arm's-length basis, the deductions for expenses attributable to rendering the services are considered related to the amounts charged and are allocated accordingly.[60]

.03 Legal and Accounting Fees

Fees for legal and accounting services are ordinarily definitely related and allocable to specific classes of gross income. For example, accounting fees for the preparation of a study of manufacturing costs will ordinarily be definitely related to the class of income from such manufacturing. However, depending on the nature of the services rendered, the fees may be allocated to all of the taxpayer's gross income.[61]

.04 Income Taxes

Generally the deduction for state, local and foreign income; war profits; and excess profit taxes ("state income taxes") is considered definitely related and allocable to the gross income on which the state income taxes are imposed.[62] In allocating and apportioning the deduction, the income upon which the state income tax is imposed is determined by reference to the laws of the state. For example, if the state imposes tax on income which includes foreign source income, the portion of the state income tax attributable to such foreign source income is definitely related and allocable to foreign source income.[63]

Example 17-8.[64] Zalon, Inc. is a domestic corporation which has branches in states A, B, and C. It also has a branch in The Netherlands which manufactures and distributes the same type of electronic equipment. In 2000, Zalon has taxable income from these activities before deduction of state income taxes of $1,000,000. Of that, $200,000 is foreign source general limitation income, and $800,000 is U.S. source income. A, B, and C each determine state taxable income by making adjustments to Zalon's federal taxable income, and then apportioning such adjusted taxable income on the basis of the relative amount of

---

[58] Reg. § 1.861-8(e)(4).
[59] *Id.*
[60] *Id.*
[61] Reg. § 1.861-8(e)(5).

[62] Reg. § 1.861-8(e)(6).
[63] *Id.*
[64] Adapted from Reg. § 1.861-8(g), Example 25.

Zalon's payroll, property, and sales within each state compared to Zalon's worldwide payroll, property, and sales. None of the states exempt foreign source income in making the calculations. Zalon is determined to have taxable income of $550,000, $200,000, and $200,000 in the three states respectively. The respective tax rates are 10 percent, 5 percent, and 2 percent. Thus, it has state tax expense of $55,000 + $10,000 + $4,000 = $69,000. The state income tax must be apportioned between foreign source general limitation gross income and U.S. source income. Since the three states do not specifically exempt foreign source income from taxation and the three states tax $950,000 of Zalon's income (while only $800,000 is domestic source income), it is presumed that the state income taxes are imposed on $800,000 of U.S. source income and $150,000 of foreign source general limitation income. Therefore, the state income tax apportioned to foreign source income is $69,000 × ($150,000/$950,000) = $10,895. The remaining state income taxes of $58,105 are apportioned to U.S. source income.

Example 17-9.[65] Assume the same facts as in Example 17-8 except that state A specifically exempts foreign source income from taxation. Therefore, state A's tax is wholly allocable to U.S. source income. States B and C impose tax on $400,000 of Zalon's income, of which only $250,000 ($800,000 − $550,000) is presumed to be from domestic sources. Therefore, the amount of state income taxes apportioned to foreign source income is $14,000 × ($150,000/$400,000) = $5,250. The remaining $8,750 is apportioned to U.S. source income.

.05 Losses on Sales and Exchanges of Property

The deduction for capital and Code Sec. 1231 losses on the sale or exchange of an asset is considered a deduction which is definitely related and allocable to the class of gross income to which such asset ordinarily gives rise.[66] If an apportionment is necessary, the deduction is apportioned between the statutory grouping (or among the statutory groupings) of gross income (within the class of gross income) and the residual grouping (within the class of gross income) in the same proportion that the amount of gross income within such groupings bears to the total amount of gross income within the class of gross income.[67] Apportionment will be necessary, for example, where the class of gross income to which the deduction is allocated consists of gross income attributable to an intangible asset used both within and without the U.S., or where gross income is attributable to a tangible asset used both within and without the U.S.[68]

---

[65] Adapted from Reg. § 1.861-8(g), Example 26.

[66] Reg. § 1.861-8(e)(7)(i).

[67] Reg. § 1.861-8(e)(7)(ii).

[68] Id.

.06 Net Operating Losses

A net operating loss deduction is allocated and apportioned in the same manner as the deductions giving rise to the net operating loss deduction.[69]

.07 Interest Expense

The method of allocating and apportioning interest is based on the concept that generally money is fungible and that interest expense is attributable to all activities and property regardless of any specific purpose for incurring an obligation.[70] Generally, the deduction for interest is considered related to all income-producing activities and assets of the taxpayer, and therefore allocable to all the gross income which the assets of the taxpayer have generated or could have reasonably expected to have generated.[71] However, see below for exceptions to this rule.

Certain items are treated as interest for this purpose. Any expense or loss incurred in a transaction in which the taxpayer secures the use of funds for a period of time is subject to the allocation and apportionment rules if the expense is substantially incurred because of the time value of money.[72]

> **Example 17-10.**[73] Hyglow Co. borrows 1,000 ounces of gold when the spot price is $300 per ounce. Hyglow agrees to return the gold within three months. It sells the 1,000 ounces of gold for $300,000. It then enters into a contract to purchase 1,000 ounces of gold three months into the future for $310,000. In exchange for the use of $300,000, Hyglow has sustained a loss of $10,000. This loss is treated as an interest equivalent.

Losses on the sale of trade receivables are allocated and apportioned as interest expense unless at the time of sale the receivable bore an interest rate at least 120 percent of the short-term applicable federal rate, or if denominated in foreign currency, its equivalent in foreign currency.[74] Bond premium amortization by the holder of the bonds is allocated and apportioned solely to interest income derived from the bond, and an amount of interest expense equal to the amortized premium is allocated and apportioned solely to the amortized premium derived by the issuer.[75] The use of other financial products (e.g., interest rate swaps, options, forward contracts, caps and collars) may result in gains that effectively reduce apportionable interest expense. These gains and losses may be netted with interest expense.[76]

---

[69] Temp. Reg. § 1.861-8T(e)(8).

[70] Temp. Reg. § 1.861-9T(a).

[71] *Id.*

[72] Temp. Reg. § 1.861-9T(b)(1).

[73] Adapted from Temp. Reg. § 1.861-9T(b)(ii), Example 1.

[74] Temp. Reg. § 1.861-9T(b)(3)(i).

[75] Temp. Reg. § 1.861-9T(b)(5).

[76] Temp. Reg. § 1.861-9T(b)(6).

Apportionment Rules for Individuals, Estates, and Certain Trusts

Individuals generally apportion interest expense according to the type of interest expense incurred. However, if the individual's foreign source income (including income excluded from gross income under Code Sec. 911) does not exceed $5,000, the entire amount of interest expense may be allocated to U.S. source income.[77] Interest expense incurred by a nonresident alien is considered connected with income effectively connected with a U.S. trade or business only to the extent that interest is incurred with respect to liabilities that are either entered on the books of the U.S. business or are secured by assets that generate such effectively connected income.[78]

Partnerships

A partner's distributive share of the interest expense of a partnership that is directly allocable under Temp. Reg. § 1.861-10T to income from specific partnership property is treated as directly allocable to the income generated by such partnership property. However, a partner's distributive share of the interest expense of a partnership that is not directly allocable generally is considered related to all income-producing activities and assets of the partnership and is subject to apportionment by reference to the partner's interest in partnership income for the year.[79]

Corporations

Domestic corporations apportion interest expense under the asset method. In the application of the asset method, the domestic corporation shall take into account the assets of any foreign branch and shall combine with its own interest expense any deductible interest expense incurred by a branch.[80]

The interest expense of a controlled foreign corporation may be apportioned by using either the asset method or the modified gross income method. However, the gross income method is not available to any controlled foreign corporation if a U.S. shareholder and the members of its affiliated group constitute controlling shareholders of such controlled corporation and such affiliated group elects the fair market value method of apportionment.[81]

Under the asset method, the taxpayer apportions interest expense to the various statutory groupings based on the average total value of assets within each such grouping for the tax year under the asset valuation rules of Temp. Reg. § 1.861-9T(g) and under the asset characterization rules of Temp. Reg. § 1.861-9T(g)(3) and Temp. Reg. § 1.861-12T.[82] Except for qualified residence interest, taxpayers must apportion interest expense only on the basis of asset values and are not allowed to apportion any interest deduction on the basis of gross income.

---

[77] Temp. Reg. § 1.861-9T(d)(1).
[78] Temp. Reg. § 1.861-9(d)(2).
[79] Temp. Reg. § 1.861-9T(e)(1).

[80] Temp. Reg. § 1.861-9T(f)(1) and (2).
[81] Temp. Reg. § 1.861-9T(f)(3).
[82] Temp. Reg. § 1.861-9T(g)(1)(i).

A taxpayer may elect to determine the value of its assets on the basis of either their tax book value or the fair market value.[83]

> **Example 17-11.** Exportum, Inc., a domestic corporation, has deductible interest expense in 2001 of $900,000. It apportions its expenses according to the tax book value method. The adjusted basis of Exportum's assets is $8,000,000, $6,000,000 of which generate U.S. source income, and $2,000,000 of which generate foreign source general limitation income. No portion of the $900,000 is directly allocable solely to identified property. Therefore, the interest expense apportioned to foreign source income is $900,000 × ($2,000,000/$8,000,000) = $225,000. The remaining $675,000 of interest is attributable to U.S. source income.

¶ 1707 Transactions Involving Computer Programs

There are four categories of transfers of computer programs:[84]

1.   A transfer of a copyright right in the computer program,

2.   A transfer of a copy of the computer program (a copyrighted article),

3.   The provision of services for the development or modification of the computer program, or

4.   The provision of know-how relating to computer programming techniques.

Any transaction consisting of more than one category of transactions is to be treated as separate transactions. A transaction that is *de minimis* will not be treated as a separate transaction but instead will be treated as part of another transaction.[85]

.01 Definition of Computer Program

For this purpose, a computer program is defined as a set of statements or instructions to be used directly or indirectly in a computer in order to bring about certain results. Included in the definition is any media, user manuals, documentation, database or similar items if these items are incidental to the operation of the computer program.[86]

.02 Transfer of Copyright Rights

The transfer of a computer program is a transfer of a copyright right if the transferee acquires any of the following four rights:[87]

1.   The right to make copies of the computer program for purposes of distribution to the public by sale or other transfer of ownership, or by rental, lease, or lending;

---

[83] Temp. Reg. § 1.861-9T(g)(1)(ii).
[84] Reg. § 1.861-18(b)(1).
[85] Reg. § 1.861-18(b)(2).

[86] Reg. § 1.861-18(a)(3).
[87] Reg. § 1.861-18(c)(1) and (2).

2.   The right to prepare derivative computer programs, based on the copyrighted computer program;

3.   The right to make a public performance of the computer program; or

4.   The right to publicly display the computer program.

.03 Transfer of Copyrighted Article

If a person acquires a copy of a computer program but does not acquire any of the copyright rights described above (or only acquires a *de minimis* grant of such rights), the transfer is classified solely as a transfer of a copyrighted article.[88] A copyrighted article includes a copy of a computer program from which the work can be perceived, reproduced, or otherwise communicated, either directly or with the aid of a machine or device. Such copy may be fixed in a floppy disk, or in the main memory or hard drive of a computer or any other medium.[89]

> **Example 17-12.**[90] Danube Valley Co., an Austrian corporation, enters into an agreement with Benevolent Software, Inc., a U.S. corporation, to purchase copies of a software program for resale purposes. The disks are shipped in boxes covered by shrink-wrap licenses. Under the license, no reverse engineering, decompilation, or disassembly of the computer program is permitted. Danube Valley Co. has acquired copyrighted articles.

.04 Classification of Transfers of Copyright Rights and Copyright Articles

The facts and circumstances test will be applied to determine whether a transfer of a copyright right or copyright article is a sale or a lease. For this purpose, the principles of Code Secs. 1222 and 1235 are applied.[91]

The site of where title passes is determinative for whether income from the sale of copyrighted articles where the computer program is considered purchased inventory is U.S. source or foreign source income. If the computer program is deemed to be produced inventory, sales will be sourced under Code Secs. 863 and 865.

If the computer program is considered personal property, its sale will constitute U.S. source or foreign income according to the residence of the seller. Income from the sale of a copyright right is sourced under the rules applicable to noninventory personal property sales. If a computer program or copyright is leased, the location of the property (in the case of rents) and the place where the property is used (in the case of royalties) determines whether the income is U.S. source or foreign source.[92]

[88] Reg. § 1.861-18(c)(1)(ii).
[89] Reg. § 1.861-18(c)(3).
[90] Adapted from Reg. § 1.861-18(h), Example 7.
[91] Reg. § 1.861-18(f).
[92] *Id.*

.05 *Provision of Services*

Whether a transaction involving a newly developed or modified computer program is treated as the provision of services or as another transaction depends on all the facts and circumstances of the transaction.[93]

.06 *Provision of Know-How*

The provision of information with respect to a computer program will be treated as the provision of know-how only if the information is:[94]

- Information relating to computer programming techniques;

- Furnished under conditions preventing unauthorized disclosure, specifically contracted for between the parties; and

- Considered property subject to trade protection.

¶ 1709 Income from Sources Outside the U.S.

The following items of gross income are treated as being income from sources without the U.S.:[95]

- Interest that is not derived from sources within the U.S.;

- Dividends that are not derived from sources within the U.S.;

- Compensation for labor or personal services performed outside the U.S.;

- Rentals or royalties from property located outside the U.S. or from any interest in such property, including rentals or royalties for the use of, or for the privilege of using outside the U.S., patents, copyrights, secret processes and formulas, goodwill, trademarks, trade brands, franchises, and other like property;

- Gains, profits, and income from the sale of real property located outside the U.S.;

- Gains, profits, and income derived from the purchase of personal property within the U.S., and its sale outside the U.S.;

- Underwriting income other than that derived from sources within the U.S.;

- Gains, profits, and income from the disposition of a U.S. real property interest (as defined in Code Sec. 897(c)) when the real property is located in the Virgin Islands.

.01 *Taxable Income from Sources Outside the U.S.*

Against the gross income listed above, a deduction is allowed for expenses, losses, and other deductions that are properly apportioned or

---

[93] Reg. § 1.861-18(d).
[94] Reg. § 1.861-18(e).

[95] Code Sec. 862(a); Reg. § 1.862-1(a)(1).

allocated to such income. In addition a deduction is allowed for a ratable part of any other expenses, losses, or deductions that cannot definitely be allocated to some item or class of gross income.[96]

¶ 1711 Special Rules for Determining the Source of the Income

Code Sec. 863(a) gives authority to the Treasury to promulgate regulations governing the allocation or apportionment of deductions to sources within or without the U.S.

.01 Mixed-Source Rules

The following items of gross income are treated as mixed-source income:[97]

- Income from services rendered partly within and partly outside the U.S.;

- Gains from the sale or exchange of inventory property produced (in whole or in part) by the taxpayer within the U.S. and sold outside the U.S., and gains from inventory property produced outside the U.S. and sold inside the U.S.; and

- Gains derived from the purchase of inventory property within a possession of the U.S. and its sale or exchange outside the U.S.

"Transportation income" which begins and ends in the U.S. is treated as derived from sources within the U.S.[98] "Transportation income" is defined as any income derived from, or in connection with, either the use (or hiring or leasing for use) of a vessel or aircraft, or the performance of services directly related to the use of a vessel or aircraft.[99] Generally 50 percent of all transportation income attributable to transportation which is not described in the preceding sentences and begins or ends in the U.S. is considered U.S. source income.[100]

.02 Source Rules for Space and Ocean Activities

Generally any income derived from a space or ocean activity is U.S. source income if derived from a U.S. person, and is foreign source income if derived by a person other than a U.S. person.[101] The term "space or ocean activity" refers to any activity conducted in space and any activity conducted on or under water that is not within the jurisdiction of any country.[102] However, the term does not include any activity giving rise to transportation income; nor to international communications income; nor to mines, oil and gas wells, or other natural deposits if located within any country.[103]

---

[96] Code Sec. 862(b).
[97] Code Sec. 863(b).
[98] Code Sec. 863(c)(1).
[99] Code Sec. 863(c)(3).

[100] Code Sec. 863(c)(2).
[101] Code Sec. 863(d)(1).
[102] Code Sec. 863(d)(2)(A).
[103] Code Sec. 863(d)(20(B).

.03 International Communications Income

For any U.S. person, 50 percent of international communications income is U.S. source income. The other 50 percent is sourced outside the U.S. If the person is not a U.S. person, the international communications income will be sourced outside the U.S. However, any international communications income that is attributable to an office or other fixed place of business in the U.S., is considered U.S. source income.[104]

"International communications income" is defined as:[105]

- All income derived from the transmission of communications or data from the U.S. to any foreign country or possession of the U.S., and

- All income derived from the transmission of communications or data from any foreign country or possession of the U.S. to the U.S.

.04 Natural Resources

The Internal Revenue Code does not discuss sourcing rules for natural resources. However, the regulations to Code Sec. 863 provide rules. Generally, gross receipts from the sale outside the U.S. of natural resources are allocated between sources within the U.S. and outside the U.S. based on the fair market value of the product at the export terminal.[106] If a taxpayer does additional production activities after shipment, the gross receipts in excess of the fair market value at the terminal are sourced under the rules for inventory.

If additional production activities are performed before the product is shipped from the export terminal, the gross receipts are allocated between sources within and outside the U.S. based on the fair market value of the product immediately prior to the additional production activities. The source of the gross receipts in excess of fair market value before the additional production activities is determined under Reg. § 1.863-3.[107]

> **Example 17-13.**[108] Webe Mining, Inc. a U.S. corporation, operates a zinc mine in Chile. Webe Mining transports the ore to a terminal where it is shipped to purchasers in the U.S. Because title of the property passes in the U.S., and the company does not engage in additional production prior to the export terminal, gross receipts equal to the fair market value of the ore at the export terminal will be from sources outside the U.S., and excess gross receipts will be from U.S. sources.

---

[104] Code Sec. 863(e)(1).
[105] Code Sec. 863(e)(2).
[106] Reg. § 1.863-1(b)(1).

[107] Reg. § 1.863-1(b)(2).
[108] Adapted from Reg. § 1.863-1(b)(7), Example 1.

Example 17-14.[109] Assume the same facts as in Example 17-13 except that Webe Mining also operates a smelter in Chile. The smelted zinc is exported to purchasers in the U.S. Gross receipts equal to the fair market value of the ore at the smelter will be from sources outside the U.S. The conversion of the ore into zinc constitutes an additional production activity, the income from which is apportioned under the rules of Reg. § 1.863-3 (discussed below).

.05 Allocating Cross Border Sales of Inventory Between the U.S. and a Foreign Country

The regulations in § 1.863-3 provide for three methods of determining the source of inventory that is either produced in the U.S. and sold outside the U.S., or is produced outside the U.S. and sold in the U.S. The methods are:

1. The 50/50 method;

2. The independent factory price (IFP) method; and

3. With IRS approval, the books and records method.

The 50/50 Method

The 50/50 method is the default method (used unless another method is elected). Under this method, 50 percent of the taxpayer's gross income is considered attributable to production. The remaining 50 percent of gross income is considered attributable to sales activity.[110]

Example 17-15.[111] Mr. Tea, Inc., a U.S. corporation, produces electric teapots in the U.S. Mr. Tea sells the teapots for $15 to a distributor in a foreign country. Mr. Tea's cost of goods sold is $7, and its gross income is $8. Under the 50/50 method, $4 of gross income is considered attributable to production and $4 is considered attributable to sales.

The IFP Method

If an independent factory price (IFP) can be fairly established, a taxpayer may elect this method. An IFP is considered fairly established based on a sale by the taxpayer only if the taxpayer regularly sells part of its output to wholly independent distributors or other selling concerns in such a way as to reasonably reflect the income earned from production.[112] If the taxpayer elects the IFP method, the amount of the gross sales price equal to the IFP will be treated as attributable to production, and the excess of the sales price over the IFP will be treated as attributable to sales activity.[113]

---

[109] Adapted from Reg. § 1.863-1(b)(7), Example 5.
[110] Reg. § 1.863-3(b)(1)(i).
[111] Adapted from Reg. § 1.863-3(b)(1)(ii), Example.

[112] Reg. § 1.863-3(b)(2)(i).
[113] Reg. § 1.863-3(b)(2)(ii).

The IFP will only be applied to sales that are reasonably contemporaneous with the sale that fairly establishes the IFP. An IFP cannot be applied to sales in other geographic markets if the markets are substantially different.[114] The portion of the cost of goods sold attributable to the production activity is deducted from the gross receipts from production to determine gross income. The portion of the cost of goods sold attributable to the sales activity is similarly deducted from gross receipts from sales to determine gross income.[115]

>   **Example 17-16.**[116] National Grain Co., a U.S. corporation, purchases wheat in the U.S. and processes it into flour. National Grain sells the flour to a foreign distributor for $50. The cost of goods sold, entirely attributable to production is $40. National Grain does not engage in significant sales activity. Therefore, the $10 of gross income is entirely attributable to the production activity. The gross income attributable to sales activity is zero.

>   **Example 17-17.**[117] National Grain Co., from Example 17-16, also sells flour in the foreign country to a retailer for $55. Because National Grain elected the IFP method and the flour is substantially identical to the flour sold to the distributor, the IFP fairly established in the sales to the distributor must be used to determine the amount attributable to production activity in the sale to the retailer. Accordingly, $50 of the gross sales price is attributable to production activity and $5 ($55 − $50) is attributable to sales activity. After reducing the gross sales price by the cost of goods sold, $10 of the gross income is attributable to production activity and $5 is attributable to sales activity.

Books and Records Method

In order to use the books and records method, the taxpayer must establish to the satisfaction of the IRS that the taxpayer, in good faith and unaffected by considerations of tax liability, will regularly employ in its books of account a detailed allocation of receipts and expenditures which clearly reflects the amount of income from production and sales activities.[118] If a taxpayer receives permission to use the books and records method, but does not comply with a material condition set forth by the IRS, permission to use the method may be revoked.[119]

Determination of Source of Income

Production activities for this purpose are activities that create, fabricate, manufacture, extract, process, cure, or age inventory.[120] If the production assets are located entirely either within or outside the U.S., the location

---

[114] *Id.*
[115] Reg. § 1.863-3(b)(2)(iii).
[116] Adapted from Reg. § 1.863-3(b)(2)(iv), Example 1.

[117] *Id.*
[118] Reg. § 1.863-3(b)(3).
[119] *Id.*
[120] Reg. § 1.863-3(c)(1)(i)(A).

of the assets determines the source of the income.[121] However, if production assets are located both within and outside the U.S., foreign source income is determined by multiplying income from the production activity by a fraction whose numerator is the average adjusted basis of production assets located outside the U.S. and whose denominator is the average adjusted basis of all production assets within and outside the U.S.[122] The average adjusted basis is computed by averaging the adjusted basis of the assets at the beginning and end of the year, unless such average does not fairly represent the average for the year.[123]

Example 17-18.[124] Widgets R Us, a U.S. corporation, produces widgets that are sold both within and outside the U.S. The initial manufacture of all widgets occurs in the U.S. The second stage of production of widgets that are sold within a foreign country is completed in such foreign country. The company's U.S. plant and machinery which makes the widgets has an average adjusted basis of $4 million. The company also owns warehouses used to store work in process. The company owns foreign equipment with an average adjusted basis of $1 million. The company's gross receipts from all sales of widgets is $10 million. Its gross receipts from export sales of widgets is $2 million. The cost of goods sold from sales of widgets in foreign countries is $1.2 million. Therefore, its gross income from widgets sold in foreign countries is $.8 million. The company uses the 50/50 method to divide its gross income between production activities and sales activities. The company's production gross income from sources outside the U.S. is obtained by multiplying one half of its $.8 million of gross income from sales of widgets, or $.4 million by a fraction, the numerator of which is all relevant foreign production assets ($1 million), and the denominator of which is all relevant production assets. All relevant production assets is equal to $1 million + the U.S. assets of $4 million × (gross receipts from exports ($2 million)/all gross receipts ($10 million). Thus, all relevant production assets = $1million + $.8 million = $1.8 million. Gross production from sources outside the U.S. = $.4 million × ($1 million/$1.8 million) = $.22 million.

The source of gross income attributable to sales activity is determined under the place of sale rules as delineated in Reg. § 1.861-7(c).[125] Generally, a sale is consummated where the property rights pass to the buyer. However, if goods are sold in the U.S., title passes in a foreign country, but the goods are then sold to U.S. customers, the income is U.S. source income.[126]

---

[121] *Id.*

[122] Reg. § 1.863-3(c)(1)(ii)(A).

[123] Reg. § 1.863-3(c)(1)(ii)(B).

[124] Adapted from Reg. § 1.863-3(c)(1)(iv), Example 1.

[125] Reg. § 1.863-3(c)(2).

[126] T.D. 8687, 1996-2 CB 47.

Election and Reporting Rules

If a taxpayer does not elect to use the IFP method or the books and records method, it must use the 50/50 method. The election is made by using the method on a timely filed original return. Permission from the IRS must be obtained to use the books and records method. A taxpayer must obtain permission to change methods.[127]

.06 Income Partly from Sources Within a U.S. Possession

Income from sources partly within a U.S. possession includes inventory produced in the U.S. and sold in a possession as well as inventory produced in a possession and sold in the U.S. Such sales are termed possession production sales. Also included is income where inventory property is purchased in a possession and sold within the U.S. These are termed possession purchase sales.[128]

Possession Production Sales

Taxpayers who have possession production sales can use one of three methods to allocate gross income between production and business sales activities:[129]

1.   The possession 50/50 method,

2.   The independent factory price method, and

3.   The books and records method.

Possession 50/50 Method

Under the possession 50/50 method, 50 percent of the gross income is allocated to production activity and 50 percent is allocated to business sales activity.[130] The source of the gross income attributable to production is determined under the rules of Reg. § 1.863-3(c)(1) as discussed above, i.e., the income is apportioned according to the location of the production assets.[131]

Gross income from the business sales activity is sourced in the possession in the same proportion that the amount of business sales activity within the possession for the taxable year bears to the amount of the business sales activity for the taxable year both within and outside the possession. The remaining income is sourced in the U.S.[132]

Business sales activity is defined as the sum of:[133]

●   Amounts paid for wages, salaries, and other compensation of employees;

---

127 Reg. § 1.863-3(e).
128 Reg. § 1.863-3(f)(1).
129 Reg. § 1.863-3(f)(2).
130 Reg. § 1.863-3(f)(2)(i)(A).

131 Reg. § 1.863-3(f)(2)(ii)(A).
132 Reg. § 1.863-3(f)(2)(ii)(B)(1).
133 Reg. § 1.863-3(f)(ii)(B)(2).

- Other expenses attributable to possession production sales (other than nondeductible Code Sec. 263A amounts, interest, and research and development); and
- Possession production sales for the taxable period.

Business sales activity is attributed to either the U.S. or the possession. Gross sales income is allocated as provided by Reg. § 1.863-3(c)(2) discussed above. Generally, a sale is considered consummated where the property rights pass to the buyer. Regulations § 1.861-8 through Temp. Reg. § 1.861-14T, as discussed above, provide the rules for allocating expenses.

Independent Factory Price (IFP) Method

The taxpayer may elect to allocate gross income from possession production sales by using the IFP rules of Reg. § 1.863-3(b)(2) as discussed above. The source of gross income attributable to production activity under the IFP method is, as provided by Reg. § 1.863-3(c)(1) discussed above, generally based on the location of the production assets.

The source of gross income attributable to sales activity under the IFP method is generally based on the place of sale rules as provided in Reg. § 1.861-7(c).

Books and Records Method

A taxpayer may elect to allocate gross income using the books and records method as provided in Reg. § 1.863-3(b)(3) discussed above. To use this method, it is necessary to obtain permission from the District Director having audit responsibility over the return.[134] The source of income attributable to production and sales activities is determined the same way as under the IFP method.

Possession Purchase Sales

Possession purchase sales may be allocated under either the business activity method or the books and records method.

Business Activity Method

Gross income from the taxpayer's business activity is sourced to the possession in the same proportion that the amount of the taxpayer's business activity for the taxable year within the possession bears to the amount of business activity both within and outside the possession, with respect to possession purchase sales. The remaining income is sourced in the U.S.[135]

Business activity is defined as the sum of:[136]

- Amounts paid for salaries and other compensation of employees and other expenses attributable to possession purchase sales

---

[134] Reg. § 1.863-3(f)(2)(i)(C).
[135] Reg. § 1.863-3(f)(3)(ii)(A).

[136] Reg. § 1.863-3(f)(3)(ii)(B).

¶ **1711.06**

(other than amounts that are nondeductible under Code Sec. 263A, interest, and research and development);

- Cost of goods sold attributable to possession purchase sales; and

- Possession purchase sales.

Books and Records Method

A taxpayer may elect to allocate gross income using the books and records method as provided in Reg. § 1.863-3(b)(3) discussed above. To use this method, it is necessary to obtain permission from the District Director having audit responsibility over the return.[137] The source of income attributable to production and sales activities is determined the same way as under the IFP method.

.07 Partnerships

The production and sales activity of a taxpayer generally does not include such activities of a partnership of which the taxpayer is a partner.[138] However, for purposes of determining the source of the partner's distributive share of partnership income or determining the source of the partner's income from the sale of inventory property which the partnership distributes to the partner in kind, the partner's production or sales activity includes an activity performed by the partnership.[139] Also, the production activity of a partnership includes the production activity of a taxpayer that is a partner directly or through one or more partnerships, to the extent that the partner's production activity is related to inventory that the partner contributed in a Code Sec. 721 transaction.[140]

A partner is treated as owning its proportionate share of the partnership's productive assets only to the extent that the partner's activity includes production conducted through a partnership.[141]

Example 17-19.[142] Rotel, Inc., a U.S. corporation, forms a 50/50 partnership with Nextrom, Ltd., a Canadian corporation. The partnership manufactures electronic components for cellular phones. The components are manufactured in the U.S., but sold outside the U.S. In determining the source of its distributive share of partnership income from the export sales of the components, Rotel is treated as carrying on the activity of the partnership and as owning a proportionate share of partnership assets.

Example 17-20.[143] Assume the same facts as in Example 17-19, except that the partnership distributes the components to Rotel and Nextrom. Rotel then further processes the components before selling them outside the U.S. In determining the source of income earned

---

[137] Reg. § 1.863-3(f)(3)(i)(B).
[138] Reg. § 1.863-3(g)(1).
[139] Reg. § 1.863-3(g)(2)(i).
[140] Id.
[141] Reg. § 1.863-3(g)(2)(ii).

[142] Adapted from Reg. § 1.863-3(g)(3), Example 1.

[143] Adapted from Reg. § 1.863-3(g)(3), Example 2.

outside the U.S., Rotel is treated as conducting the business of the partnership. Therefore, the source of gross income from the sale of the components is determined under Code Sec. 863 and the regulations. Rotel applies the 50/50 method to determine the source of income from the sales. Rotel is treated as owning its proportionate share of the partnership's production assets based on its distributive share of partnership income.

¶ 1713 Source Rules for Personal Property Sales

Sourcing rules for personal property sales depend on whether or not the personal property is inventory.

.01 Inventory Property

Inventory from the sale of inventory property purchased by the taxpayer for resale is generally sourced according to where title passes or where beneficial ownership passes. Income from the sale of property that was produced by the taxpayer or purchased in a possession and sold in the U.S. is sourced by allocating the income between the country where the property was produced and the country where it was sold.

.02 Noninventory Personal Property Sales

Generally, income from the sale of noninventory personal property is sourced according to the residence of the seller.[144] However, see the discussion of business offices below. There are three exceptions to general rule of sourcing according to residence:

1. *Depreciable personal property.* The portion of the gain from the sale of depreciable property that is attributable to previously claimed depreciation deductions is considered to come from U.S. source if the deductions were taken against U.S. income.[145] On the other hand, gain attributable to previously claimed depreciation that was taken against foreign source income is considered to come from foreign sources. Gain in excess of depreciation taken is sourced according to the general source rules for noninventory personal property.

2. *Intangible property.* Two different source rules exist for intangibles. Income is first allocated according to the source of the accumulated amortization. Then to the extent that income exceeds such accumulated amortization, the source of the excess income depends on whether or not the payments from the sale are contingent on the productivity or use of the intangible. Contingent payments are sourced the same as royalties[146] (i.e., according to the location of the property generating the royalty[147]). Noncontingent payments generally are sourced in ac-

---

144 Code Sec. 865(a).
145 Code Sec. 865(c).
146 Code Sec. 865(d)(1)(B).
147 Code Secs. 861(a)(4) and 862(a)(4).

cordance with the residence of the seller.[148] However, a special rule exists for sales through offices or fixed places of businesses. If the sale is by a U.S. resident who maintains an office or other fixed place of business in a foreign country, the income is foreign source income, provided that the foreign country levies a tax of at least 10 percent on such income.[149] If a nonresident maintains an office in the U.S., the income is sourced in the U.S., unless an office or other fixed place of business in a foreign country materially participated in the sale.[150] A different rule exists for goodwill. Payments for goodwill are considered to be derived from sources in the country where the goodwill is generated.[151]

3. *Stock of affiliates.* If a U.S. resident sells stock in an affiliate which is a foreign corporation, the gain is considered foreign source income if:

   a. The sale occurs in a foreign country in which the affiliate is engaged in an active trade or business, and

   b. More than 50 percent of the gross income of the affiliate for the three-year period ending with the close of the affiliate's taxable year immediately preceding the year in which the sale occurred was derived from the conduct of such trade or business.[152]

.03 Gains from Sales of Certain Stocks or Intangibles or Certain Liquidations

The following gains are considered foreign source income:[153]

1. Gain from the sale of stock in a foreign corporation or from an intangible which would otherwise be sourced under the U.S., provided that:

   a. Under a treaty obligation the gain would be foreign source income, and

   b. With respect to which the taxpayer chooses such benefit.

2. Gains derived from the receipt of any distribution in liquidation of a corporation, provided that:

   a. The corporation is organized in a possession of the U.S., and

   b. More than 50 percent of the corporation's gross income during the three-taxable year period ending with the close of the taxable year immediately preceding the taxable year in which the distribution is received is from the active conduct of a trade or business in the possession.

---

[148] Code Secs. 865(a) and 865(d)(1)(A).
[149] Code Sec. 865(e)(1).
[150] Code Sec. 865(e)(2).

[151] Code Sec. 865(d)(3).
[152] Code Sec. 865(f).
[153] Code Sec. 865(h).

.04 Rules for Stock Losses

In general, losses from the sale of stock are allocated to the class of income with respect to which gain from the sale of such stock would give rise in the hands of the seller.[154] For example, loss recognized by a resident of the U.S. on the sale of stock generally would be allocated to reduce U.S. source income. However, a loss on the sale of stock by a U.S. resident that is attributable to an office or other fixed place of business in a foreign country is allocated to reduce foreign source income, provided that:[155]

1. A gain on the sale of the stock would have been taxed by the foreign country, and

2. The highest marginal income tax rate in the foreign country on such gains is at least 10 percent.

If a U.S. citizen or resident alien has a foreign tax home, the loss reduces foreign source income if requirements 1 and 2 above are met.[156] If the U.S. citizen or resident alien is a bona fide resident of Puerto Rico during the entire taxable year, the loss reduces foreign source income.[157]

Loss recognized by a nonresident alien shareholder on stock that constitutes a U.S. real property interest is allocated to reduce U.S. source income.[158]

Exceptions to General Rules for Stock Losses

Three exceptions exist for the above stock loss rules. The above rules do not apply to losses from stock that constitutes inventory as well as stock in an S corporation.[159] Also, if a taxpayer recognizes a loss with respect to shares of stock, and the taxpayer included in income a "dividend recapture amount," the loss is allocated to the same class of income as the "dividend recapture amount."[160] A "dividend recapture amount" consists of actual dividends, dividends that are foreign personal holding company income and that result in inclusion of subpart F income under Code Sec. 951(a)(1)(A)(i), as well as earnings invested in U.S. property under Code Sec. 956 that result in an inclusion of subpart F income under Code Sec. 951(a)(1)(B).[161]

The recapture period is the 24-month period preceding the date that a taxpayer recognizes a loss with respect to the stock. The recapture period is increased by any period of time in which the taxpayer has diminished its risk of loss through the use of options or other positions that substantially diminish the taxpayer's risk of loss from holding the stock as described in Code Sec. 246(c)(4).[162]

---

154 Reg. § 1.865-2(a)(1).
155 Reg. § 1.865-2(a)(2).
156 Reg. § 1.865-2(a)(3)(i).
157 Reg. § 1.865-2(a)(3)(ii).
158 Reg. § 1.865-2(a)(4).

159 Reg. § 1.865-2(b)(2) and (3).
160 Reg. § 1.865-2(b)(1).
161 Reg. § 1.865-2(d)(2).
162 Reg. § 1.865-2(d)(3).

Exceptions to the dividend recapture rules exist for *de minimis* amounts (dividend recaptures of less than 10 percent of the recognized loss).[163] In addition, the passive-basket dividend exception generally exempts dividend recapture amounts that would be treated as passive income.[164]

Example 17-21.[165] Sam, Inc. is a domestic corporation. It is a shareholder of Far East Co., a foreign corporation. Far East Co. has never had any subpart F income and all of its E&P are described in Code Sec. 959(c)(3). On July 11, 1999, it distributes $5,000 in dividends to Sam, Inc. The dividend gives rise to a $250 foreign withholding tax, and Sam, Inc. is deemed to have paid an additional $1,250 of foreign income tax with respect to the dividend. Under the look-through rules of Code Sec. 904(d)(3), the dividend is general limitation income. On April 2, 2001, Sam, Inc. sells its shares of Far East Co., and recognizes an $8,000 loss. In 2001, Sam, Inc. has $20,000 of foreign source income that is general limitation income as well as $25,000 of foreign source capital gain income that is passive income, and $18,000 of U.S. source income. The $5,000 dividend paid in 1999 is a dividend recapture amount. Therefore, $5,000 of the loss must be allocated to the foreign source general limitation income. The remaining $3,000 loss is allocated to U.S. source income. After the allocation, Sam, Inc. has $15,000 of general limitation foreign source income and $25,000 of foreign source passive income.

.05 Personal Property (Other Than Stock) Loss Rules

Rules for personal property (other than stock) losses incurred after January 10, 1999, and before January 8, 2002, are contained in Temp. Reg. § 1.865-1T. Generally, losses are allocated to the class of gross income to which gain from a sale of such property would give rise in the hands of the seller. Therefore, loss recognized by a U.S. resident on the sale of a bond generally is allocated to U.S. source income.[166]

Losses of a U.S. resident on sales of property that is attributable to an office or other fixed place of business in a foreign country generally are allocated to reduce foreign income. This is so if a gain would have been taxed by the foreign country, and the highest marginal rate of tax on such gains in the foreign country is at least 10 percent.[167] However, such losses will be foreign source losses if the gain would be sourced under the depreciation recapture rules of Code Sec. 865(c), or if sourced under the

---

[163] Reg. § 1.865-2(b)(1)(ii).

[164] Reg. § 1.865-2(b)(1)(iii).

[165] Adapted from Reg. § 1.865-2(b)(1)(iv), Example 1.

[166] Temp. Reg. § 1.865-1T(a)(1).
[167] Temp. Reg. § 1.865-1T(a)(2).

intangible source rules for contingent payments under Code Sec. 865(d)(1)(B), or if sourced under the goodwill rules of Code Sec. 865(d)(3).[168]

If U.S. citizens or resident aliens have foreign tax homes, the loss is allocated to foreign source income. This is so if a gain would have been taxed by the foreign country, and the highest marginal rate of tax on such gains in the foreign country is at least 10 percent.[169]

A partner's distributive share of loss recognized by a partnership with respect to personal property is allocated as if the partner has recognized the loss. If the losses are attributable to a partnership's office or fixed place of business, the office or fixed place of business is considered to be an office of the partner.[170]

If the item sold is depreciable property, the portion of the gain that represents previously claimed depreciation is sourced according to the source of the income. The depreciation deductions are allocated to the country of predominant use.[171]

Loss with respect to a contingent debt instrument is generally allocated to the class of gross income with respect to which interest income from the instrument would give rise.[172]

Exceptions to the Loss Rules

The above rules do not apply to:[173]

- Foreign currency transactions,

- Inventory,

- Interest equivalents and trade receivables,

- Unamortized bond premium,

- Accrued but unpaid interest.

¶ 1715 Taxation of Nonresident Alien Individuals

The distinction between resident aliens and nonresident aliens is crucial because resident aliens, like U.S. citizens, are taxed on worldwide income. However, nonresident aliens are generally taxed only on certain income from U.S. sources and foreign source income that is effectively connected with a U.S. trade or business.[174]

.01 Determination of Residency Status

Residency may be determined under an applicable tax treaty. However, if there is no applicable treaty, Code Sec. 7701(b) and the regulations

---

[168] Temp. Reg. § 1.865-1T(a)(2).
[169] Temp. Reg. § 1.865-1T(a)(3).
[170] Temp. Reg. § 1.865-1T(a)(5).
[171] Temp. Reg. § 1.865-1T(b)(1).

[172] Temp. Reg. § 1.865-1T(b)(2).
[173] Temp. Reg. § 1.865-1T(c).
[174] Reg. § 1.871-1(a).

determine residency. An alien individual is treated as a resident only if one of the following three conditions are met:[175]

1. The individual is a "lawful permanent resident" of the U.S. at any time during the calendar year,

2. The individual meets the "substantial presence test," or

3. The individual elects to be treated as a resident alien.

An alien is a resident alien if at any time during the year the alien is a "lawful permanent resident." A "lawful permanent resident" is one who has been granted the privilege of residing permanently in the U.S. (issued a green card).[176]

The "substantial presence test" is met if the individual has been present in the U.S. on at least 183 days during a three-year period that includes the current year. In determining the 183 day test, each day in the current year is counted as a full day. However, each day of presence in the first preceding year is counted as one-third of a day. Each day of presence in the second preceding year is counted as only one-sixth of a day. Fractional days are not rounded up for this purpose.[177]

If an individual is not physically present for more than 30 days during the current calendar year, the substantial presence test will not be applied for that year. However, an individual need not be present for more than 30 days during either of the two preceding years.[178]

Example 17-22. Jack Hofstedder, an alien individual, is present in the U.S. for 175 days during the current year. He was present in the U.S. for 18 days in the first preceding year, and 24 days in the second preceding year. To determine the substantial presence test, he adds 175 + 6 + 4 = 185. Therefore, the substantial presence test is met.

Example 17-23. Kimberly Wong, an alien individual, was present the entire year in both 1999 and 2000. In 2001, the current year, she was present for 27 days. Because she was present for less than 31 days in the current year, the substantial presence test is not met.

Rules for First and Last Years of Residency

If an alien individual becomes a resident of the U.S. during the current year, he or she will be treated as a resident only for the portion of the calendar year which begins on the "residency starting date."[179] The residency starting date is the first day in the calendar year in which the individual was present in the U.S. while a lawful permanent resident. However, if the "substantial presence test" (discussed previously) is met,

---

[175] Code Sec. 7701(b).
[176] Reg. § 301.7701(b)-1(b)(1).
[177] Reg. § 301.7701(b)-1(c)(1).

[178] Reg. § 301.7701(b)-1(c)(4).
[179] Code Sec. 7701(b)(2)(A)(i).

the residency starting date is the first day during the calendar year in which the individual is present in the U.S.[180]

An alien individual will not be considered a U.S. resident during any portion of a calendar year if:[181]

- Such portion is after the last day in such calendar year on which the individual was present in the U.S.;

- During such portion, the individual has a closer connection to a foreign country than to the U.S.; and

- The individual is not a resident of the U.S. at any time during the next calendar year.

Closer Connection Exception to the Substantial Presence Test

An alien individual who meets the substantial presence test may still be considered a nonresident alien if:[182]

- The individual is present in the U.S. for less than 183 days,

- The individual maintains a tax home in a foreign country during the current year, and

- The individual has a closer connection to a single foreign country in which he or she maintains a tax home.

If an individual's residency starting date does not fall on the first day of the tax year, or an individual's residency termination date does not fall on the last day of the tax year, his or her income tax is computed under the rules of Reg. § 1.871-13.[183] These rules provide that the tax liability is computed under two different sets of rules, one relating to resident aliens for the period of residency, and the other relating to nonresident aliens for the period of nonresidency.[184]

An individual's tax home is the location of his or her principal place of business. If the individual has no principal place of business, his or her tax home is his or her regular place of abode.[185]

Election to Claim Residency Status

An alien is allowed to elect residency status provided that he or she:[186]

- Was not a resident in the calendar year immediately preceding the calendar year,

- Is not a resident in the current calendar year,

---

[180] Code Sec. 7701(b)(2)(A)(ii) and (iii).
[181] Code Sec. 7701(b)(2)(B).
[182] Code Sec. 7701(b)(3)(B); Reg. § 301.7701(b)-2(a).

[183] Reg. § 301.7701(b)-4(c)(2).
[184] Reg. § 1.871-13(a)(1).
[185] Reg. § 301.7701(b)-2(c)(1).
[186] Code Sec. 7701(b)(4)(A).

- Is present in the U.S. for at least 31 consecutive days in the current calendar year and will meet the substantial presence test in the next tax year,

- Is present in the U.S. for 75 percent of the days in the period beginning with the first day of the 31-day period and ending with the last day of the election year.

.02 *Taxation of Nonresident Alien Individuals*

Income of a nonresident alien individual that is not connected with a U.S. trade or business but is received from U.S. sources is generally taxed at either a flat 30 percent rate, or if lower, the applicable treaty rate.[187] Such income includes: interest, dividends, rents, salaries, wages, premiums, annuities, compensations, remunerations, emoluments, and other fixed or determinable annual or periodical gains, profits, and income.[188] Also included are timber, coal, and iron ore royalties.[189] Taxpayers have a choice with respect to rental income from realty. They may either have it treated as passive income (subject to the flat 30 percent rate), or they may elect to treat the income as effectively connected with a U.S. trade or business.[190]

Income that is effectively connected with the conduct of a trade or business is taxed at the regular U.S. tax rates.[191]

.03 *Exception for Certain Interest and Dividends*

The flat 30 percent tax is not imposed on the following items of income received by a nonresident alien individual:[192]

- Interest on deposits held by banks if the interest is not effectively connected with the conduct of a trade or business in the U.S.

- A percentage of any dividend paid by a domestic corporation that meets the 80 percent control requirement of Code Sec. 861(c)(1) (at least 80 percent of the gross income is active foreign business income). The percentage excludable is the ratio of the corporation's gross income from sources outside the U.S. to total gross income.

- Income derived by a foreign central bank of issue from banker's acceptances.

.04 *Portfolio Debt Investments*

In general, "portfolio interest" received by a nonresident alien individual from U.S. sources is exempt from the flat 30 percent tax.[193] "Portfolio interest" is defined as any interest except for certain contingent interest.

---

[187] Code Sec. 871(a)(1).
[188] *Id.*
[189] *Id.*
[190] Code Sec. 871(d).

[191] Code Sec. 871(b).
[192] Code Sec. 871(i).
[193] Code Sec. 871(h)(1).

The security may be either registered or bearer form. Original issue discount is included in the definition.[194] However, the term portfolio interest does not include interest received by a 10 percent shareholder.[195] Therefore, such interest is subject to the flat 30 percent tax.

.05 Personal Service Income

Personal services performed in the U.S. may constitute a "trade or business." However, not included are personal services performed for a nonresident alien individual, foreign partnership, or foreign corporation that is not engaged in trade or business within the U.S. at any time during the taxable year. Also not included are personal services for an office or place of business maintained in a foreign country or in a possession of the U.S. by an individual who is a citizen or resident of the U.S. or by a domestic partnership or a domestic corporation if two conditions are met:[196]

1. The services are provided by a nonresident alien who is temporarily present in the U.S. for less than 91 days during the taxable year, and

2. Whose compensation for the services does not exceed $3,000.

.06 Capital Transactions

Net capital gains of a nonresident alien that are "effectively connected" with the trade of a U.S. trade or business are taxed the same as are U.S. citizens. However, net capital gains that are not included in the definition of "fixed or determinable, annual or periodic income" and that are not U.S. property gains under Code Sec. 897 and are not "effectively connected" with a U.S. business are exempt from tax. This is so if the nonresident alien is not present in the U.S. for at least 183 days during the tax year.[197] However, if the nonresident alien's presence in the U.S. exceeds the required time period, the capital gains are subject to the flat 30 percent rate.

.07 Election for Income from Realty

In general, a nonresident alien who has income from real property that is held for the production of income and that is located in the U.S. may elect to treat all the income as being effectively connected with a trade or business in the U.S.[198] Included are gains from the sale of realty as well as rents or royalties from mines, wells, or other natural deposits as well as timber, coal, and iron ore royalties.[199] If the election is not made, no deductions are allowed, and the gross income is taxed at the flat 30 percent rate.

---

[194] Code Sec. 871(h)(2) and (4).

[195] Code Sec. 871(h)(3).

[196] Code Sec. 864(b)(1); Reg. § 1.864-2(b)(1).

[197] Reg. § 1.871-7(d)(2)(ii).

[198] Code Sec. 871(d)(1).

[199] *Id.*

.08 Deductions Taken by Nonresident Alien Individuals

In general, nonresident alien individuals may take deductions only for expenses related to income that is effectively connected with a trade or business in the U.S.[200] However, there are several exceptions.

Casualty losses not compensated by insurance are allowed to the extent allowed by Code Sec. 165(c)(2) or (3) if the loss is of property located in the U.S. Losses allowed under this provision are deducted in full, as provided by Reg. § 1.861-8 and Reg. § 1.863-1 from the items of gross income described in Code Secs. 861(a) and 863(a) as being derived in full from sources within the U.S. However, if the losses are greater than the sum of such items, the unabsorbed loss is deducted from the income apportioned under Reg. § 1.863-3 to sources within the U.S.[201]

For rules governing charitable contributions and personal exemptions, see Reg. § 1.873-1(c)(2)(iii) and Reg. § 1.873-1(c)(3).

.09 Credits Allowed to Nonresident Aliens

Nonresident alien individuals are allowed the credit for tax withheld on wages (Code Sec. 31), the earned income credit (Code Sec. 32), the credit for tax withheld at the source (Code Sec. 33), the gas tax credit (Code Sec. 34), and the credit for taxes paid by a regulated investment company (Code Sec. 852(b)(3)(D)(ii)). Other than the above, a nonresident alien individual is allowed credits on income which is effectively connected with the conduct of a trade or business within the U.S.[202]

.10 Partnership and Beneficiaries of Estates and Trusts

A nonresident alien individual or foreign corporation is considered as engaged in a U.S. trade or business if the partnership is so engaged.[203] A similar rule applies to nonresident aliens or foreign corporations who are beneficiaries of estates or trusts which are engaged in a U.S. trade or business.[204] A partnership for this purpose is as defined in Code Sec. 7701(a)(2) and the regulations.[205] The test of whether a partnership is engaged in trade or business within the U.S. is the same as in the case of a nonresident alien individual as provided by Reg. § 1.871-8.[206]

¶ 1717 Tax on Income of Foreign Corporations Not Connected with U.S. Business

In general, a flat 30 percent tax rate is applied to sources received within the U.S. by a foreign corporation for the following items of income which are not effectively connected to a U.S. trade or business:[207]

- Interest (other than original issue discount), dividends, rents, salaries, wages premiums, annuities, compensations, remunera-

---

[200] Code Sec. 873(a).
[201] Code Sec. 873(b)(1); Reg. § 1.873-1(c)(2)(ii).
[202] Code Sec. 874; Reg. § 1.874-1.
[203] Code Sec. 875(1).
[204] Code Sec. 875(2).
[205] Reg. § 1.875-1.
[206] *Id.*
[207] Code Sec. 881(a).

tions, emoluments, and other fixed or determinable annual or periodical gains, profits, and income;

- Gains described in Code Sec. 631(b) or (c) (gains from the disposal or timber or coal or iron ore); and

- Gains from the sale or exchange of patents, copyrights, secret processes and formulas, goodwill, trademarks, trade brands, franchises and other like property, or of any interest in such property, to the extent such payments are contingent on the productivity, use or disposition of the property that is sold or exchanged.

No deductions are allowed except for the charitable contributions deduction.[208]

Special rules exist for original issue discount.[209] Certain corporations created or organized in Guam, American Samoa, the Northern Mariana Islands, or the Virgin Islands may not be treated as foreign corporations.[210]

.01 Exception for Portfolio Interest

"Portfolio interest" received by a foreign corporation from U.S. sources is exempt from the flat 30 percent tax.[211] "Portfolio interest" does not include:[212]

- Contingent interest,

- Interest received by a bank on an extension of credit made pursuant to a loan agreement entered into in the ordinary course of a bank's trade or business,

- Interest received by a 10 percent shareholder,

- Interest received by a controlled foreign corporation from a related person. In addition, special rules exist for portfolio interest received by a controlled foreign corporation.[213]

.02 Exception for Certain Interest and Dividends

The flat 30 percent tax is not imposed on the following items of income received by a foreign corporation:[214]

- Interest on deposits held by banks if the interest is not effectively connected with the conduct of a trade or business in the U.S.

- A percentage of any dividend paid by a domestic corporation that meets the 80 percent control requirement of Code Sec. 861(c)(1) (at least 80 percent of the gross income is active

---

[208] Code Sec. 882(c)(1)(B).
[209] See Code Sec. 881(a)(3).
[210] See Code Sec. 881(b)
[211] Code Sec. 881(c)(1).

[212] Code Sec. 881(c)(3) and (4).
[213] See Code Sec. 881(c)(5).
[214] Code Sec. 881(d).

foreign business income). The percentage excludable is the ratio of the corporation's gross income from sources outside the U.S. to total gross income.

- Income derived by a foreign central bank of issue from banker's acceptances.

.03 Conduit Financing Arrangements

Regulations permit the IRS to disregard the participation of one or more entities in a conduit financing arrangement where such entities are acting as conduits.[215] A financing arrangement generally is defined as a series of transactions by which one person (the financing entity) advances money or other property, or grants rights to use property, another person (the financed entity) receives money or other property, or rights to use property, the advance and receipt are effected through one or more other persons (intermediate entities), and there are financing transactions linking the three entities.[216]

.04 Capital Gains

For this purpose, capital gains comprise one of four types. Certain capital gains theoretically could qualify as "fixed or determinable periodical income. Such gains are subject to the flat 30 percent rate.[217] U.S. real property gains are treated as being effectively connected with a U.S. trade or business, and thus are taxed at U.S. rates.[218] Other capital gains that are effectively connected with a U.S. trade or business are taxed at U.S. rates. Finally, capital gains that do not fit any of the three criteria are not subject to tax.

¶ 1719 Taxation of Foreign Corporations Connected with U.S. Business

Foreign corporations engaged in a U.S. business are taxed at the regular U.S. corporate rate on all income which is "effectively connected" with the U.S. trade or business.[219] Gross income for this purpose includes only gross income which is effectively connected with the conduct of a U.S. trade or business.[220] Therefore, a foreign corporation can be taxed at regular U.S. rates on:[221]

- Gross income which is derived from sources within the U.S. and which is not effectively connected with the conduct of a U.S. trade or business, and

- Gross income which is effectively connected with the conduct of a U.S. trade or business.

---

[215] Reg. § 1.881-3(a)(1).
[216] Reg. § 1.881-3(a)(2).
[217] Code Sec. 871(a)(1).
[218] Code Sec. 897(a)(1).

[219] Code Sec. 882(a).
[220] Code Sec. 882(a)(2).
[221] Code Sec. 882(b).

Foreign corporations to which the above is applicable are required to separate their income into the effectively connected income and the income which is not effectively connected, and compute a separate tax on each category of income.[222]

.01 Election to Treat Real Property Income as Connected to a U.S. Business

A foreign corporation having income from real property located in the U.S. that is not effectively connected to a U.S. business may nonetheless elect to treat such income as being effectively connected with a U.S. business.[223] Such election will enable the corporation to deduct expenses attributable to the income. If expenses from such realty exceed the gross income, the foreign corporation is then enabled to offset the net loss against other income from a U.S. trade or business.[224]

.02 Deductions and Credits

Foreign corporations are allowed deductions for expenses connected with income which is effectively connected with the conduct of a U.S. trade or business.[225] Except for interest expense, expenses are allocated and apportioned as provided by Reg. § 1.861-8. The interest expense deduction is determined under rules of Reg. § 1.882-5.[226]

Foreign corporations are also entitled to credits which are attributable to income effectively connected with the conduct of a U.S. trade or business.[227] However, the foreign corporation must file a timely return in order to receive deductions and credits.[228]

.03 Credit for Foreign Taxes

A foreign corporation may have income from foreign sources that is effectively connected with the conduct of a U.S. trade or business. In such case, if the foreign corporation incurs a foreign tax, it is entitled to the foreign tax credit.[229] Code Sec. 904 limits the foreign tax credit to the U.S. tax multiplied by the ratio of foreign source taxable income to total taxable income.[230] For this purpose, the total taxable income includes only the income that is effectively connected with the U.S. trade or business.[231]

Example 17-24. Foren Corp. is incorporated under the laws of Germany. In 2001, it had $2,000,000 of taxable income effectively connected with a U.S. trade or business. Of that amount, $1,200,000 was U.S. source income, and $800,000 was from sources within France. Assume that it paid a tax to Germany of $500,000 and a tax to France of $100,000, and that its U.S. tax before the foreign tax credit was $408,000. The potential foreign tax credit of $600,000 is limited to $408,000 × ($800,000/$2,000,000) = $163,200. If instead of taking

---

222 Reg. § 1.882-1(a).
223 Code Sec. 882(d)(1).
224 Rev. Rul. 92-74, 1992-2 CB 156.
225 Code Sec. 882(c)(1); Reg. § 1.882-4.
226 Reg. § 1.882-4(b)(1).

227 Reg. § 1.882-4(a)(1).
228 Code Sec. 882(c)(2); Reg. § 1.882-4(a)(2).
229 Code Sec. 906.
230 Code Sec. 904(a).
231 Code Sec. 906(b)(2).

the credit, Foren deducted the foreign taxes, the U.S. tax saved would be $600,000 \times .34 = \$204,000$.

.04 Exclusions from Gross Income of Foreign Corporations

The following items of income of a foreign corporation are exempt from taxation:[232]

- Gross income derived from the international operation of ships, provided that the foreign country grants an equivalent exemption to U.S. corporations.

- Gross income derived from the international operation of aircraft, provided that the foreign country grants an equivalent exemption to U.S. corporations.

- Earnings derived from payments by a common carrier for the temporary use (not expected to exceed 90 days in any tax year) of railroad rolling stock owned by a foreign corporation, provided that the foreign country grants an equivalent exemption to U.S. corporations.

- Earnings derived from the ownership or operation of a communications satellite system by a foreign entity designated by a foreign government to participate in such activity. This is so if the U.S. government participates in such system pursuant to the Communications Satellite Act of 1962.[233]

The above exemptions for ships and aircraft do not apply to any foreign corporation if 50 percent or more of the value of the stock of such corporation is owned by individuals who are not residents of the foreign country or another foreign country that grants a reciprocal exemption.[234] However, the preceding statement does not apply to controlled foreign corporations (corporations where more than 50 percent of either the total combined voting power of all classes of voting stock or the total value of the stock is owned by U.S. shareholders).[235]

.05 Branch Profits Tax

A tax rate of 30 percent (or lower if provided by treaty) is imposed on the "dividend equivalent amount" considered received by a foreign corporation.[236] This is in addition to the U.S. corporate income tax. The "dividend equivalent amount" is defined as the foreign corporation's "effectively connected earnings and profits" (E&P) for the tax year with two adjustments:[237]

1. They are reduced by any increase in "U.S. net equity" for the tax year,

---

[232] Code Sec. 883(a).
[233] Code Sec. 883(b).
[234] Code Sec. 883(c)(1).

[235] Code Sec. 883(c)(2).
[236] Code Sec. 884(a).
[237] Code Sec. 884(b); Reg. § 1.884-1(b).

2.　　They are increased by any decrease in "U.S. net equity" for the tax year.

The increase in the dividend equivalent resulting from a decrease in net U.S. equity is limited to the "effectively connected E&P" accumulated after 1986.

"U.S. net equity" is defined as "U.S. assets" minus "U.S. liabilities."[238]

U.S. Assets

The term "U.S. assets" includes both money and the total adjusted bases of property connected with the conduct of a U.S. trade or business. Special rules exist for determining whether the following assets are U.S. assets:[239]

- Depreciable and amortizable property,

- Inventory,

- Installment obligations,

- Receivables,

- Bank and other deposits,

- Debt instruments,

- Securities held by a foreign corporation engaged in a banking or similar business,

- Federal income taxes,

- Losses involving U.S. assets,

- Property that is involuntarily converted.

A foreign corporation that is a partner in a partnership engaged in a U.S. business must take into account its interest in the partnership (and not the partnership assets) in determining its U.S. assets. In determining the proportion of the partnership interest that is a U.S. asset, the partnership may elect to use either the asset method or the income method.[240] If the asset method is used, a partner's interest in a partnership is treated as a U.S. asset in the same proportion that the partner's proportionate share of the adjusted bases of all of the partnership's assets that would be treated as U.S. assets if the partnership were a foreign corporation bears to the partner's proportionate share of the adjusted bases of all of the partnership's assets.[241] Under the income method, a partner's interest in a partnership is treated as a U.S. asset in the same proportion that its distributive share of partnership effectively connected income for the partnership's tax

---

[238] Code Sec. 884(c).
[239] Reg. § 1.884-1(d)(2).
[240] Reg. § 1.884-1(d)(3)(i).
[241] Reg. § 1.884-1(d)(3)(ii).

year that ends with the partner's tax year bears to its distributive share of all partnership income for that taxable year.[242]

A foreign corporation may elect to treat marketable securities that are not U.S. assets as U.S. assets. This election can be made for a maximum of two years. The purpose of this election is to allow foreign corporations that intend to reenter a U.S. trade or business to avoid the branch profits tax.[243]

U.S. Liabilities

"U.S. liabilities" are defined as the amount of U.S. connected liabilities computed using the assets and liabilities of the foreign corporation as of the determination date.[244] The preceding amount is increased by required insurance reserves that are not otherwise treated as liabilities, and decreased by the amount by which a foreign corporation has elected to reduce its liabilities under Reg. § 1.882-5.[245]

Effectively Connected Earnings and Profits

"Effectively connected earnings and profits" are earnings and profits before dividend distributions which are attributable to income that is effectively connected to the conduct of a U.S. trade or business.[246] However, the term does not include:[247]

- Income that is excluded under Code Sec. 883(a)(1) or (2) (i.e., ships and aircraft operated by foreign corporations),

- Income of a foreign sales corporation (FSC) that is treated as effectively connected with the conduct of a trade or business within the U.S.,

- Gain on the disposition of a U.S. real property interest,

- Insurance income treated as effectively connected with the conduct of a trade or business within the U.S. because of an election under Code Sec. 953, or

- Interest (other than portfolio interest) on U.S. obligations received by banks organized in possessions (Code Sec. 882(e)).

The tax imposed by Code Sec. 884 is coordinated with tax treaties.[248]

.06 Interest Paid That Is Allocable to Effectively Connected Income

In general, if a foreign corporation is engaged in a U.S. trade or business or has gross income treated as effectively connected with such, any interest paid by the business in the U.S. is treated as if paid by a domestic corporation.[249] To the extent that the interest allocable to U.S. trade or

---

[242] Reg. § 1.884-1(d)(3)(iii).
[243] Temp. Reg. § 1.884-2T(b).
[244] Code Sec. 884(c)(2)(B); Reg. § 1.884-1(e)(1).
[245] Reg. § 1.884-1(e)(2) and (3).

[246] Code Sec. 884(d)(1).
[247] Code Sec. 884(d)(2).
[248] See Code Sec. 884(e); Reg. § 1.884-1(g).
[249] Code Sec. 884(f)(1)(A).

business income exceeds the interest actually paid by the U.S. trade or business, the excess is treated as interest paid by a U.S. subsidiary to a foreign corporation.[250] Such excess interest is subject to the flat 30 percent tax, unless exempted by treaty.

.07 Tax on Gross Transportation Income

Foreign corporations are subject to a four percent tax on "U.S. source gross transportation income."[251] "U.S. source gross transportation income" is defined as gross income which is transportation income to the extent such income is treated as from U.S. sources. However, the term does not include income that is effectively connected to a U.S. trade or business. The term also does not include income that is exempt under Code Sec. 883(a)(1) or (2) (exemptions for ships and aircraft operated by foreign corporations).[252]

¶ 1721 Income Affected by Treaty

The Internal Revenue Code "shall be applied to any taxpayer with due regard to any treaty obligation of the U.S. which applies to such taxpayer."[253] Therefore, income is not included in gross income to the extent required by treaty.[254]

One objective of tax treaties is to eliminate double taxation. The treaties provide for each treaty partner to limit its right to tax income earned from its country by residents of the other country. The treaties also require the granting of credit for taxes paid to source countries. Treaties typically provide, among other items, a definition of the term "resident." Treaties typically also provide for treatment of personal service income and passive income. Generally, U.S. tax treaties reduce the 30 percent withholding rate on interest and dividends to lesser rates. Generally treaties will exempt profits of a nonresident alien or nonresident foreign corporation unless the profits are derived from a permanent establishment. Permanent establishments are fixed places of business (e.g., offices, factories, branches, mines, etc.). Other treaty provisions may cover such items as income from realty, and gains from the disposition of property.

¶ 1723 Adjustment of Tax—Foreign Taxpayers

If a foreign country imposes a tax on U.S. citizens or residents which is considered burdensome or discriminatory, the President has the authority to issue a proclamation correcting the inequity. A tax is considered burdensome if:[255]

1. Under the laws of any foreign country, U.S. citizens who are not residents of such country or domestic corporations are subject to more burdensome taxes on any item of income from sources within the foreign country than the taxes imposed by the U.S.

---

[250] Code Sec. 884(f)(1)(B).
[251] Code Sec. 887(a).
[252] Code Sec. 887(b).
[253] Code Sec. 894(a).
[254] Reg. § 1.894-1.
[255] Code Sec. 896(a).

on residents or corporations of the foreign country having similar income derived from U.S. sources;

2.   The foreign country, when requested by the U.S. to eliminate the higher effective tax rates, refuses; and

3.   It is in the public interest to adjust the tax.

A discriminatory tax exist where U.S. citizens or domestic corporations pay a higher rate of tax on income than do the citizens or residents or corporations of the foreign country, and requirements 2 and 3 above are also met.[256]

The President cannot issue the proclamation until Congress has been given at least 30 days' notice of the President's intention.[257] The President can revoke the proclamation after finding that the burdensome or discriminatory taxes have been removed by the foreign country.[258]

¶ 1725 Disposition of Investments in U.S. Realty

Gains or losses on the disposition of "U.S. real property interests" incurred by a nonresident alien individual or by a foreign corporation are treated as if the taxpayer were effectively engaged in a U.S. trade or business.[259] The result is that the nonresident alien or foreign corporation is taxed on its sales and other taxable dispositions as if it were a citizen or domestic corporation. However, for purposes of the alternative minimum tax on a nonresident alien individual, the taxable excess is not less than the lesser of:[260]

- The individual's alternative minimum taxable income, or

- The individual's net U.S. real property gain for the taxable year.

.01 U.S. Property Real Interest

A "U.S. property real interest" is:[261]

- An interest in realty located in the U.S. or the Virgin Islands, and

- Any interest (other than solely as a creditor) in any domestic corporation unless the taxpayer establishes that the corporation at no time was a "U.S. real property holding corporation" during the shorter of the period ending after June 18, 1980, in which the taxpayer held an interest, or the five-year period ending on the date of disposition.

Realty includes: land, growing crops, timber, mines, wells, and other natural deposits; improvements on land such as buildings and other inher-

---

[256] Code Sec. 896(b).
[257] Code Sec. 896(d).
[258] Code Sec. 896(c).

[259] Code Sec. 897(a)(1).
[260] Code Sec. 897(a)(2)(A).
[261] Code Sec. 897(c)(1).

ently permanent structures; and personal property associated with the use of real property such as movable walls.[262]

A corporation is a "U.S. real property holding corporation" if the fair market value (FMV) of its U.S. realty is at least 50 percent of the FMV of the sum of its U.S. realty plus its interests in realty outside the U.S. plus any other assets used or held for use in a trade or business.[263] However, an exception exists for stock regularly traded on an established securities market. In that event, such stock will be treated as U.S. realty only if a person during the shorter of the period after June 18, 1980, or the five-year period ending on the date of disposition held more than five percent of the stock.[264]

¶ 1727   Repeal of Foreign Sales Corporations

To encourage exports, Congress allowed the formation of foreign sales corporations (FSCs). Several favorable tax benefits were granted to FSCs. An FSC's income was partially exempt from U.S. income tax since its exempt foreign trade income was treated as foreign source income not effectively connected with the conduct of a U.S. trade or business. A U.S. corporation generally was not subject to U.S. income tax on dividends distributed from certain earnings of the FSC because of the dividends-received deduction.

However, the FSC Repeal and Extraterritorial Exclusion Act of 2000 repealed the FSC laws. Instead, there is a new exclusion for extraterritorial income provided by Code Sec. 114. The new Code Sec. 114 excludes from gross income "extraterritorial income" that is qualifying foreign trade income.[265] The term "extraterritorial income" is defined as the gross income of the taxpayer attributable to foreign trading gross receipts. "Qualifying foreign trade income" is the amount of gross income which if excluded will reduce the taxable income of the taxpayer from such transaction by the greatest of:[266]

1.   30 percent of the "foreign sale and leasing income" derived by the taxpayer from the transaction,

2.   1.2 percent of the "foreign trading gross receipts" derived by the taxpayer from the transaction (however, this amount may not exceed 200 percent of the calculation in 3 below), or

3.   15 percent of the "foreign trade income" derived by the tax-payer from the transactions.

---

[262] Reg. § 1.897-1(b).

[263] Code Sec. 897(c)(2).

[264] Code Sec. 897(c)(3).

[265] Act Sec. 3(a), FSC Repeal and Extraterritorial Income Exclusion Act of 2000 (P.L. 106-519) (adding Code Sec. 114(a) and (b)).

[266] Act Sec. 3(b), FSC Repeal and Extraterritorial Income Exclusion Act of 2000 (P.L. 106-519) (adding Code Sec. 941(a)(1)).

A taxpayer is not required to use the method that results in the greatest reduction in taxable income.[267]

The term "foreign sale and leasing income" is defined in general as "foreign trade income" from the lease or rental of qualifying foreign trade property for use by the lessee outside the U.S.[268]

In general, "foreign trading gross receipts" are gross receipts:[269]

1.   From the sale, exchange, or other disposition of qualifying foreign trade property;

2.   From the lease or rental of qualifying foreign trade property for use by the lessee outside the U.S.;

3.   For services which are related and subsidiary to:

   a.   Any sale, exchange, or other disposition of qualifying foreign trade property by the taxpayer; or

   b.   Any lease or rental of qualifying foreign trade property.

4.   For engineering or architectural services for construction projects outside the U.S.; or

5.   For the performance of managerial services for a nonrelated person in furtherance of the production of foreign trading gross receipts.

The term "foreign trading gross receipts" does not include receipts if the property or services are for ultimate use in the U.S., or for use by the U.S. government or U.S. instrumentality and such use is required by law, or if the transaction is accomplished by a subsidy granted by the government of the country where the property is produced.[270] Taxpayers may also elect to exclude gross receipts from foreign trading gross receipts.[271]

Taxpayers generally may treat receipts as being foreign trading gross receipts only if economic processes with respect to the transaction take place outside the U.S.[272] A transaction is considered to take place outside the U.S. if the following requirements are met:[273]

1.   The taxpayer has participated outside the U.S. in the solicitation (other than advertising), the negotiation, or the making of the contract relating to the transaction,

---

[267] Act Sec. 3(b), FSC Repeal and Extraterritorial Income Exclusion Act of 2000 (P.L. 106-519) (adding Code Sec. 941(a)(2)).

[268] Act Sec. 3(b), FSC Repeal and Extraterritorial Income Exclusion Act of 2000 (P.L. 106-519) (adding Code Sec. 941(c)).

[269] Act Sec. 3(b), FSC Repeal and Extraterritorial Income Exclusion Act of 2000 (P.L. 106-519) (adding Code Sec. 942(a)(1)).

[270] Act Sec. 3(b), FSC Repeal and Extraterritorial Income Exclusion Act of 2000 (P.L. 106-519) (adding Code Sec. 942(a)(2)).

[271] Act Sec. 3(b), FSC Repeal and Extraterritorial Income Exclusion Act of 2000 (P.L. 106-519) (adding Code Sec. 942(a)(3)).

[272] Act Sec. 3(b), FSC Repeal and Extraterritorial Income Exclusion Act of 2000 (P.L. 106-519) (adding Code Sec. 942(b)(1)).

[273] Act Sec. 3(b), FSC Repeal and Extraterritorial Income Exclusion Act of 2000 (P.L. 106-519) (adding Code Sec. 942(b)(2)).

2. Foreign direct costs incurred by the taxpayer are at least 50 percent of the total direct costs.

Alternatively, with respect to each of at least two subparagraphs of Code Sec. 942(b)(3), the foreign direct costs incurred by the taxpayer attributable to activities described in that subparagraph equal or exceed 85 percent of the total direct costs attributable to activities described in that subparagraph. Those activities are (a) advertising and sales promotion, (b) the processing of customer orders and the arranging for delivery, (c) transportation outside the U.S. in connection with delivery to the customers, (d) the determination and transmittal of a final invoice or statement of account or the receipt of payment, and (e) the assumption of credit risk.

Expenses attributable to exempt income are generally not deductible. Therefore, expenses allocable to qualifying foreign trade income are not allowed.[274]

The effective date of the repeal of the FSC rules and the new extraterritorial income exclusion is generally for transactions entered into after September 30, 2000. However, a transition rule allows FSC rules to apply in transactions occurring before January 1, 2002.

The World Trade Organization (WTO) ruled on August 20, 2001, that the Foreign Sales Corporation Replacement Act is still a prohibited export subsidy. The U.S. is expected to appeal this ruling, but the ultimate outcome is uncertain as of this writing.

---

[274] Act Sec. 3(a), FSC Repeal and Extraterritorial Income Exclusion Act of 2000 (P.L. 106-519) (adding Code Sec. 114(c)).

Chapter 18

Estate Planning

¶ 1801 Introduction

Before estate planning concepts, tactics, and strategies are discussed, it is necessary to cover the basics of federal transfer taxation.

Federal transfer taxes are excise taxes imposed on the right to transmit property. As such they are levied on the transferor (the donor if the transfer is *inter vivos* and the decedent if the transfer is by reason of death) rather than the transferee. The executor is responsible for paying the tax.[1] *Inter vivos* transfers are subject to gift taxes, and transfers via death are subject to the federal estate tax. However, a unified transfer tax that applies to both has been in effect since 1976.

The Economic Growth and Tax Relief Reconciliation Act of 2001[2] (Tax Relief Act of 2001) repeals the estate tax, but not the tax on gifts, effective for deaths after 2009.[3] In the interim, the unified rate schedule is reduced and the unified credit is increased gradually (see the discussion below).

However, the Economic Growth and Tax Relief Reconciliation Act of 2001 contains a sunset provision which provides that all estate, gift, and generation-skipping provisions of the bill do not apply after December 31, 2010.[4] Whether or not the estate tax will be permanently repealed is problematic at this point.

---

[1] Code Sec. 2002.
[2] P.L. 107-16.
[3] Economic Growth and Tax Relief Reconciliation Act of 2001, Act Sec. 501(a), adding Code Sec. 2210(a).

[4] Economic Growth and Tax Relief Reconciliation Act of 2001, Act Sec. 901.

¶ 1803   Unified Rate Schedule; Unified Credit

For gifts made and for decedents dying after 1983 but before 2002, the following unified rate schedule is in effect.

Amount to which the tax applies			
Lower Amount (Over)	Upper Amount (Not Over)	Tax on Lower Amount	Tax on Excess Over Lower Amount*
$ 0	$ 10,000	$ 0	18%
10,000	20,000	1,800	20%
20,000	40,000	3,800	22%
40,000	60,000	8,200	24%
60,000	80,000	13,000	26%
80,000	100,000	18,200	28%
100,000	150,000	23,800	30%
150,000	250,000	38,800	32%
250,000	500,000	70,800	34%
500,000	750,000	155,800	37%
750,000	1,000,000	248,300	39%
1,000,000	1,250,000	345,800	41%
1,250,000	1,500,000	448,300	43%
1,500,000	2,000,000	555,800	45%
2,000,000	2,500,000	780,800	49%
2,500,000	3,000,000	1,025,800	53%
3,000,000		1,290,800	55%

* Code Sec. 2001(c)(1).

The tentative tax determined under the unified rate schedule must be increased by 5% of the amount above $10,000,000, but below $21,595,000 (for 2001).[5]

.01   Reduction in Rate Schedule

Effective for estates of decedents dying after 2001 and for gifts made after 2001, the top marginal rate is reduced to 50 percent. The five-percent surtax is also repealed.[6]

Additional rate reductions are scheduled for the years 2003 through 2009. The maximum rates will be as follows:[7]

---

[5] Code Sec. 2001(c)(2).

[6] Economic Growth and Tax Relief Reconciliation Act of 2001, Act Sec. 511(a) and (b), amending Code Sec. 2001(c)(1), and striking Code Sec. 2001(c)(2).

[7] Economic Growth and Tax Relief Reconciliation Act of 2001, Act Sec. 511(c), adding Code Sec. 2001(c)(2)(B).

Calendar Year	Maximum Rate
2003	49 percent
2004	48 percent
2005	47 percent
2006	46 percent
2007, 2008 and 2009	45 percent

The unified credit may be used to reduce the tax on both transfers during lifetime and transfers at death. However if used to reduce gift taxes, there is only one unified credit (for the year 2001 and prior years) to apply to the two types of transfers. The credit amount for the years 1997 through 2001 is shown below.

Year of Death	Unified Credit	Applicable Exclusion Amount
1997	$192,800	$600,000
1998	$202,050	$625,000
1999	$211,300	$650,000
2000	$220,550	$675,000
2001	$220,550	$675,000

The Tax Relief Act of 2001 increases the unified credit for estate (but not gift) tax purposes to the following applicable exclusion amounts:[8]

Year of Death	Applicable Exclusion Amount
2002 and 2003	$1,000,000
2004 and 2005	$1,500,000
2006, 2007, and 2008	$2,000,000
2009	$3,500,000

Effective for gifts made after 2001, the applicable credit amount for gifts is raised to $1 million.[9] For gifts made in 2010 and beyond, the amount of the credit allowed against the gift tax equals the tentative tax that would be determined under the new gift-tax-rate-only schedule if the amount with respect to which such tentative tax is to be computed was $1 million, reduced by the sum of the amounts allowable as a credit for all preceding calendar periods.[10]

¶ 1805 Gross Estate—Valuation

All property that is includible in the gross estate is reported at its fair market at the date of death unless the alternate valuation date is used.[11] Fair market value is "the price at which the property would change hands between a willing buyer and a willing seller, neither being under any compulsion to buy or to sell and both having reasonable knowledge of relevant facts."[12]

---

[8] Economic Growth and Tax Relief Reconciliation Act of 2001, Act Sec. 521(a), amending Code Sec. 2010(c).

[9] Economic Growth and Tax Relief Reconciliation Act of 2001, Act Sec. 521(b)(1), amending Code Sec. 2505(a)(1).

[10] Economic Growth and Tax Relief Reconciliation Act of 2001, Act Sec. 521(b)(2), amending Code Sec. 2505(a)(1).

[11] Reg. § 20.2031-1(b).

[12] Id.

.01 Alternate Valuation Date

For deaths after July 18, 1984, the alternate valuation date may be used only if the election will both reduce the value of the gross estate, and reduce the estate tax.[13] Filing requirements (see the section on filing requirements) are coordinated with the deduction equivalency of the unified credit. For example, if death occurred in 2001, the gross estate would have to exceed $675,000 before the alternate valuation date could be used.

The alternate valuation date is generally exactly six months from the date of death.[14] However, there are two exceptions. If the property is sold, distributed, exchanged, or otherwise disposed of within the six-month period, the date of valuation is the date of the sale, etc.[15]

> **Example 18-1.** Two tractors were among the assets in the gross estate of Kurt Hampton. Kurt died on May 4, 2001, and the executor elected the alternate valuation date. The first tractor was sold on August 3 and the second tractor was sold on December 13. The first tractor would be included in the estate at its value on August 3; the second tractor would be included at its value on November 4.

The second exception to the six-month rule involves assets the value of which are affected by the passage of time.[16] Included would be patents, life estates, remainder and reversionary interests, and similar assets. These assets would be valued as of the date of death, but would be adjusted for any change in value not due to the passage of time as of the alternate valuation date.

Tax Tips and Pitfalls

Electing the alternate valuation date is not always wise. The drawback to the alternate valuation date is that its use results in a lower income tax basis to the recipients of the property. Although currently the lowest marginal estate tax brackets for a taxable estate are higher than the capital gains tax rate, if estate tax rates were to be lowered, the higher capital gains tax resulting from the alternate valuation date might more than offset the estate tax. This could be especially true if the property is to be sold soon after its receipt.

The election to use the alternate valuation date must be made by the executor within one year of the due date of the return (including extensions). Once made, the election is irrevocable.[17]

.02 Special Valuation Methods for Family-Owned Businesses and Farms

Three procedures are available to mitigate the liquidity problems of farms and closely held businesses:

---

[13] Code Sec. 2032(c).
[14] Code Sec. 2032(a)(2).
[15] Code Sec. 2032(a)(1).

[16] Code Sec. 2032(a)(3).

[17] Code Sec. 2032(d).

1. Special use valuation,

2. The qualified family-owned business interest deduction,

3. The 5-year, 10-year installment payment provision.

¶ 1807 Special Use Valuation

The special use valuation replaces fair market value as the amount to include in the estate. The special use value is designed to approximate the value of the property as used in the farm or business, rather than its highest value, which might be for real estate development, recreation, speculation, or the like.

Special use valuation is elective; the executor makes the ultimate decision as to its use. The decrease in the gross estate resulting from special use valuation was originally limited to $750,000.[18] However, the limit is adjusted for inflation. For deaths in 2001, the limit is $800,000.[19]

> **Example 18-2.** Tina Bowman died in 2001. Her estate included farm land near a city which could be sold for $1,800,000. Its value as farm land was only $700,000. If the executor elects special use valuation, the farm land would be included at the greater of $700,000 or ($1,800,000 − 800,000), or $1,000,000.

.01 Requirements to Elect

Six very specific criteria must be met before the estate is eligible to elect special use valuation. They are:

1. At least 50 percent of the adjusted value of the gross estate consists of the adjusted value of real or personal property which on the date of death was used by the decedent or a "family member" for a "qualified use."[20] Qualified use means used in a closely held business or as a farm for farming purposes.[21] Family members are defined as ancestors of the decedent, spouses, lineal descendants of the decedent or the decedent's spouse, or of a parent of the decedent, or the spouse of any lineal descendant.[22] Thus family members for this purpose includes grandparents, parents, wives, husbands, children, grandchildren, brothers, sisters, nieces, nephews, and descendants of nieces and nephews.

2. At least 25 percent of the adjusted value of the gross estate consists of the adjusted value of real property that is used for a qualifying purpose.[23]

---

[18] Code Sec. 2032A(a)(2).
[19] Rev. Proc. 2001-13, IRB 2001-3, 337.
[20] Code Sec. 2032A(b)(1).

[21] Code Sec. 2032A(b)(2).
[22] Code Sec. 2032A(e)(2).
[23] Code Sec. 2032A(b)(1).

As commentators have pointed out, mineral rights cannot be combined with farm land to achieve the 50 percent and the 25 percent tests.[24] Payments for mineral rights do not meet the qualified use test.

3.   On the date of death, the property was being used for a qualified use by the decedent or by a family member.[25]

4.   The property passes to a qualified heir (a family member as defined above).[26] If successive interests, i.e., a life estate and remainder interests, are devised, the IRS has taken the position that all successive interests must pass to a qualified heir.[27]

5.   Five out of the eight years ending on the date of death the real property was owned by the decedent or a family member and was used for the qualified purpose.[28] A decedent's ownership in a corporation owning farm land is eligible for special use valuation if the requirements of Code Sec. 6166(b)(1) are met (20 percent or more of the value of the corporate stock is included in the gross estate and the corporation had 45 or fewer stockholders).[29]

6.   For the same time period as in item 5, the decedent or a family member materially participated in the business.[30]

The time period for requirement 6 is altered if the decedent was, for a continuous period ending on the date of death, either receiving Social Security benefits or "disabled." In either case, the eight-year period ends on the date of retirement or disability.[31]

Example 18-3. Richard Spear farmed continuously from 1956 to 1996. In early 1996, he retired and rented out his farm. In 2001, he died. Since he farmed continuously during the eight-year period ending with his retirement, his estate is eligible for special use valuation assuming that all other requirements are met.

"Retired" means drawing Social Security benefits. "Disabled" is defined as one who has a mental or physical impairment which would prevent him or her from materially participating in the operation of the farm or business.[32]

If a surviving spouse is passed real property from a deceased spouse, and the surviving spouse later dies while still in possession of the property,

---

[24] See Goggans and Hartman, "Current Application of Special Use Valuation Under Section 2032A," TAXES, July 1985, p. 518.

[25] Code Sec. 2032A(b)(1).

[26] Id.

[27] See Reg. § 20.2032A-8(a)(2). Also see, Bruce Bringardner, "Planning to Qualify Nonfarm Busi- ness Real Estate for Special Use Valuation," The Journal of Taxation, March 1986, p. 131.

[28] Code Sec. 2032A(b)(1).

[29] Code Sec. 2032A(g); Reg. § 20.2032A-3(b)(1).

[30] Code Sec. 2032A(b)(1).

[31] Code Sec. 2032A(b)(4).

[32] Code Sec. 2032A(b)(4)(B).

the estate of the second spouse would qualify for special use valuation if the surviving spouse had "actively managed" the farm or business.[33]

Definitions and Special Rules

The terms "qualified heir" and "family member" have been defined above. Other special definitions are listed below.

Qualified Real Property. In addition to farm land, qualified real property includes residential buildings and other structures occupied or used regularly by either the owner or the lessee, or by their employees.[34] Roads, buildings, and other structures and improvements are also included provided that they are functionally related to the qualified use.[35]

Farm. The term "farm" is defined rather liberally to include stock farms, dairy farms, poultry farms, fruit orchards, fur-bearing animal farms, truck farms, plantations, ranches, nurseries, ranges, greenhouses, or similar structures used primarily to raise agricultural or horticultural products, and orchards and woodlands.[36]

Farming Purposes. This is defined as cultivating the soil, raising or harvesting any agricultural or horticultural commodity, handling, drying, packing, grading, or storing any agricultural commodity in its unmanufactured state (but only if the owner, tenant, or operator of the farm regularly produces more than one-half of the commodity so treated), plus the planting, cultivating, caring for, or cutting of trees or the preparation of trees for market.[37]

Material Participation. Criteria similar to those that are used to determine if a person is subject to self-employment tax are used to determine "material participation."[38] The regulations also provide some guidance. Generally, if the individual works 35 hours a week or more managing the farm, such work would constitute material participation.[39] However, working less hours would also suffice so long as the necessary functions are being performed. Normally, the payment of Social Security tax on self-employment income is required, but is not itself conclusive as to the presence of material participation. If the land is used by any nonfamily member, and the involvement of the individual (person who qualifies under item 6) is less than full-time, an oral or written arrangement is necessary.[40]

The principal factors to be considered in determining if there is material participation are physical work and participation in management decisions.[41] At the least, the individual should regularly advise or consult with respect to the operation of the business. The individual should also participate in a substantial number of managerial decisions.[42] Production activities should be regularly inspected, and the individual should assume

---

[33] Code Sec. 2032A(b)(5).
[34] Reg. § 20.2032A-3(b)(2).
[35] Code Sec. 2032A(e)(3).
[36] Code Sec. 2032A(e)(4).
[37] Code Sec. 2032A(e)(5).

[38] Code Sec. 2031A(e)(6).
[39] Reg. § 20.2032A-3(e)(1).
[40] *Id.*
[41] Reg. § 20.2032A-3(e)(2).
[42] *Id.*

financial responsibility for a substantial portion of operation expenses. Furnishing machinery and livestock for the farm operation would go far toward determining material participation.[43] Maintaining a residence on the premises is a positive factor.

Partners in a partnership are required to pay self-employment tax on their share of earnings. However, if the partner is not an active participant in the business, the requirements of Code Sec. 2032A are not met even if the individual is considered self-employed for income tax purposes.[44] If a corporation owns the property (and the decedent's interest is therefore indirect), the individual would be an employee rather than self-employed. In that event, individuals are to be viewed as if they were self-employed (i.e., the relevant test is whether their duties, if in a sole proprietorship, would constitute self-employment income).[45] In all cases where the ownership is indirect (as through corporation, partnerships, and trusts), there must be an arrangement calling for material participation in the business by the individual and specifying the services to be performed.[46] A formal arrangement is not always necessary; holding a corporate office in which material participation is inherent in the job duties may suffice.[47] On the other hand, merely holding corporate office will not constitute material participation if the duties are merely nominal.

The term "material participation" is interpreted fairly liberally by the IRS in the regulations. One example in the regulations concerns a decedent who leased the land to another but who consulted with the tenant on where crops were to be planted, supervised marketing of the crop, and shared equally in expenses and income with the tenant. The decedent was present at planting time for consultation. Once planting was completed, the decedent left for his retirement cottage; he did not return until late summer when he supervised marketing of the crops. This decedent was deemed to have materially participated in the business.[48] In another example, a qualified heir, living in town, contracted with another person to manage a farm for him. The heir supplied all machinery and equipment and was responsible for all expenses. The manager submitted a crop plan and a budget for the heir's approval. The heir also inspected the farm regularly and approved all expenditures over $100. The heir visited the farm weekly during the growing season and helped decide what fields to plant and how to utilize the subsidy program. The heir was considered to have materially participated. His actions were regarded as more than merely managing an investment. But merely assuming financial responsibility and reviewing annual crop plans would not constitute material participation.[49]

As previously mentioned, the criteria to determine coverage under the self-employment tax (Code Sec. 1402(a)) are important in determining

---

[43] *Id.*
[44] Reg. § 20.2032A-3(f)(2).
[45] *Id.*
[46] Reg. § 20.2032A-3(f)(1).

[47] *Id.*
[48] Reg. § 20.2032A-3(g), Example 1.
[49] Reg. § 20.2032A-3(g), Example 4.

material participation. The Farmer's Tax Guide provides some guidance in landlord/tenant situations, stating that material participation is achieved if one out of the following four tests is met:[50]

1. The landlord does any three of the following:

    a. Pays, using cash or credit, at least half of the direct costs of producing the crop or livestock;

    b. Furnishes at least half the tools, equipment, and livestock used in the production activities;

    c. Consults with the tenant; and

    d. Inspects the production activities periodically.

2. The landlord regularly and frequently makes, or takes an important part in making, managerial decisions which substantially contribute to or affect the success of the enterprise.

3. The landlord works 100 hours or more spread over a period of at least five weeks in activities connected with agricultural production.

4. The landlord does things which in the aggregate indicate a material and significant involvement in the production of the farm commodities.

Special Material Participation Rules for Surviving Spouses and Lineal Descendants

Effective for leases entered into after December 31, 1976, both surviving spouses and lineal descendants of the decedent may lease land to a relative on a net cash basis and still qualify under the material participation requirements.[51]

.02 The Qualified Use Test

In defining qualified use, the regulations contrast active businesses with property rentals, stating:

> Under Section 2032A, the term "trade or business" applies only to an active business such as a manufacturing, mercantile, or service enterprise, or to the raising of agricultural or horticultural commodities, as distinguished from passive activities. The mere passive cash rental of property to a party other than a member of the decedent's family will not qualify.[52]

The prohibition of passive rentals appears to be in accordance with the intent of Congress. The House report noted that the "mere passive rental of property will not qualify."[53] Similarly, the Senate noted that "during any period when the decedent leases the real property to a nonfamily member

---

[50] IRS Publication 225, "Farmer's Tax Guide" (2000), p. 80.

[51] Code Sec. 2032A(c)(7), as amended by Act Sec. 504(a) of the Taxpayer Relief Act of 1997 (P.L. 105-34).

[52] Reg. § 20.2032A-3(b)(1).

[53] House Ways and Means Committee, H.R. Rep. No. 1380, 94th Cong., 2d Sess. 755-758.

for use in a qualified use pursuant to a lease under which the rental is not substantially dependent upon production, the qualified use test is not satisfied.[54]

The "qualified use" and "material participation" tests are interrelated and easily confused. The Seventh Circuit contrasts them in this way: the qualified use test focuses on *how* the property is used, while material participation focuses on the *activities* performed by the decedent or his or her family.

.03 Valuation Methods

Two methods may be used to determine the special use valuation: a method which capitalizes annual rents, and a method which combines five factors.[55]

.04 Recaptures

There are two instances in which the tax savings from the special use valuation must be recaptured, i.e., paid back, if occurring within a specified time period.

1.   If the qualified heir disposes of any interest in the qualified real property. Sales or other dispositions to a family member (as defined previously) do not result in recapture.

2.   If the qualified heir ceases to use the qualified real property for the qualified use.[56]

Dispositions

Obviously a sale constitutes a disposition for this purpose, as would a taxable exchange. Presumably, a gift to a nonqualified heir would also count as a disposition. The Code specifically exempts nontaxable exchanges (Code Sec. 1031) from recapture if the property received in exchange is "qualified exchange property."[57] "Qualified exchange property" is defined as real property which is to be used for the qualified use under which the real property exchanged for it qualified for special use valuation.[58] Often, however, exchanges which are essentially tax-free also involve the receipt of cash or other property which renders the exchange partly taxable. In that event there will be a partial recapture. It is computed as follows:

1.   A tax to be recaptured is computed assuming that the exchange is fully taxable.

2.   From the tax determined in step 1, an amount is subtracted. The amount is the tax computed in step 1, multiplied by the ratio of the fair market value of the qualified exchange property

---

[54] Senate Finance Committee, S. Rep. No. 144, 97th Cong., 1st Sess. 412, 464 (1981).

[55] For a detailed discussion of valuation methods as well as other considerations involved in special use valuation, see Maydew, Gary L., *Agribusiness Accounting and Taxation*, 2nd ed., CCH Incorporated, 1997.

[56] Code Sec. 2032A(c)(1).
[57] Code Sec. 2032A(i).
[58] Code Sec. 2032A(i)(3).

received, to the fair market value of the property exchanged. For purposes of step 2, fair market value is as of the time of the exchange.[59]

Example 18-4. In 2001, Jane McGuire inherited real property from her husband which was valued at $500,000 under special use valuation rules. The special use value reduced the estate tax by $75,000. Two years later, Ms. McGuire exchanged the property for other qualified exchange property with a fair market value of $400,000 and for $200,000 cash. The recapture tax would be $75,000 − ($400,000/$600,000) × ($75,000), or $25,000.

Generally, an involuntary conversion of special use property also does not result in recapture. In order to avoid any recapture, an amount equal to the amount realized on the involuntary conversion must be reinvested in "qualified replacement property."[60] Property that is to be used for the qualified use that the converted property is used for constitutes "qualified replacement property."[61] If the reinvestment is less than the proceeds, there is a partial recapture. The recapture is reduced by the tax multiplied by the ratio of the qualified replacement to the amount realized on the conversion.[62]

Example 18-5. Scott Hawkins inherited farm land which was valued at the special use valuation. The land was condemned for a lake and he was awarded $200,000. He reinvested $250,000 in qualified replacement farm land. The special use valuation had saved $50,000 in federal estate tax. None of the $50,000 would have to be recaptured.

Example 18-6. Assume the same facts as Example 18-5 except that Hawkins reinvested only $120,000. The amount of estate tax to be recaptured is $50,000 − ($120,000/$200,000) × ($50,000) = $20,000.

The law is less clear on other exchanges. Some exchanges that normally qualify as tax-free could nonetheless result in a recapture of the estate tax savings from special use. For example, the transfer of property to a corporation is tax-free if the corporation is "controlled" by the transferors. The IRS has ruled that the incorporation of a farm or ranch did not constitute a recapture where the qualified heir owned 100 percent both before and after the corporation.[63] However, the result is less certain where the qualified heir receives less than 100 percent of the stock. At the very least, the shares received would have to be proportionate; otherwise there would be a gift, which would constitute a partial disposition.

---

[59] *Id.*
[60] Code Sec. 2031A(h)(1)(A).
[61] Code Sec. 2032A(h)(3)(B).

[62] Code Sec. 2032A(h)(1)(B).
[63] Ltr. Rul. 8109073, December 8, 1980; and Ltr. Rul. 8218073, February 8, 1982.

Property Ceases to be Used for the Qualified Use

The instances in which there is a cessation of qualified use are as follows:

- *The property is used for a different purpose other than the use that qualified for special use valuation.*[64]

  Example 18-7. John Gray II, in 2001, converted ranch land into recreational campgrounds. When his father had died in 1991, the land was valued as special use property. The estate tax savings must be recaptured.

  The qualified heir has two years after the decedent's death to begin using the property. In that event, the recapture period does not begin until the property is used for the qualified purpose.[65]

- *The material participation requirement is not met.* This requirement provides that for any eight-year period ending after the decedent's death and before the death of the qualified heir, there cannot be periods totaling more than three years during which there was no material participation. For the portion of the eight-year period before death, material participation must have been by the decedent or a family member. For the portion of the eight-year period after death, material participation must be by the qualified heir, or by a family member of the qualified heir.[66] Note that the person must be a "relative" of the qualified heir, not merely a relative of the decedent. The IRS has ruled that there was no material participation where a son-in-law was the qualified heir but a son of the decedent materially participated. The son was not a "relative" of the son-in-law (as defined by Code Sec. 2032A(e)).[67]

  There will be eight separate eight-year periods during which both the decedent's participation and the heir's participation could be a factor. After that, there are an indefinite number of eight-year periods, depending on how long the heir lives.

The requirement of material participation is relaxed somewhat for certain "eligible qualified heirs." Instead of material participation, all that is needed is "active management." This term is defined as the making of the management decisions of a business (other than the daily operating decisions).[68] Unlike "material participation," active management can be established even though the activity is not subject to self-employment tax. The House Committee Report states that ". . . Among the farming activities, various combinations of which constitute active management, are

---

[64] Code Sec. 2032A(c)(6)(A).
[65] Code Sec. 2032A(c)(7)(B).
[66] Code Sec. 2032A(c)(6)(B).

[67] Ltr. Rul. 8218008, January 28, 1982.

[68] Code Sec. 2032A(e)(12).

inspecting growing crops, reviewing and approving annual crop plans in advance of planting, making a substantial number of the management decisions of the business operation, and approving expenditures for other than normal operating expenses in advance of the time the amounts are expended."[69] Examples of management decisions are decisions such as: what crops to plant or how many cattle to raise, what fields to leave fallow, where and when to market crops and other business products, how to finance business operations, and what capital expenditures the trade or business should make.[70] The "eligible qualified heirs" are qualified heirs who are:

- The surviving spouse of the decedent,

- Under the age of 21,

- Disabled, or

- A full-time student (as defined in Code Sec. 151(c)(4)).[71]

Specified Time Period

For deaths after 1981, there is a flat 10-year recapture period.[72]

Heir's Liability for the Tax

The qualified heir is personally liable for the additional tax unless the heir furnishes a bond.[73] If the qualified heir dies, the tax savings is not recaptured, but rather the potential recapture shifts to the heirs of the qualified heir.[74] The disposition of the property by a qualified heir to a family member is not a disposition requiring recapture.[75] The family member is treated as a qualified heir and picks up the recapture potential.[76]

.05 Mechanics of the Election

The election is made on Form 706. Once made, it is irrevocable.[77] The election is made by attaching a completed Schedule A-1 to Form 706. Schedule A-1 requires the following information:

1. The decedent's name and identification number.

2. The relevant qualified use.

3. The items of real property on Form 706 to be specially valued. These must be identified by schedule and item number.

4. Both the fair market value and the special use value of the real property.

---

[69] H.R. Rep. No. 201, 97th Cong., 1st Sess. 170 (1981).
[70] *Id.*
[71] Code Sec. 2032A(c)(7)(C) and (D).
[72] Code Sec. 2032A(c)(1).
[73] Code Sec. 2032A(c)(5).

[74] Code Sec. 2032A(c)(1).
[75] Code Sec. 2032A(c)(1).
[76] Code Sec. 2032A(e)(1); Ltr. Rul. 8115085, January 16, 1981.
[77] Code Sec. 2032A(d)(1); Reg. § 20.2032A-8(a)(1).

5. The adjusted value (fair market value less mortgages or other indebtedness against the property) of all real property which is used in a qualified use and which passes from the decedent to a qualified heir and the adjusted value of all real property to be specially valued.

6. The items of personal property shown on the estate tax return that pass from the decedent to a qualified heir and are used in a qualified use under Code Sec. 2032A (identified by schedule and item number) and the adjusted value of such personal property.

7. The adjusted value of the gross estate.

8. The method used in determining the special value based on use.

9. Copies of written appraisals of the fair market value of the real property.

10. A statement that the decedent and/or a member of his or her family has met the requirement of having owned all specially valued real property for at least five years of the eight immediately preceding the date of the decedent's death.

11. Any periods during the eight-year period preceding the death of the decedent in which the decedent or a member of his or her family did not own the property, use it in a qualified use, or materially participate in the operation of the farm or other business.

12. The name, address, taxpayer identification number, and relationship to the decedent of each person taking an interest in each item of specially valued property, and the value of the property interests passing to each such person based on both fair market value and qualified use.

13. Affidavits describing the activities constituting material participation and the identity of the material participant or participants.

14. A legal description of the specially valued property.[78]

Protective Election

If the executor thinks that there is a possibility that the estate may qualify for special use valuation, but is not certain of qualification at the time of the due date of Form 706, he or she may file a protective election. This has the effect of keeping open the possibility of using special use valuation while more information is gathered, pending values as finally determined after examination of the return and the satisfying of all of the requirements of special use valuation.[79] The protective election should be

---

[78] Reg. § 20.2032A-8(a)(3).   [79] Reg. § 20.2032A-8(b).

filed by the due date of the return and should be made by computing the appropriate parts of Schedule A-1 and attaching the schedule to Form 706. The following information is required for a protective election:[80]

1. The decedent's name and taxpayer identification number as they appear on the estate tax return.

2. The relevant qualified use.

3. The items of real and personal property shown on the estate tax return, identified by schedule and item number, which are used in a qualified use and which pass to qualified heirs. Once the executor decides that the estate qualifies, he or she must file an additional notice of election within 60 days. The notice must contain the 14 items previously discussed.

Lack of Required Information

If the executor makes a timely election and substantially complies with the information required under the regulations, but omits some required information, the election is considered valid. In that event, the executor has a reasonable period of time (not exceeding 90 days) to provide the information.[81]

Agreement by the Heirs

All parties having an interest in the property must sign an agreement consenting to the special use election. The qualified heir(s) must agree to bear personal liability for any recapture of the tax. All parties who are not qualified heirs must consent to the collection of any recapture from the qualified property. The required agreement is set forth as Part 3 of Schedule A-1 for Form 706.

The definition of interested parties is rather widespread. Thus, the executor needs to take a broad view of the term. The regulations state that any interest which could be asserted under local law must be considered.[82] Persons who have present, future, vested, or even contingent interests must sign the agreements. Such persons include:[83]

- Remainder and executory interests;

- Holders of general or special powers of appointment;

- Beneficiaries of a gift over in default of exercise of any such power;

- Co-tenants, joint tenants and holders of other undivided interests when the decedent held only a joint or undivided interest or when an undivided interest is specially valued;

- Trustees of trusts holding an interest in the property.

---

[80] *Id.*
[81] Code Sec. 2032A(d)(3).

[82] Reg. § 20.2032A-8(c)(2).
[83] *Id.*

Creditors of an estate are not interested parties "solely by reason of their status as creditors."[84]

If the interested party cannot sign because of infancy, other incompetency, or death, the agreement will have to be signed by a representative authorized under local law (a conservator) on behalf of the incompetent, etc. party.[85]

The agreement must designate an agent who will have authority to represent the interested parties before the IRS. The agent is required to inform the IRS if there is an action requiring recapture.[86]

.06 Special Lien on Special Use Property

A lien in favor of the U.S. government is imposed on all qualified real property equal to the tax savings resulting from the special use valuation.[87] The lien arises at the time an election is filed and continues until the 10-year recapture expires or until the tax is recaptured or until some other event which satisfies the IRS that no additional tax liability will arise.[88]

The district director may issue a certificate of discharge of the lien after receiving a bond or other security.[89]

The lien is also subordinate to a number of other liens.[90]

.07 Basis of Special Use Property

The income tax basis of special use property reflects the special use value included in the estate.[91] This basis may be for deaths in the year 2001 as much as $800,000 less than the fair market value at the date of death (the maximum reduction permitted). Upon recapture, however, the qualified heir (if death of the decedent occurred after 1981) has a choice of staying with the lower basis, or paying interest on the recaptured amount and thus receiving a higher basis, i.e., the fair market value at date of death. An election must be made in order to achieve the higher basis. Once made, it is irrevocable.[92]

> **Example 18-8.** Jim Patterson inherited property in 1997 from his father. The property was worth $900,000 at the death of his father, but was valued at the special use valuation of $600,000. Four years later, the property was sold and Patterson recaptured estate tax of $80,000. Interest on the recapture amounted to $38,000. Patterson elected to pay the interest as well as the additional estate tax ($118,000) and to adjust the basis of the property. Therefore, the basis of the property sold is $900,000.

---

[84] *Id.*

[85] Reg. § 20.2032A-8(c)(3).

[86] Reg. § 20.2032A-8(c)(1) and (4).

[87] Code Sec. 6324B(a).

[88] Code Sec. 6324B(b).

[89] Reg. § 20.6324B-1(c).

[90] Reg. § 20.6324B-1(d).

[91] Code Sec. 1014(a)(3).

[92] Code Sec. 1016(c)(5).

Special use valuation interacts in an interesting fashion with gift plans. Generally, special use reduces the incentive to make gifts since one prime advantage of gifts—freezing the amount that is subject to estate tax—is lessened. This is true because special use valuation removes some of the speculative element of valuation and will result in a lower amount includible in the estate. In fact, if the time period between the gift and death is short, the gift may result in the imposition of more transfer taxes than if the property was left in the estate.

> **Example 18-9.** Ben Severson makes a gift of 300 acres of land in 1997 to his son. Although the special use value is only $400,000, the fair market value is $700,000. When Severson dies, in 2001, the special use value has increased to only $450,000, and the fair market value is $780,000. Since there is no special use value for gifts, Severson's gift subject to tax is $700,000, while if he had retained the land, it would have only been included in the estate at $450,000.

To summarize, there are many aspects to plans involving special use valuation. All factors should be identified, all requirements examined, and as many variables as possible should be quantified before reaching a decision.

¶ 1809 Qualified Family-Owned Business Interest Deduction

The Taxpayer Relief Act of 1997[93] (TRA '97) introduced a new and very important estate tax relief for family-owned businesses and farms: the qualified family-owned business interest (QFOBI) exclusion. To cure some of the technical problems with the original law, the exclusion was modified and converted into a deduction by the IRS Restructuring and Reform Act of 1998[94] (IRR '98).

The deduction is effective for decedents dying after December 31, 1997. However, the Economic Growth and Tax Relief Reconciliation Act of 2001 repeals the deduction for decedents dying after December 31, 2003.[95]

.01 The Law as Originally Passed

In TRA '97, Congress added the QFOBI as an exclusion from the gross estate. The QFOBI was in addition to the special use valuation, but it was intended to interact with the deduction equivalency (hereafter called the "applicable exclusion amount") of the unified credit in such a way as to set the maximum total exclusion at $1,300,000.

---

[93] P.L. 105-34.
[94] P.L. 105-206.
[95] Economic Growth and Tax Relief Reconciliation Act of 2001, Act Sec. 521(d), adding Code Sec. 2057(j).

.02 Congress Responds to the QFOBI Confusion

To address various questions that had arisen about the law, Congress retroactively changed the exclusion to a deduction from the value of the gross estate.[96] The maximum deduction for a QFOBI is now set at $675,000.[97] To coordinate the QFOBI deduction with the unified credit, Congress provided that whenever the QFOBI is used, the applicable exclusion amount generally is maximized at $625,000, regardless of the level at which it might actually be.[98] However, this general rule would penalize estates without enough QFOBI to qualify for the maximum deduction. Therefore, the applicable exclusion amount is increased up to its maximum level by the excess of $675,000 over the amount of the QFOBI deduction allowed.[99]

> **Example 18-10.** Good Eats Cafe is owned by Samuel Shaw who dies in 2001. His gross estate includes property with a value of $900,000 that qualifies for the QFOBI. Shaw has not previously used any of his unified credit. The QFOBI deduction is $625,000. The applicable exclusion amount is $675,000 (the maximum set by Code Sec. 2010).

> **Example 18-11.** Assume the same facts as in Example 18-10 except that Shaw's death occurs in the year 2002. The QFOBI deduction is $675,000, and the applicable exclusion is limited to $625,000, even though the maximum set by Code Sec. 2010 is $1,000,000.

> **Example 18-12.** Assume the same facts as in Example 18-11 except that the QFOBI property has a value of only $620,000. The QFOBI deduction is $620,000 and the applicable exclusion is $680,000 [$625,000 + ($675,000 − $620,000)].

> **Example 18-13.** Assume the same facts as in Example 18-11 except that the QFOBI property has a value of only $250,000. The QFOBI deduction is $250,000 and the applicable exclusion is $1,050,000 [$625,000 + ($675,000 − $250,000)], but limited to the maximum 2002 exclusion of $1,000,000.

.03 Eligible Estates

To be eligible for the QFOBI deduction, the estate must meet three tests:[100]

1. The decedent must have been a citizen or resident of the U.S. at the time of death;

---

[96] Code Sec. 2057, as amended and redesignated by the IRS Restructuring and Reform Act of 1998 (P.L. 105-206).
[97] Code Sec. 2057(a)(2).
[98] Code Sec. 2057(a)(3)(A). The unified credit deduction equivalency is scheduled to increase to $3,500,000 by 2009.
[99] Code Sec. 2057(a)(3)(B).
[100] Code Sec. 2057(b)(1).

2. The sum of the "adjusted value" of the QFOBI plus "includible gifts" of QFOBIs exceeds 50 percent of the adjusted gross estate; and

3. For at least five out of the eight years preceding death, the decedent, or the decedent's "family," must have both owned the QFOBIs and "materially participated" in the operation of the business to which the QFOBIs relate.

The term "adjusted value" of the QFOBI is the amount that would be included in the gross estate (generally fair market value at the date of death), reduced by the excess of:[101]

1. All claims against the estate and unpaid mortgages and other indebtedness with respect to property included in the decedent's gross estate,[102] over

2. The sum of:

   a. Any qualified residence debt;[103]

   b. Any debt, the proceeds of which were used for the payment of educational and medical expenses of the decedent, the decedent's spouse, or the decedent's dependents;

   c. Any other debt to the extent that such indebtedness does not exceed $10,000.

Example 18-14. Dawn Allen died in 2001. Her estate included business property qualifying as QFOBI in the amount of $580,000. Total claims against the estate and other debt amounted to $200,000, $60,000 of which was a mortgage on her personal residence. The adjusted value of her QFOBI is $440,000 [$580,000 − ($200,000 − $60,000)].

Tax Tips and Pitfalls

The executor of farm estates qualifying for the QFOBI should allocate a portion of a mortgage to the farmhouse. Such an allocation will reduce the amount of debt which must be subtracted in order to determine the allowable QFOBI deduction.

.04 The 50 Percent Threshold

Successful business people and farmers often give away a substantial portion of their wealth to their family as part of an estate planning strategy. To the extent that the business remained in the family, Congress did not wish such gifts to result in the loss of eligibility for QFOBI treatment. Therefore, in applying the 50 percent threshold, gifts of QFOBIs made after 1976 to family members are added to the adjusted value of the

---

[101] Code Sec. 2057(d).
[102] These are deductions from the gross estate allowed by Code Sec. 2053(a)(3) and (4).

[103] This is acquisition debt and home equity debt, the interest on which is deductible under Code Sec. 163(h)(3).

QFOBI property. Such gifts include taxable gifts as well as gifts under the $10,000 annual exclusion, provided that the family members (other than the decedent's spouse) held the property continuously from the date of the gift until death.[104]

The term "adjusted gross estate" for this purpose is defined as the gross estate:[105]

1. Reduced by deductible claims against the estate and by unpaid mortgages and other indebtedness with respect to property included in the decedent's gross estate, and

2. Increased by the excess of:

    a. The amount of includible gifts of QFOBIs, plus

    b. The amount of other transfers (if more than *de minimis*) from the decedent to the decedent's spouse (determined at the time of the transfer) within 10 years of the decedent's death, plus

    c. The amount of other gifts within three years of death, except for gifts to family members excluded because of the gift tax annual exclusion, over

3. The amount of gifts in item 2 above which are already included in the decedent's gross estate.

Example 18-15. Amy Smithson's gross estate upon her death in 2001 is $2,000,000. Claims against the gross estate and unpaid mortgages of the decedent amounted to $500,000. At death, her estate included business property qualifying as QFOBI in the amount of $800,000. In 1983, she gave $150,000 of qualifying business property to her daughter, reporting a taxable gift after the annual exclusion, of $140,000. She also gave $80,000 of common stock to her husband in 1996 and gave an auto worth $7,000 to her son in 1999. For purposes of the 50 percent test, the numerator of the fraction is $800,000 + $140,000 + $10,000 = $950,000. The denominator is $2,000,000 − $500,000 + ($140,000 + $10,000 + $80,000 − 0) = $1,730,000.

Therefore the 50 percent test is met ($950,000/$1,730,000) > 50 percent.

Tax Tips and Pitfalls

Congress left much ambiguity here, leaving to the Secretary the authority to define what "*de minimis* gifts" will be in this context.

.05 *Property Included as QFOBIs*

In general, a QFOBI includes an interest in a trade or business carried on as a proprietorship by the decedent or by any member of the decedent's

---

[104] Code Sec. 2057(b)(3).   [105] Code Sec. 2057(c).

family.[106] If the decedent owned an interest in an entity (partnership, corporation, limited liability company, etc.), the interest qualifies if either:[107]

1.	At least 50 percent of the entity is owned (directly or indirectly) by the decedent and the decedent's family, or

2.	The decedent and his or her family owned at least 30 percent of the entity, and

    a.	At least 70 percent is owned by two families, or

    b.	At least 90 percent is owned by three families.

However, Congress listed three types of family-owned businesses that do not qualify for QFOBI treatment:[108]

1.	Businesses where the principal place of business is located outside the U.S.;

2.	Any entity, the stock or debt of which was readily tradable on an established securities market or a secondary market at any time within three years of the decedent's death;

3.	Any business if more than 35 percent of its adjusted ordinary gross income would qualify as personal holding company income if the business were a corporation.[109]

.06 Interests Not Included as QFOBIs

Two other categories of interests cannot be QFOBIs. The portion of an interest in a trade or business that is attributable to the sum of cash and marketable securities in excess of the "reasonably expected day-to-day working capital needs of such trade or business" is not a QFOBI.[110] Working capital needs are to be computed using an analysis similar to the *Bardahl* formula.[111] Accumulations intended for capital acquisitions are not to be considered "working capital" for this purpose.[112]

The other portion of an interest in a trade or business that may not be a QFOBI is that portion attributable to assets that are not used in the active conduct of a trade or business and that produce or are held for the production of personal holding company income or foreign personal holding company income described in Code Sec. 954(c)(1). These would include

---

[106] Code Sec. 2057(e)(1)(A).

[107] Code Sec. 2057(e)(1)(B).

[108] Code Sec. 2057(e)(2).

[109] For this purpose, PHCI is as defined in Code Sec. 543, (i.e., dividends, interest, annuities, royalties, amounts received from personal service contracts, and rents, except that rents are not included in PHCI if the adjusted income from rents is at least 50 percent of the AOGI). Note that the "dividends paid" test described in Code Sec.

543(a)(2)(B) need not be met in order to exclude rent income from PHCI.

[110] Code Sec. 2057(e)(2)(D).

[111] H.R. Conf. Rep. No. 1 05-220, at 80; Joint Committee on Taxation, General Explanation of Tax Legislation Enacted in 1997, (the "Blue Book,"), JCS-23-97, at 67. *Bardahl Mfg. Corp.*, CCH Dec. 27,494(M), 24 T.C.M. 1030, TC Memo. 1965-200.

[112] *Id.*

assets producing dividends, interest, rents, royalties, annuities and other types of passive assets described in Code Sec. 543.[113]

Tax Tips and Pitfalls

Practitioners who work with closely held corporations are aware that documentation of working capital needs is important in avoiding the accumulated earnings tax. It will now be equally important for all closely held businesses (whether corporations, partnerships or sole proprietorships) to document working capital needs if the QFOBI deduction is to be maximized upon the death of their owners.

.07 How Entity Ownership Is Determined

In determining corporate ownership, the decedent and the decedent's family must own the relevant percentage of both the total *combined voting power* of all classes of stock and the total *value of all* classes of stock.[114] However, for partnerships, the partner must own the relevant percentage of the capital interest in the partnership.[115] Backward attribution is proportionate, i.e., an interest owned, directly or indirectly, by an entity is considered to be owned proportionately by the owners.[116]

.08 Material Participation and Definition of Family Member

For at least five out of the eight years preceding death, the decedent or the decedent's "family" must have owned the business and "materially participated" in the operation of the business. "Material participation," for this purpose, is defined by Code Sec. 2032A(e)(6) (the special use valuation rules).[117] The term "family member" has the meaning given that term by Code Sec. 2032A(e)(2).[118]

.09 Recapture of Estate Tax Savings

Four different events, if occurring within 10 years from the date of death and before the qualified heir's death, can trigger a recapture of the estate tax savings that results from using the QFOBI deduction:[119]

1. The qualified heir or a member of the qualified heir's family no longer meets the material participation requirements;

2. There is a disposition of any portion of a QFOBI. Dispositions to a qualified heir's family or a disposition through a qualified conservation contribution[120] do not trigger the recapture;

3. The qualified heir loses U.S. citizenship and the heir does not transfer the QFOBI to a "qualified trust;"[121] or

---

[113] Code Sec. 2057(e)(2)(D).
[114] Code Sec. 2057(e)(3)(A)(i).
[115] Code Sec. 2057(e)(3)(A)(ii). For rules regarding the ownership of tiered entities, see Code Sec. 2057(e)(3)(B).
[116] Code Sec. 2057(e)(3)(C).

[117] Code Sec. 2057(b)(1)(D).
[118] Code Sec. 2057(i)(2).
[119] Code Sec. 2057(f)(1).
[120] Code Sec. 170(h).
[121] See Code Sec. 2057(g) for a definition of a "qualified trust."

4. The QFOBI's principal place of business ceases to be located in the United States.

The additional estate tax resulting from recapture is computed using rules similar to the special use valuation recapture rules of Code Sec. 2032A.[122] The estate tax savings resulting from a QFOBI deduction is multiplied by the portion of the original QFOBI that no longer qualifies.

> **Example 18-16.** Assume the same facts as in Example 18-14 and that Allen's $440,000 QFOBI saved the estate $189,200 of federal estate tax. Three years later, her heirs sell one fourth of the QFOBI. The amount of tax recaptured is $47,300 (i.e., $189,200 × .25 = $47,300).

The recapture rules are not as harsh for QFOBIs as they are for special use valuation. The recapture is phased out over a 10-year period. After six years have elapsed, the recapture is reduced 20 percent per year until the interest has been held for more than 10 years (e.g., a disposition in the seventh year would require an 80 percent recapture).[123]

Tax Tips and Pitfalls

Although Congress attempted to pattern the QFOBI deduction after special use valuation, the fact that a QFOBI includes all business or farm property, rather than merely realty, adds additional confusion, especially with regard to what constitutes a disposition. In the TRA '97 Conference Report, Congress added a statement that a sale or disposition, in the ordinary course of business, of assets such as inventory or a piece of equipment used in the business (e.g., the sale of crops or a tractor) would not result in the recapture of the benefits of [a QFOBI deduction]. However, what if a business permanently reduces its inventory by 75 percent? What if a farm business decides to sell its farm machinery and lease machinery instead? Tax preparers should encourage their farm and business clients who conduct a QFOBI to document reasons for making nonroutine sales of inventory or fixed assets. The QFOBI deduction is an extremely important estate planning tool for owners of farms and closely held businesses. Obtaining optimal results from this complicated provision will require careful planning during three stages: the decedent's life, the estate administration period, and the ensuing 10 years.

¶ 1811 General Valuation Concepts

The fair market value of an item is the retail value rather than the wholesale value.[124] It is not the price that a forced sale would produce, but the price under orderly conditions of sale. There are specific rules applied to different types of assets.

---

[122] Code Sec. 2057(f)(2)(A).
[123] Code Sec. 2057(f)(2)(B).

[124] Reg. § 20.2031-1(b).

.01 Stocks and Bonds

The value to be used for stocks and bonds is the fair market value at the applicable valuation date.[125] If the stock was sold on the exchanges or over-the-counter on the valuation date, the value used is the mean between the highest and lowest quoted selling prices.[126] If the stock was not traded that day, but was traded within a reasonable period both before and after the valuation date, an inversely weighted average (based on the number of trading days before and after the valuation date) is taken of the mean of the highest and lowest sales prices.[127]

> **Example 18-17.** Stuart Darrow died on August 13, a Tuesday. He owned stock in Consolidated, Inc. and BPZ Company. The Consolidated stock hit a high of 40½ and a low of 40 on the date of death. The BPZ stock did not trade on Tuesday or Wednesday, but on Monday hit a high of 18 and a low of 17¼, and on Thursday had a high of 18¼ and a low of 17⅞. The Consolidated stock would be valued at 40¼. The BPZ stock value would be: $((17\frac{5}{8} \times 2) + (18\frac{1}{16}) \times 1)/3 = 17\frac{37}{48}$, or 17.77.

Bid and ask quotation may be used in lieu of sales prices if sales prices are not available.[128]

Mutual funds are valued at the public redemption price (bid price) as of the valuation date. If the valuation date is a Saturday, Sunday, or holiday, the bid price used is the last price quoted by the company for the first day preceding the valuation date for which there is a quotation.[129]

Effective for transfers and deaths after June 18, 1984, Public Housing Authority Bonds are subject to federal estate and gift taxes.[130]

Notes

Notes are valued at fair market value. This is presumed to equal face value plus accrued interest unless the executor establishes otherwise.[131] Three factors indicating a value less than face would be a below market interest rate, a long period to maturity, or an uncollectible note. The executor should submit evidence justifying the discount from face value.

.02 Life Insurance

Insurance policies on the life of the decedent, if included in the gross estate, are valued at the amount received or receivable by or for the benefit of the estate.[132] Normally, this would be the face value of the policy plus indemnity benefits, accumulated dividends, returned premiums and other items. The insurance company is required to fill out IRS Form 712 and to disclose the value of the policy.

---

[125] Reg. § 20.2031-2(a).
[126] Reg. § 20.2031-2(b)(1).
[127] Reg. § 20.2031-2(b)(1).
[128] Reg. § 20.2031-2(c).

[129] Reg. § 20.2031-8(b).
[130] Act Sec. 641, TRA '84.
[131] Reg. § 20.2031-4.
[132] Reg. § 20.2042-1(a).

Insurance policies on the life of another are included at the sales price of the issuing company for a comparable policy, i.e., it is not the face value of the policy, or its cash surrender value, but its replacement cost. Again, the value would be specified by the insurance company.

.03 Annuities, Life Estates, Remainders, and Reversions

If the annuity was issued by a company regularly engaged in selling annuities contracts, the value is the replacement cost, as is true of insurance policies.[133] However, for deaths after April 30, 1989, the fair market value of noncommercial annuities, life estates, terms of years, remainders, and reversionary interests is their present value determined by standard or special Code Sec. 7520 actuarial factors. These factors are derived by using an interest rate which changes monthly (rates are published in Revenue Rulings), and if applicable, the mortality component for the valuation date of the interest that is being valued.[134] IRS Publication 1457 contains various actuarial factors. If this publication is not available, Reg. § 20.2031-7 contains information on how to use Tables B and Tables S to arrive at the needed valuations.

> **Example 18-18.** Eric Sampson died in January 2001. The Code Sec. 7520 rate for deaths in that month is 6.8 percent.[135] At the time of his death, he or his estate was entitled to receive the income from farm land worth $200,000 for as long as his father was alive. Upon the death of his father, the remainder was to go to his sister. His father's nearest age in January was 62. The coefficient for a remainder interest at age 62 from Table S of Reg. § 20.2031-7(d)(7) is .33892. Therefore, the income interest is $1 - .33892 = .66108$. Hence, $200,000 × .66108 = $132,216 is included in Sampson's estate.

Remainder interests are valued similarly to life interests.

> **Example 18-19.** Assume the same facts as in Example 18-18 except that Sampson had the remainder interest. The value would be $200,000 × .33892 = $67,784. Obviously, the life interest and the remainder interest have to add to the total value of the property.

Reversionary interests may be relatively straightforward, in which case they are treated the same as remainder interests. Reversionary interests that are subject to a number of likely contingencies are not subject to valuation according to the tables.[136] Instead, one would go back to fair market value as a general rule, i.e., determine what the reversionary interest is worth to a buyer.[137]

.04 Real Estate

There are no specific regulations governing valuation of real estate (other than special use valuation). The general rules covering valuation in

---

[133] Reg. § 20.2031-8(a).
[134] Reg. § 20.2031-7(d).
[135] Rev. Rul. 2001-3, Table 5.

[136] Reg. § 20.2031-9.

[137] Reg. § 20.2031-1.

Reg. § 20.2031 provide the only guidance.[138] Obviously, real estate is among the more difficult items to value. An IRS Revenue Procedure does give some guidance for unimproved real property (land without buildings or other improvements). The best valuation method according to the IRS is the market data (comparable sales) approach. Comparable sales may be obtained from tax assessors, real estate brokers, appraisers, the recorder of deeds, and so on.[139] The comparable properties should be inspected to determine if they have characteristics similar to the property being appraised. The following factors should be taken into account.[140]

- Location, including proximity to roads, schools, shopping, transportation, and other amenities;

- Configurations, topographic features, and total area;

- Restrictions as to land use or zoning;

- Road frontage and accessibility;

- Available utilities and water rights;

- Existing easements, rights of way, leases, etc.;

- Soil characteristics;

- Vegetative cover, such as grass, brush, trees, or timber;

- Status of mineral rights;

- Riparian rights;

- Other factors affecting value.

Other necessary information includes: names of the buyer and seller, deed book and page number, date of sale and sales price, details of mortgages, property descriptions, property surveys, the assessed value, assessor's appraised fair market value, and the property tax rate.[141]

The most commonly encountered approaches to valuation are the actual sales method, comparable sales method, capitalization of income method, and replacement cost method.[142]

The actual sale of property, if sold close to the valuation date, would obviously represent the best measure of value. Such factors as the volatility of the real estate market, type of property, and general economic conditions would influence the decision as to whether the sale was sufficiently recent to be relevant.

Sales of comparable property, if available, will provide realistic estimates of the value of property. Adjustments must be made for different

---

[138] Reg. § 20.2031-1(b).
[139] Rev. Proc. 79-24, 1979-1 CB 565.
[140] *Id.*

[141] *Id.*
[142] For a detailed discussion of these methods see Chalmers, 229 T.M. Valuation of Real Estate.

features of property. The IRS cautions that "only those sales having the least adjustments in items and/or least total adjustments should be considered . . ."[143] Rather than average a large array of values, the appraiser should "conclude that two or three adjusted sales furnish the most reliable estimate of fair market value of unimproved real property."[144]

The capitalization approach is the primary method used to obtain the special use valuation of land. However, it is generally not used to determine the fair market value of farm land. Certainly it would be an inappropriate method if a significant portion of the land's value is due to anything other than income returns and general speculation. For example, if the land is in close proximity to a city, the capitalization method would not be appropriate. The writer feels that the use of this method is appropriate only where cash rentals are widespread and the property involved has been cash rented.

The replacement cost method is not applicable to farm land but could be used to value improvements.

Determining the value of real estate is usually outside the expertise of either the executor or the preparer of the estate tax return. The hiring of competent professionals to appraise the property is generally essential.

.05 Interests in Closely Held Corporations, Partnerships, and Sole Proprietorships

These three types of assets present special valuation problems. Each will be considered in turn.

Closely Held Corporations

Closely held corporations have been defined by the IRS as corporations which are owned by a relatively limited number of shareholders, such that the stock trading, if any, is so infrequent as to not be a measure of fair market value.[145] The IRS has listed the following factors as being fundamental in the valuation process:

- The nature of the business and the history of the enterprise from its inception.

- The economic outlook in general and the condition and outlook of the specific industry in particular.

- The book value of the stock and the financial condition of the business.

- The earning capacity of the company.

- The dividend-paying capacity.

---

[143] Rev. Proc. 79-24, 1979-1 CB 565, 566.
[144] *Id.*

[145] Rev. Rul. 59-60, 1959-1 CB 237.

- Whether or not the enterprise has goodwill or other intangible value.

- Sales of the stock and the size of the block of stock to be valued.

- The market price of stocks of corporations engaged in the same or a similar line of business having their stocks actively traded in a free and open market, either on exchange or over-the-counter.[146]

An additional factor in determining the value of stock held by a decedent is the proceeds of a corporate-owned life insurance policy covering a sole or controlling stockholder that are received by a corporation or a beneficiary of the corporation. In that event, the ownership by the corporation is not attributed to the stockholder, but instead the life insurance proceeds are considered a nonoperating asset of the corporation in determining the value of the corporate stock included in the decedent's estate.

The weight of these factors depends on the circumstances in each case. In some cases, earnings may be the most important factor, while in other cases, asset value will be weighed most heavily. Assets would be weighed heavily in investment or holding companies,[147] while earnings would be heavily weighed in service concerns.

In general, options, restrictive sale agreements, or buy-sell arrangements are disregarded in determining the value of property in the gross estate.[148] However, if all three conditions listed below are met, the options, etc. are considered in determining the value to be included in the gross estate:[149]

1. It is a bona fide business arrangement;

2. It is not a device to transfer the property to the decedent's family members for less than full and adequate consideration in money or money's worth; and

3. Its terms are comparable to similar arrangements entered into by persons in an arm's-length transaction.

A right or restriction is considered to meet each of the three requirements above if more than 50 percent by value of the property that is subject to the right or restriction is owned directly or indirectly by individuals who are not members of the transferor's family.[150] However, to meet this exception, the property owned by those individuals must be subject to the right or restriction to the same extent as the property owned by the transferor.[151]

---

[146] *Id.*
[147] Rev. Rul. 59-60, 1959-1 CB 237.
[148] Code Sec. 2703(a).
[149] Code Sec. 2703(b).
[150] Reg. § 25.2703-1(b)(3).
[151] *Id.*

A right or restriction that is substantially modified is treated as a right or restriction created on the date of the modification.[152]

Example 18-20. Ted Roberts died in 2001 owning a building. In 2000, Roberts and his daughter entered into a lease of the building on terms that were not comparable to leases of similar buildings entered into among unrelated parties. The lease is a restriction in valuing property that will be disregarded in valuing the property for federal estate tax purposes.

Preferred stock held in a closely held corporation presents somewhat different valuation problems. Usually the most important factors in estimating the value of preferred stock are its yield, dividend coverage, and protection of its liquidation preference.[153] The yield should be compared with the dividend rate of high-grade publicly traded preferred. A comparison of the prime rate with the rate charged the corporation provides input as to whether yield should be as high as that on the publicly traded preferred.[154]

The adequacy of the dividend coverage can be determined by computing ratios such as the number of times dividends are earned.[155] Comparisons can then be made with publicly held companies.

The ability of the company to pay preferred stock its liquidation value may be determined by measuring the ratio of the net assets upon liquidation to the amount due preferred on liquidation. The net assets upon liquidation would equal market value of assets less liabilities.[156] This ratio should also be compared with that of publicly held companies.

Partnerships and Sole Proprietorships

Interests in partnerships and proprietorships should be valued at the fair market value, as previously defined. Some relevant factors in determining fair market value are:[157]

- An appraisal of all of the assets of the business—tangible, intangible, and goodwill;

- The demonstrated earning capacity of the business;

- Factors used in valuing corporate stock, to the extent applicable.

Most of the factors affecting the valuation of closely held corporations are present in varying degrees in partnerships and sole proprietorships. The value of a partnership or sole proprietorship is often considerably diminished by the loss of the decedent's entrepreneurial and managerial abilities.

---

[152] Reg. § 25.2703-1(c)(1).
[153] Rev. Rul. 83-120, 1983-2 CB 170.
[154] *Id.*
[155] *Id.*
[156] *Id.*
[157] Reg. § 20.2031-3.

This should be recognized if the value is determined by capitalizing earnings or if goodwill is appraised.

.06   Other Assets

A discussion of all of the other property that may be valued on the estate return is outside the scope of this book. Instead, coverage will be given to households and personal effects, farm products, growing crops and livestock, and machinery and automobiles.

Household Goods and Personal Effects

A room-by-room itemization of household and personal effects is desirable, but articles contained in the same room which do not exceed $100 may be grouped. Instead of an itemized list, the executor may furnish a statement setting forth the total value determined by a dealer in household goods or by a competent appraiser.[158]

Absent some unusual circumstances, this alternative is the more practical of the two.

An appraisal of an expert under oath is necessary for articles having an artistic or intrinsic value in excess of $3,000. Examples would be: jewelry, furs, silverware, paintings, etchings, engravings, antiques, books, statuary, vases, oriental rugs, and coin or stamp collections.[159]

Farm Products, Growing Crops, and Livestock

Growing crops are a part of the gross estate and must be included at fair market value.[160] If a crop is in the ground and growing at the date of death, it must be included in the gross estate even if the crop is later plowed under, or (presumably), destroyed by drought, disease, or the elements.[161] Growing crops are not considered to be income in respect of a decedent; rather the crops are items of property.[162] Hence, the crops are not subject to income tax of a cash basis taxpayer until sold.[163] Since crops are items of property, if the six-month alternate valuation date is used, the value used would be fair market as of the alternate date, or fair market value at the date of disposition, whichever date is earlier.[164]

> **Example 18-21.** At the time of her death (July 15), Jill Sawyer owned land which contained a growing crop of soybeans. The crop was harvested and sold in October. The crop was appraised at $4,000 as of July 15, but it was sold for $10,000. The amount included in the gross estate would be $10,000 if the alternate valuation date is used.

Livestock are also considered to be items of property rather than income in respect of a decedent. Furthermore, the gain or appreciation in

---

[158] Reg. § 20.2031-6(a).
[159] Reg. § 20.2031-6(b).
[160] *Est. of L. Pryor*, 5 BTA 386, CCH Dec. 1887 (acq).
[161] *Est. of R.E. Tompkins*, 13 TC 1054, CCH Dec. 17, 325 (acq).

[162] Rev. Rul. 58-436, 1958-2 CB 366.
[163] *Id.*
[164] Rev. Rul. 68-154, 1968-1 CB 395.

value from the date of death until the alternate valuation or until sold (if earlier) is not property earned or accrued. Therefore, the increment in value must be included in the estate, provided that the alternate valuation date is used.[165] The grain, hay, or other feed on hand at the date of death is to be valued at the date of disposition, if the feed is fed to the livestock.[166] The date of disposition is considered to be the date fed to the livestock. There is a double counting of the feed, i.e., the feed is included in the gross estate and is also reflected in the higher value of the livestock. To mitigate the double counting, the value of feed fed to the livestock is deductible on the federal estate tax return as administrative expenses.[167] Livestock should be valued net of freight costs and commission costs. The weight on the farm should be reduced by estimated shrinkage to the market.

Harvested farm products are also not income in respect of a decedent but are items of property. They should be measured at fair market value. Freight and other costs of disposal makes the farm value less than the value of an elevator or terminal market.

Machinery and Automobiles

The fair market value of property is to be determined by the sale price in a market in which the item is generally sold to the public.[168] The value of an automobile, for example, would be the retail value, not the wholesale value.[169] Used machinery is acquired by farmers both from implement dealers and from public auctions of farmers retiring or otherwise going out of business. Thus either market should be appropriate for valuing farm machinery.

If the automobile or machinery is sold at a public auction or through a newspaper ad within a reasonable time after the date of death (or six months later) the price received will be acceptable for estate valuation if market conditions have not changed markedly.[170]

¶ 1813   Gross Estate—Inclusions

The estate tax code provides a widesweeping definition of the gross estate, stating that ". . . all property, real or personal, tangible or intangible, wherever situated"[171] shall be included to the extent of the interest that the decedent had in the property at the time of his or her death.[172]

Therefore, virtually all property owned by the decedent at the time of his or her death is includible. Even though interest on state and local bond interest is excludable from income tax, the securities and any accrued interest at the date of death are includible in the gross estate.[173] Certain foreign real estate if acquired by gift or inheritance may not be includ-

---

[165] Rev. Rul. 58-436, 1958-2 CB 366.
[166] *Id.*
[167] *Id.*
[168] Reg. § 20.2031-1(b).
[169] *Id.*

[170] Rev. Proc. 65-19, 1965-2 CB 1002.
[171] Code Sec. 2031(a).
[172] Code Sec. 2033.
[173] Reg. § 20.2033-1(a).

ible.[174] Cemetery lots are includible only to the extent that the value represents that part of the lot which is not designed for the interment of the decedent and the members of his or her family, but which is salable.[175]

.01 Dower or Curtesy Interests

The full value of property is included in the gross estate, without regard to a dower or curtesy interest of the surviving spouse, or any statutory interest in lieu of or in modification of a dower or curtesy interest.[176] Further, there is no deduction for a dower or curtesy interest.

.02 Gifts Within Three Years of Death

Before the unification of the estate and gift tax rates, wealth holders had a great incentive to make gifts of property before death. The incentive arose primarily from the lower gift tax rates. To prevent abuse of this tax-saving opportunity, gifts within three years of death were considered to be "in contemplation of death" and were included in the gross estate of the decedent/donor. The unification of gift and estate tax rates contained in the Tax Reform Act of 1976[177] decreased the incentive to make gifts; hence the three-year rule was changed by that Act and was further changed by the Economic Recovery Act of 1981[178] (ERTA). Generally, for deaths after 1981, the three-year rule does not apply, and the gifts will not be included in the gross estate.[179] The gifts will be added to the taxable estate to arrive at the total tax base if made after December 31, 1976. The significant difference, however, is that property included in the gross estate is included at fair market value at the date of death, while gifts are valued at their fair market value at the time of the gift. The gift tax paid on gifts within three years of death must be added to the gross estate, i.e., gifts within three years of death must be "grossed up."[180]

Some gifts within three years of death must still be included in the gross estate. Required to be included are transfers with a retained life estate, transfers taking effect at death, revocable transfers, and proceeds of life insurance.[181] Also, all gifts within three years of death are included to determine the eligibility for capital gain treatment on the redemption of stock (the 35 percent of gross estate requirement), special use valuation (the 25 percent and 50 percent requirements), and tax liens.[182] Also, the deferral of time to pay estate taxes provided by Code Sec. 6166 is met only if the estate meets the 35 percent requirement, computed both with and without the inclusion of gifts within three years of death.[183]

---

[174] Reg. § 20.2031-1(c).

[175] Reg. § 20.2033-1(b).

[176] Code Sec. 2034; Reg. § 20.2034-1.

[177] P.L. 94-455.

[178] P.L. 97-34.

[179] Code Sec. 2035.

[180] Code Sec. 2035(b).

[181] Code Sec. 2035(a).

[182] Code Sec. 2035(c)(1).

[183] Code Sec. 2035(c)(2).

.03 Transfers with Retained Life Estate

If the decedent has transferred property during his or her lifetime for less than adequate consideration, the property must be included in the gross estate if the decedent retained:[184]

- The use, possession, right to the income or other enjoyment of the property; or

- The right, either alone or with any other person, to designate who shall possess or enjoy the property or the income from the property.

Retention of the right to vote (directly or indirectly) shares of a "controlled" corporation is considered to be a retention of the enjoyment of property. A "controlled" corporation is one where the decedent (either alone or with any person) at any time after the transfer but within three years of the decedent's death owned or had the right to vote stock having at least 20 percent of the total combined voting power of all classes of stock.[185] Thus, the stock would have to be included in the decedent's estate.

Enjoyment of the property is deemed to be retained by the decedent/transferor if the property, or income from the property, is used to pay his or her legal obligations. This includes a legal obligation to support a dependent.[186]

Example 18-22. Tim Jarvis established a trust for his 14-year-old son. Income from the trust is to be used to pay tuition, board, and books for attendance at a boarding school. At age 19, his son is to receive the trust corpus. Jarvis dies when his son is 16. The trust property is includible in the gross estate.

.04 Transfers Taking Effect at Death

Lifetime transfers that are intended to take effect at death may have to be included in the gross estate of the decedent/transferor. If both of the following conditions are met, the property must be included:[187]

1. Possession or enjoyment of the property can, through ownership, only be gotten by surviving the decedent.

2. The decedent has retained a "reversionary interest" in the property which, immediately before death, exceeded five percent of the value of the property.

For these purposes, "reversionary interest" includes a possibility that the transferred property may either return to the decedent or his or her estate, or may be subject to a power of disposition by him or her.[188] A reversionary interest in the income alone does not meet condition 2

---

[184] Code Sec. 2036(a); Reg. § 20.2036-1(a).
[185] Code Sec. 2036(b).
[186] Reg. § 20.2036(b)(2).

[187] Code Sec. 2037(a).

[188] Code Sec. 2037(b).

above.[189] Thus, such reversionary interest would not cause the property to be included in the gross estate. If a life tenant to the property had general powers of appointment exercisable immediately before the decedent's death, the property is not included in the decedent's estate, regardless of whether or not the power was exercised.[190]

Example 18-23. Rob Thurman transferred property to a trust. Income was to be distributed each year to his adult children. At his death, the trust corpus was to be paid to his grandchildren. His wife had unlimited powers to alter, amend, or revoke the trust. The property would not be includible in Thurman's gross estate.

.05 Revocable Transfers

Transfers by a decedent during his or her lifetime for less than adequate consideration are included in the decedent's estate if the transfer was revocable, i.e., if the decedent had the power to alter, amend, revoke, or terminate the transfer either at the date of death or if the power was relinquished, within three years of death.[191]

Generally, a transfer of property under a state Uniform Gifts to Minors Act will relieve the transferor of income tax on the income. However, if the transferor of the property is the custodian, the property will be included in the transferor's gross estate if he or she was either still custodian at the date of death or if he or she relinquished the custodianship within three years of death.[192] On the other hand, if the transferee reached maturity before the transferor's death and the custodianship was ended, the property would not be includible in the gross estate.

Tax Tips and Pitfalls

An elderly transferor transferring property to a minor may prefer to have another adult designated as the custodian. This will prevent the property from being included in the estate.

.06 Annuities

Annuities that end on the death of the decedent are not included in the estate since nothing of value can pass to the heirs. However, annuities which are payable to a beneficiary by reason of the beneficiary's surviving the decedent are generally includible in the gross estate.[193] The portion of the value of annuity to be included is determined by multiplying the value of the annuity by a fraction. The numerator of the fraction is the purchase price furnished by the decedent. The denominator is the total purchase price.[194]

---

[189] *Id.*
[190] Reg. § 20.2037-1(b).
[191] Code Sec. 2038(a)(1).
[192] Rev. Rul. 57-366, 1957-2 CB 618 and Rev. Rul. 70-348, 1970-2 CB 193.

[193] Code Sec. 2039(a).
[194] Code Sec. 2039(b).

Example 18-24. Andrew Bates and his wife purchased a joint and survivorship annuity for $50,000: Bates paying $40,000 and his wife $10,000. Upon Bates' death, the annuity was valued by the insurance company at $80,000. The amount includible in the estate is $80,000 × ($40,000/$50,000), or $64,000.

Employee Annuities

For deaths prior to 1985, if the employee annuity qualified for exemption from income taxes under Code Sec. 401 or Code Sec. 403, a limited exclusion for the portion of the value attributable to the employer's cost was available. The exclusion was limited to $100,000, and was allowed only if the estate was not the recipient and only if the beneficiary was paid in installments rather than in a lump sum.[195]

For deaths after 1984, generally no exclusion is available, i.e., the entire value of the annuity is included in the gross estate.[196] However, there are two exceptions to this rule. If the interest in the annuity is created solely by interests in community income arising from community property laws, and the spouse of the employee dies before the employee, none of the value of the annuity need be included in the spouse's estate. Also, the $100,000 exclusion is still available to the estate of a decedent who:[197]

- Was a participant in any plan,

- Was in pay status on December 31, 1984, and

- Irrevocably elected before July 18, 1984, the form of benefit.

Keogh (HRIO) Plans and IRAs

For deaths after 1984, the entire value of IRA and Keogh Plans must be included.[198]

.07 Joint Interests

Joint ownership of property can take several different forms. For purposes of this discussion, four forms of joint ownership will be considered: joint tenancies of spouses, joint tenancies of nonspouses, tenancies in common, and community property interests.

Joint Tenancies of Spouses

If spouses own property as joint tenants with rights of survivorship or as tenants by the entirety, then only one-half of the value of the property is included in the estate, regardless of who furnished the purchase price.[199]

Example 18-25. Joel Harmon and his wife purchased farm land in 1970, registering it as joint tenants with the right of survivorship. Harmon furnished $30,000 of the purchase price and his wife furnished

---

[195] Code Sec. 2039(c) and (g); Reg. § 20.2039-4(a) (prior to amendment by TRA '84).
[196] Code Sec. 2039(a) and (b).

[197] Act Sec. 525, TRA '84.
[198] Code Sec. 2039(a).
[199] Code Sec. 2040(b).

$10,000. Upon his death in 2001, the land was worth $180,000. Only $90,000 is included in his estate.

Joint Tenancies of Nonspouses

The rules are considerably more harsh for nonspousal joint tenancies. The entire value of property that was acquired by purchase will be included in the gross estate unless it can be established that the survivor paid for part of the cost.[200]

> **Example 18-26.** Assume the same facts as in Example 18-25 except that Harmon purchased the property with his sister. If Harmon precedes his sister in death, $135,000 [$180,000 × ($30,000/$40,000)] is included in his estate. If his sister dies first, $45,000 is included in her estate.

If the property was acquired by gift, devise, bequest, or inheritance, then the property is presumed to be owned equally and only the decedent's fractional share is included.[201]

Jointly held property covered by these rules includes, in addition to realty and personalty, joint bank accounts, stocks, bonds, and other instruments. The above rules do not apply to tenancy in common.[202]

Tenancies in Common and Community Property

Only the fractional interest of a tenancy in common is included in the decedent's estate.

> **Example 18-27.** Toby Wright and his two brothers inherited an equal interest in their mother's farm when she died. They held the land as tenants in common until 1995 when Wright died. The land was worth $120,000 at the date of death. The gross estate would include $40,000 of farm land.

Since the decedent can pass to his or her heirs only one-half of community property, only one-half of the value is included in his or her estate. This is true regardless of who paid the cost, or how the property is registered.

.08 Powers of Appointment

Inclusion in the estate of property over which the decedent had powers of appointment depends on whether the power was created before October 22, 1942 or on or after that date. In this discussion, it will be assumed that all powers were created after October 21, 1942. Another relevant factor is whether the power created is a general power or a limited power of appointment.

---

[200] Code Sec. 2040(a).
[201] Reg. § 20.2040-1(a)(1).

[202] Reg. § 20.2040-1(b).

A general power of appointment is a power that can be exercised in favor of the decedent, his or her estate, his or her creditors, or the creditors of his or her estate.[203] Essentially then, a general power gives the holder the ability to benefit personally from the property. However, there are limited instances in which a holder may benefit personally from the exercise of a power, but the power will not be considered a general power.

- A power to consume, invade, or appropriate property for the benefit of the decedent which is limited by an ascertainable standard relating to the health, education, support, or maintenance of the decedent is not considered a general power of appointment.

- If the power is exercisable only in conjunction with another person who has a substantial interest in the property, and who would find the exercise of the power adverse to his or her interest, the power is not considered a general power.[204]

If the decedent holds a general power of appointment at his or her death, the value of such property must be included in his or her estate.[205] This is true whether or not it is exercised by will.

Generally, limited or special powers of appointment are not includible in the gross estate of the decedent holding the power.

> **Example 18-28.** Shelley Eaton's will created a trust which named her husband as the life tenant and her children as the remaindermen. Eaton's husband can designate in his will how the children are to share the trust, but cannot invade the trust for his benefit. The property will not be included in his gross estate.

.09 Life Insurance

Life insurance on the life of the decedent may be either payable to the estate (directly or for the benefit of the estate), or to a beneficiary. The decedent may also own life insurance on the life of another. Rules for inclusion in the gross estate differ according to these varying circumstances.

Proceeds Payable to the Estate

If the proceeds are payable to the estate, the entire value of the life insurance policy is includible in the gross estate.[206] Even if not payable to the estate, if payable for the benefit of the decedent, the policy value must be included in the gross estate. Thus, for example, the proceeds of credit life insurance, though paid to the creditor, must be included in the estate. If the insurance policy is community property, only one-half of the proceeds will be includible.[207]

---

[203] Code Sec. 2041(b).
[204] *Id.*
[205] Code Sec. 2041(a).

[206] Code Sec. 2042(l).

[207] Reg. § 20.2042-1(b).

Proceeds Payable to Another Beneficiary

The decedent must have possessed any of the incidents of ownership for the proceeds to be includible in his or her gross estate if the proceeds are payable to one of his or her beneficiaries.[208] If the decedent is merely the insured but does not possess any incidents of ownership, the proceeds will not be includible in his or her gross estate.

Example 18-29. Keith Gibson purchased a policy on his life in 1980 and immediately transferred all the incidents of ownership to his daughter. His daughter paid the premiums on the policy. In 1995 he died, and the proceeds were paid to his daughter. The amount is not included in his gross estate.

The incidents of ownership includes the power to change the beneficiary, to surrender or cancel the policy, to assign the policy, to revoke an assignment, to pledge the policy for a loan, or to borrow against the policy.[209]

If the decedent controls a corporation (owns over 50 percent of the voting power), and the corporation owns a policy on the decedent's life, whether or not it is includible in the decedent's estate depends on the beneficiary of the policy. If the beneficiary of the policy is the corporation or a third party, the policy proceeds are not included in the gross estate.[210] However, if any part of the proceeds are not payable to the corporation or for the benefit of the corporation, the proceeds are includible in the gross estate.[211]

Since policies in which the decedent is only the insured and has no incidents of ownership are generally excludable from the gross estate, there is some incentive to transfer the ownership of policies. However, if the policy is transferred within three years of death for less than adequate consideration, the proceeds of the policy must be included in the gross estate.

.10 Qualified Conservation Easements

Effective for the estates of decedents dying after December 31, 1997, the executor of an estate can elect an exclusion from a decedent's gross estate the lesser of "the applicable percentage" of the value of the land subject to the "qualified conservation easement" or the "exclusion limitation."[212] The "applicable percentage" is 40 percent reduced by 2 percentage points for each percentage point (or fraction) by which the value of the qualified conservation easement is less than 30 percent of the value of the land (determined without regard to the value of the easement and reduced by the value of any retained development right).[213] The "exclusion limitation" begins at $100,000 for deaths in 1998 and increases by $100,000 each

---

[208] Reg. § 20.2042-1(c).
[209] Reg. § 20.2042-1(c)(2).
[210] Reg. § 20.2042-1(c)(6).

[211] *Id.*
[212] Code Sec. 2031(c)(1).
[213] Code Sec. 2031(c)(2).

year, reaching a maximum at $500,000 in the year 2002 and thereafter.[214] The exclusion is not allowed to the extent that the property is debt-financed property.[215]

Land subject to a "qualified conservation easement" is land that is located:[216]

- In or within 25 miles of a metropolitan area as defined by the Office of Management and Budget;

- In or within 25 miles of a national park or wilderness area, unless the IRS determines that such land is not under significant development pressure;

- In or within 25 miles of an Urban National Forest.

In addition, the land must have been owned by the decedent or a decedent's family at all times during the three-year period ending on the date of the decedent's death. Also, the land must be subject to a qualified conservation easement granted by the decedent or a member of the decedent's family.[217] Use of the conservation easement is not restricted to individuals; it also applies to an interest in a partnership, corporation, or trust if at least 30 percent of the entity is owned (directly or indirectly) by the decedent.[218]

The term "qualified conservation easement" means a qualified conservation contribution (as defined in Code Sec. 170(h)(1)) of a qualified real property interest. A qualified real property interest means a restriction (granted in perpetuity) on the use which may be made of the real property (including a prohibition of more than a *de minimis* use for a commercial recreational activity).[219]

The granting of a conservation easement does not affect specially valued property under Code Sec. 2032A, i.e., the property can qualify for special use valuation as well, and the granting of an easement is not a disqualifying disposition.

Tax Tips and Pitfalls

Owners of farms and ranchers within the required 25 mile radius of a metropolitan area, national park, etc. who wish to continue using the land for farming or ranching and who have environmental interests should consider the conservation easement. The combination of the easement exclusion and special use valuation can effect significant estate tax savings.

---

214 Code Sec. 2031(c)(3).
215 Code Sec. 2031(c)(4).
216 Code Sec. 2031(c)(8).
217 *Id.*

218 Code Sec. 2031(c)(10) (as amended by TTREA '98).
219 Code Secs. 2031(c)(8)(B) and 170(h)(2)(C).

¶ 1815 Deductions Against the Gross Estate

In computing the taxable estate, four basic categories of deductions are provided by the Code. These broad categories are: expenses, indebtedness and taxes; losses; transfers for public, charitable, and religious uses; and bequests to surviving spouses.

.01 Expenses, Indebtedness and Taxes

Code Sec. 2053 provides for the deduction for funeral expenses, administration expenses, and claims against the estate (including unpaid mortgages and taxes).[220] Each will be discussed in some detail.

Funeral Expenses

Essentially all expenses involved with the preparation of the deceased, the cost of the funeral, and the burial are deductible if reasonable in amount. Included are the cost of transporting the body from the place of death to the area where buried (transportation costs of the person bringing the body back are included), the undertaker's charges (this would normally include the cost of preparing the body, the casket, the service, and in some instances flowers and the gravesite), and expenditures for a tombstone, monument, or mausoleum.[221] Only one-half of the deductions may be permitted in those community property states that regard the funeral expenses to be an expense of the entire community property. This is true regardless of what the will may provide.[222] Most community property states permit all of the funeral expenses to be deducted from the decedent's estate; if so, the expenses would be deductible in full for federal estate tax purposes.

Social Security death benefits and veterans' death benefits are not included in the gross estate, but they are subtracted from the funeral expenses to arrive at the net amount deductible, if the proceeds are not paid to the surviving spouse. If the proceeds are paid directly to the surviving spouse, the proceeds do not reduce allowable funeral deductions because the spouse is not required to use the money for that particular purpose.[223]

Administration Expenses

For administration expenses to be deductible, they must be actually and necessarily incurred in the administration of the estate, i.e., incurred while collecting the assets, paying debts, and distributing property to the rightful recipient. Expenditures incurred for the individual benefits of the heirs, legatees, or devisees are not deductible. Administrative expenses fall into three categories: executor's commissions, attorney fees, and miscellaneous expenses.[224]

---

[220] Code Sec. 2053.
[221] Reg. § 20.2053-2.
[222] Rev. Rul. 78-242, 1978-1 CB 292.

[223] Rev. Rul. 66-234, 1966-2 CB 436.

[224] Reg. § 20.2053-3(a).

Executor's Commissions. A deduction may be taken for executor's commissions which have been paid, or for the amount reasonably expected to be paid, such determination to be made at the time the estate tax return is filed.[225] Often the local court of jurisdiction will have fixed the total commissions, but if not, the amount expected to be paid is deductible if:[226]

- The district director is reasonably satisfied that the commissions will be paid.

- The deduction claimed does not exceed the maximum amount allowable under state and local law.

- The amount claimed agrees with accepted practice in the jurisdiction to allow such an amount for comparable estates.

If the executor receives a bequest or devise in lieu of a commission, such amount is not deductible. However, the decedent can fix the commissions by will, and the amount is deductible to the extent that it does not exceed the maximum allowable by law or local practice.[227] It has been suggested that the will should clearly state that the executor's commissions are not intended as a gift or bequest.[228]

Attorney Fees. The amount of attorney fees that at the time of the filing of the estate tax return have actually been paid or may be reasonably expected to be paid are deductible.[229] If additional attorney fees are included as a result of contesting a deficiency assessment or claiming a refund, the deduction should be claimed at that time.[230]

Attorney fees incurred by beneficiaries in litigating their respective interests are not deductible unless the litigation is essential to the proper settlement of the estate.[231] If more than three years have expired since the estate tax return was filed, the attorney fees are deductible only if the additional fees are allowed by the Tax Court in the final decision.[232]

Miscellaneous Administration Expenses. This category of expenses includes such expenses as court costs, surrogate's fees (fees of the local court having jurisdiction over the estate), accountant's fees, appraiser's fees, clerk hire, and so on.[233] Expenses that are necessary to preserve and distribute the estate are deductible. This includes the cost of storing or maintaining property provided that immediate distribution cannot be made to the beneficiaries.[234] Two types of expenditures are not deductible: any expenditure that should be capitalized, and expenses incurred because the executor has kept the property longer than was reasonably required.[235]

---

[225] Reg. § 20.2053-3(b).
[226] Id.
[227] Id.
[228] *Jetter,* 243-2nd T.M., Estate Tax Deductions—Sections 2053, 2054, and 2057, p. 13.
[229] Reg. § 20.2053-3(c)(1).
[230] Reg. § 20.2053-3(c)(2).
[231] Reg. § 20.2053-3(c)(3).
[232] Rev. Rul. 78-323, 1979-2 CB 240.
[233] Reg. § 20.2053-3(d)(1).
[234] Id.
[235] Id.

For income tax purposes, expenses of selling property are normally an offset against the sales price. However, when an estate sells property in order to pay the debts of the decedent, expenses of administration, or taxes, or sells to preserve the estate, or to effect a distribution, the selling expenses are deductible as administration expenses.[236] This regulation has been interpreted variously by the courts. The Sixth and Seventh Circuits have ruled that none of the three reasons need be present, while the Second Circuit, Ninth Circuit, Eleventh Circuit and the Tax Court have upheld the regulations.[237]

If the sale is for less than fair market value, and is to a dealer, a deduction is permitted for the lessor of:[238]

- The excess of the fair market value on the valuation date over the proceeds of the sale, or

- The excess of the fair market value on the date of sale over the proceeds of sale.

Deducted on Which Return?

Funeral expenses are deductible only on the estate tax return. However, administration expenses may be deducted on either the fiduciary income tax return or on the federal estate tax return. The choice is up to the executor. If the executor decides to take the deductions on the income tax return, a statement must be filed in duplicate stating that the items have not been deducted on the estate tax return, and that all rights to the deductions are waived.[239]

Only the items specified on the waiver are deductible for income tax purposes and nondeductible for estate tax purposes. Thus, expenses can be separated between the two tax forms in any allocation deemed appropriate.[240]

Tax Tips and Pitfalls

The executor should carefully assess the result of taking the deduction on the fiduciary income tax, taking into account tax rates and the date the tax is due. In many small- and medium-sized estates, there will be no estate tax due. In that case, the waiver should definitely be filed and the deduction taken on the fiduciary income tax return. The fiduciary can select the accrual income tax accounting method even if the decedent was on a cash basis; the accrual method may make it easier to deduct various administration expenses in the most advantageous tax year. In addition, the executor may be able to

---

[236] Reg. § 20.2053-3(d)(2).

[237] See *Estate of Park v. Commr.*, 73-1 USTC ¶ 12,913, 475 F.2d 673 (6th Cir., 1973); *Estate of Jenner v. Commr.*, 577 F.2d 1100, 78-2 USTC ¶ 13,251 (7th Cir. 1978); *Marcus v. Dewitt*, 83-1 USTC ¶ 13,521, 704 F.2d 1227 (11th Cir. 1983); *Estate of Smith v. Commr.*, 75-1 USTC ¶ 13,046,

510 F.2d 479 (2nd Cir. 1975); *Hibernia Bank*, CA-9, 78-2 USTC ¶ 13,261, 581 Fd 741; *Estate of Posen v. Commr.*, 75 T.C. 355 CCH Dec. 37,450 (1980).

[238] Reg. § 20.2053-3(d)(2).

[239] Code Sec. 642(g); Reg. § 1.642(g)-1.

[240] Reg. § 1.642(g)-2.

maximize the value of these deductions by choosing the optimum number of months in the first tax year of the fiduciary.

Claims Against the Estate

The amounts that may be deducted as claims against a decedent's estate are limited to those personal obligations of the decedent existing at the date of death. Accrued interest on the debt is also allowable. The amount of accrued interest for this purpose is unaffected by the executor's election of the alternate valuation date, i.e., only the accrued interest to the date of death may be deducted.[241] Generally, the claim is deductible only if the liability is bona fide and was contracted for adequate consideration.[242]

The IRS has ruled that a claim which was not filed within the time specified by local law (and is therefore not enforceable) is not deductible.[243]

Claims against the estate, funeral expenses, administration expenses, and mortgages and liens may exceed the value of "property subject to claims." If so, deductions are limited to such amount, except to the extent that they are attributable to amounts paid before the due date of the estate return.[244] "Property subject to claims" denotes property includible in the gross estate of the decedent which, or the profits and proceeds of which, under state and local law bear the burden of such deductions in the final adjustment and settlement of the estate. However, the value of the property is reduced by the deduction for losses provided by Code Sec. 2054.[245]

Transfers for less than adequate considerations are required to be included in the gross estate to the extent that the fair market value at death exceeds the consideration given to the decedents.[246] For estates of decedents dying after July 18, 1984, transfers of property in connection with a divorce settlement are considered to be for adequate consideration,[247] provided that they are made pursuant to a written agreement, and that divorce occurs within one year before or two years after the date of the agreement.[248]

If death occurs before the property settlement has been made, the assets would be included in the decedent's estate but a deduction is now permitted, since the provisions of Code Sec. 2053(c) (requiring that adequate and full consideration have been given) are now met.[249]

Taxes. Generally, taxes are deductible against the gross estate of a decedent only if they represent a claim against the estate.[250] Usually, the tax must have been a liability at the date of death; however, see the subsequent discussion.

---

[241] Reg. § 20.2053-4.
[242] *Id.*
[243] Rev. Rul. 60-247, 1960-2 CB 272.
[244] Code Sec. 2053(c).
[245] *Id.*

[246] Code Sec. 2043(a).
[247] Code Sec. 2043(b).
[248] Code Sec. 2516.
[249] Code Sec. 2053(e).
[250] Reg. § 20.2053-6(a).

Property taxes are not deductible unless they have accrued before the decedent's death. "Accrual" in this instance does not refer to an accounting definition; instead, the taxes must be an enforceable obligation of the decedent at the date of death.[251] Usually, property taxes are an enforceable claim against the estate if they constitute a lien against the property at the date of death. However, state law governs.

"Death taxes" such as estate, succession, legacy, or inheritance tax payable because of the decedent's death are generally not deductible. However, in certain instances, state death taxes that are imposed on charitable transfers are deductible.[252] Also, there is a tax credit for state death taxes.[253]

Unpaid gift taxes on gifts made before the decedent's death are deductible as a claim against the estate.[254] Often an election is made to have one-half of the gift treated as being made by the spouse. If the decedent in fact made the gift, the full gift tax is deductible. However, if the decedent's spouse made the gift, the gift tax is deductible only to the extent that the obligation is enforced against the decedent's estate and the estate has no effective right of contribution against the spouse.[255]

Unpaid income taxes are deductible provided that they apply to the income property includible in an income return of the decedent up to the date of death.[256] Usually, a joint return will be filed if the decedent was married at the time of death. In that event, the tax deduction is limited. The regulations provide a formula to use to compute the deduction.[257]

Mortgages. The estate may take a deduction for the unpaid mortgage on property or any other indebtedness pertaining to any property of the gross estate. This includes interest accrued to the date of death.[258] If the decedent's estate is liable for the debt, the full value of the property is included in the estate and the debt is taken as a deduction. If the estate is not liable to pay the mortgage, then the mortgage is offset against the value of the property and the net amount is included in the gross estate.[259]

.02 Losses

A deduction against the value of the gross estate is allowed for certain losses incurred during the settlement of the estate. These losses must be from fires, storms, shipwrecks, or other casualties, or from theft; ordinary losses are not deductible.[260] The loss must not be compensated for by insurance; if partly compensated for by insurance, only the excess of the loss over the insurance compensation is deductible.[261]

---

[251] Reg. § 20.2053-6(b).
[252] See Reg. § 20.2053-9.
[253] See Code Secs. 2011, 2014 and 2058.
[254] Reg. § 20.2053-6(d).
[255] Id.
[256] Reg. § 20.2053-6(f).

[257] Id.
[258] Reg. § 20.2053-7.
[259] Id.
[260] Code Sec. 2054; Reg. § 20.2054-1.
[261] Id.

As in the case of administration expenses, losses can be claimed on either, but not both, the federal estate tax return or the fiduciary income tax return.[262]

.03 Transfers for Public, Charitable, and Religious Uses

A deduction against the gross estate is permitted for all bequests, devises, legacies, or transfers:[263]

- To the United States or any state or local government.

- To any corporation organized and operated exclusively for religious, charitable, scientific, literary, or educational purposes. Included is the encouragement of art and the prevention of cruelty to animals or children.

- To certain veterans organizations.

The estate of a decedent holding a general power of appointment over property may, if the property is included in his or her estate, take a charitable deduction if the property is passed to the donee.[264] The property may pass by reason of the exercise, failure to exercise, release, or lapse of a power of appointment.[265]

The will of the decedent may specify that all or part of the estate and/or death taxes be paid out of the charitable bequest. Alternatively, state law may require part of the tax to be paid out of the bequest. If either is the case, the charitable deduction is reduced by the taxes so applied.[266] The reduction for taxes further reduces the charitable deduction. Either the use of a formula or a trial and error method involving successive iterations is necessary to determine the ultimate deduction.[267]

There are complex rules and limitations on transfers to private foundations and transfers of only part of the interest in property, e.g., reversionary interests. These are outside the scope of this book.[268]

In order to substantiate the deduction, the executor must submit with the estate tax return:[269]

- A copy of the will, or other instrument, if the transfer was not made by will.

- A written statement by the executor, under oath, stating whether any action has been taken that would affect the charitable deduction claimed.

---

[262] Reg. § 20.2054-1.
[263] Code Sec. 2055(a).
[264] Code Sec. 2055(b).
[265] Reg. § 20.2055-1(b).

[266] Code Sec. 2055(c).
[267] Reg. § 20.2055-3.
[268] See Code sec. 2055(e); Reg. § 20.2055-2.
[269] Reg. § 20.2055-1(c).

.04 Bequests, Etc. to Surviving Spouses

Congress created an unlimited marital deduction in 1981 as a part of the Economic Recovery Tax Act of 1981 (ERTA). In effect, husbands and wives are now one tax entity with respect to estate and gift taxes. Any complete transfers between spouses are nontaxable, effective for transfers after 1981.

Generally, a marital deduction is now allowed for the value of any property passing to the surviving spouse, provided that the property is included in the gross estate of the decedent.[270]

Life Estates and Other Terminable Interests

Generally, a transfer of a "terminable interest" to a surviving spouse is not eligible for the marital deduction.[271] The rationale for not allowing a marital deduction is that since the holder of a terminal interest may not have to include it in his or her estate at death, the transfer would escape tax twice. A "terminal interest" is an interest which will end or fail due to the lapse of time or the occurrence (or failure to occur) of a contingency. Examples of terminable interests are life estates, terms for years, annuities, patents, and copyrights.[272]

If both conditions below are met, the terminal interest is generally a nondeductible terminal interest:[273]

- Another interest in the same property (e.g., a remainder interest) passed from the decedent to a person other than the surviving spouse for less than adequate consideration.

- Because of its passing, the other person or his or her heirs or assigns may possess or enjoy any part of the property after the spouse's interest ends or fails.

There are five exceptions to the above rules, i.e., five instances in which a terminal interest may qualify for the marital deduction.[274] They are discussed below.

Interest of Spouse Conditioned or Survived for Limited Period

A deduction may be allowable for a terminal interest if:[275]

- The only condition causing it to terminate is the death of the surviving spouse within six months after the decedent's death, or simultaneous deaths (they both die in a common disaster); and

- The condition does not in fact occur.

---

[270] Code Sec. 2056(a).
[271] Code Sec. 2056(b); Reg. § 20.2056(b)-1(a).
[272] Reg. § 20.2056(b)-1(b).

[273] Reg. § 20.2056(b)-1(c).
[274] Reg. § 20.2056(b)-1(d).
[275] Code Sec. 2056(b)(3); Reg. § 20.2056(b)-3.

Example 18-30. Stephen Sharp bequeathed his entire estate to his wife on condition that she should survive him for four months and that they not die together in a common disaster. In the event that she does not survive him, his son is to receive the estate. His wife lived for seven months. His estate is entitled to the marital deduction.

Life Estates with General Powers of Appointment

Since the holder of a life estate with general powers of appointment must usually include it in the estate, there is no particular reason for denying a marital deduction to the creator of the life estate. Hence, terminal interests with general powers of appointments are generally eligible for the marital deduction.[276]

These trusts are known as "marital deduction trusts" because the main purpose is to qualify the transfer for the marital deduction. There are five specific requirements.[277]

1. The surviving spouse must be entitled for life to all of the income from the entire interest or a specific portion of the entire interest, or to a specific portion of all the income from the interest.

2. The income must be payable to the surviving spouse at least annually, if not more frequently.

3. The surviving spouse must have the power to appoint the entire interest or the specific portion to either himself or herself or the estate.

4. The power in the surviving spouse must be exercisable by him or her alone and must be exercisable in all events.

5. The entire interest or the specific portion must not be subject to a power by any other person if that person could appoint somebody other than the surviving spouse.

Example 18-31. Julia Graham's will created a trust in which her husband was the life tenant with general powers of appointment exercisable by his will. No other person has appointment powers. The income is required to be distributed to him semi-annually. The value of the property transferred to the trust qualifies for the marital deduction.

Certain Life Insurance or Annuity Payments

When property passes from the decedent to the surviving spouse in the form of life insurance or annuity payments which are then paid out in the form of installments to the surviving spouse, or if interest is paid to the surviving spouse, then generally the property will be eligible for the marital

---

[276] Code Sec. 2056(b)(5); Reg. § 20.2056(b)-5.

[277] Reg. § 20.2056(b)-5.

deduction.[278] Five requirements similar to those for life estates must be met.[279]

Qualified Terminable Interest Trusts

As previously mentioned, surviving spouses holding a life estate must have general powers of appointment before the transfer from the decedent is eligible for the marital deduction. However, many decedents would be reluctant to give their spouse that degree of control over the property. For example, the spouse may be a second wife and the decedent may have wished to ensure that children by his first wife be provided for.

Congress provided for such possibilities in ERTA when it permitted "qualified terminable interest property" to qualify for the marital deduction.[280] The term "qualified terminal interest property" means property:[281]

1.   Which passes from the decedent,

2.   In which the surviving spouse has a "qualifying income interest for life,"

3.   For which an election has been made.

A "qualifying income interest for life" exists if:

1.   The surviving spouse is entitled to all of the income from the property, payable at least annually; and

2.   No person has a power to appoint any part of the property to any person other than the surviving spouse.[282]

However if the power is exercisable only at or after the death of the surviving spouse, requirement two is not applicable.[283]

Example 18-32. Ted Woodward died in 2001. His will established a trust to which $700,000 of farm land was transferred. His wife has a life estate. Upon her death, the remainder interest passes to his two daughters. The transfer to the QTIP trust qualifies for the marital deduction. An election must be made to claim the marital deduction for the passing of terminable interest property. The election is irrevocable.[284]

This property will ultimately be subject to a transfer tax, either when the surviving spouse exercises a power during his or her lifetime, or when the property passes upon the death of the surviving spouse. In the former instance, a gift tax is imposed;[285] in the latter instance, the property must be included in the surviving spouse's gross estate.[286]

---

[278] Code Sec. 2056(b); Reg. § 20.2056(b)-6.
[279] *Id.*
[280] Act Sec. 403(d) of the Economic Recovery Tax Act of 1981, adding Code Sec. 2056(b)(7).
[281] Code Sec. 2056(b)(7).

[282] *Id.*
[283] *Id.*
[284] Code Sec. 2056(b)(7).
[285] Code Sec. 2519.
[286] Code Sec. 2044.

Charitable Remainder Trusts

A deduction can be taken for transfers of terminable interests to surviving spouses if the remainder interest is a "qualified charitable remainder trust."[287] This is a trust described in Code Sec. 664 for a purpose (charitable, educational, etc.) described in Code Sec. 170. A deduction can also be taken against the gross estate for a transfer to a charity. Annuity tables are used to determine how much of the value of the property is a marital deduction (the life estate) and what portion is a charitable bequest (the remainder interest).

¶ 1817 Credits Against the Tax

There are five credits which serve to reduce the estate tax: the unified credit, the credit for state death taxes, the gift tax credit, the tax on prior transfers, and the credit for foreign taxes. The unified credit has previously been discussed. The foreign tax credit is outside the scope of this book. The other three credits are discussed in this section.

.01 *Credit for State Death Taxes*

A credit is allowed for any estate, inheritance, legacy, or succession taxes actually paid to any state as well as the District of Columbia.[288] The credit is limited to the lesser of the tax paid or the amount allowed in a table set forth by the Code.[289] In no event can the credit exceed the estate tax less the unified credit.[290] The amount allowable per the table is based on the "adjusted taxable estate." The "adjusted taxable estate" is the taxable estate reduced by $60,000.[291] The credit is taken on only the excess of the adjusted taxable estate over $40,000.

The Tax Relief Act of 2001 begins, effective in 2002, a gradual phaseout of the state death tax credit. The credit is reduced by 25 percent for deaths in 2002, 50 percent for deaths in 2003, and 75 percent for estates of decedents dying in 2004. It is repealed completely for decedents dying in 2005 and beyond.[292] Effective for deaths after 2004, the credit is replaced with a deduction from the gross estate.[293] The Act imposes a limitation period for the deduction. The deduction is allowed only for such taxes actually paid and the deduction therefore claimed before the later of:[294]

1. Four years after the filing of the estate tax return,

2. 60 days after a decision of the Tax Court becomes final,

---

[287] Code Sec. 2056(b)(8).
[288] Code Sec. 2011(a).
[289] Code Sec. 2011(b).
[290] Code Sec. 2011(f).
[291] Code Sec. 2011(b).
[292] Economic Growth and Tax Relief Reconciliation Act of 2001, Act Sec. 531(a), amending Code Sec. 2011(b); and Act Sec. 532(a), adding Code Sec. 2011(g).

[293] Economic Growth and Tax Relief Reconciliation Act of 2001, Act Sec. 532(b), adding Code Sec. 2058.
[294] Economic Growth and Tax Relief Reconciliation Act of 2001, Act Sec. 532(b), adding Code Sec. 2058(b).

3.   The date an extension for payment of the estate tax or a deficiency expires, or

4.   If a timely claim for a refund has been filed, the latest of the expiration of:

   a. 60 days from the mailing of a notice of disallowance of the claim,

   b. 60 days after a court decision becomes final, or

   c. Two years after a notice of waiver of disallowance is filed.

.02   Gift Tax Credit

Gift taxes that have been paid by the decedent reduce the liability for estate taxes. However, depending on whether the gift was made after December 31, 1976, the gift tax is either subtracted from the tentative tax or is taken as a credit.

If the gift was made after December 31, 1976, there is no credit allowable.[295] In that event, the tax payable on the gift(s) is deducted from the tentative tax.

The gift tax on gifts made before January 1, 1977, is taken as a credit, provided that the property is included in the gross estate. However, the credit is subject to a limitation. The credit is the lesser of:[296]

- The gift tax paid on gifts included in the gross estate, or

- The amount of estate tax attributable to the inclusion of the gift in the decedent's gross estate.

The purpose of the credit for gift taxes is to prevent double taxation.

.03   Tax on Prior Transfers

If the heir of a decedent dies within a short time after the death of the decedent, the property included in the first decedent's gross estate is taxed twice within a short time frame. The total tax burden could then border on confiscatory. To mitigate this burden, Congress has provided for a credit for the tax on prior transfers.

The credit applies to the estate of a decedent who was passed properly by a transferor who died within 10 years before, or within two years after, the decedent's death.[297] The credit allowed decreases 20 percent for every two full years that the decedent outlives the transferor. Thus the credit is:[298]

- 100 percent, if the decedent dies within two years of the transferor.

---

[295] Code Sec. 2012(e).
[296] Reg. § 20.2012-1(b).

[297] Code Sec. 2013(a).
[298] *Id.*

- 80 percent, if the decedent dies within the third or fourth year.

- 60 percent, if the decedent dies within the fifth or sixth year.

- 40 percent, if the decedent dies within the seventh or eighth year.

- 20 percent, if the decedent dies within the ninth or tenth year.

- Zero, if the decedent outlives the transferor by over 10 years.

The credit allowed is the smaller of two computations:

1. The portion of the transferor's "adjusted federal estate tax" that is attributable to the inclusion of the property transferred,[299] or

2. The additional tax to the decedent's estate resulting from the inclusion of the transferred property.[300]

The computations of the credit are made on Form 706–Schedule Q.[301]

¶ 1819 Computation, Filing, and Payment of the Tax

This section covers the computation of the tax, the filing requirements, and the paying of the tax. Each is considered in turn.

.01 Computing the Tax

After the gross estate and allowable deductions are determined, the taxable estate is computed by subtracting the various deductions from gross estate. Next, the "adjusted taxable gifts" are added to the taxable estate to get to the amount subject to tax. "Adjusted taxable gifts" are taxable gifts (those in excess of the annual donee exclusion) made after December 31, 1976, other than those that have already been included in the gross estate. The tentative tax is then computed on the amount subject to tax. Next, the total gift tax paid on gifts after 1976 is deducted to get to the gross estate tax (the tax before credits). Finally, the various credits, including the unified credit, are subtracted to arrive at the net estate tax.

.02 Filing the Return

Filing requirements for Form 706 are based on the gross estate reduced by "adjusted taxable gifts" and the specific exemption used to reduce the tax on gifts made during the transition period of September 9, 1976, through December 31, 1976. Filing requirements for various years are as follows:[302]

---

[299] Reg. § 20.2013-2.
[300] Reg. § 20.2013-3.
[301] Also see the examples in Reg. § 20.2013-6.
[302] Code Sec. 6018(a).

Year	Gross Estate (as Adjusted)
1998	$ 625,000
1999	$ 650,000
2000 and 2001	$ 675,000
2002 and 2003	$1,000,000
2004 and 2005	$1,500,000
2006, 2007 and 2008	$2,000,000
2009	$3,500,000

As previously discussed, the federal estate tax is scheduled to expire in 2010, but is to be reinstated in the year 2011.

The return is due nine months after the date of the decedent's death.[303] A maximum six-month extension of time for filing may be granted by the IRS upon a timely filing of Form 4768.[304] The return should be filed with the service center for the state where the decedent was domiciled at the date of death.[305]

.03 Payment of the Tax

Absent the use of the installment method to pay the tax, the tax is normally due when the return is due.[306] However, there are two installment plans provided for in the Code for which the estate may qualify.

The 5-Year, 10-Year Installment Method

Estates having an "interest in a closely held business" which at the date of death exceeded 35 percent of the value of the "adjusted gross estate" may elect the 5-year, 10-year installment method.[307] Effective for decedents dying after December 31, 1997, interest on the tax on the first $1,060,000 (for 2001) of taxable estate attributable to a closely held business the payment of which is deferred under the 5-year, 10-year installment method is reduced from four percent down to two percent.[308] Interest in excess of the portion of the tax eligible for the two percent rate is 45 percent of the rate applicable to underpayments of tax.[309] No deduction is allowed for estate tax or income tax purposes for the interest paid on the deferred estate tax.[310]

Tax Tips and Pitfalls

The 5-year, 10-year installment method is a tremendous boon to the estates of closely held businesses and farmers. In addition to greatly mitigating the liquidity problem that farm and ranch estates often have, the deferral also saves significant interest costs. Assuming that the estate (or the heirs) would face an eight percent interest rate

---

[303] Code Sec. 6075(a).
[304] Reg. § 20.6081-1.
[305] Reg. § 20.6091-1.
[306] Code Sec. 6151.
[307] Code Sec. 6166(a)(1).
[308] Code Sec. 6601(j)(1)(A) (as amended by the Taxpayer Relief Act of 1997 (P.L. 105-34).

[309] Code Sec. 6601(j)(1)(B) (as amended by the Taxpayer Relief Act of 1997 (P.L. 105-34).
[310] Code Sec. 163(k) (as amended by the Taxpayer Relief Act of 1997 (P.L. 105-34).

if the money was borrowed to pay the estate taxes, a savings of six percent interest is achieved on the first $412,000 of estate tax attributable to the farm or ranch. This would amount to a $24,720 savings each year for five years. The present value of that savings at an eight percent discount rate is $98,707. Additional savings will result from the 45 percent rate applied to the excess tax and to the remaining nine years of partial deferral.

After the five-year period is up, the tax must be paid in not more than 10 annual installments. The first payment of tax is due five years after the due date for filing the return.[311]

Not all of the tax may be deferred. Only the portion of the tax that is attributable to the inclusion of the closely held business may be deferred and paid in installments.[312] This is determined by multiplying the estate tax after credits by a fraction, the numerator of which is the value of the closely held business, and the denominator of which is the adjusted gross estate (gross estate less expenses, indebtedness, taxes and losses).

> **Example 18-33.** Ivan Nichols died in 2001. His gross estate was $2,500,000; deductions for expenses, debt, taxes, and losses amounted to $500,000. His farm land, machinery, and livestock totaled $800,000; he had no other closely held business. The estate tax after credits amounted to $400,000. The amount of tax which may be paid in installments is $400,000 × ($800,000/$2,000,000), or $160,000.

Although the tax on more than $1,060,000 (for 2001) of closely held business property may be deferred, the two percent interest rate previously mentioned is limited to the first $1,060,000 (for 2001) of estate tax value ($370,000 of tax). Interest on the remaining deferral is payable at 45 percent of the rate applicable to underpayments of tax.[313]

An "interest in a closely held business" means:[314]

1. Any trade or business carried on as a sole proprietorship.

2. An interest in a trade or business carried on as a partnership if:

   a. 20 percent or more of the capital interest in such partnership is included in the gross estate of the decedent, or

   b. The partnership had no more than 15 partners.

3. Stock in a corporation carrying on a trade or business if:

   a. 20 percent or more of the value of the voting stock is included in the gross estate of the decedent, or

   b. The corporation had 15 or fewer shareholders.

---

[311] Code Sec. 6166(a)(3).
[312] Code Sec. 6166(a)(2).

[313] Code Sec. 6601(j).
[314] Code Sec. 6166(b).

The determination shall be made as of the time immediately before death.

Attribution rules also apply. For purposes of the 15-partner or 15-shareholder rule, all property that the decedent owns with his or her spouse under community property laws, as joint tenants, tenants by the entirety, or tenants in common is treated as owned by one partner or one shareholder.[315] In addition, all partnership interests and corporate stock owned by spouses, brothers, sisters, ancestors, and lineal descendants are included. Property owned, directly or indirectly, by a corporation, partnership, estate, or trust is considered as being owned proportionately by its shareholders, partners, or beneficiaries.[316]

Effective for deaths after 2001, the number of allowable partners and shareholders is increased from 15 to 45.[317]

A farmhouse or other residential structures can be included for purposes of the 35 percent test so long as either the decedent or lessee (or their employees) regularly occupied the buildings for purposes of operating or maintaining the farm.[318]

There is a special attribution rule that can help decedents achieve the 20 percent test, if the executor so elects. Capital interests in a partnership and "nonreadily tradeable" stock if owned by a family member or by a corporation, partnership, estate, or trust can be added to the decedent's interest to determine if the 20 percent test is met.[319]

If this provision is elected, both the five-year deferral and the two percent interest rate are not available. In effect, there is a 10-year installment method, the first payment being due on the date the estate tax would normally be due.[320]

The term "nonreadily tradeable stock" is defined as stock which was not traded on a stock exchange or in an over-the-counter market. Time of determination is date of death.[321]

If the decedent has an interest in two or more closely held businesses, each of which meets the 20 percent test, they are treated as one business. They could be then added together to determine if the 35 percent test is met.[322]

If the decedent had previously operated the business, inability to manage the business for several years before death due to physical and/or mental incapacities will not disqualify the estate, i.e., the business will be considered an "interest in a closely held business."[323]

---

[315] *Id.*
[316] Code Sec. 6166(b)(2).
[317] Economic Growth and Tax Relief Reconciliation Act of 2001, Act Sec. 571(a), amending Code Sec. 6166(b)(1).
[318] Code Sec. 6166(b)(3).

[319] Code Sec. 6166(b)(7).
[320] *Id.*
[321] *Id.*
[322] Code Sec. 6166(c).
[323] Ltr. Rul. 8327009, March 29, 1983.

The tax deferral ends, and the unpaid portion of the tax becomes due, if:

- The sum of the distributions, sales, exchanges, or other dispositions of the interest in a closely held business and the money or property withdrawn from the business exceed 50 percent of the value of the interest.

- A payment of interest or tax is not paid within six months of the due date. There are penalties and extra interest levied if a payment is not timely, but is paid within six months of the due date.[324]

The first instance listed above is not applicable if the transfer is to a person entitled to receive the property under the decedent's will, the applicable laws of descent and distribution, or a trust created by the decedent. Subsequent transfers because of the death of the first transferee will also not accelerate the tax payment, provided that each transfer is to a family member (as defined by Code Sec. 267(c)(4)).[325]

Stock redemptions qualifying under Code Sec. 303 do not count as distributions or withdrawals and thus do not accelerate the tax payment.[326]

Indirect Ownership

Previous to the Tax Reform Act of 1984[327] (TRA '84), only directly owned stock in corporations was eligible for the Code Sec. 6166 installment method. Hence, the estate of a decedent who owned a holding company in turn owning stock in a subsidiary conducting an active business could not use the 5-year, 10-year method. Congress felt that liquidity problems (what the 5-year, 10-year method is designed to mitigate) could exist whether closely held businesses were owned directly or indirectly.[328]

For decedents dying after July 18, 1984, the executor may elect the use of the 10-year installment method.[329] However, neither the five-year deferral for principal, nor the two percent interest rate on the deferral may be used.[330]

It is crucial to meet the 35 percent test and, where applicable, the 20 percent test. If an individual has a farm and/or closely held business, but is below the tests, an additional investment in the farm or business may be warranted. If the individual has a terminal illness, or is elderly, selling or making gifts of nonbusiness assets may be appropriate. Unlike the special use valuation rules, there are no five-out-of-eight-years-before-death requirements. Thus a purchase of an interest in a closely held business shortly before death might qualify the decedent's estate for the deferral unless the IRS could establish that the transaction was merely to avoid taxes.

---

[324] Code Sec. 6166(g).
[325] Id.
[326] Code Sec. 6166(g)(1)(B).
[327] P.L. 98-369.
[328] Senate Finance Committee Rept. P.L. 98-169, Vol. I, p. 712, April 2, 1984.
[329] Code Sec. 6166(b)(8).
[330] Id.

Discretionary Extension of Time

The IRS may, for "reasonable cause," extend the time to pay estate tax for a reasonable period not in excess of 10 years.[331] Although the regulations have not, as of this edition, been updated to reflect P.L. 97-34 and P.L. 97-448, presumably "reasonable cause" will still include the following:[332]

- An inability to immediately marshall the liquid assets.

- The estate is comprised in substantial part of assets such as accounts receivable, annuities, copyright royalties, or contingent fees.

- Substantial assets cannot be collected without litigation.

- The estate lacks enough funds to pay the tax and also provide for the surviving spouse and children and to pay the claims.

- The estate has a closely held business or farm that does not qualify for the 5-year, 10-year method.

- The assets would have to be sold in a depressed market.

This extension of time to pay does not carry a favorable rate of interest; the interest rate is that due on underpayments. The extension must be applied for in writing. It must be made under penalties of perjury and must provide a statement of reasonable cause.[333]

¶ 1821 Generation-Skipping Transfer Tax

Property that is transferred to a later generation (e.g., children) and that is in turn transferred to the next generation (e.g., grandchildren) is subject to federal transfer taxes twice. One obvious way to avoid the transfer tax on one generation would be to make gifts or transfers at death to grandchildren. In order to prevent this avoidance, a generation-skipping transfer tax (GSTT) is imposed on transfers that skip a generation.[334] The tax on such transfers is levied at the maximum estate tax rate.[335]

The GSTT is, along with the estate tax, scheduled to expire for generation-skipping transfers made after December 31, 2009. However, as is true of the estate tax, under current law it is scheduled to be reinstated for the year 2011.

The tax is levied on "taxable distributions" and "taxable terminations" as well as on "direct skips."[336] A "taxable termination" is defined as the termination by way of death, lapse of time, release of power, or otherwise of an interest in property held in trust to a "skip person."[337]

---

[331] Code Sec. 6161(a)(2).
[332] Reg. § 20.6161-1(a).
[333] Reg. § 20.6161-1(b).
[334] Code Sec. 2601.

[335] Code Sec. 2602.
[336] Code Sec. 2611(a).
[337] Code Sec. 2612(a).

Example 18-34. Joe Higgins establishes an irrevocable trust under which the income is to be paid to his daughter, Eliza II, for life. On the death of Eliza II, the trust principal is to be paid to Higgins' grandson, Norris. If Eliza II dies survived by Norris, a taxable termination occurs at Eliza II's death because her interest in the trust terminates and thereafter the trust property is held by a skip person who occupies a lower generation than Eliza II.

A "taxable distribution" is a distribution from a trust to a skip person.[338]

Example 18-35. Al Affluent establishes an irrevocable trust under which the trust income is payable to his child, Larry, for life. When Al's grandchild, Henry, attains 35 years of age, he is to receive one-half of the principal. The remaining one-half of the principal is to be distributed to Henry on Larry's death. Larry is still alive when Henry receives the one-half distribution. The distribution is a taxable distribution because it is a distribution to a skip person.

A "direct skip" is a transfer of an interest in property to a skip person.[339] Only one direct skip occurs when a single transfer of property skips two or more generations.[340]

Example 18-36. I.B. Older transferred land to his great granddaughter. Although two generations are skipped, the transfer is subject to the GSTT only once.

A "skip person" is either a natural person two or more generations below the generation of the transferor, or a trust if all interest in the trust is held by skip persons or if there is no person holding an interest in the trust and transfers cannot be made to nonskip persons.[341]

.01 Taxable Amounts of GSTTs

The taxable amount of a GSTT taxable distribution is the value of the property at the time of distribution reduced by any expenses incurred by the transferee in connection with the GSTT.[342] If the GSTT is paid by the trust in connection with a distribution, the tax paid is treated as a taxable distribution.[343]

In the case of a taxable termination, the taxable amount is the value of all property with respect to which the taxable termination has occurred, less deductions for expenses, debt, and taxes attributable to the property to which the taxable termination has occurred.[344]

The taxable amount of a direct skip is the value of the property received by the distributee.[345]

---

[338] Code Sec. 2612(b).
[339] Code Sec. 2612(c).
[340] Reg. § 26.2612-1(a)(1).
[341] Code Sec. 2613.

[342] Code Sec. 2621(a).
[343] Code Sec. 2621(b).
[344] Code Sec. 2622.
[345] Code Sec. 2623.

Generally, the value of the property is fair market value at the time of the generation-skipping transfer.[346] However, in the case of a direct skip of property included in the transferor's gross estate, if the value is determined by the alternate valuation date or by special use valuation, such value is used for the GSTT.[347] In addition, if a taxable termination occurs at death, the alternate valuation date may be used.[348]

.02 GSTT Exemption

Every individual has a GSTT exemption. For the year 2001, the exemption is $1,060,000.[349] Effective for GSTT transfers after 2003, the GSTT exemption is equal to the applicable exclusion amount for that year.[350] Therefore, the GSTT exemption in the years 2004 and beyond will be:[351]

Year of Transfer	GSTT Exemption
2004 and 2005	$1,500,000
2006, 2007, and 2008	$2,000,000
2009	$3,500,000

¶ 1823 Gift Tax

The gift tax is an excise tax levied on the right to make lifetime transfers of property for less than full and adequate consideration. Since it is levied on the right to transmit property, the nature of the property transferred has no hearing on the gift tax. For example, interest on municipal bonds is not subject to income taxes, but the transfer of the bonds is nonetheless subject to the gift tax.[352]

.01 Elements of a Gift

To constitute a gift under state law, a transfer must meet four requirements:

1. There must be on the part of the donor, gratuitous intent, i.e., an intent to make a gift;

2. A capability, on the part of both the donor and the donee, to transfer and receive the property;

3. Delivery of the gift from the donor to the donee;

4. Acceptance of the gift by the donee.

Federal law does not correspond exactly to state laws with respect to gifts. For example, donative intent is not an essential element in the

---

[346] Code Sec. 2624(a).
[347] Code Sec. 2624(b).
[348] Code Sec. 2624(c).
[349] Code Sec. 2631.
[350] Economic Growth and Tax Relief Reconciliation Act of 2001, Act Sec. 521(c), amending Code Sec. 2631.

[351] Economic Growth and Tax Relief Reconciliation Act of 2001, Act Sec. 521(a), amending Code Sec. 2010.
[352] Reg. § 25.2511-1.

application of the gift tax to the transfer.[353] One of the more crucial elements is that of delivery to the donee. If there has not been a cessation of donor's dominion and control, it is not taxable.[354] Thus, for example, where the donor has reserved any power over the disposition of the property, the transfer may not be complete.[355]

¶ 1825 Valuation of Gifts

Gifts are valued at fair market value at the time of the gift.[356] The six month alternate valuation date is not available for gifts. Fair market value is defined as the price at which a property would trade between a willing buyer and a willing seller, neither being under any compulsion to sell, and both having reasonable knowledge of relevant facts.[357]

.01 Joint Tenancies—Spousal

For gifts made after 1981, a joint tenancy created by gift between spouses is not subject to tax.[358] This is because of the unlimited marital deduction that has been in effect since that date. If the tenancy was created before 1982, different rules applied to personal property and real property. In the case of real property, if the creation of the joint tenancy was treated by the donor as a gift, one-half of the property was taxed at death. If the donor elected not to treat the creation of the joint tenancy as a gift, a gift was deemed to have occurred at the time of the termination of the tenancy, if it occurred before 1982. For personal property, there must have been a completed gift for the creation to be treated as a gift.

.02 Joint Tenancies—Nonspousal

If an individual creates a joint tenancy, the value of the gift equals one-half of the difference between the contributions of the parties.

> **Example 18-37.** Kevin McCartney purchased farm land for $120,000 and registered it jointly with his son. He is deemed to have made a gift of $60,000 to his son.

> **Example 18-38.** Assume the same facts as in the previous example except that his son paid $20,000 of the cost. The gift = .5 (100,000 − 20,000) = $40,000.

.03 Reversionary Interests and Remainder Interests

If the donor has a remainder or reversionary interest in the property, the value of the interest is determined by consulting actuarial tables which also incorporate present value.[359] The table for a single life remainder factor (published in Reg. § 20.2031-7(d)(7)) contains valuation factors for a series of interest rate categories. The interest rate to be used is 120 percent of the federal midterm rate in effect for the month in which the valuation

---

[353] Reg. § 25.2511-1(g)(1).
[354] Reg. § 25.2511-2(b).
[355] Id.
[356] Code Sec. 2512(a).

[357] Reg. § 25.2512-1.
[358] Code Sec. 2523(a).
[359] Reg. § 25.2512-5(d).

takes place.[360] The applicable rates are published monthly via a Revenue Ruling.

> **Example 18-39.** In January 2001, Laura Mason transferred by gift property worth $100,000 which she is entitled to receive on the death of her brother, age 62. The Code Sec. 7520 rate for deaths in that month is 6.8 percent.[361] The value of the remainder interest from Table S of Reg. § 20.2031-7(d)(7) is .33892. Thus, the value of the gift is $33,892.

.04   Annuities and Life Insurance Contracts

If a policy has been issued by a company that regularly issues such contracts, the value of the contract would be the cost of a comparable contract. However, if a private annuity is issued, the value is determined by reference to valuation tables established in the regulations.[362] When the gift is of a contract which has been in force for some time and on which further premium payments are to be made, the value may be approximated. This is achieved by adding to the interpolated reserve at the date of the gift the proportionate part of the gross premiums last paid before the date of the gift which covers the period extending beyond that date.[363]

¶ 1827   Types of Gifts

Gifts may be effected by:[364]

- The creation of a trust,

- The forgiveness of a debt,

- The assignment of a judgment,

- The assignment of an insurance policy,

- The transfer of cash or property.

.01   Powers of Appointment

A power of appointment is the right to enjoy the benefits of the property subject to the power. The power must be received by person other than the "donor" of the power. A creation of a power of appointment is taxable only if the power created is a general power. The creation of special or limited powers normally does not constitute a gift.

A general power is created when it can be exercised in favor of the possessor, his or her estate, his or her creditors, or the creditors of his or her estate.[365] However, the following items are not general powers:[366]

- A power to consume, invade, or appropriate property for the benefit of the possessor which is limited by an ascertainable

---

[360] Code Sec. 7520(a).
[361] Rev. Rul. 2001-3, Table 5.
[362] Reg. § 25.2512-6.
[363] *Id.*

[364] Reg. § 25.2511-1.
[365] Code Sec. 2514(c).
[366] *Id.*

standard relating to the health, education, support, or maintenance of the possessor.

- A power of appointment created on or before October 21, 1942, which is exercisable only in connection with another person.

- A power exercisable only in conjunction with the creator of the power.

- A power exercisable only in conjunction with another person who has an interest adverse to the individual.

Example 18-40. Carlos Green established a trust that provided income to his sister for her life and the remainder interest to his children. His wife cannot invade trust corpus, but can change the amount of remainder interest allocated to each child. She has only limited powers of appointment.

Example 18-41. Assume the same facts as in Example 18-40 except that Green's wife may invade trust corpus for any purpose. She possesses a general power of appointment.

.02 Revocable Gifts

If the donor reserves any power over the disposition of the property, the gift may be wholly incomplete, or partially complete, depending on the circumstances.[367] One must examine the terms of the power to determine its scope, in order to determine whether a gift has occurred.[368]

A gift is not considered complete if the donor reserves the power to take back title to the property. It is also incomplete if the donor retains the power to name new beneficiaries or change the interests of beneficiaries.[369] If the donor releases or terminates the retained powers, a gift occurs at that point.

When a trust is deemed revocable, no taxable gift occurs at the time the trust is created, but rather gifts occur each year as the income from the trust is paid out to the donee/beneficiaries.

Effective for gifts made after 2009, a transfer in trust is to be considered a taxable gift unless the trust is treated as wholly owned by the donor or spouse under the grantor trust rules of Code Sec. 671 *et seq.*[370]

.03 Gift-Splitting Provisions of Spouses

If both spouses consent, the gift by one to a third party may be treated as being made half by each spouse.[371] This is of considerable advantage since the annual exclusion and the unified credit are thereby doubled.

---

[367] Reg. § 25.2511-2(b).

[368] *Id.*

[369] *Id.*

[370] Economic Growth and Tax Relief Reconciliation Act of 2001, Act Sec. 511(e), amending Code Sec. 2511(c).

[371] Code Sec. 2513(a).

Example 18-42. Russell Hailey gave his son $18,000 in 2001. His wife consents to having the gift treated as being made half by her. Each is considered to have given $9,000. Since this is less than the $10,000 annual exclusion, no gift tax will result. However, Hailey would have to file a gift tax return.

¶ 1829 Deductions and Credits

When calculating the amount of a donor's taxable gifts, reductions are allowed for the annual exclusion, transfers to charity, transfers to the donor's spouse, and the unified credit. They are discussed in turn.

.01 Annual Exclusions

For taxable gifts made after 1981, a donor may exclude up to $10,000 per year of gifts to any one donee.[372] The $10,000 annual exclusion for gifts is indexed annually for inflation, effective for gifts made after 1998.[373] However, the annual exclusion for gifts made in 1999–2001 remains at $10,000. The exclusion is available only for gifts of present interests; gifts of "future interests" do not qualify. The term "future interests" includes reversions, remainders, and other interests or estates, whether vested or contingent, and whether or not supported by a particular interest or estate, which are limited to commerce in use, possession, or enjoyment at some future date or time.[374]

Example 18-43. Wendy McCall transferred property in trust, the income to go to her daughter for life, and the remainder interest to her grandson. The value of the life estate was $8,000; the remainder interest was worth $17,000. The life estate is eligible for the annual exclusion; the remainder interest is not.

Transfers for the Benefit of Minors

It is possible to transfer property in trust to a minor and have the gift be treated as a present interest even if the minor does not have immediate enjoyment of the property. The following conditions must be met:[375]

1.   Both the property itself and its income may be expended by or for the benefit of the donee before he or she attains the age of 21.

2.   Any portion of the property and its income not disposed of in condition 1 will pass to the donee when he or she attains 21.

3.   Any portion of the property and its income not disposed of under condition 1 will be payable either to the estate of the donee or as he or she may appoint under a general power of appointment if he or she dies before 21.

---

[372] Code Sec. 2503(b).
[373] Code Sec. 2503(b)(2), as amended by the Taxpayer Relief Act of 1997 (P.L. 105-34).

[374] Reg. § 25.2503-3.

[375] Code Sec. 2503(c); Reg. § 25.2503-4.

A gift which does not satisfy the above three requirements may either be a present or a future interest. For example, a transfer of property in trust with income required to be paid annually to a minor beneficiary and corpus to be distributed at age 25 is a gift of a present interest with respect to the income, but a gift of a future interest with respect to the corpus.[376]

Uniform Gifts to Minor Acts

Gifts made under the Uniform Gifts to Minors Act and Uniform Transfers to Minors Act are considered gifts of present interests and are eligible for the annual exclusion. Even though title is held by the custodian, the minor is considered to have enjoyment and possession of the property. However, the gift will not always enable the donor to escape estate tax on the property. If the donor is custodian of the property and dies before the minor is of legal age, the property must be included in his or her gross estate.[377]

Transfers for Educational Expenses or Medical Expenses

There is an unlimited annual exclusion (the gifts are not taxable) for "qualified transfers."[378] "Qualified transfers" are those paid on behalf of an individual as tuition or to any person who provides medical care to such individual.[379]

Application of the Annual Exclusion Rules

The annual exclusion is applied to each donee. Thus, if a donor makes gifts to four donees, there is not necessarily a $40,000 exclusion, but rather the exclusion is the lesser of $10,000 or the amount of gifts to each donee.

> **Example 18-44.** Renee VanDorf gave $8,000 to her first son, $9,000 to her second son, and $15,000 to her third son. The annual exclusion is $8,000 + $9,000 + 10,000, or $27,000. Thus, $5,000 is taxable.

.02 Charitable, Public, and Religious Transfers

The taxpayer is allowed to deduct certain gifts for charitable, public, and religious purposes. Permitted deductions are allowed for gifts to or for the use of:[380]

- The United States, any state, or any political subdivision thereof, or the District of Columbia, for exclusively public purposes.

- A corporation, trust, community chest, fund or foundation, organized and operated exclusively for religious, charitable, scientific, literary, or educational purposes, or to foster national or international amateur sports competition (but only if no part

---

[376] Reg. § 25.2503-4(c).
[377] Rev. Rul. 59-357, 1959-2 CB 212.
[378] Code Sec. 2503(e).

[379] Id.

[380] Code Sec. 2522(a).

of its activities involve the provision of athletic facilities or equipment), including the encouragement of art and the prevention of cruelty to children or animals. No part of the net earnings of such entity may inure to the benefit of any private shareholder or individual; the entity must not be disqualified for tax exemption under Code Sec. 501(c)(3) by any reason of attempting to influence legislation; and the entity may not participate in, or intervene in (including the publishing or distributing of statements), any political campaign on behalf of (or in opposition to) any candidate for public office.

- A fraternal society, order, or association, operating under the lodge system, but only if such gifts are to be used exclusively for religious, charitable, scientific, literary or educational purposes, including the encouragement of art and the prevention of cruelty to children or animals.

- Posts or organizations of war veterans, or auxiliary units or societies of any such posts or organizations, if such posts, organizations, units, or societies are organized in the United States or any of its possessions, and if no part of their net earnings inures to the benefit of any private shareholder or individual.

Generally, the deduction for a charitable remainder interest is not permitted.[381] However, remainder interests may be deducted if they are in farms and personal residencies, annuity trusts or unitrusts described in Code Sec. 664, and pooled income funds described in Code Sec. 642(c)(5).[382]

Example 18-45. The Detweillers transferred a life estate of their farm to their aunt, with the remainder interest to their church. The value of the remainder interest is eligible for the charitable deduction.

.03 Marital Deduction

There are three important dates with respect to the marital deduction. The marital deduction was only 50 percent for gifts prior to 1977. For gifts after 1976 but before 1982, the deduction was 100 percent for gifts up to $100,000, nothing for gifts from $100,000 to $200,000, and 50 percent for gifts over $200,000. The annual exclusion at that time was only $3,000. For example, a gift of $123,000 would be taxable to the extent of $20,000 ($123,000 − 3,000 − 100,000).

For gifts after 1981, an unlimited marital deduction exists. However, for the marital deduction to apply, the interest must not be a terminable interest, such as a life estate.

Example 18-46. Wayne Campbell transferred real property to his wife for life, with remainder interest to his son. No marital

---

[381] Code Sec. 2522(c).   [382] Reg. § 25.2522(c)-3.

deduction is allowed since the wife's interest terminates upon her death.

However there are two exceptions to the terminable interest rule. If the spouse receiving the life estate has a general power of appointment, the marital deduction is permitted.

Example 18-47. Assume the same facts as in Example 18-46 except that Campbell's wife may invade corpus to an unlimited extent for her or for others' benefit. The marital deduction is permitted.

The other exception pertains to qualified terminable interest property (QTIP). QTIP is property:[383]

- Transferred by the donor spouse,

- In which the donee spouse has a qualifying interest for life, and

- To which an election has been made.

Tax Tips and Pitfalls

A QTIP is an excellent device for the accomplishment of several objectives. The grantor may wish to make a gift to his or her spouse that will qualify for the marital deduction yet still limit the action of the spouse. For example, the trust could provide for a remainder interest to children of a first marriage. The one drawback is that upon the death of the donee spouse, the property is includible in the estate of such donee spouse. Thus, if the donee spouse already has a large estate, the QTIP may not be the best alternate.

.04 The Unified Credit

Prior to 1977, a donor was permitted to deduct (in a lifetime) $30,000 against gifts. This deduction was called the specific exemption. The Tax Reform Act of 1976 substituted a tax credit (called the unified credit) for the specific exemption. The unified credit may be used to reduce the tax on both transfers during lifetime and transfers at death. However, if used to reduce gift taxes, there is only one unified credit (for the year 2001 and prior years) to apply to the two types of transfers. The credit amount for the years 1997 through 2001 is shown below.

Year of Death	Unified Credit	Applicable Exclusion Amount
1997	$192,800	$600,000
1998	$202,050	$625,000
1999	$211,300	$650,000
2000	$220,550	$675,000
2001	$220,550	$675,000

---

[383] Code Sec. 2523(f).

Effective for gifts made after 2001, the applicable credit amount for gifts is raised to $345,800 (determined as if the applicable exclusion amount were $1 million).[384] For gifts made in 2010 and beyond, the amount of the credit allowed against the gift tax equals the tentative tax that would be determined under the new gift-tax-rate-only schedule if the amount with respect to which such tentative tax is to be computed was $1 million, reduced by the sum of the amounts allowable as a credit for all preceding calendar periods.[385]

The unified credit in 2001 of $220,500 is equivalent to deductions of $675,000 (shields from taxation that amount).

¶ 1831 Computing and Paying the Tax

The gift tax is a cumulative tax. It is computed by adding up all of the taxable gifts made (gifts in excess of the annual exclusion for all years). From that tax, two items are deducted: the tax (before the unified) credit on all gifts made prior to the current year, and the unused unified credit.

Example 18-48. Martha Kumple made taxable gifts (after the annual exclusion) of $250,000 in 1980, $350,000 in 1983, and $300,000 in 1996. The tax for 1996 is as follows:

Tax on (gifts through 1996 of $900,000)		$306,800
Less: tax on gifts before 1986 of $600,000		192,800
Tax on 1996 gifts		114,000
1996 unified credit	$192,800	
Less: credit used in prior years	79,300	
		113,500
Tax due		$ 500
Tax on 1980 gift	$ 70,800	
Unified credit available in 1980	42,500	
Lesser of the two		$ 42,500
Tax on 1983 gift	$122,000	
Unused 1983 credit ($79,300 − $42,500)	36,800	
Lesser of the two		36,800
Total credits used in prior years		$ 79,300

The tax could also have been computed by deducting the taxes previously paid ($28,300 + $85,200), or $113,500 and the 1996 unified credit of $192,800 from $306,800. This will yield $306,800 − 113,500 − 192,800 = $500.

---

[384] Economic Growth and Tax Relief Reconciliation Act of 2001, Act Sec. 521(b)(1), amending Code Sec. 2505(a)(1).

[385] Economic Growth and Tax Relief Reconciliation Act of 2001, Act Sec. 521(b)(2), amending Code Sec. 2505(a)(1).

.01 New Tax Rate Schedule Solely for Gifts

Effective for gifts made after 2009 (when the estate tax is to be repealed), a new rate schedule for gifts will be in effect. The tax on the cumulative gifts is to be:[386]

Amount	Tentative Tax
Not over $10,000	18%
$10,000 to $20,000	$1,800 plus 20% of excess over $10,000
$20,000 to $40,000	$3,800 plus 22% of excess over $20,000
$40,000 to $60,000	$8,200 plus 24% of excess over $40,000
$60,000 to $80,000	$13,000 plus 26% of excess over $60,000
$80,000 to $100,000	$18,200 plus 28% of excess over $80,000
$100,000 to $150,000	$23,800 plus 30% of excess over $100,000
$150,000 to $250,000	$38,800 plus 32% of excess over $150,000
$250,000 to $500,000	$70,800 plus 34% of excess over $250,000
Over $500,000	$155,800 plus 35% of excess over $500,000

The gift tax return is filed annually and is due on April 15 following the year of the gifts. (The gift tax return was filed quarterly from 1977 through 1981.) If a taxpayer files an extension request for individual income taxes, he or she may also obtain an extension for the gift tax return by checking the appropriate box on Form 4868.

If the statute of limitations has expired for a gift made in a preceding year, the gift's value (for computing the cumulative gift tax) is what was reported in that preceding year. This is effective for gifts made after August 5, 1997.[387]

¶ 1833 Estate Planning Strategies

.01 Objectives of Estate Planning

Most individuals have both financial and nonfinancial estate planning objectives. Objectives could include:

- Maximizing after-tax wealth,

- Providing financial support for loved ones,

- Ensuring that "spendthrift" relatives are taken care of,

- Providing for children of a previous marriage,

- Providing for one's grandchildren,

- Ensuring adequate wealth to last during a lifetime,

- Ensuring that the details of one's estate remain private,

---

[386] Economic Growth and Tax Relief Reconciliation Act of 2001, Act Sec. 511(d), amending Code Sec. 2502(a).
[387] Code Sec. 2504(c), as amended by the IRS Restructuring and Reform Act of 1998 (P.L. 105-206), and the Taxpayer Relief Act of 1997 (P.L. 105-34).

- Preventing or minimizing conflict among family members over the disposition of the estate,

- Provide beneficiaries protection against creditor's claims.

The focus of this section will be on fulfilling financial estate planning objectives; however, certain of the strategies also achieve one or more of nonfinancial objectives.

.02 Use of Lifetime Gifts

The annual exclusion is a tremendous benefit in estate planning. Currently, a married couple can give $20,000 per year per donee without any transfer tax consequences. Suppose a married couple has three children, all in stable marriages, and five grandchildren. The couple could give $220,000 per year without using the unified credit. Two advantages are achieved. The transfers are at a zero transfer tax rate. The transfers also reduce the transfer tax base. Gifts in excess of the annual exclusion freeze the transfer tax base.

> **Example 18-49.** In the year 2002, Tom and Mary Smith give their two children stock worth a total of $1,440,000. They had not previously used any of their unified credits, so the transfer tax after the unified credits is zero. The stock appreciates in value at the rate of 10 percent per year. Ten years later, Tom and Mary die. At that time, the stock is worth some $3,735,000. Assume that transfer tax rates before the Tax Relief Act of 2001 are in effect. If Tom and Mary had transferred the stock at death, the estate tax would have been slightly less than $600,000, assuming both unified credits are fully used. Thus, the children gain almost $600,000 from receiving the stock by gift rather than at the death of the parents.

.03 Impact of Tax Relief Act of 2001 on Freezing the Transfer Tax Basis

The unified credit (applicable exclusion amount) for estates is gradually, but sharply, increased for estates of decedents dying in the time period 2002–2009. Therefore, except for very large estates, freezing the transfer tax base during that time period will not be as important. Assuming the estate tax repeal is not rescinded, death in 2011 will not generate an estate tax. Thus, the freezing benefits of gifts are lost, and the drawback of loss of basis step-up will remain (see below).

If the donees are in a lower income tax bracket than the donor, gifts also save income tax.

> **Example 18-50.** Assume the same facts as in Example 18-49. Also assume that the stock pays a 5 percent dividend each year, and that the children are in the 15 percent income tax bracket while the parents are in the 35 percent bracket. Each year there is $14,400 in income tax savings [($1,440,000 × .05) × (.35 − .15)]. At the end of 10

years, that tax savings, if invested at an 8 percent after-tax rate, would grow to $208,605.

Once the annual exclusion and unified credits are used up, gifts become taxable. The main disadvantage of making taxable gifts is that the transfer tax is paid in the current year, instead of in the later year(s) of death. Thus, time value of money is working against the taxpayer. However, two factors work in favor of taxable gifts: the transfer tax freeze as mentioned above, and a more subtle difference. Although the transfer tax rates remain unified until 2010, the estate tax is grossed-up (there is an estate tax on the estate tax), whereas the gift tax is not (so long as the gift is not made within three years of death). This gross-up feature makes the effective rate on transfers at death much higher than on gifts. If t = the unified transfer tax rate, and g = the effective gift tax rate, then $g = t \times [1/(1 + t)]$. For example, if the unified transfer tax rate is 25 percent, the effective rate on gifts is only 20 percent $(.25 \times [1/(1 + .25)])$.

However, a second disadvantage of gifts (whether taxable or not) is that the income tax basis to the recipient will usually be lower than if the asset is transferred at death. For income tax purposes, the donor's basis carries over to the donee in the case of a gift, while transfers at death are "stepped up" to fair market value. For transfers by death after 2009, there is a partial loss of stepped-up basis. However, all estates will be able to step up the basis of assets by $1,300,000, and property passing to a surviving spouse will be eligible for an additional $3,000,000 step-up in basis. Therefore, the stepped-up basis feature of transfers at death will continue to be attractive, except for large estates.

.04 Use of Marital Deduction and Bypass Trusts

To see the value of married couples using trusts as an estate planning tool, the following three examples have been provided.[388]

Example 18-51. Philip Brown, having used none of his unified credit during lifetime, dies in the year 2002 and leaves his entire estate of $2,000,000 to his wife. The unlimited marital deduction reduces his taxable estate to zero and he therefore is not able to use his unified credit of $229,800. When his wife dies (assuming the estate value remains at $2,000,000), estate tax of $551,000 (after deducting her unified credit) will be due. The unused unified credit of Mr. Brown, $229,800, will have been wasted.

Example 18-52. Christina Jones, having used none of her unified credit during lifetime, dies in the year 2002 and leaves all of her $2,000,000 estate to a limited power of appointment trust that gives her husband income for his life and the children the remainder interest. After using her unified credit, her estate pays a tax of $551,000.

---

[388] The calculations for examples 1–3 assume unified credit and tax rates in effect before the 2001 Act. The illustrative impact of the examples remains intact.

When her husband dies, he has no taxable estate and therefore cannot use his unified credit. Again, $229,800 of estate tax is paid unnecessarily.

The problem with the above two scenarios is that in both instances only one unified credit was utilized. Example 18-53 offers a different scenario.

Example 18-53. Corey Roberts dies in the year 2002, having used none of his unified credit. He leaves his $2,000,000 estate in two trusts. He funds the marital deduction trust with $1,300,000, giving his wife general powers of appointment over it. The remaining $700,000 is placed into a bypass trust. His wife has only limited powers of appointment over this trust (she is entitled to the income from the trust, but can invade corpus only in limited circumstances).[389] The first trust qualifies for the marital deduction, leaving his taxable estate at $700,000, exactly equal to the exemption equivalency of his unified credit. Therefore, his estate tax is zero. Assuming the asset values remain unchanged, when his wife dies, the value of the first trust is included in her estate; the value of the second trust is not. Therefore, her taxable estate is $1,300,000, the tax before the unified credit is $469,800, and after deducting the unified credit, the tax is $240,000.

Tax planning with respect to the unified credits for married couples is to transfer, either outright or through a trust, at least the deduction equivalency of the unified credit to a relative other than one's spouse. Assets should be transferred, again either outright or through a trust, to the spouse so that the spouse's estate can fully utilize its unified credit. Beyond that, optimal division of assets between the spouse and other relatives depends on a number of factors, among them expected future transfer tax rates, expected appreciation in assets, and life expectancy of the surviving spouse.

Tax Tips and Pitfalls

The scheduled increases in the unified credit (applicable exclusion amount) will require the revision of testamentary documents so as to fully utilize the increases in the unified credit. Bypass trusts will need to be funded with more assets. Many smaller estates will no longer need federal estate planning as the increase in the unified credit will effectively remove them from taxation. But for larger estates, close and constant attention will need to be paid to the estate planning implications of the stair-step increases in the unified credit.

For the marital deduction trust discussed above to qualify for the marital deduction, the surviving spouse must have general powers of

---

[389] See Code Sec. 2041(b) for a list of powers which are considered limited.

appointment over the trust. However, the decedent may not consider this desirable. The decedent may have children from a second marriage that he or she wishes to provide for. Or the decedent may be concerned about the financial acuity of the surviving spouse. In that event, the decedent may set up a qualified terminable interest trust (QTIP). A QTIP trust qualifies for the marital deduction, and the value of the trust upon death of the surviving spouse must be included in his or her estate at death.

.05 Use of Grantor Retained Interest Trusts (GRATs, GRUTs, and GRITs)

Because the grantor retains an interest in these trusts, all three are subject to being included in the gross estate of the grantor under Code Sec. 2036. However, if the grantor has an income interest for a term of years that ends before the grantor's death, the property will not be included in his or her gross estate provided that the grantor does not have a remainder interest in the trust. Upon creation of a grantor retained annuity trust (GRAT) or a grantor retained unitrust (GRUT), a taxable gift is created for the discounted present value of the remainder interest. Assuming that the grantor outlives the term of the trust, there are no additional transfer tax considerations. Therefore, appreciation of the trust assets during the term of the trust escapes transfer taxation. However, if the remainder interest goes to a relative (as would almost always be the case), the income interest of the grantor must be a "qualified interest" as defined in Code Sec. 2702. If it is not a qualified interest, the income interest is valued at zero, thus making the full value of the assets transferred into the trust subject to gift tax.

.06 Grantor Retained Income Trusts (GRITs)

Income payments are not required if the assets transferred to the trust are the grantor's residence, adjacent land, or nondepreciable tangible property.[390] Typically these assets generate no income; hence, they are also termed grantor retained use trusts. As is true of GRATs and GRUTs, if the grantor outlives the term of the trust, there are no additional transfer tax considerations, i.e., appreciation of the trust assets during the term of the trust escapes transfer taxation.

.07 Use of Irrevocable Life Insurance Trusts

Life insurance policies are included in a decedent's gross estate only if the decedent is the owner or if the decedent's estate is the beneficiary. Therefore, if an irrevocable trust is the owner of a life insurance policy on the life of the decedent, when the proceeds are paid because of death, the excess of the policy proceeds over the premium costs not only escapes income taxation, but avoids transfer taxation.

---

[390] See Reg. § 25.2702-2.

Payments of the annual premiums constitute a taxable gift that is not eligible for the annual exclusion (the payments are not considered a gift of a present interest). The unified credit can be used to absorb such gifts. Alternatively, it is possible to give the trust *Crummey* powers, in which case the premium payments do qualify for the annual exclusion.[391]

.08 Use of Charitable Remainder Trusts (CRTs)

When a charitable remainder trust (CRT) is used, the grantor transfers property into an irrevocable trust which will pay the donor (or another beneficiary) regular payment for life or for a term certain not to exceed 20 years. At the end of the time period, the charity receives the remainder interest in the trust.[392] The grantor takes a charitable deduction for the present value of the remainder interest. The trust may sell appreciated assets and is not taxed on the capital gains. No gift tax is incurred when the property is transferred to the trust if the grantor is the income beneficiary. In addition, the death of the grantor does not trigger an estate tax with respect to the trust. However, the noncharitable beneficiary (usually the grantor or a relative) is taxed on distributions to him or her.

.09 Types of Charitable Remainder Trusts

A charitable remainder annuity trust (CRAT) provides a fixed annuity to the grantor for a period of years (not in excess of 20) or for the life of the grantor or other beneficiary.[393] The annual fixed payment must be at least 5 percent and not more than 50 percent of the fair market value of the trust principal when first established.[394] Additional contributions to the CRAT after the original creation are not allowed.

A charitable remainder unitrust (CRUT) provides for a fixed percentage of the fair market value (determined annually) of the trust property. The payout must be at least 5 percent of the net fair market value of the assets, but not in excess of 50 percent.[395] Thus, the CRUT payout may increase or decrease each year according to the results inside the trust. A CRUT payout can take three forms:[396]

1. A fixed percentage of the net fair market value is paid out regardless of the income generated by the trust.

2. A payout equal to the lesser of the fixed percentage or the net income of the trust is made.

3. The payout is as described in 2. However, if the fixed percentage payout exceeds the trust net income, it is paid in later years in which the trust income exceeds the fixed payout (referred to as a NI-CRUT or a NIMCRUT).

---

[391] See a discussion of *Crummey* trusts.
[392] Code Sec. 664.
[393] Code Sec. 664(d)(1)(A).

[394] *Id.*
[395] Code Sec. 664(d)(2)(A).
[396] See Reg. § 1.664-3.

Additional contributions may be made to a CRUT after it is established.

From the standpoint of the income interest, a CRUT gives the recipient more protection against inflation, while the CRAT does not expose the recipient to market risk.

Since the trust principal is held for the benefit of the charity, the establishment of the trust does not result in a gift tax on the transfer of the remainder interest. However, if the income interest goes to an individual other than the grantor or the grantor's spouse, a gift equal to the present value of the income interest is created.

As previously mentioned, the distributable net income of the trust, to the extent distributed, is taxed to the noncharitable income beneficiary. One advantage of a CRT is that capital gains are not taxed to the trust. Therefore, commentators often recommend transferring highly appreciated capital assets to the CRT.[397] Capital gains can be taxed to the income beneficiary, however. This will occur when the trust makes distributions in excess of its cumulative undistributed net income and also has cumulative undistributed capital gains. The queuing order for distributions from the trust are:

1. Ordinary taxable income to the extent of the cumulative undistributed ordinary taxable income of the trust—taxed as ordinary income to the beneficiary.

2. Capital gains to the extent of cumulative undistributed capital gains of the trust—taxed as capital gains to the beneficiary.

3. Cumulative undistributed other income of the trust (e.g., exempt bond interest)—taxed or exempt to the beneficiary according to its characteristic.

4. A distribution of corpus—not taxed to the beneficiary.

Tax Tips and Pitfalls

The grantors of a CRT must be careful not to run afoul of the assignment of income doctrine. In *Jorgl*, a husband and wife transferred stock in a closely held corporation to a CRUT which sold the stock. However, the owner insisted that a covenant not to compete be signed by the couple. The Tax Court held that the portion of the sales price allocated to the covenant not to compete was taxable to the couple under the assignment of income doctrine.[398]

.10   Charitable Lead Trusts (CLTs)

A charitable lead trust (CLT) is an irrevocable trust created either at death or during lifetime in which the charity receives the income interest,

---

[397] See, e.g., Bart I. Fooden, "Charitable Remainder Trusts," 66 CPA Journal No. 9 (Sept. 1996).

[398] *Jorgl v. Commr.*, 79 TCM 1318, TC Memo 2000-10, CCH Dec. 53,711(M).

and others (e.g., children or grandchildren) receive the remainder interest. The income payments to the charity can be made either for a term certain or for the life of a named individual. As is true of CRTs, the payment may take the form of an annuity or a unitrust. In a CRT, the grantor always receives a charitable deduction for income tax purposes. However, in a CLT, an income tax charitable deduction is permitted only if:[399]

- The trust is structured to be a grantor trust.

- The income interest (charitable beneficiary) receives either an annuity or a unitrust payout.

Because a grantor trust is taxed to the grantor as if no trust exists, the impact of a CLT that qualifies for the income tax charitable deduction is to create a charitable deduction in the year of creation, but income in subsequent years.

Tax Tips and Pitfalls

If the grantor's income tax bracket in the year that the trust is created equals or is greater than in subsequent years, the time value of money will render the contribution deduction more valuable than the income that will be reported in later years.

If the trust is treated as a separate entity (is not a grantor trust), the grantor receives no charitable deduction for income tax purposes. However, a gift tax charitable deduction (or estate tax deduction if created by will) is allowed for the actuarial value of the income interests.[400]

The time period requirements are more flexible for a CLT than for a CRT. There is no minimum percentage payout requirement, nor a maximum time period.

Although a CRT's income is not taxed to the trust (unless it has unrelated business income), a CLT has taxable income (it is treated as a complex trust) and a corresponding deduction for charitable payouts. Therefore, income in excess of the charitable deduction would result in the trust paying income tax.

The main advantage of a CLT is that the grantor's gross estate is reduced substantially due to the discounted value of the remainder interest. Since this value is determined at the time the trust is funded, creation of a CLT effectively freezes the amount to be included in the estate.

Tax Tips and Pitfalls

A CLT incorporating a unitrust payout can be an important generation-skipping transfer (GST) tax tool. If the unused GST exemption at the time the trust is funded is at least equal to the excess of the value of the property transferred reduced by the charitable gift tax

---

[399] Code Sec. 170(f)(2).   [400] Code Secs. 2055(e)(2)(B) and 2522(c)(2)(B).

deduction, the trust will escape the GST. However, if the trust payout takes the form of an annuity, this determination is not made until the trust ends.[401]

.11 Use of Private Annuities

Private annuities are useful vehicles for transferring property to heirs without incurring a transfer tax while continuing to receive income. In a private annuity contract, the transferor (the annuitant) transfers property to the transferee (obligor) in return for the obligor's unsecured promise to make periodic payments to the annuitant (generally for the life of the annuitant).

The annuity payments consist of three possible parts: a return of cost, which is excludable from income; capital gains, consisting of the excess of the value of the property over the adjusted basis; and ordinary income. No gift results so long as the value of the annuity is at least as much as the value of the property. If the annuity is a joint and survivor annuity, death of the first spouse results in inclusion of the value of the annuity in the gross estate. However, the marital deduction will shield it from federal estate tax. There are no estate tax ramifications upon the death of the second spouse (there is no asset to transfer).

The income tax implications of a private annuity, while favorable to the transferor (annuitant), are less favorable to the transferee (obligator). The obligator gets no interest deduction from the periodic payments. In addition, the income tax basis and depreciable basis of the obligator are subject to complex and not necessarily favorable rules.

.12 Use of Self-Canceling Installment Notes

If assets are to be transferred to heirs, an alternative to private annuities is the use of a self-canceling installment note (SCIN). Upon the death of the seller, the unpaid balance is automatically canceled. Therefore, such unpaid balance is not included in the seller's gross estate. In order for there to be no gift tax consequences, the SCIN must contain a risk premium, either a sales price in excess of fair market value, or an interest rate in excess of the market rate.

In order for the SCIN to be treated as an installment sale, the seller's life expectancy must exceed the installment term. Otherwise, the SCIN is treated as a private annuity.[402]

Although there are no estate tax consequences from the SCIN, the IRS has ruled that the cancellation at death creates income in respect of a decedent (IRD) to the estate.[403]

---

[401] See, Jonathan G. Blattmachr, "A Primer on Charitable Lead Trusts: Basic Rules and Uses," Trusts and Estates (April 1997); and Robert P. Connor, "CLTS: An Important Tool in the Right Situation," Trusts and Estates (Sept. 1997).

[402] GCM 39503 (5/17/86).
[403] See Rev. Rul. 86-72, 1986-1 CB 253; *Estate of Frane*, 93-2 USTC ¶ 50,386, 998 F.2d 567 (8th Cir., 1993), aff'g in part 98 TC 341 (1992), CCH Dec. 48,115.

The SCIN has a major advantage to the buyer over a private annuity. Although none of the buyer's payments in a private annuity are deductible as interest, the interest paid by the buyer in a SCIN is deductible.[404]

.13 Use of Valuation Discounts

The case for valuation discounts for closely held business rests on the lack of decision-making ability a minority owner possesses. Minority owners are not in a position to influence dividend policy, set salaries, or, depending on their ownership percentage, may not even be able to prevent liquidation of the business. Thus, courts have allowed sizable discounts for minority owners of closely held corporations and partnerships. Commentators have observed that discounts allowed in recent years have increased.[405] For example, in *Estate of Brookshire*, the Tax Court allowed a 40 percent discount for lack of marketability in valuing the stock of a grocery chain. Factors cited by the court included the lack of a ready market to sell the stock, a restrictive buy-sell agreement, the fact that the stock constituted a large block, and that the stock owned by the decedent was a minority interest.[406]

The IRS has often asserted that family limited partnerships lack economic substance and therefore fail to qualify as a partnership under federal law. However, the Tax Court has not given credence to this argument as long as the partnerships were in accordance with state law.[407]

---

[404] For a more detailed discussion of SCINs, see Scott H. Malin, "Self-Canceling Installment Notes Maintain Estate Planning Usefulness," Practical Tax Strategies, Sept. 2000.

[405] See, Reed W. Easton, "Give More and Pay Less Tax by Claiming Valuation Discounts," Practical Tax Strategies, Feb. 2000.

[406] *Estate of Brookshire v. Commr.*, 76 TCM 659, TC Memo. 1998-365, CCH Dec. 52,911(M).

[407] See *Knight v. Commr.*, 115 TC 506 (2000), CCH Dec. 54,136 and *Est. of Strangi v. Commr.*, 115 TC 478 (2000), CCH Dec. 54,135.

Index

References are to paragraph (¶) numbers.

A

Accelerated cost recovery system (ACRS) . . . 805–805.13. *See also* Modified accelerated cost recovery system (MACRS)

    accumulated and future depreciation under straight-line rates and . . . 1603.07

    applicability to and restrictions for assets of . . . 805.01

    for automobiles used primarily for business . . . 805.05, 807.02

    for automobiles used primarily for personal purposes . . . 805.06

    class lives for . . . 805.13

    for listed property . . . 805.07

    for luxury automobiles . . . 805.04

    mixed-use (business and personal) assets limited for . . . 805.02

    for real property . . . 805.09

    recovery periods of personal property under . . . 805.03

    for substantial improvements to buildings . . . 805.12

Accelerated depreciation of real property . . . 319

Accounting fees allocable to classes of gross income for deductions . . . 1705.03

Accounting methods . . . 507

    in corporate reorganizations . . . 1209.05

    permitted by IRS . . . 507.01

    selection of . . . 1603.05

Accrual accounting method . . . 507.01, 507.04

    claim of right doctrine applied with . . . 509.02

    deducting bad debts under . . . 609.04

    deductions of expenses under . . . 621.02

    deferred reporting of prepaid services under . . . 517.02

    to report OID . . . 515.08–.11, 515.14

    tax planning for . . . 1603.05

Accumulated adjustments account (AAA) . . . 423

Accumulated earnings, justifying . . . 1501

Accumulated earnings, need of business for . . . 1105–1105.07

    acquisition of business enterprise as . . . 1105, 1105.02

    contingencies as . . . 1105, 1105.05

    debt retirement as . . . 1105, 1105.03

    expansion of business or replacement of plant as . . . 1105, 1105.01

    investments or loans to suppliers or customers as . . . 1105, 1105.04

    product liability losses as . . . 1105, 1105.05

    regulations for reasonable grounds of . . . 1105

    working capital requirements as . . . 1105, 1105.07

Accumulated earnings tax . . . 1103–1105.07

    burden of proof as shifting to IRS for certain cases of . . . 1103.05

    computing . . . 1103.03

    computing accumulated taxable income for . . . 1103.01–.02

    documentation of need for retained earnings to avoid . . . 1105.01

    interpretation of tax avoidance for . . . 1103.04

    liquidating corporation as alternative to paying . . . 1501

    organizations not subject to . . . 1103

    safe harbor threshold for . . . 1103.01

    stock redemptions from estate matched to Code Sec. 303 purposes as . . . 1105, 1105.06

Accumulated earnings tax credit . . . 1103.01

Acquisition, corporate . . . 1203, 1203.02–.03

Active foreign business income defined . . . 1703.01

Actual useful life of business asset . . . 817.01–.02

Adjusted basis, computing . . . 901

Adjusted current earnings (ACE) defined . . . 323

Adjusted gross estate defined . . . 1809.04

ADJ

COR

Expenses—continued

prepaid to accelerate deductions . . .
1603.03, 1605.02

prepaying deductible personal,
accelerating deductions by . . .
1603.03

recognition of . . . 621–621.02

related to tax-exempt interest . . . 625.03

Extraordinary dividends of corporations
. . . 353.02

Extraterritorial income exclusion, Code
Sec. 114 . . . 1727

F

Fair market value

of assets contributed to partnership,
difference between partner's basis and
. . . 207

of assets of liquidating subsidiary . . .
1517.03

as basis of inherited property . . . 905,
1605.04

of gifts . . . 1825

of leased listed property . . . 807.05

for purchased property . . . 903–903.03

replaced with special use valuation for
estate valuation of farm or closely held
business . . . 1807

as retail value under orderly conditions of
sale . . . 1811

of stock redeemed to pay death taxes,
income tax basis revalued
to..l.1411.06

of stock rights . . . 1409.04

Family-owned businesses

qualified family-owned business interest
(QFOBI) deduction for estates of . . .
1809–1809.09

special valuation methods for estates of
. . . 907.10, 1805.02

Farm products and growing crops,
valuation of . . . 1811.06

Farmers, debt relief for . . . 521.04

Farmland

sale of . . . 515.13

transfer of, using special use valuation
under Code Sec. 2032A . . . 907.10

Farms

defined for special use valuation . . .
1807.01

installment payment methods for estate
tax on . . . 1819.03

Farms—continued

qualified family-owned business interest
(QFOBI) deduction for . . .
1809–1809.09

special valuation methods for . . . 907.10,
1805.02, 1807–1807.07

Federal Food, Drug, and Cosmetic Act . . .
739

Federal transfer taxes . . . 1801

50/50 method for sourcing inventory
across borders . . . 1711.05

Fines, government, as nondeductible . . .
625.01

Five-year averaging for lump-sum
distributions repealed . . . 1025.04

Foreign central bank, tax rate exception
for banker's acceptances of . . .
1715.03, 1717.02

Foreign corporations

bank interest received by . . . 1717.02

as beneficiaries of estates or trusts . . .
1715.10

branch profits tax for . . . 1719.05

capital gains of . . . 1717.04

charitable contribution deduction for . . .
1717

conduit financing arrangements of . . .
1717.03

connected with U.S. business, taxation of
. . . 1719–1719.07

deductions allowed to . . . 1719.02

dividend equivalent amount received by
. . . 1719.05

dividend exclusion for . . . 1717.02

dividends from . . . 1703.02

as exempt from PHC tax, certain . . . 1107

gains of, tax rates for . . . 1717

gross income exclusions for . . . 1719,
1719.04

gross transportation income tax for . . .
1719.07

as ineligible for S corporation status . . .
403.01.

income not connected with U.S. business
of . . . 1717–1717.04

interest expense of controlled . . .
1705.07

interest paid by . . . 1719.06

interest received by, tax rate on types of
. . . 1717–1717.02

as partner . . . 1719.05

personal services performed for . . .
1715.05

real property income of . . . 1719.01

requirements for filing returns for . . .
1719.02

EXT